THE
AMERICAN
SLAVE COAST

THE
AMERICAN
SLAVE COAST

A HISTORY OF THE

SLAVE-BREEDING INDUSTRY

NED *and* CONSTANCE SUBLETTE

Lawrence Hill Books
Chicago

Copyright © 2016 by Ned Sublette and Constance Sublette
First hardcover edition published 2016
First paperback edition published 2017
Published by Lawrence Hill Books
An imprint of Chicago Review Press Incorporated
814 North Franklin Street
Chicago, Illinois 60610
ISBN 978-1-61373-893-1

The Library of Congress has cataloged the hardcover edition as follows:
Sublette, Ned, 1951-
    The American slave coast : a history of the slave-breeding industry / Ned Sublette,
Constance Sublette. — First edition.
        pages cm
    Includes bibliographical references and index.
    ISBN 978-1-61374-820-6 (hardback)
1. Slave-trade—United States—History. 2. Slave traders—United States—History.
3. Slavery—Economic aspects—United States. 4. Slaves—United States—Social
conditions. 5. Slaves—United States—Sexual behavior—History. 6. Slaveholders—Southern States—History. 7. Southern States—History—1775-1865. 8.
Slave-trade—Southern States—History. 9. Slave traders—Southern States—History. I. Sublette, Constance. II. Title.
    E442.S82 2015
    331.11'7340973—dc23
                                    2015002493

Cover design and illustration: Natalya Balnova
Interior design: PerfecType, Nashville, TN

Printed in the United States of America
5 4 3

Although it is a record of horror it has an odd, matter-of-fact air about it simply because the infamies that are described were so completely taken for granted.

—Bruce Catton, reviewing the 1965 edition of
*Documents Illustrative of the
History of the Slave Trade to the Americas*

Contents

Part Six: The Revolution

NEGROES WANTED,

 We at all times wish to purchase any number of negroes, of both sexes; either slaves for life or a term of years, that are sound and healthy, and good titles, for which we will pay more money in gold than any other Maryland traders. We are permanently located at this place, where we have fitted up a place for the safe keeping of negroes, at 25 cents per day. Persons having servants to dispose of, will do well to see us, as we are at all times buying and forwarding to the different Southern markets, and will always pay the highest prices the Southern markets will justify. All communications, (post-paid, and not otherwise,) will be promptly attended to, if addressed to

JOHN N. DENNING & CO.

Centreville, Queen Ann's county,

May 27, 1843.   1y   Maryland.

Kent News, *Chestertown, Maryland.*

Introduction

THIS IS A HISTORY of the slave-breeding industry, which we define as the complex of businesses and individuals in the United States who profited from the enslavement of African American children at birth.

At the heart of our account is the intricate connection between the legal fact of people as property—the "chattel principle"—and national expansion. Our narrative doubles, then, as a history of the making of the United States as seen from the point of view of the slave trade.

It also traces the history of money in America. In the Southern United States, the "peculiar institution" of slavery was inextricably associated with its own peculiar economy, interconnected with that of the North.

One of the two principal products of the antebellum slave economy was staple crops, which provided the cash flow—primarily cotton, which was the United States' major export. The other was enslaved people, who counted as capital and functioned as the stable wealth of the South. African American bodies and childbearing potential collateralized massive amounts of credit, the use of which made slaveowners the wealthiest people in the country. When the Southern states seceded to form the Confederacy they partitioned off, and declared independence for, their economic system in which people were money.

Our chronology reaches from earliest colonial times through emancipation, following the two main phases of the slave trade. The first phase, *importation,* began with the first known sale of kidnapped Africans in Virginia in 1619 and took place largely, though not entirely, during the colonial years. The second phase, *breeding,* was the era of the domestic, or interstate, slave trade in African Americans. The key date here—from our perspective, one of the most important dates in American history—was the federal prohibition of the "importation of persons" as of January 1, 1808. After that, the interstate trade was, with minor exceptions, the only slave trade in the United States, and it became massified on a previously impossible scale.

The conflict between North and South is a fundamental trope of American history, but in our narrative, the major conflict is intra-Southern: the commercial antagonism between Virginia, the great slave breeder, and South Carolina, the great slave importer, for control of the market that supplied slave labor to an expanding slavery nation. The dramatic power struggle between the two was central to the Constitutional Convention in Philadelphia in 1787 and to secession in 1860–61.

Part One is an overview, intended as an extended introduction to the subject.

Part Two, which begins the main chronological body of the text, describes the creation of a slave economy during the colonial years.

Part Three centers on the US Constitution's role as hinge between the two phases of slave importation and slave breeding.

Parts Four through Six cover the years of the slave-breeding industry, from the end of the War of 1812 through emancipation: the rise, peak, and fall of the cotton kingdom.

Note: This book describes an economy in which people were capital, children were interest, and women were routinely violated. We have tried to avoid gratuitously subjecting the reader to offensive language and images, but we are describing a horrifying reality.

Part One

The Capitalized Womb

1

The Mother of Slavery

"VIRGINIA WAS THE MOTHER of slavery," wrote Louis Hughes.

It wasn't just a figure of speech.

During the fifty-three years from the prohibition of the African slave trade by federal law in 1808 to the debacle of the Confederate States of America in 1861, the Southern economy depended on the functioning of a slave-breeding industry, of which Virginia was the number-one supplier. When Hughes was born in 1832, the market was expanding sharply.

"My father was a white man and my mother a negress," Hughes wrote.[1] That meant he was classified as merchandise at birth, because children inherited the free or enslaved status of the mother, not the father. It had been that way in Virginia for 170 years already when Hughes was born.

Partus sequitur ventrem was the legal term: the status of the newborn follows the status of the womb. Fathers passed inheritances down, mothers passed slavery down. It ensured a steady flow of salable human product from the wombs of women who had no legal right to say no.

Most enslaved African Americans lived and died without writing so much as their names. The Virginia legal code of 1849 provided for "stripes"—flogging—for those who tried to acquire literacy skills. A free person who dared "assemble with negroes for the purpose of instructing them to read or write" could receive a jail sentence of up to six months and a fine of up to a hundred dollars, plus costs.[2] An enslaved person who tried to teach others to read might have part of a finger chopped off by the slaveowner, with the full blessing of law.

So it was an especially distinguished achievement when in 1897 the sixty-four-year-old Louis Hughes published his memoir, titled *Thirty Years a Slave: From Bondage to Freedom: The Institution of Slavery as Seen on the Plantation and in the Home of the Planter*. Like the other volumes collectively referred to as slave narratives, it bears witness to a history slaveowners did not want to exist: the firsthand testimony of the enslaved.

By the time Hughes was twelve, he had been sold five times. The third time, he was sold away from his mother to a trader. "It was sad to her to part with me," he recalled, "though she did not know that she was never to see me again, for

Louis Hughes's author photograph.

my master had said nothing to her regarding his purpose and she only thought, as I did, that I was hired to work on the canal-boat, and that she should see me occasionally. But alas! We never met again."

The trader carried the boy away from the Charlottesville area that had been his home, down the James River to Richmond. There he was sold a fourth time, to a local man, but Hughes "suffered with chills and fever," so the dissatisfied purchaser had him resold. This time he went on the auction block, where he was bought by a cotton planter setting up in Pontotoc, Mississippi—a booming region that had recently become available for plantations in the wake of the delivery of large areas of expropriated Chickasaw land into the hands of speculators.

Slaves were designated by geographical origin in the market, with Virginia- and Maryland-born slaves commanding a premium. "It was held by many that [Virginia] had the best slaves," Hughes wrote. "So when Mr. McGee found I was born and bred in that state he seemed satisfied. The bidding commenced, and I remember well when the auctioneer said: 'Three hundred eighty dollars—once, twice and sold to Mr. Edward McGee.'"[3]

McGee had plenty of financing, and he was in a hurry; he bought sixty other people that day.[4] A prime field hand would have commanded double or more, but even so, the $380 that bought the sickly twelve-year-old would be more than $10,000 in 2014 money.[5]

Like the largest number of those forcibly emigrated to the Deep South, McGee's captives were all made to walk from Virginia to Mississippi, in a coffle.

Southern children grew up seeing coffles approach in a cloud of dust.

A coffle is "a train of men or beasts fastened together," says the Oxford English Dictionary, and indeed Louis Hughes referred to the coffle he marched in as "a herd."[6] The word comes from the Arabic *qáfilah*, meaning "caravan," recalling the overland slave trade that existed across the desert from sub-Saharan Africa to the greater Islamic world centuries before Columbus crossed the Atlantic. With the development in the late fifteenth century of the maritime trade that shifted the commercial gravity of Africa southward from the desert to the Atlantic coast, coffles were used to traffic Africans from point of capture in their homeland to point of sale in one of Africa's many slave ports.

But the people trudging to Mississippi along with Louis Hughes were not Africans. They were African Americans, born into slavery and raised with their eventual sale in mind. Force-marched through wilderness at a pace of twenty or twenty-five miles a day, for five weeks or more, from can't-see to can't-see, in blazing sun or cold rain, crossing unbridged rivers, occasionally dropping dead in their tracks, hundreds of thousands of laborers transported themselves down south at gunpoint, where they and all their descendants could expect to be prisoners for life.

Perhaps 80 percent of enslaved children were born to two-parent families—though the mother and father might live on different plantations—but in extant slave-traders' records of those sold, according to Michael Tadman's analysis, "complete nuclear families were almost totally absent." About a quarter of those trafficked southward were children between eight and fifteen, purchased away from their families. The majority of coffle prisoners were male: boys who would never again see their mothers, men who would never again see wives and children. But there were women and girls in the coffles, too—exposed, as were enslaved women everywhere, to the possibility of sexual violation from their captors. The only age bracket in which females outnumbered males in the trade was twelve to fifteen, when they were as able as the boys to do field labor, and could also bear children.[7] Charles Ball, forcibly taken from Maryland to South Carolina in 1805, recalled that

> The women were merely tied together with a rope, about the size of a bed cord, which was tied like a halter round the neck of each; but the men . . . were very differently caparisoned. A strong iron collar was closely fitted by means of a padlock round each of our necks. A chain of iron, about a hundred feet in length, was passed through the hasp of each padlock, except at the two ends, where the hasps of the padlocks passed through a link of the chain. In addition to this, we were handcuffed in pairs, with iron staples and bolts, with a short chain, about a foot long, uniting the handcuffs and their wearers in pairs.[8]

As they tramped along, coffles were typically watched over by whip- and gun-wielding men on horseback and a few dogs, with supply wagons bringing up the rear. In the country coffles slept outdoors on the ground, perhaps in tents; in town they slept in the local jail or in a slave trader's private jail. Farmers along the route did business with the drivers, selling them quantities of the undernourishing, monotonous fare that enslaved people ate day in and day out.

Sometimes the manacles were taken off as the coffle penetrated farther South, where escape was nearly impossible. But since the customary way of disposing of a troublesome slave—whether criminally insane, indomitably rebellious, or merely a repeated runaway—was to sell him or her down South, drivers assumed that the captives could be dangerous. Coffles were doubly vulnerable, for robbery and for revolt, so security was high.

The captives were not generally allowed to talk among themselves as they tramped along, but sometimes, in the midst of their suffering, they were made to sing. The English geologist G. W. Featherstonhaugh, who in 1834 happened upon the huge annual Natchez-bound chain gang led by trader John Armfield, noted that "the slave-drivers . . . endeavour to mitigate their discontent by feeding them well on the march, and by encouraging them"—*encouraging* them?— "to sing 'Old Virginia never tire,' to the banjo."[9] Thomas William Humes, who saw coffles of Virginia-born people passing through Tennessee in shackles on the way to market, wrote: "It was pathetic to see them march, thus bound, through the towns, and to hear their melodious voices in plaintive singing as they went."[10]

Sometimes coffles marched with fiddlers at the head. North Carolina clergyman Jethro Rumple recalled them stepping off with a huzzah: "On the day of departure for the West the trader would have a grand jollification. A band, or at least a drum and fife, would be called into requisition, and perhaps a little rum be judiciously distributed to heighten the spirits of his sable property, and the neighbors would gather in to see the departure."[11] Rumple was speaking, needless to say, of "heightening the spirits" of young people who had just been ripped away from their parents and were being taken to a fate many equated, not incorrectly, with death.

A coffle might leave a slave jail with more people than it arrived with. The formerly enslaved Sis Shackleford described the process at Virginia's Five Forks Depot (as transcribed by the interviewer):

> Had a slave-jail built at de cross roads wid iron bars 'cross de winders. Soon's de coffle git dere, dey bring all de slaves from de jail two at a time an' string 'em 'long de chain back of de other po' slaves. Ev'ybody in de village come out—'specially de wives an' sweethearts and mothers—to see dey solt-off chillun fo' de las' time. An' when dey start de chain a-clankin' an' step off down de line, dey all jus' sing an' shout an' make all de noise dey can tryin' to hide de sorrer in dey hearts an' cover up de cries an' moanin's of dem dey's leavin' behin'.[12]

An enslaved person could always be sold to another owner, at any time. When Louis Hughes's coffle reached Edenton, Georgia, McGee sold twenty-one of his newly purchased captives, taking advantage of the price differential in the Lower South to post an immediate profit on a third of his Virginia transaction and thereby hedge his debt to his financier.

Charles Ball described a deal that took place on the road in South Carolina:

> The stranger, who was a thin, weather-beaten, sunburned figure, then said, he wanted a couple of breeding wenches, and would give as much for them as they would bring in Georgia. . . . He then walked along our line, as we stood chained together, and looked at the whole of us—then turning to the women; asked the prices of the two pregnant ones.
>
> Our master replied, that these were two of the best breeding-wenches in all Maryland—that one was twenty-two, and the other only nineteen—that the first was already the mother of seven children, and the other of four—that he had himself seen the children at the time he bought their mothers—and that such wenches would be cheap at a thousand dollars each; but as they were not able to keep up with the gang, he would take twelve hundred dollars for the two. The purchaser said this was too much, but that he would give nine hundred dollars for the pair.

This price was promptly refused; but our master, after some consideration, said he was willing to sell a bargain in these wenches, and would take eleven hundred dollars for them, which was objected to on the other side; and many faults and failings were pointed out in the merchandise. After much bargaining, and many gross jests on the part of the stranger, he offered a thousand dollars for the two, and said he would give no more. He then mounted his horse, and moved off; but after he had gone about one hundred yards, he was called back; and our master said, if he would go with him to the next blacksmith's shop on the road to Columbia, and pay for taking the irons off the rest of us, he might have the two women.[13] (paragraphing added)

Women with babies in hand were in a particularly cruel situation. Babies weren't worth much money, and they slowed down coffles. William Wells Brown, hired out to a slave trader named Walker, recalled seeing a baby given away on the road:

Soon after we left St. Charles, the young child grew very cross, and kept up a noise during the greater part of the day. Mr. Walker complained of its crying several times, and told the mother to stop the child's d——d noise, or he would. The woman tried to keep the child from crying, but could not. We put up at night with an acquaintance of Mr. Walker, and in the morning, just as we were about to start, the child again commenced crying. Walker stepped up to her, and told her to give the child to him. The mother tremblingly obeyed. He took the child by one arm, as you would a cat by the leg, walked into the house, and said to the lady,

"Madam, I will make you a present of this little nigger; it keeps such a noise that I can't bear it."

"Thank you, sir," said the lady.[14]

From the first American coffles on rough wilderness treks along trails established by the indigenous people, they were the cheapest and most common way to transport captives from one region to another.

The federally built National (or Cumberland) Road, which by 1818 reached the Ohio River port of Wheeling, Virginia (subsequently West Virginia), was ideal for coffles. It was the nation's first paved highway, with bridges across every creek. Laying out approximately the route of the future US 40, its broken-stone surface provided a westward overland transportation link that began at the Potomac River port of Cumberland, Maryland. From Wheeling, the captives could be shipped by riverboat down to the Mississippi River and on to the Deep South's second-largest slave market at Natchez, or further on to the nation's largest slave market, New Orleans.

Beginning after the War of 1812 and continuing up through secession, captive African Americans were trafficked south and west by every possible method, in an enormous forced migration. "A drove of slaves on a southern steamboat, bound for the cotton or sugar regions," wrote William Wells Brown in his 1849 autobiography, "is an occurrence so common, that no one, not even the passengers, appear to notice it, though they clank their chains at every step."[15]

As railroads extended their reach, captives were packed like cattle into freight cars, shortening the time and expense to market considerably. Some passenger trains had "servant cars," though a cruder term was more commonly used. On his first trip to the South, in January 1859, the twenty-one-year-old New Englander J. Pierpont Morgan noted: "1000 slaves on train."[16]

They were trafficked by sea in oceangoing vessels that sailed the hard passage from the Chesapeake around the Florida peninsula to New Orleans, as well as in shorter voyages within that route. Ocean shipment was more expensive than a coffle, but it was quicker, so it turned the capital-intensive human cargo over more efficiently. Though exact figures do not exist, it is safe to say that tens of thousands of African Americans made the coastwise voyage from the Chesapeake and from Charleston to New Orleans and up the Mississippi to Natchez, as well as to Pensacola, Mobile, Galveston, and other ports. Maryland ports alone (principally Baltimore) shipped out 11,966 people for whom records exist between 1818 and 1853, and an unknown number of others before, during, and after that time.[17]

More slave ships came to New Orleans from the East Coast of the United States than from Africa. In a shorter recapitulation of the Middle Passage of a century before, the captives were packed into the hold with ventilation slats along the side to keep them from suffocating. Upon arrival, they were discharged into one or another of New Orleans's many slave pens, where they were washed, groomed, and fed, their skin was oiled, and their gray hairs, if they had any, were dyed or plucked out. On sale day, they were put into suits of the finest clothes many of them would ever wear, with perhaps even top hats for the men. Most would be sent to the cotton fields, where inhuman levels of work would be extracted from them through torture, or to Louisiana's death camps of sugar.

Following the precedent set by the Europeans, who referred to the coastal regions of Africa by their exports—the Ivory Coast, the Gold Coast, the Slave Coast—some writers have referred to the Chesapeake region as the Tobacco Coast.

But it would also be appropriate to call it the American Slave Coast.

2

Protectionism, or, The Importance of 1808

Industry: A particular form or branch of productive labour.

—Oxford English Dictionary

By HEMISPHERIC STANDARDS, THE African slave trade to English-speaking North America was petty.

According to database-backed estimates by David Eltis and David Richardson, only about 389,000 kidnapped Africans were disembarked in the ports of the present-day United States, the majority of them before independence. We say "only": that's an enormous number of captives to be dragged across the ocean, but Africans trafficked to the United States territory account for less than 4 percent of the estimated hemispheric total. An estimated 10.7 million Africans arrived alive to the Americas—out of an estimated 12.5 million embarked, leaving 1.8 million dead at sea.[1]

There is no way to figure the collateral damage to African populations from slave-raiding with even a rough level of accuracy. Slave-raiding, which was typically conducted by Africans, was notoriously wasteful of life, since only the young were taken and often the rest were killed. If one died for every one taken captive in slave raids—a speculative and possibly conservative number—that would mean the transatlantic slave trade killed or enslaved some twenty-five million Africans. It may have been double that; there's no way to know.

10

Barbados, an island about the size of the New York City borough of Queens, appears to have taken in more Africans than the entire territory of the present-day United States—493,000, according to Eltis and Richardson.[2]

Region	Estimated number of African captives
Chesapeake (Virginia and Maryland)	129,000
Lowcountry (South Carolina and Georgia)	211,000
New England and Mid-Atlantic	27,000
Gulf Coast	22,000
Total present-day US	**389,000**
Barbados	**493,000**

Estimates vary, of course; historian James McMillin believes that the number for the United States and its colonial predecessors exceeded 500,000. But that difference is not an order of magnitude.[3] Some captives were brought to North America from Barbados and other places in the West Indies, especially in the seventeenth century; while documentation is scarce, the numbers were small by comparison.

Africans were only the seed. By 1860, those few hundred thousand Africans had given way to four million African Americans. Each birth was, as Thomas Jefferson described it, "an addition to the capital."[4] The South did not only produce tobacco, rice, sugar, and cotton as commodities for sale; it produced people.

Virginia had been slave breeding since the seventeenth century. It had the oldest, most deeply rooted African American population, and the largest. With far more slaves than any other state, and with much of the land already burned out for tobacco farming by the time of the Declaration of Independence, the agricultural productivity per laborer in Virginia was low. The most profitable thing for Virginia planters to do with their growing slave population was to sell young people to traders for shipment down South.

The existence of slavery in the United States was taken for granted by the delegates to the Constitutional Convention in 1787; there was little or no discussion of abolishing it. The African slave trade, however, was very much in contention.

None of the delegates assembled at the Constitutional Convention could know that there would soon be a revolution in Saint-Domingue (the future Haiti), much less that as a consequence Napoleon Bonaparte would make a snap decision to sign his claim to Louisiana over to the United States in 1803. But it was commonly understood that territorial expansion was coming. Everyone knew that the upriver hinterlands of New Orleans were being invaded by Anglo-American settlers who would eventually take the territory over through force of numbers. Charleston merchants had a long-established web of overland trade that spread a thousand miles, across Georgia and what we now call Alabama and Mississippi into Louisiana. The frontiersmen of Kentucky and Tennessee were itching to drive the Native Americans out of Alabama and take their rich, black land. Spanish Florida had from the beginning been a security threat to South Carolina and Georgia; it, too, would come under US control. The market for slaves was about to explode in volume, and everyone knew it.

The question of who would have the concession to supply slave labor to this plantation-empire-to-come was an obstacle to unity at the Constitutional Convention. Slaveowners in Virginia, and in smaller numbers Maryland, were uniquely positioned to sell slaves into the emerging markets. Unlike the sugar slaves in the rest of the Americas or the rice slaves of South Carolina, the tobacco slaves of the Chesapeake didn't die off. It was an unprecedented phenomenon in the hemisphere: their numbers increased every year.

Prohibiting the African trade, as the New England delegates wanted to do, would create a grand bonanza for Virginia slaveholders—at the expense of South Carolina. But the delegates from Virginia had to compromise if they wanted South Carolina and Georgia to be part of the nation instead of an independent, belligerent, slave-importing competitor for power next door—one, moreover, whose territory was the overland gateway to territorial expansion into the Deep South.

Charleston, meanwhile, was the major receiving port in North America for kidnapped Africans, and South Carolina's delegates wanted no federal interference in their market-driven opening and closing of the trade. Chesapeake slaveowners, who were the only ones with sufficient surplus labor to sell off, wanted the African trade permanently closed. They compromised on a twenty-year guarantee that the foreign slave trade could exist on a state-by-state basis.

Accordingly, Article 1, Section 9 of the United States Constitution reads:

This 1762 map portrays Virginia, Carolina, and Georgia as extending all the way out to Louisiana, across densely forested territories held by different Native American confederations.

The Migration or Importation of such Persons as any of the States now existing shall think proper to admit, shall not be prohibited by the Congress prior to the Year one thousand eight hundred and eight, but a tax or duty may be imposed on such Importation, not exceeding ten dollars for each Person.[5]

"Importation of persons" was a euphemism; the framers were not so indelicate as to use the word *slave*. It was an anomalous provision, containing as it did the only date in the Constitution, and moreover the only price—the ten-dollar duty limit, which guaranteed that the African slave trade could not be taxed out of existence but implied that the slave trade might contribute revenue to the federal budget.*

That constitutionally stipulated deadline of January 1, 1808, is, from our perspective, one of the most important dates in American history, signaling as it does the transformation of the United States slavery industry.

---

*The ten-dollar duty was never imposed; South Carolina congressmen reacted with such fury when a Northern legislator proposed it that the measure was killed, and slave importation remained tax exempt.

For this reason, 1808 is also an essential date for understanding the making of African American culture. Kidnapped Africans had been arriving for almost two hundred years, repeatedly re-Africanizing American culture. No longer. The child was separated from the ancestors. With the changeover to a domestic slave trade, the long-established Afro-Chesapeake culture of Virginia and Maryland was diffused southward over several decades. Meanwhile, there was an overland march westward of the more recently Africanized Lowcountry of Carolina and Georgia across Alabama and into Mississippi and Louisiana, as well as vessels sailing around Florida to New Orleans. The two collided with each other in the presence of the smaller but potent creolized culture of Catholic Afro-Louisiana.

While the forces involved were greater than any single historical figure, individuals do make a difference in history. We will interpret key events and figures of American history in the light of their relationship to the profit-seeking machine African Americans were caught in. In particular, three slaveowning politicians loom large in our narrative as principal enablers of the territorial expansion of slavery and, consequently, of the slave-breeding industry: Thomas Jefferson, Andrew Jackson, and James K. Polk—a Virginian and two Tennesseans. All three were slaveholders, and like all slaveholders, their wealth was primarily stored in the form of captive human beings, so their entire financial base—personal, familial, social, and political—depended on high prices for slaves. To that end, they restricted the supply of captives by keeping the African trade closed; by opening new territory for US slavery to expand into, they expanded the demand for that restricted supply, greatly increasing as they did so the wealth and political power of the slaveowning class.

Fourteen years after the Constitution went into effect, on December 20, 1803, the territorial area of the new nation approximately doubled when French governor Pierre Clément de Laussat handed New Orleans over to President Jefferson's men, the Virginia-born W. C. C. Claiborne and the Maryland-born James Wilkinson. From that date until Louisiana became a state in 1812, the territory was effectively a colony of Virginia.

Jefferson's pointedly undemocratic rule of the Louisiana Territory assured favorable regulatory treatment for Virginia slaveowners. He asked Congress for, and got, monopolistic commercial restrictions on the slave trade into Louisiana:

importation into Louisiana of slaves from outside the United States was prohibited, but importation into Louisiana of slaves from within the United States was allowed.

With the Constitution having set the rules of the match, Virginia and South Carolina were in direct competition to supply the growing Louisiana slave market. It was an enormous business opportunity for Charleston's slave dealers, but time was running out. The twenty-year constitutional guarantee of protection for the African slave trade that South Carolina had insisted on had only four years to run. While Jefferson proactively worked to be sure that window was closed at the first possible moment, the Carolina merchants scurried to take maximum advantage of it.

South Carolina legislators knew full well that the prohibition of the African slave trade by federal law was on President Jefferson's action list; accustomed to turning the trade on or off as economic conditions dictated, they rescinded their previous ban against the African trade as soon as the news of the acquisition of Louisiana arrived at the end of 1803. Disregarding the anger the move provoked elsewhere, they opened the port of Charleston to cargoes of kidnapped Africans. Louisiana couldn't legally import Africans but South Carolina could, and could then resell the Africans to Louisiana via the domestic trade. Even with a substantial markup, they could still undercut the price Virginia farmers charged for African Americans.

The Constitution did not require the federal prohibition of importation of persons as of 1808; it merely stipulated that federal law could not prohibit it before that date. But Jefferson, who legally owned more than six hundred people during his lifetime, proactively made sure that importation of persons would indeed be prohibited as of the earliest constitutionally permissible date. So as not to have slave importation one day more than necessary, on December 2, 1806, he gave his Sixth Annual Message and asked Congress for a measure to end the African trade—more than a year before it could become effective. It was a move that was to his personal financial advantage as a Virginia slaveowner and to the disadvantage of South Carolina's wholesale slave importers.

To be sure, Jefferson framed ending importation of persons as a humanitarian act, and many historians have treated it that way, but it was not. Ending the African slave trade was protectionism on behalf of Virginia. It kept out the cheaper African imports so as to keep the price of domestically raised people high. Nobody in Chesapeake politics wanted more Africans coming in and devaluing their most significant assets. Over the long term, ending the African trade was a business coup on behalf of the slaveowners of Virginia, who were Jefferson's most loyal constituents throughout his increasingly disastrous second term as president (1805–1809).[6]

Moreover, ending the foreign slave trade to the United States was popular among other groups as well. Few white people wanted more black people in the country. Antislavery people wanted the African trade suppressed. The Southern public approved of ending the foreign slave trade as an antiterrorism measure: they were alarmed by the discovery of Gabriel's planned uprising in 1800, terrified by the bloody chain of events that had produced the newly declared nation of Haiti, and always frightened of the ever-present possibility of slave rebellion at their door.

But not everyone was happy about the prohibition of the African trade. Louisiana and Mississippi's burgeoning planter population wanted all the slave labor it could get, but once foreign sources were shut off pursuant to Jefferson's signature, no states besides Virginia and Maryland had quantities of laborers ready to sell. The French Creoles of Louisiana were particularly angry at having to pay high prices to the Virginians for English-speaking slaves when they could have gotten Africans much cheaper via Havana. But the United States shifted over to an entirely domestic slave trade in African Americans as of 1808—albeit with some ill-documented smuggling of captives from outside for ten more years or so, particularly by the Lafitte brothers' operations in Louisiana and Spanish Texas.

In a frenzy of last-minute stocking-up during the last legal year, in 1807 South Carolina merchants imported the highest one-year volume of Africans in the history of the North American trade, with the result that the market became glutted and captives from diverse parts of Africa died on Gadsden's Wharf awaiting sale.

Though the end of the African slave trade was a major commercial shift, its immediate impact was eclipsed by a mercantile catastrophe. Only a few days before the African trade ban went into effect, in one of the most radical economic actions ever taken by a president, Jefferson put an embargo on *all* foreign commerce rather than respond militarily to naval aggression by the British and the French. From then until 1815, American business was paralyzed—first by embargo, then by war—during which time the large-scale domestic slave trade could not develop. But it grew spectacularly after that.

❈

With the African trade halted, those slaves that continued to be bought and sold brought profit to US slaveowners, speculators, and slave trading firms instead of to British syndicates and African royals.

Slavery required a slave trade, and with the trade in kidnapped Africans shut off, there was no slave trade without slave breeding. By deliberately creating a scarcity of slave labor from which profit could derive for those who could supply it, the 1808 cutoff of the African trade created an economic incentive for farmers to deliver as many homegrown laborers to market as possible, as fast as possible.

The Maine-born Episcopal clergyman Joseph Holt Ingraham, writing under deep cross-gendered cover as Kate Conyngham, reported from Virginia in the 1850s that:

> So necessary is the annual decimation of slaves by sale to support these old decayed families, that it has become a settled trade for men whose occupation is to buy slaves, to travel through the "Old Dominion", from estate to estate. . . . Here he gets one, there another, and in a few weeks he enters Lynchburg, Alexandria or Richmond with a hundred or more. . . . As it is, slaves are raised here more as a *marketable* and money-returning commodity than for their productive labor.[7]

For Virginia's African Americans, Jefferson's legacy was unspeakably cruel. When the prohibition of importation of Africans made a massive business out of the already existing interstate slave trade in African Americans, black Virginians and Marylanders were trafficked in mass quantities to the newly opened territories, destroying family ties with every sale. The human cargoes that were driven in coffles and loaded onto ships were assembled by a network of traders' agents who fanned out through the farming territories of the Chesapeake, combing the slave-producing region to buy—one could say harvest—young people from farmers, often one at a time.

With the acreage under cultivation vastly expanding, the slave-selling industry touched the lives of everyone in the slave-trade zone, free or enslaved. It put a price on everyone—including on slaveowners, whose wealth was stored in the bodies of their always-liquidatable slaves and whose available credit was a function of the size of their slaveholdings. In the absence of a domestic supply of coin, slaves collateralized the credit that created new money.[8]

The growing nation of fortune hunters exerted a popular pressure to wrest more cotton-growing land from the Native Americans, a mission notably carried out by General Andrew Jackson under cover of the War of 1812, creating the land-and-slaves boom remembered as "Alabama Fever." Jackson's subsequent taking of Florida by military conquest and removing the South's remaining Native Americans from their ancestral lands—we now call it "ethnic cleansing"—made the entire Deep South safe for plantation slavery and further increased the demand for slave labor.

President James Monroe—a Virginian, as were all his predecessors in the office except John Adams—cracked down on what remained of the clandestine African trade, signing into law in 1820 a bill that declared participation in the foreign slave trade to be piracy and, as such, punishable by death. For the next forty-five years, the enslaved population of the United States was a closed system that expanded its numbers through sexual reproduction, more politely referred to as "natural increase." As W. E. B. DuBois described it, "slaves without [the African] slave trade became more valuable; with cotton culture their value rose still further, so that they were fed adequately and their breeding systematically encouraged."[9] Over time, more states, including South Carolina, got into the business of exporting African Americans to new territories.

While the North developed cities and industry, the South failed to build an infrastructure through which consumer goods could be distributed, and thus furnished no domestic market; instead, its profitable system of plantation-prisons expanded to new lands through imperial and military effort. After the worst depression the nation had yet suffered, President James K. Polk prosecuted the Mexican War to annex Texas for the Southern cotton kingdom, an action hotly contested by John Quincy Adams in the House and generally unpopular in the North. Once Texas was in the Union, Southern slave prices continued to climb, with only brief dips, until secession.

Polk's success in extending the Southern slave regime to Texas instantly— and predictably—revalued slaveowners' human portfolios upward. Including his own: Polk bought slaves in secret from his office in the White House on an ongoing basis during his presidency in the hope of building up his nest egg while he worked to extend the reach of American slavery.[10]

A century and a half later, what vocabulary to use in talking about this is still something of a work in progress.

It's hard to describe business without employing a business vocabulary. That said, economists who have written on the subject have sometimes used the antebellum business vocabulary too readily, as in the 1958 study that made the hypothetical assumption that "each prime field wench produced five to ten marketable children during her lifetime."[11] The history of slavery is a study in euphemisms, beginning with the near-universal use by refined whites of the polite term "servant" to refer to the individuals they legally owned. The colloquial term of choice used by slave traders, more often spoken than written, was, of course, "nigger," or, more politely, "Negro," which was considered synonymous with "slave"; judging from available evidence, the n-word was used by the enslaved themselves as freely as it is on playgrounds today, even as the vocabulary of slavery times echoes in colloquial black speech: *bitch, buck*, and the ultimate curse, *motherfucker.**

A number of people presently prefer to say "enslaved person" or some similar construction instead of "slave," arguing that Africans and African Americans never accepted their enslaved condition. This phrasing can become cumbersome in an extended discussion, and in talking about our subject, it can lead to a paradox of parallel constructions. If one was not a slave, then one had no owner, and one could not be sold. True enough on a moral level, but unfortunately, what we are describing is precisely the legal ownership and sale of slaves. We have chosen generally, and perhaps not entirely consistently, to use the words "enslaved" or "captive" to refer to people in their human aspect and "slave" to refer to their economic function and social position, and we hope the reader will cut us some slack.

The term "slave breeding" was much in use when it was happening—hurled as a charge on the floor of Congress and denounced as a damned lie by

---

*Unlike the words *funk, the blues*, or, for that matter, *nigger* (in its one-g form, *Niger*), the formerly unprintable *motherfucker* doesn't seem to have come from Britain. It's not clear how far back it goes, but it probably reaches back to slavery days as part of a vocabulary that ultimately became hipster lingo and emerged into print and recordings only slowly. The earliest written forms cited by the Oxford English Dictionary are two court cases from the South: in 1889 in Texas, "that God damned mother-fucking, bastardly son-of-a-bitch!" and, even more provocatively, in 1918, when the twenty-two-year-old African American soldier Sidney Wilson of Tennessee was court-martialed and sentenced to ten years at hard labor for having written a letter to the Memphis *Commercial Appeal* that said, "You is a line Mother Fucker, an' don't think the boys from Memphis is the onlyest one said that. We is goin' to straiten up this country, just as soon as we get some amonation," and another letter to his draft board that said, "you low-down Mother Fuckers can put a gun in our hands but who is able to take it out?" See Ellis, 89–90.

slaveowners.* But it wasn't merely an allegation: "slave breeding" was an ugly term that described a horrific reality.

Our ambivalence about terminology extends to the naming of wars, which is a highly political pursuit. Slavery ended as a consequence of what American history generally chooses to remember by the name of the Civil War, and which in official US documents was called the War of the Rebellion. But revolutions generally are civil wars, and vice versa; we argue that, depending on one's perspective, the most common names for the two great national conflicts—the Revolutionary War and the Civil War—could be flipped.

In recent years, it has become more common for scholars to speak of the War of Independence from Britain (commonly memorialized as the Revolutionary War) as a civil war, as indeed it was frequently described during the independence struggle. We will argue that the War of Independence not only did not intend to end slavery, but was fought in part to protect slavery from the growing power of British abolitionism. From the perspective of the enslaved, meanwhile, the war usually called the Civil War was the revolutionary war, because it ended chattel slavery and, in removing the appraised resale value of human beings from the balance sheets, remade the basis of American money.

---

*The general usage of the word "breeding" in reference to people was more common than it is today, as per the still occasionally heard phrase "well-bred."

A Literature of Terror

Were I about to tell you the evils of Slavery . . . I should wish to take you, one at a time, and whisper it to you. Slavery has never been represented; Slavery never can be represented.[1]

—William Wells Brown, address to the Female Anti-Slavery
Society of Salem, Massachusetts, 1847

"SLAVERY IS TERRIBLE FOR men; but it is far more terrible for women," wrote Harriet Jacobs, under the pseudonym Linda Brent. "Slaveholders have been cunning enough to enact that 'the child shall follow the condition of the *mother*,' not of the *father*; thus taking care that licentiousness shall not interfere with avarice."

Jacobs's memoir, *Incidents in the Life of a Slave Girl. Written by Herself,* describes her abuse by "Mr. Flint," whose real name was James Norcom of Edenton, North Carolina. One of only a few nineteenth-century slave narratives written by a woman, it is perhaps the frankest in its treatment of sexual exploitation:

> The slave girl is reared in an atmosphere of licentiousness and fear. The lash and the foul talk of her master and his sons are her teachers. When she is fourteen or fifteen, her owner, or his sons, or the overseer, or perhaps all of them, begin to bribe her with presents. If these fail to accomplish their purpose, she is whipped or starved into submission to their will. . . . Resistance is hopeless.[2]

Like Louis Hughes's memoir, Jacobs's was one of more than a hundred slave narratives published in book form in the nineteenth-century United States. All but forgotten until the 1960s, these testimonies have now become more familiar

$100 REWARD

WILL be given for the apprehension and delivery of my Servant Girl HARRIET. She is a light mulatto, 21 years of age, about 5 feet 4 inches high, of a thick and corpulent habit, having on her head a thick covering of black hair that curls naturally, but which can be easily combed straight. She speaks easily and fluently, and has an agreeable carriage and address. Being a good seamstress, she has been accustomed to dress well, has a variety of very fine clothes, made in the prevailing fashion, and will probably appear, if abroad, tricked out in gay and fashionable finery. As this girl absconded from the plantation of my son without any known cause or provocation, it is probable she designs to transport herself to the North.

The above reward, with all reasonable charges, will be given for apprehending her, or securing her in any prison or jail within the U. States.

All persons are hereby forewarned against harboring or entertaining her, or being in any way instrumental in her escape, under the most rigorous penalties of the law.

JAMES NORCOM.
Edenton, N. C. June 30

A runaway ad for Harriet Jacobs placed by James Norcom in the Norfolk Daily Beacon of July 4, 1835. This description of an abused slave makes clear the abuser's close familiarity, and stalker's fascination, with her, while affirming that the enslaved girl "absconded" without "any known cause or provocation."

outside specialist circles and are understood not only as an essential body of historical witness, but also a fundamental corpus of American literature. Frederick Douglass and William Wells Brown, foundational figures of African American letters, both wrote autobiographies detailing their experiences in slavery. Solomon Northup's *Twelve Years a Slave* (1853)—one of the best-written of the slave narratives, specific in its details, well-authenticated by scholars, and forgotten until the 1960s—is now well known because of the 2013 movie version, but there are many others. The narratives participate in literary tropes and publishing conventions of the day, and many bear the influence of editors and cowriters. But even discounting for occasional possibly exaggerated or invented scenes in some of them, their composite picture of the workings of the regime of slavery is remarkably consistent, mutually corroborating, and credible. They speak up for one another.

Bethany Veney, from Paige County, Virginia, reinforced the testimony of Jacobs when she wrote in her 1889 memoir:

> My dear white lady, in your pleasant home made joyous by the tender love of husband and children all your own, you can never understand the slave mother's emotions as she clasps her new-born child, and knows that a master's word can at any moment take it from her embrace; and when, as was mine, that child is a girl, and from her own experience she sees its almost certain doom is to minister to the unbridled lust of the slave-owner, and feels that the law holds over her no protecting arm, it is not strange that, rude and uncultured as I was, I felt all this, and would have been glad if we could have died together there and then.[3]

Also essential to our understanding is the collection of more than twenty-three hundred oral histories of formerly enslaved elders taken under the general direction of folklorist John A. Lomax by the Federal Writers' Project of the Works Progress Administration between 1936 and 1938, and by earlier researchers from Fisk and Southern University in 1929 and 1930. These twentieth-century narratives are of variable quality and reliability. There are some issues of mistrust of white interviewers by black subjects (though some interviewers were black); questions of reliability without recording (though a few were recorded); questions of memory (interviewees were recalling seventy years previously, and some were too young to remember their lives in slavery, though older respondents could recall events as early as the 1840s); and a heavily dialectized transcription style (though the emphasis on phonetic precision is not without value). But even so, this collection provides the most extensive description extant of slavery from the inside, and, as with the nineteenth-century slave narratives, the many voices corroborate each other over and over again. It has served as a significant source for many books about slavery published since the 1970s and has a major advantage over the nineteenth-century narratives in the much higher percentage of women represented. Unfortunately, about half the Virginia interviews were lost or destroyed, and there are no interviews from Louisiana at all.[4]

The silence from the eighteenth century is deafening. There were no slave narratives published in North America during the colonial era; there is only one known diary by a white indentured servant.[5] With only a few exceptions, the essential witness of the enslaved is largely missing from the historical record for the colonial years, which is why there will be few black voices in that section of our book.

No less than any other form of capitalism, American slavery capitalism was premised on continual expansion. The growth of the Southern economy was tied directly to the productivity of the capitalized womb, a term we use to refer to the way enslaved women's bodies functioned as the essential production engine of the slave-breeding economy, which in turn fueled a global economy that processed slave-grown cotton into mass-produced cloth.

That individual plantation owners practiced slave-breeding through the rape of enslaved women is attested to repeatedly in the testimony of the formerly enslaved and elsewhere. But beyond that, we argue, with the importation of African captives shut off, antebellum slavery was in the aggregate a slave-breeding system.

One of the functions of this slave-breeding machine was to chew up the black family, systematically, in every generation. Why might elite whites want a machine with which to destroy the black family? Most immediately, because the family was the strongest unit of social cohesion and resistance to slavery. But longer term, because destroying family webs systematically in every generation was the best way to guarantee the perpetual existence of an abject underclass whose labor and upkeep would remain as cheap as possible.

With every generation, the American elite became collectively more entrenched as its family structures expanded while the enslaved became collectively more entrenched as an underclass as its family ties were systematically, recursively cut.

For enslaved women, who could be freely violated in the cellar, the barn, the field, or anywhere else a captor chose, it was a system of terror. Beyond the purely venal incentive of unrestrained sexual activity, the existence of a market in young people created a financial incentive for slaveowners to intrude into the reproductive lives of enslaved women, leading to what Richard Follett calls an "intrusive policy of demographic engineering."[6] A blunter way of saying it is forced mating: enslaved women could be assigned to enslaved men by slaveowners, or impregnated by white men who had access to them.

Forced mating was sufficiently widespread to be documented in a surfeit of examples, from the presidential-slaveholder level on down. During James K. Polk's presidency, his brother-in-law Robert W. Campbell, who was watching the plantation for him, promised the president in a letter to purchase "young girls" for him with the purpose of force-mating them with Polk's "young men":

> when I go down [to the plantation] I [will] act according to my best Judgment about the husbands & wives of your people[.] I want to take down likely young girls for wives for your young men as there are to[o] gr[e]at a proportion of men on your farm for the women.[7]

The formerly enslaved Lueatha Mansfield of Bastrop, Louisiana, recalled that if a slaveowner "saw a fine woman or man on another plantation, he would buy him or her for breeding purposes in order to continue to have good able workers. If he didn't bring them on the same farm, he would arrange for them to breed from each other."[8]

Charles Grandy, enslaved in Virginia, recalled that "Marsa would stop de ole nigger-trader and buy you a woman. Wasn't no use tryin' to pick one, cause Marsa wasn't gonna pay but so much for her. All he wanted was a young healthy one who looked like she could have children, whether she was purty or ugly as sin."[9]

James Green, half Native American and half African American, sold away from his mother at the age of twelve for $800, recalled at the age of ninety-seven in 1938 in San Antonio, Texas, that "no one had no say as to who he was goin' to get for a wife. All de weddin' ceremony we had was with Pinchback's [the slaveowner's] finger pointin' out who was whose wife."[10] Much less did the "wife" have any say.

Before abolitionists made the term too notorious to use beginning in the 1830s, slave-sale advertisements might bluntly extol one or another woman as a "breeder," meaning that she had proven her ability to give birth to healthy children and recover to reproduce again at a time when many women died from childbirth. "If a woman wern't a good breeder she had to do work with de men," said Green, "but Pinchback tried to get rid of women who didn't have chillen."[11]

Fannie Moore, interviewed in North Carolina in 1937, recalled that (as transcribed): "De 'breed woman' always bring mo' money den de res', [even the] men. When dey put her on de block dey put all her chillun aroun her to show folks how fas she can hab chillun."[12] Mary L. Swearingen of Bastrop, Louisiana, paraphrasing her enslaved grandmother, said, "Whenever a woman was an extraordinary breeder, she was mated by the master to his own accord. Only sometimes the couples were happily married, and occasionally when a couple was happy, the master separated them by selling one or the other."[13]

Resistance to forced breeding was described by Mary Gaffney, enslaved in Texas, who described chewing cotton root as a contraceptive (as transcribed):

> Fact is, I just hated the man I married but it was what Maser said do. When he came to Texas he took up big lots of land and he was going to get rich. He put another negro man with my mother, then he put one with me. I would not let that negro touch me and he told Maser and Maser gave me a real good whipping, so that night I let that negro have his way. Maser was going to raise him a lot more slaves, but still I cheated Maser, I never did have any slaves to grow and Maser he wondered what was the matter. I tell you son, I kept cotton roots and chewed them all the time but I was careful not to let Maser know or catch me, so I never did have any children while I was a slave.[14]

We can't quantify forced mating; Eugene Genovese, who tried, estimated that "forced marriages affected perhaps one out of ten."[15] Every slaveowner was free to set his own rules; just as some provided better material conditions for their captives than others, some allowed them leeway in choosing partners, and some did not. According to quantitative historian Daniel Scott Smith, the "average slave" lived on a plantation with forty-one slaves; on larger plantations, there would presumably have been somewhat more choice of mates while on smaller ones there were fewer options.[16] But by virtue of being enslaved, no slave had fully free choice.

Most Americans' familiarity with the notion of slave breeding comes from popular fiction—in particular, from the 1957 Southern gothic novel *Mandingo,* set on an imaginary slave-breeding plantation.

The general reputation of *Mandingo* among critics is as a benchmark for bad writing. The first novel by the Illinois-born Kyle Onstott (1887–1966), previously the author of *The New Art of Breeding Better Dogs,* it was published by Denlinger's, an independent publisher of dog books in—where else?—Richmond, Virginia. Though it has been out of print for years as of this writing, *Mandingo* sold more than five million copies, mostly in mass-market paperbacks that sold for under a dollar at a time when strict controls on movie and television content made books the place to go for explicit material. It generated a franchise of fourteen novel-length sequels by various writers over thirty years; a Broadway play with Adolphe Menjou and Dennis Hopper that opened in May 1961 for eight performances; and, in the heyday of blaxploitation pictures, two big-budget movies with remarkably hateful dialogue.[17]*

With its fictional stud-farm plantation—Falconhurst, it was called—that bred and raised people for market, *Mandingo* disseminated an inaccurate and exaggerated vision, to say nothing of the stereotypes it promoted.

Not that *Mandingo* got it all wrong. As antebellum historical fantasy goes, its brutal, lascivious dystopia was closer to the truth of slavery than the nostalgic *Gone With the Wind* of a generation earlier, in which slaves were never sold and captive women loved their masters' children more than their own. But much is missing from *Mandingo*'s fetishistic gaze.

A generation of scholarly search has turned up no confirmed documentation of plantations devoted exclusively to breeding slaves, and some scholars have concluded they did not exist as such.[18]

There is a compelling reason why such a plantation wouldn't make economic sense: human beings grow too slowly to raise them as a cash-producing monocrop. The overwhelming majority of the enslaved on such a plantation would be children, but children brought very little money on the market, so they would have to be raised to maturity. Meanwhile, most of the adults would have been women weakened from pregnancy, so the farm would not be able to produce income from the sale of staple commercial crops. It would take seventeen to twenty years of raising the farm's children until they reached peak sale age, adding up to a huge barrier to entry for all but the very well capitalized.

Some farmers seem to have tried it. Drawing on a data sample from 1860 on farms in the Deep South—not even including the major slave-selling states of Virginia and Maryland—of 9,185 enslaved women between the ages of fifteen and forty-four and of 9,098 men, the economist Richard Sutch in 1972 identified

---

Mandingo (1975), starring James Mason; and *Drum* (1976), starring Warren Oates. Boxer Ken Norton played the title roles of each. Reviewer Vincent Canby described *Drum* as "nasty, lascivious, sadistic, mean, rude, evil, and supposedly erotic" (Talbot, 97, 207).

forty-seven "suspected breeding farms" on which enslaved women and children substantially outnumbered enslaved men. A farm in Drew County, Arkansas, had only two men but twenty-two women and twenty-seven children. Another in Wake County, North Carolina, counted 28 men, 38 women, and 120 children.[19] Michael Tadman, whose *Speculators and Slaves* is the landmark study of the demographics of the interstate slave trade, suggests that there might be other explanations for the gender imbalance of Sutch's data; "abroad marriages" to another plantation, for example, were common, though it seems unlikely that that could explain away the Drew County farm.[20] The meaning of Sutch's data, suggestive as it is, remains within the realm of speculation. But perhaps the most plausible explanation for the Drew County farm is that it *was* a slave-raising plantation, possibly relying on what several Federal Writers' Project interviewees called "stock" men—"portly" men who were used as studs for large numbers of women, as dramatized in *Mandingo*, and who did not have to do as much fieldwork.

There is some testimony—although not a lot—from diverse parts of the South that at least a few such "breeding men" existed. Jeptha Choice, born in 1835 in Texas, noted that (as transcribed) his "master was mighty careful about raisin' healthy nigger families and used us strong, healthy young bucks to stand the healthy nigger gals. When I was young they took care not to strain me and I was as handsome as a speckled pup and was in demand for breedin'. Later on we niggers was 'lowed to marry."[21] West Turner of Whaleyville, Virginia, told of a "stud man": "Joe was 'bout seven feet tall an' was de breedinges' nigger in Virginia. Didn't have no work to do, jus' stay 'round de quarters sunnin' hisself 'till a call come fo' him."[22] Ida Blackshear Hutchinson, born enslaved in Alabama in 1865 and interviewed in Arkansas in 1937, recalled family lore:

> My grandfather on my father's side, Luke Blackshear, was a "stock" Negro . . . six feet four inches tall and near two hundred fifty pounds in weight. . . . Luke was the father of fifty-six children and was known as the GIANT BREEDER. He was bought and given to his young mistress in the same way you would give a mule or colt to a child. Although he was a stock Negro, he was whipped and drove just like the other Negroes.[23]

There was one particularly horrible kind of operation in which this kind of slave breeding would have been profitable, and it appears to have been an inspiration to Onstott, who as a teenager met "Uncle Bob"—Robert Wilson, the direct inspiration for his character of Mede the Mandingo.[24]

According to Wilson's April 12, 1948, obituary in the *Elgin (IL) Daily Courier-News*, the accuracy of which we could not independently verify, he was 112 years old when he died in the Elgin State Hospital for Veterans and was a black veteran who had served in the Virginia Infantry—which was to say, the Confederate army—in 1862 and 1863. (There are already two unusual, perhaps suspect, features to this story: Wilson's extreme longevity, and the very rare situation of a black soldier in the Confederate army.) The obituary did not mention Wilson's local-legend status for allegedly having fathered hundreds of children at different plantations, but Wilson himself talked about it freely. While it's not possible to confirm or deny Wilson's tales of being used vocationally as a rapist of enslaved women, it's clear that: 1) Onstott did not make Wilson or his story up; 2) Wilson told his story to a number of people; and 3) there are mentions, albeit not very many, in oral histories from diverse locations in the South of such stock men. Certainly there was no reason that such an arrangement could not be put into practice, and it is consistent with the dehumanizing logic of the slave market.

Illinois journalist-historian Jon Musgrave fills in some details: though it was not legal to own slaves in Illinois, people did. Moreover, slaves were rented (or "hired") from Kentucky, sometimes more than a thousand of them, to work in the saltworks near Shawneetown. The Carolina-born John Hart Crenshaw, who began working as a young man in the violent, lawless environment of the saltworks, apparently raised his capital to get into business by kidnapping free people of color and illegally selling them away. He subsequently leased saltworks from the US government and became a very wealthy man, renting large numbers of slaves to do the brutal work of saltmaking.

Over a criminal career that lasted from the mid-1820s (when he was indicted for kidnapping) until secession, Crenshaw appears to have kidnapped hundreds of free black people, including in 1842 his cook Maria Adams and seven or eight of her children, whom he sold for $2,000 to John G. Kuykendall, a slave trader based in the then-independent Republic of Texas, and his father, Lewis.[25] He was said to have kept his victims in holding-pen cubicles on the upper floor of his mansion called Hickory Hill—still standing today and known as the Old Slave House—outside the ironically named town of Equality, Illinois.*

---

*Hickory Hill subsequently became a popular tourist stop as a haunted house and has been designated by the National Park Service as part of its Underground Railroad Network to acknowledge the existence of a "Reverse Underground Railroad" of kidnappers' networks that funneled people from free territories into slavery.

According to Musgrave (and Onstott, who wrote an article about it in the October 1959 issue of *True: the Men's Magazine*), that's where Robert Wilson came in. Crenshaw purchased Wilson, apparently in Virginia at the age of twenty in 1856. He put him to work, so goes the story, to impregnate the women held captive at Hickory Hill—a vocation Wilson claimed to have performed previously on other plantations—either to sell the children into a record-high market or because pregnant women and mothers brought a higher price than women whose reproductive abilities had not been proven. That Crenshaw was a kidnapper-trader and that Wilson was Crenshaw's captive between 1856 and 1859 seems to be well established. Was the third floor of Hickory Hill a rape room, or was that a lurid tall tale?

Perhaps this problematic, unverifiable, but possibly true story became the basis of a mega-bestseller in segregated 1957 because its narrative lent itself so conveniently to stereotypical libels of the black male and the black family. Although women, who had to do both field work and bear children, were doubly enslaved, it bears emphasizing that forced mating was a violation of enslaved men as well. The evidence—and common sense—suggests that enslaved men and women overwhelmingly worked as partners when they could and were emotionally devastated when their marriages were broken by sale.

That is not the story *Mandingo* tells. Nor the corollary: forced mating was a violation of the most basic notions of genealogy, which is a basic element of much African religion, and of economic legacy, which is the accumulated consequence of family.

For all the anecdotal testimony, circumstantial evidence, and creepy local lore, no one has proved with documents the existence of a single full-time specialized slave-breeding farm with a monocrop of fatherless children, much less a network of such farms constituting a supply chain. The best argument, pretty much a clincher, against the existence of such businesses on any significant scale is that there seems to be no mention of them in existing slave traders' letters. If such farms existed, they would have existed to supply traders, and mentions of them would presumably have turned up in traders' records—which, so far, they have not.

So, to be clear about the subject of our book: we do not contend that slave breeding was conducted by means of businesses specializing solely in human reproduction, though such operations may have occasionally existed. But that doesn't mean slave breeding didn't take place on a broad scale, only that it wasn't practiced as an isolated profession.

Slaves weren't the same kind of cash crop as tobacco or cotton; domestically raised slaves and staple crops functioned together, complementing each other's economic function to bring financial stability to a farm operation. For a farmer, slave breeding commonly functioned as a long-term play to stabilize his finances, while adult slaves' labor produced the price-volatile monocrops that provided cash flow. The proportion of revenue deriving from the sale of crops versus the sale of young people varied from farm to farm. In Virginia and Maryland, where tobacco crops were increasingly poor and wheat needed fewer hands, it appears that many farms needed to raise tobacco in order to grow slaves, rather than the other way around.

Every farm where the enslaved had children was a slave-breeding farm, if only because every newborn slave child increased an estate's net worth. But some farms were net consumers of slaves, as was the case in the rest of the hemisphere, where the enslaved died more often than they were born: in the United States, the rice plantations of South Carolina and Georgia and the sugar plantations of Louisiana were slave-consuming areas. And there was a conversion cycle: as new land was cleared and farms established, territories that formerly bought slaves from settled areas joined the growing ranks of sellers of slaves to the frontier, becoming slave breeders instead of slave consumers. Slave breeding was premised on continual expansion.

It is unsurprising that a planter who denied the humanity of the people he held captive for life would have thought of his laborers as breeding stock. Farms were, and are, all about increase: the creation and sale of a surplus. A handful of seeds brought bushels, out of which a farmer fed his family and sold or bartered the surplus for things he could not produce. Animals were expected to perform reproductively: mares, heifers, sows, nanny goats, or ewes that did not breed were sold off or were eaten by the family as a matter of basic farm management. The stallion, bull, boar, billy goat, or ram that didn't do its job would suffer the same fate. Runts were killed without a second thought so that the mother's nourishment could go to the stronger offspring. Slaves, whose legal status was comparable to that of livestock, were expected to provide a farm owner with marketable children.

There are occasional mentions of inducements for women who hit a pro-creation target: a frock, a piglet, a few weeks off from field labor. Before laws prohibiting manumission were passed, the grand prize was emancipation, as in John Guthrie's 1761 will in Virginia, which stipulated that "if Jeany brings ten live children" she would be freed.*[26] Slave breeding was premised on continual expansion.

But the real incentives were negative. "I have known a great many negro girls to be sold off, because they did not have children," wrote an unnamed slave owner to Frederick Law Olmsted.[27] The girl who tried to refuse being bred might be beaten, and, in the end, the girl who wasn't a "good breeder" could expect to be sold south, which was commonly understood to be the worst thing that could happen. There she would work among strangers under an overseer's lash in the cotton fields, or finish out her life after a few years on one of Louisiana's sugar plantations.

If, however, she was a good breeder, her children would suffer that fate instead.

Breeding seems to have been something of an obsession for men of property, who wanted to create the fastest horses, the best dogs, the cotton bolls that most perfectly fit the human hand, and the strongest slaves. From African slave raids forward, marketing people was a process of selection for desirable traits as well as survival of the fittest, with clear eugenic implications.

Some oral histories recall eugenic practices by slaveowners. Eighty-two-year-old Charlotte Martin, interviewed in Live Oak, Florida, recalled, as summarized by the interviewer, that her captor, Judge Wilkerson, "selected the strongest and best male and female slaves and mated them exclusively for breeding. The huskiest babies were given the best of attention in order that they might grow into sturdy youths, for it was those who brought the highest prices at the slave markets. Sometimes the master himself had sexual relations with his female slaves, for the products of miscegenation were very remunerative. These offsprings were in demand as house servants."[28]

Henry H. Buttler—born in Virginia, transported in a group to Arkansas in 1863 to escape Union forces, subsequently educated, and interviewed in Fort

---

*Manumission: the voluntary freeing of an enslaved person by his or her captor.

Worth, Texas, at the approximate age of eighty-seven—recalled that "the slaves were allowed to marry but were compelled to first obtain permission from the master. The main factor involved in securing the master's consent was his desire to rear negroes with perfect physiques."[29]

Above all, masters wanted bigger, stronger laborers. The Alabama-born Thomas Johns, interviewed in Cleburne, Texas, at the age of ninety, recalled that

> If a owner had a big woman slave and she had a little man for her husban'
> and de owner had a big man slave, or another owner had a big man slave,
> den dey would make the woman's little husban' leave, and dey would make
> de woman let de big man be with her so's dere would be big children,
> which dey could sell well. If de man and de woman refuse to be together
> dey would get whipped hard and maybe whipped to death. . . . Course
> even if it did damage de sale of a slave to whip him, dey done it, 'cause dey
> figured kill a nigger, breed another—kill a mule, buy another.[30]

The formerly enslaved Cornelia Andrews, interviewed in North Carolina at the age of eighty-seven, recalled a castration policy for eugenic purposes: "Yo' knows dey ain't let no little runty nigger have no chilluns. Naw sir, dey ain't, dey operate on dem lak dey does de male hog so's dat dey can't have no little runty chilluns."[31]

African Americans have been uncomfortably aware of the issue of eugenics all along, as when *Saturday Night Live* comedian Leslie Jones, responding to *People*'s designation of *Twelve Years a Slave* star Lupita Nyong'o as the world's "most beautiful person," stirred up a tweetstorm during the May 2, 2014, broadcast with what was surely one of the few mentions of forced mating on network television, let alone in the context of comedy. Nyong'o, born in Mexico City to Kenyan parents—in other words, not descended from American slavery—had recently won the Academy Award for her role in *Twelve Years a Slave*, in which she was stripped naked and whipped on camera. Jones, from Memphis and descended from slavery, contrasted her large physique with Nyong'o's petite one, drawing on the enduring power of the *Mandingo* franchise to make her point:

> See, I'm single right now, but back in the slave days? I would have *never*
> been single. I'm six feet tall and I'm *strong*! I mean, look at me, I'm a *Mandingo*! . . . I'm just saying that back in the slave days, my love life would have
> been way better. Master would have hooked me up with the best brother
> on the plantation, and every nine months I'd be in the corner havin' a
> superbaby!

It was an attempt at transgressive humor: presenting herself as a product of a eugenic process achieved through recursive rape and euphemized as "love life," she hurled the image of the blatantly exploitative *Mandingo* at the studiedly artistic *Twelve Years a Slave*. After ebony.com senior editor Jamilah Lemieux (among others) took offense at what she saw as Jones's minstrelsy, Jones tweeted back, "I would have been used for breeding straight up. That's my reality."[32]

When Sherry George of Birmingham, Alabama, was discovered in 2012 to be a distant white cousin of First Lady Michelle Obama, she responded to the news by saying, "I'm appalled at slavery. . . . I know that times were different then. But the idea that one of our ancestors raped a slave . . . I would not like to know that my great-grandfather was a rapist. I would like to know in my brain that they were nice to her and her children. It would be easier to live with that."[33]

Her tormented words express the difficulty of coming to terms with the reality of antebellum American slavery. The idea that one's ancestor was "nice" to the people he kept imprisoned has comforted many slaveowner-descended families—and, indeed, some were less cruel than others. But in the days when First Lady Michelle Obama's great-great-grandmother had a child fathered by the slaveowner's son, it was legal nonsense to speak of raping a slave.

To own a slave was to have a license for libertine behavior, because sexual violation was intrinsic to slavery. The slaveowner had the full legal right to do with his property as he saw fit, and sexual use was part of the portfolio of privileges. The oral-history interviewees described forced mating between the enslaved less frequently than they did sex forced on enslaved women by white men.[34] Perhaps a rough index for quantifying sex between enslaver and enslaved is the census, which in 1860 counted 588,352 "mulattoes," rating them as "13.25 per cent. of the whole colored class."[35] The census also attempted to explain why there were more mulattoes in the free states even though they were increasing faster in the slave states. It concluded that they were more likely to be manumitted (a phenomenon observable in the rest of the enslaved Americas as well): "the greater number of mulattoes in the condition of freedom has arisen chiefly from the preference they have enjoyed in liberation from slavery." The census's summary further noted "that of every 100 births of colored about 17 are mulattoes, and 83 are blacks," then went on to deplore the morals not of the white men who were impregnating captive black women, but of the free colored class.[36]

With new additions to the gene pool entering via intercourse with white men, an increasing portion of the enslaved population became lighter-skinned with every passing generation. "The time has passed by when African blood alone is enslaved," wrote the formerly enslaved Austin Steward in his 1857 memoir. "In Virginia as well as in some other slave States, there is as much European blood in the veins of the enslaved as there is African; and the increase is constantly in favor of the white population."[37]

Nor did enslaved women have legal protection against sexual abuse from enslaved men. In the 1859 case of *George v. the State of Mississippi*, in which an enslaved man was accused of raping an enslaved female child, the Mississippi supreme court noted that "a slave can only commit rape upon a white woman" and held that "the regulations of law, as to the white race, on the subject of sexual intercourse, do not and cannot, for obvious reasons, apply to slaves; their intercourse is promiscuous, and the violation of a female slave by a male slave would be a mere assault and battery."[38]

There was, then, legally no such thing as the rape of an enslaved woman. A Missouri court effectively affirmed that rape was legally what Saidiya Hartman calls the "normative condition" for enslaved women in that state when it sentenced the slave Celia to death in 1855.[39] Celia, who had no last name, was hung for having at the age of nineteen killed the man who had been raping her repeatedly since the day he purchased her at the age of fourteen.[40]

Slaveowners in the antebellum United States enjoyed full legal impunity for any sexual aggression they might commit against their human property. Concubinage with the master, the most privileged form of sexual servitude, tantalized enslaved women with the possibility of better living conditions and perhaps even the prospect of freedom, but it rested on the routine perpetration of atrocities, which often included selling the concubines, along with their children, after a few years. Enslaved concubines bedded down by the master watched their bastard daughters, lighter-skinned by half, grow up to do the same—raised to the office, as it were. The stories mostly went untold. Thomas Jefferson's second-generation family concubine Sally Hemings must have strongly resembled his deceased wife, Martha, since, according to Madison Hemings (Jefferson's son by Sally Hemings), the two women had the same father (the slave trader John Wayles), but there is no portrait extant of either woman, nor did either one leave a record of her thoughts.

If a slaveowner wanted to enjoy the adolescent daughters of his work force, he had absolute authority over them. No one would say no—not even his wife, who had few legal rights and who had perhaps grown up ignoring her own resemblance to the enslaved half sister who served her.

Slavery was rape. A person who has no right to refuse has no consent to give, so even absent the use of physical force at the moment of the sex act, an enslaved woman could not have consensual sex with a white man. The lack of consent was explained away by what has become known as the Jezebel libel, which characterized black women as incorrigibly licentious, always willing, and irredeemably dishonored from birth.

The logic of capital required safeguarding the slaveowners' human assets by dividing society into two rigidly defined, inescapable, color-coded castes—one of which was expected to reproduce according to moral protocols, and the other promiscuously. It was a common social understanding that did not need to be explained out loud, though visiting Northerners noticed and commented on it. The intermediate caste of free people of color, so prominent in other slave societies of the hemisphere, was very small in the slave societies of the United States, though in Louisiana and in the small Southern cities in general, their presence was acutely felt.

But whether a woman was white and respectably married, or black and laboring in the field, she was expected to reproduce as much as possible. Neither woman had the right to say no; Virginia law didn't even recognize spousal rape as a crime until 1986.

Jefferson, who by all accounts loved his wife, Martha Wayles Jefferson, dearly, nevertheless bred her to death with repeated pregnancies that killed her. John Quincy Adams nearly did the same: Louisa Catherine Johnson Adams, his cosmopolitan British-born wife, suffered depression and was in chronic poor health from her reproductive regime of fourteen pregnancies (Adams referred to them as "illnesses"), in which she miscarried nine times (five of them within the three and a half years before her first live birth). She had one stillborn child and four live children, one of whom died at the age of two.[41]

But those women at least got to choose their husbands, and their children were not sold. If that was the fate of the wives of the great men of the land, imagine how the lowest of the low fared. The slave narratives give us a glimmering of an idea, but they have to stand in as paradigms for the unheard testimonies of millions.

Natural Increase

CASH FOR NEGROES.

WANTED to purchase fifteen or twenty likely young NEGROES, for which I will give more than any Georgiaman in Baltimore. Apply at Anthony Egan's, opposite the Circus, Old Town, to
june 20—d4t   AUSTIN WOOLFOLK.

One of slave trader Austin Woolfolk's early advertisements. Baltimore Patriot and Mercantile Advertiser, *June 27, 1817.*

CASH FOR NEGROES, shouted the advertisements that ran in the newspapers of Virginia and Maryland.

The ads were running as early as 1810, but the War of 1812 brought them to a temporary halt.[1] After the Battle of New Orleans in January 1815 put a final victorious stamp on the war that had ended before the battle was fought, they proliferated as the economy began a ferocious expansion. An 1818 item in the New York–published *National Advocate* reports traders going around the streets of the Shenandoah Valley town of Winchester, Virginia, with labels reading CASH FOR NEGROES displayed on their hats.

There was always a market for "Negroes" in an expanding country of uncleared agricultural land. The key word was "cash." Slave traders dealt in cash, which could mean specie (silver or gold coins) but typically meant high-quality paper that could be readily exchanged for specie. That made their offers compelling in an environment where "money"—almost always meaning not coins, but credit—was otherwise hard to come by. In the antebellum plantation economy, slaves were far and away the easiest property to convert to cash that a farmer might have; when a crop failed or prices dived, slaveowners could cover their debts by selling some of their laborers. Land, by contrast, had little cash value. Traders often sold slaves on time-payment plans, but they paid cash when buying, so they were important financial intermediaries in the Southern agricultural economy, dispensing liquidity as they bought children and enlarging the overall supply of credit—which was to say, of money—through the terms they gave their customers. In other words, staple crops were a credit business, but slaves were a cash business; the Southern economy was the result of the way the two worked together.

As the United States threw itself into what has been retroactively called the "market revolution," transitioning from commerce based on imports to an ever more broadly based domestic market of producers and consumers, the domestic slave trade was the expression of that movement in the South. Addressing the American Anti-Slavery Society in 1839, Connecticut abolitionist Henry Stanton used the common business-textbook metaphor of cash flow as blood circulation to describe the system that carried human chattels from the Upper South to the expanding Deep South: "The internal slave trade is the great jugular vein of slavery; and if Congress [would] . . . cut this vein, slavery would die of starvation in the southern, and of apoplexy in the northern slave states."[2]

The rest of the world was well aware of this commerce. Writing in *Die Presse* of Vienna on October 25, 1861, the former *New York Daily Tribune* columnist Karl Marx noted "the transformation of states like Maryland and Virginia, which formerly employed slaves on the production of export articles, into states which raised slaves in order to export these slaves into the deep South."[3]

We can't quantify the domestic slave trade with any certainty, but we have a rough idea. Local transactions, not interstate trades, were likely the majority of slave sales; Stephen Deyle believes that at least two million people were sold in all, two-thirds of them in local transactions.[4] Tadman declines to put a total number on the interstate trade, but based on Tadman's work Deyle estimates that during the four decades or so prior to the end of slavery in the United States at least 875,000 enslaved people were taken southward, 60 to 70 percent of them trafficked in commercial transactions and the rest brought as a consequence of planter migration.[5] More anecdotally, Illinois-born Frederic Bancroft, the path-breaking historian of the domestic slave trade, wrote in 1921 of trips he took to the "Southwest" in 1902 and 1907: "I made it my business to inquire of every ex-slave I met as to how he or she came South, if not a native. In fully four cases out of five, they were brought literally by the traders."[6]

The southward trafficking of domestically raised slaves from what we will call the Upper South (Chesapeake and inland) and the Lower South (Carolina, Tennessee, Georgia) down into the "Southwest," or Deep South (western Georgia, Alabama, Mississippi, Louisiana, Arkansas, Texas), accompanied by a flow of money in the opposite direction, bound these distinct geographical regions together into a commercial circuit that made it possible to speak of "the South" as a single entity.

That in turn led members of the Southern elite to imagine themselves leaders of a nation built on the economic system of slavery, which thrived with a balance of cash crops and human property value. In the widely reproduced March 1861 words of Alexander Hamilton Stephens, the exultant, newly named vice president of the Confederate States of America, slavery was "the chief stone of the corner in our new edifice."[7]

Antebellum slavery was, in Gavin Wright's essential phrase, "a set of property rights."[8] In a collision of the ancient institution of slavery with free-market capitalism, the modern nineteenth-century American slavery industry made laborers into financial products: merchandise, cash, productive capital, collateral, and, even, at the end of the chain, bonds.

Besides working for the people who legally owned them, the enslaved could be "hired"—rented—out, generating an income stream that could pay off a mortgage on them. "Negroes are a kind of capital which is loaned out at a high rate, and one often meets with people who have no plantation, but who keep negroes to let and receive very handsome sums for them every month," wrote a German visitor to Savannah in 1860.[9] Enslaved children were often rented out, among them Frederick Douglass.

But revenue from slave labor was only part of the profitability of slavery. Selling slaves was part of the commerce at every little Southern junction. Most farmers who had slaves bought or sold them at one time or another. "In slavery, niggers and mules was white folk's living," recalled an unnamed formerly enslaved woman in Tennessee, who said that her former master "would sell his own children by slave women just like he would any others. Just since he was making money. . . . My mother sold for $1,000."[10]

The most obvious method of profit-taking in the slave market was by selling one or a few people at a time, as a plantation's younger captives came of age while working on the staple crop with which the farm was at least nominally identified. Typically that crop was tobacco, in the case of Virginia and Maryland; the twin industries of slave raising and tobacco raising went on as complements to each other, but slave raising was for many the more lucrative.

The sale of surplus laborers wasn't as explosive a cash-flow generator as a bumper crop, but it was more dependable, and the profits were significant. Financial and legal historian Richard Holcombe Kilbourne Jr. writes that "slaves represented a huge store of highly liquid wealth that ensured the financial stability and viability of planting operations even after a succession of bad harvests, years of low prices, or both."[11] Meanwhile, the seller had the important social distinction of being a planter instead of a slave breeder.

But neither were slaves merely labor to be jobbed out and merchandise to be sold for cash; they were also collateral with which to generate credit. Planters were chronically indebted, perpetually a year behind. They lived on credit, financing their operations with loans to be paid off by next year's crops. The security pledged for such arrangements was most commonly the planters' slaves, who were seen by lenders as largely risk-free collateral, even as they provided the labor that made the crop. If the crop failed, the laborers could be seized and sold on the open market. Meanwhile, the debt they collateralized added to the wealth of the slaveholding South; it was bundled into bonds that were sold to investors in New York, London, and beyond.

The financialization of enslaved people made them fundamental to the economy of the credit-driven slave society. The value of slaves, said James Gholson in the great Virginia slavery debate of 1832, "regulate[s] the price of nearly all the property we possess." Children born into slavery, blandly referred to as "increase," were capital assets at birth. They were the only way a planter's assets could grow as inexorably as his debts compounded.

With human capital shoring up balance sheets as collateral for mortgages in a heavily indebted society, reproductive potential was factored into the price of enslaved women as part of a farm's value as assessed by creditors. A slaveholder wrote to Frederick Law Olmsted that "a breeding woman is worth from one-sixth to one-fourth more than one that does not breed"; the ratio would presumably have been higher had women not died in childbirth so frequently.[12]

"Planters mortgaged their plantations, livestock, and slaves," writes Russell R. Menard of the colonial Lowcountry, "to expand their estates by purchasing additional land, livestock, and slaves."[13] Most of this value was in the slaves, who as human collateral were constantly exposed to the risk of sale away from their families and community.

That's how Thomas Jefferson funded the renovation of Monticello, by mortgaging the labor force that did the work. After he died in debt, his laborers were sold at auction. Often the decision was out of the slaveowner's hands. In Jefferson's case, the bitter end took the form of an estate liquidation after his death, so he never saw the human consequences of his impractical showpiece mansion and his extravagantly acquisitive ways: families separated forever on the auction block.

Much like a house mortgaged to a bank today, mortgaged slaves were security for those who put up the money for the mortgage, to whom the slaves were "conveyed." A mortgage financier might be a merchant, a church with an investment portfolio, a college, a bank, or, commonly, a wealthy individual with a large slavehold. A slave put up for sale had to be warranted not only of "good character" (not criminal-minded or rebellious) but "free of all incumbrance" (not already mortgaged).[14] Slaveowners had physical possession of, and legal title to, the enslaved, but to speak only of the slaveowners is to underestimate how broad was the stakeholding.

It is common today to hear people protective of the antebellum legacy go on the defensive by pointing out that the North profited from slavery too.

Certainly people and businesses in the North profited from slavery. Northern slaveowners sold off slaves to the West Indies and the South as slavery was ending in their territories, cashing in and diffusing their black population southward, though the numbers were tiny compared with those of the Chesapeake. New York monopolized the shipping of plantation products across the Atlantic. Northern banks captured the credit and foreign exchange generated by slave-driven agriculture, and bought and resold bonds collateralized by slaves. Hartford insurance companies, including the still-existing Aetna, sold policies to slave shippers and slaveowners, as Lloyd's of London had done before. After the African slave trade was declared piracy, Northern merchants illegally financed and equipped expeditions to supply industrial quantities of African captives to the plantations of Cuba and Brazil.

But the capital invested in the expansion of the agricultural South does not seem to have mostly come from the North. Slavery created its own distinct circuit in the American economy, since its most valuable commodity, slaves, had no value outside the slavery bloc. By the last three decades of slavery, the South was largely funding itself, or, as Kilbourne puts it, despite the "despair-filled declarations of Southern commercial boosters and conventions . . . most of the internal investment in the region was funded with savings that had been accumulated over several generations in numerous wealthy households throughout the Cotton Belt."[15] Those "savings" overwhelmingly took the form of slaves, who were the basis of this massive intra-Southern credit-circulation system.

The Constitution gave Congress the power to coin money but in 1804, when Jefferson annexed Louisiana, the only US coins in common circulation were copper pennies.[16] There was a chronic shortage in the South of "Spanish dollars"—the silver *pesos* minted in Mexico, also known as "pieces of eight," which were accepted as legal tender in the United States, because until the discovery of gold in California in 1848, there were no large money mines in the United States. What little specie there was in circulation before the Gold Rush was rapidly pulled to the centers of banking in the North and, especially in colonial days, was sucked across the ocean by the manufacturing and commercial heavyweight of the world, Britain. The workhorse of Southern commerce was bank-issued paper money, but it entailed the risk that the bank might fail and it lost its value with distance from the issuing bank.

Enslaved people were the savings accounts. In lieu of coin or trustworthy paper, people were money in the slaveholding South. Most economists will tell you, with variations in the wording, that three conditions must be met for a commodity to be considered money:

1) a means for conducting transactions ("medium of exchange");

2) retention of its worth over time ("store of value"); and

3) a way to keep accounts ("unit of account").[17]

Slaves easily fit the first two criteria. They were a unique kind of money—a "money thing," economists today might call it. They weren't a convenient medium of exchange the way coins were, but coin was rare and when no reliable bank paper was available for a transaction a store debt could be paid with a child, whether through transfer of ownership or hiring out. A slave might be handed over in lieu of a debt from a land purchase or lost to a cardshark as a thousand-dollar bet in a high-stakes game.

Slaves satisfied the second condition of being money as well. As a store of value, they were the most trusted form in which a slaveowner might save his money. They not only retained their value over time by maintaining their value through reproduction, but they increased that value by reproducing frequently, which is why slaveowners insisted on owning the children: people paid flesh-and-blood interest when they reproduced. This was a modern adaptation of an ancient concept, as David Graeber notes: "in many Mediterranean languages, Greek included, the word for 'interest' literally means 'offspring.'"[18] Frederic Bancroft wrote that:

> A stock-raiser indifferent to enlarging his herd was not so rare nor so absurd as a large planter that did not count the annual births and values that grew with the slave children. This increase alone was conservatively estimated to yield a net annual profit of from five to eight per cent after deducting all losses from age, illness or death. And even careless and spendthrift planters had such a passion to increase the number of their slaves that this human interest was regularly added to the principal, and thus compounded. A slaveholder twenty-five years old having 40 slaves might reasonably hope, without buying any, to become the owner of 150, or perhaps 200, slaves by the time he reached the age of sixty.[19]

If people were money, children were interest. That's why the rigidly enforced color-coded caste system of slavery offered no path to freedom even over multiple generations: no escape from the asset column could be permitted.

At first glance, it might seem that slaves didn't satisfy the third condition of being money, a unit of account. They were not what economists call a "sovereign currency." No government accepted them for taxes, duties, fines, licenses, or fees. That honor went to the dollar, a denomination that Thomas Jefferson had (in the absence of any domestic sources of silver) modeled on the Spanish dollar combined with a French-inspired decimal system of cents, all in pointed contradistinction to the British pounds-and-shillings system.[20]

But in another way, slaves *were* a unit of account. The white South kept score in slaves. A rule of thumb for estimating a Southerner's wealth was the number of slaves he had. And, as we will discuss, the Constitution's notorious three-fifths clause* was explicitly designed to allow the South to vote that kind of wealth, making slaves a unit of account for what was literally political capital.

---

*Article 1, Section 2, Clause 3 of the Constitution, subsequently invalidated by the Thirteenth Amendment, allows for the counting of three-fifths of "persons bound to service," i.e. slaves, in determining a state's representation in the House of Representatives, and, by extension, in calculating representation in the electoral college.

But if slaves were a kind of money, they were a nonconvertible domestic money, usable only inside the slave-trade zone. New York merchants wouldn't accept slaves in payment for manufactured goods from Britain. They did frequently become slaveowners via control of slaves pledged as collateral, but if slaves had to be seized in satisfaction of a debt, they could only be sold in the regions that used slave labor. Since slaves couldn't be used in trade outside the area of their circulation, they defined the economy of the region where they were traded.

For a money to be continually valuable, it must at times be defended by the government, even if the government is not the issuer. That happened in the case of slavery; Southern politicians were obsessively dedicated to preserving the monetary value of slaves, culminating in the cataclysmic war that ended the slave economy.

Owning people entailed risk: the person claimed as property might die, escape, or rebel. Those possibilities were best absorbed by large fortunes; slaveholding, the ultimate in inequality, was dominated by the wealthy. But taking on risk was essential for those who wanted to grow their fortunes fast. The Southwest was a magnet for high-spirited gamblers, especially in the Jacksonian era of wildcat banks. Young men in the South wanted to get rich *now*, before they died of some fever or distemper, so they went into cotton, plunging into debt to buy as many slave laborers, plant as much acreage, and get as fast a return as possible, then plow the profits into more land and slaves. But cotton acreage could only expand as fast as labor could be acquired to clear and cultivate it.

The reason slaves could not legally be created equal was not merely that appropriating one hundred percent of their labor was wildly profitable. Nor was it the many forms of comfort and pleasure they afforded their owners, nor even the owners' routinely expressed fear that if freed, the blacks would do to the whites what the whites had done to them.

It was that attributing fully human characteristics to the enslaved would have debased the coin of the Southern realm.

The four million enslaved in 1860 were not merely a labor force; they were the South's capital stock. Fanny Kemble quoted the words of "a very distinguished Carolinian" in her 1838–39 journal: "I'll tell you why abolition is impossible: because every healthy negro can fetch a thousand dollars in Charleston at this moment."[21]

Whether a slave child was ever sold in the market or not, his or her birth *created* money, in the form of credit, so the growth to four million enslaved people was in itself an economic expansion. The bottleneck in the creation of this unique form of sentient money was the capitalized womb.

Large landowners often preferred a strategy of buying slaves whenever they could get a good deal but never selling, whereas smaller farmers were more likely to need to sell an enslaved adolescent for cash to a regional trader's representative. The kingpin of the Jackson-era slave trade, Tennessean Isaac Franklin, grew his fortune by accumulating people, and then put the money they collateralized to work in the credit market of his place and time by lending to smaller fry, whose slaves were in turn pledged to him as collateral. An 1847 accounting of the deceased Franklin's estate valued the infants Andrew, George, Eliza, Larienia, Little Ann, Cynderrilla, Betsy, Shadrach, Sylvia, Lewis Edward, Noah, Isaac, Randolph, Washington, William, another Isaac, Meshac, and Matilda, along with "an infant child of Tracy Butler," at $75 each (more than $2,000 each in 2014 dollars). They were not being priced for immediate sale, but expertly appraised for estate valuation.[22]

Older slaves were depreciated. Minerva Granger, who had produced nine children while enslaved by Thomas Jefferson, was at the age of fifty-five appraised as being worth nothing.[23] Historian Caitlin Rosenthal explains that planters "appraised their inventory [of slaves] at market value, compared that with its past market value to assess appreciation or depreciation, calculated an allowance for interest, and used this to determine their capital costs. In a sense they were marking slaves to market."[24] The on-paper value of a child increased as he or she survived and grew, picking up around the age of eight, when he or she could begin to do a day's work. The price peaked in the late teens, when the full-grown laborer could do a long day's work and be advertised for sale as a "likely young Negro."

That now-archaic word "likely," ubiquitous in slave sale advertisements, had a cluster of converging meanings: vigorous, strong, capable, good-looking, attractive, promising—in other words, likely to reproduce.

5

Little Shadows

Common sense will tell us, that the consumption of a slave must be less than that of a free workman. The master cares not if his slave enjoy life, provided he do but live . . . even the soft impulse of sexual attraction is subject to the avaricious calculations of the master.[1]

—Jean Baptiste Say, *A Treatise on Political Economy*
(1803; 1821 translation)

CAPITAL IS USELESS IF it is not being put to work, and slaveholders in every era were diligent in extracting the maximum return from their human capital.

Slaves were not allowed to be idle. Black men, women, and adolescents worked long days under the punishing sun doing hard labor that would have killed a white man, or so said the white men who expropriated their labor. In cold weather, they shivered in the rain and froze their fingers in the ice and snow.

In the early days of Chesapeake colonization, working alongside indentured English, Scotch, and Irish paupers and convicts, the enslaved cut down the hardwoods, pulled up the stumps, turfed the slopes of the plantations, and manicured the grounds of the master's estate. They plowed, planted, weeded, harvested, and cured tobacco, rolled it in hogsheads down to docks they had built, and loaded it onto boats that enslaved boatwrights had constructed, piloted by enslaved navigators.

They fired the bricks with which they built the great houses that they painted, maintained, and staffed. Enslaved laborers built the stone walls, the zigzagging "worm" fences, and the roads, barns, sheds, smokehouses, and cesspools, as well as the cabins where they lived, six or eight or ten to a room. They forged the decorative ironwork, made the furniture, and except for hoes, chains, and a few other items, they even made the tools they made everything else with. "Almost all the implements used on the plantation were made by the slaves," recalled Louis Hughes. "Very few things were bought."[2]

They were most commonly employed in repetitive monocrop farming, the kind that is most destructive to the land. Every future Confederate state except Virginia raised quantities of cotton, and there were regional monocrops of tobacco in the Chesapeake, rice in the Sea Islands and Tidewater of South Carolina and Georgia, and sugar in south Louisiana. From London, Karl Marx succinctly described the practice in an October 25, 1861, newspaper column:

> The cultivation of the Southern export articles, cotton, tobacco, sugar, etc., carried on by slaves, is only remunerative as long as it is conducted with large gangs of slaves, on a mass scale and on wide expanses of a naturally fertile soil, that requires only simple labor. Intensive cultivation, which depends less on fertility of the soil than on investment of capital, intelligence and energy of labor, is contrary to the nature of slavery.[3]

On this matter, which was more or less conventional wisdom, Marx agreed with his ideological adversary the *Economist*, which had printed in 1859:

> The truth is, that Slavery *could* only be profitable on rich, large, and sparsely populated soils. The profit it yields it can only yield while the first fertility of a soil is unexhausted, and, therefore, where land is unsettled, and the labour need not be of a very earnest or skilful kind.[4]

When utilized this way, slave laborers were known for being utterly unenthusiastic workers. In some plantation regimes, the work was deliberately kept heavy so as to leave the labor force too tired to revolt. A note accompanying a hoe on display at Edisto Island Museum explains: "Until after the Civil War, even large tracts of land on Edisto were cultivated primarily by slaves using hoes, not animal-drawn plows. With the natural increase in the slave population, it was considered 'good management' to keep the work force as busy as possible."

Perhaps neither Marx nor the *Economist* realized that slaves' labor was not only crude. They brought a wide variety of expertise to skilled work. Enslaved craftsmen were the artisan class of both the colonial and the antebellum South. They helped build the White House and the US Capitol. Their knowledge, together with the forced labor of enslaved muscle, transformed forest, bramble, and swamp into the Anglo-American idea of civilization.

Planters and merchants arranged for their particularly talented artisans to be taught special skills by European craftsmen, which had the side effect of establishing a knowledge base among the community of the enslaved. It enhanced their monetary value: slaves deemed to be "skilled" brought more money in the market for both renting-out and sale. They worked as mechanics and tradesmen, discouraging white tradesmen from immigrating. Skilled slaves did cabinetry, woodworking, ironworking, tailoring, dressmaking, and jewelry-making; they were usually better than white craftsmen, if only because white craftsmen, if they were any good, often quit their trade as quickly as possible to go into planting rather than compete economically with slaves, or bought a slave to do the work for them.

Knowledge from Africa was basic to planters' fortunes, nowhere more than in the cultivation of rice. In the unhealthy marshes of the Lowcountry of South Carolina and Georgia, teams of enslaved laborers with interconnecting jobs—specialized task labor, not gang labor like cotton—operated complex plantations they had built with skills that were unknown to Europeans. They did this mostly in the absence of the masters, who fled their plantations in mortal fear of disease during the hot months, leaving only an overseer to run an all-black plantation.

The great rice plantations of the Lowcountry could never have been built and staffed with free labor. No one would have done that work voluntarily. Attacked by clouds of stinging insects in rattlesnake-ridden swamps, the rice slaves built dams, dug miles of ditches, burned the ground cover in spectacular nocturnal conflagrations, pulverized the earth, spent their days standing barefoot and waist-high in foul-smelling stagnant water, hoed endless rows of rice, regulated how much of the heavier salt water versus how much of the lighter fresh water to allow into the sluice gates they had designed and built, chased away the thick flocks of migrating bobolinks that could devastate a crop, winnowed the rice in baskets they had woven according to African practice, pounded the husks off with African-style tall pestles in mortars, and cut and hauled wood to build the barrels with, while also raising or catching much of the food they ate.

The homes of the enslaved brought little comfort after the work day. Josiah Henson, who published several iterations of his autobiography—the bestselling of the slave narratives, because Henson was said to be the inspiration for Harriet Beecher Stowe's character of Uncle Tom—recalled in the earliest (1849) and possibly most accurate version that:

> Our lodging was in log huts, of a single small room, with no other floor
> than the trodden earth, in which ten or a dozen persons—men, women,

and children—might sleep, but which could not protect them from dampness and cold, nor permit the existence of the common decencies of life. There were neither beds, nor furniture of any description—a blanket being the only addition to the dress of the day for protection from the chillness of the air or the earth. In these hovels were we penned at night, and fed by day; here were the children born, and the sick—neglected.[5]

Old age was especially miserable for the enslaved. When Jefferson's slaves got too old to work, he routinely cut their rations in half.[6] Aged slaves were a drag on a planter's profits, at which point it was cheaper to turn them loose and let them die off premises. The Virginia code of 1849 provided a fine of fifty dollars for "any person who shall permit an insane, aged or infirm slave . . . to go at large without adequate provision for his support," which perhaps attests to how common the practice was.[7] Isaac Mason, born enslaved in 1822 in Kent County, Maryland, recalled in his memoir that

> My grandfather, in consideration of his old age and the time being past for useful labor, was *handsomely* rewarded with his freedom, an old horse called the "old bay horse"—which was also past the stage of usefulness— and an old cart; but, alas! no home to live in or a place to shelter his head from the storm.[8] (emphasis in original)

They labored and reproduced and died and were replaced, without retaining the proceeds of their labor for their own needs, while the people who claimed to be their owners generally spent as little as possible on their maintenance. Field laborers, who had little or no direct contact with the master and his family, wore rough, cheaply manufactured "negro shoes," and covered their bodies with osnaburg, or "negro cloth," of jute or flax, a little softer than burlap. George White of Lynchburg, Virginia, recalled that "Dat ole nigger-cloth was jus' like needles when it was new. Never did have to scratch our back. Jus' wiggle yo' shoulders an' yo' back was scratched."[9] They perhaps, but not necessarily, got summer and winter varieties. "Do you recollect

Isaac Mason's author photograph.

that you have not given your Negroes Summer clothing but twice in fifteen years past[?]" wrote Georgia Sea Island plantation manager Roswell King to his boss, Constitution framer and absentee gentleman farmer Pierce Butler, at Butler's mansion in Philadelphia.[10] Thomas Jefferson's captives got one blanket per family every three years, but when Monticello was leased out during his presidency, an overseer failed to distribute blankets for five years.[11]

They did hard labor in the same clothes all day, every day. When 225 enslaved people asserted their freedom by escaping into the custody of British rear admiral George Cockburn during his invasion of the Chesapeake in the War of 1812, Cockburn feared that the dirty rags they came clothed in might spread disease. He issued the men bright red jackets, which, said his commanding officer, Admiral Alexander Cochrane, might "act as an inducement to others to come off," and he gave them military training, which they had previously been kept away from.[12]

Sometimes they worked without clothes at all. Enslaved children and sometimes even post-pubescent adolescents commonly were naked or barely clothed. Charles Ball recalled his first workday in a South Carolina cotton field after being trafficked from Virginia:

> More than half of the gang were entirely naked. Several young girls, who had arrived at puberty, wearing only the livery with which nature had ornamented them, and a great number of lads, of an equal or superior age, appeared in the same costume. . . . [O]wing to the severe treatment I had endured whilst traveling in chains, and being compelled to sleep on the naked floor, without undressing myself, my clothes were quite worn out, I did not make a much better figure than my companions; though still I preserved the semblance of clothing so far, that it could be seen that my shirt and trowsers had once been distinct and separate garments.[13]

Denied basic hygiene, the laborers' funk bothered masters enough to become a conversational commonplace among slaveholders, who typically attributed it to a racial characteristic, referring if necessary to Thomas Jefferson's racist pseudo-factbook *Notes on the State of Virginia*: "they secrete less by the kidnies, and more by the glands of the skin, which gives them a very strong and disagreeable odour."[14]

Enslaved women made the soap the slaveowner washed with. They carded, combed, spun, weaved, knitted, cut out, sewed, mended, washed, starched, and ironed the fine clothes the master's family wore, and they worked into the night after a long day's labor to dress their own families a little better, though at times there were difficult to enforce laws that forbade slaves from dressing above their station. Domestics, who were on display to guests, typically dressed much better than field laborers, often in hand-me-downs of the master or mistress.

In eighteenth-century Maryland, liveried coachmen drove the imported "chariots" in which the masters rode. In wealthy antebellum Mississippi, they wore velvet topcoats in the heat as they drove the masters' barouches. Enslaved blacksmiths forged iron shoes for the horses that enslaved grooms put up at night. Enslaved fiddlers played at the Saturday night dances, and when the masters hunted foxes, enslaved houndsmen blew the hunting horns.

The enslaved brought to the masters' table the food they supplied and prepared, and they kept everything the guests saw spotless, all on an unforgiving schedule. Urban slaves generally had a better diet than those on the plantations, and African Americans seem to have generally eaten better than slaves did on Antillean sugar plantations. But the quality and availability of food varied sharply from plantation to plantation, and most had an insufficient diet by modern standards.

The enslaved laborers who built the University of Virginia were fed the basic slave diet: greasy fat bacon and cornmeal, purchased in industrial quantities. A hogshead of bacon could weigh 900 pounds or more, and plantations bought commensurate quantities of molasses. "Some slaves enjoyed a wide variety of foods," write Kenneth Kiple and Virginia King, "[but] others suffered from a seldom if ever supplemented hog-and-corn routine, while most existed on a basic meat-and-meal core with some supplementation."[15] That monotonous diet of "hominy and hog" was the mainstay for the enslaved, as well as for poor whites, in much of the South, though the enslaved of the Chesapeake and Lowcountry generally ate better than those in the Deep South. Unfortunately, the Southern-raised white corn, the most commonly eaten variety, contained no vitamin A.[16] Milk was in short supply in the South, so the enslaved often got little or no calcium. They shocked doctors with their high rate of geophagy—eating clay or dirt, a malnutrition-related behavior especially associated with pregnant women—which caused a range of health problems.[17] Arguing in favor of feeding the enslaved in a way he considered adequate, the overseer Roswell King Jr. of Butler Island, Georgia, wrote of the plantation's 114 enslaved children in an 1828 letter published in the *Southern Agriculturalist* that "it cost less than two cents each per week, in giving them a feed of Ocra soup, with Pork, or a little Molasses or Hommony, or Small Rice. The great advantage is, that there is not a *dirt-eater* among them."[18]

Black cooks knew how to work with the animal parts the master's family didn't want—the offal—and they also knew how to prepare grand Christmas feasts. It was common for the enslaved to tend a garden patch after a long day of work, and Sundays, usually a day off, could be spent hunting or fishing if owners allowed it. But even so, slaves were often malnourished and therefore sickly; the typical food expenditure for an enslaved laborer in Virginia was about a quarter that of a free laborer. Henry Watson, born in 1813 near Fredericksburg, Virginia, who was sold six times and whose experience was especially harsh, recalled the routine he knew in 1820s Mississippi:

> In the morning, half an hour before daylight, the first horn was blown, at which the slaves arose and prepared themselves for work. At daylight another horn was blown, at which they all started in a run for the field, with the driver after them, carrying their provisions for the day in buckets. . . . [They] worked until such time as the driver thought proper, when he would crack his whip two or three times, and they would eat their breakfasts, which consisted of strong, rancid pork, coarse corn bread, and water, which was brought to them by small children, who were not able to handle the hoe.
>
> As soon as Harry, the driver, has finished his breakfast, they finish likewise, and hang up their buckets on the fence or trees, and to work they go, without one moment's intermission until noon, when they take their dinner in the same manner as their breakfast; which done, they go again to work, continuing till dark. They then return to their cabins, and have a half hour to prepare their food for the next day, when the horn is again blown for bed. If any are found out of their cabins after this time, they are put in jail and kept till morning, when they generally receive twenty-five or thirty lashes for their misdemeanor.[19] (paragraphing added)

Charles Ball recalled a scene he witnessed while accompanying his master on travels in South Carolina:

> After it was quite dark, the slaves came in from the cotton-field, and taking little notice of us, went into the kitchen, and each taking thence a pint of corn, proceeded to a little mill, which was nailed to a post in the yard, and there commenced the operation of grinding meal for their suppers, which were afterwards to be prepared by baking the meal into cakes at the fire.
>
> The woman who was the mother of the three small children, was permitted to grind her allowance of corn first, and after her came the old man,

and the others in succession. After the corn was converted into meal, each one kneaded it up with cold water into a thick dough, and raking away the ashes from a small space on the kitchen hearth, placed the dough, rolled up in green leaves, in the hollow, and covering it with hot embers, left it to be baked into bread, which was done in about half an hour.

These loaves constituted the only supper of the slaves belonging to this family for I observed that the two women who had waited at the table, after the supper of the white people was disposed of, also came with their corn to the mill on the post and ground their allowance like the others. They had not been permitted to taste even the fragments of the meal that they had cooked for their masters and mistresses.[20] (paragraphing added)

Slave cabins did not have kitchens; cooking, if done indoors, was done in the fireplace. On some plantations children were fed out of troughs, eating with their hands or improvised spoons out of a communally served mush of cornbread, molasses, or whatever else was customary.[21]

Beginning with maternal, fetal, and infant malnutrition, it's hardly surprising that the enslaved were more susceptible than free people to most infirmities, including crib death, infant mortality of all kinds (including infanticide), death in childbirth, and injuries and deterioration to the mother from repeated childbirth, along with typhoid, cholera, smallpox, tetanus, worms, pellagra, scurvy, beriberi, kwashiorkor, rickets, diphtheria, pneumonia, tuberculosis, dental-related ailments, dysentery, bloody flux, and other bowel complaints. The health conditions of the enslaved were aggravated by overwork, accidents, and work-related illnesses such as "green tobacco sickness," today known as nicotine poisoning, which plagued tobacco workers.[22] The heavy work regimes they endured wore down their bodies and aged them prematurely, with childbirth-related fatalities limiting women's life spans even more than the men's.

The enslaved had a greater immunity to some diseases than the whites, though: the sickle-cell trait is believed to have evolved as a defense against malaria, to which many of the enslaved were immune, though they might become ill from sickle-cell disease. Some Africans were also immune to the yellow fever that on occasion killed large numbers of whites in fierce epidemics.

Africans brought a vast lore of medicines (and poisons) from Africa, and on occasion learned the use of local herbs and roots from the Native Americans. Attentive slaveowners learned from the medical knowledge of the enslaved, as in the case of smallpox vaccination, which spread in the hemisphere through the knowledge of Africans.[23] In colonial Boston, Cotton Mather heard of smallpox vaccination from the enslaved Onesimus, whom Mather's congregation had given him as a present: "Enquiring of my Negro-man *Onesimus*, who is a pretty Intelligent Fellow, Whether he had ever had ye *Small-Pox* he answered, both, *Yes*, and, *No*; and then told me, that he had undergone an Operation, which had given him something of ye *Small-Pox*, & would forever preserve him from it." Onesimus had been vaccinated for the disease in Africa, and told Mather it was a common practice among the "Gurumantese" (Akan or Twi people of the Gold Coast, now called Ghana), "& who ever had ye Courage to use it, was forever free from ye fear of the Contagion. He described ye Operation to me, and shew'd me in his Arm ye Scar, which it had left upon him."[24]

Especially in colonial days, slaveowners sometimes doubled as doctors. William Byrd II, the founder of Richmond, had a large medical library and gave his enslaved frequent "vomits" and "purges." The enslaved were used as guinea pigs for experimental treatments that advanced the practice of medicine in the United States. An aspiring doctor or dentist in the South might buy an old or infirm slave to practice on. The nation's first teaching hospital, at the Medical College in Charleston, used live enslaved people for demonstrations and dead ones for dissection. The "father" of modern gynecology, generally portrayed in medical historiography as an innovative figure, was the South Carolina surgeon J. Marion Sims, whom one historian refers to as "the Architect of the Vagina." Sims refined his innovations by operating experimentally on the genitals of enslaved women he kept for that purpose. In this way, he developed a surgical repair for vesico-vaginal fistulas, using an infection-resistant silver suture, and more generally he popularized the use of surgery for gynecological problems, becoming quite wealthy in the process. In a "hospital" he built in his backyard in Montgomery, Alabama, he operated on a woman named Anarcha thirty times, sewing her insides without anesthesia and giving her opium afterward. He also kept women named Lucy and Betsy for this purpose, describing the expense of their maintenance as a research cost. After perfecting his treatment, he subsequently moved to New York, where he founded the Woman's Hospital and continued experimenting surgically; since there was no slavery in New York, he practiced on poor Irish women, performing thirty surgeries on one Mary Smith.[25]

Later, there was an entire lucrative branch of "slave medicine" dedicated to "negro diseases," in which naming a disease could be the road to prestige and higher fees for a physician. The Virginia-born Dr. Samuel A. Cartwright described at a professional conference a medical condition he had discovered called *drapetomania*, in a paper reprinted in *DeBow's Review* in 1851. Drapetomania's victims were "Negroes," and its chief symptom was an irresistible urge to run away. When milder therapy failed, Dr. Cartwright prescribed "whipping the devil out of them." He also described another purported disease, *dysæsthesia æthiopica*, or "hebetude of mind," whose symptom was commonly described by overseers as "rascality," and which was "much more prevalent among free negroes living in clusters by themselves, than among slaves on our plantations, and attacks only such slaves as live like free negroes in regard to diet, drinks, exercise, etc."[26] Dr. Cartwright was serious; the Southern medical profession had taken up the call to demonstrate the purportedly separate and inferior physical and mental characteristics of what was considered to be the "Negro race."

Slaveowners had the power of life and death, and despite slaves' monetary value as human property, death came to some from "punishments"—torture— and other violence inflicted by the owner or his agents, as Fannie Berry recalled in Petersburg, Virginia: "sometimes if [you rebelled], de overseer would kill yo'."[27] Others committed suicide.

It was much preferable to be enslaved in town. The urban enslaved generally enjoyed better material conditions than those on the plantation, as well as more independence of movement and association, more chances to make money, and, especially in port towns, a better chance to escape to free territory. Most of the work in Southern towns was done by "hired" slaves; the urban South developed in direct proportion to the amount of slave-rental that went on. Such Southern industrial work as there existed was mostly done by the enslaved, who sometimes managed to collect a bit of incentive pay.

Robert S. Starobin estimates that there were between 160,000 and 200,000 industrially employed slaves by the 1850s, 80 percent of them owned by the businesses' owners and the rest rented.[28] Ironworking was heavily dependent on enslaved labor. Slaves mined lead, salt, and coal. Turpentine production, a large industry, was almost entirely done by enslaved laborers. They manufactured rope, tanned leather, baked bread, cut lumber out of the Dismal Swamp till all the trees were gone, and operated gristmills and printing presses. In shipyards and textile mills, they worked side by side with poor whites in a sometimes violently uneasy coexistence that worked to the disadvantage of the enslaved.[29]

Enslaved workers cleaned and repaired Southern streets, laid down turn-pikes, and dredged canals. They marked twain, shoveled coal, and sometimes were scalded to death or blown up in boiler explosions on the riverboats, with the more dangerous jobs going to older, less salable men. They built almost all the railroads in the South, as a March 30, 1852, advertisement in the *Southern Recorder* of Milledgeville, Georgia, illustrates:

IMPORTANT SALE OF NEGROES, MULES, &C.
ON THE 27TH DAY OF APRIL NEXT.

The undersigned having nearly completed their contract on the South Carolina Railroad, will positively sell, without reserve, on TUESDAY, the 27th day of April next, at Aiken, South Carolina to the highest bidder –

130	NEGROES
85	MULES,
3	HORSES,
90	CARTS and HARNESS,
25	WHEELBARROWS
190	SHOVELS,

Railroad PLOWS, PICKS, Blacksmith's, Carpenter's and Wheel-right's Tools, &c.

These Negroes are beyond doubt the likeliest gang, for their number, ever offered in any market, consisting almost entirely of young fellows from the age of twenty-one to thirty years, some few boys, from twelve to sixteen years of age, and four women.

Among the fellows are first rate Blacksmiths, Carpenters, Coopers, Brick-moulders, Wheel-rights and Wagoners.

Among the women, one excellent Weaver and Seamstress, another one, a good Cook. All well trained and disciplined for Rail and Plank-road working. . . .

Terms Cash. J.C.SPROULL & CO., Aiken, S.C., immediately on the Railroad, 16 miles from Hamburg.[30]

In the towns and cities no less than on the plantations, virtually all domestic servants were enslaved; a white Southern woman who hired out as a maid had fallen on hard times indeed. In some cities, notably New Orleans and Charleston, enslaved women were major vendors of foodstuffs, whose customers were typically enslaved domestics doing the mistress's shopping.

Slaves learned the hard way to anticipate the master and mistress's slightest wishes. Having their ears boxed would be the least of it; they could be exposed naked to be brutally whipped with a knotted cowhide, leaving their backs and buttocks bloody raw. Slave narratives commonly contain accounts of severe punishment resulting in horrible scarring, maiming, or even death, for minor or even imagined infractions, for domestics no less than for field hands. A single example, selected almost at random from the literature, is J. D. Green's testimony: "When I was fourteen years old my master gave me a flogging, the marks of which will go with me to my grave, and this was for a crime of which I was completely innocent."[31]

Whether the victims were female or male, the torture of the enslaved also had a sexual component. There is little or no documentation of male-on-male intercourse, something unspeakable in that era, but there is much testimony about slaves being stripped naked and flogged, which today we would call sexual abuse. There are many stories of deliberate sadism in the slave narratives. After Henry Watson was trafficked to Natchez, he was sold to a man who beat him daily:

The first morning I was severely flogged for not placing his clothes in the proper position on the chair. The second morning I received another severe flogging for not giving his boots as good a polish as he thought they had been accustomed to. Thus he went on in cruelty, and met every new effort of mine to please him with fresh blows from his cowhide, which he kept hung up in his room for that purpose.[32]

Isaac Mason recalled that

whenever I did anything that was considered wrong . . . I had to go to the cellar, where I was stripped naked, my hands tied to a beam over head, and my feet to a post, and then I was whipped by master till the blood ran down to my heels. This he continued to do every week, for my mistress would always find something to complain of, and he had to be the servant of her will and passion for human blood. At last he became disgusted with himself and ceased the cruel treatment. I heard him tell her one day—after he had got through inflicting the corporal punishment—that he would not do it any more to gratify her.[33]

The enormous rawhide bullwhips were designed to lacerate; accounts mention whips cutting flesh to bone. Solomon Northup used the word "flaying."[34] "Many a time I've heard the bull-whips a-flying," recalled Lizzie Barnett, a centenarian interviewed in the 1930s, "and heard the awful cries of the slaves. The flesh would be cut in great gaps and the maggots would get in them and they would squirm in misery."[35] These beatings—and other tortures too numerous to mention—could, and occasionally did, kill.

The enslaved had no right to refuse intimate services to the people who could order them beaten. Harriet Jacobs writes of her great-aunt Nancy, who "slept on the floor in the entry, near [the mistress's] chamber door, that she might be within call" through six of Nancy's pregnancies, all resulting in premature births.[36]

Sometimes enslaved concubines got special treatment, but sometimes not. Henry Watson's owner had taken an enslaved woman "to wife" and had two children by her; she was "out in the field all the day, and in his room at night."[37] James Green recalled that "de nigger husbands weren't the only ones dat keeps up havin' chillen. De mosters and the drivers takes all de nigger girls day want. One slave had four chillen right after the other with a white moster. Their chillen was brown, but one of 'em was white as you is. But dey was all slaves just de same, and de niggers dat had chillen with de white men didn't get treated no better."[38]

The brutality of forced concubinage took place within the more fundamental brutality of being property: even the nicest master might be forced to pay his debts by selling his favorite slave, along with his children by her.

It mattered not whether white women disliked this state of affairs, since they had little or no legal standing themselves. The South Carolina plantation mistress Mary Boykin Chesnutt, author of a widely read diary and a good friend of Confederate First Lady Varina Davis, wrote angrily in 1861,

[O]urs is a *monstrous* system and [full of] wrong and iniquity . . . Like the patriarchs of old our men live all in one house with their wives & their concubines, & the Mulattoes one sees in every family exactly resemble the white children—& every lady tells you who is the father of all the Mulatto children in every body's household, but those in her own, she seems to think drop from the clouds or pretends so to think.[39]

Harriet Jacobs said it even more bluntly:

Southern women often marry a man knowing that he is the father of many little slaves. They do not trouble themselves about it. They regard such children as property, as marketable as the pigs on the plantation; and it is seldom that they do not make them aware of this by passing them into the slave-trader's hands as soon as possible, and thus getting them out of their sight. I am glad to say there are some honorable exceptions.[40]

There is much testimony like that of Savilla Burrell, interviewed at the age of eighty-three in Winnsboro, South Carolina, who recalled (as transcribed) that "Old Marse wus de daddy of some mulatto chillun. De 'lations wid de mothers of dese chillun is what give so much grief to Mistress. De neighbors would talk 'bout it and he would sell all dem chillun away from dey mothers to a trader. My Mistress would cry 'bout dat."[41]

Enslaved women were used for milk extraction, in the common case of wet nurses, or "sucklers"—women whose own babies had died or were pushed aside. Isabella Van Wagenen, better known as Sojourner Truth, born enslaved in New York in 1797, was said to have exposed her breasts to a proslavery crowd in Indiana that had questioned her gender while shouting that "her breasts had suckled many a white babe, to the exclusion of her own offspring."[42] Since enslaved women were pregnant so often, there was little need for a slaveowning white woman to feed her own baby, with the result that baby cotton planters grew up sucking from black women's breasts. Nursing women might be lent out to a family member, or rented out to a stranger. In the latter case, the slaveowner was selling the protein and calcium out of the woman's body.

While a "prime field hand"—young, healthy, strong, and male—was the benchmark of the slave market, the premium-priced captives were young female sex slaves, or "fancy girls," who were light skinned or even passable as white. A teenaged "fancy girl" purchasable either for private sexual use or pressed into commercial service by a pimp could bring a multiple of what even a "prime field hand" might command.

A number of reports from the later days of slavery mention blond-haired, blue-eyed slaves on sale—the children of enslaved women, despite their phenotype. Fredrika Bremer, the Swedish novelist who visited Richmond in 1851 as part of an extended journey, wrote in her widely read *Homes of the New World* of visiting "some of the negro jails, that is, those places of imprisonment in which negroes are in part punished, and in part confined for sale." She visited one "where were kept the so-called 'fancy girls,' for fancy purchasers," and yet another where "we saw a pretty little white boy of about seven years of age, sitting among some tall negro-girls. The child had light hair, the most lovely light-brown eyes, and cheeks as red as roses; he was nevertheless the child of a slave mother, and was to be sold as a slave. His price was three hundred and fifty dollars."[43]

The enslaved caste grew with every generation. Escape, whether by flight or by manumission, was difficult to achieve; the census counted 1,011 escaped slaves in 1850, "about 1/30 of one percent" of the enslaved.[44] People in the Chesapeake might escape to free territory in the North, but in the Deep South, that was practically impossible. The lighter-skinned an enslaved person was, the greater the possibility that he or she might be able to steal away, escape the dragnet that routinely captured unaccompanied black people, and pass for white under a new identity; Thomas Jefferson allowed two of his four children by Sally Hemings to do so, under which cover they disappeared from the historical record.

Notwithstanding the severity of the whippings that occupy such a prominent role in slave narratives, the threat of sale was the most powerful coercive weapon in the slavemaster's arsenal. As Isaiah Butler of Hampton County, South Carolina, put it: "Dey didn't have a jail in dem times. Dey'd whip 'em, and dey'd sell 'em. Every slave know what 'I'll put you in my pocket, sir!' mean."[45] No aspect of slavery was more emblematic of its horror than forced separation of families, which took place regularly and publicly in the theater of the slave auction.

Slave marriages were not binding on the slaveowner, and forced mating was always possible, sanctioned by law and by custom. Even those whose families remained together knew that the fortunes of a slave could change in a heartbeat. The enslaved lived with the knowledge that they or a loved one—a mate, a sibling, a child—might at any moment be removed without warning from their familiar world and taken away from their family without so much as a fare-thee-well.

The slave trade routinely destroyed marital relationships, along with all other family ties, by selling one or the other partner away. Robert H. Gudmestad estimates that "forced separation . . . destroyed approximately one-third of all slave marriages in the Upper South."[46] Marriage between slaves was sometimes solemnized and celebrated on the plantation ("jumping the broomstick"), but it was a charade: there was no such thing as legal marriage for slaves. As Matthew Jarrett, born in 1848 and interviewed in Petersburg, Virginia, put it, "don't mean nothin' lessen you say 'What God done jined, cain't no man pull asunder.' But dey never would say dat. Jus' say, "Now you married."[47]

An individual slaveowner might respect slave marriages, but when he died, the heirs would have to divide up the estate at auction.

Masters often tried not to let slaves know in advance they were going to be sold, since they tended to run away if they knew. They ran away in any case, everywhere there was slavery. Among the many fragmentary song lyrics collected as part of the Federal Writers' Project oral histories, none appears more frequently than *Run, nigger, run / Patter-roller* catch you*, a song sung by both white and black in the South. The surveillance society was a reality to African Americans in slavery—not that people didn't run away anyway. Maroons often hid out in their home region, sometimes hiding for years in underground dugouts or hard-to-access places, sometimes returning to the plantation surreptitiously at night for food and on occasion returning to the workforce after negotiating conditions for their return.

Men ran away more than women, who might be gang-raped if caught, as described by the fugitive Lewis Clarke in 1842: "They know they must submit to their masters; besides, their masters, maybe, dress 'em up, and make 'em little presents, and give 'em more privileges, while the whim lasts; but that ain't like having a parcel of low, dirty, swearing, drunk, patter-rollers let loose among 'em, like so many hogs."[48]

Masters grew up with "little shadows," personal child servants who did everything for them, were not allowed to fight back when they were abused, and were in deep trouble if anything happened to their young master. The three-quarters white William Wells Brown was an enslaved "playmate" at the age of nine for a five-year-old master to whom he was related. The position carried the privilege of wearing a white linen suit; he had to audition for it against "some fifteen" others by doing gymnastics. After the family moved to Missouri, Brown recalled that

> William had become impudent, petulant, peevish, and cruel. Sitting at the tea table, he would often desire to make his entire meal out of the sweetmeats, the sugarbowl, or the cake; and when mistress would not allow him to have them, he, in a fit of anger, would throw any thing within his reach at me; spoons, knives, forks, and dishes would be hurled at my head, accompanied with language such as would astonish any one not well versed in the injurious effects of slavery upon the rising generation.[49]

When masters became older, they sometimes bet and lost their childhood companions to strangers in card games, or they might be sold to pay an extraordinary expense. In Roswell, Georgia, a town founded by Pierce Butler's former

---

*patteroller = patroller

manager Roswell King as a summer refuge for the wealthy, James Stephens Bull-och sold off four enslaved people to pay for his younger daughter Mittie's grand wedding at Bulloch Hall on December 22, 1853.[50] Bulloch did not sell Mittie's personal slave, whose too-appropriate name was Toy. Nor could the "shadow" of Mittie's troubled half brother Daniel Stuart Elliott be sold, because Daniel had previously shot and killed him in a fit of temper.[51] But Bess, the attendant of Bulloch's older daughter Anna, was sold together with her son John for $800. Anna, who had no husband and was therefore of no economic importance, sub-sequently became governess to Mittie's children, one of whom was the future president Theodore Roosevelt Jr.

"When your marster had a baby born in his family," recalled an unnamed formerly enslaved woman in Tennessee, "they would call all the niggers and tell them to come in and 'see yur new marster.' We had to call them babies 'Mr.' and 'Miss' too."[52] If a little white boy with a Roman-numeraled name said up was down, his captive black playmate had better agree. Once the boy was grown into a planter, if he said up was down, who dared correct a man who was accustomed to punishing disagreement with torture? Virtually all of the members of the Southern aristocracy that seceded from the United States grew up with such a regime, going back ten generations for the oldest families among them.

Up became more down with every passing decade, and more incompatible with the outside world. The build out of the slavery ideology became more elabo-rate, more radical, and more delusional as each generation began from a more doctrinally inbred point of departure. Meanwhile, it became more belligerent, accompanied by a vigilant suppression of dissent.

Antislavery opinions were not to be expressed publicly in the slave states. That was considered traitorous and was repressed with violence that was some-times spontaneous and sometimes organized. Any perceived slight to the system of slavery could provoke a hair-trigger response. There was not even a pretense of free speech on the subject of slavery in the South, nor did slavery's defenders want anyone in the North to criticize, or even mention, slavery. The enslaved were, needless to say, not to speak against their captivity. They were to be happy, or else. They loved their master, or else.

Unlike Africans—or, more horrifying to slaveowners, the "French Negroes" of Haiti—African Americans were believed to be docile, since scrupulous atten-tion was paid to keeping them ignorant of military technique. That was one of the attractions of "Virginia and Maryland Negroes" in the market—they had been raised to an unquestioning submission to the work regime, or so it was believed.

That belief was disproved daily. For all their powerlessness and the almost unimaginable degree of their exploitation, the enslaved were social actors—of course they were—who, despite their great disadvantages, had some ability to negotiate their conditions. They also had the dangerous power that stemmed from slaveholders' fear of them.

Rebellions existed wherever there was slavery, in every era, because everywhere, always, the enslaved were at war with their condition. Rebellions happened on the slave ships, on the plantations, and in the towns. Herbert Aptheker, writing in 1943, found "records of approximately two hundred and fifty revolts and conspiracies in the history of American Negro slavery," defining such incidents as involving ten slaves or more and with the intention of obtaining freedom.[53]

Smaller rebellions were ubiquitous. Every runaway was a rebel, and there were runaways at almost every plantation. Often escape attempts were unsuccessful and violently repressed, while others were temporary with a negotiated end, and some were successful and permanent. Twenty-two-year-old Ona Judge, who was Martha Washington's personal servant, escaped from the President and First Lady of the United States in Philadelphia in 1796 after learning she was to be given away as a wedding gift. She married a free black man in Portsmouth, New Hampshire, and managed to avoid falling prey to the attempts at recapture that George Washington attempted against her until he died in 1799.[54]

Every slave who got into a suicidal, or perhaps murderous, fight with an intolerable overseer was a rebel. Every slave who took something from the master (called "stealing," as if the master were not the one stealing from his captives) was a rebel. Every enslaved person who learned to read was a danger. The now-common term "day-to-day resistance," proposed by Raymond A. and Alice H. Bauer in 1942, expresses the ongoing inconformity of the enslaved with their status.[55]

The larger rebellions, small though they were in military terms, were extraordinarily effective at bringing the war on slavery forward: the Stono rebellion (1739), the alleged New York conspiracy (1741), Gabriel's conspiracy (1800), the German Coast rebellion (1811), Denmark Vesey's alleged conspiracy (1822), Nat Turner's rebellion (1831), and others were sensational news when they happened. To slaveowners, they were a portent of apocalypse.

Major foreign wars were also occasions of slave rebellion, though it was folded into the larger context. Collectively the enslaved formed a Fifth Column in every war, siding with those who promised to deliver them from the death-in-life of slavery. In Saint-Domingue, black generals fought with the Spanish against the French, with Toussaint Louverture crossing over to the French once France had declared emancipation in North America. The enslaved of Virginia and points south defected to the British during the War of Independence and again during the War of 1812. Then in 1860 they supported the Union against the Confederacy, first as "contrabands" who decamped en masse, and then as soldiers. After they were allowed to fight against the Confederacy pursuant to the Emancipation Proclamation, the war was won.

Abolitionist books and publications by David Walker, Benjamin Lundy, William Lloyd Garrison, Frederick Douglass, and others cast a long shadow. In the eyes of slaveowners, they were multiplied manyfold into a giant "San Domingo," with the aid of demonized figures like John Quincy Adams, William Seward, Salmon P. Chase, and Charles Sumner. This was the much-decried "Northern aggression," whose forces were, in the minds of the South's political class, gathering to swoop down on the defenseless South, when purportedly savage "Negroes," would, it was believed, be let loose to rape, pillage, and kill, with nothing less than the destruction by murder and amalgamation of the white race as their object.

A letter to a Fredericksburg, Virginia, paper in 1800 declared that "if we will keep a ferocious monster in our country, we must keep him in chains."[56] In other words, the omnipresent, entirely legal violence of slavery was an ongoing state of war.

6

Species of Property

Slavery was not the beautiful state of love and confidence between masters and slaves that we often see pictured in books.[1]

—Judge O. P. Temple, Knoxville, Tennessee,
letter to Frederic Bancroft, 1904

SLAVERY WAS THE CENTRAL fact of Southern life.

Slaveowners formed the whole of the Southern political class and controlled Southern governments from top to bottom, with South Carolina the most proudly antidemocratic of all. The pro-slavery plutocracy of 1860—the Slave Power, abolitionists not incorrectly called it—had the full weight of American legal history behind it in claiming as its property 38.9 percent of the people of the slaveholding states (57 percent in South Carolina).

The legal systems of the Southern states were organized around maximizing slaveholder profit. In the towns, repressing the enslaved population was the principal goal of the policing system, which was not one of beat cops on patrol but of military-style squads that made street sweeps. In Charleston, these sweeps were done nightly by twenty to thirty officers at a time, which required much higher levels of manpower than Northern police forces.[2]

With their enslaved assets fully capitalized, slaveowners were not merely wealthy; they were spectacularly wealthy. At the time of secession, two-thirds of the millionaires in the country lived in the slave states, with most of their wealth in the form of slaves.[3] The Slave Power became wealthier with every territorial annexation for slavery: new territories meant new slave markets, which jacked up the resale value of existing slaveholdings.[4]

65

Protecting and developing enslaved assets—most definitely including reproductive value—was slaveowners' first, second, and third political order of business. With the leisure provided by living on the proceeds of slave labor and in the absence of other profitable ventures in the largely nonindustrial South, they had plenty of time to pursue politics, in which they competed to be the most faithful to the ideal of slavery and its concomitant philosophy of states' rights.* Thanks to the compromises brokered at the Constitutional Convention and to the slaveowners' bloc-voting fraternity, they exercised disproportionate political power at the national level, right up through the collapse of their system.

Slaveowners were an elite within their own geographically and ideologically isolated societies, with those who owned the most slaves at the apex of the social and political order. According to the detailed US census of 1860, which enumerated slaves and slaveholders in its "Agriculture" supplement, the 347,525 owners of one or more slaves constituted only 4.3 percent of the 8,039,000 "whites" in the fifteen slaveholding states (eleven of which would shortly secede) and 2.86 percent of the population of those states as a whole. If, as Frederic Bancroft did, we count the population of slaveholding families as five times the number of slaveowners, some 14 percent of the population of the slave states were of the slaveholding class. Perhaps one-half of 1 percent of the population of the slaveholding states owned a hundred slaves or more, and a few owned a thousand or more. It has been suggested that the 1860 census numbers might have underreported large slaveowners, but it's unlikely that large slaveholders—again, almost the entire political class of the South—amounted to even 1 percent of the population of their states.

The South's 1860 population of 3,953,742 enslaved people comprised or made viable an estimated four billion dollars' worth of private property, as per Mississippi's declaration of secession: "Our position is thoroughly identified with the institution of slavery. . . . We must either submit to degradation and to the loss of property worth four billions of money, or we must secede from the Union."[6]

This figure, which turns up in other contemporary writings, was an estimate of the South's capitalization. It apparently valued slaves at a blunt average of $1,000 per human being, or maybe something like $800 per human being and $200 for the land he or she worked on. Slaves were not all the property involved in that quick-and-dirty computation, but they were most of it, the rest

---

*"States' rights" was not implicitly a slaveholders' project at first; Massachusetts nearly seceded during the War of 1812. But a states' rights slaveholders' doctrine can be traced from Patrick Henry to John Randolph to John C. Calhoun, who more than anyone made it the boilerplate of slavery.[5]

being land and equipment that Southerners insisted would be valueless without slave labor. Some estimates said three billion dollars, and some said two billion; sporadic sales reports in Southern newspapers during the final years before the war, at the dizziest peak of the market, suggest that a thousand a head for a total of four billion dollars might not have been too high a figure to put on it. At the beginning of 1860, the *Albany (GA) Patriot* reported an estate liquidation of 536 people—one of the largest slave sales ever—that brought an average price of $1,025 per person sold, making the total sale worth more than $15 million in 2014 dollars. Another estate sale from Columbus brought an average of $1,084. The *Mobile Daily Advertiser* of January 18, 1860, reported a Mississippi sale with an average price of $1,145.[7]

Four billion dollars in 1860 was equivalent to about a hundred billion in 2010. It was more than 20 times the value of the entire cotton crop that year and 17.5 times all the gold and silver money in circulation in the United States ($228.3 million, most of it in the North). It was more than nine times the $435.4 million of currency in circulation—which, pursuant to the dismantling of the national banking system by President Andrew Jackson, was issued by local banks whose notes depreciated over distance.

Four billion dollars was more than double the $1.92 billion value of farmland in the eleven states that seceded.* Without labor Southern land lost what value it had, but even with labor Southern land in 1860 still was worth much less than land in the free states. In the census of that year, farmland in the mid-Atlantic states was valued at $28.08 an acre, and in New England at $20.27 an acre, but in the Southern states it was only worth $5.34—even though the South was producing the big export crops.[8] Farms in Pennsylvania, New York, Ohio, and Illinois were more improved, more diversified, better tended, more mechanized, better connected to market by infrastructure, and were worked by family or wage labor instead of by capital-intensive slaveholdings.

It was almost a laboratory experiment: two mutually exclusive economic systems competing for territorial expansion and financial supremacy, each one having at the start about the same number of inhabitants—but one allowing enslaved human property and the other not. Slave societies were caught in a downward spiral. Slavery brooked no competition from free labor, and without

---

*Notwithstanding the thirteen stars on the Confederate battle flag, there were only eleven Confederate states (in order of secession: South Carolina, Mississippi, Florida, Alabama, Georgia, Louisiana, Texas, Virginia, Arkansas, North Carolina, Tennessee). The other two stars represented Kentucky and Missouri, slave states that did not secede, though a Confederate government proclaimed itself in Missouri in addition to the Union government.

a broad consuming class of wage laborers, the slavery bloc furnished no domestic market for the products of industry. Moreover, industrial working conditions involving complicated machinery proved a more problematic situation than field labor for workforce discipline, which often had to be resolved with some kind of incentive pay for the enslaved, something the politics of plantation slavery was resolutely opposed to. Without industry, the South slid further and further behind while the North modernized and grew in population.

Meanwhile, the South had no foreign outlet for its other main product besides cotton: slaves. With slaveowners' encouragement, and sometimes their participation, the enslaved population was increasing by 25 percent or more every decade, even in the face of high mortality among the generally unhealthy enslaved.

With domestic labor needs being met, the South looked to territorial expansion for the growth of its slavery business. By 1860 North Carolina, South Carolina, Georgia, Kentucky, Tennessee, and Missouri—and even Alabama and Mississippi—were no longer importing enslaved laborers from their neighbors to the north but were exporting coffles as far west as they could go. As more states became slave sellers, having new territories to sell slaves into became a matter of ever greater urgency.

From President Jefferson's time forward, the grand prize of territorial expansion was Cuba. In his first year of retirement from political office, ex-president Jefferson rhapsodized in a letter to his protégé, President James Madison, about his imperial dream that the United States would acquire Cuba with Napoleon Bonaparte's blessing, and would conquer Canada in war: "We should have such an empire for liberty as she has never surveyed since the creation: & I am persuaded no constitution was ever before so well calculated as ours for extensive empire & self government."[9] Then he described the weather and the condition of his gardens, and thanked Madison for the squashes he had sent.

When a "founding father's" remarks about "liberty" don't seem to make sense, substitute the word "property" and they do. Taking over Havana would have created an empire of liberty, all right—for slaveowners. Jefferson wasn't fantasizing about freeing the two hundred thousand or so slaves who were being systematically worked to death on Cuba's sugar plantations and replaced by new arrivals from Africa. Cuba was at that time a fantastically productive sugar machine that was still in the early phase of its multi-decade peak of importation of kidnapped Africans. Acquiring Cuba would have been a windfall for Virginia slave breeders and would have added two reliably pro-slavery senators.

In 1861, slaveowners went to war with the North over slavery, as South Carolina's planter class had been inciting them to do for decades. The idea that the South fought a war so that it could be left in peace to have slavery merely within its settled boundaries is sometimes voiced as a cherished myth today, but it does not fit the facts on the ground, nor did anyone think so at the time. Quite the contrary: the war was fought over the expansion of slavery. Southern rulers feared being restricted to the boundaries they then occupied. The dysfunctional-from-the-beginning Confederate States of America was set to have an aggressively annexationist foreign policy.

Premised on infinite reproduction into an ever-expanding market, the slave-breeding economy was like a chain letter or a Ponzi scheme: sooner or later someone would be left holding the bag. Expansion into other territories was thus presented as a demographic imperative; in the last days of 1860, two Alabama "secession commissioners" sent to pitch secession to the North Carolina legislature announced that:

> [Alabama's black] population outstrips any race on the globe in the rate of its increase, and if the slaves now in Alabama are now to be restricted within the present limits, doubling as they do once in less than thirty years, the [white] children are now born who will be compelled to flee from the land of their birth, and from the slaves their parents have toiled to acquire as an inheritance for them, or to submit to the degradation of being reduced to an equality with them, and all its attendant horrors.[10]

Though the Jeffersonian "empire for liberty"—which, like we said, meant slavery—never managed to annex Cuba, it confiscated vast amounts of Native American territory as it pushed into western Georgia, Florida, Alabama, Mississippi, Louisiana, Arkansas, Missouri, and, after an international war of territorial conquest, Texas. Slaveowners fought bitterly but unsuccessfully to have slavery in New Mexico, California, and, in an 1854 armed confrontation of national dimensions, Kansas and Nebraska. Until Lincoln, they were used to having the president on their side.

The clash between slave labor and free-soil—the "irrepressible conflict," to use William Seward's phrase of 1858—resulted in the overthrow of slavery. But it was not merely a clash between labor systems; it was a clash between monetary systems.

When slavery was abolished and the on-paper value of flesh-and-blood capital disappeared from the balance sheet, the wealth of the South evaporated.

Since the South's economy had been built entirely on a foundation of slavery, there was nothing to substitute for it. There were as many laborers as before, but they could no longer be coerced. There was nothing to pay labor with, because the labor had been the money. The security for hundreds of millions of dollars in debt walked away, leaving the obligations valueless, the credit structure imploded, the hundred-dollar Confederate notes trampled in the mud, and the planters owning worthless land.[11]

Emancipation destroyed an entirely legal form of property, which is why it was a revolution.

Before achieving independence, the thirteen quarrelsome colonies were already well along with the process of cleaving into two interdependent but hostile economies. As each new territory came into the Anglo-American system, its policies regarding slavery and slave trading occasioned a shifting of the balance of power in the economy. The tension was there all along, and it formed arguably the greatest obstacle to union at the Constitutional Convention. The difference was not merely one of large states versus small states, or protective tariffs versus free trade, or even wage labor versus enslaved labor; it went directly to the issue of property rights in people. Within that framework, however, there was a sharp competition between the two major centers of power in the slave societies: Virginia and South Carolina. The commercial and political antagonism between the two went back to colonial days.

We're going to turn back to the sixteenth century now, in order to describe the formation of the states of the Chesapeake and the Lowcountry, each in their differing social and political particulars. We begin just before the establishment of an English colony in North America, when the first known group of enslaved Africans brought to live in the present-day territory of the United States rebelled and escaped.

next page: John Smith's map of Virginia, showing the "Virginian Sea," dated 1606 on the legend. North is to the right; the four major rivers on the western shore of the Chesapeake can be seen clearly.

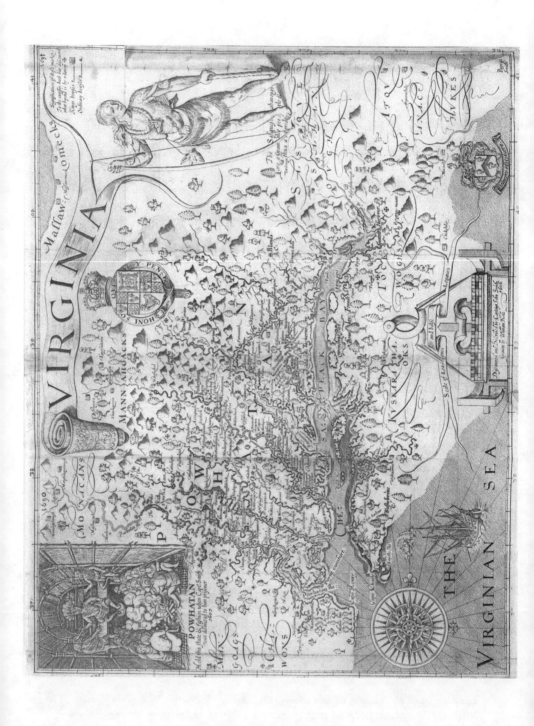

Part Two

The Chesapeake
and the Lowcountry

7

Rawrenock

It will rather hasten ye Spaniards rage, then retard yt; because he will see it, to grow every day harder for him to defeat us.[1]

—*A Justification for Planting in Virginia Before 1609*,
Records of the Virginia Company

Those who are now boastfully called popes, bishops, and lords [have issued from] such a pompous display of power and such a terrible tyranny that no earthly government can be compared to it . . . we have become the slaves of the vilest men on earth.[2]

—Martin Luther, *Concerning Christian liberty* (1520),
trans. R.S. Grignon

TODAY THE LAND AROUND Sapelo Sound is part of Georgia, but in 1526 the Spanish considered it part of the vaguely bounded territory Juan Ponce de León had named in 1513: Florida.

It was probably somewhere near Sapelo Sound that the conquistador Lucas Vázquez de Ayllón established a Spanish colony in 1526, bringing some six hundred people from Santo Domingo in six vessels—including an unknown number of enslaved Africans, whose precise point of origin is also unknown, along with eighty or perhaps a hundred horses.

It was a mighty undertaking, the first since Ponce de León had left the region, and Ayllón carried a commission from Holy Roman Emperor and King of Spain Carlos V. Unfortunately, Ayllón's short-lived town of San Miguel de Guadalpe became that archetypal horror of colonial history: a failed settlement

75

in the wilderness. Ayllón died of disease; the Africans rebelled, burning down the colonial prison; and one hundred fifty or so surviving Spanish colonists made their way back to the island of La Española (or Hispaniola).

The Africans appear to have been left behind to live or die among the Guale Indians, beginning Florida's tradition of marronage, a state of outlaw freedom for a self-emancipated slave.* Their ultimate fate is unknown.[3]

In his explorations, Ayllón had discovered the major watercourses of North America's east coast, including the Chesapeake Bay, which first appears on a map with the name Bahía de Santa María. After various failed ventures, including a brief reign of slaughter and enslavement of Native Americans under Hernando de Soto in 1539, Spain gave up trying to colonize Florida. But the Spanish king's hand was forced by the appearance of a colony of heretics.

Martin Luther's revolution (October 31, 1517) never took hold in militantly Catholic Spain. But in northern Europe, where dissident mobs attacked churches and monasteries, destroying statues and images in iconoclastic riots, what came to be called Protestantism was an active political project. It was a new kind of movement, disseminated by the booming technology of moveable-type printing, which thrived in northern Europe on Bible sales, creating as it did so a new political medium—the printed tract—that gloried in a rhetoric of freedom versus slavery that would carry forward into the coming centuries.

African slavery, introduced into Iberia by Portugal in 1441 or so, had not yet developed on a large scale in the Americas, nor did it exist in most of Europe, where slavery was associated with Spain and Portugal—as were black people, who in England were called *blackamoors*, reflecting their Iberian provenance. But though Martin Luther had no personal contact with slavery, he used the term frequently, describing conditions of the soul and of the church in terms of liberty versus slavery. In his theology, freedom was associated with reading the Bible in one's own language, and slavery was associated with Catholic ritual.

As Europe divided into Catholic and Protestant camps, a series of civil wars paralyzed France for four decades. Huguenots, followers of Jean Calvin who numbered at their peak a little more than a tenth of the French population, were mostly urban people, many of them tradesmen, at odds with a mostly rural,

---

*In Spanish the self-emancipated were called *cimarrones*, a word deriving from the Taíno language that became *marron* in French and *maroon* in English.

agricultural country. When they declared their church an established institution with a national synod in 1559, a crisis began.[4]

Then, the following year, a ten-year-old was crowned king of France—Charles IX, whose affairs were guided by his Italian mother, Catherine de Medici, acting as regent. Catherine saw the growth of Protestantism as a threat to the state, and allied the French throne with Spain against it, while the Huguenots sought English and German support.

On February 18, 1562, the Huguenot sea captain Jean Ribaut embarked on a French colonizing mission across the Atlantic, which meant creeping into territory claimed by Spain. Flying the banner of his Catholic child-king, he founded the settlement of Charlesfort, at present-day Parris Island, in what later came to be called South Carolina.

Ribaut found the indigenous people* to be friendly, and when one of them showed the French the best place to land their vessel, Ribaut had him "rewarded with some looking glases and other prety thinges of smale value"—the beginning of a long cycle of trade between Native Americans and Europeans in the area.[5] As the richness of the unplowed land became apparent, and after Ribaut presented more gifts, he asked the question most on Europeans' minds:

> we demaunded of them for a certen towne called Sevola [Cibola], wherof some have written not to be farr from thence. . . . Those that have written of this kingdom and towne of Sevolla . . . say that ther is great aboundaunce of gould and silver, precious stons and other great riches, and that the people hedd ther arrowes, instedd of iron, with poynted turqueses.[6]

Ribaut kidnapped two of the natives but, to his apparent surprise, they did not want to be captives, and they escaped: "We carried two goodly and strong abourd our shippes, clothing and using [treating] them as gentlly and lovingly as yt was possible; but they never ceassed day nor nyght to lament and at length they scaped away."[7]

Leaving twenty-eight men behind at Charlesfort, Ribaut returned home to raise money, but he found France's ports closed. Two weeks after he had embarked from France, the Duc de Guise had massacred a group of Huguenots at worship, and in Ribaut's absence, a religious civil war had begun. He went instead to London, a city he knew well and whose language he spoke, where in May 1563 he published a forty-four-page pamphlet whose short title is *The whole and true discovery of Terra Florida*. In it, he noted that the natives would trade

*Which group Ribaut encountered is unknown.

for "littell beades of glasse, which they love and esteme above gould and pearles for to hang them at there eares and necke."[8]

The pamphlet brought Ribaut to a meeting with England's Queen Elizabeth, who wanted to mount an English expedition to Florida. She briefly gave Ribaut "a salary of three hundred ducats and a house," as the Spanish ambassador duly reported to the Hapsburg monarch Felipe (Philip) II, but then she had him imprisoned in the Tower of London after he tried to escape with four French hostages Elizabeth was holding.[9]

By then, the desperate, quarreling men Ribaut had left behind at Charlesfort had resolved to sail home. Running out of food and water on the voyage, they drank their own urine and turned to cannibalism, killing and eating an unfortunate outcast of their number before they were picked up by a British ship.[10]

A second, much larger, colonizing voyage from France brought both women and men to Florida when René Goulaine de Laudonnière, Ribaut's former second-in-command, established the Huguenot colony of Fort Caroline (also named for Charles IX) on June 22, 1564, near the site of present-day Jacksonville, Florida. Laudonnière brought an official expedition painter along, who depicted the sixteenth-century aristocrat dressed in "a crimson, yellow, and blue costume," in yellow boots with red linings, and three colors of plumes in his hat.[11] His colonists recorded eight births during the short life of their community.[12] Unfortunately, they neglected to plant sufficient crops in the fall, so when famine struck they took an Indian chief hostage for a food ransom.[13]

Even more unfortunately, they were in the high-security Gulf Stream corridor.

Ponce de León noted in his journal of 1513 that his three ships encountered a current they could not go against, despite favorable winds. He had discovered the strongest current in all the world's oceans—a one-way express lane in the sea, where the water was warm even when the air was cold. More than two centuries later, Benjamin Franklin named it the "Gulf Stream."

Driven in a west-to-east direction by the Earth's rotation and intensified by the temperature differential between equatorial and polar latitudes, the Gulf Stream is stronger in the summer than in the winter. It originates after the waters of the Caribbean pass northward through the Straits of Yucatán, pouring into the Gulf of Mexico and making the clockwise circuit in the Gulf now

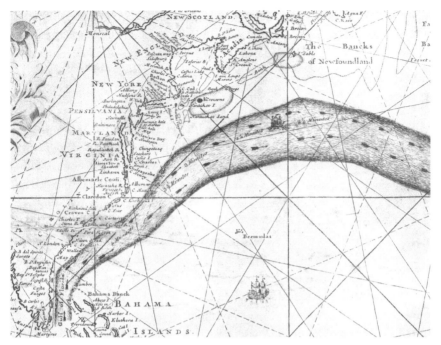

Detail of the 1768 Franklin-Folger map showing the Gulf Stream, which diverges from the mainland off the coast of North Carolina.

known as the "loop current." The current is amplified again, and the waters become more turbulent, when it shoots eastward through the constricted passage of the Straits of Florida. Following along the eastern coast of the United States, it reaches its closest point to land near present-day Cape Hatteras, North Carolina, before gradually veering away from the coastline and out into the Atlantic. There it divides into two main branches, with one continuing up the North Atlantic along the "great circle" route to Europe, while another branch curves off eastward, leading to Spain.

Every year, a Spanish fleet bound for Sevilla sailed up the Gulf Stream out of the port of Havana, packed full of silver and gold ripped out of the bowels of Mexico and Perú. The volume of silver sharply increased as of 1557, when the Spanish mines began using an amalgamation refining process that involved indigenous slaves tromping in a toxic slurry of mercury, a labor force that was soon to be augmented with Africans.

When the Spanish king Felipe II learned that French Protestants had established a colony on the mainland at a potential choke point for the route his treasure ships took, he commissioned the militantly Catholic Don Pedro Menéndez de Avilés as *adelantado* (governor) of Florida, instructing him to establish a Spanish presence on the North American mainland that would remove the interlopers.

William Hawkins made what was probably the first African trading voyage—but not a slave-trading one—from England in 1536, traveling from England to "Guinea" (Africa) and then to Brazil. The first English company to finance commercial ventures to Africa seems to have been a London syndicate founded in 1540, but there was little further action until a highly lucrative voyage brought back gold, ivory, and hot peppers in 1553. It was followed by more expeditions, and Queen Elizabeth became an African-venture partner in 1561. These voyages, which did not entail carrying off kidnapped people, created good relations with the African traders, but Hawkins's son John changed that.[14]

There are two previous documented incidents of Englishmen engaging in commerce of small numbers of slaves, but John Hawkins was the first to make a profitable "triangular," or clockwise, slave trade. Moreover, he not only traded in slaves but participated in raiding for them, burning a town on the Gold Coast during his first voyage. He also seized them from other slave traders through piracy—or rather, as a privateer.

Privateering—the state endorsement of commercial piracy against vessels of other flags in furtherance of military and political objectives—was an early form of capitalism as war. "The setting forth of a privateer required considerable capital," writes Kenneth R. Andrews. "Even in ventures consisting of one small ship, the joint-stock system of investment was used more often than not."[15] In England, the partners were *adventurers*, a word implying joint-investor commercial enterprise, as in the Company of Merchant Adventurers of London, apparently already in existence when it was chartered by Henry VII in 1407. Freelance piracy by English captains flourished during Queen Mary's reign (1551–58), but Queen Elizabeth, Mary's half sister and successor, gave the former pirates letters of marque to become privateers and used them as a tool of policy—"a privileged criminal class," in the words of Hugh F. Rankin.[16]

Investment in privateering ventures was facilitated by the improved quality of English money during Elizabeth's long reign (1558–1603). Henry VIII had imposed what is remembered as the Great Debasement on his coinage as a money-making trick, sabotaging the value of the monarch's money. But Elizabeth's financial advisor Thomas Gresham accomplished the considerable feat of calling in the debased coinage and replacing it with newly minted gold sovereigns within a year (1560–61). Restoring value to the money created the conditions for a credit market to thrive, without which no long-distance trade could function. Gresham also impressed on Elizabeth the wisdom of raising money domestically from England's own internal commerce instead of from foreign bankers as the Spanish crown did. From Elizabeth's time forward, England was a financial center.

Backed by a syndicate of investors, Hawkins took three ships to Sierra Leone in 1562 with the intention of capturing Africans to sell in La Española and thereby to violate the Spanish trade monopoly. Once arrived on the African coastline, he plundered Portuguese traders and made a slave-raiding alliance with an unnamed African king. He had some three hundred captives to sell by the time he arrived at La Ysabela, Columbus's now-vanished first settlement near present-day Puerto Plata in the Dominican Republic. Arriving with more soldiers than the Spanish had, he said he'd behave if he got to do business. After selling the Africans to eager customers, he acquired two more ships and loaded all five up with sugar, hides, ginger, and pearls for the return voyage to Europe, ultimately turning a profit for his investors.[17]

Hawkins's second triangular voyage, heavily subscribed by merchant adventurers in 1564, brought back gold, silver, and pearls. On his return in August, he stopped at Fort Caroline in need of fresh water. There, in a gesture of Protestant solidarity against the Spanish, he saved the remaining Huguenot colonists by trading them food and a ship he didn't need in exchange for a Spanish brass cannon they had captured. During the months Hawkins remained there, Jean Ribaut arrived; released from the Tower of London, he had brought a fresh colonizing expedition of five hundred men and two hundred women.

In Spain, Menéndez's huge expedition to Florida was already in preparation when the news of Hawkins's arrival at

Design for Sir John Hawkins's crest, depicting an African woman, bare-breasted and bound, 1568.

Fort Caroline arrived. To the Spanish king, it seemed proof of an international alliance to break his control of the Americas, and he ordered Menéndez to speed up his departure.

Menéndez had Felipe's trust. He had fought against the forces of the French Valois king François I under Felipe's father, Carlos V, and he had successfully escorted Felipe to London in 1554 for Felipe's short-lived royal marriage to his Catholic second cousin, the English Queen Mary Tudor.*[18] He was captain general of the Carrera de Las Indias, the transatlantic treasure route, during what is remembered as Spain's *Siglo de Oro*, its Golden Age. With the security for Spain's entire money supply and commerce on his shoulders, as well as a fantastically lucrative upside should his franchise thrive, he took his responsibilities to God, king, and silver seriously. At enormous personal expense, he brought to Florida an armada of ten ships carrying 995 people, 300 of whom were veteran soldiers, along with 200 horses. They landed on the day of San Agustín (August 28, 1565), founding the town that today is still called St. Augustine—the oldest continually occupied European-style city in the United States, though there are older Native American communities.

Shortly after Hawkins departed Fort Caroline, Menéndez captured it in a surprise attack.[19] As the massacre began, he gave an order to spare women and children under fifteen (though some were apparently dispatched before the order to spare them was communicated).[20] One hundred forty-three men were killed, according to one source, although Laudonnière escaped.[21] Others were slaughtered in the countryside as they fled. The Spanish caught some two hundred of them, who had to be confirmed as members of the *nueva religión* before being executed, because they could escape death if they declared themselves Catholics. When they refused, they were taken behind a sand hill in groups of ten with their hands bound, and their throats were cut.

The Spanish found six cases of the Huguenots' gilt-edged Bibles, which they burned. Ribaut got away with some 350 of his people, but their boat was shipwrecked near St. Augustine and Menéndez caught them. Gonzalo Solís de Merás, Menéndez's official chronicler and brother-in-law, noted that Ribaut offered a ransom to spare their lives, but Menéndez spared only "the fifers, drummers, trumpeters, and four more who said that they were Catholics, in all

---

*The daughter of Henry VIII, she acquired the nickname "Bloody Mary" by burning 283 Protestants at the stake in 1555 during the revolt that followed her marriage to Felipe; Felipe effectively left the marriage in 1556 when he assumed the throne of Spain, leaving Mary without an heir and thus halting her project of re-Catholicizing England.

sixteen persons: all the others had their throats cut," including Ribaut.[22] One town had exterminated another town thirty miles away. The site is still known today as Matanzas (Massacre) Inlet. It was a small massacre, however, compared to the St. Bartholomew's Day massacre of August 1572, when the gates of Catholic Paris were closed and three days of killing of Huguenots began, followed by similar massacres in twelve other French cities that claimed an unknown number of thousands of victims.

With the Huguenots of Florida annihilated, the Spanish Fleet of the Indies continued its annual treasure runs from Havana through the Straits of Florida. To Christianize the natives, Menéndez established a mission system that was the first interconnected circuit of European settlements in North America. He established firm military control over the region, sending a detachment up north to build a fort where the Charlesfort community had been, calling it Santa Elena (St. Helena in English). One of his captains, Juan Pardo, built Fort San Juan in western North Carolina, near present-day Morganton, the ruins of which were unearthed by archaeologists in the first decade of the twenty-first century.[23] The area north of St. Augustine would remain a zone of conflict between Protestant and Catholic states for almost two centuries more.

Hawkins made his third and final slave-trading voyage in 1567, taking between four and five hundred captives, but Spain mounted effective resistance, and his expedition lost money.[24] The English did not immediately continue the slave trade, but John Hawkins had started them in it.

By this time, Spain had purchased tens of thousands of Africans from Portuguese slavers to work in its silver and gold mines in Mexico and Perú. It was becoming clear how vulnerable the Spanish American possessions were to slave rebellion, given how badly outnumbered the whites were, and how vulnerable they were to attack from free black people whose arrival in the hemisphere predated that of the English. With the help of numerous maroons, as well as Huguenot privateers, Hawkins's nephew Francis Drake captured a fortune in gold—he had to leave the silver behind for lack of vessels to carry it—when he attacked one leg of the Spanish treasure fleet at Nombre de Dios, Panamá, in 1573.

England's Queen Elizabeth knew well the traps that awaited women in royal marriage. She was the ex-sister-in-law of Spain's Felipe II, from his marriage to her half sister Mary Tudor. Her father, Henry VIII, had beheaded her mother,

Anne Boleyn. For her refusal to subordinate herself, she became known as the Virgin (meaning unmarried) Queen.

According to the writer remembered as John Taylor the Water-Poet, John Hawkins was the first person to bring tobacco to England, but it was popularized by Elizabeth's favorite, Sir Walter Raleigh.[25] An Englishman who owned extensive tracts of land in Ireland, Raleigh was the fashionable figure who popularized "tobacco-drinking," as it was called at first, puffing away on his long-stemmed silver pipe even in the presence of the snuff-dipping queen. When the Virgin Queen awarded Raleigh a charter in 1584 to a broadly defined area of North America, he named it Virginia in her honor.

Unlike the Spanish colonies, which were developed as state projects and were often named for saints, Virginia was a commercial enterprise from the start, and its first colony, Roanoke, was named for money. *Rawrenock*, as Captain John Smith spelled it, was the medium of exchange used by the Pamunkey people who lived there: "white beads that occasion as much dissention among the salvages, as gold and silver amongst Christians," Captain Smith wrote.[26] The settlement was founded in 1585 on an uninhabited island off the coast of present-day North Carolina that gave signs of having previously been the site of a massacre.

Virginia was a challenge to Spain's hegemony in the Americas. Pushed by a "war party" among her advisers—advocates of North American colonization who were locked out of commerce in the Americas by the Spanish monopoly— Elizabeth authorized Francis Drake to conduct a 1585–86 raiding expedition to the West Indies. To accomplish his mission, Drake outfitted a large fleet of some twenty-five sailing ships and at least eight pinnaces (smaller oar-and-sail combos, used for boarding and reconnaissance). He press-ganged some of his crew, but captains were eager to serve under England's great sailor, warrior, profiteer, and anti-papist.

Shortly after setting out, a fever killed hundreds of Drake's men, but his surviving force sacked towns on the Cape Verde islands. Then, according to one sailor's account, on New Year's Day 1586 he landed a thousand men some "9 or 10 miles distant from the Towne of Saint Domingo, the same day our men (by Gods helpe) tooke and spoyled the Towne."[27] To dramatize their ransom demand, the English burned between half and two-thirds of Santo Domingo, starting with the poorest parts of town. They hanged two friars, took everything of value, and remained there a month before pushing on to Cartagena de las

Indias in Nueva Granada (today Colombia), which they likewise "spoyled," tormenting the Cartagenans for six weeks before moving on.

In both Santo Domingo and Cartagena, they burned Spanish galleys; a Mediterranean naval artifact out of place in the Caribbean, the ships were slower-moving and clumsier than Drake's vessels. They freed hundreds of galley slaves, some of whom joined Drake's forces—a motley crew that included Africans, Turks, Frenchmen, and Greeks.[28] Coming up the Gulf Stream along the coast of Florida, Drake spotted the watchtower of San Agustín, established twenty-one years before, and paused to allow his two thousand or so men to sack and burn the town.

Proceeding north, Drake's final stop on his American tour was the queen's colony of Roanoke. But when he arrived there, the colony was failing. He carried 105 dejected colonists home to England, so when Admiral Richard Grenville arrived with a supply ship shortly after, he found the colony abandoned. Leaving behind fifteen men, Grenville returned to England. When a second attempt at colonization with 150 colonists arrived in 1587, they found the colony abandoned yet again.

Drake's campaign was not a profitable expedition for its joint-stock investors but it was costlier still for Spain, systematically dismantling as it did Spain's defenses and ports. After his assault, "every sail upon the horizon conjured up the memory of Drake" for the Spanish in their system of fortresses that they called *llaves* (keys).[29] It was the beginning of eighteen years of war between the two countries, during which England was allied with the Dutch.

Bent on retaliation for Drake's depredations, the Invincible Armada of Spain sailed for England in 1588, but it went down to humiliating defeat. First there was a devastating storm that was widely seen in England as God's intervention against popery and the Irish, then a battle in which England's use of signaling beacons, constructed at strategic points along the coast, revolutionized naval communications. The defeat of the armada marked the ascension of England to the status of world power and brought a knighthood for John Hawkins. An innovative shipwright, he was effectively the founder of the English navy, which grew out of picking at Spain piecemeal.

One casualty of the Anglo-Spanish war was the Roanoke settlement: no supplies could be shipped to the colonists. By the time a ship arrived in 1590, three years after the previous supplies had landed, they had disappeared once again. There has been much speculation over the centuries about the fate of the mysterious "lost colony," but the simplest explanation is that they were killed by the Pamunkeys under Chief Powhatan, whose territory they were invading; according to Samuel Purchas, Powhatan "confessed" to Captain John Smith "that he had bin at the murther of that Colonie."[30]

Virginia had failed on its first try.

In the wake of Drake, Spain began building up its American fortifications to withstand future assaults. But in defending its positions on the mainland and the "vital artery of the treasure route," writes Kenneth R. Andrews, most significantly meaning Havana as well as Lima, Portobelo, Cartagena, and Veracruz, "this inevitably meant that eastern Cuba, Jamaica, Hispaniola, Puerto Rico and the Lesser Antilles, though by no means abandoned, were more and more exposed to all forms of infiltration and attack."[31] Menéndez launched a newly formalized Spanish treasure fleet in 1566; that same year the Protestant Dutch, who had been under occupation by the Hapsburgs since 1482, launched a war for independence from Spain that dragged on in one form or another for some eighty years.

Spain claimed a monopoly on commerce and shipping in the Americas, but its fortress colonies were increasingly being visited by freelance merchant-warriors from other nations, who often acquired their goods by piracy and wanted in on the mercantile action, drilling into the Spanish monopoly like so many termites. The Dutch, who with their shipping industry were creating the world's most dynamic economy in the Netherlands, made a grand business of attacking Spanish shipping. As the Anglo-Spanish war heated up, English privateers hammered at Spanish merchants and treasure ships, with profits accruing to the underwriters, who were often London merchants.

Drake and Hawkins made the mistake in 1595 of attacking the early version of San Juan's formidable, well-defended Morro Castle, whose gunners and cannoneers had every possible angle of fire. The two despoilers of cities died in the aftermath of the assault, apparently of dysentery.

Elizabeth unified church and state under her sovereignty, formalizing the existence of the Church of England (or Anglican, or Episcopal church), which Henry VIII had broken out from the Catholic Church in 1534. The Anglican church retained much from Catholicism, but without the pope, without saints, and without the veneration of the Virgin Mary. The Lutherans and Calvinists thought the Anglicans corrupt, and the Catholics thought them heretical. While

Elizabeth prioritized the avoidance of religious civil war in England, she brutally completed the conquest of Catholic Ireland that Henry had left unfinished, in a campaign that saw Spain side with its Irish co-religionists against England.

Elizabeth became alarmed by a small but increasing number of black people visible on London streets, and she ordered them deported in 1601, decrying the "great numbers of Negars and Blackamoors" in her kingdom and characterizing them as "Infidels." She did not succeed in removing them, but she did establish a precedent in England for separating black people from others.[32]

Elizabeth died—unmarried, as per her vow, and without issue—in 1603 after a forty-four-year reign. She took no part in choosing her successor, but advisor Sir Robert Cecil had negotiated a succession pact in favor of her second cousin, James Stuart, who had been crowned James VI, King of Scotland at the age of thirteen months. James had been raised as an Anglican; his Catholic mother, the conspiratorial Mary Stuart, Queen of Scots, had been beheaded on Elizabeth's reluctant orders in 1567 after eighteen years of imprisonment, in a botched execution that required three ax strokes to completely sever her head. James was considered a foreigner by the English, but no matter: at the age of thirty-seven he succeeded Elizabeth as King James I of England.

Elizabeth bequeathed James a much more powerful country than the one Henry VIII had left her. Elizabethan England had beaten Spain, finished the subjugation of Ireland, and—not the least of its achievements—stabilized the pound sterling. The House of Stuart, however, proved to be, as one historian succinctly put it, "Europe's most hapless dynasty."[33] Unifying the English and Scottish crowns, James was the first of a line of Stuart monarchs who would enrage Parliament.

Despite the black people of London having been singled out as a distinct and undesirable class by Elizabeth, their presence was changing notions of style in the city. A fashionable white fascination for blackness was particularly visible in the worlds of art and music, as on Twelfth Night, January 6, 1605, when James's court attended *The Masque of Blackness*, written by Ben Jonson at the request of James's wife, Queen Consort Anne of Denmark. "It was her majesty's will to have them blackmoors at first," wrote Jonson by way of introduction; the ladies of the court who performed in the cast were dressed in high style—which was the point of the exercise—as Africans, with their faces blacked.

8

A Cargo of Shining Dirt

Seagull, a sea captain. *Come, boys, Virginia longs till we share the rest of her maidenhead.*

Spendall, adventurer bound for Virginia. *Why, is she inhabited already with any English?*

Sea. *A whole country of English is there, man . . . the Indians are so in love with 'em that all the treasure they have they lay at their feet.*

Scape. *But is there such treasure there, Captain, as I have heard?*

Sea. *I tell thee, gold is more plentiful there than copper is with us; and for as much red copper as I can bring, I'll have thrice the weight in gold. Why, man, all their dripping-pans and their chamber pots are pure gold; and all their chains with which they chain up their streets are massy gold; all the prisoners they take are fetter'd in gold; and, for rubies and diamonds, they go forth on holidays and gather 'em by the seashore, to hang on their children's coats, and stick in their caps, as commonly as our children wear saffron gilt brooches and groats with holes in 'em.*

Scape. *And is it a pleasant country withal?*

Sea. *As ever the sun shin'd on; temperate, and full of all sorts of excellent viands: wild boar is as common there as our tamest bacon is here; venison, as mutton. And then you shall live freely there, without sergeants, or courtiers, or lawyers, or intelligencers . . . . You may be an alderman there, and never be a scavenger; you may be a nobleman, and never be a slave.*

—from *Eastward Hoe* (1605), a comedy by Ben Jonson, George Chapman, and John Marston, who were briefly imprisoned for their impudence (emphasis added)

ANYONE WHO GREW UP in the southern United States knows that Jesus spoke seventeenth-century English.

That's because the King James Bible is the Word of God, at least as far as the English language goes. More or less concurrently with William Shakespeare, and together with the Anglican Book of Common Prayer, it effectively codified written English.*

Having a vernacular Bible was a matter of some urgency to King James. A connoisseur of theological argument and a self-proclaimed expert on witches, he believed that by the divine right of kings he was sitting on Jesus's throne on earth. He was, in short, blessed with no less beatific a vision of his own grandeur than the Spanish monarchs he hated. The English-language Bible he commissioned on behalf of the Church of England was begun in 1604, the first year of his reign as king of England, and was completed in 1611.

Religion was politics in the post-Lutheran world, and commissioning this new Anglican Bible was a political act. An extremist group that enjoyed increasing power in Parliament, called "Puritans" by their enemies, aggressively opposed the monarch. In *Basilikon Doron*, a how-to-be-a-king book that James wrote for his toddler son, Henry, subsequently published in Edinburgh (1599) and then in London, we read: "as to the name of Puritanes, . . . they thinke themselves onely pure, and in a maner without sinne, the onely true Church, and onely worthy to be participant of the Sacraments, and all the rest of the world to be but abomination in the sight of God."

As the Bible was being translated, James chartered the joint-stock Virginia Company, whose first corporate settlement was, predictably, to be named Jamestown. No Puritans would be welcome there. Jamestown signified the exportation to America of the Church of England. Clergymen who wanted to come to Virginia had to audition, giving a trial sermon for the Virginia Company. If successful, their reward would be a terrifying weeks- or months-long voyage that might carry them to death from some combination of massacre, starvation, or any of a number of diseases.

As land-granted through latitude descriptions by King James to the venture capitalists of the Virginia Company on April 10, 1606, the Virginia territory comprised about 80 percent of the present continental United States. It

---

*The King James Bible drew heavily on the vocabulary of William Tyndale's translation, which was published in the early days of Lutheranism, the 1520s and '30s. Tyndale was burned as a heretic in 1536. See Tombs, 196–9.

extended all the way west across the unexplored continent, a distance seventeenth-century Englishmen did not comprehend. The directors of the company thought Virginia was an island and that on the other side of the mountains would be the ocean, which would provide the fabled passage to the riches of the Orient.

By the time the English in Virginia began privatizing land previously used as a commons, or "enclosing" it, they had had plenty of experience doing it at home. The planting of the Jamestown colony took place as political radicalism was growing in England in response to the mass dispossession of the people of the commons—the "commoners"—by enclosure.

The year Jamestown was founded, 1607, was the year of anti-enclosure riots in the English Midlands, erupting out of Northamptonshire. The rioters erased the boundaries of enclosure, filling in ditches and tearing down hedges, for which action they began to be called "levellers." The social implication of the name was obvious; though they were not a forward-looking movement, the tendency the levellers represented, toward erasing social and financial distinctions in society, using violence if necessary, anticipated Marx's idea of communism by over two hundred years. The rioters were repressed on James's orders; dozens were killed, some by slow-death torture.

As the dispossessed, masterless people arrived in the cities, that liveliest and most squalid of slums was created: greater London. A huge city of two hundred thousand in 1600, when England's population was four million, it teemed with idle poor, far more than were needed as weavers by England's woolens industry, for whom the prospect of seven years' servitude in the New World could seem a rescue from freezing and starving.

For the English capital class, the colonies were a handy way to deal with a social problem by shipping it elsewhere. Besides finding gold and producing luxury goods, another of the intended functions of the foreign plantations was to draw down the excess laboring population that had become a drag on English society. Class tension, occasionally flaring into armed conflict, was a permanent fixture of English political life and was exported to Virginia with the first generation, along with a tradition of taverns.

Meanwhile, another colonization scheme was occupying King James: the Ulster plantations in Northern Ireland. These were not "plantations" in the later sense of large staple-producing farms; this prior sense of the word meant (quoting the Oxford English Dictionary): "the settling of people, usually in a conquered or dominated country; *esp.* the planting or establishing of a colony."

Before colonies could be planted with crops, they had to be planted with people, who were called "planters" simply for being there.

For feudal Scotland, where land ownership was even more concentrated than that of England, northern Ireland was an escape valve. With the aim of securing the sparsely populated northern part of Ireland as a zone of British loyalty, it was Protestantized with planters. Vast tracts of confiscated land in the Ulster region were given to English (mostly Anglicans) and to Scots (mostly Presbyterian) who were being rewarded en masse by their countryman King James for their loyalty, or at least for their general political affiliation with him.

The thick woods of Ulster had to be cleared. Land was given to those bringing English and Scotch laborers, who had to be certified as Protestant. There was a racial mythology to go with this, one that cast the Scots as superior to the Celtic Irish.

By the time the English arrived in what they called Virginia, the Chesapeake Bay watershed had been populated for some eleven thousand years. An enormous estuary that connects North America's most complex river system to the Atlantic Ocean, it was created by global warming some twelve thousand years ago, when rising temperatures melted the last ice sheet and flooded the meteoric basin that had been an ancient riverbed.

About 180 entirely navigable miles long from south to north, and about 30 miles across at its widest point, the Chesapeake is fed by nineteen principal rivers, all of them navigable, and by four hundred or so lesser creeks and streams, many of them navigable. The big rivers are on its western shore, carrying the force of continental drainage. Though the English didn't know it yet, this huge riverine system offered unrivaled possibilities as a transportation—which meant, a communications—network. The superstructure erected atop it became a global capital of power and influence: in the twentieth century, the world's most powerful military command center, the Pentagon, was built on a lagoon of the Potomac River, seventeen miles below the fall line, using sand dredged from the river.

The Spanish never occupied the Chesapeake. Since it was north of the Gulf Stream's bend away from the continent, it was safely out of the range of Spanish security concerns. But they went there as explorers, spreading diseases that killed natives who had never had face-to-face contact with Europeans.

From that contact with the Spanish, the Pamunkey knew something of European culture, religion, and politics years before the English began referring to Pamunkey territory as Virginia. The seven-year-old son of a Pamunkey *werowance*, or chieftain, had traveled with Spanish explorers to Mexico and on to Madrid, where he received a Jesuit education. Baptized as Don Luís de Velasco, the young man returned in 1571 after ten years away, arriving via Havana with nine Spanish Jesuits who hoped to plant a colony. The Indians killed the Jesuits, apparently with Velasco's help.

The Pamunkey had long been at war with other natives of the region, and they may well have seen the English newcomers as one more variable in a complex scenario—one more ally or one more enemy, and not necessarily always one or the other. But neither the Pamunkey nor the Virginia Company could have foreseen that they were the first point of encounter in a continent-wide war of enclosure.

Captain John Smith—the rank referred to his onetime position in the Transylvanian army—was the best negotiator with the indigenous people that Virginia ever had, and as such he was a key figure in the survival of the Jamestown colony. A bona fide war hero, he had fought against the Spanish both for the French and the Dutch, continued on to the Mediterranean, then went to the Balkans where he fought the Ottoman Turks. His coat of arms had three turbaned heads on it, representing the Turkish champions he had slain and ritually decapitated in three tournaments of mortal combat fought in lieu of confrontation between armies.

Smith was an escaped former slave—a white man who had worn an iron collar around his neck. Captured and enslaved by the Tatars, he ultimately escaped and was decorated, commissioned, and given a sinecure by Transylvanian prince Sigismund Báthory. Leaving his comfortable position at Báthory's court he returned to England, and then, at the age of twenty-seven, arrived at Jamestown with the first colonists on board the *Susan Constant*. He thereafter not only devoted himself to the mission of colonization but also became an outspoken advocate of the laboring colonist, to the point of being accused of being a leveller.

The colonists needed an advocate. From the beginning of the Virginia colony through the Boston Tea Party 166 years later, English policy-makers demonstrated over and over again an utter incomprehension of American realities. The tension between colony and metropolis that was to characterize

Anglo-American relations was present from the first generation in Virginia, in the form of resistance to corporate governance. Not following foolish instructions was essential for survival, such as when the company sent to Virginia a disassembled ship. The colonists were to carry the five ship parts over the Blue Ridge Mountains, assemble them, and sail on into the ocean.[1]

Returning to England in October 1609 following a gunpowder explosion that apparently damaged his manly organs, Smith became a writer, and a good one at that. It was Smith who named New England and first described it, in 1610. His various books and pamphlets are full of firsthand historical information; he was one of the first autobiographers in England. In his masterwork, a classic of early hemispheric literature titled *Generall Historie of Virginia, New England, and the Summer Isles* (1624), Smith described the Chesapeake region as "a country that may have the prerogative over the most places knowne for large and pleasant navigable rivers, heaven and earth never agreed better to frame a place for man's habitation. . . . Here are mountaines, hils, plaines, valleyes, rivers, and brookes, all running more pleasantly into a faire bay, compassed but for the mouth, with fruitful and delightsome land."[2]

Smith was an autodidact cartographer. His maps did much to get Englishmen interested in North America; the *Mayflower* Pilgrims who established the Plymouth colony relied on Smith's map when they crossed the Atlantic in 1620. An early example of Virginia branding, his map of the area labeled the region of the Atlantic Ocean outside the Chesapeake as the "Virginian Sea." The colonists briefly tried calling their grand estuary Virginia Bay, but the name Chesapeake was already established, deriving from the Algonquian *chesapioc,* "village at big river," which implies the rivers' communicative function.

As with the Cuban hardwoods that built ships in Havana for the royal silver fleet of timberless Spain, the availability of Chesapeake lumber facilitated shipbuilding. Not only were there extensive stands of timber, they were located next to water—which was necessary to make the lumber useful, since there was no practical way to haul it over land. The first members of the Shipwright's Guild arrived in Virginia in 1610, three years after the establishment of Jamestown. Over the next two centuries, the region became known for its innovative vessel design. A number of specialized craft were designed for the conditions of the shallow Chesapeake, which has an average depth of twenty-one feet but can be six feet or less. The number of vessels documented as sunk there over time exceeds three thousand, an indication of how much activity there was constantly on this vast aquatic highway system.[3]

With so many rivers and streams, the Chesapeake abounded in rich alluvial deposits that were ideal for farming. Food could be fished, trapped, hunted, foraged, cultivated, or traded along the river system. The region was hospitable to horses and dairy animals. The Chesapeake ranges between freshwater and salty, so it supports both kinds of marine life in complex interlocking lifecycles. Crabs and oysters, the latter growing on giant underwater "bars," could be harvested in quantities. There were terrapins, which in the nineteenth century would supply the kitchens of grand hotels in Baltimore, Philadelphia, New York, Boston, and other cities. There were so many waterfowl that in the early twentieth century commercial hunters illegally mass-harvested them using Gatling guns, bringing down dozens with a single volley.

Jamestown, however, was terribly situated. Colonist Thomas Gates described it as being

> in somewhat an unwholesome and sickly air, by reason it is in a marish ground, low, flat to the river, and hath no fresh-water springs serving the town but what we drew from a well six or seven fathom deep fed by the brackish river oozing into it; from whence I verily believe the chief causes have proceeded of many diseases and sicknesses which have happened to our people, who are indeed strangely afflicted with fluxes and agues.[4]

No one knew what crops might grow or how to grow them. The colony was expected to provide England not only with gold and silver, but also with wine, olives, oranges, and almonds. These fancy foods grew in the Mediterranean on the same latitudes as Virginia, so the plan was to supply England with them from America. Unfortunately, the planners neglected to factor in America's colder climate. Moreover, since England wanted agricultural products that did not grow at home, the English had no knowledge of how to cultivate them. A period of desperate experimentation began to find a staple crop for the colony, involving repeated experiments with King James's personal hobbyhorse, silkworms. While Virginia did ultimately produce some silk, in the main the colony seemed destined to produce nothing finer than masts, pitch, tar, turpentine, hemp, flax, woad (a blue dye, later replaced by indigo), and madder (a red dye).

The Indians fed themselves easily, but the Jamestown colonists were frequently at the brink, and sometimes over the line, of starvation. Once they were disembarked into the deadly wilderness, the Virginia Company's "planters" attempted to replicate the bureaucratic and social structure of England. Idle, wealthy aristocrats kept tables for the colony's too-numerous gentlemen of fashion, attended by footmen who were themselves strangers to labor; meanwhile, others starved. There was a jeweler and a perfumer, but only one competent carpenter. During an investigation in 1623, Smith recalled that the company was at fault for "maintaining one hundred men [servants and guards] for Governour, one hundred for two Deputies, fifty for the Treasurer, five and twenty for the Secretary, and more for the Marshall and other Officers who were never there nor adventured any thing, but onely preferred by favour to be Lords over them that broke the ice and beat the path, and must teach them what to doe."[5]

After Smith left Virginia, Jamestown hit its low point: the "starving time" of the winter of 1609–10 under the fatally inept administration of Smith's enemy, John Ratcliffe. Smith had managed to trade with the Indians, but after he left, Powhatan seems to have deliberately starved the colony, and settlers resorted to cannibalism as the population dwindled to sixty. Refugees who returned to England on board the *Swallow* in 1610 brought tales that all London heard, though the Virginia Company denied them. The horrific stories were substantially true; a recent archaeological discovery indicates that a fourteen-year-old girl who died was subsequently butchered and eaten by other colonists.[6]

The capitalistically named *Sea Venture*, a vessel bringing colonists to Jamestown, was shipwrecked on the Bermuda archipelago, off the Florida coast, in 1609. The misadventure occasioned a ten-month island interlude for the colonists; some found it pleasant, spurning rescue to remain there.[7] A publication about the experience, titled *A True Reportory of the Wracke, and Redemption of Sir Thomas Gates, Knight, upon, and from the Islands of the Bermudas*, which begins with the words "A most dreadful tempest," appears to have been one of the inspirations for Shakespeare's *The Tempest*, performed in the presence of King James on November 1, 1611, and repeated the following winter.

Among the castaways rescued from Bermuda who went on to Virginia, arriving in the aftermath of the starving winter, was the young farmer John Rolfe, born in Norfolk, England, in 1585. Rolfe's experience on Bermuda had been cruel; he left buried there an infant daughter named Bermuda; his wife also apparently died, though her death is not noted in the historical record.

Rolfe was an "ardent" smoker who seems to have come to Virginia with the intention of trying tobacco cultivation. That wasn't in the Virginia Company's playbook. It certainly wasn't what King James wanted.

9

Our Principall Wealth

A custome lothsome to the eye, hatefull to the Nose, harmefull to the braine, dangerous to the Lungs, and in the blacke stinking fume thereof, neerest resembling the horrible Stigian smoke of the pit that is bottomelesse.

—King James I on smoking, *A Counterblaste to Tobacco* (1604)

CHEW IT, SNORT IT, smoke it—any way you use it, tobacco gets you high.

Native Americans used it for ceremonial and medicinal purposes, but now an increasing number of Englishmen and women wanted regular doses of this addictive drug, imported or smuggled in from Spanish territories and sold in small quantities for a high price.

Londoners began getting hooked on what they called sot-weed, for the way it intoxicated the smoker. So much money was spent on it that the balance of trade between Spain and England was affected. Spain guarded its tobacco monopoly jealously, but John Rolfe obtained the seed of a strain that grew in the Spanish colonies of Venezuela and Trinidad. It was industrial theft: Rolfe convinced a sea captain, who would have been hung by the Spanish had he been discovered, to smuggle the tiny seeds to him from Trinidad. Once Rolfe was himself planted in Virginia, he began raising his crop, naming his plantation Varina after the tobacco strain; it is still a working farm in Virginia today.

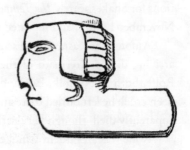

Indian tobacco pipe from Virginia. From Fairholt.

With Rolfe's first successful crop of tobacco in 1612, Virginia found its staple. Instead of providing delicacies for England's wealthy with olive groves and vineyards, the Virginians began supplying cheap, strong-smelling, habit-forming weed to the plebes. The tobacco the Virginians grew was universally accounted inferior to the leaf of Hispaniola, Cuba, Trinidad, Puerto Rico, or Venezuela, but it cost less.

Colonists quickly went over to cultivating the leaf. Tobacco required land and labor but not a fortune to get started, and it remained the most important American cash crop throughout the colonial years. The market was at first modest, but it swelled. Virginia's production reached thirty million pounds by the end of the seventeenth century, and one hundred million pounds fifty years later.

Its widespread availability created a mass consumer culture in England. People were willing to work to have the money to buy tobacco, although, as the anti-tobacco King James ruefully (and correctly) noted, many a man had been

Rotterdam 1623: expelling smoke through the nose was the fashionable way to smoke. From Fairholt.

known to "smoke himselfe to death with it." James hated tobacco no less than he hated Raleigh, whom he ordered beheaded in 1618. Meanwhile, the English consumers' new nicotine habit sustained the colonial economy that brought it to them.

When the new "partners" of the Virginia Company arrived in America, they found to their dismay that they were conscripts, coerced into gang labor under martial law. Everything they produced was to belong to the company, so they had no incentive to work.

Half or more of them died shortly after arrival. As word got out that Virginia was a death trap, agents, popularly known as "spirits," went combing the streets for potential indentured servants for the colony—a process that included abducting children, bringing the phrase *spirited away* into popular usage, as well as the word *kidnap*.[1] Some two hundred boys were taken from London in 1618, while groups of young women were dispatched in 1619 to provide wives for colonists; company officials were instructed to see that the women were not married against their will.[2]

Many of the desperately poor who went to Virginia were urbanites from London or Bristol, England's second city.[3] There were indentured servants in England, but their term was a year and they received a wage. In Virginia, the term was between four and seven years, and the wages were paid up front in the form of a ticket for a transatlantic crossing.[4]

The conditions of those crossings were described in a 1623 letter from Virginia that, according to the Oxford English Dictionary, provides the first known instance of the much older word *funke* as meaning "a strong smell or stink": "Betwixt decks there can hardlie a man fetch his breath by reason there ariseth such a funke in the night that it causes putrefaction of bloud."[5] This was not a description of a slave ship; they smelled even worse.

Realizing that there was little reason to come to Virginia and little incentive beyond mere survival to work hard once arrived, Virginia governor Thomas Dale threw open the door to private land acquisition in 1616, hoping to stimulate growth. He offered a good deal: the "old planters" who were already there got a hundred acres each, along with another hundred acres if they were company shareholders. Newcomers got fifty acres.

The colony had begun as a commons under military discipline, but by changing its regime to one in which individual colonists could become landowners, Dale created a real estate market, which in turn quickly became a land grab.[6] But the land was worthless without labor. It now fell to individual entrepreneurs, not the Virginia Company, to address the labor problem in Virginia, and by 1617 the company was allowing semi-independent plantations, called "hundreds," which transported their own labor.

Indentures were probably under way in Virginia by 1617, but the first extant contract of indenture that has come down to us, issued by the Virginia partnership called the Berkeley Hundred, is dated September 17, 1619. That year, the colony's secretary John Pory wrote to London: "All our riches for the present doe consiste in Tobacco, wherein one man by his owne labour hath in one yeare raised to himselfe to the value of 200£ sterling; and another by the meanes of six servants hath cleared at one crop a thousand pounds English."

Then, as if thinking it through as he was writing, Pory corrected himself in the same paragraph:

"Our principall wealth (I should have said) consisteth in servants."[7]
Workers were already capital assets.

Planters rarely imported specific indentured servants. Upon arrival, the survivors of the voyage were displayed in a market and—they used the word—"sold." John Harrower, the Scottish indentured servant who left a journal of his tragically short life in Virginia, recalled the scene on May 16, 1774, still aboard the ship that brought him to Fredericksburg, Virginia; interestingly, he used the term "soul driver," more commonly associated with the slave trade:

> This day severalls came on board to purchase servts. Indentures and among them there was two Soul drivers. They are men who make it their bussines to go on board all ships who have in either Servants or Convicts and buy sometimes the whole and sometimes a parcell of them as they can agree, and then they drive them through the Country like a parcell of Sheep untill they can sell them to advantage.[8]

This manner of labor distribution uncomfortably reminded some of the slave markets of the Muslim world, which those with military backgrounds might possibly have encountered (or, as in the case of Captain John Smith, been sold in).

Planters had a sweet deal, known as the "headright" system: they were given fifty acres of land for every indentured servant whose passage they paid—so they not only got the benefit of several years of wageless labor, but also received the land to do it on. This facilitated the acquisition of large tracts of land by those with even modest amounts of capital. Headrights could be sold; by the 1650s, they were being traded for as little as forty or fifty pounds of tobacco.[9] A real estate market had been created out of enclosed Virginia land, with any claims of sovereignty by Native Americans instantly discarded.

The urban poor who came as laborers were unskilled and unaccustomed to agricultural work. The descendants of multiple malnourished generations, they were not physically strong enough for the backbreaking task of clearing what George Washington would call "this wooden Country," and their mortality rates after arrival were dreadful.[10] They were, however, sufficient to amass large landholdings from headrights for those with the capital to sponsor them as land speculation began.

⋙⋘

John Rolfe is most remembered in popular history not for his pioneering of Virginia's great staple crop but for having married Pocahontas, a daughter of the Pamunkey chief Powhatan.

Pocahontas had learned English after being kidnapped by the Jamestown settlers in 1613, during which time she was Christianized and renamed Rebecca. As a prosperous tobacco farmer, Rolfe traveled to London in 1618 together with Rebecca/Pocahontas and their infant son, Thomas, but she fell ill and died while preparing to return to Virginia. Fearing his son would not survive the voyage, Rolfe reluctantly left him in England and returned to America.

Back in Virginia, Rolfe documented, rather off-handedly, the first known sale of African slaves in Anglo-America, from a passing Dutch vessel. One day "about the latter end of August" in 1619, as Rolfe described it in his historic letter of January 1620 (modern calendar) to Sir Edwin Sandys of the Virginia Company:

> a Dutch man of Warr of the burden of a 160 tunnes arriued at Point-Comfort. . . . He brought not any thing but 20. and odd Negroes, wch the Governor and Cape Marchant bought for victualls (whereof he was in greate need as he pretended) at the best and easyest rates they could.[11]

It was a good deal for the purchasers, and, since the seller got some much-needed food, perhaps a good deal for the seller as well. But if it was a win-win for buyer and seller alike, it was at the expense of those who were bought and sold.

Historians ever since have wished Rolfe had provided more detail. These were not, as has sometimes been claimed, the first black people to come to Virginia; a census five months earlier counted thirty-two.[12] Nor were they the first slaves whose sale was documented. Already in *The Generall Historie of Virginia, New England, and the Summer Isles*, John Smith had noted an inter-Indian slave trade of sorts, though it overlapped with the concept of marriage. Powhatan, Pocahontas's father, had sold a daughter of his, and Smith chided him for underpricing:

> [Powhatan said,] "I have sold [my daughter] within this few days to a great Werowance, for two bushels of rawrenoke, three days journey from me."
> I replied . . . she was but twelve years old . . . he should have for her three times the worth of the rawrenoke in beads, copper, hatchets, &c.[13]

The supremacy of Dutch maritime commerce was a mark of shame for the English. In a report submitted to King James, Sir Walter Raleigh had noted that the Dutch "have a continual trade into this kingdom with five hundred or six hundred ships yearly with merchandize of other countries . . . and we trade not with fifty ships into their country in a year."[14]

"The establishment of the American settlements," writes Philip A. Bruce, "was the first step on the part of the English people towards a successful competition with the Dutch merchant marine."[15] England was a heavy importer of raw materials from other European nations, for which it had to pay in scarce specie. Opening up North American colonies would make a whole array of products cheaply available to them: tar and pitch, salt and potash, iron and timber, hides and pelts.

It was not unusual for the Dutch to be nosing around the Chesapeake. In flagrant violation of England's rules, they carried Virginia and Maryland tobacco to their market in Amsterdam and gave better prices for peltry. The Dutch merchant fleet and credit services were far and away the world's most advanced. But as their commercial power grew globally, carrying goods was no longer enough for them, and they moved toward vertical integration.

The Dutch, who were not yet trading in slaves on an industrial scale, could not attack the Portuguese under the terms of their Twelve Years' Truce with Spain (1609–1621), because Portugal was under the Spanish crown between 1581 and 1640. But they occasionally sold slaves who had been taken as prizes from Portuguese slavers by English privateers. John Thornton argues that the "20. and Odd Negroes" were Kimbundu-speaking soldiers from Angola, captured during the large, formalized military campaigns of a war waged by the Portuguese against the kingdom of Ndongo.[16] Historian Engel Sluiter provides evidence that they were nabbed by an English corsair in a raid on a Portuguese ship on its way to Veracruz.[17] The raided cargo was then presumably swapped over for commercial liquidation to that "Dutch man of warr" (with an English "Pilott") that visited Jamestown in August 1619.

If so, the "20. and Odd" would have been Catholic, at least nominally. Some of them probably spoke some Portuguese.

Ruin of the Catholic church of São Salvador do Congo, known in Kikongo as kulu mbimbi, *"strong place," built in 1491 at the royal seat of Mbanza-Kongo, in present-day northern Angola. July 2012.*

Central Africa was Catholicized in 1491—before Columbus crossed the Atlantic —when the *manikongo* (Kongo king) Nzinga a Nkuwu at his hilltop capital of Mbanza-Kongo converted—not at sword's point, but enthusiastically and immediately upon the arrival of two missionaries. The *manikongo*, who ruled the largest empire in Africa at the time,* accepted baptism and became King João I.

João seems to have grasped immediately the political uses of Catholicism. Converting his territory gave him a powerful new set of tools to establish his hegemony over the freelance priesthood of traditional Kongo religion, as well as allying him with powerful European patrons and giving him access to previously unknown manufactured goods, most especially including guns.[18] Building churches throughout his vast kingdom, he established diplomatic relations with the Vatican.

The symbols and beliefs of Catholicism merged well with the symbols of traditional Bakongo religion, creating a syncretized version of Catholicism that was compatible with existing Kongo cosmology and continued ancient practices,

---

*Reaching from present-day Gabon to present-day Zambia.

which were arguably no more superstitious or magical than fifteenth-century Catholicism. The Bakongo already had a cross—the *dikenga*—a cosmogram that signified the meeting in time of the land of the living with the land of the dead on the other side of the water. It was a midpoint cross, not a chest-high crucifix, but it was recognizable. The Bible that the priest revered was, to the Bakongo, clearly an *nkisi*—a power object.

As Central Africans became the most numerously slaved people of the African trade, the Kongo-Catholic syncretization— a "fully Africanized" Christianity, in Thornton's words, which came into existence *before* the Middle Passage—was transported to all points of the Americas, serving as a fundamental backbone of African culture in the Americas.[19] It took root easily in the Catholic territories established by Spain and Portugal, which would lead to enslaved Bakongo being suspected in the English colonies as potential allies of the Spanish.

Rolfe went on in his "20. and odd" letter to describe the colonists' fear of Spanish attack in the coming spring:

> wee have no place of strength to retreate unto, no shipping of certeynty (wch would be to us as the wodden walles of England) no sound and experienced souldyers to undertake, no Engineers and arthmen to erect works, few Ordenance, not a serviceable carriadge to mount them on; not Ammunycon of powlder, shott and leade, to fight 2. wholl dayes, no not one gunner belonging to the Plantaccon.[20]

By that time, the Anglo-American tobacco economy in Virginia was well into a debt-driven boom, with interest typically at 6 percent per annum. With credit, people drank up the profits, then ordered another round. "The first legislative assembly in Virginia in 1619 felt obliged to pass acts against excess in apparel and also against drunkenness," writes Edmund S. Morgan. "The thirst of Virginians became notorious in England. . . . The ships that anchored in Virginia's great rivers every summer were, as one settler observed, moving taverns, whose masters, usually private traders, got the greater part of the tobacco that should have been enriching the colonists and the shareholders of the company. . . . There were sometimes as many as seventeen sail of ships to be seen at one time in the James River."[21]

The colonists on occasion starved. Maybe it was self-destructive depression under the harsh conditions, or maybe the sheer ineptitude of their gentry-heavy colonial population. But you could also blame it on the weed: they were so determined to grow tobacco that they neglected to grow food. Colonists were officially required to cultivate a plot of corn, but many ignored the law and relied instead on the Native Americans to do the base labor of raising corn while they chased tobacco riches, but the natives didn't always want to sell their corn to the colonists, so sometimes the Virginians went and took it.

The income that in theory accrued to the Virginia Company was being systematically drained away by its shamelessly corrupt officials, who repressed dissent brutally as its investors lost money and colonists died of diseases, mysterious distempers, and violence. A massacre commanded by Pocahontas's uncle Opechancanough killed about a third of the colonists and kidnapped twenty women in more than thirty separate surprise attacks on March 22, 1622, with the aim of driving the English out. The ailing John Rolfe was a victim of the campaign: one of the raids destroyed his plantation, after which he died, though whether from violence or from illness is unknown.

That massacre, along with the concomitant destruction of productive facilities, was followed by yet another starving time. With fewer than a thousand colonists still alive, King James rescinded the Virginia Company's charter, reverting the colony to royal status—a decision that earned James the vituperation of future Virginia historians. Edmund S. Morgan, in his landmark history of slavery in Virginia, responded: "Because the Stuart kings became symbols of arbitrary government and because Sir Edwin Sandys [one of the proprietors of the Virginia company] was a champion of Parliamentary power and was even accused at the time of being a republican, historians for long interpreted the dissolution of the Virginia Company as a blow dealt to democracy by tyranny. Modern scholarship has altered the verdict and shown that any responsible monarch would have been obliged to stop the reckless shipment of his subjects to their deaths."[22]

Colonial development in Virginia was going to be a long-term investment, far longer than the timetables of profit could hold out for. By the time the rescission of the Virginia Company's charter became final in 1624, investors in the company had lost £200,000 and more than three-fourths of the six thousand or so people who had emigrated since 1607 were dead.[23]

And by the following year, so was King James. But not before he empowered an enemy of Virginia.

In his capacity as King James's secretary, George Calvert was the monarch's man in Parliament to defend the proposed "Spanish match," the never-achieved royal marriage of James's second son, Charles, to Hapsburg princess Maria Ana, daughter of Felipe III. The idea that Charles might take a Spanish-Austrian Catholic bride horrified the Puritans in Parliament. King James's older son, Henry, known for his upright Protestant morality, had been the great popular hope of the Puritans, but he died in 1612 at the age of eighteen, leaving younger brother Charles in line for the throne.

In the end the Spanish princess would not marry a Protestant, and though Charles traveled to Spain to court her, he would not convert to Catholicism, so the marriage never came to pass. But the fallout from the affair led to a deterioration of relations between England and Spain, followed by war. It also left Calvert on the outs politically. He resigned his position and came out of the closet as a Catholic. James rewarded Calvert for his services, and got him out of the way, by awarding him a barony in northern Ireland and a title in the Irish peerage: Lord Baron of Baltimore.

Then Charles, the future king of England, scandalized the Puritans by marrying a French Catholic Bourbon princess, Henrietta Maria de Medici. That's Maria as in the Virgin Mary, and also as in the territory that was named for the new queen consort: Maryland.

10

Maria's Land

Does my hair trouble you?[1]

—King Charles I to his executioner, January 30, 1649

IN HER MARRIAGE CONTRACT, the fifteen-year-old Queen Consort Henrietta Maria was guaranteed the full practice of her Roman Catholic religion, which enraged the Puritans.

Born in 1609, nine years after her father King Henri IV's Edict of Nantes provided civil guarantees for French Protestants, Henrietta Maria came from France to England with a mission of spearheading Catholic power by means of strategic marriage. She had learned the art of queening at the knee of her mother, Marie de Medici, who commissioned a series of twenty-six allegorical paintings depicting her life from the prolific Peter Paul Rubens.

She brought with her from France eleven liveried musicians and three singing boys, who performed sacred music composed for her. The English crown was considerably less affluent than the French, and Henrietta Maria's retinue was smaller than the Bourbons were accustomed to in France, but it was large enough that her household staff included a "keeper of the parrots" and two dwarves, Jeffrey and Sarah, both of whom had servants.[2] "Pet" dwarves were common figures in royal courts, but in the case of Charles and Henrietta Maria, they had the function of making the monarchs look bigger: Charles was five foot four, and Henrietta Maria was so short she only came up to his shoulder.

England began its slide to civil war in 1629 when Parliament, with strong Puritan representation, refused to convene. For the Puritans, having a Catholic queen was a dreadful infamy; they saw Charles as soft on popish Spain. By that time, England's monarch had deferred to Parliament for over three hundred years, but now Charles attempted to run England without Parliament, a standoff that lasted eleven years. During that period the royals also had a tense relationship with William Laud, the Archbishop of Canterbury, who persecuted both Puritans and Catholics while discharging his responsibilities as head of the twelve-member Lords Commissioners for Foreign Plantations.

The ensuing migration of Puritans to America defined one of the principal power blocs of future American politics, as approximately twenty thousand dissenters came to the Massachusetts Bay Colony in the 1630s. Unlike most other immigrants to the Americas, these were not single young men, but families. Many were relatively prosperous, and the community they built was stable, productive, and repressive.

Puritan New England, a culture of literate, industrious, small farmers, was on guard against tyranny and against witchcraft—which, for them, included Catholicism. There was no doubt: the Antichrist was the pope, and the Spanish were his henchmen. Immigrants had to be formally admitted to New England: the Puritans required letters of recommendation for potential colonists, who could only be part of the Calvinist New England Congregationalist Church. They were anti-episcopal (didn't have bishops), and they were intolerant of the episcopal Anglicans, as well as of the Quakers, to say nothing of Catholics.

In 1629, the same year that Puritans began fleeing to New England, George Calvert, now titled Lord Baron of Baltimore, asked Charles I for a land grant. His short-lived Avalon colony in Newfoundland had been defeated by a harsh winter. Now he wanted the territory belonging to Virginia on both the western and eastern banks of the upper Chesapeake, as mapped out by Captain John Smith. He pitched the charter as providing a buffer zone to protect His Majesty's grand Chesapeake Bay from encroachment by the Dutch and Swedish. The former had founded Nieuw Amsterdam in 1625, while the latter, colonizing parts of what later became Delaware and Pennsylvania, named a river and a settlement after the Swedish Queen Christina.

If the Swedish queen had a settlement named in her honor, what homage befit the queen of England?

Calvert died only weeks before his land grant was finalized, but it was bestowed on his son Cecil Calvert, who inherited his title. Writing in Latin, a priest gave an account of the colony in 1633, before the first colonists had sailed: "The Most Serene King of England desired that it should be called the land of Maria or Maryland, in honor of Maria, his wife. The same Most Serene King, out of his noble disposition, recently, in the month of June, 1632, gave this Province to the Lord Baron of Baltamore and his heirs forever."[3]

Praying to the Virgin Mary was a razor-sharp dividing line between Catholics and Protestants, the former of whom saw it as a mystical experience and the latter of whom saw it as idolatry. Virginia had been named for the Virgin Queen, Elizabeth, whose Church of England had removed the worship of the Virgin Mary from its liturgical calendar. Now there would be another Virgin-inspired queen-named colony in the typhoidal swampland—this one appropriate for Catholic pioneers, for whom Marianism was at once a religious and political imperative.

Mary's Land was to be tolerant, but Maryland would not be Catholic turf the way the Spanish domains were. Quite the contrary: Maryland was officially Anglican, the majority of its colonists were Anglican or Protestant, and no Catholic church was actually established there, though Jesuits manned missions.

Never again would the Chesapeake be under the control of a single entity. Its division into upper (Maryland) and lower (Virginia) affected everything from the cultivation of tobacco—the two colonies could never coordinate how much they would produce or even what the standard measure was—to the two territories' opposing status in 1861, when Virginia went Confederate while Maryland remained in the Union.

The first Maryland colonists arrived in 1634 on the *Ark*, traveling via the Antilles. The priest Andrew White, who crossed the Atlantic with them, wrote in his journal that "we came before [the island of] Monserat, where is a noble plantation of Irish Catholiques whome the virginians would not suffer to live with them because of their religion."[4] This first known written instance of the word "virginian" was, significantly, used in connection with Virginia's intolerance. Virginia was officially Anglican and remained intolerant until independence, although Virginia was not settled by religious dissenters and was not particularly pious. "With no resident bishop and only a handful of ministers to watch over its rowdy, scattered populace," writes Paul Lucas, "seventeenth-century Virginia became noted for its lack of religiosity."[5]

"As for Virginia, we expected little from them but blows," wrote Father White. When they arrived, he was impressed by the "Patomecke" (Potomac)

River, which the new colonists attempted to rename St. Gregory's; it was, he wrote, "the sweetest and greatest river I have seene, so that the Thames is but a little finger to it."[6]

Father White brought with him a Portuguese-surnamed indentured servant of African descent, Mathias de Sousa, described as a "molato," along with another "molato" named Francisco, so free men of color—albeit indentured—were among the founders of the colony. Father White assigned his headrights to one Ferdinando Pulton, who claimed land grants based on the importation of twenty-one people.[7]

The Virginia colonists were already insolent. In a 1634 letter written from Jamestown, Captain Thomas Yong of the Maryland expedition wrote, "I have bene informed that some of the [Virginia] Councellors have bene bold enough in a presumptuous manner to say, to such as told them that perhaps their disobedience might cause them to be sent for into England, That if the King would have them he must come himself and fetch them."[8]

Virginia was by that time relatively stable. Its food problem had largely been solved by the successful establishment of large herds of cattle and especially hogs, which can have two or more litters a year of up to a dozen piglets at a time. With so much land available for pasturage, raising meat animals was practical, and the easy availability of high-quality protein from meat and dairy products may have been the salvation of the Virginia colony.

Virginia was impresarial, its founding the work of a corporation with investors, but Maryland was a proprietorship. Lord Baltimore *owned* it. A number of counties in Maryland are named for his family members: Calvert (the family name), Cecil (for Cecil Calvert, the second Lord Baltimore), Charles (for Charles Calvert, the third Lord Baltimore), Anne Arundel (Cecil Calvert's wife, Charles Calvert's mother), and Talbot (Lady Grace Talbot, Cecil Calvert's sister).

Written in Latin, King James's charter granted to Lord Baltimore the *hactenus inculta*, or uncultivated lands, "partly occupied by Savages, having no knowledge of the Divine Being." As compensation, the king and his heirs and successors were to receive (according to contemporary translation) "TWO INDIAN ARROWS of those Parts, to be delivered to the said Castle of *Windsor*, every Year, on Tuesday in Easter-week; and also the fifth Part of all Gold and Silver Ore, which shall happen from Time to Time, to be found within the aforesaid Limits."

The Maryland charter covered both shores of the upper Chesapeake, creating a territory divided into two parts by water. The "western shore" and the "Eastern Shore" of Maryland do not meet, but must connect across water.* The Virginians had the Chesapeake's four great rivers in their territory, though they were not yet fully navigable—from south to north, the James, the York, the Rappahannock, and the Potomac. Maryland occupied the northern bank of the Potomac, but never attempted to navigate it commercially.

Calvert's territory did, however, have a grand harbor on its western shore. It would not be of much use for transatlantic traffic, but would later be the commercial powerhouse of the Chesapeake's communication with the westwardly expanding domestic market: Baltimore.

The Virginians were too few in number to have occupied the Maryland territory, but William Claiborne (or Clayborne, or Clairborne), a Virginian from Kent, England, was already invested in the territory and opposed Baltimore's plan. Claiborne, a member of the Virginia Council, had named and claimed proprietorship of Kent's (or Kent) Island, which sits in the middle of the Chesapeake adjacent to the Eastern Shore. He focused not on planting tobacco but on fur trading, which obliged him to have good relations with the Native Americans. Claiborne insisted that the charter's language could not apply to Kent Island, to which he asserted ownership rights. Planning for the island to be the hub of a mercantile empire he would build, he had convinced settlers to move there and plant it with orchards and vines. He set up a shipyard, where he had the pinnace *Long Tayle* built in 1631, three years before the arrival of Lord Baltimore's colony—"the first boat built solely on the bay," writes Frederick Tilp.[9]

The first naval battle in the Anglo-American colonies took place in 1635 between Maryland and Virginia, when Lord Baltimore's pinnaces defeated Claiborne's vessels at the entrance to the Pocomoke River.[10] Claiborne attempted various times to get back what he considered his land, through military conflict and diplomatic wrangling, but he ultimately relinquished the struggle in 1657 after an intra-Chesapeake hostility that lasted more than twenty years. Remembered as the champion of Virginia's former grandeur, he was the founder of a

---

*By custom "Eastern Shore" is capitalized, but "western shore" is not.

still-prominent family line of politically connected American bluebloods that includes his great-great-grandson W. C. C. Claiborne (the Virginian who was the first American governor of Mississippi and Louisiana).

Perhaps it was Calvert's experience with the failed colony at Newfoundland that led him to issue and enforce instructions to his colonists to grow food crops for themselves: "that they cause all the planters to imploy their servants in planting of sufficient quantity of corne and other profision of victuall and that they do not suffer them to plant any other comodity whatsoever before that be done in a sufficient proportion wch they are to observe yearely."[11]

Plantations were anything but self-sufficient in food. As John Smith explained to a royal commission, "Corne was stinted [valued] at two shillings six pence the bushell, and Tobacco at three shillings the pound; and they value a mans labour [in tobacco] a yeere worth fifty or threescore pound, but in Corne not worth ten pound."[12] The capital-intensive nature of a plantation required the dedication of all land to maximum financial return, with supplies imported and paid for on credit. But Lord Baltimore's insistence that "Mary's Land" raise its own "victuall" implanted from the beginning a culture of expert and varied cultivation in the colony, with long-range consequences for the state's high-quality food supply.

Maryland put itself to the cultivation of tobacco from early days, with the result that Virginia planters had competitors who could be expected to increase production if they held back.

New England (Connecticut, Rhode Island, Massachusetts, New Hampshire, and, later, Vermont and Maine) never developed a staple crop, or a plantation system. New England had slavery in the colonial years, but unlike Virginia, it never became a slave society, in which all social and economic relations revolve around slavery. One of the first slaveowners in Massachusetts, Samuel Maverick, was the object of a complaint from a captive African woman whom he had force-mated with an African man; but without plantations, and cooped up in the limited space of houses in town, New Englanders did not engage much in slave breeding.[13] New Englanders bought slaves, but mostly in small numbers: Africans (or creoles) from the Antilles and, later, Native Americans from Carolina, who were generally destined to be household, urban, or small-farm workers. Nor was New England a heavy consumer of indentured labor.

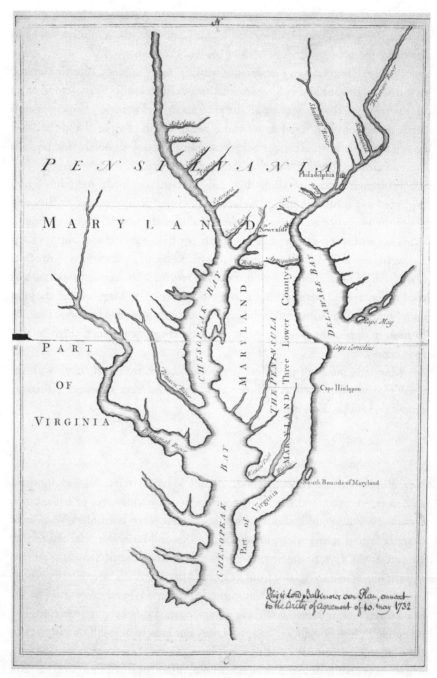

The Eastern Shore is prominent in this depiction of Lord Baltimore's Maryland in 1732.

New England survived in its early days the way the French did in Canada: on the fur trade. Beaver pelts were a principal export, and King Charles provided a market for them all by himself. He particularly liked silk-lined beaver hats, worn with brightly colored hatbands, and bought them not only for himself but for his retinue. According to Nick Bunker, he bought "sixty-four beaver hats in 1618, fifty-seven in 1619, forty-six in 1623, and forty-three in 1624." Bunker estimates that as the beaver hat became popularized as "an emblem of status" for the peerage and the landed gentry, a minimum of twenty-three thousand of them a year were needed to accommodate the demand.[14]

The small farmers of New England exported a variety of food and commodities, especially corn, and they diversified into becoming fishermen, lumberjacks, and shipbuilders, then developed into shippers, merchants, bankers, and insurers.

David Hackett Fischer's tracing of four English folkways in America provides a model for appreciating the cultural contrast: 1) the Puritans of southeast and northeast of London, who moved to New England; 2) the Royalists of the south and west, who moved to Virginia; 3) the up-country Quakers, to Pennsylvania; and 4) the "Scotch-Irish," to the Appalachians. Fischer surveys the demographics of England from which each migration came and demonstrates strong cultural continuity between locales on either side of the Atlantic, each of which would develop into a distinct political tendency in the independent American republic.

Slavery was not a new idea in English culture, particularly in the area from which the largest number of Virginia's early populators came. "Virginia's recruiting ground," writes Fischer, "was a broad region in the south and west of England" of scarce urban development and large rural manors—an area where slavery had earlier (though no longer) existed for centuries, going back to the Roman era. "During the eighth and ninth centuries," writes Fischer, "the size of major slaveholdings in the south of England reached levels comparable to large plantations in the American South. When Bishop Wilfred acquired Selsey in Sussex [in the late seventh century], he emancipated 250 slaves on a single estate. Few plantations in the American South were so large even at their peak in the nineteenth century."[15]

The Puritans of New England and the Royalist Virginians, opposed to each other from the start, struggled to establish their respective colonies in America as the hatred between "Roundheads" (Puritans, so called because they cut their hair short, who in popular telling were commoners descended from Saxons) and

In this woodcut tobacconist's card from ca. 1700, Virginia
cavaliers drink and smoke while black slaves labor behind them.
Images of Africans at work appeared in a variety of English
tobacco advertising materials in the late seventeenth century,
along with (not depicted here) Indians depicted with black skin,
in tobacco-leaf skirts and headdress, overtly promoting as part
of the product's public image its origin as an "Indian weed"
cultivated by slave labor in Virginia. From Fairholt.

"Cavaliers" (Anglicans, who wore their hair long and were said to be aristocrats
descended from French Normans, who were in turn the descendants of Norse-
men, or Vikings) erupted in 1642 into what has been remembered in England as
the Civil War, which had a strong echo in America.

The Puritans versus the Cavaliers: not coincidentally, in North America these
words connoted the two power bases of New England and Virginia. The Royalist
Virginia gentry, who were largely descendants of English family webs transferred
to America, believed in aristocracy, hierarchical society, luxury, idleness, and servants. Their identification as "Cavaliers"—a word meaning "horsemen," or, more
broadly, "knights"—links them with the Spanish *caballeros* and the French *cheva-
liers*. Like them, the Cavaliers had the opposite of the Puritans' work ethic. "Many

Virginians of upper and middle ranks aspired to behave like gentlemen," writes Fischer. "The words 'gentleman' and 'independent' were used synonymously, and 'independence' in this context means freedom from the necessity of labor."[16]

The stringently religious Puritans did not gamble, but Virginia planters gambled compulsively. The Puritans suspected them of being Catholic sympathizers. By the 1630s, the more affluent Virginians were buying African slaves from Dutch traders on an ongoing basis, while Virginia frontier traders, who were something of a renegade element in the colony, enslaved and sold Native Americans.[17]

Henrietta Maria opened her chapel at Somerset House in 1636, after seven years of work. It was a safe place to attend Mass, and thousands did. It was also the height of fashion. The chapel hummed with motets commissioned from the queen consort's preferred composers. Marian imagery was everywhere. "Visitors thronged to see the mesmerizing decorative scheme," writes Erin Griffey, "replete with paintings and a special sacristy. Conversions of prominent courtiers and aristocrats, ladies in particular, were not uncommon in 1637. [Archbishop] Laud was incensed by the public scandal."[18] But pursuant to an anti-superstition act of the Puritan Parliament, Henrietta Maria's chapel was destroyed by a mob of iconoclasts in 1643.[19] They tore its crowning work, Rubens's *Crucifixion*, into bits and threw the pieces into the Thames, along with the rest of the painting and sculpture the chapel contained.

By then, the English Civil War was under way. The Puritans, whose New Model Army was the first modern army in England, beat the forces of King Charles in 1645 and established the Commonwealth of England in 1649. Parliament carried out one of the most radical acts in all of European history when it tried, convicted, and, on January 30, 1649, killed the king. Remembering the botched execution of his grandmother, Mary Queen of Scots, Charles Stuart put his long Cavalier hair away from his neck into a cap to allow his executioner (a professional, brought from France for the occasion) a clean shot at his neck, and was successfully beheaded with a single stroke.

Once Puritans no longer feared persecution in England, out-migration to New England stopped as suddenly as it had begun. The region would not receive another mass migration for nearly two centuries. There was even a reverse migration back to England, since previously closed doors were now open to well-connected Puritan businessmen.

The Puritan regicide further poisoned the relations between Catholic and Protestant Europe. The designation of the ambitious New Model Army leader and king-killer Oliver Cromwell as Lord Protector of England, Wales, Scotland, and Ireland in 1653 began an era of intolerance, during which the execution of heretics increased and theaters remained shut down.

In Maryland, the colonial assembly passed the Act of Toleration in 1649 at the Calverts' urging. The first law in the colonies concerning religious tolerance, it reiterated the tolerant policy that had been part of Lord Baltimore's instruction from the beginning. But after a ten-man Puritan council headed by Maryland's old nemesis William Claiborne took charge of Maryland in post-Cromwell 1654, a new law prohibited open practice of the Catholic faith.[20] In 1658, Calvert managed to get the Act of Toleration reinstated. Still, on July 23, 1659, the council issued a directive to "Justices of the Peace to seize any Quakers that might come into their districts and to whip them from Constable to Constable until they should reach the bounds of the Province."[21]

Quakers, who were antislavery and were therefore unwelcome, presented a new social and political problem for the nominally Anglican Cavaliers.[22] The first seed of Quakerism was planted in Virginia in 1656 by the Londoner Elizabeth Harris, who remained in Virginia for a year or so and proselytized. Quaker George Wilson, who had been whipped from constable to constable through three different towns and banished from Massachusetts, arrived in Virginia in 1661 and was imprisoned until "his flesh actually rotted away from his bones," in the words of a chronicler.[23]

Under the Puritans, Royalists fled England for Virginia and Maryland, an exodus that continued even after the Restoration of 1660. "From 1645 to 1665," writes Fischer, "Virginians multiplied more than threefold and Marylanders increased elevenfold, while New Englanders merely doubled."[24]

Other Cavaliers fled hostile Puritan England for the island of Barbados, where a different kind of revolution was in progress: sugar.

11

Barbados

The genterey here doth live far better then ours doue in England; thay have most of them 100 or 2 or 3 of slaves apes [apiece] whou they command as they pleas: hear they may say what they have is thayer oune; and they have that Libertie of contienc [conscience] which wee soe long in England have fought for: But they doue abus it.[1]

—Henry Whistler, Barbados, 1655

THE ATLANTIC SUGAR PLANTATION system took shape in the late fifteenth century on the previously uninhabited island that the Portuguese called São Tomé, off the coast of Calabar, in the crook of Africa.

Settled by explorer Álvaro Caminha in 1493—the same year Columbus brought experimental sugar seedlings to the present-day Dominican Republic—São Tomé built on the previous model of Mediterranean sugar plantations but employed previously unthinkable quantities of labor to produce sugar on a new, large scale.[2] The labor was available via São Tomé's ready access to slave markets; it was a transshipment point for slaves headed to the Americas. By the 1550s, São Tomé had sixty sugar mills grinding, with individual plantations boasting workforces of as many as three hundred slaves.

The Portuguese applied the São Tomé model to create the first great sugar industry of the Americas in northeastern Brazil, where a full-scale planters' aristocracy had entrenched itself by the mid-sixteenth century. There was one major difference, however: the labor force in Brazil was mostly made up of enslaved indigenous Brazilians, who quickly proved to be unsatisfactory laborers. In a pattern later replicated throughout the hemisphere, a transition began in Brazil to African slave labor.

Wanting in on the sugar plantation action, the Dutch captured São Tomé in 1598–99. While paused from attacking Spanish and Portuguese merchant vessels during the Twelve Years' Truce (1609–1621), they built up their navy. They established Dutch outposts in North America, beginning in 1615 with Fort Nassau on the Hudson River and including, as of 1625, Fort Amsterdam—the future New York City—at the tip of Manhattan Island. With its defensive battery positioned on the site of present-day Battery Park, Fort Amsterdam

The relative closeness of Africa and Brazil is depicted in this detail from the first map of the hemisphere, a 1562 collaboration between Spanish cartographer Diego Gutiérrez and Dutch engraver Hieronymous Cock. In the ocean between the two, the Portuguese fleet is depicted on its way to "Calicute" (India). In the lower portion of the image, a naval battle is depicted.

provided protection for Dutch families who had been consolidated there from around the region.

Nieuw Amsterdam was from the beginning dense, secular, tolerant (with Jews both Sephardic and Ashkenazi), and multilingual. The colony's first shipment of slaves, eleven in all, came in the colony's second year, making it the second colony (after Virginia) in the present-day United States to import African slaves.

Slaves in Nieuw Amsterdam were corporately owned by the Dutch West India corporation. With time, they were manumitted and given land of their own, though they had to give a portion of their proceeds back to the company. On July 14, 1645, the free African Paulo d'Angola was granted a parcel of land on present-day Washington Square Park. Antony Congo was granted a parcel on the east side of the Bouwerie (from a point between present-day Houston and Stanton Streets to Rivington) on March 25, 1647. Francisco and Simon Congo were given nearby plots.[3] They were exposed pioneers in a bad neighborhood, forming the buffer zone between the Dutch at the lower tip of Manhattan and the Native Americans to the north who might decide to raid.

As Dutch commercial policy became more aggressive, the Dutch fleet assaulted Portugal's markets in Asia, then in the 1620s began a war for the European sugar market, which was principally supplied at that time by the two Brazilian centers of Salvador da Bahia and Recife in Pernambuco. They took Recife in 1641, though they could not hold Salvador.

From their vantage point in Brazil, the Dutch saw a double commercial opportunity nearby, on the English-controlled island of Barbados. In taking advantage of it, they created the Antillean sugar industry.

Barbados was easy for a seventeenth-century navigator to miss. Located in the Atlantic a hundred or so miles to the east of the arc of the rest of the Lesser Antilles, it's a patch of land comprising only some 166 square miles. Off the main sea road, it was the farthest from the major Spanish bases in the Americas, and it offered a relatively easy sail to Europe.

Barbados means "bearded ones" in Spanish, though why the island was called that is a mystery. The Spanish had claimed the unoccupied island in 1511, but it was abandoned by the time the English occupied it in 1627, just as the Dutch were making their move into Brazil. Sent by a commercial syndicate in London, the English expedition to settle Barbados paused on the way to "capture

*In this detail from a 1639 Dutch map by Joan Vinckeboons, Barbados
is the island sticking out to the east of the arc of the Lower Antilles.*

a prize"—i.e., plunder another country's vessel. They stole ten "negro slaves,"
who were taken to Barbados along with the eighty settlers that disembarked on
February 17, 1627.

The island had no native population, but Captain Henry Powell induced
thirty-two agriculturally knowledgeable native people from Dutch-held Guy-
ana to come to Barbados, then enslaved them once they were there.[4] Starvation
would not be an immediate problem: the island teemed with wild hogs, the
legacy of a long-gone Spanish presence. The colonists killed them off in three
years flat.[5]

The Barbadian colonists tried raising tobacco at the same time it was being
developed in Virginia and Maryland. But their product was of even poorer quality than the Chesapeake's, and they had problems getting labor because Barbados's checkered reputation in England made recruiting difficult. As happened
over and over in the Americas, crooks and whores were sent as colonists, but they
were far from satisfactory as plantation workers.

The trade balance between England and its colonies was projected to be even, via barter, without a need for settling accounts by a transatlantic flow of silver and gold that was wanted elsewhere. Since London made the rules and set the prices, London could tinker with the numbers as it liked. But just as the London planners were caught by surprise when Virginia became a tobacco exporter, they didn't count on the Dutch setting up English colonists in Barbados in the sugar business, from a base in Brazil.

It happened in the 1640s, while England was embroiled in the civil war between Roundheads and Cavaliers. Barbados had both political tendencies present but neither controlled the society definitively, and the island was practically independent during those years, enjoying what was effectively free trade with vessels of various flags.[6]

The Dutch, not the English, made the Barbadians rich. Fueled by a substantial injection of Dutch capital—something strictly forbidden by London—the Barbadians learned how to make sugar, via Dutch intermediaries and also by firsthand observation from traveling to Brazil.[7] The Dutch had a lot to offer the Barbadians, and they could take a profit at every step of the process. They provided the Barbadians with Europe's cheapest credit to get started making a fortune in sugar and waited until the sugar was on the market to collect and refinance.[8] They sold them the machinery and technology. They refined the molasses into sugar in Europe, and sold the sugar in the lucrative Dutch markets.

The Dutch could also provide the crucial and most expensive element: the labor. As a complement to taking Brazil, in 1637 they took the Portuguese slave castle of Elmina, offshore from the Gold Coast. They established posts on the Slave Coast (present-day Benin) that were controlled from Allada (or Ardra). For a time the Dutch controlled Luanda and Benguela in Angola as well. The strategic reason to occupy the slave ports was to support the Dutch sugar venture in Brazil, where the labor force died or escaped to the wilderness in large numbers even as acreage under cultivation was increasing. As a consequence of their move into Africa, the Dutch had plenty of slave-trading capacity with which to service the English, who were not yet engaged in the commercial African slave trade.

The Dutch didn't rule the Brazilian northeast for long. The Brazilian planters rebelled against them in 1645, but by the time they drove the Dutch out definitively in 1654, the Barbadians had copied their techniques for making sugar and were making fortunes.[9]

The sugar revolution transformed Barbados. Among the skills the Barbadians learned from the Dutch and the Brazilians was the management of hundreds of slaves on a single plantation. When they converted Barbados to slave labor, they did it massively and quickly. Barbados, then, became the first place where Englishmen surrounded themselves with large numbers of enslaved Africans. The Barbadian planters had been purchasing indentures of white servants, but they made an abrupt transition to purchasing the legal rights to the bodies and the future "increase" of black laborers. They imported large numbers of kidnapped Africans, because, as with later sugar regimes, their labor force was not self-reproducing: "though we breed both Negroes, Horses, and Cattle," wrote Richard Ligon in Barbados, "yet that increase, will not supply the moderate decays which we find in all those."[10]

Along with the changeover to a slave society came accumulation by dispossession, with the mortgage as a primary tool.* The Dutch were conservative about whom they extended credit to, making for a concentration of large planters. The wealthy then extended credit to the less wealthy by means of a mortgage, and foreclosed when they could not pay, as land ownership consolidated. Many former indentured servants had been given small patches of ground at the end of their tenure; now the small farmholds of forty different farmers became the eight hundred acre property of a single sugar baron, one Captain Waterman.[11]

The new Barbadian sugar planters quickly developed, in Richard S. Dunn's words, "a code of conduct that would never be tolerated at home. . . . In the islands there were no elders, the young were in control, and many a planter made his fortune and died by age thirty. In short, Caribbean and New England planters were polar opposites; they represented the outer limits of English social expression in the seventeenth century."[12] But these two outer limits did business with each other, as Barbados was dependent on New England for much of its food.

Barbados's sugar revolution was well under way in 1645, when the island's black population was 5,680. Guadeloupe and Martinique, belonging to the enemy commercial system of France, quickly followed in the conversion to sugar with the help of Dutch exiles from Brazil. On the other side of the Atlantic, some of Glasgow's first factories were rum distilleries, which added value to the molasses Glaswegian merchants were importing from the Antilles already in the 1640s.[13]

---

*The term "accumulation by dispossession" was suggested by David Harvey, who proposes it as an update to Marx's "primitive accumulation." Harvey, 137.

As Barbados was experiencing its first rush of sugar prosperity, the execution of King Charles in 1649 sent Cavaliers fleeing to the island. They seized control of its government following a pamphlet war and armed action, making the island into a Royalist stronghold. By the following year, Barbados had declared itself for Charles II, who was in French exile. Austere, regicidal, militarized, religious extremists: the Puritan government was unpopular at home, but Barbados was in open rebellion.

More consequentially, Barbados's practice of free trade with the Dutch antagonized the politically powerful London merchants and shippers, who were not happy about losing their captive market to foreign competition. An embargo, the Act of 1650, froze all English trade with Barbados as well as with the other Royalist colonies, including Virginia, and authorized the confiscation of all merchandise headed there. That became a hot issue in New England, whose trade with Barbados was its most profitable commercial activity.

Barbados issued what was essentially a declaration of independence on February 18, 1651, charging Parliament with placing it in a state of "slavery"—a word that would resound through pro-independence polemics on the North American mainland in the eighteenth century. Barbadian Cavaliers confiscated the lands of Barbadian Roundheads; according to an anguished letter written from Barbados, they had "Sequestred 52 Gallandt plantations, who are Werth as all ye island besydes."[14] Meanwhile, Barbadian royalists' lands in England, Scotland, and Ireland were confiscated by Parliament.

The Puritan Parliament passed a Navigation Act in 1651 that forbade trading with foreigners, requiring the use of English ships and captains for all commerce. That quickly led to war between England and the Netherlands, leaving Barbadian planters' Dutch business contacts on the wrong side of hostilities. Believing, perhaps not incorrectly, that Cromwell was out to destroy them, the Barbadian planters openly favored their Dutch commercial partners over their English colonial masters, effectively committing treason during wartime.

With instructions to seize Dutch merchantmen, Cromwell's admiral Sir George Ayscue blockaded the island in 1652. Then, despite having only a small force, he attacked with the support of scurvy-ridden troops who had detoured from their mission of subduing Virginia. He bluffed the Barbadian royalists into surrendering and established a government loyal to Parliament. But the damage was done to the British colonial system: Barbados had experienced independence and free trade.[15]

Ayscue's victory was only the beginning of Cromwell's military designs. After making peace with the Dutch in 1654, he began a project—the Western Design, it was called—to drive the Spanish out of the Americas. Unfortunately, Cromwell sent an untrained, incoherent expedition of conquest to base itself in Barbados in 1655—there to provision itself, on an island dependent on importation for its food.[16] Depleting the island's scant resources, the English fleet funded itself by laying high duties on the island's imports.

That there was already a nascent slave-breeding business of sorts in Barbados is suggested by the journal of a member of the Western Design expedition, a Puritan named Henry Whistler, who noted in 1655 that children had a cash value at birth and that there was a market in them:

> This Island is inhabited with all sortes: with English, french, Duch, Scotes, Irish, Spaniards thay being Iues [Jews]; with Ingones [Indians] and miserabell Negors borne to perpetuall slavery thay and thayer seed: these Negors they doue alow as many wifes as thay will have, some will have 3 or 4, according as they find thayer bodie abell; our English heare doth think a negor child the first day it is born to be worth 5[11] [five pounds eleven shillings], they cost them nothing the bringing up, they goe all ways naked: some planters will have 30 more or les about 4 or 5 years ould: *they sele them from one to the other as we doue shepe*.[17] (emphasis added)

The principle of *partus sequitur ventrem* was already in place. "By 1650 certainly, and probably a good bit earlier," writes Dunn, "slavery in Barbados had become more than a lifetime condition. It extended through the slave's children to posterity."[18] The idea that one caste of people, visibly different, could be born into bondage conflated the condition of slavery with the concept of "race."

Before leaving Barbados on its mission of conquest, the English fleet recruited the island's dispossessed whites to join its soldiery, a job that entailed risking one's life but also brought the possibility of plunder, or even land. When the expedition sailed away on March 31, 1655, it took away some four thousand white Barbadians, mostly formerly indentured servants, who were never to return. In their wake were sent a rougher class: defeated Scotch and Irish soldiers captured in battle, sent as laboring prisoners, along with troublemakers, Catholics, and former landowners.

The Western Design expedition's attack on Santo Domingo was a murderous failure, repulsed definitively by the Spanish. But then the expedition turned its sights more successfully on Jamaica. Cromwell's navy invited pirates into

Jamaica's gaudy, raunchy, now-disappeared capital of Port Royal, beginning a golden age of piracy in the Caribbean.* While England launched attacks against Spanish coastal towns, the pirates (most infamously Henry Morgan) attacked Spanish shipping, provoking a two-fronted war that expelled the Spanish from Jamaica in 1655, though it took another five years for the English to subdue the insurgency.

This first dislodging by force of Spain from an established colony sparked a new rush for riches as politically connected merchants jockeyed for position in Jamaica. Few if any of the former Barbadian yeomen who had come to Jamaica with the fleet benefited, however; most died of disease. Some surviving soldiers received land grants and became planters, amassing large fortunes through the use of slave labor and achieving that rare, coveted condition: class mobility.

After Cromwell died in 1658, probably of a bacterial infection, the Round-heads in England deteriorated into bickering factions and the Cavaliers retook power. The extravagant, lecherous, French-raised Charles II, son of the beheaded Charles I, ascended to the English throne in 1660. Amid widespread rejoicing at the departure of the unpopular regime, the theaters of England, shuttered by the Puritans, reopened. In what has been remembered as the Restoration, London once more began to have a public life after more than a decade of Puritan sobriety, as an age of coffeehouses began.

With the Restoration came an aggressive new commercial policy designed to project an image of grandeur by maximizing the royal share of the world. Charles II was not much interested in governing, but he was attuned to the importance of the colonies; many places in the New World had been named for his father, and Maryland bore the name of his mother. In appreciation of Virginia's loyalty, he bestowed on the colony the title of Dominion, a name that persists as Virginia's nickname of "Old Dominion."

Ownership of Barbadian land was quite concentrated by this time, and sugar production increased precipitously. There were twenty thousand black captives on Barbados by 1660, twenty times as many as in Virginia. By 1676, the number had grown through importation to 32,473, and 46,602 in 1684.[19] The island became one of the most densely populated areas in the world.

---

*Port Royal was permanently submerged by earthquake and tsunami in 1692.

Now that the labor force was mostly black, the situation required legal clarification. Barbados had a comprehensive slave code by 1661 that differentiated indentured servants from slaves, with provisions that were highly disadvantageous to the enslaved: killing an enslaved person was punishable only by a fine.[20] The code came just in time to be useful to Jamaican lawmakers; Charles II formally annexed Jamaica for England in 1661.

Parliament passed another Navigation Act in 1660, requiring exclusivity of trade by the colonies, who could conduct commerce only with English ships that were captained by Englishmen and three-fourths of whose sailors were English. Subsequent Navigation Acts were passed in 1662 and 1663 and were followed up in 1673 and 1696, defining a policy that would in one form or another endure through the Napoleonic era. The Navigation Acts were highly consequential; by denying the Dutch access to American markets controlled by England, they consolidated England's position as the number-one commercial power.

They also empowered the New England colonists, though that was an unintended consequence. New England had been conducting some hemispheric trade since the 1630s. Now, since colonial ships counted as English, the Navigation Acts stimulated the New England shipping industry, turning the New Englanders into "the Dutch of England's empire."[21] New England's territorial advancement to the north was blocked by French Canada. Especially in the case of the Rhode Island colony, founded in 1636 by Massachusetts dissident Roger Williams, New England had little in the way of a hinterland. Rhode Island was like Portugal in that both places consisted mostly of coastline; like the Portuguese, Rhode Islanders turned to the sea to make money.

The colonists weren't allowed to manufacture, but New England ships could run down to the West Indies and exchange their farm and fishing products for molasses, which they brought home and distilled into great quantities of rum. The New Englanders also sold the Barbadians kidnapped Native Americans as slaves, but since New England was hemmed in by French Canada, their supply was limited.

Charles II was more interested in trying to find gold than slaves when he chartered the Governor and Company of the Royal Adventurers Trading to Africa on January 10, 1662.[22] Most of Africa had no gold, but the Gold Coast had for centuries provided a money supply to the Muslim world. Its gold, traded overland up through the Maghreb and into Europe, had been turning up in English commerce since at least the thirteenth century, when the Royal Mint was established. Though the Gold Coast's resources were partly depleted by the time of the Restoration, it was still a gold producer.

At that time, the Gold Coast was not an exporter of African slaves, but an importer: an intra-African coastal slave trade conducted by Portuguese captains brought laborers kidnapped from Calabar to labor in the Akans' gold works.[23] Under pressure from the colonies to supply labor, English traders began to insist on taking slaves from the Gold Coast as well as gold and ivory. The company instructed its traders not to pay for slaves with gold but with barter, because the idea was to bring gold home. But African traders quickly began demanding gold for at least part of the price of slaves, the rest being made up of manufactured goods.

The Royal Mint began striking a new gold piece in 1663, the first machine-minted English coin, intended to be worth twenty shillings (actual exchange rates were different). A tiny elephant embossed on each one—sometimes an elephant and castle—let the world know that England's money was made with Africa's gold. The coins became known almost immediately as "guineas," from the name of the long coastal stretch of West Africa between the mountain ranges of Sierra Leone and the Bight of Biafra. Elephant and elephant-and-castle guineas were minted until 1726, though later non-African-themed guineas were minted until 1813, the monarch pictured on the "heads" side changing with the throne.

Detail of a guinea.

The castle was a direct image of England's growing importance in the slave trade, while the coin's elephant image depicted another of the sources of wealth of the African trade: ivory, used in all manner of fine manufactures, notably including musical instruments. Ivory comes from killing a male animal (only the males have big tusks) of five tons or so in order to harvest the approximately 1 percent of its body weight that is dentine mass, while leaving the carcass for carrion eaters. As keyboards appeared all over Europe and America, the intelligent animals were slaughtered in large numbers so their teeth could produce ivory for the fingers of well-bred young ladies to caress, the market picking up when the piano began to be mass-produced in the nineteenth century. Ivory toothpicks became a necessary gentleman's item in Europe. In Africa, where hunting elephants was basic to survival and hunting lore was remembered in the form of song, the animal was consumed after slaughter and the tusks used as ceremonial trumpets across a wide range of the continent.

England's creation of the guinea spearheaded an offensive in which it squared off against the Netherlands. Charles II's brother James (the future King James II), who bore the king's brother's traditional title of Duke of York, prosecuted a second Anglo-Dutch war, fought on multiple fronts in different parts of the world. The English attacked Dutch slave-trading positions on the African coast, and in 1664, they took control of Nieuw Amsterdam, renaming it New York in honor of the city's new royal master. But they were otherwise badly beaten in the war, which ended in 1667 with England's humiliating defeat. In the treaty negotiations, the English offered to trade New York back to the Dutch in exchange for the sugar-producing, moneymaking South American colony of Surinam, but the Dutch refused the offer. The English kept Manhattan, locking in their control of the Atlantic seaboard from New England down to Virginia.

That stretch of the North American Atlantic coast formerly claimed by the Dutch became property of the Duke of York, James Stuart; Charles II gave him all the land between New England and Maryland. James in turn dealt out the territory between the Hudson and Delaware Rivers to John Lord Berkeley and Sir George Carteret, never mind that people already lived there. It was divided into East Jersey and West Jersey, with the whole collectively known as, according to the document signed by James, "New Caeserea or New Jersey," whose birth was thus pure cronyism.[24] Up the Hudson, the Dutch Fort Nassau was renamed Albany, for James's Scottish title. Located on the Mohawk River, in the gap between the Catskills and the Adirondack Mountains, Albany was perfectly positioned for commerce with the West.

The Anglo-Dutch war badly damaged the ineffective Company of Royal Adventurers Trading to Africa, which was reorganized and renamed the Royal African Company in 1672. But the new company was also badly managed, and it made no attempt to get North American slaveowners the labor they wanted. The gap was filled by independent entrepreneurs.

><

As soon as there were slaves, there were conspiracies to rebel—sometimes involving indentured whites as well, sometimes together with Native Americans. Herbert Aptheker lists the first "serious conspiracy involving Negro slaves" in English North America as occurring in Virginia in 1663, when there were still relatively few black people in Virginia and they had only just been declared to be slaves.[25] The Virginia Assembly, in passing a 1672 act that authorized the killing of maroons, with reparations made at public expense to the individual slaveowners thus deprived of property, noted, "it hath beene manifested to this grand assembly that many negroes have lately beene, and now are out in rebellion in sundry parts of this country and that noe meanes have yet beene found for the apprehension and suppression of them from whome many mischeifes of very dangerous consequence may arise to the country if either other negroes, Indians or servants should happen to fly forth and joyne with them."[26] A similar authorization was passed in 1680, suggesting that the problem continued to vex the Virginians.

A plot to murder the masters, neither the first nor the last, was discovered on Barbados in 1674. Whether it existed in reality or not is hard to say, since slave societies were particularly alert to potential uprisings, to the point of sometimes executing people for imagined crimes. According to a pamphlet published in London in 1676, the conspiracy was led by the "Cormantee"—Akan people from the Gold Coast. The pamphlet's text is notable for its description—complete with, supposedly, elephant-tusk trumpets—of the artistry and artisanship attendant to Gold Coast royal pageantry, of which some seventeenth-century Barbadians would have had firsthand knowledge from slaving voyages. It also includes an early occurrence of the word *Baccararoe*, i.e., *buckra*, which would become a black term for whites throughout the English-speaking Americas:

> This Conspiracy first broke out and was hatched by the Cormantee or Gold-Cost Negro's about Three years since, and afterwards Cuningly and Clandestinely carried, and kept secret, even from the knowledge of their own Wifes.
>
> Their grand design was to choose them a King, one Coffee an Ancient Gold-Cost Negro, who should have been Crowned the 12th of June last past in a Chair of State exquisitely wrought and Carved after their Mode; with Bowes and Arrowes to be likewise carried in State before his Majesty their intended King: Trumpets to be made of Elephants Teeth and Gourdes to be sounded on several Hills, to give Notice of their general Rising, with a full intention to fire the Sugar-Canes, and so run in and Cut

their Masters the Planters Throats in their respective Plantations where-unto they did belong.

Some affirm, they intended to spare the lives of the Fairest and Hand-somest Women (their Mistresses and their Daughters) to be Converted to their own use. But some others affirm the contrary; and I am induced to believe they intended to Murther all the White People there, as well Men as Women: for Anna a house Negro Woman belonging to Justice Hall, overhearing a Young Cormantee Negro about 18 years of age, and also belonging to Justice Hall, as he was working near the Garden, and discoursing with another Cormantee Negro working with him, told him boldly and plainly, He would have no hand in killing the Baccaroroes or White Folks; And that he would tell his Master.

All which the aforesaid Negro Woman (being then accidentally in the garden) over-heard, and called to him the aforesaid Young Negro Man over the Pales, and enquired and asked of him What it was they so ear-nestly were talking about? He answered and told her freely, That it was a general Design amongst them the Cormantee Negro's, to kill all the Baccararoes or White People in the Island within a fortnight. Which she no sooner understood, but went immediately to her Master and Mistris, and discovered the whole truth of what she heard, saying withal, That it was great Pity so good people as her Master and Mistriss were, should be destroyed.[27]

This account exemplifies what was already a well-worn conspiracy theory, combining as it does three major tropes of white narratives of slave rebellion:

1) decisions taken by a council of slaves from various plantations to stage an organized rebellion (as would in fact happen more than a century later in Saint-Domingue/Haiti);

2) the assertion by the chronicler of the intention of the black rebels to kill white men and take white women for sexual use; and

3) the salvation of the whites by the intercession of a faithful domestic slave who betrays the conspiracy of the black rank-and-file out of love for her master's family.

These elements recur in masters' accounts of conspiracies throughout the hemispheric history of slavery, both black and indigenous. The following excerpt from the same pamphlet concludes with the characteristic final trope of the slave rebellion narrative, portrayed as a happy ending: the torture and massacre by the masters of a number of the enslaved. It also reports a common belief of Africans, reported in various parts of the Americas, that the enslaved would return to Africa upon death.

> Six burnt alive, and Eleven beheaded, their dead bodies being dragged through the Streets, at *Spikes* a pleasant Port-Town in that Island, and were afterwards burnt with those that were burned alive. . .
>
> The spectators . . . cryed out to *Tony, Sirrah, we shall see you fry bravely by and by.* Who answered undauntedly, *If you Roast me to day, you cannot Roast me tomorrow*: (all those *Negro's* having an opinion that after their death they go into their own Countrey). Five and Twenty more have been since Executed.[28]

In this telling from a colonist, the death of Africans was only of importance as the cost of doing business.

12

The Anglo-Saxon Model

*It was not necessary to pretend or to prove that the enslaved were a differ-
ent race . . . Anyone could tell black from white, even if black was actually
brown or red. And as the number of poor white Virginians diminished, the
vicious traits of character attributed by Englishmen to their poor could in
Virginia increasingly appear to be the exclusive heritage of blacks.*[1]

—Edmund S. Morgan

THE FIRST LARGE LAND distribution in Virginia was overseen by William
Berkeley, royal governor as of 1642. A wit and playwright from the court of
Charles I, he "encouraged the cavaliers to come over in large numbers," wrote
Philip A. Bruce, and made his cronies into large landholders.[2] Berkeley remained
as governor over a thirty-five year period, although he was out during the years
of the Civil War and the Puritan reign. His years in power were on the whole
prosperous ones, but his governorship ended badly with the suppression in 1676
of Nathaniel Bacon's rebellion, the largest colonial-era uprising in the territory
of the future United States.

Bacon's Rebellion was a class war, in which "the ambitions and fears of
frontier planters clashed with the desire of the royal governor to maintain a
monopoly of trade with the Indians."[3] A tiny number of families—the gentry—
had quickly come to control the affairs of each county, and they had the good
coastal land locked up. The leading edge of the economy was on the west, pushing out into the wilderness. In a pattern that would be repeated in various forms
during the long westward expansion across the continent, the pioneers made war
on the Native Americans in order to enclose the land the "salvages" lived on. To

that end, they wanted to get rid of the Indians as fast as possible—abduct them and sell them to Barbados, thereby profiting, or simply kill them and consider the expropriated land adequate profit.

Bacon, recently arrived in Virginia, led a group that attacked the Pamunkey and then led an uprising against Berkeley in which he promised slaves their freedom if they would fight with him. Bacon was put down by Berkeley after a battle involving a thousand Redcoats sent from London; a battalion of eighty slaves and twenty indentured servants was one of the last to surrender.[4] In the course of suppressing the rebellion, Berkeley heavy-handedly massacred a number of the rebels, and hung some as well, confiscating the property of anyone he deemed an enemy. Ebenezer Cook, the London-born Maryland poet remembered for his satirical poem "The Sot-Weed Factor," composed his longest poem about Bacon's Rebellion. He described the rebels as "Bullies, Ruffians, Debauchees, Cheats, Gamesters, Pimps, and Raparees," and characterized Berkeley's force as a mercenary one:

> *Berkley, whom the Mob detested,*
> *In Bacon's Absence had invested;*
> *Transporting from the Eastern Shore*
> *(T'augment the Force he had before)*
> *Of Arms and Ammunition Store,*
> *And Men, who fought for ready Pay,*
> *Twelve Pence a Head, for ev'ry Day;*
> *With Plunder of all that had taken*
> *Rebellious Oath to Col'nel Bacon.*

There had been uprisings of the poor in England, but Bacon's Rebellion brought a new element into the mix that would become a permanent feature of American clashes: guns. Unlike England, Virginia was a gun culture. "Whereas in England, only men with estates valued at above one hundred pounds sterling were allowed to own guns," writes Kathleen M. Brown, "English men in Virginia at all levels of property ownership were *expected* to own them, especially after the succession of Dutch threats to the colony during the late 1660s and early 1670s."[5] Guns and slavery were intimately associated with each other; all slave-raiding relied on guns, and all slaveholding relied on armed repression.

One of the messages of Bacon's Rebellion as received by the Virginia gentry was that new poor freedmen emerging from indenture every year created a social problem. Enslaving them was not possible: Englishmen would not countenance enslaving other Englishmen. The solution was to shift over to African laborers.

By replacing English laborers with African ones, they could, in Edmund S. Morgan's memorable phrase, "enslave the poor," transforming the underclass from a political threat to a security issue with a color-coded caste system.[6]

Locked up and dispersed across isolated tobacco plantations, enslaved Africans were easier to control than indentured English, Scottish, and Irish freemen. Slavery was for life: manumission, common in Spanish territories, would not become so in Virginia. It was widely assumed that if slaves were freed, they would be a danger to the public at large, an assumption that drew on (and fed) a common belief that Africans were naturally more violent than Europeans and would become vicious if not repressed.

Though tobacco required much less startup capital than sugar, Virginia nonetheless became a magnet for capital, much of which went into acquiring slaves. With slave labor, Virginia produced more tobacco than ever before.[7] "In the three generations that followed Bacon's Rebellion," writes Bernard Bailyn, "a hierarchy of the plantation gentry emerged in stable form, dominated by a social and economic leadership whose roots can be traced back to the 1650s and whose dominance in politics was largely uncontested."[8] The fact that this politicized gentry was principally invested in slaves would determine the course of policy for subsequent generations.

Leaving future generations to deal with the consequences of a society divided into white masters and black slaves, the great planters of late seventeenth-century Virginia established dynasties of wealth in English North America, some of which continue into the present day. They locked the need for slavery into place by making it such a central part of the economy that, once implemented, it could not be eradicated—at least, not without the destruction of the economic structures they had put in place and the erasure of their accumulated wealth. Future generations were born into a system they felt powerless to dismantle.

The move to a slave society in Virginia bound rich and poor whites together through the privilege of skin color. Landowning Virginians would be free to experiment with democracy, since their enslaved working class had no rights or vote. Lesser whites would identify with the masters, whose caste they were privileged to belong to, and not with the slaves. This implied a considerable commitment to the policing of caste boundaries, since this category of the poor would have to remain repressed and enslaved in perpetuity.

By the time of independence, some two-thirds of freemen were landowners. Their society was necessarily organized along different lines than that of England, nurturing the republican tendencies already present in English society and fostering an ideology of liberty that was taken to extremes, with guns aplenty. It was a frontier society, in which the most brazen won out.

A Virginia slave regime was implemented by 1640, the earliest date at which "surviving Virginia county records began to mention Negroes," writes Winthrop Jordan, who adds, "sales for life, often including any future progeny, were recorded in unmistakable language."[9] There was now a clear distinction between slave and indentured servant—necessary not only in terms of civil and criminal law, but in terms of the market for their services: a transfer of indenture was considerably less valuable than a slave sale. While the changeover from indentured to chattel labor offered political and labor advantages, the greatest benefit for slaveowners was the property rights it conferred.[10] It was the profitability of owning slaves as capital, added to their capacity for labor, that made slavery foundational to Virginia's economy.

There was "no body of English law to invoke," writes James A. Rawley. "Slavery may be considered a colonial invention, abetted by the English traders in slaves."[11] A legal framework appeared in Virginia for dealing with slavery, one law and ordinance at a time, beginning in the 1650s. In 1662 the *partus sequitur ventrem* passed to Virginia children the free or enslaved legal status of the mother, thus extending slavery to all future matrilineal generations, in perpetuity. Another law seven years later, headed *An Act about the Casuall Killing of Slaves,* exempted slaveowners from being charged with felony murder if one of their slaves should die during "correction," noting the difference in types of punishment dealt to indentured servants and slaves: "The only law in force for the punishment of refractory servants resisting their master, mistris or overseer cannot be inflicted upon Negroes." In other words, since indentured servants could have their term extended as a punishment but slaves in perpetuity could not, it was necessary to use violence on slaves. The law even provided a philosophical justification that noted the value of slaves as multigenerational property: "it cannot be presumed that prepensed malice (which alone makes murther ffelony [*sic*]) should induce any man to destroy his owne estate."[12]

Management of slave labor in the Americas generally took one of two forms. One, which Jacob M. Price calls the Latin model, protected the integrity of the plantation by treating slaves as immovable assets, or real estate, which could not be separated from the plantation as a whole.[13] This model, employed in the

Spanish, Portuguese, and French territories, tended toward maintaining family ties among the enslaved and may well have contributed to the rootedness of the Afro-Louisianan population that is notable into the present day.

The other, the Anglo-Saxon model, protected the creditor by treating slaves as chattel, or disposable personal property, like furniture, and allowed the dismantling of a plantation for the instant conversion of its labor force into cash, breaking family relations among the enslaved whenever it was financially expedient.

The Barbadian code at first considered slaves to be real estate but was amended in 1668 to reclassify them as chattel alienable from the land, conforming with facts on the ground. That quickly became part of Virginia law as well, where the forward-looking knew that massive importation of Africans would come soon. The logical consequence of capitalizing slaves as chattel was that creditors felt more secure investing in slaves.[14] As the international slave market became stronger, the chattel principle also supported the creation of a locally traded market in slaves, who were a self-increasing source of riches—an important domestic business during those days of restricted foreign trade.

By the time slave ships began to disgorge hundreds weekly into Virginia, a legal framework for slavery was already in place. This legal infrastructure would be subject to constant revision, but the basic questions were settled by the time of the great wave of African arrivals in the last days of the seventeenth century. By 1690 or so, perhaps a little earlier, Virginia's labor force was majority enslaved, not indentured.[15] The society became even more unequal as large landowning slaveholders became very wealthy men and the formerly indentured were shut out of participation in the economy and from landowning.

Despite the glamour of the Royalist Cavalier image, most British emigrants to Virginia were indentured servants, most of them young men. In marked contrast to Puritan New England, which was more middle-class and more egalitarian, Virginia received rich and poor, exalting the former and exploiting the latter.

Many of the Virginia colonists confronting the daunting physical problems of clearing and planting wilderness land never bothered to establish formal title, and did not necessarily know how. Many would move on; their relentless, unrotated farming of tobacco exhausted the soil of the necessary nutrients after a few years, and the West was always beckoning with the promise of more land. Old Dominion became concentrated in large holdings, which ultimately facilitated the cultivation of tobacco and the importation of slaves.

The consequences for American society were permanent. "During a brief period in the late seventeenth and early eighteenth century," writes Anthony S. Parent in his study of the creation of Virginia's slave society between 1660 and 1740, "a small but powerful planter class, acting in their short-term interest, gave America its racial dilemma."[16] A miserably fed, clothed, and housed force of enslaved black laborers was what planters wanted, and that's what they bequeathed.

Only the wealthy could afford to own an enslaved work force, so the influx of slaves created an additional competitive advantage for the larger planters, even as the enslaved people themselves counted as wealth for them. "The workers who produced the crops," writes Lorena S. Walsh, sounding a note repeatedly expressed by writers on the subject, "were almost invariably the most valuable asset that planters possessed." The rich of Virginia became richer, and the super-rich, or "great planters holding thousands of acres and exceptionally large labor forces" probably "increased from fewer than a dozen in 1640 to around eighty at the close of the Seven Years' War [1763]."[17]

While generally the colonial wealthy had unimpressive fortunes compared with the income English lords had, the Virginians had them beat in terms of luxurious living: they had slaves, who made the planters' lives comfortable in every detail.

The planters had to superintend their affairs closely, though; unlike the island confines of sugar-producing Barbados and Jamaica, the extensive tobacco lands of Virginia were not conducive to absentee ownership. Planter William Fitzhugh wrote about a proposed land deal in 1689: "it is not worth two pence to anyone that is not actually upon the Spot."[18]

Not all farmers understood the importance of legal documentation, but it made a fortune for those with English legal training and connections. Holding public office in early Virginia was a direct path to personal enrichment on a drastic scale. Members of the oligarchy who knew best how to appropriate land helped themselves to large tracts. Claimed and commodified by England, this newly fenced land was given to individuals who were in a position to use it to create wealth. The laws were crafted so as to make rights of property—both the enclosed land and the human labor—sacrosanct at a foundational level to the society built atop the Chesapeake, creating a network of property owners whose descendants have traditionally been of high social importance in the region.

Writing of the nineteenth century, Steven Deyle notes that white births were recorded in a Bible, black ones in a ledger.[19] It was that way already when the big ships began sailing from Africa to Virginia. Black servitude was to be perpetual, including all future children of the enslaved person, and their children, and their children's children, founding a fortune of human property within a few generations through the power of what came to be called "natural increase."

Consider a hypothetical example of the economic power of the capitalized womb: if an enslaved girl brought from Africa in 1695 survived long enough to give birth to four children who survived long enough to be of reproductive age (which typically entailed giving birth to a number of other children who died), and if two of those four surviving children were girls and each similarly produced four surviving children, recursively over 165 years (twelve generations, supposing fifteen years to be a generation), a first-generation enslaved woman's womb would thus engender a population of 2,048 people by 1860, all of them legally considered property, each with a cash value.

The only thing hypothetical about that scenario is the numbers. Apart from that, it in fact happened: enslaved women began having children as soon as their bodies were able, and their children were handed down as inherited property from generation to generation. There was a white family's fortune to be accumulated from the "increase" of a single African kidnap victim. That Virginia planters understood this is clear from the records of one of the first planters for whom we have much documentation, who was also a lawyer.

On the strength of his correspondence, the English-born William Fitzhugh was a pioneer not only in the use of an enslaved labor force in Virginia, but also in comprehending the value of owning the laborers' children and descendants in perpetuity. Anthony S. Parent writes:

> He did not have to purchase laborers; he could grow his own. He thought of his blacks as stock, not unlike cattle, that could be bred indefinitely. He boasted in 1686 that most of his twenty-nine enslaved workers were Virginia-born, and the Africa-born were as "likely as most in Virginia."[20]

In a 1681 letter about a slave cargo (the place of origin is not noted) expected to arrive into York, Virginia, Fitzhugh requested a colleague there "to buy me five or six, whereof three or four to be boys, a man and woman or men and women, the boys from eight to seventeen or eighteen, the rest as young as you can procure them, for price I cannot direct therein because boys according to there age and growth are valued in price."[21]

He used the word *breeders*. Writing of his holdings, Fitzhugh anticipated cheerfully that "the Negroes increase being all young, & a considerable parcel of breeders, will keep that Stock good for ever."[22] He does not appear ever to have purchased any more Africans. Were more documentation extant of the thoughts and actions of seventeenth-century colonists, one would presumably find more examples of this line of thinking, as per the 1696 deed in Hampton, Virginia, turning over "one negro Lad nam'd Will and one Gray Mare & their Increse to him & his heirs for ever."[23]

Educated in England as a lawyer and elected to the Virginia House of Burgesses in 1676, Fitzhugh used his office to acquire vast parcels of land through abuse of the headright system. He had labor to work it, his workforce increasing as the long-range value of owning people's perpetual descendants worked its actuarial magic. When Fitzhugh died in 1701 at the age of fifty—not an uncommonly early age to die in colonial Virginia—he was a very wealthy man. He had not only been a highly successful accumulator of land, but had also watched his holdings of human beings increase on their own, or perhaps with his or his sons' help, as household sexual abuse of servants by gentlemen was common.

Fitzhugh's informative will makes clear the ideal of legacy in Virginia. Dividing out his possessions among his widow and five sons (his married daughter Rosamond was not included), it begins with bequests of land, awarding five parcels containing a total of 30,918 acres to his eldest son, also named William Fitzhugh, "to have and to hold the said Tracts and parcels of Land to him & the heirs of his Body Lawfully begotten for ever."[24] Dividing among his remaining sons and his widow a total of twenty-seven parcels comprising 49,500 acres, he described precisely from whom each parcel had been acquired and any details and conditions attaching to it, e.g., "all that Tract or parcel that I bought to Mr. Waugh conta. 400 acres lying upon Rappahannock one half thereof being now Leased [to] William Yates."[25]

Once the lands were bequeathed, Fitzhugh divided up his slaves. His style of disposition made clear that he saw them as the most valuable of his family's heirlooms, parceling out to different households in the region his fifty-one "Negroes and Mulattoes," providing inadvertent witness that the multigenerational skin-lightening process had already begun in Virginia.

> *AND* as for what Personal Estate God Almighty hath been graciously pleased to Endow me with I Give and bequeath as followeth[:] *Item* I Give to my Dear and well beloved wife seven Negroes – (to say) Harry & his wife Katherine Kate Will and his wife Peggy, Hanna & her youngest child

to her & her dispose forever . . . I Give to my said beloved Wife one silver Bason three silver Plates one of the Lesser silver Candlesticks a silver Salt half my silver Spoons in the house the second Best silver Tankard a silver Porringer & a large silver Ladle the Great silver Tumbler to her & her heirs forever [etc.] . . .

The enslaved Hanna left no record of her thoughts, so we do not know how she responded to the news that she was being bequeathed to Mrs. Fitzhugh along with her youngest child only, while her children Clory, Rose, and Robin went to one of Fitzhugh's sons, her family divided up like so many silver spoons. Still, there was some consolation: Hanna would be in the same county as her children, and perhaps they would see each other from time to time or could at least hear news of each other.

Virginia's enslaved population grew its own extended communities through fragile webs of kinship that paralleled those of the masters, with the grapevine as a means of communication. Despite the regime of dehumanization that confronted the enslaved, a multigenerational African American community was forming in Virginia, which was as much home to Hanna's children as it was to Fitzhugh's heirs.

Sugar in Barbados, tobacco in the Chesapeake: following the whirl of the ocean gyre, a global production cycle, still in its early stages, took slave labor from Africa to raise crops in the Americas that were consumed in Europe.

But Barbados was full. Population pressures were already palpable there in the 1640s. After the Restoration, the Barbadian Royalists who had been loyal to Charles II during his years of exile, and who were now influential in his court, successfully petitioned the king to be allowed to create a colony in southern Virginia that would be christened with the Latin version of his name.

Carolina wouldn't cost the king anything. It would be a buffer between Virginia and the Spanish territories, and it was the perfect expansion slot for Barbados.

13

Carolina

Formerly when beavor was a comodity they sold about 1200 skins a year but no imployment pleases the Chicasaws so well as slave Catching. A lucky hitt at that besides the Honor procures them a whole Estate at once, one slave brings a Gun, ammunition, horse, hatchet, and a suit of Cloathes, which would not be procured without much tedious toil a hunting.[1]

—Thomas Nairne, *Journalls to the Chicasaws
and Talapoosies*, 1708

THE PRIME MOVER OF the idea to seek an American concession from Charles II for a proprietary colony was John Colleton, a Cavalier who had fled to Barbados after Charles I's execution.[2] Returning to England after the Restoration, Colleton was knighted in return for the loyalty that had cost him the confiscation of his property by the Roundheads. He got a plum position: named to the Council for Foreign Plantations, he came into contact there with the heavy players of economic expansion for the revitalized monarchy, all of them happily and openly using their positions to enrich themselves.

Colleton joined with seven other power brokers, five of whom were members of the Council for Foreign Plantations. Together the eight asked His Highness for a royal charter, which was granted in 1663, of the territory to be owned by the eight True and Absolute Lords Proprietors.

Carolina's north-to-south reach was described as being from 31° to 36° latitude, blithely ignoring Spanish or Native American claims to the territory. Its boundaries were expanded both northward and southward by a second charter two years later, including areas that were already colonized—to the north, the Albemarle colony that had been settled by Virginians; to the south, the Spanish fortification of St. Augustine, even though that was unoccupiable by the English. To the west, the Carolina territory was defined as stretching all the way across the unexplored continent, and the Carolinians took that seriously; Carolina as natural master of the continent became part of an enduring ideology.

A colony attempted by Barbadian adventurers at Cape Fear failed in 1667. It took until 1669 for the Carolina project to begin to take off, which it did after one of the lords proprietors, Baron Anthony Ashley-Cooper, took active charge, persuading the others to put up £500 sterling each in seed money for a settlement at Carolina's Port Royal.

In support of his utopian project of proprietary colonialism, Ashley-Cooper created an ambitious document, the Fundamental Constitutions of Carolina (1669). Though unsigned, it was largely drafted by John Locke, who was secretary to the lords proprietors and an investor in the Royal Adventurers and the Royal African Company, and who lived in Ashley-Cooper's house and tutored his children. Locke's *Two Treatises of Government*, which popularized the notion of a social contract between governed and governors and established him as a founding philosopher of modern liberalism, was still twenty years away.[3]

After the trauma of a king beheaded, a Puritan interregnum, and a new king reseated on the throne, Carolina would exemplify royal grandeur amid separation of powers. Though the Fundamental Constitutions were never formally ratified and were roundly ignored by the colonists, they served as a kind of mission statement, sketching out in some detail how a system of nobility could function in Carolina and how a freeman might join that nobility. It proposed an elaborate structure, heavy on theory: though it hoped to "avoid a numerous democracy," there would be a sort of system of checks and balances between the power of the nobles in the metropolis and the new nobility in the colony. Carolina would have representative government, elected by an oligarchy, with a parliament, a council, and a complicated court system to settle the many disputes that occur when an entire society is simultaneously engaged in land-grabbing.

At the head of it would be a hereditary aristocracy. Carolina would be a "palatinate": the eldest lord proprietor was designated the palatine, the direct representative of the king whose functions might be exercised by a local deputy called a landgrave or a lesser figure called a cazique.* Locke was named a landgrave in 1671, though he never traveled to America.[4]

---

*The word "landgrave," previously associated with the Holy Roman Empire, referred to an officer of the border guard, which was indeed Carolina's strategic buffer-zone function; "cazique" was a Taíno word for chieftain that apparently crept into the vocabulary via Spanish.

The colonists, the theory went, would pay the costs of establishing themselves in exchange for generous land grants—though there were Native Americans living on the granted land—and policies facilitating slaveowning, which was to be the economic backbone of the new colony. The proprietors, who in theory owned a fifth of the unsurveyed land, were assigned "baronies" of twelve thousand acres, and nobles received another fifth, but any intrepid colonist with even a little capital could acquire land, thanks to a generous headrights system that awarded 150 acres per servant imported—triple what Virginia had offered. It must be a large territory indeed to be able to give away so much land, and indeed, they claimed all the land to the west.

In response to a request for clarification, the lords proprietors agreed that the headright for importation of servants would apply to slaves as well. They had a motive: with four of the eight lords proprietors having also been founders of the Royal African Company, Carolina was founded by slave traders. It was created to be slaveowners' heaven. Bring in a slave, get a hundred fifty acres free. Bring twenty, fifty, a hundred! Colonists could own their slaves securely, because, as in Barbados, these slaves would have *no rights at all*. Ashley-Cooper, writes M. Eugene Sirmans, "inserted in all drafts of the Fundamental Constitutions a provision which became of crucial importance in shaping the development of Carolina. 'Every Freeman of Carolina,' it was stipulated, 'shall have absolute power and authority over his Negro Slaves, of what opinion or Religion soever.'"[5]

Conversion to Christianity would not free them. Carolina was not a religiously motivated colony, nor was it founded by refugees from persecution. Needing to attract settlers, it was relatively tolerant of religion; the Fundamental Constitutions included a limited guarantee of religious freedom, though Catholics were not welcome. The utopian vision of Carolina was the pursuit of individual profit by any means necessary.

For an aggressive young man starting out, it was as good a deal as could be, if he didn't die of the numerous diseases. The lords proprietors published pamphlets "praising [South Carolina] as a healthy and temperate location, indeed a paradise for English bodies," writes Peter McCandless, but in reality, Carolina was even more unhealthy than Barbados.[6] Malaria was not common in Barbados, but the Lowcountry had it, and yellow fever too, as well as parasitic worms and diarrheal diseases.[7]

Buffeted and blown off course by storms, the first South Carolina colonists spent seven grueling months at sea before arriving in March 1670. The travel experience was sufficiently horrible from the beginning that four colonists deserted when the ship stopped in Ireland.[8] Stopping at Barbados on the way, they picked up the Royalist landowner John Yeamans, who brought his slaves with him, with the result that black people participated in the founding of Carolina, as they previously had in Barbados. Once landed, they planted their settlement, naming it after their king and patron: Charles Town. Yeamans, who had been instructed to choose a governor for the territory, chose himself and was proclaimed governor in 1672.

Virginia received some Barbadian immigrant planters, but South Carolina was defined by them. It was, in Peter H. Wood's phrase, "the colony of a colony." "By the second summer of settlement," Wood writes, "almost half of the whites and considerably more than half of the blacks in the colony had come from Barbados."[9] It was even less polite than Virginia, as the colonists jockeyed to game the system and take profit at gunpoint. It was combative; with Florida to its south, it was the most exposed of any of England's territories to Spanish attack.

The largest immigration to South Carolina in the 1670s was a movement of Barbadian planters to a community near Goose Creek, off the Cooper River, which became a power base that dominated South Carolina politics throughout the proprietorship. Practiced hands at colonial survival, the "Goose Creek men" had no intention of being subject to the lords proprietors, and they quickly acted to take control of the fledgling colony's elaborate governing structure of council and parliament. There was a religious schism as well: the Goose Creek men were part of Carolina's Anglican contingent, which wanted the Church of England to be an official religion, with favoritism for its members and themselves running it.[10]

Carolina's business policies were from the beginning hostile toward Virginia, some of whose colonists had to a degree been trading with the Native Americans and in native slaves. As soon as the Carolinians arrived, they went directly to work at cutting the Virginians out of the Indian trade, and they were favorably located to do so. Virginia's natural connection was not to the southern part of the eastern seaboard but to the line of colonies to its north. By land, Virginia was hemmed in by the Appalachians on the west and the Dismal Swamp to the south. By sea, a vessel going south from Virginia would have to cross the rough Cape Fear barrier and go against the Gulf Stream. So Virginia's easiest commerce was to the north and with Europe; it had little maritime contact with Charles Town and points south.

The northern part of Carolina was hemmed in worse than Virginia—blocked by barrier islands along the coastline, the Dismal Swamp on the north, and the Appalachians to the west. Forming a large buffer zone between Charles Town and Virginia, it would be formally partitioned as North Carolina in 1712. It was physically impossible to govern both Carolinas from a single seat; sea travel was the only practical access between them. But Charles Town was in charge commercially: North Carolina had no major seaport, and never developed a colonial aristocracy.

The two Carolinas were quite different from each other. Whereas North Carolina was settled principally from the north by frontiersmen and became mainly a domain of small farms, South Carolina was settled principally by sea, via immigration from England, Scotland, Ireland, and Barbados, and became a regime of large plantations. Its west and southwest were located below the Appalachians, leaving the way clear for overland travel on trails through thick forests to the vast region that we now call the Deep South—the home of a complex, interlocking network of related native cultures that anthropologists call the Mississippian, which dated back to the innovation of maize cultivation and storage in the region around 1000 BC.[11]

Not only was North Carolina where the South began; South Carolina was where the Southwest began. South Carolinians fought the Native Americans and drove westward expansion. From South Carolina's earliest days, it saw itself as extending all the way out to New Mexico, where the first Spanish settlement had been established in 1598.

The indigenous peoples had long fought internecine wars among each other. The arrival of the Europeans increased the pressure of war that was already forcing the Native Americans into confederations, including:

- the Choctaw, who inhabited the Mississippi River region;
- the Chickasaw in present-day northern Mississippi and western Tennessee;
- the powerful Creek confederation, loosely divided into Upper Creeks (present-day Georgia) and Lower Creeks (Alabama);
- the mountain-dwelling Cherokee in eastern Tennessee and parts of South Carolina; and
- others: the Natchez of Mississippi, the Catawba of the Carolinas, the Tuscarora of North Carolina; as well as
- two that would play important roles in the South Carolina native slave trade: the Yamasee of South Carolina and the Shawnee (or Savannah) of the Savannah River area, where the town of Savannah was later founded.[12]

Meanwhile, the picture was complicated considerably by the entry into Louisiana of the French, who were strategically focused on the Mississippi River. The French, the Spanish, the English: three contenders for the same large Native American territory that later became the cotton kingdom, all enslaving the natives. But it was Carolina traders—many of them Scots—who massified the Native American slave trade.

Coming from Barbados, the Carolinians had ample knowledge of the workings of the global slave trade, and they also had business contacts on the island. They knew that there were no indigenous people on Barbados, but Carolina abounded with Native Americans, and the settlers immediately began trafficking in them to supply Barbados's, and the other English colonies', slave markets. They also exported kidnapped natives to England's enemy colonies of Saint-Domingue, Martinique, and Guadeloupe.

Formerly, when Native Americans defeated rival tribes they tortured the men to death over a period of days and took the wives and children. Now, the losers could instead be sold to South Carolina traders. The Carolinians, in other words, paid Native American warriors with consumer goods to annihilate each other, escalating an already existing circle of recriminative violence whose origin predated the arrival of the Europeans. Carolina, then, took its first steps toward having an economy by building a Native American slave trade that would then fund the growth of a plantation system using black labor.

The lords proprietors had not contemplated this; like the Virginia Company previously, they wanted to reserve the trade in hides for themselves, for which reason they wanted good relations with the natives. Though African slavery was central to the proprietors' design, they were furious when Carolina's first industry became a trade in enslaved Native Americans. For one thing, they didn't get a cut from that business since the colonies, not the Royal African Company, supplied the market.

The merchants of Britain, the slaveowners of Barbados, and the traders of Carolina worked together through commerce to create a revolution against the lords proprietors. New England and Virginia had previously sold some native slaves, but the Carolinians had access to a much larger supply, and they set about it with a will. This Native American slave trade was completely illegal under the laws of the colony, in which free people were not to be enslaved except in "just war." (Africans, however, were deemed to have been already enslaved at the time of purchase in Africa.) A set of additional rules for Carolina, written in Locke's hand in December 1671, specifically prohibited enslaving the natives.[13] Too late. Traders in the two-year-old colony were already fomenting war among the local tribes for the purpose of slave-raiding, accumulating wealth by dispossession.

The Native Americans needed little encouragement from the English and Scottish to kill and enslave each other, and the Carolinians were eager to help them do it. The methodology had already been worked out by African slave traders. To create slave exports, the entrepreneurs producing slave-raiding wars had to create an arms race among the native people, whether they were the indigenous peoples of Mississippi or of Ouidah. As in Africa, slave-raiding in greater Carolina was done by the natives: the traders armed their Indian allies and bought the slaves they captured.

From its earliest years, Carolina sought to extend its control over the entire region by means of its superior trading goods, which most especially meant guns and ammunition. In the last two decades of the seventeenth century, Carolina traders built a network that extended through the territories later known as Georgia, Alabama, Mississippi, and Louisiana. It was all South Carolina, at least in the minds of the Carolinians.

There were two main export products from this commercial wilderness trading circuit. One was deerskins, which were exported by the tens of thousands annually to European markets. Fashions in London changed with the availability of the new commodity, which was cheaper than New England beaver: stylish Englishmen began wearing breeches made of the comfortable, soft leather, and women wore deerskin gloves. But the more lucrative, and primary, commodity that Carolina traders sold was native slaves, who were exported to the Antilles as well as to New England. The farther west the traders penetrated—by the 1690s they were operating in present-day Mississippi and Louisiana—the less likely they were to be handling deerskins. The Native Americans preferred slaves as their long-distance export; they were more valuable and, unlike deerskins, which were a burden to be carried, captives could walk themselves to market.

Generally the Carolinians preferred to sell the Native Americans away rather than keep them as slaves locally; for one thing, the natives knew the territory better than the Carolinians did, and they had allies outside, so the potential for escape was high. But also, Africans were much preferred as workers.

"That slavery would be the accepted labor system of South Carolina was unquestioned from its earliest settlement," writes Elizabeth Donnan. "Coming from Barbados, Jamaica, Antigua, and St. Kitts, slavery was the accustomed order, the bringing of slaves into the province the natural and desirable practice."[14] Even before South Carolina was able to establish a major staple crop, it quickly developed a two-way slave trade: first, exporting Native Americans, then plowing the profits into importing Africans.

The flow of captives among the Anglo-American markets was a complex circuit in the years after South Carolina became a power in Native American slave trading.

In the late seventeenth century, there was a market for slaves at every port in the English colonies. Every colony wanted labor, and if it didn't come from the Royal African Company, so much the better. Boston, New York, Philadelphia—they all bought slaves when they could get them, though the market was smaller in the North. The plantations of Virginia were an especially good market for any trader with laborers to sell, because the territory received few Africans.[15] Barbados, Jamaica, Antigua—the first stops after Africa on the trade routes of the clockwise loop—were almost always ready to buy Africans, so there was no need for a slaver who could sell his cargo there to continue for weeks more to Virginia with prisoners who could erupt into violence or die in an epidemic. (Much the same thing would happen later with French slavers, who could always sell their cargo in Saint-Domingue and had no need to continue on the perilous way to Louisiana.)

So vessels packed with enslaved Africans came into the sugar islands in the 1660s, albeit in insufficient quantities to please the planters, but only rarely to North America, where slaves accordingly sold for high prices. The scarcity created business opportunities: needing desperately to diversify from the monocrop of sugar, Barbadians developed a minor trade in exporting small quantities of slaves to the mainland. Right up until the War of Independence, vessels coming to North America from the West Indies might carry a few slaves along as part of the cargo, generally new arrivals from Africa. A captain could buy them on his own account, paying with the gold coins the Barbadians otherwise had such a hard time getting. He would sell them for deerskins—or, later, rice—in Carolina or to Virginians for tobacco, then take that commodity to London, sell it for paper exchangeable for gold, and continue on another round with a new supply of coins. Alternatively, black slaves from the Antilles were exchanged for native slaves from Carolina, sometimes at a two-for-one exchange rate that reflected both the Carolinians' desire to rid their territory of Native Americans and their eagerness to acquire black slaves.

The sugar boom on Barbados thus indirectly provided a labor supply for the Chesapeake, even as the Barbadians bought Carolina natives. While presumably most of the black slaves trafficked to the Chesapeake were African-born, others were born in Barbados, or were what historians have begun to call "Atlantic creoles"—a new cosmopolitan people who, writes Ira Berlin, "might bear the features of Africa, Europe, or the Americas."[16]

The native slave trade was not a small business; Alan Gallay, whose scholarship has informed our treatment of this topic, estimates that the Carolinians trafficked between thirty and fifty thousand Native Americans off to slavery.[17] Perhaps ten to twenty thousand of them came from the Florida peninsula, which was largely depopulated as a result. There is little documentation of the traffic of either native slaves out of Carolina or of black slaves from the Indies up to the mainland. Gallay concludes that during the years of the Native American slave trade (until the Yamasee War put an abrupt stop to it in 1715), more native slaves were exported from Charles Town than African slaves were imported.[18]

Whatever the precise numbers, the direction was clear: over a period of more than 150 years, culminating in the Native American removals of the 1830s, the free, sovereign, native population of the entire Deep South was hollowed out and gradually replaced by an imprisoned African, then African American, population.

The creation of a voracious external market in abducted Native Americans was a much different proposition than pre-Columbian indigenous enslavement of natives by natives had been. It altered forever the political and social relations among indigenous people, none of whom could remain unaffected as Indian slave trade routes emerged across the densely forested Deep South. Tribal groups became well-armed colonial clients, racing toward each other's destruction.

This Charles Town trade web reached as far as Louisiana. Even before the Canadian Pierre Le Moyne, Sieur d'Iberville, brought his force to the Gulf Coast to establish the Louisiana colony in 1699, South Carolinian traders had already begun depopulating the region, removing enslaved indigenous people through their already well established frontier posts.[19] On February 28, Iberville wrote that two Englishmen were leading Chickasaw war parties "among all the other nations to make war on them and to carry off as many slaves as they could."[20]

These Carolina traders, with their organized circuits, were the first Europeans to learn, however crudely, something of the political complexity of the indigenous Mississippian culture. They were also the first English to comprehend the plan of "encirclement," by which the French hoped to control the entire circuit from the St. Lawrence in Canada down the continental backbone of the Mississippi River to the Gulf of Mexico, with the ultimate aim of driving the English out of the coastal Atlantic areas.

The Mississippi River did not figure much in the Native Americans' strategy; they dominated the land. Presumably they could have exterminated the European settlements had they not been so at odds with each other. Instead, they made alliances with the Europeans for protection against other tribes and for the guns and other consumer goods that the Europeans brought. Rarely did Europeans fight Native Americans directly, and though the European forces on occasion attacked each other's strongholds, in general they fought their wars through native clients, who attacked each other.

The French made allies of the Choctaw, whose enemies, the English-allied Chickasaw, were by then completely given over to a slaving economy. When the Chickasaw attacked the Choctaw, it was England attacking France. The large Creek confederation managed the feat of never allying with any of the three European powers in the vicinity, and thus became power brokers.

This early Carolina trading economy was the work of perhaps two or three hundred traders, some of whom were cattlemen as well. Trade was war: like the privateers of Elizabeth's time, these were merchant-warriors, known for their brutality.

The traders established "factories" in the wilderness and in the Native American towns. A word with roots in slavery, *factory* derives from *factor*, referring to the financial agents who, in the absence of banks in America, settled colonial accounts on behalf of the London syndicates. That's what they called the trading posts in Native American territories, as well as the hellish installations that similarly swapped merchandise for people along the West African coast: factories.*

---

*Muscle Shoals, Alabama, famous in the annals of recorded music, was at one time the site of such a Native American–trading factory.

In Africa, slave-ship captains assembled a live cargo over a period of weeks as local traders came downriver, sometimes waiting for a nearby battle to end so that war captives would be available for purchase. The captives' heads were shaved before they were packed belowdecks, a precaution against lice that also de-individualized them, along with stripping them of their names, identities, and culture. Likewise their clothes went: most were shipped naked, in violation of the traditional modesty of many African societies.

The modern sense of a *factory* was already implicit, then, in what the slave trade did. Through a series of dehumanizing procedures, it processed the raw material of people into a value-added industrial product: slaves. As the American plantation system emerged, planters did not have to capture and enslave people; they bought African slaves, offered to them as a product by a slave factory.

The systematic crushing of the black family by the later antebellum slave-breeding industry began with the severance of African family ties. The elite of the Americas, whose successive generations tended to remain elite, and who had in many cases come from Europe with the advantage of family connections, did everything possible to make sure that the family structures of Africa, which in some cases included royalty, high priests, and military heroes, did not transfer their webs to the Americas.

Ripped from the families that had always been their strength, the captives were intended to be as close to human blanks as the slave traders could deliver—though, as scholars have detailed in recent decades, there is abundant evidence to confirm what common sense suggests: that the enslaved struggled against their condition all along, and never accepted their captivity. Slave traders couldn't remove the Africans' heads, and in those heads the captives brought culture and knowledge, which in turn became their defense after they were sold—captured, bound, imported, naked, packaged in chains, nameless, and, in the Duke of York's heyday, complete with corporate logo.

When we speak of "branding" today, we should remember that it was at one time literal: with a hot iron pressed against human flesh. York literally put his name on his merchandise: many thousands of people were branded RAC, for Royal African Company, while thousands more were branded DY, for Duke of York. The brand functioned as a tax stamp, signifying that the person was to be considered a legally imported factory product.

⇒⇐

In modern commentary, one sometimes hears the term "feudal" applied to the slaveholding South. That is incorrect;* instead of following a feudal model as prescribed by the Fundamental Constitutions, South Carolina agricultural slavery was capitalism in action. Enslaved black people in English North America did not have the advantages of serfs, who were attached to specific pieces of land and could at least remain with their families and communities.* Carolina slaves were, like Barbadians, chattel—a different category of property, which allowed them to be separated from their family members and redistributed as necessary for financial advantage to the master or his creditors.

A color-caste system of forced laborers to produce export crops for sale on the global market was as modern a notion as a new sugar factory, a more efficient sailing vessel, an insurance policy, or a London bill of exchange. It was based not on tradition—English involvement in African slavery was still a recent phenomenon—but on empirical, market-driven experience: African slaves had been proven in both Barbados and Virginia to be more profitable than indentured Englishmen.

Not only through custom, but also as stipulated by law, the enslaved were routinely treated as if they were less than fully human. As such, they could be fed inhumanely: a low grade of Indian corn, imported from New England, would suffice, so that the maximum amount of land and agricultural labor could be devoted to cash crops.

Income from plantation produce arrived not in the form of coins but as credit, always leading production by a year, giving the perennially indebted planter an urgent incentive to produce, which was transmitted to his overseer, who in turn used his whip to communicate the economic imperative to the people in the field.

Introducing firearms, ammunition, and consumer goods, conspicuously including rum, into native societies had the effect of making the natives dependent on their Carolina allies. Meanwhile, the slave trade in indigenous people increased the collective temperature of rage among the tribes, who in the aggregate greatly outnumbered the Carolinians. The Europeans' dealings with the natives were thus highly political: these were not unions of tribes but confederations whose ancestrally distinct factions could turn hostile against each other and whose

---

*Though there was later an idealized affinity in the antebellum South for the fantasy medieval life depicted by Walter Scott in his 1820 novel *Ivanhoe*.

antagonisms could be stoked and played off against each other. Some tribes were eradicated entirely, as in the case of the small but violent Westo.[21]

The Westo, who acquired that name only when they got to Carolina, had endured two forced migrations in fifteen years. First displaced from New York and Pennsylvania by the Iroquois Confederation—the most highly organized of the native governments—they went to Virginia, where they slave-raided on behalf of Virginia traders until the Pamunkey, who were themselves being displaced by the Virginia colonists, pushed them out. The Westo migrated down to Carolina, where they terrorized other tribes and sold the captives to traders, doing much business between 1675 and 1680.[22] But they too were killed and enslaved when the Carolinians found a stronger trading partner, the Savannah, who would in turn be replaced by a confederation called the Yamasee, whose fighting men numbered perhaps twelve hundred and whose origins are unclear.[23]

It was a deliberately genocidal business model. In Louisiana, Iberville told a Choctaw council in 1702 that, as summarized by Vernor W. Crane, "within the last decade the Chickasaw had taken five hundred Choctaw prisoners at English instigation and had killed more than three times that many."[24] By giving Native Americans a mercantile incentive to assassinate and capture one another, the English facilitated the murderous process of depopulation. So killing was the traders' business, and business was good, especially because credit could now be had. British business took enormous steps toward modernization during the period of the native slave trade out of Carolina, and the Carolina economy took full advantage of the financial innovations.

The Royal African Company was founded in 1672, a disastrous year for British business. The finances of the extravagant Charles II, who was supported by Louis XIV, were in such disarray that England defaulted on its debts. Carolina's earliest days, therefore, coincided with the rise of private banking in the face of Charles's default.

Private banks issued readily transferable debt in the form of bills of exchange. These were something like checks that could be traded; their expansion came along just in time to play a key role in fueling South Carolina's economic growth. Bills of exchange had been used in England as early as the fourteenth century, arriving there as part of the credit footprint of Italian bankers. In the intervening centuries, they had played a key role in the humbling of monarchs by empowering the bourgeoisie. They allowed for the production of money without the intervention of the king, although—and here's the catch—the system required a stable sovereign currency to function well.[25]

An individual bill of exchange might be passed around from hand to hand many times before being redeemed at the office of the original issuer. It was a lot easier than passing around pieces of gold, especially since there was rarely gold to be had in the colonies. In writing up a bill of exchange, the merchant in effect created money in the form of new debt. This system, as elaborated in late seventeenth-century England, created the conditions necessary for capitalism to thrive; it was copied throughout Europe.[26]

Charles Town, which was in close contact with London over the years, developed a powerful mercantile economy based on bills of credit. The increased availability of credit from London merchants facilitated Carolina's import/export slave trade that in effect exchanged Native Americans for Africans, who then served as collateral for the creation of more credit.

The position of bills of exchange in commerce was illustrated by a report made to Thomas Starke, one of the first importers of African slaves direct to the Chesapeake (as of 1692) and one of London's largest tobacco importers. When in 1697 he sent an apprentice to Maryland to collect a large sum owed him by indebted tobacco planters and to sell dry goods, Barbadian rum, and slaves, the apprentice reported back that indentured servants were being paid for with tobacco (meaning tradable paper notes redeemable in tobacco), whereas slaves were being paid for with bills of exchange—meaning that slaves were more valuable than indentured servants and had to be purchased with a higher-quality money.

When Charles II died in 1685 without an heir, his younger brother James, the Duke of York and of Albany, became King James II. Though it was an orderly succession, it alarmed Protestant politicians. James, who like Charles had spent his formative years in exile in France, had converted to Catholicism in 1669—more or less in secret at first, while continuing to attend Anglican services. A believer in a strong monarchy, James dissolved Parliament twice during the three years he was in power. When his Italian wife, Mary of Modena, gave birth to a Catholic heir in 1688, tensions grew until James was deposed by his own Protestant daughter Mary, who had married the Dutch prince Willem van Oranj (William of Orange).

William and Mary took power in 1688 at the invitation of the Protestants and in collusion with the Dutch, who had ample reason to hate James. Their anti-Catholic coup d'etat has been remembered as the "Glorious Revolution," a term that put a halo and a political spin around the word "revolution," which also described the movement of the heavens.

Virginia and Massachusetts both exulted at the Glorious Revolution, though otherwise they rarely agreed on anything. The days of absolute monarchy—and, they hoped, of rule by Catholics—were definitively over. And so were the days of Catholics being able to hold office, or even vote, in Maryland, a situation that would not change again until independence.

The discontent that led to the Glorious Revolution stemmed in part from Charles's fiscal profligacy. Now there would be no more Stuart spendthrifts. King William III was placed on an allowance and had to go to Parliament for money. Meanwhile, under its Dutch king, English finance was penetrated by Dutch systems, the most modern of the day. The Bank of England was created in 1694, and a stock exchange came into being in London. Making use of Dutch innovations that were not available to or, apparently, understood by the French, English commerce flourished, with merchant-created "credit-money" (Geoffrey Ingham's term) becoming "the most common means of transacting business," even as England created "the strongest metallic currency in history."[27] The merchants' bills of exchange were pegged to that now-solid currency.

All of this augured a more dramatic projection of England as a world power. After the accession to the throne of Mary's Protestant sister (and Charles II's niece) Queen Anne in 1702, the Union of Crowns in 1707 brought England and Scotland together into the new nation of Great Britain—a powerful free-trade zone that did not include Ireland, which would remain an exploited colony.

Neither Catholics nor Quakers were welcome in Virginia, but both thrived in Maryland and Pennsylvania. Meanwhile, not all the white settlers in Virginia were English, Scottish, Welsh, or Irish. There were Palatines, as German immigrants were called.

And there were French Huguenots. By the beginning of the eighteenth century, after Louis XIV removed civil guarantees for Protestants in 1685 and began torturing them and confiscating their wealth following eighty-five years of tranquility, a migration was under way that made the Huguenots the largest continental group in the English colonies at that time. Iberville's strong military presence in Louis XIV's Catholic Louisiana foreclosed on the possibility of the hundreds of Huguenot refugees going to the Gulf Coast in 1700, and instead they established the colony of Manakin Town, some twenty miles north of Richmond, on the James River fall line.* Others went to South Carolina.

By this time the commercial struggle between South Carolina and Virginia for control of the Native American trade was well under way. South Carolina harassed the Virginians with duties on skins and on occasion seized traders' inventories.[28] But South Carolina had much hotter conflicts on its hands; its founding inaugurated a border war with Spanish Florida that lasted more than a century. For the first decades, it looked as though one colony might annihilate the other, the way the Spanish had exterminated the French Fort Caroline. The Carolinians carried out an effective campaign of burning Spanish missions in the area.

In San Agustín, chronically underfunded by the Spanish, shortages were a way of life. But thinking there was a hoard of silver bars there, the English pirate Robert Searles attacked the town in 1668, burning it and killing some sixty people. The Spanish responded by fortifying their defenses, breaking ground on a fourteen-year construction project that began in 1672. Built by native and black slaves, convicts, and Spanish soldiers, the Castillo de San Marcos is today under the management of the United States National Park Service. Like similar, larger structures that can be seen in Havana, Santiago de Cuba, San Juan, Cartagena, Luanda, and other places around the former Iberian empire, it's still impressive. During multiple attacks on the city, its formidable walls were never breached. When a 1702 attack by the South Carolina governor (and Goose Creek Indian slave trader) James Moore razed the town of San Agustín and besieged the castle for two months, the population retreated to safety within its walls.[29]

By contrast, a Scottish settlement in South Carolina, at present-day Beaufort, was annihilated. Stuart's Town (or Stuart Town), established in 1684, competed with Charles Town for the Native Americans' alliances. But after the Yamasee attacked a Spanish mission, Santa Catalina de África, killing some fifty people and taking away indigenous and African people to sell to Stuart Town traders, the Spanish attacked and burned Stuart Town in retaliation, destroying it in 1686.

Besides direct assault, the Spanish had a powerful ultimate weapon to use against Charles Town: the lure of freedom for those who wanted to accept Catholicism or who, like the Bakongo, had been baptized Catholic in Africa. This allowed manumission to be part of what Gerald Horne calls "leverage" for the enslaved that resulted from the Catholic-Protestant enmity.[30] The Spanish were not, of course, motivated by kindness; offering freedom to those who would defect was a tactic.

---

*Disclosure: the Sublette (or Soblet) family arrived in America as part of this migration.

The Castillo de San Marcos as seen from the town of St. Augustine, Florida. June 2013.

The first recorded instance of defection was in 1687 when, writes Jane Landers, "Florida's governor, Diego de Quiroga, reported to Spain that eight men, two women, and a nursing child had escaped from Carolina to San Agustín and were requesting baptism into the 'True Faith.'"[31] In the succeeding years, more groups of escapees arrived, occasioning a complaint to San Agustín's governor by John Colleton.

Spanish Florida made use of slave labor, but it was a military outpost, not a plantation empire. The territory's de facto status as a haven for enslaved people wishing to be baptized Catholic was formalized by a November 7, 1693, edict from the feeble Spanish king Carlos II. The last Hapsburg king of Spain, he was believed to be bewitched but was actually the product of generations of royal inbreeding; his decisions, presumably including this one, were largely made by his regent mother, the Austrian queen Mariana.

Offering freedom was an effective measure: the promise of a safe haven for slaves within marching distance kept South Carolinians afraid of domestic revolt, to say nothing of their fear of nearby Spanish armies, which commonly had black soldiers.

With the death of Carlos in 1700, the Bourbons took the Spanish throne, with Louis XIV's grandson Philippe d'Anjou becoming Felipe V. This union of French and Spanish crowns alarmed the rest of Europe. The War of Spanish

Succession, known in America as Queen Anne's War, began in 1701 with England, the Netherlands, and the Austrian-centered Hapsburg Empire as allies against France and Spain. In local terms, that meant intensifying the conflict between South Carolina and Florida, between South Carolina and Louisiana, and between the English-allied Chickasaws and the French-allied Choctaw.

Iberville formulated a plan for a joint French-Spanish expedition against Charles Town, which would in theory continue on to Virginia and New York. He was perhaps the most able military man in the Americas at the time, and it is possible he could have taken Charles Town, but he died before he could carry out the assault, apparently of yellow fever, in Havana in July 1706. It went on without him in September, launched from Havana, with both black and indigenous troops joining the combined French and Spanish forces. But the invaders were defeated with the substantial participation of citizen militia, and the assault failed miserably.

14

The Separate Traders

Most of the wealth consists in slaves or negroes. . . . These negroes are brought annually in large numbers from Guine and Jamaica (the latter of which belongs to England) on English ships. They can be selected according to pleasure, young and old men and women. They are entirely naked when they arrive, having only corals of different colors around their necks and arms. They usually cost from 18 to 30 pounds [between about $3,900 and $6,500 in 2014 dollars]. They are life-long slaves and good workmen after they have become acclimated. Many die on the journey or in the beginning of their stay here, because they receive meagre food and are kept very strictly. Both sexes are usually bought, which increase afterwards.[1]

—A Swiss visitor to Virginia, 1702

In the face of the Royal African Company's continued inability to provide planters with all the slave labor they wanted, independent entrepreneurs ignored the royal monopoly, rushing contraband slave ships to Africa in numbers.

The West Indian planters, who were influential in Parliament, wanted the Royal African Company's monopoly broken. After experimentation with individual licenses, the African trade was deregulated in 1698. Independent merchant syndicates (called "separate traders") could now trade, provided they paid a 10 percent duty to the company on merchandise they exported or brought back, except for "red-wood" (a dyestuff, with a duty of 5 percent) and for the significant exception of "Negroes," on whom no duty was charged.

The separate traders were also allowed to maintain their own factories in Africa, where they spread rumors that the RAC was bankrupt and lured factors away from the company into their service.[2] Many were based in Bristol, which began its ascent as a major slaving port after the deregulation. The RAC had established itself at some thirty to forty factories along the African coast, from Elmina to Luanda, and many of these were taken over by separate traders, whose competition drove up prices at the African source.[3]

Another financial innovation of the time was an insurance sector. The investors of Lloyd's coffeehouse in London began insuring in 1688, and, since the transatlantic slave trade was a high-risk enterprise, the rise of separate trading grew Lloyd's business considerably.

Deregulation was effective at stimulating the traffic in kidnapped Africans. The black population of Virginia approximately tripled over the twelve years after the opening of separate trading, and only with separate trading did large-scale trafficking of Africans to South Carolina begin.[4] By the end of that period, the arrival of large numbers of African laborers had, predictably enough, raised Virginia and Maryland's production levels dramatically, causing a glut of tobacco on the market. The price plunged to crisis levels, causing numerous defaults on payments for slaves bought on credit from the RAC. Cutting its losses, the company stopped voyages to Virginia in 1706, but the separate traders continued pouring in Africans, as this comparison for the years between 1698 and 1707 shows:[5]

	Jamaica	Virginia	Maryland
Separate traders	35,718	5,692	2,938
Royal African Company	6,854	679	0

The separate traders' aggressive importation consolidated the power of the slave plantation in the Chesapeake, making Virginia into a full-blown slave society. As planters reinvested their profits in more slaves, they ran up a trade deficit sufficiently alarming to cause the Virginia assembly in 1710 to levy a five-pound duty on each imported captive—Virginia's first domestically generated tariff— with the result that for five years only a few slaves entered the territory, until the balance of payments problem eased.

The large slaveowners who made up the Virginia assembly were in favor of restricting the entry of new slaves. Not only did they have all the captive laborers they needed to run their plantations at peak efficiency, but the laborers were surviving and reproducing instead of dying off, creating capital gains for them. A slaveholder's on-paper worth, and therefore his credit, was based on the price he could command if he sold his surplus labor; as the century rolled on, Virginians complained frequently of the English slave trade, which drove down the value of their enslaved assets. The simple device of keeping the price of domestically born enslaved human property artificially high through import restriction was to be fundamental to the economy of Virginia, right up through emancipation.

Virginia and Maryland charged duties to each other's vessels. Scofflaws could find their slaves confiscated and sold for the commodity money of tobacco to the colonial government's benefit. After Maryland relocated its capital away from the upper bank of the Potomac and needed a statehouse at its new site of Annapolis,* the Maryland Assembly in 1695 imposed a per-slave import duty of ten shillings to pay for it, and doubled the duty the following year.

Across the Chesapeake from Annapolis, slavery was the first order of business for the new port of Chestertown. It was right up top, in the language the Maryland Assembly used when it created the little town on April 19, 1706, designating a plantation waterfront on the Chester River as one of a number of official customs posts where "all Ships and Vessells trading into this Province shall unlade and put on shoare all Negroes Wares goods merchandizes and Comodities."

That the first dutiable item mentioned in the creation of the new town was "Negroes" reflected the growing importance of the slave trade as a source of revenue for colonial government. That the law specified "Negroes" rather than "servants," "slaves," or even "Africans" reflected that the criterion for enslavement was a two-tone caste system, because "Negroes" was a color word, from the Spanish and Portuguese *negro*, meaning black. That "Negroes" were separately broken out on the list implied that although the enslaved were being sold along with "Wares goods merchandizes and Comodities," there was something different about selling human beings.

The importation of indentured English, Scotch, and Irish paupers, who had previously constituted the Chesapeake labor force, had slowed after the Glorious Revolution of 1688. A large-scale importation of convict laborers was still in the future. The trade was in Africans.

---

*Named in 1694 for Princess Anne, who became Queen Anne in 1702.

A "servant" could be any of several different classes of people; one writer has discerned "nine or ten varieties of servitor," with indentured whites at the top of the hierarchy and "negro slaves" at the bottom.[6] The term applied equally to indentured Irish, Scottish, or English paupers and to African slaves, to people doing brutally hard field labor and to artisans, valets, cooks, or tutors. What they all had in common was that they did not generally receive wages. The trade that shuttled them to their destinations was as bare-knuckles a business as could be, and constantly provided a fat target for taxation.

The new separate-trading legislation empowered Bristol, whose captains made fortunes in pauper, convict, and African labor; and the new high-volume capital of the African trade, Liverpool, whose captains would trade as many slaves as Bristol and London together.

The business transformed with the arrival of the biggest commercial contract of the day: the *asiento*, a word literally meaning "seat" that refers to a contract between the government and a private concern. Spain had been purchasing slaves by means of the *asiento* since the sixteenth century, mostly from the Portuguese, without developing a major slaving industry of its own. As the long War for the Spanish Succession was ending, Spain in 1713 sold the *asiento* to Britain to supply 4,800 African slaves a year to its colonies, and it was then awarded in turn to the recently created South Sea Company by Queen Anne Stuart, James II's younger daughter.*[7]

Anne died the following year at the age of forty-nine. Gout was the stated cause of her death, but she had been weakened by the eighteen pregnancies she experienced before becoming queen; eleven were miscarriages and none of them resulted in a surviving heir to the throne.[8] She was succeeded by her second cousin, King George I, a Protestant descendant of the Stuarts from the house of Hanover, whose first language was German.

Hugh Thomas calls the *asiento* the "El Dorado of commerce."[9] Not only was it a thirty-year monopoly to sell slaves, but since it allowed British ships into Spanish ports, it gave British merchants practical, though not legal, access to all sorts of other commerce.

---

*"South Sea" referred to the South Atlantic.

The resulting investor hysteria in London culminated in the South Sea bubble, infamous in business history, when a mania for shares in the company drove prices sky-high, with the inevitable crash. Many of London's best-known figures—Alexander Pope, John Gay, and Sir Isaac Newton, among thousands of others—were burned when their investments in the slave trade went sour.

But the slave trade itself continued being profitable as the age of large-scale British slaving got under way. About 4,000 Africans arrived in Virginia between 1715 and 1718, and then 5,170 came on thirty-five ships between 1719 and 1721.[10] The problem of tobacco overproduction predictably returned, and prices for the commodity were depressed throughout the 1720s. Complicating the market further was that the wide-open competition of freelance traders to supply slaves bid the price up in Africa even as it fueled intra-African wars that fed the trade in captives, depopulating some areas (especially in Central Africa), and creating ever wealthier, ever more rapacious African elites—and, as economist Warren Whatley argues, promoting polygyny in Africa and the development of small, fragmented African states over large ones.[11]

With the advent of high-volume freelance slave trading, colonial assemblies levied duty after duty on what the US Constitution would later politely call "importation of persons." Not that cash actually changed hands at the customs post: as the colonists had no gold or silver, tobacco was used as money—"commodity money" is the economist's term. But passing around hogsheads of tobacco was impractical; paper notes backed by tobacco were issued as early as 1727, and perhaps earlier, in Virginia. Around the Chesapeake, duties, fines, commissions, and prices of all sorts were quoted in pounds of tobacco and paid by tobacco notes. When the Kent County courthouse in Chestertown was torched by an arsonist in 1719, a new one was built at the cost of fifty-five thousand pounds of tobacco and was renovated in 1750 at the cost of fifty thousand pounds more.[12]

Once planters had enough slaves for themselves, they were happier if no one else did, especially not their emerging competitors to the west. The colonies were political battlefields of conflicting interests with constant tension between settled areas and the newer communities on the western frontier. The planters and merchants of the former tended to have control of colonial assemblies, while the farmers of the latter constituted a market to exploit. Meanwhile, the African slave trade—not to be confused with slavery itself—made many in the colonies uneasy, because it was seen as introducing a dangerous population into the colonies. It also had another deleterious effect: it sucked specie out of the colonies and put colonists in debt to British merchants, who for their part were very pro–slave trade.

London's policy was to encourage importation of enslaved and indentured labor whether the colonists liked it or not. The more labor, the more profit: there was profit in the agricultural commodities that were produced, but also in shipping them; in financing, selling, and shipping the labor; and in taxing the sales.

Prohibitively high duties on slave importation were laid at times by colonial assemblies, but the laws they made could always be overridden by London, where slave-trade interests, sometimes including the king, prevailed time and again to roll the duties back. A group of Liverpool merchants successfully lobbied for a rollback of a 1728 Virginia duty, while a similar effort resulted in the denial of South Carolina's attempt to impose a duty of £10 per head in 1731.[13]

Slaves were frequently purchased on credit, typically twelve months or less but sometimes as long as three years, by means of the planter's giving a postdated bond with one or two cosigners. As the colonial legislatures began erecting a fence of measures to protect planters against debt collection by British merchants, the traders of Liverpool, Bristol, and London brought pressure to bear on Parliament to pass the Colonial Debts Act of 1732, which allowed creditors to seize "lands, houses, chattels, and slaves" in satisfaction of debts. This new law, abhorred by the colonial planters, strengthened the merchants' hand: their factors working in the colonies could collect on a planter's bond if he could not pay it when due.

By clarifying that slaves could be seized and sold in satisfaction of obligations, the Colonial Debts Act expanded significantly the available credit for slave purchasers, and made the use of planters' bonds the most common credit instrument in the Virginia slave trade. It also provided for the legal, forcible separation of the enslaved from their families by a debt collector. The logical consequence was that creditors felt more secure investing in slaves.[14]

Sugar—the crop for which most of the 12.5 or so million Africans were embarked in chains to the Americas—systematically brought death to its laborers. Cutting cane is backbreaking labor, but that was not the worst of it. Cane had to be boiled and reduced to molasses on the spot, as it was too bulky and perishable to transport, so sugar plantations were full-scale factories. They were hot, smoky, and physically dangerous, but even so, the deadliest factor was the unbearably long hours the laborers were forced to work.

Sugar-making was both labor intensive and seasonal. Rather than work a full complement of laborers ten hours a day and have to maintain them during the "dead time" when there was nothing for them to do, it was cheaper to make half as many workers go for as many as twenty hours a day in the peak periods, replacing them with newly arrived Africans when they finally expired.

The system of sugar plantation management that the English sugar planters learned from the Dutch and the Brazilians followed the logic of free-market capitalism: x pounds for equipment, y number of African laborers who cost z pieces of gold and live m years, to get n amount of molasses that brought p amount of money in q time. The result of these multivariable calculations, which pushed the limits of eighteenth-century accountancy, was that self-interested rationally acting plantation owners with no moral scruples could make the most money by working laborers to death.

Compared with sugar, cultivating and packing tobacco was milder work. Tobacco was a less intensely seasonal crop; it did not require as many hands, and its planters had no financial incentive to work their slaves to death. In the off time, when hands were not needed for tobacco, they were put to work raising food crops and doing artisanal and construction work. "Planters placed few demands on the outside world, in these respects, and supplied little to the outside world," write Anderson and Gallman.[15]

Fernando Ortiz, who wrote what was perhaps the first work of structural anthropology, *Cuban Counterpoint of Tobacco and Sugar,* described the distinct lifestyles associated with those two crops as constituting the poles of the Cuban personality. About sugar, he wrote, "capital was needed to buy slaves, to bring in experts and administrators and all the machinery for milling, boiling, evaporating, and decanting. Even aside from the land required, sugar production was necessarily a capitalist enterprise."[16]

Above all, sugar required access to slave labor. To facilitate the capitalist enterprise of sugar, there was another capitalist enterprise at work: procuring and selling the laborers that produced the sugar. That required financing, credit, international contacts, political contacts, market information, insurance, ships, shore facilities, and crews.

Sugar plantation populations typically had fewer women than men. Wherever in the hemisphere enslaved laborers were applied to sugar, they had negative reproduction rates. But in the milder climate of Virginia, with the relatively milder work of tobacco, with more women among the enslaved population and more adequate food, the numbers increased. By the 1710s, Virginia's enslaved population was growing by reproduction—an "unprecedented event for any New World slave population," writes Philip D. Morgan. Despite the arrival of so many Africans, "natural increase" was such that by 1720 Virginia-born slaves accounted for about half the colony's total.[17] (It would take about another thirty years for gender balance of the enslaved to even out.) This was something that did not happen elsewhere in the Americas, and it was the key to Virginia's developing a slave-breeding industry.

In South Carolina, it was very different.

Charles Town

You ain't got no supper in Beaufort unless you got some rice. You ain't
finished cookin' yet, until you've cooked a pot of rice.[1]

—Sea Island folklorist Anita Singleton-Prather in her
performance persona as Aunt Pearlie Sue

Question. I see it hazardous for a man to give so much Money for a Slave,
and that Slave may soon die, then all his Money is lost. . . .

[Answer]. Is it not so here If a Man purchase Cattle or Horses, how can
he be assur'd of their Lives? Yet we have a greater Encouragement to buy
Slaves, for with good Management and Success, a Man's Slave will, by his
Labour, pay for his first Cost in about four Years at most, besides his Maintenance, so, the Remainder of his Life, you have his Labour as free Gain,
we esteem their Eating and Wearing as little, for that rises on the Plantation, and is little cost out of Pocket.[2]

—John Norris, Profitable Advice for Rich and Poor,
promotional London pamphlet pitching emigration
to South Carolina, 1712

THE GROWING CONDITIONS OF Virginia and Carolina were as different as their
topographies, necessitating different crops.

It took Virginia between sixty and a hundred years to become a slave society, but South Carolina began as one. "By the late seventeenth century," writes
Philip D. Morgan, "Virginia had a plantation economy in search of a labor force,
whereas South Carolina had a labor force in search of a plantation economy."[3]
Virginia had defined its staple crop for decades before massive importation of

Africans began, staffing the fields mostly with indentured servants, whereas South Carolina, founded by slave traders, began as a slave society that had not yet found its staple crop.

A 1708 census of the Carolina colony, which did not count free Native Americans, gave the population as 9,580—with a distribution of 42.5 percent white, 42.5 percent black, and 15 percent enslaved Native Americans.[4] Most of the captives brought to the colony in the late seventeenth century were "seasoned" slaves, brought up from the West Indies. But Carolina colonization began as England was beginning to get involved in the African trade on an industrial scale. The first known slave ship to travel from Africa to South Carolina arrived in 1696, about the same time quantities of African captives were beginning to come to Virginia and Maryland.

After that, the floodgates opened. "The first quarter of the eighteenth century saw the enactment of numerous laws laying import duties on the incoming slaves," Elizabeth Donnan writes, "the reason offered being sometimes 'the great importation of negroes,' which threatened the safety of the province, and sometimes the need for a revenue, easily provided by a duty on slave importations. . . . Despite occasional outbursts of anxiety over the menace of a [']barbarous['] population greatly outnumbering the planters themselves, the lure of profit which slave labor held out prevented the success of any consistent policy of limitation."[5]

Sugar, chocolate, and coffee came from the warmer latitudes. Virginia and Maryland were growing tobacco. But what would Carolina produce? So far, it was an exporter of Native American slaves and deerskins. It took some decades of experimentation, but by the beginning of the eighteenth century Carolina had found its principal staple crop: rice. Tradition has it that the first crop was made with seed from Madagascar, brought in by a privateer.[6]

Investing in the Madagascar trade from East Africa—a striking exception to the flow of slaves from West and Central Africa—was a New York specialty, though others were in it too. During the Royal African Company's monopoly (through 1698), wealthy New Yorkers made fortunes doing an end run around it, trading

next page: Scottish trader and Indian agent Thomas Nairne's 1711 map, made for the lords proprietors, shows South Carolina's territory as including present-day Georgia, Alabama, much of Florida, and part of Mississippi. The only named towns are Charles Town, Port Royal, and Augustine; the "South Bounds of Carolina" is shown as well south of Augustine. Native American locations are precisely described, with a count of the warriors: "Chicasa 600 Men," etc.

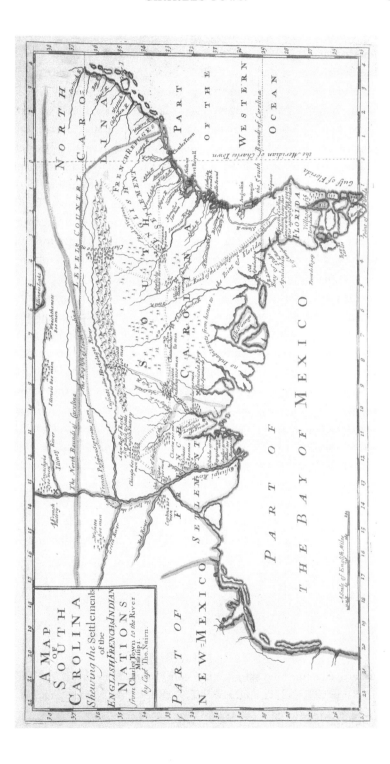

illegally in slaves and other African merchandise by opening a commercial corridor to Madagascar, where the RAC's vessels did not go.

The Scottish-born merchant Robert Livingston was one of a number of New York merchants who became rich investing in African trading expeditions. The son of a Scottish Presbyterian minister who had fled Charles II's compulsory Anglicanism in 1663 for Rotterdam, he ultimately emigrated to America. After marrying the wealthy Albany Dutch widow Alida Schuyler Van Rensselaer in 1679, Livingston became the head of a family that came to own about a million acres of land. With the disappearance of Dutch commerce from New York after the definitive English takeover in 1674, the established merchant families of the former Nieuw Amsterdam took greater control, consolidating commercial dynasties headed by the city's old money, and by 1690, Livingston was a half-partner in the *Margriet*, a ship that traded slaves, sugar, and tobacco on an illegal trading voyage to Madagascar, Barbados, and Virginia.[7]

The first rice seed may have come to Carolina from Madagascar, but the cereal grain was grown across a wide area of Africa. Rice was indigenous to Africa as well as to other places, and an African strain was domesticated there; Mande people had built the Malian empire in part on the technical achievement of cultivating it.[8] The Europeans did not know how to produce rice, but West Africans were familiar with its complicated cultivation, and they brought their knowledge to Carolina. Virginia had unsuccessfully attempted to grow rice during Berkeley's governorship, but its climate was not hot enough.[9] Planters competed to buy slaves from a vaguely defined part of West Africa referred to in slave-sale advertisements as the Rice Coast—a name it received not because Africa exported rice, but because it exported kidnapped farmers who knew how to grow it.

The "Rice Coast" often meant the Windward Coast, but could mean anywhere from Senegal down to present-day Ghana. A slave-sale advertisement from the *South Carolina Gazette* of March 18, 1769, makes clear the involvement of Africans in rice culture:

TO BE SOLD
On Wednesday the 29th Instant
A CARGO of Two Hundred and Ninety
SLAVES
REMARKABLY HEALTHY
Just arrived in the Ship Sally, Capt. George Evans, from CAPE MOUNT
A RICE COUNTRY on the WINDWARD COAST, after a SHORT
Passage of Five Weeks.

That these captives were from "a rice country" (in present-day Liberia) was an incentive for rice farmers to purchase them.

Carolina quickly became the largest supplier of rice in the world. In his landmark study *Black Majority*, which called attention to the African genesis of the Carolina rice industry, Peter H. Wood observes that "during precisely those two decades after 1695 when rice production took permanent hold in South Carolina, the African portion of the population drew equal to, and then surpassed, the European portion."[10] As South Carolina out-imported Africans over any other territory, becoming a black majority society, the Sea Islands off its coast became not only black but diversely so, with people from disparate regions of Africa.

Both South Carolina rice and, a little later, indigo relied on African agricultural and processing knowledge. That was also the case in Louisiana, where the first slave ships brought rice seedlings and Senegambians who knew how to grow it, and where indigo was also grown and processed into dye.[11]

Imports of Africans increased dramatically as diversified farming gave way to a plantation society in South Carolina. Big operators gobbled up freeholds; as planters became wealthy, small farmers became impoverished, and the population became blacker. "Put simply," write McCusker and Menard, "rice brought the demographic regime of the sugar islands to South Carolina. . . . In long-settled plantation districts spread along the tidewater in both directions from Charleston, the black share of the population approached 90 percent by 1740, roughly the proportion in the sugar islands."[12]

Rice was a miserable crop to tend. It had to be weeded constantly, which meant bending over all day long while standing in mud. Disease thinned the laborers' numbers constantly. The standing water of the rice plantations incubated mosquitos that bore maladies usually associated with more tropical climates, while the density of workers rendered rice plantation slaves especially vulnerable to epidemics.

Rice wasn't for small family farms; it required an operation of at least thirty workers to be profitable.[13] The fatality of the environment was a disincentive to voluntary immigration. Rice could only be produced on a commercial scale in the Lowcountry with slaves, who lived unspeakably miserable lives.

The enslaved population of the rice plantations exhibited characteristics seen in the sugar islands with mortality exceeding births as laborers were worked to death. Africans in South Carolina had a negative growth rate, and the burned-out laborers would have to be replenished by new arrivals. It took until the 1770s for African Americans to become the majority of the black enslaved in South

Carolina, fifty years after it happened in Virginia and more than a century after black slaves had first been brought there.[14]

A boosterish book by John Norris, published in London in 1712 to stimulate emigration, contrasted the two ethnic slaveries that coexisted in South Carolina. Norris mentioned perpetual enslavement of Native American slaves' descendants while pointing out their provenance from "French" (Louisiana) or "Spanish" (Florida) territories:

> Those we call Slaves are a sort of Black People, here commonly call'd Blackmoors, some few kept here in England by Gentry for their Pleasure . . . but their proper Names are Negroes. . . . When these People are thus bought, their Masters or Owners, have then as good a Right and Title to them during their Lives as a Man has here to a Horse or Ox after he has bought them. . . .
>
> There is also another sort of People we buy for Slaves, call'd Indians, bred on the Continent, but far distant from us, belonging to the French and Spanish Territories in America. They are a sort of Red Dun, or Tan'd Skin'd People, who are also Sold us by Merchants or Traders that deal with several Nations of our Native Indians, from whom they first buy these People, whom we then make Slaves of, as of the Negroes . . . they are never Free-Men or Women during their Life, nor their Children after them, who are under the same Circumstances of Servitude as their Parents are, during their Lives also.[15]

Norris described how a hypothetical £1,500 investment should be spent to yield a plantation producing £400 annually. His first item of expense was "Fifteen good Negro Men at £45 each," followed by "Fifteen Indian Women to work in the Field at £18 each," "Three Indian Women as Cooks for the Slaves, and other Household-Business," and "Three Negro Women at £37 each, to be employ'd either for the Dairy, to attend the Hogs, Washing, or any other Employment."[16]

The many twists and turns of the conflict between slave-raiding South Carolina and the shifting alliances of Native Americans with the French and Spanish are beyond the scope of this volume. Suffice it to say that Carolina's slave trade in

Native Americans was ended by a full-scale war between the Carolinians and an alliance of native tribes that lasted for two years, an enormously long campaign in the context of indigenous struggles against the Europeans.

On the morning of April 15, 1715, the Yamasee, in alliance with the Creeks, struck in a coordinated attack and massacred the frontier traders. Thomas Nairne, the Scottish trader who had led an expedition to the Mississippi and was the most capable frontiersman in South Carolina, was captured and slowly roasted to death by means of burning splinters stuck into his body over a period of days.[17] The Indians did not attack Charles Town, which became a citadel for frightened people from the countryside.

Remembered by the Carolinians as the Yamasee War, the uprising changed direction with the entry of the Cherokees as South Carolina's allies against the Creeks, and it was over by 1717. The remaining Yamasee fled to Florida; the Creeks, the most powerful of the confederations, migrated west and retained their status as a crucial regional power while nursing a special hatred of the Cherokees.

"This war," writes Alan Gallay, "marked the birth of the Old South, just as Appomattox later marked its death."[18] The turning point in the consolidation of the rice-plantation economy, it led to the end of the proprietorship and the reversion of Carolina to royal colony status.

It is worth underscoring that the end of trading in native slaves came about as the direct result of a focused attack by Native American alliances, and also that this native rebellion was a black rebellion as well. Black soldiers fought together with Native Americans in the Yamasee War; the Carolinians, meanwhile, were so desperate that they armed some of their slaves.

South Carolina's war with Native Americans underscored how exposed the English were on their southern flank. With the flight of the remaining Yamasee to Florida and the Creeks' move west, the southern frontier was depopulated, even of Native Americans, which represented a grave security issue. And the land that the Yamasee had abandoned was prime rice-growing land.

The lords proprietors' claims to own the land to the southwest had foreclosed on the possibility of settlers there, but now, under the pressure of the Spanish threat from Florida, a convention of colonists (with the militia's support, expressed by flying colors) rose against the lords proprietors. After fifty years of proprietary government, what South Carolina remembered as the Revolution of 1719 led ten years later to the final return of the colony to crown status.

After the Carolinians successfully petitioned to change the colony's status in 1729, the lords proprietors took a lowball buyout.

The Yamasee War made the Native Americans more powerful relative to the South Carolina colonists than they had previously been and diminished England's influence against the Spanish and French in the region. But the French colony had arrived at its own crisis with the Native Americans. On November 28, 1729, Natchez Indians attacked Fort Rosalie, the nucleus of the later town of Natchez and the hub of the fledgling French agricultural effort, worked by enslaved natives and Africans. They killed much of the town's population—between 230 and 240 settlers, mostly men—and kidnapped 62 more, mostly women and children, and 106 slaves, and they destroyed all the crops. On April 10, according to Marc-Antoine Caillot, a clerk for the Company of the Indies, "a Natchez Indian woman whom the Tunicas had captured" was slow-tortured, dismembered, and burned to death by the Tunicas in New Orleans, Indian-style, with the permission of the French, in reprisal for the Natchez torture of their captives.[19] The destruction of the colony's agriculture signaled the end of the active French colonization effort in Louisiana, as that colony reverted to crown status in 1731, two years after South Carolina had done so.

The Carolina economy had to be rebuilt after the Yamasee War, something that took most of the 1720s to accomplish, during which time the transition to a rice-plantation economy based on African labor was consolidated. Once again, the importation of Africans increased the threat of slave rebellion, both real and imagined. An "anonymous letter addressed to a Mr. Boone in London, and dated 'Carolina June 24, 1720'" mentions a purported slave conspiracy:

> I am now to acquaint you that very lately we have had a very wicked and barbarous plott of the designe of the negroes rising with a designe to destroy all the white people in the country and then to take the town [Charles Town] in full body but it pleased God it was discovered and many of them taken prisoners and some burnt some hang'd and some banish'd.[20]

Records from the period are scanty, but there is reason to believe that this slaughter of "negroes" was far from the only one in South Carolina. A letter from Charles Town dated August 20, 1730, describes a purported plan for an uprising much like the purported 1674 Barbados conspiracy and not unlike the one successfully executed sixty-one years later in Saint-Domingue, the future Haiti. This one was organized around a dance:

a bloody Tragedy which was to have been executed here last Saturday night (the 15th Inst.) by the Negroes . . . some of them propos'd that the Negroes of every Plantation should destroy their own Masters; but others were for Rising in a Body, and giving the blow at once on surprise; and thus they differ'd. They soon made a great Body at the back of the Town, and had a great Dance, and expected the Country Negroes to come & join them; and had not an overruling Providence discovered their Intrigues, we had been all in blood.[21]

By this time, more than two thousand Africans a year were coming into Charles Town. Samuel Wragg testified before the board of trade in 1726 that he

had been a Trader to Carolina Seventeen or Eighteen years. That that Country formerly had but very few Negroes, but that now they employd near 40,000. That they now usually import 1,000 per Ann: whereas they formerly imported none, and sometimes 2 or 300. At the same time Mr. Platt, also of Carolina, reported that the colony imported about 1000 negroes per annum, at prices ranging from £30 to £35 sterling.[22]

"Even though Wragg were greatly exaggerating both the yearly importation and the number of slaves in Carolina," writes Elizabeth Donnan, "it is evident that by this decade the trade had become of sufficient importance to merit the fostering care of the home government and the constant solicitude of British and Carolina merchants, foremost among whom were the Wraggs, Joseph and Samuel."*[23]

The frontier between Carolina and Florida had never been agreed on, much less defined. Carolina's colonists, who were influential in London, pressed for a new boundary colony that would buffer them against the Spanish, the French, and the Native Americans. Promotional literature began circulating in London in favor of a new colony below South Carolina. The first one to circulate, in 1717, continued the feudal fantasy of the still extant proprietorship, proposing a colony that would be headed by a hereditary official called a margrave. The name of the new colony was to be the Margravate of Azilia.

It took fifteen more years for a colony to be planted there. When it was, it was named for King George II: Georgia.

There was to be no slavery in Georgia.

---

*When Joseph Wragg died in 1751, the obituary in the *South Carolina Gazette* called him "an eminent Merchant of this Town, who formerly dealt pretty largely in the Slave Trade."

16

Savannah and Stono

As the staples of Carolina were valuable, and in much demand, credit was extended to that province almost without limitation, and vast multitudes of negroes, and goods of all kinds, were yearly sent to it. In proportion as the merchants of Charlestown received credit from England, they were enabled to extend it to the planters in the country, who purchased slaves with great eagerness, and enlarged their culture.[1]

—Alexander Hewatt, 1779

If We allow Slaves we act against the very Principles by which we associated together, which was to relieve the distressed. Whereas, Now we Should occasion the misery of thousands in Africa, by Setting Men upon using Arts to buy and bring into perpetual Slavery the poor people who now live free there.[2]

—James Oglethorpe to the Trustees, January 17, 1738/9

LONDON NEWSPAPERS HAILED THE initiative to found Georgia. It was the product of humanistic and philanthropic movements in London, and also of public relations. The colony's visionary founder, James Oglethorpe, spent two years directing the colony's promotional campaign before sailing for America.[3]

Oglethorpe was an aristocrat formerly allied with the Stuarts. He had studied classical antiquity at Oxford's Corpus Christi College, then went to military school in Paris and fought against the Turks in the 1717 siege of Belgrade.[4] Becoming radicalized after his scholar friend Robert Castell died in debtor's prison, Oglethorpe wanted to help the poor better themselves in the autocratic, militarized utopia he would build.[5] Georgia was intended to be a site of relief where debtors could have a fresh start—though in practice, no debtors were among the colonists—while functioning as the avant-garde of England's North American empire, protecting South Carolina from Florida.

Drawing on his studies of Greece and Rome, Oglethorpe devised a unique plan for a city: a matrix of connected rectangular plazas—twenty-four were built—each one serving as a commons around which were to be housed ten families, with garden plots for subsistence located within walking distance. Because of that plan, and with help from the lush vegetation, historic Savannah today is one of the most beautiful urban environments in the United States.

The colonists carved out their plots from a densely wooded area on a bluff overlooking the Savannah River, beginning the construction of Oglethorpe's meticulously planned community of 240 freeholders. He also founded several other communities in Georgia: Darien; Frederica; James Brown's future home town of Augusta, on the South Carolina border; and Ebenezer, a community of persecuted Protestants from Salzburg who were dead set against slavery. A group of forty-one Jews, all but seven of them Sephardic Portuguese, arrived on July 11, 1733, and founded a short-lived congregation in 1735. After checking with lawyers in Charles Town as to whether Jews could be admitted to Georgia, Oglethorpe was advised that they could be, since they weren't papists. Their arrival upset the trustees in London, but they were powerless to do anything about it.[6]

Oglethorpe, who had been deputy-governor of the Royal African Company, saw slavery as a bad system that would lead to problems in Georgia—and not only because the ever-present potential for rebellion was aggravated by San Agustín's offer of freedom directly to the south. He also saw it as a corrupting influence on white colonists. Oglethorpe felt the same way about rum, prohibiting its sale, though wine and beer were permitted. Nor did he want a real estate market; in Oglethorpe's Georgia, land given to colonists was passed on by entail: it could not be sold, only inherited, and only by men.

As the first houses of Savannah were being built and moved into, Oglethorpe lived in a tent to set an example of self-sacrifice for the others. But there was trouble from the beginning, and in an isolated community riven by vicious personal rivalries and much disagreement, slavery was a divisive issue.

Charles Town did more to destroy Oglethorpe's utopia than Florida. Carolina merchants ran trade routes all through the area, and Savannah was dependent on them for many kinds of supplies. But Oglethorpe didn't want his colony buying the supplies the Carolinians most wanted to sell: slaves. Moreover, Georgia's resistance to rum impeded the Carolinians' business of selling it to the

Native Americans along with the guns and ammunition they were selling them, which created friction.[7]

As slaveowners would do more than a century later in Missouri and Kansas—and would even attempt to do in Southern California—the South Carolinians infiltrated pro-slavery colonists into Georgia. The Carolinians who moved down into Georgia had no more respect for Oglethorpe's restrictions than they previously had for the lords proprietors'. From South Carolina, Eliza Lucas Pinckney complained in a September 1741 letter of Oglethorpe's "Tyrannical Government in Georgia," presumably because its residents were denied the freedom to own slaves, plant large plantations with staple monocrops, deal in rum, or buy and sell land.[8] Noting ill treatment of indentured servants in Savannah that had caused some to desert, colonist Thomas Jones wrote: "The Carolina Temper, of procuring Slaves, and treating them with Barbarity, seems to be very prevalent among us."[9]

Charles Town merchants thus began making money importing Africans from British slave traders for re-export into Georgia, a market that would keep them rich for generations. Prosperity reigned; in 1732, the year Georgia was planted, Benjamin Franklin's ex-apprentice Lewis Timothy founded the *South Carolina Gazette*, with Franklin as a silent partner. The South's second newspaper to appear, it was as strategic a media rollout as the times afforded: South Carolina's economy, heavily centralized in Charles Town, was booming. By 1735 Charles Town was sufficiently wealthy and cultured to found the St. Cecilia concert society. Its fast-growing wealthy elite consumed luxury goods. It was *the* prime underserved advertising market.

Meanwhile, another migration to North America was picking up: the so-called Scotch-Irish, whose Presbyterianism made them a dissenting sect in

A view of Charles Town, as depicted in 1739 by artist Bishop Roberts and etcher W. H. Toms, emphasizes the constant activity in its port.

Anglican Ulster. They had to settle to the west, because the good coastal land was taken. After the first such colony moved to South Carolina to receive land grants near the Santee River, establishing Williamsburg in 1732, they were in "low and miserable circumstances," wrote Alexander Hewatt, until they too bought slaves from the Charles Town merchants and their lands "in process of time became moderate and fruitful estates."[10]

The border was still dangerous. Having Georgia as a buffer between South Carolina and Florida made Carolina that much more secure. But England and Spain were still facing off in the region; the Spanish responded by inducing more of the English colonists' slaves to escape.

There were already small communities of free blacks around San Agustín, but in October 1733 a Spanish edict reiterated that people reaching Florida and accepting the Catholic faith would be free, increasing the flow of runaways. To further bedevil the Carolinians, a free black garrison town, called Gracia Real de Santa Teresa de Mose, was established in 1738 about two miles north of San Agustín, providing a first line of defense for the Spanish.* Its governor was Francisco Menéndez, the leader of Florida's black militia. A Mandinga who was born a Muslim, Menéndez had been kidnapped to Barbados as a boy and then taken to South Carolina. He defected to the Yamasee Indians at the time of the Yamasee War in 1715 and ultimately escaped to Florida, where he accepted Catholicism and was baptized with his Spanish name.[11] There was a price on his head in South Carolina, but no matter: he was fighting for the Spanish, and he had weapons. The news traveled: a free black town on the side of the Spanish, with Bakongo soldiers among its residents, within marching distance.

In 1738, the Spanish at San Agustín announced that runaways would be given freedom and land, sweetening the attraction the Florida territory already had for Carolina slaves. Benjamin Franklin's *Pennsylvania Gazette*, with its good contacts in South Carolina, ran the following item on October 8, 1739:

> Extract of a Letter from Charlestown in South Carolina.
>
> The Spaniards of St. Augustine near Georgia, have issued a Proclamation, giving Freedom to all white Servants and Negro or Indian Slaves, belonging to Carolina, Parrisburg or Georgia, that will go over to them, and have allotted them Land near St. Augustine, where upwards of 700 have been receiv'd to the great Loss of the Planters of those Parts, which

---

*The site of Gracia Real de Santa Teresa de Mose was found in a 1986 architectural dig and is now a Florida state park.

will prove their Ruin if a Stop is not put to such a villanous Proceeding. This is a certain Proof of their Intent to attack Georgia, in which Case these Servants and Slaves are to be their Pilots and our worst Enemies.

The feared uprising had already happened but word of it hadn't reached Philadelphia yet. Remembered as the Stono Rebellion, it erupted about twenty miles from Charles Town on September 9, 1739. The anonymous sole firsthand description of the event is not too long to reproduce in its entirety.

AN ACCOUNT OF THE NEGROE INSURRECTION IN SOUTH CAROLINA

Sometime since there was a Proclamation published at Augustine, in which the King of Spain (then at Peace with Great Britain) promised Protection and Freedom to all Negroes Slaves that would resort thither. Certain Negroes belonging to Captain Davis escaped to Augustine, and were received there. They were demanded by General Oglethorpe who sent Lieutenant Demere to Augustine and the Governour assured the General of his sincere Friendship, but at the same time showed his Orders from the Court of Spain, by which he was to receive all Run away Negroes.

Of this other Negroes having notice, as it is believed, from the Spanish Emissaries, four or five who were Cattle-Hunters, and knew the Woods, some of whom belonged to Captain Macpherson, ran away with His Horses, wounded his Son and killed another Man. These marched f [sic] for Georgia and were pursued, but the Rangers being then newly reduced [sic] the Countrey people could not overtake them, though they were discovered by the Saltzburghers, as they passed by Ebenezer. They reached Augustine, one only being killed and another wounded by the Indians in their flight. They were received there with great honours, one of them had a Commission given to him, and a Coat faced with Velvet.

Amongst the Negroe Slaves there are a people brought from the Kingdom of Angola in Africa, many of these speak Portugueze [which Language is as near Spanish as Scotch is to English,] by reason that the Portugueze have considerable Settlement, and the Jesuits have a Mission and School in that Kingdom and many Thousands of the Negroes there profess the Roman Catholic Religion. Several Spaniards upon diverse Pretences have for some time past been strolling about Carolina, two of them, who will give no account of themselves have been taken up and committed to Jayl in Georgia.

The good reception of the Negroes at Augustine was spread about, Several attempted to escape to the Spaniards, & were taken, one of them was hanged at Charles Town. In the later end of July last Don Pedro, Colonel of the Spanish Horse, went in a Launch to Charles Town under pretence of [taking] a message to General Oglethorpe and the Lieutenant Governour.

On the 9th day of September last being Sunday which is the day the Planters allow them to work for themselves, Some Angola Negroes assembled, to the number of Twenty; and one who was called Jemmy was their Captain, they suprized a Warehouse belonging to Mr. Hutchenson at a place called Stonehow [Stono]; they there killed Mr. Robert Bathurst, and Mr. Gibbs, plundered the House and took a pretty many small Arms and Powder, which were there for Sale. Next they plundered and burnt Mr. Godfrey's house, and killed him, his Daughter and Son. They then turned back and marched Southward along Pons Pons, which is the Road through Georgia to Augustine, they passed Mr. Wallace's Ta[v]ern towards day break, and said they would not hurt him for he was a good Man and kind to his slaves, but they broke open and plundered Mr. Lemy's House, and killed him, his wife and Child. They marched on towards Mr. Rose's resolving to kill him; but he was saved by a Negroe, who having hid him went out and pacified the others.

Several Negroes joined them, they calling out Liberty, marched on with Colours displayed, and two Drums beating, pursuing all the white people they met with, and killing Man Woman and Child when they could come up to them. Collonel Bull Lieutenant Governour of South Carolina, who was then riding along the Road, discovered them, was pursued, and with much difficulty escaped & raised the Countrey. They burnt Colonel Hext's house and killed his Overseer and his Wife. They then burnt Mr. Sprye's house, then Mr. Sacheverell's, and then Mr. Nash's house, all lying upon the Pons Pons Road, and killed all the white People they found in them. Mr. Bullock got off, but they burnt his House, by this time many of them were drunk with the Rum they had taken in the Houses.

They increased every minute by new Negroes coming to them, so that they were above Sixty, some say a hundred, on which they halted in a field, and set to dancing, Singing and beating Drums, to draw more Negroes to them, thinking they were now victorious over the whole Province, having marched ten miles & burnt all before them without Opposition, but the Militia being raised, the Planters with great briskness pursued them and when they came up, dismounting; charged them on foot. The Negroes were soon routed, though they behaved boldly several being killed on the Spot, many ran back to their Plantations thinking they had not been missed, but they were there then taken and Shot, Such as were taken in the field also, were after being examined, shot on the Spot, And this is to be said to honour of the Carolina Planters, that notwithstanding the Provocation they had received from so many Murders, they did not torture one Negroe, but only put them to an easy death.

All that proved to be forced & were not concerned in the Murders & Burnings were pardoned, And this sudden Courage in the field, & the Humanity afterwards hath had so good an Effect that there hath been no farther Attempt, and the very Spirit of Revolt seems over. About 30 escaped from the fight, of which ten marched about 30 miles Southward, and being overtaken by the Planters on horseback, fought stoutly for some time and were all killed on the Spot. The rest are yet untaken. In the whole action about 40 negroes and 20 whites were killed.

The Lieutenant Governour sent an account of this to General Oglethorpe, who met the advices on his return from the Indian Nation[.] He immediately ordered a Troop of Rangers to be ranged, to patrole though Georgia, placed some Men in the Garrison at Palichocolas, which was before abandoned, and near which the Negroes formerly passed, being the only place where Horses can come to swim over the River Savannah for near 100 miles, ordered out the Indians in pursuit and a Detachment of the Garrison at Port Royal to assist the Planters on any Occasion, and published a Proclamation ordering all the Constables &c. of Georgia to pursue and seize all Negroes, with a Reward for any that could be taken. It is hoped these measures will prevent any Negroes from getting down to the Spaniards.[12]

A brief account of this uprising in the *Pennsylvania Gazette* on November 8 read:

We hear from *Charlestown* in *South-Carolina*, that a Body of Angola Negroes rose upon the Country lately, plunder'd a Store at *Stono* of a Quantity of Arms and Ammunition, and murder'd 21 white People, Men, Women and Children before they were suppress'd: That 47 of the Rebels were executed, some gibbeted and the Heads of others fix'd on Poles in different Parts, for a Terror to the rest.

John Thornton underscores the probable military background of the "Angola Negroes." They were likely not Kimbundu-speaking Angolans, relatively few of whom came to North America, but their immediate neighbors to the north, who were Bakongo. The term "Angola," Thornton writes, "surely meant the general stretch of Africa known to English shippers as the Angola coast," though the possibility exists that some people from various central African origins were mixed in.[13] In a world divided by religion, that these Africans were Catholic made them instant allies of the Spanish.

As the slave trade created business opportunities in Africa, African despots formed regularly organized armies and battled each other, the losers being sold into slavery. The result was that the ranks of the enslaved in the Americas included increasing numbers of combat-seasoned veterans of gun-toting African armies. In her history of Kongo Catholicism, Cécile Fromont identifies the ceremony that preceded the Stono uprising as "a typical central African *sangamento*, a martial performance in preparation for battle, in a manner similar to that used by contemporary Kongo armies."[14] The mention of drums and singing ties the Stono rebellion in with later rebellions as well as with Kongo military and spiritual influence, in Saint-Domingue and Cuba. African drums were a means of military communication, as the British well understood. Since 1699 the law in Barbados had stipulated that

> Whatsoever Master, &c., shall suffer his Negro or Slave at any time to beat Drums, blow Horns, or use any other loud instruments, or shall not cause his *Negro-Houses* once a week to be search'd, and if any such things be there found, to be burnt . . . he shall forfeit 40 s. Sterling.[15]

The *South Carolina Gazette* ran no articles about the Stono uprising, apparently fearing even to mention the subject where the black majority might learn of it. But a Charles Town merchant wrote in a letter of December 27 of that year, "We shall Live very Uneasie with our Negroes, while the Spaniards continue to keep Possession of St. Augustine."[16] "For several years after [Stono]," writes Peter H. Wood, "the safety of the white minority, and the viability of their entire plantation system, hung in serious doubt."[17]

Believing foreign slaves to be the most dangerous, South Carolina raised the duty on slave importation from £10 to a prohibitive £50. But that made for considerable lost income for local government in a territory where slaves had accounted for two-thirds of customs revenues in 1731, so in 1744 the duty was lowered back to its previous level. Previously, South Carolina had imposed double duties on slaves *not* coming from Africa, apparently in order to discourage the unloading of incorrigible West Indian slaves into their territory.[18]

The author of an 1825 pro-slavery pamphlet in Charles Town noted that the Stono rebellion was also remembered as the Gullah War.*[19] In recent years, Y. N. Kly has been arguing for the use of the term "Gullah War" as a blanket name for the ongoing black resistance struggle in South Carolina, Georgia, and Florida that lasted from Stono until 1858, with the end of what is usually called the Third Seminole War.[20] This Gullah War can be seen as part of the larger war against slavery, fought in ways large and small by the enslaved. From this perspective, slave rebellions reveal themselves not to be isolated struggles, as they have been frequently characterized, but rather as eruptions of a widespread, ongoing state of resistance. Their tactics ranged from day-to-day resistance, to absconding, to full-out uprising, to actions taken by the enslaved in major wars.[21]

In the wake of Stono, the South Carolina legislature on May 10, 1740, passed a detailed new slave code. "An act for the better ordering and governing Negroes and other slaves in this province," or, more simply, the Negro Act, had long been in preparation but some had thought it severe; its passage was catalyzed by the crisis atmosphere. Under its regulations, teaching a slave to write[†] became punishable by a fine of one hundred pounds; masters had to apply to the legislature for permission to manumit; and it even forbade slaveowners to allow their slaves to dress in "clothes much above the condition of slaves."

Aimed at making impossible the kinds of public assemblies that could turn into mobs or hatch conspiracies, Article 36 (out of 58) paraphrased the existing Barbadian regulation to stipulate that "whatsoever master, owner or overseer shall permit or suffer his or their Negro or other slave or slaves, at any time hereafter, to beat drums, blow horns, or use any other loud instruments or whosoever shall suffer and countenance any public meeting or feastings of strange Negroes or slaves in their plantations, shall forfeit ten pounds, current money, for every such offence." One long-term consequence of this and similar legislation was that African hand drums, so rigorously prohibited by the British colonists, do not turn up in popular African American music until they came into the United States via the Cubans in the mid-twentieth century. That African drums were

---

*The name of the creolized African American people called "Gullah" in South Carolina likely derives from "Ngola," or Angola, though there are other theories; in Georgia, the population is known as "Geechee," the name presumably deriving from the indigenous-named Ogeechee River.

†Writing was taught separately from reading in those days. Slaveowners feared that slaves who could write would forge the passes that every slave traveling alone was required to carry and thus escape.

played on some Southern plantations is documented, but they do not seem to have flourished outside their immediate context.

Another clause of the Negro Act forbade slaves from engaging in sales, and yet another restricted gatherings of "great Numbers of Negroes, both in Town and Country, at their Burials and on the Sabbath Day." All this was in marked contradistinction to New Orleans, where Sunday gatherings were already taking place at the commons later known as Congo Square.

The Negro Act was not discussed in the *South Carolina Gazette*. Days after the legislature adjourned, a slave conspiracy was uncovered (or perhaps imagined) in June 1740 among plantation slaves planning to strike in some numbers against Charles Town. The undoing of that conspiracy—also unreported in the *Gazette*, though other colonial newspapers took up the slack—resulted in the hanging of fifty people, in daily batches of ten. The following year, after a purportedly murderous slave conspiracy was uncovered in New York, the second largest black city after Charles Town, magistrate Daniel Horsmanden executed or exiled over one hundred people. Horsmanden, who may have dramatically exaggerated an existing plot or may have even imagined it all, linked the never-realized black insurrection to an alleged Catholic plot involving the Spanish.[22] Between 1730 and 1760 there were twenty-nine slave revolts reported in North America, about one a year, with an unknown number of others of smaller dimensions going unreported.[23]

When a calamitous fire in Charles Town on November 18, 1740, "in a very short time laid the fairest and richest part of the town in ashes, and consum'd the most valuable effects of the merchants and inhabitants," it was said at first that the fire had been set by slaves, though this apparently was not true.[24] The clergyman Josiah Smith preached a sermon, subsequently published with the title "The Burning of Sodom," that spoke of the fire as God's punishment for wickedness. Smith excoriated the whites of the town for defiling themselves by having sex with their slaves—not because they were taking unfair advantage of their captives but because they were cohabiting with inferiors. Reverend Smith insisted there was a great deal of fornication going on:

> there has been too much *Affinity* in *our Sins* and those of *Sodom*, as there has been in *our Punishment*.—Whether we have any *Sodomites* in our Town strictly so, I can't say.—Such abandon'd Wretches generally curse the *Sun*, and hate the *Light*, lest their Deeds should be reproved.—But in some Respects and Instances we declare our Sin as *Sodom*; we hide it not—We have proclaim'd on the *House-Top* what we should be asham'd

of in *Secret* . . . Let us enquire seriously, Whether our Filthiness be not found in our Skirts?—Whether our *Streets, Lanes* and *Houses*, did not burn with *Lust*, before they were consumed with *Fire*? . . . That unnatural Practice of some *Debauchees*, that Mixture and Production, *doubly spurious*, of WHITE AND BLACK; and taking those to our *Bed* and *Arms*, whom at another Time we set with *the Dogs of our Flock*, ought to stand in *red Capitals*, among our *crying* Abominations! I know not, if *Sodom* had done *this*![25]

The news of Stono arrived in Georgia concurrently with the confirmation that, as rumored, England and Spain were at war yet again. It was especially unhappy news because tensions along the disputed Georgia-Florida border had been the catalyst for the hostilities.

Britain's enduring, disingenuous name for the resulting war was applied to it much after the fact, in 1858, by Thomas Carlyle: the War of Jenkins' Ear. This referred to an incident that occurred off the coast of Florida in 1731, eight years before the war began. A Spanish coast guard patrol boat from San Agustín boarded a British brig, during which action the Spanish officer Juan de León Fandiño cut off the ear of the British captain Thomas Jenkins, taking in vain the name of the British king as he did so; the pickled ear was subsequently exhibited on the floor of Parliament.

Remembering the conflict as the War of Jenkins' Ear might suggest that the war was somehow trivial or silly. In Spain, however, the war was remembered not by that anecdotal incident but by its underlying financial cause: the *Guerra del Asiento*. British merchants commonly used their slave shipments to the Spanish colonies as trojan horses to smuggle in all sorts of other prohibited goods. Worse, the British government had stopped making its payments for the *asiento* to Spain as called for.

With England and Spain at war, Oglethorpe led a monthlong siege of San Agustín in 1740 but failed to take it; its defenders included about a hundred black militiamen from Gracia Real de Santa Teresa de Mose, led by Yamasee War veteran Francisco Menéndez.[26] Meanwhile, a dissident faction in Georgia, dubbed the Malcontents, were uninterested in small, self-sufficient, inalienable farms. They wanted to get rich via large, debt-driven, plantation slavery, and they wanted a functioning real-estate market so that they could buy out or seize the farms of others. Oglethorpe thought them in league both with the Charles

Town merchants (which they were) and the enemy in San Agustín (perhaps not). Oglethorpe wrote the trustees on May 28, 1742:

> The Mutinous Temper at Savannah now shows it self to be fomented by the Spaniards, & that the Distruction of that Place was but part of their Scheme for raising a general Disturbance through all North America. . . . They found three Insuperable obstacles in their way in driving out the English from this Colony. 1st. The People being white & Protestants & no Negroes were naturally attached to the Government. 2dly. The Lands being of Inheritance, as Men could not Sell, they would not leave the Country so easily, as new commers would do, who could Sell their Emprovements. 3^{d}. Distilled Liquors were prohibited which made the Place Healthy.
>
> Their Partizans laboured to get those who Perhaps intended no ill to bring about what they Desired. 1st. To Obtain Negroes being secure that Slaves would be either Recruits to an Enemy or Plunder for them. 2dly. Land Alianable which would bring in the Stock Jobbing Temper, the Devill take the Hindmost. 3^{d}. Free Importation of Rum & Spirits which would Destroy the Troops & Laboring People here.[27] (paragraphing added)

The war with Spain made Savannah's Jewish community particularly nervous, since they had fled the Inquisition. The community collapsed in 1741, and some of its members relocated to Charles Town where a congregation was organized in 1749, with the community divided between "Portuguese" (Sephardic) and "German" (Ashkenazi).[28]

Oglethorpe defeated a Spanish invasion of St. Simons Island in the descriptively named Battle of Bloody Marsh on July 6, 1742, effectively consolidating Britain's ownership of the Spanish-claimed territory of Georgia. The force that attacked St. Simons Island was a large one: about a thousand Spanish regulars and five hundred or so black militiamen from Cuba, where a quarter or more of the soldiery was *pardo* (mulatto) or *moreno* (black). Alexander Hewatt, a Scottish Presbyterian minister who wrote the first history of South Carolina and Georgia (after being expelled from Charles Town as a Loyalist in 1777), recalled the frightening impression made by the presence of uniformed black soldiers:

> Among their land forces they had a fine company of artillery, under the command of Don Antonio de Rodondo, and a regiment of negroes. The negro commanders were clothed in lace, bore the same rank with white officers, and with equal freedom and familiarity walked and conversed with

their commander and chief. Such an example might justly have alarmed Carolina. For should the enemy penetrate into that province, where there were such numbers of negroes, they would soon have acquired such a force, as must have rendered all opposition fruitless and ineffectual.[29]

The war was mostly over by 1742, after an attempted occupation of Cartagena by some thirty thousand British troops was repulsed, though hostilities continued through 1748. During the war, Spanish ships (joined in 1741 by French ones) preyed on shipments bringing American tobacco to London, denying the Chesapeake's tobacco farmers access to their market in Britain. This further encouraged the farmers in their ongoing switch to wheat, which had a domestic market, took fewer weeks of labor than tobacco, and needed less tending as it grew.[30]

Meanwhile, the British were cut off from their supply of indigo in the French West Indies, spurring the development of indigo production in South Carolina.

The first crop of indigo was brought in 1744 about five miles from the site of the Stono Rebellion by the twenty-one-year-old Eliza Lucas. A true godmother of American slavery, Lucas had lived most of her life in Antigua, where her father was the lieutenant governor. After trying her hand at raising ginger, alfalfa, cotton, and cassava at her father's South Carolina plantations, which she managed in his absence, she found she could grow indigo with seeds of the West Indian variety that her father sent her—but she could not process the plant into dye until her father sent her a "negro man" who knew how.[31] After the success of her crop, she distributed seed to her neighbors and married Charles Pinckney of Charles Town, becoming Eliza Lucas Pinckney.

Britain paid a bounty for indigo cultivation in order to have a supply of dye for its growing textile manufactures, though the South Carolina product was inferior in quality to the indigo they had been receiving from India. Indigo was the perfect complement to rice. Both called for large amounts of labor and, most importantly, they grew in different seasons, allowing for one overworked labor force to produce two different staple crops in a year. Both crops required disagreeable, unhealthy work.

Accounts of indigo production describe the terrible stench it gave off as the plants decomposed after infusion. It attracted grasshoppers and clouds of flies, was toxic to the workers, depleted the soil, and ruined the surrounding land for

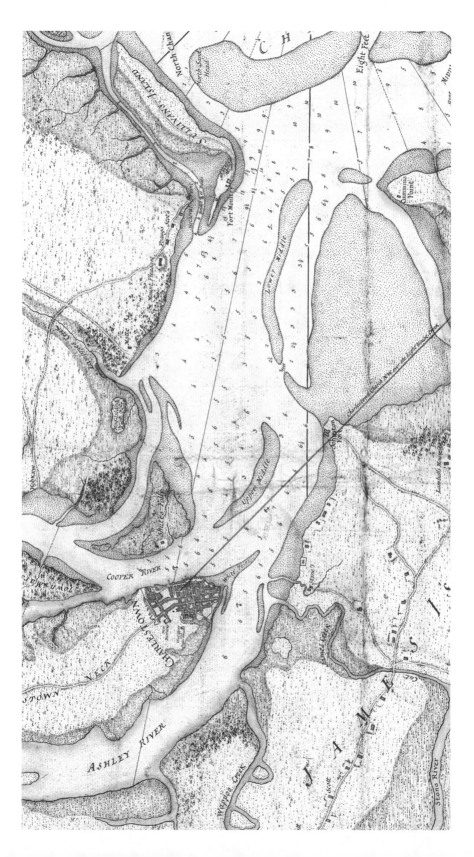

cattle, which were needed to provid basic nourishment for the region. But once processed, it was a perfect long-distance export: a small amount of the concentrated, solid dyestuff had a high value. It was even more profitable than rice. The success of indigo made South Carolina much more profitable, further stimulating British trade, most especially the slave trade, to the colony.

Oglethorpe returned to England for good in 1743, leaving behind William Stephens as governor. Stephens followed Oglethorpe's principles—at tremendous personal cost, since his son Thomas had become a leader of the Malcontents—but in 1749 he admitted defeat, advising the trustees that the prohibition against slavery was no longer enforceable. Slavery was legalized in Georgia as of January 1, 1751, and by 1752 the trustees had washed their hands of the place as the territory reverted to crown colony status. The itinerant traders who brought slaves in from South Carolina became known by a name that would outlive them: Georgiamen.

Twenty years after its founding as the first free-soil territory in the nascent British Empire, Georgia was firmly established as a satellite of South Carolina's world of plantation slavery. Though slaveowners frequently accused Britain of having forced the system of slavery on them, the case of Georgia offered an unambiguous model to the contrary: the British who established the colony wanted no slavery, but some of the colonists—and the South Carolina merchants—did.

previous page: Charles Town, at the confluence of the Ashley and Cooper Rivers, at the end of a defensible channel behind barrier islands, as depicted in a 1780 map by William Faden. Sullivan's Island, to the right, was the entry and quarantine point for upwards of a hundred thousand Africans.

following page: The coast of Georgia as depicted in a British map of 1780, showing the Sea Islands down to Amelia Island, claimed by Florida. Savannah is in the upper right.

PARISH

Fort Argyle

SAVANNAH

SAVANNAH
TOWNSHIP

WILMINGTON
ISLAND

Coanooche River

Opetchee Ferry

HARDWICK

SKEDWAY
ISLAND

GREAT
WASSAW
ISLAND

S⁹ JOHN'S PARISH

OSSABAW or
HOSABA SOUND

Fresh Water Bluff
Indian Camp Bluff
Bengchon'a Bluff

SUNBURY
Fort

HOSABA
ISLAND

S⁹ ANDREW'S PARISH

Bermuda
Island

Makkar'ie
Island

S⁹ CATHERINES SOUND

South *Newport*

S⁹
CATHERINES
ISLAND

Donofo'd Ferry

Barber's I
Wilson I

Outer I⁹ SAPOLLA or
SAPELLO SOUND

S⁹ DAVID'S   PARISH

Fort Barrington

North Branch of Sapola or Sapello River
Jo⁹ Smith's Island

Phœnahalloway Creek

Alatamaha River

Sapello River *Cockspur*

SAPELLO ISLAND

S⁹ PATRICK'S PARISH

DARIEN

Doboy

Wolf Is

S⁹ THOMAS'S   PARISH

Turtle River

Doboy Inlet
Wolf Island
Inlet
Island

ALATAMAHA SOUND

Little Satilla River

S⁹ SIMONS
ISLAND

Lookout
Frederica
Dunbar's Cr
Hawkins I
Ilriver &
Cap Vincengut
Bluff

Great Satilla River Newark

Williss or
Bluff Isl

Cara River

S⁹ SIMONS SOUND

S'S PARISH

JEKYL
ISLAND

Slafeangafee, or Crooked River

CUMBERLAND SOUND

Ferry S⁹ Mary's River

S⁹Andrew's
Fort

Dondingo Creek

CUMBERLAND ISLAND

Johnson's

Prince Williams F⁹

Tyger Island

AMELIA SOUND
or S⁹ MARY'S INLET

Little S⁹ Mary's River

AST   FLORIDA

New Town

AMELIA
ISLAND

West Longitude from London.

17

A Rough Set of People, but Somewhat Caressed

. . . that Cargo Sold at pretty good prices tho they were a month about it . . .
it was a most butifull Cargo of the Sort chiefly young People from 15 to 20
which are not accustom'd to destroy themselves like those who are older.[1]

—Henry Laurens, letter to Liverpool slave trader John Knight,
May 28, 1756

THROUGHOUT GEORGE WASHINGTON'S CAREER, it would never be forgotten by the British, the French, or the Spanish that when the young land speculator was a twenty-one-year-old lieutenant colonel in the British army, he played a key role in starting the war that deprived France of its North American real estate.

As French troops from Louisiana made incursions into the unexplored Ohio Valley, trying to connect France's Canada positions with Louisiana and thus box the British in on the Atlantic coast, they were ambushed on July 3, 1754, in what is now southwestern Pennsylvania, by a detachment led by Washington, with one column of British troops and one column of Native Americans. The British troops had been sent there by Virginia governor Robert Dinwiddie, in part to protect the land claims of the Ohio Company of Virginia, of which Washington's half brother Lawrence was a cofounder.

After a skirmish that led to the death in captivity of the French commander Jumonville at the hands of Washington's indigenous ally Tanacharison, Washington was captured and released after signing a confession in French, which he could not read. The Ohio Valley conflict escalated into a global war, with

London and Paris as the principal belligerents. In America it became known as the French and Indian War, and in Europe as the Seven Years' War. Its outcome drastically altered the course of hemispheric history, driving the French out of North America and giving control to Britain of New France, or Canada.

In the final phase of that war, after Spain's Bourbon king Carlos III foolishly entered the conflict on the side of his cousin, Louis XV of France, Britain occupied the great harbor of Havana, the hub of Spain's gold- and silver-shipping empire, for about ten months. At war's end, victorious Britain, in another net territorial gain, returned Havana to Spain in exchange for Florida.*

After 198 years as a Spanish Catholic town, San Agustín was now to become St. Augustine, a British Protestant town. Britain promptly divided Florida into West and East, with the Apalachicola River as the eastern boundary between the two. Pensacola, founded as a fort in 1698, was the capital of West Florida, which had the Mississippi as its western boundary abutting French Louisiana and controlled the access to the sea for the Gulf Coast hinterland. St. Augustine was the capital of East Florida, which included the entire peninsula.

London began giving away—mostly to politically connected Scots—massive amounts of the depopulated Florida land it now claimed, as well as large tracts in Georgia. It was the first, but not the last, boom in Florida real estate: "during the great speculation in American lands that preceded the American Revolution," writes George C. Rogers Jr., "there was more interest in the real estate of East Florida than in the property of any other region of British America." In the years from 1764 to 1770, 2,856,000 acres of East Florida were distributed.[2]

Virginia's tobacco was the largest American export, but the Lowcountry's rice and indigo was the second largest. Moreover, Virginia's exports were declining, while shipments from Charles Town's harbor, one of the colonies' busiest, were increasing. As plantations proliferated in South Carolina, Georgia, and Florida, Charles Town was the great mercantile supplier to all of them, with slaves far and away the highest-value merchandise supplied. Debts incurred purchasing slaves mounted up so fast that importation of Africans was suspended from 1766 to 1769, and disputes over taxation with England depressed importation in 1770–1, but in 1772 and especially 1773, importation was enormous. These slaves were often sold in gangs, with the result that, as in the sugar territories,

---

*Britain wanted the island of Guadeloupe, but had to keep Canada—which was producing much less revenue—instead.

people from a single African point of origin wound up on the same plantation, a consciousness that has remained in black Sea Island folkways, where different islands are understood to have different African cultural influences.[3]

Florida was to embody, once again, the British dream of enormous land-holdings. One of the first in the door was a leading British capitalist: the Scottish slave trader, commodity trader, shipping magnate, army contractor, planter, and stock market investor Richard Oswald, who was one of six owners who built Bance (or Bunce) Island in the Sierra Leone River into a major slave-trading factory. Oswald received twenty thousand acres in 1764, almost as soon as Florida was open for business. African slaves were brought directly to Florida for the first time, and Oswald soon had a hundred of them on his plantation.

A dinner at a meeting of the East Florida Society of London, founded in 1766, brought together a group of men that included Richard Oswald and Benjamin Franklin, who thought Oswald an "honest" man. Oswald's firm was at the time on the first year of its unprecedented five-year contract with a French society to bring regular shipments of slaves to the war-damaged plantations of Saint-Domingue and Guadeloupe from their Sierra Leone River base at Bance Island—a job only achievable by a modern factory, requiring as it did the coordination of regular supplies of people captured in slave raiding and war, with shipping schedules and cash flow, year in and year out. This type of venture marked a new level of professionalization in a business that had largely been the province of individual merchants working with captains who assembled cargoes as best they could. By the time Grant, Oswald & Co.'s French contract expired in 1770, they had delivered 4,847 people.[4] Oswald had a remarkable record of picking winners, but his venture in Florida was a bust, as were most of the others: the land was unsuited for rice or for sugar.

With the handover of Florida to Britain, more than three thousand of the Spanish colony's people evacuated, most of them fleeing to Cuba, where many established themselves in the communities of Guanabacoa and Regla, now part of metropolitan Havana. Residents of the free black town of Gracia Real de Santa Teresa de Mose founded the community of San Agustín de la Florida in Matanzas province. The western part of Cuba, meanwhile, was being reconfigured by sugar. Control of the sugar market had been a major object of contention during the Seven Years' War, and after the abrupt British withdrawal from Cuba the island entered into its era of sugar prosperity. During its ten months as an occupier in Havana, Britain had begun aggressive slave importation there, giving new life to Cuba's moribund sugar industry. Cuba had been home to

Africans for almost two and a half centuries at that point but had not had massive plantation slavery; now that began to change. Liverpool slave captains serviced much of this new Cuban market, bringing large numbers of captives supplied by their African trading partners in the Bight of Biafra, the region known as Calabar. The African traders of Bonny and Old Calabar were particularly powerful and did not allow the establishment of factories by Europeans, giving them a trade advantage.[5]

Removing the Spanish antagonist from St. Augustine was a godsend for Carolina and Georgia slaveowners. Meanwhile, in compensation for the loss of Florida, the French Louis XV gave Louisiana (in secret, at first) to the Spanish Carlos III. Spain was occupied with reasserting Spanish authority in Cuba, where planters had tasted British commerce and weren't going back, so no Spanish governor was sent to Louisiana until 1768, during which time the French and Creole elite of New Orleans further developed its already pronounced independent streak.

Spain had no choice but to take Louisiana when the French king handed it over. Though Louisiana produced little of value, it was an essential buffer zone for protecting Spain's Mexican silver mines from the English. So, for approximately the last third of the eighteenth century, the governor of Louisiana reported to the captain general in Havana, with enormous cultural consequences for the town of New Orleans, which under the Spanish took on the structure of a city and started to be a port of importance.

The London economy suffered a panic in 1772, which, coupled with a quickly withdrawn incentive plan to encourage poor Protestant immigrants, brought in thousands of desperate Scots, Irish, and especially Scotch-Irish to South Carolina. In the four days between December 19 and 22, 1772, four ships from Northern Ireland disgorged more than a thousand people into Charles Town.[6] These were poor and uneducated Ulsterpeople, nominally Presbyterians but in fact barely churched. Henry Laurens, who dealt in indentured servants as well as slaves, wrote of a group of them:

> I have been largely concerned in the African trade . . . yet I never saw an instance of Cruelty in ten or twelve Years experience in that branch equal to the Cruelty exercised upon those poor Irish . . . Self Interest prompted the Baptized Heathen in the first case to take care of the wretched Slaves for a Market, but no other care was taken of those poor Protestant Christians from Ireland but to deliver as many as possible alive on Shoar upon

the cheapest terms, no matter how they fared upon their Voyage or in what condition they were landed.[7]

The coastal land was taken, so most of the new arrivals went upcountry.

The little more than a decade between the end of the Seven Years' War and the Declaration of Independence was a time of great political transformation and opportunity for enterprise. With peace and stability, the Lowcountry plantation economy boomed. The growth of rice cultivation expanded enormously owing to the adoption of a new method of irrigation that used sluices to bring in sea water mixed with fresh to make aquaculture possible in the Tidewater, instead of merely in the inland swamps.

South Carolina was the opposite of the decentralized Chesapeake: it was highly centralized in Charles Town, an empire whose commercial relations extended for hundreds of miles. The only place in South Carolina that could be described as a city, it traded via small oceangoing vessels with coastal North Carolina, Georgia, and Florida, and by land, selling the native confederations and the new arrivals upcountry guns to kill each other with, as well as having its own prosperous residents to import goods for. Leila Sellers described it as "a sort of city-state, drawing to itself all the wealth of the surrounding country, which gave it a prestige the memory of which has never faded."[8]

The easy upward social mobility the slave society offered white men was described by Alexander Hewatt in 1779, in the course of explaining why he thought (correctly) that industry would not develop in South Carolina:

> Nor is there the smallest reason to expect that manufactures will be encouraged in Carolina, while landed property can be obtained on such easy terms. The cooper, the carpenter, the brick-layer, the shipbuilder, and every other artificer and tradesman, after having laboured for a few years at their respective employments, and purchased a few negroes, commonly retreat to the country, and settle tracts of uncultivated land. . . . Though the wages allowed them are high, yet the means of subsistence in towns are also dear, and therefore they long to be in the same situation with their neighbours, who derive an easy subsistence from a plantation, which they cultivate at pleasure, and are answerable to no master for their conduct.

Even the merchant becomes weary of attending the store, and risking his stock on the stormy seas, or in the hands of men where it is often exposed to equal hazards, and therefore collects it as soon as possible, and settles a plantation. Upon this plantation he sets himself down, and being both landlord and farmer, immediately finds himself an independent man. Having his capital in lands and negroes around him, and his affairs collected within a narrow circle, he can manage and improve them as he thinks fit.

He soon obtains plenty of the necessaries of life from his plantation; nor need he want any of its conveniences and luxuries. The greatest difficulties he has to surmount arise from the marshy soil, and unhealthy climate, which often cut men off in the midst of their days. Indeed in this respect Carolina is the reverse of most countries in Europe, where the rural life, when compared with that of the town, is commonly healthy and delightful.[9]

Hewatt wrote that Charles Town "may be ranked with the first cities of British America." He estimated its 1765 population to be between five and six thousand white inhabitants and between seven and eight thousand "negroes," while his estimate for South Carolina as a whole was forty thousand whites and eighty to ninety thousand blacks.[10] When the Declaration of Independence was signed, Charles Town was the fourth largest city in the colonies, far behind Philadelphia and New York in population and somewhat behind Boston. It was a town of young people, as Hewatt noted: "There are few old men or women to be found in the province, which is a sure sign of the unhealthiness of the climate. We cannot say that there are many in the country that arrive at their sixtieth year."[11]

In Charles Town, slaves were crucial to a merchant's offerings, since they drew customers who might then purchase their dry goods from him. "Before the Revolution," writes Elizabeth Donnan, "at least one hundred [Charles Town] firms had offered [slave] cargoes for sale, some advertising but one, others one a year for a number of years, while Brailsford and Chapman, in the year 1765, handled nine cargoes, two of which numbered four hundred slaves each."[12] That was exceptional: a big cargo was a lot to handle, and even a large merchant would normally not handle more than two or three in a year. But there were a lot of merchants.

Henry Laurens was the number-one dealer in Africans. During 1760, his firm Austin, Laurens, and Appleby advertised 1,010 slaves for sale; for purposes of comparison, 3,573 slaves were sold in all of Charles Town for the year beginning November 1, 1759.[13] In surveying accounts of duties paid, Daniel J. McDonough identifies Laurens as involved in the importation of some 6,900 people.[14] That was synonymous with being well capitalized; Charles Town's slave distribution network reached North Carolina, upcountry South Carolina, Georgia, Florida, and beyond, but only very wealthy merchants could lay out the sums necessary for such operations.[15] Since the trade was highly seasonal (April to November, primarily because the cold months killed too many of the captives), capital drain was concentrated in time. On the sale end, the trader had to extend credit and collect, a process that sometimes took years; Laurens estimated that he often had more than £10,000 sterling out. Advising a pair of young brothers who were hoping to get started as slave traders, Laurens wrote, "We experimentally know that a large Capital is requisite to negotiate a Trade in this Country for 7 or 800 Negroes a Year in the way we take them."[16] He took his profits in slaves; by 1776 he owned 797 of them, and plantations for them to work on.[17]

But smaller, less-capitalized merchants could also participate in this chain of value creation. The 1,108 slave cargoes known to have been brought to colonial Charles Town (almost no place else in South Carolina received Africans) were received by 405 different merchants and factors.[18] There was no business easier to make a profit in. Slaves were sold everywhere commerce was conducted in Charles Town, from Gadsden's Wharf, large merchants' warehouses, auction houses, plantation grounds, and the "Negro yard," to small dry goods stores and on many public occasions that included, in Leila Sellers's description, "at the race course between the heats of the races."[19] Slaves were still coming in from Barbados and Antigua, and occasionally Jamaica, in one- and two-digit quantities, but most of the vessels by now were from Africa, perhaps making a stop in the West Indies first, and bringing hundreds at a time.

The traders had a paper money supply that facilitated their commerce. There was little specie in South Carolina for cash purchases, but bills of exchange from reputable London merchants were circulating in some numbers, though the supply was subject to sharp fluctuation. Carolina's paper money, first issued in 1703 when North and South Carolina were still one polity, "established a security and stability rare in the colonies," writes John J. McCusker; the seven-to-one rate of exchange between South Carolina currency and London pounds sterling remained in effect from the 1730s until shortly before South Carolina's declaration of independence from the British Empire.[20]

Henry Laurens's letter to a London trading firm on August 25, 1763 noted a spectacular ninefold markup realized in a slave sale that mixed people from two disparate regions of Africa: "Negroes have yielded great prices hitherto & will continue do so thro the Year unless the Importations should be excessive. A Cargo of Angola's lately averaged £32 Sterling round & 50 prime Gold Coast Negroes bought in Antigua at £34 per head sold in one lot at £300 round."[21]

Though we have no specific details of the settlement of that sale, it's close to impossible that a horse-cart loaded with tons of silver trudged through the streets of Charles Town. Sales were accomplished with transferable credit of one type or another, and could not have been effected at all unless London merchants were willing to extend credit to the purchasers. In effect, the profit reported by Laurens that day was money that had not previously existed, but had been written into being at the moment of sale, in the form of bills of exchange. These sales actively turned people into money. Laurens's firm may have been Charles Town's biggest factorage, but the factors' profits were small compared to those realized by the British merchant houses they were affiliated with. Laurens was proud of his association with his "worthy Friend" Richard Oswald, whose firm of Grant, Oswald, and Co. shipped 12,742 Africans across the Atlantic that are documented, and an unknown number of others, between 1748 and 1770.[22]

Arriving in Charles Town to sell a quantity of flour in 1765, the Connecticut merchant Pelatiah Webster found a town of "about 1000 houses, with inhabitants, 5000 whites and 20000 blacks"—a considerable exaggeration in the latter case, but one based on appearances. Webster wrote an enthusiastic account of his "sauntering about town as much as the great heats will permit" and dining as the guest at the magnificent tables of a succession of Charles Town merchants, all of whom sold slaves as a significant part of their business. In the course of making the social business circuit, he "passed some hours . . . with some Guinea captains, who are a rough set of people, but somewhat caressed by the merchants on account of the great profits of their commissions."

The slave ship captains may have been coarse, but according to Webster, the merchants who sold human beings by the boatload were anything but. Thomas Smith, of Brewton and Smith, was "a reputable merchant in this town & in very fine business: is an agreeable sensible kind man." His brother, Benjamin, one of the wealthiest men in South Carolina, had made a great fortune in the slave trade;

by then retired from active trading, he was "a Gent about 50" who was "cheerful, easy & generous." Thomas Shirley, of Shirley and Martin, was "a very polite English Gent. residing here in very genteel fashion: is an ingenious ready man: was bread a merchant, has traveled much, understands several modern languages." Thomas Liston was "a man of great openness and politeness, of generous sentiments and very genteel behavior"; Webster traveled with him to Sullivan's Island, the entry point for slave cargoes, where there "were 2 or 300 negro's performing quarantine with the small pox" in the local pest house. After hearing some "very fine airs on the harpsichord by Mr. _____, an English organist," he found Charles Town an "agreeable and polite place," noting that "the laborious business is here chiefly done by black slaves of which there are great multitudes."[23]

Georgia received its first cargo direct from Africa in 1766, when a Liverpool captain brought in a vessel coming from Senegal with seventy-eight kidnapped people in the hold.[24] The following year, Savannah built a pest house to quarantine new arrivals, like the one at Sullivan's Island for Charles Town, where incoming slaves were expected to remain for a minimum of ten days. But in the absence of capital to handle a sizable African cargo, a larger percentage of Georgia's imports came in smaller shipments from the Antilles—especially Jamaica, but also Antigua, Barbados, St. Christopher, St. Kitts, Grenada, Curaçao, and others.[25] Even today, you can hear in the Gullah and Geechee way of talking a marked resemblance to black speech of the British West Indies.

South Carolina was already at least occasionally exporting enslaved African Americans to neighboring regions by sea, as when Laurens shipped a "parcel" of "country Negroes" to British-controlled St. Augustine in 1768.[26]

With Jamaica and Saint-Domingue both taking large numbers of Africans, the African slave trade was reaching its hemispheric peak. Liverpool, London, Bristol, and Lancashire captains competed to open up new sources of supply in Africa.

Both forced African immigration and voluntary European immigration to the colonies reached new levels after the Seven Years' War, increasing the colonial population by 10 percent or so. There were newcomers in every town. Many were getting ready to push west, out where one could own land, albeit at the price of defending one's claim from the Indians. The moving frontier of westward expansion, still in its early stages, kept the market for slaves strong.

18

Ballast

She [Phillis Wheatley] does not seem to have preserved any remembrance of the place of her nativity [Senegal], or of her parents, excepting the simple circumstance that her mother poured out water before the sun at his rising.

—"written by a collateral descendant of Mrs. Wheatley"
for the 1834 edition of *Memoir and Poems of Phillis Wheatley,*
a Native African and a Slave

IRON WAS FUNDAMENTAL TO any kind of industrial development. England had been making iron since the Roman era, but by the beginning of the eighteenth century, British furnaces had slowed down—not for lack of iron ore, but for lack of fuel, the forests having been consumed. Britain had been importing iron from Sweden but the coronation of King George I in 1714 put an end to that because George was at war with Sweden.[1]

With commerce between Britain and Sweden frozen, Britain was eager to get iron from its colonies. Maryland made it governmental policy to encourage iron furnaces as of 1719, and the Chesapeake became a leader in colonial iron production. These ironworks produced only bars, or "pigs," because as codified in the Iron Act of 1750 the colonists were not to have rolling, plating, or slitting mills, much less to make steel of their own. The colonials were to be consumers, not manufacturers, so they weren't allowed even to work iron into the rods used in the manufacture of nails, because supplying nails to plantations was a British business. Americans were expected to buy their iron back in the form of finished nails from the West Midlands naileries, with the cost of two ocean voyages factored into the price.

By the early 1720s, the Principio Company was already up and running in Maryland from a base in Cecil County and with holdings throughout Maryland. Owned by English investors, it employed English ironmasters as well as enslaved workers.[2] Using slaves in an industrial setting was something of an experiment, but black men producing iron was not: iron was a longtime African specialty.[3]

A list of Principio's laborers enumerates twenty-six paid laborers, ten wage-less indentured laborers who had last names, and thirteen enslaved laborers who did not have last names: Ben, Cuzo, Quash, Quamini, Tantaro, Tom, Prince, Joe, James, and Pohick.[4] The enslaved laborers seem to have started at the bottom of the Principio labor chain, as woodcutters feeding the endlessly hungry furnaces, but by 1750 several of them were listed as skilled laborers and they received incentive pay of a shilling per ton of iron blooms produced.[5] Prince was still working at Principio in 1781 at the age of sixty-five, and was classed as a skilled forgeman, along with fifty-five-year-old Harry, sixty-five-year-old Dancer, and thirty-seven-year-old Ellick and Will.[6]

Even the highest-ranking white wage laborers at Principio did not necessarily receive their pay on time. Much of their salary was taken in the form of credit at that notorious institution, the company store, "which seems to have been the first part of the enterprise . . . to go into operation," writes Michael W. Robbins in his history of the company.[7] Needless to say, the black laborers were treated worse than white employees. A 1781 inventory of the facilities of one iron company, the Kingsbury Furnace, includes both a kitchen and a "Negro kitchen," suggesting that the enslaved ate separately, and, to be sure, more poorly.[8] Caloric requirements for the hard labor were high, and though they ate a monotonous diet based on corn, they had to have enough to keep moving. On their feet they wore what were listed in budget lines as "negro shoes," bought in large quantities. They lived crowded into shanties and crude cabins where privacy was unknown. They were corporately owned, in what could amount to as many as 150 enslaved laborers on an iron plantation. Large numbers of support personnel were needed to sustain the ironworkers; a few of the enslaved in the ironworks were women, who cooked and sewed—and occasionally were ironworkers as well.

Charles Carroll the Settler arrived from Ireland to Lord Baltimore's colony in 1688. Determined to become wealthy in spite of the discrimination against

Catholics in the wake of the Protestant coup of the Glorious Revolution, he became the largest landowner and the largest lender in Maryland. He began a family line that included a number of people named Charles Carroll, who then needed another name to differentiate them, so that Charles Carroll the Settler's son was Charles Carroll of Annapolis, whose only child and heir was Charles Carroll of Carrollton.

Charles Carroll of Annapolis also had a distant relative in the area, known as Dr. Charles Carroll, who was the father of Charles Carroll the Barrister. But unlike the previously named Charles Carrolls, Dr. Charles Carroll's branch of the family was not Catholic but Anglican, so in Annapolis they spoke of the Catholic Carrolls and the Anglican Carrolls.

Hoping to diversify their holdings, Dr. Carroll and four partners—including Charles Carroll of Annapolis—were eagerly looking for alternatives to tobacco as a way to put their capital to work. They started the Baltimore Iron Works (or the Baltimore Company), in 1731 on a choice plot of about thirteen hundred acres north of the Patapsco River that Dr. Carroll had purchased. The second ironworks in Maryland, it was well situated: the little village of Baltimore was next to a thick vein of iron ore and had a deep-water harbor.

Before committing to founding the company, Dr. Carroll even drew up a business plan of sorts, which concluded that profitability could be reached in a mere two years. In his operating budget, the largest single expense was the purchase of laborers, who were capital acquisitions and were resalable. This earliest of Baltimore industries used a combination of free, indentured, and slave labor, beginning the diverse mix of workers that would later characterize the city. By 1734, the Baltimore Iron Works had forty-three enslaved black laborers, eight of them cooks.

Thirty years later, when Charles Carroll of Annapolis was the richest man in Maryland, he listed his holdings for his son and heir's benefit. Valuing at £10,000 his one-fifth interest in the company 's holdings of thirty thousand acres and "150 slaves young and old," he listed as part of his estimated £88,380.97 personal wealth "20 Lots in Annapolis with the houses thereon," valued at £4,000, and "285 Slaves on my different Plantations at £30 Ster," valued at £8,550.

Twenty built-up lots in Annapolis was a substantial holding, but 285 human beings were worth more than twice as much. That letter's addressee, Charles Carroll of Carrollton, became the only Catholic signer of the Declaration of Independence, as well as the wealthiest. Charles Carroll of Carrollton was already price-conscious at the age of twenty-nine when he wrote his father's partner Walter Dulany on August 29, 1767, that "I am informed that negroes sell cheap in Virginia: as they are much wanted at the works would it not be pro[per] to direct Clt. Brooke to attend the Sales? Next Octbr. I am told will be the best time to purchase when it is probable the gentleman says from whom I had my information, young likely country born negroes may be bought at £25 or 30 Sterling."[9]

Dulany wrote back: "I shou'd be for purchasing Negroes in Virginia, since they are to be had so cheap there as Mr. carroll mentions—I know of but one Reason against doing it of this Side of Winter, which is that we shall probably have them all to cloath with Goods bought here, for it is very uncertain whether our Goods will come in in time from England; however I am willing to run the Risque."[10]

Apparently the purchasing did not go forward as Charles Carroll of Carrollton wished. He wrote a circular letter to the other four partners in 1773 complaining that, "In 1769 I procured from our Clerks a list of hirelings wages at the furnace, and at the three forges, which I have often mentioned in my Letters to the Company, to induce them to purchase Slaves to save that enormous expence, but hitherto without success." He then computed in detail the costs of purchasing slaves, concluding that an

> annual saving of 901.5.0 would not be the only Advantage the Company would reap from the purchase of 40 Slaves: the business would be carried on with more Alacrity, and fewer disappointments; we should encrease our Stock of negroes, and be greatly benefited by that encrease, in case the company should hereafter come to the resolution of selling their Lands, or leasing them, selling their Stock, and breaking up the Iron works.[11]

It was good business to own slaves instead of rent them, and the richer one became, the easier it was to do. By purchasing slaves, not only did the partners save on labor costs in day-to-day operations, they acquired human capital that could then be sold or rented out. A few years later, on December 3, 1773, the seventy-one-year-old Charles Carroll of Annapolis wrote a good-news letter to his only son and heir, Charles Carroll of Carrollton:

> I have taken a very Exact Acct of all the Negroes Here, I was Closely employed 5 Mornings from Breakfast to Dinner & two long Evenings in Comparing the last with my present List, they Amou[nt] to 330 including the 3 Jobbers with You. My Love & Blessing to You . . .

Negroes as pr List taken Decr:1st: 1773	330
Do: as pr List taken Decr:1st: 1767	<u>273</u>
Increase in 6 years	57

Carroll's return on investment in "Negroes" was almost 21 percent in six years.[12] Those extra fifty-seven people also increased Carroll's liquidity, since slaves could be disposed of more readily than any other holdings.

As the South developed what little industry it would have, slave labor was omnipresent, positing a model of industrial slavery in which either the workers and their children were corporate assets, or the workers were hired from local owners via employment agents specializing in slave labor. But slave labor was problematic in an industrial setting. Gang labor in the field was a blunt instrument, and agricultural slaves were notoriously recalcitrant. That spirit couldn't be set loose on expensive factory machinery. Enslaved factory laborers had to be paid incentives to work properly, but paying wages to slaves was seen by slaveowners as a hazardous practice. Indeed, many slaveowners believed that paying wages to *anyone* set a dangerous precedent.

The legacy of the old days is visible all over the Eastern Shore of Maryland. In Crumpton, the effects of a fine old house were auctioned one day in January 2011. Among the items the auctioneer turned over was a two-piece ring of iron, just big enough to fit around someone's neck. It was a slave collar, found in the basement of the house. When it was knocked down for ninety dollars, the ghost of slavery threw off yet another commission for an auctioneer.

Chestertown's population was 5,252 in the 2010 census, not much more than in the late eighteenth century. Like many English colonial towns, Chestertown has, besides a Queen Street, a High Street, and, adjacent to the harbor, a Water Street (also known as Front Street), where the building known as the Custom House dates to 1746 or so. Located as it is on the waterfront of the Chester River on the Eastern Shore of Maryland, the Custom House was at one time the home of a wealthy merchant who traded in slaves and convicts: Thomas Ringgold IV.*

---

*Disclosure: today the Custom House is the home of Washington College's C.V. Starr Center for the Study of the American Experience, where the first half of this volume was drafted.

In America as in England, much of the business of African slavery belonged to Roman-numeraled generations of wealth. With a surname that spoke directly to money, Thomas Ringgold I was one of many Anglicans who left England during the Puritan regime (1647–1660). Only sixteen years after the *Ark* and the *Dove* brought the first Maryland colonists, he arrived in Maryland with his two sons in 1650. He acquired an Eastern Shore estate in 1657 by marrying a widow, a common means of enrichment for men in a land of high mortality and few rights for women.

By great-great-grandson Thomas Ringgold IV's time in the mid-eighteenth century, Chestertown was the most important port on Maryland's Eastern Shore, second only to Annapolis in all of Maryland, and the Ringgolds were its leading family. Together with his son, Thomas Ringgold V, and his brother, William Ringgold, the energetic Thomas Ringgold IV imported a variety of goods besides British manufactures: the strong, sweet, fortified wine the colonists drank (from Portugal, England's oldest trading partner); West Indian molasses; and indentured servants, convict labor, and African slaves. It was his good fortune to be at his peak during the boom years for colonial merchants after the French and Indian War, when explosive, immigrant-driven population growth made for an active commercial world throughout the bustling colonies. As merchants profited from supplying the new arrivals, the newly wealthy were furnishing exquisite new mansions. Ringgold IV bought the almost-new Custom House from its tavern-keeper builder in 1749, and it became both his residence and his place of business.[13] He appears to have been the wealthiest man in Kent County, though he had competition from his next-lot neighbor Thomas Smyth, whose magnificent Georgian mansion Widehall, built in 1769, still stands on the former Water Lot #16, across High Street from the Custom House.

Eighteenth-century businessmen were necessarily diversified, and Ringgold IV was an attorney, planter, import/export merchant, and retailer. He shipped out tobacco and iron—the two went together, with the iron serving as ballast—and by the 1760s, with the Chesapeake already making a transition out of tobacco, he was loading wheat onto an increasing number of ships.

Fueled by the growth in mercantile revenues, building after solid building went up in Annapolis, the small, wealthy colonial capital that had been designed in the European style. Its peculiar baroque pattern of streets radiating outward from two circular plazas (called Church and State, they were joined by a road to symbolize the Anglican union of the two) was unlike the square grid pattern already in effect in Philadelphia and in Burlington, New Jersey. With overhead cabling and signage having been removed in the mid-twentieth century to enhance the time-capsule effect, Annapolis is today a living reminder of the Enlightenment's rational organization of space: a logical order imposed on a small, urban area.

At the peak of Annapolis's influence, about a third of its population was enslaved, mostly in domestic service. With a population of only a thousand or so, Annapolis was the most stylish town of its size in the North American colonies, the social leader of the Chesapeake. A theater opened in 1771, where Annapolitans saw what had decades before been the most popular works of the London stage: Joseph Addison's *Cato*, John Gay's *The Beggar's Opera*, and Isaac Bickerstaffe's afterpiece *The Padlock*, with its comic, Spanish-derived, black-faced character Mungo, the precursor of black minstrelsy. Annapolis even had a colonial version of "macaronis," the young, effeminate, Italianate dandies with comically big hair who burst on the London scene in 1772, as lampooned in "Yankee Doodle."

A MACARONI IN 1772.   A MACARONI IN 1773.

Fast-changing Macaroni fashions in London, from Thomas Wright, Caricature History of the Georges, *1904.*

Many of the wealthy men who founded the American nation passed through Annapolis and Chestertown, which were cheerful stops on the dreary overland route between Virginia and Philadelphia. The only road that ran south from Philadelphia divided in Delaware, one branch going to the Eastern Shore and the other to the western. The Eastern Shore branch, the quicker of the two, ran through Chestertown, from where it continued on to connect to the ferry that as of 1762 ran between the Eastern Shore's Rock Hall (later a small town, but then a terminal) across the Chesapeake to Annapolis.

Publishing magnate Benjamin Franklin, traveling home to Pennsylvania from Virginia on official business after having been appointed deputy postmaster general of the colonies, attended a January 1754 meeting of Annapolis's celebrated Tuesday Club. This was a social club in the London style where participants took on funny names (Franklin, internationally famous as a scientist, was dubbed "Electro-Vitrifrice," or electric glass-stroker), made ribald jokes ("longstanding members," that sort of thing), and sang drinking songs. In Chestertown, Franklin, whose postmaster position paid little but was of great benefit to his newspaper business, handed over his Eastern Shore accounts receivable for the *Pennsylvania Gazette* to Ringgold IV for collection.[14]

Across the bay from Chestertown, Ringgold IV's partner Samuel Galloway III (1720–1785), was one of the most important merchants of Annapolis. Galloway was a Quaker and thus a second-class citizen; there were even whispers among Anglicans that the Quaker ranks concealed Catholics in disguise. Spanning both sides ("shores") of the Chesapeake, the Galloway-Ringgold partnership was a commercial force linking Annapolis and Chestertown, locked down with strategic weddings: Thomas Ringgold V (1744–1776) married Galloway's daughter Mary, while Galloway's other daughter, Anne, in turn married into another merchant family, the Chestons.

When the Mount Vernon planter George Washington ordered from a merchant "a Pipe [about 126 gallons] of your best Lisbon Wine," the price to be drawn against an account in London, he asked that it "receive a Freight in any of Mr Galloway's, or Mr Ringold's vessels."[15] That Washington should be on friendly terms with Galloway and Ringgold was hardly surprising: the wealthy of Virginia and Maryland formed a tight society, with interlocking kinship by marriage at the heart of the business network. By marrying the widow Martha Custis, Washington had become a large slaveowner and a rich man—rich enough, in the long run, that he could wear his own custom-designed uniform when he served eight years at the head of the Continental Army without pay, and rich enough that he could be a racing enthusiast.

Thoroughbred racing, an amusement for the truly wealthy, had become popular in England after the Restoration of Charles II in 1660. It came to Virginia quickly, where it became a central social activity of the ruling class, and arrived in Annapolis in 1745. Washington's wealth wasn't sufficient to put him in the league of racehorse owners, but he traveled hundreds of miles to hobnob at Annapolis, noting in his ledger on October 10, 1772, "Cash lost on the Races 1.6 pounds."[16] On occasion he enjoyed the hospitality of Tulip Hill, Galloway's country estate, which still exists.

Galloway was the owner of Selim, "the most famous native colonial Chesapeake racer," whose heyday was at the height of the town-house era, between 1766 and 1772.[17] Wealthy slaveowners were investing in the expensive hobby of horse breeding that attends a racing culture: twenty-seven stud farms have been identified in colonial Virginia.[18] Selim had cost Galloway £178 on three years' credit, a heavy outlay at a time when an enslaved male laborer might be had for £35. Even so, Selim was profitable. Besides winning races, he earned stud fees by covering the mares of Maryland's wealthiest. As did those sired from him: in 1793, it was advertised in Chestertown that one of Selim's grandsons—named Liberty, of course—"will cover at SIX DOLLARS each mare, the season," noting that "Country produce, at market price, will be received" to pay for the stud service.[19] Galloway kept a detailed Stud Book, now in the possession of the Maryland State Archives.[20]

Galloway was diversified. He planted tobacco and wheat, invested in ironworks, and owned a stand of oak trees that "was the envy of all ship builders along the eastern seaboard," writes J. Reaney Kelly. In 1757, during the French and Indian War, he built and outfitted an eighteen-gun privateer and advertised for a crew.[21] He tried and failed at launching a distillery, which was an essential asset for going into the African slave trade from North America.

Colonial documents contain pages-long lists of the fine things and basic necessities merchants imported: horses, cheese, candles, glass, paper, carpets, overcoats, hats, shoes, and on and on, in many varieties. Merchants also imported money, in many different forms, functioning in essence as mini-banks. They had to be agile mental calculators, since the currency they handled—in a non-decimal-denominated system of twenty shillings to a pound and twelve pence to a shilling—was issued by myriad sources, each with its own exchange rate or discount reflecting varying degrees of confidence in the solidity of the issuer. Frequently, debts were collected in merchandise, which meant keeping track of commodity price trends. The merchandise then had to be resold or traded for something else; that could be done at the Ringgolds' store on the ground floor of the Front Street building.

Ringgold IV traded in real estate as well, of course, but the way to make real estate valuable was to apply labor to it. No merchandise was more urgent, or potentially more lucrative, than laborers.

In front of a house on Queen Street in twenty-first-century Chestertown, the trees are set off from the sidewalk by a perimeter of "rounded, water-worn stones," that, as Peregrine Wroth described them in 1871,

> are not natives of our alluvial district, being entirely different from any that I have ever seen in Kent [County]. . . Traditionally we are informed that they were brought to this country in ships from England which traded for Tobacco, as ballast; in the early times of the colony, tobacco being our staple crop for exportation. The stones being thrown out to take in the cargo, were afterwards used to pave the approach to the wharves.[22]

"If I can procure him iron," wrote Ringgold of an arriving sea captain, "I shall get his ballast wch I want to compleat my wharf."[23] Pigs of iron made for a profitable cargo going back to London. The commerce in question was not the notorious clockwise, or "triangular," trade, but a less efficient, colonially disadvantageous, back-and-forth monopoly circuit between North America and England. Ballast was necessary in both directions, but more of it was needed on the long westbound trip to America, because there was less cargo in the hold on the outbound voyage. Tobacco, the Chesapeake colonies' principal export, was a bulky commodity; the goods a ship would bring from London in exchange took up much less room. Freight was expensive, and shipping stones from England to Maryland was unprofitable. But the slack in a lopsided balance of trade is taken up by cheap labor, and an unprofitable cargo of ballast stones could share the hull with a profitable cargo of unfortunate people.*

That's where Ringgold and Galloway came in. They imported British convicts—a product line with a dependable supply, as there were always plenty of

---

*Ballast was needed with human cargoes, because people move around.

prisoners on hand in Britain, already processed into the penal system. A steady flow of convicts in irons was a colonial merchant's dream, and was a specialty of the English port of Bristol. Ringgold was a factor, or agent, for the Bristol firm of Sedgely, Hilhouse, and Randolph, whose deported convicts received pardons for their crimes in exchange for indentures to labor in America.[24] Some were felons, pirates, rogues, or dissenters, but others were merely indebted; and to judge from a number of advertisements in the *Maryland Gazette* for the return of various runaways described as a "Convict Servant Lad," a number of them were boys between sixteen and nineteen years of age. Convicts and paupers were in any case bundled together in the servant business, mixing the truly dangerous with the merely malnourished. While the number of convicts who were brought to America is difficult to state with any precision, the high-quality records of Annapolis indicate that by 1776, that port had handled 8,846 convicts, making the merchants who sold them rich.[25]

The difference between indentured and enslaved labor was often negligible in terms of the actual work performed by the laborer. From the beginning of indentured servitude in America, tales circulated in England about how the indentured were made to work alongside the enslaved. It was common to refer to the "purchase" of indentured laborers, as per the 1774 letter from Charles Carroll of Carrollton authorizing a Baltimore Iron Works representative "to Purchase 5 Negroes & 5 white Servants" for industrial labor.[26] But there was a significant difference between the two: the convict laborer was not bound for life, but the black slave was. Nor was the indentured servant's potential for "natural increase" part of the deal, as it was with the enslaved.

In the television miniseries *Roots*, as in Alex Haley's novel on which it was based, the fictional protagonist Kunta Kinte was brought from the Gambia and sold at Annapolis in 1767. That was when Samuel Galloway was conducting slave sales at Middleton's Tavern, like the one he advertised in 1761, presumably of captives brought up from the West Indies, since they were "seasoned":

TO BE SOLD

At the House of Mr. Samuel Middleton, in Anna-
polis, *on Saturday next, being the 22d Instant,*
A CHOICE PARCEL of Healthy Seasoned
NEGRO MEN.
. . . S GALLOWAY, and Company.

A "parcel" might be two to four dozen people, less than a "cargo," which could be hundreds. Ringgold and Galloway sold at least one cargo in 1761, but it was not a good sale.

July 29, 1761.

JUST IMPORTED

In the Snow Alexander, *Captain* Neilson, *from the*
Coast of AFRICA,

A CARGO of Choice Healthy SLAVES, and to be Sold on Tuesday next, being the 4th of *August*, at *Annapolis*, for Bills of Exchange or Cash, by   THOMAS AND WM. RINGGOLD,

SAMUEL GALLOWAY

The promise of "Choice Healthy SLAVES" was a barefaced lie. They were the wretched captives who arrived on the *Alexander*, a vessel that had been outfitted to carry 320 humans as if they were sardines.[27] The *Alexander* had met with "misfortune," Ringgold and Galloway wrote the ship's owners in Bristol afterward, resulting "in the Loss of so great a part of her Slaves. We had but 105 left alive to sell, 11 of them so bad we were glad to get £11 Ster. P Head for them, 6 of the 11 since dead and many of the others in very bad Condition."[28] It is unknown whether the "misfortune" was smallpox, typhoid, measles, or any of a number of other diseases that could carry away shiploads of people.

It took a while to work through the undesirable inventory, but slaves rarely went unsold. Ringgold wrote Galloway on August 15 of the liquidation: "We sold 14 of the Negroes yesterday very well considering the Cond'n they were in. The wenches and 1 man at 60 each, 1 man £68, 1 Boy £60, Girls at £56, 2 sickly Girls cheap, the Maits [mate's] Boy for £70, the small poor Boy died coming up. We have only The 2d Maits Fellow and 2 Girls hope they go today."

This was business correspondence—formal and decorous, in the manner of colonial merchants, and devoid of remorse for over two hundred deaths, let alone the partners' responsibility in them. Then Ringgold delivered what he saw as the really bad news: "But the worst of it twas chiefly on some Credit."[29]

No Chesapeake merchants were exclusively slave traders in those days, but the converse of that was that many merchants might handle some slave trade, and every merchant was aware that the slave trade was murderous. But then, life was precarious in the colonies, where children routinely died, childbirth was every woman's hazard, and the wealthiest citizen might take sick and be gone within hours. The crews on occasion had higher mortality rates than the people who made up the cargo; slave ships were death ships, the bottom of the employment ladder for sailors. Stephen D. Behrendt, analyzing the mortality of 58,778 crewmen on 1,709 slave voyages out of Liverpool from 1780 forward, found 10,439 deaths, or 17.8 percent, about half of them killed by the captives.[30] The "seasoning" process for newly arrived Africans was often more deadly than the crossing. Some emaciated arrivals expired dockside. Others died unattended in the pest house, where the healthy were locked up together with the dying in quarantine. Still others took mortally ill within months after sale.

Slave buyers and merchants had a definite hierarchy of desirable African ethnicities. Gambians were at the top of the list, both in the Chesapeake and in South Carolina. One reason was that the voyage from that northernmost part of the West African slaving territory was significantly shorter than from farther south, and there was less time for the captives to sicken and die. As Ringgold IV put it in a letter: "Gambia the best and generally comes in best helth as the Passage is quick from thence to this place," though the passage surely seemed to last an eternity for those chained in the hold.[31]

The cultivation of tobacco was well suited to Senegambians' existing agricultural skills.[32] Conveniently, they were at the time easy to get, an availability that peaked in the first three decades of the eighteenth century, as intra-African conflicts in that region threw war captives onto the market. The Bambara, the Wolof, the Mandinka, the Fulani: they brought with them not only agricultural skills, but all kinds of cultural skills, including music. They brought the banjo and a bowed fiddle (the latter a specialty of the nomadic Fulani), which they used to play a highly ornamented dance music. They brought a sense of swing, in which pairs of notes were not of equal length, but were long/short. They brought a bardic poetic tradition that informed their way of singing, and, not least, they brought a centuries-old history of contact with Islam. The musical styles of the Muslim world affected their way of playing music greatly, and aspects of it— melisma, pitch-bending, and heterophony (a loose sense of unison)—would surface in a new African American music.[33] Senegambians were early populators of all three major African American cultural areas: the Chesapeake, the

Lowcountry, and Louisiana. But there were people from all seven of the major slaving regions of West and Central Africa (and perhaps a few from the eighth, Southeast Africa) in Chesapeake society.

Even the biggest tobacco planters didn't purchase labor in the quantities Antillean sugar planters did. Most slaves in the Chesapeake were bought in small numbers, many in ones and twos; even large plantation workforces were assembled piecemeal out of hetergeneous sources.[34] Annapolis was a breakup point, where cargoes were separated into smaller "parcels" for local distribution.

Once the captives had been sold, they were plantation bound, so their next journey was to be shipped along the watercourse of the Chesapeake river system and possibly marched over land. In their traumatized condition, often half-dead from their ordeal, they were traded and re-traded around the waterways, along with other merchandise, traversing a web of traders and planters. They were all connected by water along the decentralized Chesapeake system's thousands of miles of fractal coastline and riverbank.

Africans had long worked as sailors in European navies. Now Africans' descendants, raised in the intricate world of Chesapeake creeks and marshes, would become its boatmen, pilots, and navigators.

By contrast with the convict trade, the African slave trade was unpredictable. It was a high-stakes venture, with a remunerative upside but facing hazards unlike those of any other business. Given the dangers of the trade, a slave ship might never return. Even on a successful run, it could be incommunicado for a year or more, collecting one or a few captives at a time on the African coast, bargaining anew for each one, on occasion waiting for slave raids or nearby battles to end so that fresh victims could be procured.

Though the upside was high, outfitting African slave-trade expeditions was a nerve-wracking business. "There are more disasters in these Voyages than any others whatever," Ringgold wrote Galloway.[35] The return on investment was at best excruciatingly slow, and, as with the other risks of slavery, it was best absorbed by large fortunes.

Colonial merchants sent their own expeditions to Africa as early as 1643, when a ship from Boston brought African captives to Barbados. But even for men of Galloway and Ringgold's wealth, it was hard to outfit an expedition to Africa from America. For one thing, the African traders who sold captives to the Guineamen wanted specific merchandise for their domestic markets in exchange, and most of it wasn't available in the colonies.

The African market was known for its "fastidiousness," both in terms of the goods it would accept and the variety of them it demanded. Willem Bosman, the Dutch West India Company's factor at Elmina, wrote in 1703 that "to trade on this Coast, about a hundred and fifty several sorts of Commodities are necessary," though he pleaded that the specific list was a trade secret.[36] African merchants' conditions had many regional variations, but generally they wanted gold and silver, guns and gunpowder, textiles, hardware, brass basins and pans, luxury goods (principally rum and tobacco), and vast quantities of copper, which was a common material for adornment and, in the form of rods or bracelets called manillas, was Africa's most common currency.[37]

Except for the rum and tobacco, none of this came from the colonies. Accordingly, rum was of central importance to the portion of the African slave trade outfitted from America. Beginning in Newport in the 1720s, Rhode Island's slaving activities grew out of its rum manufacturing; that in turn depended on molasses illegally imported from Saint-Domingue, whose syrup was cheaper than the Jamaican variety. The unusually well-documented voyage of the Providence slaver *Sally* was probably typical; it went loaded with more than seventeen thousand gallons of rum, along with tobacco and onions, to be introduced into the African market in exchange for people.[38] With its many distilleries, Rhode Island was the only North American colony to specialize in outfitting African slavers—approximately a thousand voyages, accounting for an estimated 111,000 captives over its trading life.[39]

Rhode Island ran a clockwise loop trade that carried New England rum to Africa in exchange for Africans, who were in turn taken to the West Indies (or sometimes North America) and exchanged for molasses, which was then brought to Rhode Island for distilling into rum, and so on recursively, in theory with a profit taken at every stop. In this way, Rhode Island in the eighteenth century became the largest outfitter of slaving voyages in North America, with Newport sometimes referred to as the "American Liverpool."

Conspicuously, this commercial triangle did not include England. Nor did it necessarily include much hard currency, if the African slave traders could be persuaded to accept rum and tobacco, though they usually wanted manufactured goods or money too.

South Carolina did little smuggling; its commerce largely followed British rules. But New England was a hotbed of contraband. According to Britain's routinely ignored 1733 Molasses Act, importation from the French colonies was to be prohibitively taxed. In the face of the need to raise revenue against Britain's debts from the French and Indian War, the Sugar Act of 1764 halved the molasses tax but included measures to enforce it, causing widespread alarm throughout New England, where distilling was a major business. The merchants of Providence responded by sending London a ringing defense of their right to smuggle molasses, pointing out that the rum thus produced gave them the revenues with which to pay for the British manufactures they consumed. Recalling the era, John Adams wrote in an 1818 letter, "I know not why we should blush to confess that molasses was an essential ingredient in American independence . . . these articles of molasses and sugar, especially the former, entered into all and every branch of our commerce, fisheries, even manufactures and agriculture."[40] The antislavery Adams discreetly neglected to mention the vital role molasses had played in the slave trade.

To give the devil his due, Rhode Island's slave trade was an extraordinary achievement given the obstacles to it, a feat Maryland did not replicate. The only known African slave voyage outfitted from Maryland was sent by Ringgold and Galloway in 1762, together with two other partners, though Galloway may have invested in others of which there is no record. It was a fiasco.

In an effort to stock their Africa-bound ship with commodities for trade, Ringgold traveled to Philadelphia. The decentralization of the Chesapeake had worked against the creation of urban centers in favor of widely scattered individual wharves, a situation pleasing to price-gouging English merchants. In doing so, it created a commercial vacuum for Philadelphia to exploit. Philadelphia, which had surpassed Boston as the largest city in the colonies in the 1750s, was the commercial capital, with the best-supplied marketplace. But even there, as Ringgold wrote Galloway:

> I found a great deal of Trouble and Diligence required to get anything and severel Things I did not get . . . so I was obliged to supply the Defects by Manchester Goods in Immitation as well as I coud. . . . I was put to great Difficulty ab't Gunns could not find any of the Trading Gunns but 21 in Town . . . Getting so few Gunns in Philada. I wrote to Mr. Freman to try to pick me up 100 or Less at York of the Cheap sort and send with the Rum.[41]

The Scottish slave trader Richard Oswald, by contrast, in 1754 notified the British government of his intention to ship "one hundred and twenty barrels of gunpowder, one hundred & twenty chests containing three thousand trading guns & thirty cases containing three thousand cutlasses" to Africa.[42] But even British slave traders had difficulties coming up with enough trade goods. "Assembling an export cargo normally took several months," writes Kenneth Morgan, who argues that one of the advantages Liverpool traders had over those of Bristol and London was their proximity to the Isle of Man, a duty-free zone where until 1765 Dutch shippers could transship cheap products from Asia that included cowry shells (used as money in many parts of Africa) as well as those perennial trade offerings to Africa, textiles and lethal weaponry.[43]

Coin was equally difficult for even an affluent American to obtain; merchants rarely received it. "I wrote him also as to Dollars," Ringgold's letter continued, referring to silver pesos, "not one of them to be got in Philad[elphi]a."

The partners' slave ship made it to Africa and back, but the kidnapped Gambians never reached Maryland; to their consternation, the captain stopped off in Antigua and sold them there. "If he was to go to the nearest place," fulminated Ringgold, "why did not he take Barbados? Where slaves are wanted and would have sold well."[44] Though the captain's side of the story appears to be lost to history, it might have been that much of his cargo had died and he feared losing it all if he continued any farther. At any rate, that's why Eseck Hopkins, captain of the previously mentioned *Sally*, dumped onto the Antiguan market in 1765 the 87 naked, emaciated captives who remained alive out of the 196 he had embarked from Africa with instead of bringing them father north.[45]

These were complicated deals. "Dear Sir," Ringgold wrote Galloway in 1764, "I have been looking over our Guinee Accts since I came home, and They really are almost got out of my Hand. I wish we could get them settled whilst we can understand them."[46]

Like other merchants' letters, Ringgold's correspondence is full of complaints about business, but he was making money. In 1767, he added to his portfolio the property with enclosed grounds at Water and Cannon Streets, a block upriver from the Custom House, commissioning Virginia architect William Buckland to tie together two existing structures to create a grand new mansion with a double staircase, a style that was becoming popular among the wealthy. Today it is known as the Hynson-Ringgold house, and is the presidential residence of Washington College.[47]

Charles Willson Peale's portraits of Thomas Ringgold IV, who is depicted writing, and Anna Maria Ringgold.

The Baltimore Museum of Art has portraits of the Ringgolds by American master Charles Willson Peale, but there are no portraits extant of "Sue, Fender, Milford, Betty, Sukey, Sarah, Cinthia, Darkey, and Will Harding," whom Ringgold bequeathed to his wife, Anna Maria, when he died in 1772 at the age of fifty-seven. Born into a fortune, he left a greater one to his only son.

In the tradition of the time and place, the Ringgolds were hospitable. When George Washington passed through one night in 1773, he "lodgd at Ringgolds," referring to the Hynson-Ringgold house, home of Thomas Ringgold V, who went into the family business of buying and selling, and continued the family tradition of politics. Along with his uncle William Ringgold and neighbor Thomas Smyth, Ringgold V was one of seven Kent County signers of the Maryland Declaration of Independence in Annapolis on July 26, 1775, and he was a delegate to the Annapolis Convention, which met on May 8, 1776, to draft a constitution for the state. But he died unexpectedly on October 26 of that year, at the age of thirty-two.[48] The short-lived Ringgold V left behind a will, in which he bequeathed the Chestertown mansion to his mother. He also left her his car—not a motorcar, of course, but "my imported chariot," the three-seat coach with a perch for an enslaved driver and a roost for an enslaved footman, in which she rolled up and down High Street.[49]

❖

Because Annapolis is so well documented and preserved, and because so much archaeology has been done there, we know that under the steps leading down into a basement room in Charles Carroll of Carrollton's mansion, Nanny the cook placed a spirit bundle. Known throughout a wide area of Africa in different forms, these bundles in their North American manifestation include such specific items as bent nails (Zarabanda, they call him in Cuba, the Kongo blacksmith spirit with the power secret of iron) and four-hole buttons, as well as organic ingredients that did not survive the centuries. It seems likely that more spirit materials will turn up, especially now that there is a greater awareness of their existence. They're not that easy to identify, though, because they're mostly mundane objects. It's the combination of them that gives them away as spirit materials. None have been identified from the seventeenth century in the Chesapeake; the earliest known is from Virginia in 1702, while the earliest in Maryland dates from 1790.

Christianity was a religion of the book, and slaves were not supposed to know how to read. Even as slaveowners prohibited the use of African drums on their plantations, they often preferred that the enslaved not be Christianized, and many of them never were, especially in the colonial era. But there was never a moment when the enslaved were not spiritually conscious. In the new land the Africans had been dragged to—across the ocean to the land of the dead, according to Kongo cosmology—they fashioned a set of religious practices that developed, with significant regional variations and with Native American influence, into a broadly generalized African American religion that was also a social mediator and a medicinal practice. Katrina Hazzard-Donald calls this set of practices "the old Hoodoo religion," arguing that it developed in available "safe spaces," and proposing that the mid-eighteenth century must have been a crucial time in the crystallization of this wide-reaching system.[50]

In different regional forms, this old hoodoo religion radiated outward from the three great fountainheads of African American culture—the Chesapeake, the Lowcountry, and the Gulf South. Its persistence was described by Louis Hughes in his 1897 autobiography:

> It was the custom in those days for slaves to carry voo-doo bags. It was handed down from generation to generation; and, though it was one of the superstitions of a barbarous ancestry, it was still very generally and tenaciously held to by all classes. I carried a little bag, which I got from an old slave who claimed that it had power to prevent any one who carried

it from being whipped. It was made of leather, and contained roots, nuts, pins and some other things. The claim that it would prevent the folks from whipping me so much, I found, was not sustained by my experience—my whippings came just the same. Many of the servants were thorough believers in it though, and carried these bags all the time.[51]

"Because it concerned the transformation of a variety of traditional African religions into one spiritual tradition," Hazzard-Donald writes, "Hoodoo must have involved a major confrontation of spiritual forces."[52] Mande speakers from the Islamized Sahel; Akan from the Gold Coast, Fon from the Slave Coast, Igbo from the Calabar, and many other peoples from the zone of West African traditional practice; Bakongo from Catholicized Central Africa—their cosmologies all had elements in common, and all played a part in the composite religious understanding of the enslaved.

Because Monticello has been so thoroughly scrutinized by archaeologists, we know that Thomas Jefferson's enslaved kept pits under their floors, a common practice among the enslaved of Virginia at the time.[53] What did they keep in those pits? Anything valuable. Anything they didn't want Master Tom, or the other members of their community, to see. Goods that could be considered stolen—which, since they could have no legal property of their own, might mean anything of value. Spirit materials.

The tour guide to Monticello's Mulberry Row, an entire street of slave cabins and workhouses that in Jefferson's day was hidden from the big house's view by mulberry trees, will tell you that cowrie shells—historically used as money in many parts of Africa—were "passed to later generations" by Monticello's laborers and were worn as jewelry or attached to clothing. Some of the people at Monticello wore pierced silver Spanish coins around their necks or ankles. They were not mere adornment; the formerly enslaved Silvia Witherspoon recalled in 1937, in Alabama, that (as transcribed) "sometimes I wears dis dime wid de hole in it aroun' my ankle to keep off de conjure."[54]

Portable spirit bundles were carried by nomadic and migrating Africans, in societies that counted the departed as living presences. Called by various names in different territories of Africa and the New World, a portable spirit bundle—though not containing ancestors' remains as in the motherland—was known in the southern United States as a *mojo* (*moyo*, a Kikongo word meaning something like "soul force"). Mentions of a "mojo hand" are familiar from blues lyrics, and mojo hands of one kind or another continue being made and used today.

Another version of the mojo hand was called by an English name: a *toby*. As per the first line in Charles Burnett's film *To Sleep With Anger*, about spirit combat in South Central Los Angeles: "I was looking through my trunk and I can't find my toby"—a foreshadowing that bad things are about to happen.

How did it come to be called a toby? We can't prove this, but there is some intriguing circumstantial evidence:

It was in the 1760s, the heyday of Annapolis and Chestertown, and of Galloway and Ringgold, that a modern kind of consumer item became ubiquitous: industrially produced, gaily painted, lead-glazed beer vessels from the child-labor pottery workshops of Staffordshire. Shaped in the form of a comically figured man (who was sometimes styled as a king), they were called *filpots*, but more commonly were referred to as *toby jugs*. Their popularization as household objects was preceded for several decades by what J. A. Leo Lemay characterizes as "a minor subgenre of poetry concerning drunks who were transformed into liquor containers," as per "Dear Sir, this Brown Jug that now foams with raild Ale / Was once Toby Filpot a thirsty old soul."[55] Such works as the witty Boston clergyman Mather Byles's "The Transformation of Bug-Barret into a Brandy Bottle" inspired the twenty-seven-year-old *Pennsylvania Gazette* printer Benjamin Franklin to publish his mock "Meditation on a Quart Jugg" (1733)—in which he compared the soul in the jug to an abused slave:

> Alas! what Power, or Place, is provided, where this poor Mug, this unpitied Slave, can have Redress of his Wrongs and Sufferings? Or where shall he have a Word of Praise bestow'd on him for his Well-doings, and faithful Services? . . . Poor Mug, unfortunate is thy Condition! Of thy self thou wouldst do no Harm, but much Harm is done with thee! Thou art accused of many Mischiefs; thou art said to administer Drunkenness, Poison, and broken Heads: But none praise thee for the good Things thou yieldest![56]

In the Catholic territories, iconic statues of saints abounded, and were syncretized by Africans for their own religious purposes. The *santo* that the priest called Santa Bárbara, for example, who holds a hatchet in her hand, became for the enslaved the image of Changó, the womanizing, ax-wielding warrior, apotheosis of masculinity, the greatest dancer, the owner of thunder and drums whose colors are red and white and who is called by specific rhythms that are known to millions of Cubans. This kind of syncretization is often said not to have existed in the Protestant Anglo-American territories, where saints did not exist, to say nothing of sacred statues. But the figurative power of the toby jug seems to have spoken to the African-born and to the not-yet-Christianized African Americans, who carried bound-up spirits with them.

The toby jug, it would appear, lent its name to a syncretized African practice in the eighteenth-century Chesapeake that was unseen and uncomprehended by the merchants who sold both the jugs and the people. A container that holds a soul: that needed no explanation to Africans. It fit right into the needs of the old hoodoo religion. In their captivity, the enslaved could bring nothing with them but their souls, their minds, and the bodies that contained them. While the slaveowners repurposed the ballast stones from England for wharfing, the enslaved repurposed what they found in their hostile new world, trying to protect themselves however they could—with nails, spirit bundles, cowries, coins, resistance, readiness to take flight, and rebellion.

next page: One of thirty-nine human prizes at a raffle, co-organized by twenty creditors including George Washington. Rind's Virginia Gazette, *November 23, 1769.*

110 A fine breeding Woman named *Pat*, lame of one Side, with Child, and her
three Children, *Læt*, *Milley*, and *Charlotte*.

Part Three

Silent Profit

Newspapers as Money as People

There is to be sold a very likely Negro Woman aged about Thirty Years who has lived in this City, from her Childhood, and can wash and iron very well, cook Victuals, sew, spin on the Linen Wheel, milk Cows, and do all Sorts of House-work very well. She has a Boy of about Two Years old, which is to go with her. The Price as reasonable as you can agree.

And also another very likely Boy aged about Six Years, who is Son of the above said Woman. He will be sold with his Mother, or by himself, as the Buyer pleases. Inquire of the Printer.

—Advertisement, Benjamin Franklin's *Pennsylvania Gazette*,
May 3, 1733

FROM THE BEGINNING OF newspapers in America, the forced-servitude business was a steady part of their revenue stream.

American newspapers and slavery helped grow each other. The first regularly published American newspaper—issue number one of the *Boston News-Letter* in 1704—contained an "advertisement" that read:

> This News Letter is to be continued Weekly; and all Persons who have any Houses, Lands, Tenements, Farmes, Ships Vessels, Goods, Wares or Merchadizes, &c to be Sold or Lett; *or Servants Run away*; or Goods Stoll or Lost, may have the same Inserted at a Reasonable Rate. [1] (emphasis added)

The *Boston News-Letter* was distributed at the Boston post office and printed by the colonial postmaster, a linkage that would continue into the age of postmaster-printer Benjamin Franklin. Advertisers were slow in coming to the publication, but among the earliest, in issue number seven, was a slave-sale ad:

𝔄𝔡𝔳𝔢𝔯𝔱𝔦𝔣𝔢𝔪𝔢𝔫𝔱𝔰.

TWo Negro men, and one Negro Woman & Child; to be Sold by Mr. *John Colman*, Merchant; to be feen at Col. *Charles Hobbey*, Efq his Houfe in *Bofton*.

Tens of thousands more would appear over the next 154 years. Maryland had a newspaper as of 1727, the *Maryland Gazette*. Published in Annapolis, it ceased publication in 1734; the printer, William Parks, moved to Williamsburg, the bustling port on the James River, where in 1736 he started the *Virginia Gazette*. (A second *Maryland Gazette* appeared in 1747, from a different printer.)

Then as now, the unique economics of newspapers necessarily relied on income from diverse sources. The popularity of the word *Gazette* in so many colonial newspapers' names derived from its then-current connotation of "official record," which allowed the paper to get government business printing public notices.[2] But newspapers also derived a steady, dependable income from slavery-related advertisements.

Newspapers ran two main kinds of slavery-related advertisements: for apprehension of runaways, and for sale or hiring. In the former case, the existence of this new advertising medium strengthened slavery by creating a system of vigilance that made long-term escape less of a possibility. In the latter, newspapers not only ran advertisements for slave sales but also facilitated them through brokerage, by furnishing venues for a sale to take place, and even by consignment of slaves to the paper's printer.

In turn, the soul-driving business grew and prospered with the marketing power afforded by this up-to-date medium, as per the advertisement in the *Pennsylvania Gazette* of November 18, 1731:

> To be Sold, A Likely Negro Wench, about Fifteen Years old, has had the Small-pox, been in the Country above a Year, and talks English. Enquire of the Printer hereof.

The "Printer" was twenty-five-year-old Benjamin Franklin, who bought the *Pennsylvania Gazette* in 1730 after its founder, Samuel Keimer, went to debtor's prison. Keimer, though English, was a follower of the "French prophets," a millennial sect of Huguenots in London; in an account of his sufferings he referred to himself as a "white Negro," predating Norman Mailer's use of the term by more than two hundred years. He relocated to Barbados, where he began the *Barbados Gazette*, which ran many slavery-related advertisements.[3]

With Franklin's newspaper and his retail location in Philadelphia, he brokered slave sales like the one at the beginning of this chapter for a girl at the beginning of her childbearing years. Franklin, the only one of the "founding fathers" to have been an indentured servant,* owned slaves for thirty years or so.

A concerned student of the problems of creating and retaining wealth, Franklin fused what we now call "the media" with political power in America via networking and new technology. A vegetarian in his youth (the "Pythagorean regimen," as it was called),[4] he was also an amateur avant-garde composer who invented musical instruments and, while living in France, wrote in the then-new string quartet idiom a striking, unique-sounding three-movement work played entirely on open strings.†

Franklin franchised his newspaper operation, partnering with printers in other towns. We have previously noted his silent partnership in the *South Carolina Gazette*. When William Parks was preparing to start the *Virginia Gazette*, Franklin advised him to build his own papermill—the first in the Southern colonies—and sold him the rags he needed to make the paper from.[5] "By the mid-1740s," writes David Waldstreicher, whose *Runaway America: Benjamin Franklin, Slavery, and the American Revolution* has informed this section of our narrative, "Franklin was the largest paper dealer in the colonies."[6] He controlled paper itself and saw its uses as medium and as money.

Franklin's influence as an economic theorist was all the more significant because his ideas were grounded in real-world practice. He made his *Pennsylvania Gazette* into a new kind of newspaper. "As no one quite had before," writes Waldstreicher, "he learned to make his printed manufactures—the newspaper and the annual almanacs—essential goods in the booming economy."[7] As part of that process, Franklin got himself named postmaster of Philadelphia in 1737—a significant and profitable office for a newspaperman, since newspapers constituted the bulk of what the postal system carried. He subsequently became

---

*Franklin was indentured to his older brother, a newspaper printer in Boston, from whom he ran away to the forty-one-year-old town of Philadelphia in 1723.
†There has been a question of attribution of authorship about this singular work, but there is no strong evidence in favor of any other composer. Besides the traditional attribution to him, our ultimate reason for believing it to be Franklin's is subjective: its wit, style, and above all its sense of invention.

deputy postmaster general for British North America, and ultimately postmaster of the United States, creating the US Postal System. For much of his adult life he used the post office as a base from which to dispense patronage and build his personal network as the North American economy grew.

Franklin was an anti-monetarist: in an economy where he might have to accept (and store, and sell) a quantity of tobacco as payment in lieu of silver, he was a strong proponent of paper currency. From his perspective in America, where land was cheap but labor was dear, Franklin saw wealth in terms of labor, not silver.

"Franklin's writings of the 1730s and 1740s pivot repeatedly around . . . notions of money as akin to people, and people as capital," writes Waldstreicher.[8] Karl Marx, who quoted Franklin approvingly in *Das Kapital*, described him in 1859 as the man "who formulated the basic law of modern political economy."[9] Marx was referring to Franklin's anonymously published pamphlet (in 1729, when Franklin was twenty-three) titled "A Modest Enquiry into the Nature and Necessity of a Paper-Currency":

> Trade in general being nothing else but the Exchange of Labour for Labour, the Value of all Things is . . . most justly measured by Labour. . . .
>
> By Labour may the Value of Silver be measured as well as other Things . . . Thus the riches of a country are to be valued by the *quantity of labour* its inhabitants are able to purchase.[10]

Somewhere between 6 and 10 percent of the population of Philadelphia at the time was enslaved and was therefore purchasable labor.[11] The Pennsylvania legislature dropped the duty on slaves from ten pounds to twenty shillings in the 1720s, and throughout the 1730s an ever-increasing number of kidnapped Africans were arriving.[12] Franklin owned at least two slaves, though he found them troublesome; in a 1748 letter to his elderly mother about domestic matters, he wrote of an enslaved couple that "we conclude to sell them both the first good opportunity, for we do not like Negro servants."[13]

Franklin lived to be eighty-four, and in his late years, he became a vocal abolitionist. But that was after he made his fortune with newspapers that acted as clearing houses for slave sales and runaway advertisements. Using the unpaid labor of black slaves, indentured servants, and his wife, Deborah, Franklin operated a book and stationery shop on the street level of his printing house. In a cash-poor society, Franklin frequently had to take payment in the form of South

Carolina rice or West Indian sugar, selling it at his store, and on at least one occasion accepted a slave as partial payment for a debt.

Not for nothing did 1990s rappers speak of $100 bills as "the Benjamins." Franklin saw paper money as a democratization of capital, and thereby as a broader franchise for the wider civic participation he favored—though that did not include the participation of "Negroes," to whom a cash value was assigned. In the wake of the smallpox epidemic of 1731, Franklin published a calculation in his newspaper: "The Number of those who died here of that Distemper, is exactly 288. . . . 64 of the Number were Negroes; if these be valued one with another at 30 pounds per Head, the Loss to the City in that Article is near 2000 pounds."[14]

In a sense, Franklin's newspaper and his almanac were his money, since they were paper he could exchange for commodities. But Franklin also literally printed money—more than £770,000 worth of notes for Pennsylvania between 1731 and 1764, as well as notes for Delaware and New Jersey.[15] As a newspaper publisher, he had a bird's-eye view of the variety of contemporary commerce. He routinely had to handle complex transactions entailing a mix of barter, credit, and occasionally cash, with heightened insight into the workings of the colonial credit economy. He understood clearly how "money" could take on various forms.

France had tried a disastrous experiment with paper money in 1717, urged on the Regent Duke of Orleans by John Law, the gambler son of an Edinburgh goldsmith. Law created a paper money for France, backing it with future revenues from the infant colony of Louisiana, which had neither a staple crop nor a labor force. To that end, a cedar swamp was cleared in 1718 and New Orleans was built. As he privatized France's foreign debt into a single, paper-issuing, monster corporation, there followed a speculative bubble in which Law's notes traded at ten times their face value in Paris, with the inevitable crash coming in 1721. After that, France was soured on paper money until the nineteenth century.[16] The crash was more or less concurrent with the London South Sea bubble, but Britain bounced back much better.

As Virginia, Maryland, and Delaware bulked up with slaves, South Sea Company ships from Africa pulled up into the ports of the Chesapeake. Discharged from widely disparate West and Central African slaving territories, the cargoes were sometimes very large, as per this advertisement from Williamsburg's *Virginia Gazette* on April 8, 1737, the second year of the paper's existence:

ADVERTISEMENTS.
THE Ship Johnſton, *of Liverpool, Capt.* James Gil-
dart, *is arriv'd at* York, *from* Angola, *with* 490
choice young Slaves: The Sale of them is to begin on
Tueſday *the* 12*th Inſtant, at* York *Town, by*
                                          Thomas Nelſon.

Alexander Hewatt in 1779 described the situation of South Carolina forty
years previously:

> Adventurous planters in Carolina, eager to obtain a number of negroes,
> always stretched their credit with the traders to its utmost pitch; for as
> negroes on good lands cleared themselves in a few years, they by this
> means made an annual addition to their capital stock. After obtaining this
> credit, it then became their interest to maintain their superiority in assem-
> bly, and discharge their debt to the merchants in the easiest manner they
> could. The increase of paper-money always proved to them a considerable
> assistance, as it advanced the price of those commodities they brought to
> the market, by which they cancelled their debts with the merchants; so
> that however much this currency might depreciate, the loss occasioned by
> it from time to time fell not on the adventurous planters, but on the mer-
> chants and moneymen who were obliged to take it.[17]

In other words, slaves were safer money than paper currency. This would
continue to be true in the slave territories of the United States until the end of
slavery.

The newspaper runaway ads of Virginia and Maryland in the 1730s were
more often for indentured servants than for black slaves. The descriptions of
the absconded, often quite detailed, provide the closest we have to thumbnail
sketches of the white servant population. But by the 1750s, black slaves, many of
them described as "Virginia born," dominated the runaway ads.

Slave-sale advertisements appeared in the *Virginia Gazette* from its earliest
numbers in 1736. They were numerous by the 1760s, by which time they stressed
the "Virginia-born" provenance of the human merchandise. Four advertisements

that appeared on page four of the January 8, 1767, issue of the *Virginia Gazette* offered "Sixty odd exceeding fine Negroes, all, except two, *Virginia* born"; "Sundry Valuable Virginia Born Slaves"; "About 100 choice Negroes, most of them *Virginia* born"; and "Sixty choice Virginia born Slaves."

The opposite of "Virginia-born" was "outlandish," a word that subsequently came into common use in a more general sense. "Virginia born" laborers had a number of advantages in the market over the "outlandish." They were English-speaking, were trained in plantation work, were "seasoned," i.e., had immunities to American diseases—and, importantly, they were considered to be more docile and were carefully kept away from military training. Outlandish Negroes might have military experience. The destabilization of Africa occasioned by the slave trade created a legacy of war, as well as a means of funding those wars. They provided captives for slave traders: African soldiers, captured in battle, were sold in American markets. In Virginia, a preference for slaves with no military knowledge was reflected in higher prices.

Raised from birth to a slave work regime, the Virginia-born had never known freedom. They did not file their teeth sharp, an African tradition that in the Americas became a means of defense for people who were not allowed to carry weapons. Those scary-looking filed teeth turned up in an August 20, 1761, advertisement placed in the *Maryland Gazette* by the twenty-seven-year-old George Washington, who, ever the alert commander, was prepared with precise descriptions of his servants and slaves in case any of them decamped. When he advertised for the return of four "Negroes" named Peros (perhaps Pérez?), Jack, Neptune, and Cupid, he advised that Jack had "Cuts down his Cheek, being his Country Marks," and Neptune, his teeth "fil'd sharp," and his "Back, if rightly remember'd, has many small Marks or Dots running from both his Shoulders down to his Waistband, and his Head was close shav'd." This was the British military method of identifying black soldiers, of whom there were many. Washington, an acute observer, differentiated the runaways' language skills, though he couldn't pinpoint their origins within Africa. Neptune and Cupid, he wrote, "were brought in an African ship in August 1759, and talk very broken and unintelligible English; the second one, Jack, is Countryman to those, and speaks pretty good English, having been several Years in the Country. The other, Peros, speaks much better than either, indeed has little of his country Dialect left, and is esteemed a sensible judicious Negro."

><

Quite possibly, though we do not know, an enslaved fiddler played for the dancing at the splendid ball of April 26, 1738, in Williamsburg. Surely Mrs. Degrassenreidts' guests that night were waited on by liveried black servants, even as her soirée was enlivened by a show of cruelty, a slave sale in the form of a raffle, as advertised in the *Virginia Gazette*:

> *March* 31, 1738.
>
> *THIS is to give Notice to all Gentlemen and Ladies,* That there will be a Ball on Wednesday Evening, the 26th of April next, and an *Assembly* on Friday the 28th, at the House of Mrs. Degraffenreidt, *in* Williamsburg. Tickets to be had of her.
>
> N. B. There will be set up to be Raffled for, a likely young Virginia Negro Woman, fit for House Business, and her Child.

For more than a century, slaves were occasionally sold by raffle in Virginia, where gambling was a mania. The seller hoped to realize more money from a raffle than from an auction, and the ticket buyers got the entertainment value of seeing who won the human prizes. What will you draw? The carriage? A garden tool? A couple of children? The only losers were the people being raffled for fun and profit—but then, it was a common (and convenient) belief among slaveowners that "negroes," being a lesser kind of being, did not feel the sorrows of parting from kin as deeply.

Directly below that advertisement was another one, for the following night, which combined a raffle of a young man with "Grotesque Dances":

> *THIS is to give Notice to the Gentlemen and Ladies,* That there will be a *Publick* and *Assembly*, at the Capitol, on Thursday Evening the 27th of April next : *Also* several Grotesque *Dances, never yet* perform'd *in* Virginia. Tickets to be had of Mrs. Stagg.
>
> N. B. Several valuable Goods will be put up to be Raffled for ; also a likely young Negro Fellow.

Sometimes the raffle method was even used to liquidate a large estate. Henry Wiencek calls attention to an advertisement (in one of two concurrent, competing *Virginia Gazettes*) for an estate liquidation to take place in Williamsburg, in which fifty-five slaves were announced to be raffled off in thirty-nine lots.

This form of dispersing an estate at random guaranteed the maximum degree of dismemberment of the family and community structures that had existed on the plantation prior to being liquidated. There was little chance, for example, that "A Negro Woman named *Kate*, and a young Child, *Judy*" would be won by the same person who won "A Negro Girl, *Aggy*, and Boy, *Nat*; Children of *Kate*."

George Washington was the third of twenty co-organizers listed for that raffle. The advertisement is too long to reprint in full, but suffice it to say that one of the lots offered as a raffle prize was "a fine breeding Woman named *Pat*, lame of one Side, with Child, and her three Children, *Læt, Milley,* and *Charlotte*." The advertisement ran in the April 14, 1768, issue of Rind's *Virginia Gazette*, with no date for the sale specified.

The sale apparently took more than a year and a half to pull off, being advertised once again in the issue of November 23, 1769, with a date of December 13 set for the drawing. The "fine breeding Woman" Pat was once again represented as being "with Child" a year and a half later.

It was done at a tavern, with all the conviviality that implies, and animated by the thrill—not of buying, but of *winning* Pat and her children, or maybe children who were being separated from their mother.

Washington seems to have taken part in drawing the lottery winners, to judge from his journal entry: "went to Southalls in the Evening to draw Colo. Moores Lottery," a process that took three nights. As Wiencek puts it, "Washington himself was raffling off slaves."[18] Before Wiencek's book was published in 2003, no previous biographer of George Washington had called attention to his participation in this utterly depraved practice. Wiencek then attempts to account for the transformation of Washington into the man who in his last will took the then-unusual step of freeing his (though not Martha's) slaves. Washington, it should be noted, was free to liberate his slaves: he was not under crushing debt when he died, so they were not seized and sold. He had no natural heir, having not sired any children with Martha. If he had had a son to inherit his property, it would have been seen as a betrayal to devalue his estate like that.

⤜⤛

"I think God has a Quarrel with you for your Abuse of and Cruelty to the poor Negroes," wrote English preacher George Whitefield in *A Letter to the Inhabitants of Maryland, Virginia, North and South Carolina, Concerning their Negroes.*

The cross-eyed Whitefield had a mighty voice, and he was the first big-hit performative evangelist to travel throughout the colonies.* He was one of the founders of Methodism, along with the brothers John and Charles Wesley, in approximately 1729 while they were all students at Oxford; his version was Methodist Episcopalism, a Calvinist offshoot of Anglicanism. His speaking had intrigued, though not converted, Benjamin Franklin, who after hearing him speak and making some calculations concluded that his reputation for addressing tens of thousands at a time in England was probably not exaggerated.

That was the sort of thing that caught Franklin's attention. Though he had no interest in the new sect of Methodism Whitefield intended to implant in North America, he was a media man, and he was clearly fascinated by the sense of communication this phenomenal figure created. His *Pennsylvania Gazette* published the schedule of Whitefield's high-profile journey through the colonies during the second of his seven American tours. On April 17, 1740, he devoted his front page to Whitefield's sensational open letter that said bluntly, "considering what Usage they commonly meet with, I have wondered, that we have not more Instances of Self-Murder among the Negroes, or that they have not more frequently rose up in Arms against their Owners." It was the first antislavery tract in any colonial newspaper, and the only one that would run for another thirty years.

Anglican clergymen read droning word-for-word sermons that they might not even have written themselves, but Whitefield was dynamic. He had a theatrical—which was to say, a disreputable—background, and his revivals were a kind of popular theater. In South Carolina, he was denounced by Anglican pastor and naturalist Alexander Garden. Alexander Hewatt wrote that he was

> not unlike one of those strange and erratic meteors which appear now
> and then in the system of nature. In his youth, as he often confessed and
> lamented, he was gay, giddy, and profligate; so fondly attached to the stage,
> that he joined a company of strolling actors and vagabonds, and spent a
> part of his life in that capacity. At this period it is probable he learned that

---

*Jonathan Edwards began holding revivals in the early 1730s that on one occasion paralyzed an entire Massachusetts town as it got the religious fever and on another occasion led to a wave of religiously motivated suicides, but he never left New England.

grimace, buffoonery and gesticulation which he afterwards displayed from the pulpit.[19]

With theater still in its early days in the colonies as of 1740, this evangelical "Great Awakening" (a cynic might call it the Great Wave of Superstition) was the first cultural phenomenon to tie together Northern and Southern colonies.

Methodism already had a base in Georgia. The brothers Wesley had been there since 1736, when Oglethorpe invited them to minister to his colony. The Wesleys in turn invited Whitefield to come to Savannah, where he started the Bethesda Orphanage, raising a sizable amount of funds to do so. But they differed on doctrinal issues: Whitefield's Calvinist Methodism held that God's elect would be the only ones go to heaven no matter what, but John Wesley, in what was called the Arminian heresy by its enemies, democratized salvation by insisting that anyone could attain it—a free-will doctrine that would be fundamental to African American Christian belief as well.

After Whitefield's celebrity arrival in the colony, the trustee's secretary William Stephens wrote that he hoped the clergyman would focus slaveowners' minds away from rape and incest, though he didn't use those words: "It may be hoped That Good Work is lately begun from Mr. Whitfields so daily gaining on the affections of the people: but [there remains] the practice of open Lewdness, in first making Whores of their Female Servants; then cohabiting with them and their Bastards, from whence a continuation of the same Course may be presumed."[20] Whitefield's followers had a tendency, distressing to slaveowners, to go out and convert the enslaved, who on one occasion chose the occasion of being converted to go "raving in the Woods for some time till their Masters were oblig'd to take them under Discipline."[21]

While Alexander Hewatt acknowledged grudgingly that "religion in America owed not a little to the zeal, diligence, and oratory, of this extraordinary man," he was troubled by Whitefield's converts in South Carolina who became abolitionist preachers for a time, before they were repressed: "After him a servile race of ignorant and despicable imitators sprung up, and wandered from place to place, spreading doctrines subversive of all public order and peace."[22]

The "subversive" Whitefield preached the gospel to white and black both. Methodism in its early days was doctrinally antislavery, and some black South Carolinians converted. But South Carolina had a miniscule population of free blacks, and enslaved blacks on the plantations were kept far away from evangelists. The big wave of conversion would have to wait until after independence, when religious intolerance became constitutionally prohibited and itinerant evangelists had a freer hand.

Despite his early abolitionist posture, however, Whitefield came to feel that Georgia could never be profitable without slave labor. He bought slaves to work at his orphanage, spoke up in favor of legalizing slavery in Georgia, and ultimately became a plantation owner in South Carolina. He was said to treat his slaves kindly, which is to say that he was a founding father of the school of Christian slaveowning that would later dominate Southern ideology, which historians generally refer to as paternalism.

Shockingly to many, Whitefield preached to the enslaved; in the eighteenth century, almost no effort was made to Protestantize them. Slaveowners were by and large not eager for their captive labor force to be Christianized. Kongos arrived pre-Catholicized, though their version of Catholicism was Kongo all the way down. Other captives, from Senegambia and elsewhere, practiced a sub-Saharan form of Islam. Various belief systems of West Africa were active, and the old hoodoo religion was everywhere. Hewatt wrote of South Carolina in 1779 that "the negroes of that country, a few only excepted, are to this day as great strangers to Christianity, and as much under the influence of Pagan darkness, idolatry and superstition, as they were at their first arrival from Africa."[23]

But Christianization of the enslaved was moving forward. When Whitefield died in 1770, a poem was published eulogizing him that caused a sensation. "An elegiac poem, on the death of that celebrated divine, and eminent servant of Jesus Christ, the late reverend, and pious George Whitefield," by "PHILLIS, a Servant Girl of 17 Years of Age, Belonging to Mr. J. WHEATLEY, of Boston: – And has been but 9 Years in this Country from Africa" was the poem that made Phillis Wheatley famous.

Born in Senegal, Wheatley gained a first-rate command of English in only a few years. Her spiritual poetry had an edge to it that might not be easily apparent to a modern reader. Her best-known poem, "On Being Brought from Africa to America," was practically a civil-rights demand to be allowed to participate in the evangelical movement:

Remember, *Christians*, *Negros*, black as *Cain*,
May be refin'd, and join th' angelic train.

Her ardor for Africans to achieve spiritual greatness was fully present at her debut, in her eulogy to Whitefield:

Take HIM ye Africans, he longs for you;
Impartial SAVIOUR, is his title due;
If you will chuse to walk in grace's road,
You shall be sons, and kings, and priests to GOD.

Slaveowners took pains to disabuse the notion, popular among the enslaved, that Christianity was a path to freedom. There was to be no path to freedom, not for the enslaved and not for their descendants. The South was from the beginning dependent on the economic magic of slave reproduction, deeply integrated as it was into the very basis of credit. There could be no climb-down position. "The permanent riches of the country," wrote Hewatt of South Carolina in 1779, "consisted in lands, houses, and negroes; and the produce of the lands, improved by negroes, raw materials, provisions, and naval stores, were exchanged for what the province wanted from other countries."[24]

From very early on, there were only two choices for the South. Ending slavery would have meant watching the vast on-paper wealth of its oligarchy disappear; that wasn't going to happen. The other course was to commit fully to a two-caste system: the perpetually free and the perpetually enslaved.

20

Lord Dunmore's Blackbirds

Your petitioners apprehend we have in common with all other men a natural right to our freedoms without being depriv'd of them by our fellow men as we are a freeborn people and have never forfeited this blessing by any compact or agreement whatever.

—"Petition of a grate number of blackes" to General Thomas
Gage, the recently inaugurated royal governor of Massachusetts,
May 25, 1774

The late resolution of the Quakers in Pennsylvania to set at liberty all their negro slaves may satisfy us that their number cannot be very great. Had they made any considerable part of their property, such a resolution could never have been agreed to.[1]

—Adam Smith, *An Inquiry into the Nature and Causes of the
Wealth of Nations*, 1776

WITH THE END OF the French and Indian (or Seven Years') War, Prime Minister John Stuart, the Scottish Third Earl of Bute, decided not to demobilize the army but to station ten thousand troops in America. Previously British troops had appeared in the colonies to fight the colonists' enemies, but now they were going to be a police force.

Worse, the colonists were told to pay for it. The colonies had long endured trade regulations that gave them access to British ports but cut them off from competing markets and otherwise imposed intolerable conditions on the merchants, but they had never been "internally" taxed (as opposed to "external" taxes, such as duties). Now Parliament laid a tax on them.

Boston merchant banker John Hancock denounced the Stamp Act as "slavery." Hancock, who never bought or sold slaves but grew up served by slaves in the house of his wealthy merchant uncle, was exaggerating. In reality, the 1765 Stamp Act was a tax—not, thought the British, a terrible one, given what had been expended to protect the colonists from the French and Indians, but a maddening one to colonists who had to pay with hard coin for the new stamped paper that would be used in any officially recorded transaction.

Contrived to make all levels of society pay, the Stamp Act was a serious miscalculation on the part of the clueless British officialdom. Nothing was more calculated to infuriate the legal class than the Stamp Act, since it mandated use of stamped paper for legal documents. It angered the poor: it required a one-shilling stamp on a deck of playing cards—a particular annoyance, since gambling required frequent replacement of the deck—and a whopping ten shillings on a pair of dice. And it was a call to arms as well for newspaper printers, who were expected to print on officially stamped and purchased paper, and who retaliated with all the ink at their disposal.

In Boston, where the first insurrections of colonists against Britain exploded, two distinct social levels were active, each of which had their own motives: the merchants, and the motley crew that made up the mob.[2] We speak today of "the mob" most commonly with reference to the Sicilian-style Mafia, as transplanted to America via New Orleans in the late nineteenth century. But in the 1760s another kind of mob was already well established in Boston, though it was more loosely structured. The mob culture of Boston was a principal actor in the early days of the American Revolution.

Puritan Boston didn't have any Catholic churches, nor did it celebrate Christmas or Easter, nor did it have a theater. As in Connecticut and Rhode Island, "stage-plays" were prohibited in Massachusetts and were not part of the public consciousness, so Bostonians had not seen Addison's influential *Cato*, nor did Boston have that part of social life that centered around the theater. Boston's theatrical urges played out differently: in the form of participatory mass actions in the street, as happened every year on November 5, or "Pope's Day." Known in England as Guy Fawkes Day for the radical Catholic who had tried to blow up Parliament with gunpowder in 1605, the holiday had replaced the pagan All Hallows' Eve. In Boston, some people observed it by dressing as devils and popes for a carnival of misrule that might include attacking Catholics—a practice imported from London—should any be detected.

"Rioting in Boston was almost a ritual," writes Hiller B. Zobel.[3] Boston's street culture meshed with its heritage of Protestant dissent, which had long expressed itself in resistance to the colonial government. An anti-impressment riot in 1747 lasted three days, during which a multiethnic, mutinous mob of sailors that grew to some three thousand participants battled press gangs, took hostages, burned boats, and physically confronted the governor—"literally a case," write Linebaugh and Rediker, "of the people's fighting for its liberty, for throughout the eighteenth century the crew of a ship was known as 'the people,' who once ashore were on their 'liberty.'"[4]

By the time of the Stamp Act, the Mob—they wrote it with capitals—was a focused force that took direction and had been repurposed as a political weapon. The leader of the Mob in Boston (which divided into antagonistic North and South Boston factions) was a twenty-eight-year-old shoemaker named Ebenezer Mackintosh. Zobel writes:

> During the years from 1765 to 1770 . . . although the rioters seemed uncon-
> trolled and uncontrollable, they were in fact under an almost military
> discipline. On one notable occasion, according to the Tory Peter Oliver,
> Mackintosh "paraded the Town with a Mob of 2,000 Men in two Files, &
> passed by the Stadthouse, when the general Assembly were sitting, to dis-
> play his Power: if a Whisper was heard among his Followers, the holding
> up of his Finger hushed it in a Moment: & when he had fully displayed his
> Authority, he marched his Men to the first Rendezvouz, & Order'd them
> to retire peacably to their several Homes; & was punctually obeyed."[5]

Perhaps the figure of two thousand is an exaggeration; that number represented well over half of the town's adult male population. But there is no doubt-
ing that in Boston more than anywhere else, the hatred of the British and of
those thought to collaborate with them generalized and transcended social class.
And Boston had no police force to speak of.

Mackintosh's Mob, performing some of the functions of a militia, wound
up being the street enforcers of a group called the Loyal Nine, a club of mid-level
merchants and businesspeople that included Benjamin Edes, printer of the *Boston Gazette*, as well as a ship's captain, a jeweller, and two distillers who bought
much forbidden molasses from Saint-Domingue.

Frequently present at Loyal Nine meetings, though not a member, was Harvard graduate and failed businessman Samuel Adams Jr. Possibly the most fully
committed revolutionary to appear during the entire independence process, he
was thirteen years older than his second cousin John Adams. When the Stamp

Act crisis came to a head, Adams seems to have been one of the principal ligatures between merchants and Mob, a connection that was a significant tactical achievement of the urban American insurgents. At the height of the action, he was perhaps the most powerful man in Boston.

Adams had been affected by the experience of Boston's 1747 impressment riots, and subsequently began a radical newspaper, the *Independent Advertiser.* He had come to consciousness in the midst of the fierce political struggle between the "popular" party (which dominated the Massachusetts House of Representatives) and the "court" (pro-British, aristocratic) party.

Many Americans today have the impression that the uprisings in Boston were directed solely against British occupiers, but despite his close collaboration with the crown, the Massachusetts merchant Thomas Hutchinson was as much an American as Samuel Adams. The Hutchinsons were the ruling class; they had a reputation for tight, strategic intermarriage among three clans that had literally come to be Boston's ruling family. They dedicated themselves exclusively to commerce and officeholding. After a prolonged "bank war" between a crown-associated "silver bank" and a populist-associated "land bank" went badly for the latter, Samuel Adams's family hated the Hutchinson clan obsessively—especially Thomas Hutchinson, who simultaneously served as governor, legislator, and supreme court justice.

The Loyal Nine were at the center of the first provocative actions of what came to be called the American Revolution, dispatching physical intimidation as a primary tactic. The presence of printer Benjamin Edes was critical: the first confrontations exploded amid a torrent of radical pamphleteering, which, amid the proliferation of printers and newspapers, was the new-media component of the American Revolution. The message Edes never stopped printing was that a standing military force was tyranny, and the very presence of troops an affront.

The Loyal Nine were absorbed into the Sons of Liberty, a self-appointed action group with chapters in all the colonies. The many merchants in their ranks intended to be on the winning side when their wealthy loyalist competitors had been hounded out of town, a process they eagerly threw themselves into. They hanged in effigy the wealthy merchant Andrew Oliver on the hot night of August 14, 1765, for collaborating with the Stamp Act. While that might seem relatively mild as compared with, say, breaking on the wheel, as was done to rebellious slaves in Louisiana, it was a terrifying experience for the victim.

On August 26, violence erupted as the Mob stormed Thomas Hutchinson's house, using axes to break their way into the fine house, built seventy-five years previously by Hutchinson's grandfather. Hutchinson's family, who had been having supper, fled as the Mob destroyed the furniture, took everything of value—clothes, rings, cash—and, in Bernard Bailyn's words, "destroyed or scattered in the mud all of Hutchinson's books and papers, including the manuscript of volume I of his *History* and the collection of historical papers that he had been gathering for years as the basis for a public archive." They did their best to pull the building down: "only the heavy brickwork construction of the walls prevented their razing the building completely, though they worked at it till daylight."[6]

The violence of the Boston Mob, whom the aristocrats saw as "levellers," astounded their bourgeois sponsors. They got away with it—not only with impunity, but with glory. In a systematic campaign of intimidation directed largely at merchants, the Mob enforced a nonimportation edict. To anyone suspected of not supporting nonimportation, they made life unbearable. The violence was strategic, implying both a command structure and a financed campaign.

They showed up at targets' homes en masse, carrying clubs. They beat people up, and they inflicted the signature torture of the American Revolution: tarring and feathering. They stripped their victims naked in front of a crowd, covered them first with scalding hot tar (making them black) and then with goose feathers (making them Indians), and paraded them in that condition about town for perhaps three hours to be the object of ridicule and beatings before being left half dead. As a public humiliation and street theater, tarring and feathering dates back at least to the twelfth century in England, but it seems to have made its first appearance in the colonies in the hands of the self-proclaimed Patriots.

The Mob hounded Thomas Hutchinson's nephew, the merchant Nathaniel Rogers, with more than a year's worth of attacks on his house, physical threats, and intimidation of his family, until he left Boston. Then they had their Sons of Liberty soldiers in New York hound him out of that city.[7] But New York did not mobilize like Boston had.

With its relatively homogenous population, accustomed as it was to the focus and discipline of Puritan society, Boston was unique. In New York, heterogenous and multilingual from the moment of its founding by the Dutch, coordinated movement was less likely. The Sons of Liberty tried the same tactics there, but the mobs lacked organization and merely went trashing, vandalizing the rich and on one occasion destroying a newly built theater.

The colonists' violent reaction to the Stamp Act caught the British—and some of their factors—by surprise. In South Carolina, the radical who stirred up mob action was Christopher Gadsden, a temperamental merchant who was the most aggressive local figure in defying colonial governors. Writing under the pseudonym of Homespun Freeman, Gadsden denounced the Stamp Act as a Scottish plot.[8] He went to New York in 1765 as a delegate to the Stamp Act Congress, which asserted that only colonial assemblies had the right to tax the colonies, and he returned to Charleston an ardent member of the Sons of Liberty. He was a kindred spirit and warm correspondent with Samuel Adams; their friendship was emblematic of the close ties of insurgency between New England and South Carolina. It was Gadsden who designed the "Don't Tread On Me" rattlesnake flag for John Paul Jones to hoist over the *Alfred,* the first ship of the American navy, as the "special standard" of the US Navy's first commander in chief, the former Rhode Island slave-ship captain Eseck Hopkins.[9]

Gadsden in 1767 invested his fortune in the seven-year project of building his 840-foot wharf, the largest in the colonies, which shipped out enormous amounts of rice.[10] It is notorious in American memory as the site where Africans were taken for sale after their period of quarantine at Sullivan's Island; perhaps more than one hundred thousand Africans were sold from Gadsden's Wharf before the African trade was prohibited.

The anti–Stamp Act mob in Charles Town rioted for nine days. Henry Laurens, a conservative businessman who prided himself on doing things legally, was in favor of complying with the Stamp Act, and so was targeted by the mob, which came to Laurens's house bent for, as he put it years later while confined in the Tower of London, "seizing the Stamp'd Paper just arrived in Charles Town & for awing the Officers appointed to distribute it."[11] But Laurens successfully talked the mob down, demonstrating the crowd-handling skill he subsequently deployed as president of the First Continental Congress.

Radicalism was a double-edged sword for the merchants. Many were invested in commercial alliances in England, and destabilization was not good for business. War would disrupt shipping. But being constantly at the mercy of British trade regulations seemed to them to be "slavery," the word they invariably used. Independence would give merchants ownership of their commerce—which in some cases, needless to say, included slave trading—and would put them in charge of regulation. The Loyalists weren't going to be the winning side, and knocking them out would remove competition.

As the "Patriots" seized power in all thirteen colonies, merchants who didn't dance to the broadly popular tune of revolution might be labeled Tories and find themselves the object of mob action. As Henry Laurens discovered, it was a better bet to be the one leading the mob. In Chestertown, Maryland, Thomas Ringgold IV cast his lot with change. Besides being a member of the Maryland assembly, Ringgold was a founder of the local chapter of Sons of Liberty and a member of the Stamp Act Congress. He became a slave-trading revolutionary, and not the only one.

While the repeal of the Stamp Act on March 17, 1766, temporarily averted a crisis, it was accompanied by the Declaratory Act, which held

> that the said colonies and plantations in *America* have been, are, and of right ought to be, subordinate unto, and dependent upon the imperial crown and Parliament of *Great Britain;* and that the king's Majesty . . . had, hath, and of right ought to have, full power and authority to make laws and statutes of sufficient force and validity to bind the colonies and people of *America*, subjects of the crown of *Great Britain,* in all cases whatsoever.[12]

With the Declaratory Act, London reaffirmed its right to strike down colonial law at will. "Every colony had been established by a document from the king that authorized a colonial legislature to enact laws for the colony so long as they were 'not repugnant to the laws of England,'" write Alfred and Ruth Blumrosen. "Thus the British government retained a kind of superintending power over the colony's behavior. This was well known in the colonies."[13] That was a problem: while the Declaratory Act aroused no popular protest in the colonies, its implications were clear to the colonial ruling class. Meanwhile, Southern slaveholders were become increasingly alarmed by the abolitionist movement that had been growing in Britain since the 1760s, fed by the increasing popularity of Methodism and Quakerism, both antislavery.

Nowhere did British and colonial law differ more sharply than on slavery. William Blackstone, the ranking British jurist of his day in 1765, praised liberty in terms that infuriated the Virginians: "[the] spirit of liberty is so deeply implanted in our constitution, and rooted even in our very soil, that a slave or a Negro, the moment he lands in England, falls under the protection of the laws and so far becomes a freeman."[14]

Slaveowning colonists were particularly alarmed by the 1772 *Somerset* decision. James Somerset was the slave name of a man who had been kidnapped from Africa at the age of nine. After landing in Virginia in 1749, he caught the eye of the young Scottish-born tobacco merchant Charles Stewart of Norfolk, whom he served for more than two decades as his "body servant," performing whatever personal services Stewart required.

When Stewart took Somerset along to London in 1771, Somerset escaped. Stewart recaptured him with the aid of professional slave catchers, who existed in London because there were enough enslaved people there, belonging to colonists both visiting and resident, that this kind of thing happened on an ongoing basis. The displeased Stewart avenged his humiliation by having Somerset bound and put on a ship to be sold in Jamaica—a reminder that a slave could easily be removed from the most relatively privileged urban echelons to a tropical death camp.

Before the vessel could sail, however, Somerset was dramatically rescued by the abolitionist Granville Sharp, who paid for Somerset's defense in court. The unprecedented case was a striking example of using litigation to steer social policy and was reflective of the maturity of the British justice system at the time. It put slavery on a show trial, occasioning widespread debate in the press, and it thrust the eminent, conservative jurist Lord Mansfield into the hot seat.

To the objection by Stewart's lawyer that freeing the estimated fourteen thousand slaves held in Britain would cost their owners a catastrophic £700,000, figured at £50 a head, Mansfield replied, "£50 a head may not be a high price." But he judged the case narrowly. He felt the issue was one for Parliament to take up, urging them to do so in his decision freeing Somerset: "The state of slavery is . . . so odious, that nothing can be suffered to support it but positive law. Whatever inconveniences, therefore, may follow from the decision, I cannot say this case is allowed or approved by the law of England; and therefore the black must be discharged."[15]

The decision, widely reported in colonial American newspapers, effectively prohibited chattel slavery in England (Scotland had a separate body of law), and unquestionably was a great victory for the antislavery movement.[16] At bottom, it established that Somerset had the rights of a person, which went directly contrary to the current of colonial law. Somerset was feted at a party in London attended by two hundred free people of color, an event also reported in colonial papers, including the *South Carolina Gazette*. Benjamin Franklin, who was in London in 1772 when the *Somerset* decision came down, wrote in full cry:

> *Pharisaical Britain!* to pride thyself in setting free *a single Slave* that happens to land on thy coasts, while thy Merchants in all thy ports are encouraged by thy laws to continue a commerce whereby so many *hundreds of thousands* are dragged into a slavery that can scarce be said to end with their lives, since it is entailed on their posterity![17]

The passage above has sometimes been cited as a proof of the non-plantation-owning Franklin's humanitarian bent. But if we read this with a pragmatic politician's understanding, we see less a simple cry against the immorality of slavery than that favorite trick of the political debater: changing the subject. And it was disingenuous: as Franklin well knew, Rhode Island captains had carried tens of thousands of Africans, and he himself made money from advertisements for slave sales in his newspapers, especially in South Carolina.

The British Parliament never picked up the gauntlet Lord Mansfield had thrown down. Slavery in Britain would never be made legal by affirmative law. It had been implemented in the colonies by English merchants, officials, captains, and by the colonists who had written laws to support it there, but there was never any groundswell of public opinion in its favor at home.

Stamped paper and tea are iconic in American popular history, but only recently have historians begun to consider the *Somerset* case much in the narrative of American independence. *Somerset* posed a more basic kind of threat to a slaveowner than stamped paper. It jeopardized the basis of Southerners' wealth: property consisting of human beings.

Henry Laurens was in London when *Somerset* was being argued. Before the verdict was delivered, he took a sarcastic tone in a letter of May 29, 1772: "They say that supper is ready, otherwise I was going to tell a long and comical Story, of a Trial between a Mr. Stuart and his Black Man James Somerset, at King's Bench, for Liberty."[18] Thirteen years later, he argued in a letter that "nor is it quite a decided fact that the moment a Negro sets his foot on British Ground he becomes a freeman. Lord Mansfield left this a moot point."[19] But Laurens was arguing against the tide: Mansfield's shocking decision was strongly felt, as evidenced by the 1774 newspaper advertisement in Virginia for return of a runaway that said, "He will probably endeavor to pass for a Freeman by the name of John Christian, and attempt to get on Board some Vessel bound for Great Britain, from the Knowledge he has of the late Determination of Somerset's Case."[20]

A British crackdown on smuggled molasses and tea inevitably led to confrontation. In Providence, the wealthy slave trader and rum distiller John Brown was one of the (at the time) unidentified leaders of a group of sixty or so who on the night of June 9, 1772, with their faces blacked, boarded and blew up the British blockade ship *Gaspée*, wounding the vessel's master in the struggle.* The assault on the *Gaspée* was tremendously popular among the people of Providence; no one would identify Brown or the other combatants, let alone testify.

In response to the Tea Act of 1773, which laid a threepenny duty on a vast surplus of tea that was otherwise being dumped on the American market, militants disguised with soot-blacked faces and Indian feathers on December 16 staged what later became known as the Boston Tea Party, arguably the detonating act of the American Revolution. Other anti-tea events followed in every colony, with a general boycott of tea that created a sense of revolutionary unity in the face of collective caffeine deprivation. In Annapolis, the ship *Peggy Stewart* was burned; the vessel's owner, Anthony Stewart, was compelled to torch it himself, with its load of tea. Samuel Galloway, perhaps with a there-but-for-the-grace shudder at the loss to his colleague and competitor, noted in a letter of October 24, 1774, that Stewart was not allowed even to place a handbill in the newspaper. "This is Liberty with a Vengence," Galloway wrote to Thomas Ringgold V. For his part, Ringgold insisted the whole incident was cooked up by Stewart to curry favor with London and wrote his father-in-law and merchant partner that he was "glad the people have shewn so much spirit."[21]

Philadelphia, meanwhile, was riled up by the *Centinel*, written in various issues of the *Pennsylvania Journal and Weekly Advertiser* beginning March 24, 1768, by Francis Alison, John Dickinson, and George Bryan, which warned of a plan to install an Anglican bishopric in the colonies, something that, despite the colonies' official status as Anglican, had never been done. Evangelicals and other religious dissenters, a major force in the independence struggle, feared that an "American Episcopate" would bring religious oppression to tolerant, multi-sected Pennsylvania. *Centinel* #1, which warned of the danger to religious dissenters, charged that "Enemies of America, . . . are exerting their utmost Endeavours to strip us of our most sacred, invaluable and inherent Rights; to reduce us to the State of Slaves; and to tax us."[22] Needless to say, this came from people who knew full well that the "State of Slaves" involved far more than taxation.

There was plenty to enrage the colonists, including the Quebec Act of 1774, which would have extended the province of Quebec down to the Ohio and Mississippi Rivers. But all of that aside, and allowing for the argument that the

---

*Brown, along with his abolitionist brother Moses, was later a cofounder of Brown University. See Rappleye.

colonies had in fact largely been independent since their foundation, the slave-society colonies of the South had their own compelling reason to secede from Britain: only independence could protect slavery from the growing power of British abolitionism.

The British army came with a display of intimidating grandeur. Malcolm Bell Jr. describes the arrival in 1765 of the mostly Irish Twenty-Ninth Regiment of Foot in Halifax on the ship *Thunderer*: "Ten black drummers, all former slaves captured from the French on the island of Guadeloupe, gave the band a special air. In their brilliant uniforms of scarlet pantaloons, silver-buttoned yellow jackets, Hessian boots, feathered turbans, and Persian scimitars, they won the admiration of all who saw them perform."[23]

Traveling with that regiment was Major Pierce Butler. An Irish Anglican, proud and even defensive throughout his life of his (somewhat questionable) aristocratic lineage, he was a third son and as such not in line to receive an inheritance in the age of primogeniture. The Americas were a fortune-hunting ground for younger sons; when Butler was eleven years old, his family purchased him a commission in the king's army. He came to North America at the age of fourteen during the French and Indian War, then subsequently returned to service in Ireland, and was sent again to Canada in 1765 with the rank of major.

Butler traveled to Philadelphia in 1767 with other officers to determine where best to post the regiment, then traveled alone down to Charles Town, arriving December 11, 1767, and remaining there through April 1769. During that time, in September 1768, his regiment was posted to insurgent Boston, which, with about sixteen thousand residents, was far and away the most rebellious of American towns and was the only site of resistance that British politicians were concerned about. There were no barracks in Boston to quarter the troops, who were hated as occupiers by the townspeople. Minor street beefs became confrontations between civilians and military, who otherwise mingled in various ways. Some soldiers deserted; others supplemented their regimental pay by doing casual day labor in Boston's ropeworks.

The twenty-one-year-old Major Butler (as he would be referred to throughout his life) had wider latitude. While in Charles Town, he caused a scandal by eloping with a fifteen-year-old heiress, but her stepfather intervened and thwarted the marriage, to the amusement of local society. When she married the following year, her fortune was quantified in the newspaper as "Thirty Thousand Pounds

Sterling," with an implicit mockery of Butler, who was reported in the same issue to be leaving town and who never quite lived down his reputation as a fortune hunter.

Broke and experiencing problems with receiving his pay, Butler returned to his regiment in Boston, at a time when the town was at a peak pitch of anti-colonial furor. He was apparently present, though not in uniform, on March 5, 1770, when members of his regiment killed five people after provocation, committing what was immediately trumpeted by propagandists as the Boston Massacre, and, reported Thomas Hutchinson, brought Massachusetts to the brink of—a commonly used term at the time—"civil war."[24]

Returning to Charles Town in January 1771 with only his military commission to his name—not an insubstantial holding—Butler quickly married Mary Middleton, whose deceased father, Thomas, had in the 1750s been one of the largest slave traders in Charles Town. The young heiress had received not only Middleton's legacy, but an even larger fortune from her maternal grandmother.

It was a prosperous time for South Carolina's businessmen, but Thomas Middleton left a legal mess behind, with much property and much debt. Butler became property manager for his wife's portfolio, which catapulted him into the ranks of the large planters. He now owned hundreds of slaves, many of them originally kept back from general sale by Middleton, who as a slave trader had first pick and a practiced eye.

It appears that one of the first things Butler did was to put hot-iron brands on their skins. There is nothing to suggest that Butler subsequently continued this practice, but the year after his marital windfall, he advertised in the *South Carolina Gazette* for two runaway slaves, thanks to which advertisement we know that they wore his initials for life:

RUN AWAY
From the Subscriber's Plantation in Prince William's *Parish*,
TWO NEGRO FELLOWS
Named MINOS, and CUDJOE; — they are both strong-made Fellows.
Minos appears to be near 40 Years old. Cudjoe about 26: — They are
marked a little above the right Breast with the Letters PB . . .
PIERCE BUTLER.[25]

Despite having married into the Charles Town gentry, Butler was still an officer in His Majesty's Army. The Crown was still giving away land to

settlers counted loyal to the king, and Butler managed a substantial land grab
as a Loyalist. "In the years immediately following his marriage," writes Bell,
"Pierce Butler made numerous requests for property and was awarded in excess
of ten thousand acres, of which more than eight thousand was in the Carolina back country."[26] Butler, who ultimately made a considerable fortune in
real-estate deals, was described approvingly in 1785 by no less a profiteer than
Henry Laurens as a "great Speculator" who "loves to make money."[27] There was
no question that all this land would be cleared and planted by newly arrived
Africans.

Butler maintained the fiction of loyalty as long as he could, but as his regiment was preparing to ship back out to Britain, he resigned from the British
army in 1773. Selling his military commission, he plowed the receipts from
cashiering himself into purchasing a seventeen-hundred-acre plantation on St.
Simons Island off the coast of Georgia. With his hundreds of slaves and the
excellent land he had acquired, Butler began producing rice and premium-
priced long-staple cotton. His fortune was made.

He was collaborating actively with the independentists by 1775, and with
the coming of the war, he became South Carolina's adjutant general against his
former army, charged with whipping a backwoods militia into shape as a military force. Keenly aware that South Carolina's defense was obstructed by the
reluctance of men to leave their homes and families unguarded against Native
American attack or slave insurrection, he requested a force of five thousand
troops from the North to protect the Lowcountry—from the British, officially,
but also from domestic enemies.[28]

The Scottish naturalist Alexander Garden, who arrived in Charles Town in
1752, "had not been in South Carolina very long before he was told by both
doctors and laymen of their concern that people were being poisoned by their
slaves," write Edmund and Dorothy Smith Berkeley. "It was widely believed that
plant poisons were being administered in food or drink, especially in tea. When
he inquired concerning what plants were suspected of being used, he found that
no one had a very clear idea."[29] Dr. Garden came to the conclusion that many of
the local cases of "poisoning" were actually other maladies.

It was not, however, an unfounded fear. Knowledge of poisons was the same
as knowledge of medicines; both were African specialties, and there were many

cases of terror by poison in the slave societies of the hemisphere, perhaps most notably the sorcerer-poisoner Makandal, counted as a foundational figure in Haitian political iconography. Regardless of whether the poisonings in Charles Town were real or imagined, they were vivid in white Charles Townians' imaginations, as was another perceived danger: the free black and enslaved tradesmen who formed Charles Town's artisan class had access to all sorts of potentially lethal objects. Alexander Hewatt wrote in 1779, and note the use of the word *breed*:

> From [enslaved] labourers in the field the colonies have perhaps less danger to dread, than from the number of tradesmen and mechanics in towns, and domestic slaves. Many negroes discover great capacities, and an amazing aptness for learning trades, where dangerous tools are used, and many owners, from motives of profit and advantage, breed them to be coopers, carpenters, bricklayers, smiths, and other trades.
>
> Out of mere ostentation the colonists also keep a number of them about their families, who attend their tables, and hear their conversation, which very often turns upon their own various arts, plots, and assassinations. From such open and imprudent conversation those domestics may no doubt take dangerous hints, which, on a fair opportunity, may be applied to their owners hurt.
>
> They have also easy access to fire arms, which gives them a double advantage for mischief. When they are of a passionate and revengeful disposition, such domestic slaves seldom want an opportunity of striking a sudden blow and avenging themselves, in case of ill usage, by killing or poisoning their owners. Such crimes have often been committed in the colonies, and punished; and there is reason to believe they have also frequently happened, when they have passed undiscovered. Prudence and self-preservation strongly dictate to the Carolineans the necessity of guarding against those dangers which arise from domestic slaves, many of whom are idle, cunning and deceitful.[30] (paragraphing added)

Out on the western edge of Anglo-American expansion, concerns were different. A 1772 panic in London's financial markets caused widespread hunger among the poor, triggering a translatlantic exodus of Scots, Irish, and so-called "Ulster Irish" or "Scotch-Irish," who, though often referred to simply as "Irish," were Scots from Northern Ireland. In South Carolina, the Scotch-Irish Presbyterians and the German immigrants of the rugged upcountry would have loved to have had the luxury of worrying about stamps and tea, let alone plantations full of slaves. Pillaging by bandits and annihilation by the natives were daily threats to them. They had no representation in the colonial legislature, nor were they under the protection of any state. Any policing they had, they did themselves by means of regulators, practicing vigilante justice.

South Carolina's Congress was in session in June 1775 when news of the first blood of Lexington arrived. The assembled oligarchs responded immediately; from the steps of the majestic building now known as the Old Exchange, they declared South Carolina to be the first independent provisional government. Henceforth Her Majesty's government was disregarded by Charles Town's political class, who considered this independence from Britain to be their second revolution, the first having been against the lords proprietors in 1719. Henry Laurens signed the document that created a thirteen-man Council of Safety and three committees: a General Committee; a Secret Committee of five persons with broad, vaguely defined powers; and a Special Committee, which was an extension of the Secret Committee and which had the repression of black people as its primary mission.

According to nineteenth-century South Carolina historian Edward McCrady, the rationale for the latter appears to have come from a private letter received from London, "intimating that a plan had been laid before the Royal government for instigating the negroes to insurrection, which seems to have been believed, and to have been regarded as more alarming because it was known that some of the negroes entertained the idea that the contest was for their emancipation. To meet, therefore, whatever might arise, a *Special Committee* was appointed to form such plans as they should think immediately necessary to be carried into execution 'for the security of the good people of the colony.' "[31] The Secret Committee also managed to tar and feather a couple of Roman Catholics, who, it was feared, might be in league with the "Negroes."[32]

Then came the edict that shocked the slaveowners, and made clear what was at stake for them.

"Hell itself could not have vomitted anything more black," wrote a Philadelphian in a letter published in the *Morning Chronicle and London Advertiser*.[33]

The proclamation by Lord Dunmore, the Scottish governor of Virginia, on November 5, 1775, read in pertinent part:

> I do hereby . . . declare all indented Servants, Negroes, or others, (appertaining to Rebels,) free that are able and willing to bear Arms, they joining His MAJESTY'S Troops as soon as may be, for the more speedily reducing this Colony to a proper Sense of their Duty.

I . . . declare all . . . Negroes . . . free. These were the words of slaveowners' nightmares. It did not apply to those enslaved by Loyalists. At least in theory, slaveholding colonists who were not taking up arms against the king had nothing to fear, because they could stay home and keep their slaves on lockdown. But those rebels who left their plantations to fight might first find their capital running away and then find themselves facing off against the very people they had brutalized, now with guns in their hands. The insurgents responded by raiding the plantations of those they demonized as "Tories," or Loyalists, and confiscating their slaves, who were put to military support work.

Dunmore had been thinking about this for a few years. In 1772, he had written:

> At present the Negroes are double the Number of white people in this Colony, which by the natural increase, and the great addition of new imported ones every year, is Sufficient to allarm not only this Colony, but all the Colonies of America . . . in case of War (which may probably often happen) with Spain, or indeed any other power . . . the people, with great reason tremble at the facility that an enemy would find in procuring such a body of men; attached by no tye to their Masters or to the Country . . . by which means a Conquest of this Country would inevitably be effected in a very Short time.[34]

By threatening to take away the Southerners' principal source of wealth, Dunmore's proclamation galvanized wavering elements of the white population of Virginia and South Carolina into supporting the "patriots," or, as the British called them, the "rebels," who defended the idea of enslaved property. The struggle against the British in the Southern colonies became profoundly identified with the struggle of the white population against emancipation of the black population. The newspapers printed rumors that Dunmore was paying the "savages" (Native Americans) in specie to attack. "We have a right to take up arms in self-defense," read a letter to the *Virginia Gazette*'s printer "Mr. Purdie" in the December 8 edition, "since we have been threatened with an *invasion* of *savages*, and an *insurrection* of *slaves*, and have had our *negroes* and *stocks* piratically taken from us."

Dunmore was obliged to flee, retreating offshore to a flotilla of more than a hundred vessels, where he remained while the enslaved flocked by the hundreds to seek the protection of the Union Jack. Dunmore needed them; reinforcements from Britain were not forthcoming, since for reasons inexplicable to him they were sent to North Carolina instead. Almost immediately, he formed what became known derisively as Lord Dunmore's Ethiopian Regiment. Their first skirmish was the Battle of Kemp's Landing, ten days after Dunmore's Proclamation, in which, as a correspondent for Purdie's *Virginia Gazette* wrote, "23 members of the *Scabby race* went as volunteers, with 200 regulars."[35] The British won the battle, with the result that Colonel Joseph Hutchings of the colonial militia was taken prisoner by one of his former slaves.

On December 14, the *Pennsylvania Evening Post* reported that: "Late last night, a gentlewoman, going along Second street, was insulted by a negro, near Christ church; and upon her reprimanding him for his rude behaviour, the fellow replied, "Stay you d----d white bitch, till lord Dunmore and his black regiment come, and then we will see who is to take the wall."

So it was that the rebels, patriots, insurgents, continentals, call them what you will, were at war with the British and those suspected of being loyal to them, most especially the "Negroes." An article in the March 22, 1776, issue of Purdie's *Virginia Gazette* demonstrates Dunmore's effectiveness at getting under the colonists' skins. Laden with racist scorn, the article not only notes the presence in Virginia of the balafon (a marimba-type mallet instrument known across a wide region of Africa), called in Virginia *barrafoo*, but implies that it was something familiar to the readership:*

> We hear that lord Dunmore's *Royal Regiment of Black Fusileers* is already
> recruited, with runaway and stolen negroes, to the formidable number of
> 80 effective men, who, after doing the drudgery of the day (such as acting
> as scullions, &C. on board the fleet) are ordered upon deck to perform the
> military exercise; and, to comply with their *native* warlike genius, instead
> of the drowsy drum and fife, will be gratified with the use of the sprightly
> and enlivening *barrafoo*, an instrument peculiarly adapted to the martial

---

*The indentured servant John Harrower described a "barrafou" in 1775: "The body of it is an oblong box with the mouth up & stands on four sticks put in bottom & cross the [top?] is laid 11 lose sticks upon [which?] [the player] beats." Harrower, 89.

tune of *"Hungry Niger, parch'd Corn!"* and which from henceforward is to be styled, by way of eminence, the BLACKBIRD MARCH.

The British used armed, emancipated former slaves who knew the terrain. The most prized defectors were pilots and navigators, masters of the marshy nooks and crannies in which they had been born and raised. Others were former African soldiers. In all cases, they were highly motivated in going to war against the masters they had escaped, who might kill them, torture them, or sell them away if they were recaptured. On the other side, in South Carolina and Georgia the independentists confiscated slaves from Loyalists and put them to work as military laborers. Patriot soldiers in Virginia, South Carolina, and Georgia were paid with slaves; according to Malcolm Bell Jr., in Georgia slaves were given "to public officials as salary, and were exchanged for provisions for use by military units."[36]

After a battle on December 29, 1778, the British took Savannah and held it until 1782, despite a thirty-two-day siege of the city that ended with a failed assault by French and American forces on October 18, 1779. Men of color had been serving as French soldiers on foreign missions since the beginning of French Antillean slavery, and the bloody siege of Savannah is rembered for the participation of the 750-man Chasseurs-Volontaires de Saint-Domingue, a free-black volunteer corps that provided about a third of the expedition's manpower, and in which, it is popularly believed (it may be true), future Haitian leader Henri Christophe served as a drummer boy.[37]

One sometimes reads that black soldiers fought on both sides in the War of Independence. That's technically correct, but misleading. Some did fight in Northern pro-independence regiments, but in the South, where most black people were, they ran away and joined the British if they could. Both sides used mercenaries and foreign troops: in 1780, there were more Americans fighting for the British than for the Continental Army, including a number of formerly enslaved African Americans.

In the War of Independence, as in every other conflict involving slave societies, the constant potential for slave insurrection was taken into account in every military calculation. In the plantation societies, more than anywhere else, the war between Britain and the colonists was a revolutionary war—at least on the part of the formerly enslaved black soldiers, who were fighting with the British against the slaveowning Patriots for their liberty.

21

The General
Inconvenience

*sold Sandy to Col. Chas Lewis for £100. paiable in June. from which deduct
£9.4.8 my present debt with him; leaves £90.15.4. to be received.*[1]

   —Thomas Jefferson, Memorandum Book, January 29, 1773

PATRICK HENRY WAS BY accounts a good fiddler, a singer of tavern-ballads,
and an engaging character. Jefferson, who first encountered him in 1760 when
Henry's store had failed, recalled that "his manners had something of coarseness
in them; his passion was music, dancing, and pleasantry. He excelled in the latter, and it attached everyone to him."[2] A slaveowning tobacco planter and a sedi-
tious orator, Henry strikingly personifies the fundamental paradox of the early
American experience: how liberty could be intimately bound up with slavery.

  "Give me liberty, or give me death!" Henry's hyperdramatic, rhetorical ulti-
matum, the most popular and durable slogan of the independence movement,
subsequently venerated as patriotic scripture, was in support of what was basically his own declaration of war against Britain, arguing in favor of placing the
entire state on an emergency mobilization. Henry's speech has been widely credited with moving Virginia to declare independence from Britain. It took place, so
we are told (though there is no contemporary record of it), on March 20, 1775,
from the third pew of the left central section of St. John's Church in Richmond.

  Hoping to avoid escalation of hostilities, the pro-American Irish statesman
Edmund Burke warned in a speech given in London two days after Henry's peroration that "in Virginia and the Carolinas they have a vast multitude of slaves

Interior of St. John's Church, Richmond, June 2013.

. . . these people of the southern colonies are much more strongly, and with a higher and more stubborn spirit, attached to liberty, than those to the northward . . . such will be all masters of slaves, who are not slaves themselves. In such a people, the haughtiness of domination combines with the spirit of freedom, fortifies it, and renders it invincible."[3]

It required five weeks minimum, and often much longer, for a message to travel from America to England, so Burke's speech was not a direct response to Henry, but his words described Henry perfectly. Henry's polemical evocations of liberty and slavery were framed by his concrete, daily experience of denying the most basic freedoms to an entire community of people over whom his word was law, and who lived in misery at his grudging expense.

Henry's famous line was reworked from Joseph Addison's *Cato*, a play the founders of the American republic knew well. Written in 1712 and published the following year, *Cato* might be understood as a parable: Britain, once a vassal of the Roman Empire, was now the center of an empire modeled on Rome. Addison's sober neoclassical tragedy of liberty versus tyranny was set in Mediterranean North Africa, with Roman exiles as the heroes. The word "Africa" is heard frequently in the mouths of the actors in *Cato*, perhaps for its resonant value, though the play is ambiguous about it. By Addison's time, London coffeehouses were getting coffee from Martinique; the transformation that African labor in the colonies had wrought in the metropolitan economy lurked offstage as well as on. The African character, Juba, is a figure out of history: the king of Numidia

(Algeria), then under the control of the Carthaginians. When Juba wants the hand of Cato's daughter, Marcia, Cato responds with a nonanswer to his request: "It is not now time to talk of aught / But chains or conquest, liberty or death."

Arguably the most politically consequential play in the history of British theater, *Cato* was carefully bipartisan and scrupulously inoffensive. At its premiere, Whigs and Tories competed to applaud the loudest at the mention of the word "liberty." To be a patriot, a son of liberty, a free man and not a slave—that was a British oratorical legacy, imperial in scope and carried over to the colonies. In England, writes Bernard Bailyn, "a flood of what has been called 'Whig panegyric verse' . . . poured from the presses from 1700 to 1760 and . . . echoed from the stage in play after play . . . No writer, however famous or obscure, could afford to neglect the theme of British liberty and power."[4]

The Americans saw themselves as Cato's conspirators, called to sacrifice against a British Caesar. The first professional theater companies in the colonies performed *Cato*. Excerpts of its soliloquies were printed in colonial newspapers.[5] It was staged by students at William and Mary College. Benjamin Franklin could recite chunks of it from memory. Its line "What a pity it is / That we can die but once to serve our country" proved inspirational for the martyred Nathan Hale. George Washington, who saw *Cato* various times, referred to it in letters and had it performed near the front lines at Valley Forge on May 11, 1778, within earshot of the British troops.[6]

There's a good reason modern audiences have not seen *Cato*: it's not Shakespeare. Today it would seem stiff, stilted, and interminable. A celebration of stoicism in the face of tyranny, it lacks complex characters. Cato is noble and good; Caesar, the villain, is an unseen oppressor who has no part in the drama. Amateur theatrics were popular in the isolation of plantation Virginia, and *Cato* was, writes Jane Carson, "a favorite vehicle for amateurs because it requires little acting ability; the characters simply strike an attitude and declaim noble sentiments in high-flowing oratory."[7]

Patrick Henry was something of a "ham actor," notes biographer George F. Willison, and as he gave his riveting oration in Richmond, he dramatized it.[8] Not that we know exactly what he said: unlike Jefferson, who even as president declined to speak in public but left us a massive record of his thought in written form, Henry's most famous words live today only as hand-me-downs. There is no contemporaneous transcription of the full text; what follows, likely assembled from the recollection of jurist St. George Tucker, was published seventeen years after Henry's death:[9]

It is vain, Sir, to extenuate the matter. Gentlemen may cry peace, peace; but there is no peace. The war is actually begun! . . .

Is life so dear, or peace so sweet, as to be purchased at the price of chains and slavery?

Forbid it, Almighty God!

I know not what course others may take. But as for me—give me liberty, or give me death!

When Henry shouted "Give me liberty!" he paused for effect, and poised a letter opener in his right hand, pointed at his chest—an ivory letter opener, a product of Africa. When he said "or give me death!" he thumped his right hand containing the letter opener of death against his breast, as if stabbing himself. John Roane, who was present, recalled that "When he said, 'Is life so dear, or peace so sweet, as to be purchased at the price of chains and slavery?' he stood in the attitude of a condemned galley slave, loaded with fetters, awaiting his doom. His form was bowed, his wrists were crossed, his manacles almost visible."[10]

Patrick Henry knew what a manacled slave looked like. He had received six people as a wedding present from his father-in-law, and later sold them to raise money to set himself up in an ill-fated storekeeping venture. For that matter, slaves were routinely sold in front of the Virginia House of Burgesses in Williamsburg, where a fair-weather auction outside would have been audible through the open windows of the building.

Henry's bound-slave gesture can be read as an example of how the struggle for independence from Britain branded itself as a "revolution" against "tyranny." To judge from the writings and recorded speeches of the self-proclaimed Patriots, they were obsessed with slavery, as per a New York protest of 1770, typical of the genre: "The Right of a People to tax themselves is essential to their Liberty; and the Power of imposing Taxes on them, when exercised by others, subjects that People to the most abject Slavery."[11] The word "slave" turns up repeatedly in their discourse, as the essence of what they would never allow themselves to become. This was nothing new: describing those in opposition to oneself in terms of slavery and freedom was an ingrained English trope of at least two centuries by then, heard routinely from the pulpit in the sermons of every denomination.

Henry's liberty-or-death message carried the clear blame-the-victim implication that those who submitted to slavery were unworthy of liberty. The protest against Britain thus doubled as a taunt at the colonists' enslaved laborers. It was a libel routinely asserted against African Americans: that they were complicit in their degradation.

Meanwhile, the use of *slavery* as a political fighting word continued in use in England as well. "Shall our fate be national bankruptcy, poverty, oppression and slavery?" asked a 1772 London pamphlet castigating the East India Company.[12] Looking at a dismal future as a colony, in which their sole purpose would be to enrich Britain, the wealthy North American colonial elite saw an analogy with the way the slave only existed for the benefit of the master. But the word "slavery" did not only compel colonials as an abstract metaphor; the Americans brought something different to the use of the term. For those who were born into full-fledged slave society as masters, some of their most profound, complex, and unrestrained relationships were with their slaves.

Patrick Henry owned slaves when he was a sermonizing radical, and he owned them when he was the first governor of independent Virginia, where he was second in popularity only to George Washington. Like other liberty-loving Virginians, he bewailed the necessity of having slaves. Henry acknowledged the contradiction in a 1773 letter to his Virginia planter friend Robert Pleasants. A devout Quaker, Pleasants had educated and freed his slaves at an enormous personal cost of £5,000 (more than $700,000 in 2014 dollars) and had sent Henry an antislavery book. "Would anyone believe," asked Henry rhetorically, "I am master of slaves of my own purchase? I am drawn along by the general inconvenience of living here without them. I will not, I cannot, justify it." This was, it should be emphasized, in a private letter; there is no record of his expressing such sentiments publicly. "I believe a time will come," the letter continued, "when an opportunity will be offered to abolish this lamentable evil . . . I could say many things on this subject, a serious view of which gives a gloomy perspective to future times."[13]

His gloomy perspective was well-founded. The general inconvenience of living without slaves would have meant not merely having to empty one's own slop jar. It would have meant not living on the capital they embodied. Ending slavery would have required a different kind of revolution than the one Henry championed.

The liberty Patrick Henry was willing to trade for death (not his own martyrdom, as it turned out; others did the dying) was, as his other discourses and letters bear out, the freedom to own—which inescapably meant the freedom to breed and sell—slaves. Henry's revolution did nothing to change slaves' status as chattel or creditors' valuation of them as collateral. Whether or not Henry believed, as he wrote to Pleasants, that the time for abolition would someday come, he clearly believed it had not come yet, and he worked to delay it until long after his generation had departed.

Henry argued against freeing slaves even as he dramatized the evil of slavery. "Slavery is detested," he wrote in a letter. "We feel its fatal effects, — we deplore it with all the pity of humanity . . . we ought to lament and deplore the necessity of holding our fellow-men in bondage. But is it practicable, by any human means, to liberate them without producing the most dreadful and ruinous consequences?"[14]

Was it practicable? It would indeed have been possible to free the slaves voluntarily. Thousands of slaveowners did, including Robert Pleasants, in some cases because they got religion and in others simply because they despised the slave system they had been born into as hereditary slaveowners. But it was not "practicable"—not because, as Henry, Jefferson, and most other slaveowners assumed, freeing the slaves would unleash the criminality they believed was inherent in the enslaved, but because to do so would have made their former owners poor.

To manumit one's slaves was to make a ruinous financial sacrifice. Without slaves, Virginia would be destitute; with them, she was the wealthiest of the states. With slavery having been built into the deepest levels of the colonial Virginia economy during the seventeenth century, there was no way to get rid of it by Patrick Henry's time, short of all of the slaveowners voluntarily impoverishing themselves. The historical record amply demonstrates that most slaveowners were not only not willing to do this, but would hurl the poorer class of their society against cannonballs first.

That the War of Independence resulted in the strengthening, not the termination, of slavery was not an unexpected outcome for Southerners: protecting slavery had been the point of the war for them. It was the principal Southern political goal at every moment until slavery was destroyed.

"Here's to the next insurrection of negroes in the West Indies," said the proudly anti-American Dr. Samuel Johnson as he offered a toast at Oxford.[15] In a thirteen-thousand-word pamphlet called *Taxation No Tyranny* that mocked the inflated rhetoric of the colonists in the last days before war, he wrote in the spring of 1775, "How is it we hear the loudest yelps for liberty from the drivers of Negroes?"

Patrick Henry, the loudest of all the voices for liberty, was the perfect example of the colonists being caricatured by Johnson, though no one who heard
Henry orate ever described his voice as a "yelp." Dr. Johnson continued his essay
by proposing to arm the colonists' slaves:

> It has been proposed, that the slaves should be set free, an act, which,
> surely, the lovers of liberty cannot but commend. If they are furnished
> with firearms for defence, and utensils for husbandry, and settled in some
> simple form of government within the country, they may be more grateful
> and honest than their masters.

As Dr. Johnson knew full well, though the colonial tax protestors might feel
emboldened to stand up to London, their more serious threat came from closer
to home. After Dunmore's proclamation, which put the idea espoused by Dr.
Johnson into practice, enslaved people in Virginia began voting with their feet.

By December 23, 1775, Henry was writing Edmund Pendleton, who as
president of the Virginia Committee of Safety was Virginia's highest-ranking
official, from Williamsburg: "SIR: I have the pleasure to inform you . . . that we
have taken a Vessel of the Govt. bound to the Eastern shore for provisions, commanded by Capt. Collett & manned with 16 Negroes."[16] Not only the "Govt.,"
but "Negroes," were Henry's enemies in war. The enslaved overwhelmingly sided
not with Henry's vision of liberty, which was their slavery, but with the British
who offered them freedom.

The paradox of liberty versus slavery at the nation's birth is no paradox at all.
Liberty was the right to property. Slaves were property. Liberty for slaveowners
meant slavery for slaves.

Viewed from the slaveowners' perspective, liberty *was* slavery. It was made
much easier by—indeed, almost required—believing something that resonated
with the Calvinist doctrine of predestination: those who were enslaved were
those who were naturally inferior. God had made them that way for a reason,
and they were easy to visually identify.

In Thomas Jefferson's celebrated reworking of George Mason's "all men are by
nature equally free and independent" into the catchier, more deistic "all men
are created equal," the thirty-three-year-old Virginian was not envisioning a
republic in which Barack Obama would be president. In Jefferson's society, black

people did not have the legal status as people—"personhood," we call it now—that Lord Mansfield had acknowledged in the *Somerset* case.

The later pro-slavery propagandists of the Confederacy were right in insisting that, like them, Jefferson did not intend those words to mean "all men." This is not merely a statement about Jefferson's psychology; there was an existing framework for interpretation of the phrase. When George Mason wrote his version of the phrase as part of the preamble to a new Virginia constitution, it met with objections from planters, who saw it as an incitation to slave rebellion. Donald L. Robinson writes: "Defenders of Mason's language replied that the clause could not have this effect because it did not apply to Negroes, since Negroes were not 'constituent members' of the society being formed."[17] Nor did anyone think it applied to Native Americans. "All men" did not mean *all* men, any more than it meant women, but it was a politically useful phrase, since those opposed to slavery could read into it what they wanted.

In drafting the document (his authorship of it was generally not known at the time), Jefferson needed to please the French, who wanted a political commitment on the Americans' part before they in turn would commit to an overt war against Britain in America yet again, after having gotten kicked off the continent not twenty years before. Though Britain's naval power was supreme, its army boasted nowhere near the manpower of France's, which was the largest in Europe.

Nor, despite the citation of it fourscore and seven years later in Lincoln's Gettysburg Address, was Jefferson declaring the existence of a new nation. The Declaration announced the birth of, in Garry Wills's words, "not one country, but thirteen separate ones" that were forced to form a "league" in order to attract foreign aid for the war they were fighting together.[18]

Jefferson's document was not the legal declaration of independence; that had been made by the Continental Congress on July 2, with the passage of the Virginian Richard Henry Lee's resolution that "these United Colonies" were "free and independent states," and note the plural.[19] Jefferson's Declaration, which took on a mythical glow with the passage of years, announced the passage of Lee's resolution. The French participation in the American uprising took two more years to codify, in the commercial treaty of February 6, 1778.

Despite Jefferson's expressed misgivings about slavery during his early years and his frequently quoted bits of antislavery-sounding rhetoric and philosophical reflection, his actions make it clear where he stood on the subject in practical terms: African Americans in republican Virginia were property, period. He did his best to sound like a French *philosophe* when he inserted that word: life, liberty and the pursuit of . . . *happiness.* But whether Jefferson's captives, whom he described as laboring for his "Happiness," lived at his mountaintop prison of Monticello or on one of his other parcels of land, they had no right even to keep their own children, though they were mostly allowed to.[20] Nor did Jefferson at any time express any intention of ultimately extending the franchise to them, ever.

In his draft of the Declaration, Jefferson included a complaint against the king for the slave trade:

> he has waged cruel war against human nature itself, violating it's most sacred rights of life & liberty in the persons of a distant people who never offended him, captivating & carrying them into slavery in another hemisphere, or to incur miserable death in their transportation thither. this piratical warfare, the opprobrium of infidel powers, is the warfare of the CHRISTIAN king of Great Britain. determined to keep open a market where MEN should be bought & sold, he has prostituted his negative for suppressing every legislative attempt to prohibit or to restrain this execrable commerce . . .

Then he evoked the terrorism of Lord Dunmore:

> and that this assemblage of horrors might want no fact of distinguished die, he is now exciting those very people to rise in arms among us, and to purchase that liberty of which he had deprived them, & murdering the people upon whom he also obtruded them: thus paying off former crimes committed against the liberties of one people, with crimes which he urges them to commit against the lives of another.[21]

It was slickly done. The slaveowner denied all American agency in slavery. He threw all the blame for the slave trade on Britain, thereby exonerating the slave-ship captains of Rhode Island, the many slave dealers throughout the colonies, and the eager buyers who patronized slave sales. The slave trade was an easy target: it was genuinely unpopular, and not only for its sheer ugliness. The traffic to North America was mostly conducted by British ships, with a corresponding loss of profit to Americans. It was out of the control of colonial legislatures, which at times wanted to regulate the supply of Africans on the market by shutting it off. Every slave ship lowered the resale value of slaves already in the colonies, and Virginia already had an oversupply. The arrival of so many Africans was terrifying to the nonslaveowning majority of whites, who tended to see them the way they were generally portrayed in the political discourse of the day, as a socially destabilizing and potentially violent element.

Though Jefferson cloaked his complaint in "moral dress" (Robinson's term), it was a complaint against the African slave trade, not against slavery itself; but the section was struck out at the insistence of the congressmen from South Carolina and Georgia, who were not against the slave trade at all.[22]

While Jefferson was a member of the Virginia House of Delegates between 1776 and 1779, he obtained a prohibition of the slave trade into the state—but, tellingly, not out of it. One of his best-known achievements of those years was his successful campaign to end the aristocratic institutions of primogeniture (the first son received the entire inheritance) and entail (landholdings could not be broken up) in Virginia. Georgia was the first state to ban primogeniture and entail entirely, in its constitution of 1777; all the other states prohibited them as well. Though these institutions were not vigorously in force in Virginia at the time of their prohibition, abolishing primogeniture and entail was unquestionably a democratizing move—for whites. But the resulting distribution of land among more men of the family (and thus the franchise, for only men of property could vote) meant breaking up more black families, who were divided up along with the estate.

Jefferson biographer Dumas Malone recalled in 1967 his conversation with "a traditional Virginia lady more than forty years ago. This *grande dame* began by asserting that 'Mr. Jefferson undermined the family.' Her reference was to the abolition of entails and primogeniture, which were supposed to safeguard family estates and family lines. Continuing, she said, 'he wrecked the church,' the reference being to the disestablishment in Virginia shortly after the American Revolution. 'In fact,' she triumphantly concluded, 'the only decent institution he left us was slavery.' "[23]

This flurry of lawmaking could have proceeded along a different line than it did. The Virginia delegates did not throw out the established body of law and create a new one from scratch; instead, they retained and modified the existing law regarding slavery. John Quincy Adams commented retrospectively on the process in 1831:

> The principle of setting aside the whole code of their legislation would of itself have emancipated all their slaves. In renovating their code, they must have restored slavery after having abolished it; they must have assumed to themselves all the odium of establishing it as a positive institution, directly in the face of all the principles they had proclaimed. . . .

> It was easier to abolish the law of primogeniture . . . the bill on the subject of slaves was a mere digest of the existing laws respecting them, without any intimation of a plan for a future and general emancipation. . . . Mr. Jefferson contents himself with a posthumous prophecy that [emancipation] must soon come, or that worse will follow.[24]

Partus sequitur ventrem came through the Revolution intact, as did the rest of Virginia law regarding slaves, all of which had been made by the Virginia House of Burgesses and none of which was British law.

When Patrick Henry was governor of Virginia, at war in 1777, he signed a bill written by Jefferson to regulate and discipline the militia. Every free man in Virginia was expected to join it, including indentured servants and free men of color, with a list of exceptions (professors at William and Mary, for example). Jefferson stipulated that "the free mulattoes in the said companies or battalions shall be employed as drummers, fifers, or pioneers," which meant that men of color were to be required to participate in combat, but were not to have guns.[25]

Lord Dunmore had offered freedom to the enslaved, and military commissions, but the best Jefferson could do was to put free people of color on a battlefield as "pioneers." That word may evoke covered wagons to some, but its prior military use meant those who went out in front of the army to dig trenches, one of the most dangerous of positions. *Pioneer* is etymologically related to *pawn* and to *peon*, and roughly synonymous with the French military term *avant-garde*. Virginia's militia, according to Jefferson, was to be an all-white force except for the musicians and the free black avant-garde, who would not have weapons to defend themselves with.

Writing from Charlottesville on January 20, 1779, Thomas Anburey, a lieutenant in the British army who kept an extensive journal and who was clearly not a sympathetic observer, described in detail the typical Virginia planter as an idle character, then went on to outline the work day:

> It is the poor negroes who alone work hard, and I am sorry to say, fare hard. Incredible is the fatigue which the poor wretches undergo, and that nature should be able to support it; there certainly must be something in their constitutions, as well as their color, different from us, that enables them to endure it.

They are called up at day break, and seldom allowed to swallow a mouthful of homminy, or hoe cake, but are drawn out into the field immediately, where they continue at hard labour, without intermission, till noon, when they go to their dinners, and are seldom allowed an hour for that purpose; their meals consist of homminy and salt, and if their master is a man of humanity, touched by the finer feelings of love and sensibility, he allows them twice a week a little fat skimmed milk, rusty bacon, or salt herring, to relish this miserable and scanty fare. The man at this plantation, in lieu of these, grants his negroes an acre of ground, and all Saturday afternoon to raise grain and poultry for themselves. After they have dined, they return to labor in the field, until dusk in the evening; here one naturally imagines the daily labor of these poor creatures was over, not so, they repair to the tobacco houses, where each has a task of stripping allotted which takes them up some hours, or else they have such a quantity of Indian corn to husk, and if they neglect it, are tied up in the morning, and receive a number of lashes from those unfeeling monsters, the overseers, whose masters suffer them to exercise their brutal authority without constraint. Thus by their night task, it is late in the evening before these poor creatures return to their second scanty meal, and the time taken up at it encroaches upon their hours of sleep, which for refreshment of food and sleep together can never be reckoned to exceed eight.

When they lay themselves down to rest, their comforts are equally miserable and limited, for they sleep on a bench, or on the ground, with an old scanty blanket, which serves them at once for bed and covering, their cloathing is not less wretched, consisting of a shirt and trowsers of coarse, thin, hard, hempen stuff, in the Summer, with an addition of a very coarse woollen jacket, breeches and shoes in Winter. But since the war, their masters, for they cannot get the cloathing as usual, suffer them to go in rags, and many in a state of nudity.

The female slaves share labor and repose just in the same manner, except a few who are term'd house negroes, and are employed in household drudgery.

These poor creatures are all submission to injuries and insults, and are obliged to be passive, nor dare they resist or defend themselves if attacked, without the smallest provocation, by a white person.[26]

In 1779 at the urging of Jefferson, who had at this time been elected governor of Virginia, the state's capital was moved inland from Williamsburg to

Richmond—farther away from Washington's home turf and closer to Jefferson's. In the first days of 1780, Jefferson and his family fled Richmond for Monticello—his wife Martha Wayles Jefferson had an infant in her arms—to escape Benedict Arnold's troops as they entered the new capital.

The British began a victorious forty-day siege of Charles Town on March 5, 1780, and after the city surrendered en masse, they occupied the city until the end of 1782, almost three years, with an army whose ranks included—to the white population's great discomfort—armed black men. Escaped slaves came to occupied Charles Town to seek refuge.

Lord Charles Cornwallis invaded Virginia in 1781, plundering and bringing liberated slaves along in an entourage that was larger than any town in Virginia, but from there, he went directly on to defeat at Yorktown. During that invasion, shortly after Jefferson's term as governor expired, the Jeffersons—Martha was pregnant—fled the British again, this time from their home in Monticello, to escape a troop led by Cornwallis's Lieutenant Colonel Banastre "Bloody" Tarleton. Adding to the insult, Cornwallis used Monticello as a base for a few days while the Jeffersons hid.

It was as close to being in combat as Jefferson ever came, unless you count peering through the Venetian blinds of his carriage in the streets of Paris in 1789.[27] He was subsequently called on to defend his alleged cowardice as governor in a formal proceeding, which Jefferson believed to have been instigated by Patrick Henry. Sixteen years later, when Jefferson was running for president against John Adams, his nemesis Alexander Hamilton wrote mockingly (and pseudonymously) of the occasion that the "governor of the ancient dominion dwindled into the poor, timid philosopher and, instead of rallying his brave countrymen, he fled for safety from a few light-horsemen and shamefully abandoned his trust."[28]

But then, Hamilton was a bona fide war hero. Born illegitimate in Charlestown, the capital of the tiny Antillean island of Nevis, he had distinguished himself in active military service during the long War of Independence, serving as Washington's aide-de-camp during the horrendous winter at Valley Forge. Rising through war, in 1780 he married one of the most eligible rich young women in New York—Elizabeth Schuyler, a slaveowner.

In April 1780, George Washington received word that Louis XVI was sending six thousand troops in ten ships of the line* and thirty transports, with one of France's most distinguished generals, Jean-Baptiste-Donatien de Vimeur,

---

*Ships of the line were large, heavily armed vessels that, in battle, formed a line.

Comte de Rochambeau, at the head, all to be placed under Washington's command. Financed via Havana, the white-uniformed French troops, who tripled the size of the US army, paid for their purchases in gold and silver, endearing them to local merchants.[29] Virginia was grateful to Louis XVI, and on May 1, Governor Jefferson signed the Virginia General Assembly's charter for a new port town: Louisville, on the Ohio River in the part of Virginia that would become Kentucky.*

French cannon, dated 1761, on the grounds of Yorktown battlefield, June 2013.

In the late days of the war, there were various plans and proposals to arm black regiments, as in Maryland in 1781, when Charles Carroll of Carrollton wrote his father indicating he would not oppose such a measure: "nothing but the exigency of the occasion, & the total want of money can excuse such hars[h] & violent measures."[30] Henry Laurens tried to act as though he were taking seriously his son John's proposal for a black regiment in South Carolina, but no such plan came to fruition.

One of the decisive battles of the War of Independence was not fought by Americans at all. The Battle of the Capes was a days-long encounter at sea between François Joseph Paul de Grasse's French fleet—whose expedition was financed by a substantial loan from Havana, because Spain also had an interest in defeating the British—and Sir Thomas Graves's smaller British fleet.[31] Beginning September 5, 1781, the French blockade at the mouth of the Chesapeake resulted in the British Navy's withdrawal to New York, cutting off Cornwallis and his army from escape by sea.

The decisive assault of the Siege of Yorktown, the storming of the redoubts with bayonets on October 19, was accomplished by two stealth groups of four hundred handpicked troops that included black troops from the Rhode Island Regiment on one side, commanded by Alexander Hamilton, and a French team on the other. Once the redoubts had been attacked, two columns attacked the British: George Washington led the left column, and Rochambeau the right. In that decisive campaign against the British, French soldiers formed the majority of those on the battlefield.

---

*Kentucky was entirely occupied by Native Americans until the first settlement at Harrod's Town, later Harrodsburg, on a surveying expedition ordered by Lord Dunmore in 1774.

About half of the British forces were sick with malaria. Cornwallis abandoned the escaped slaves in his train, many of whom were dying. Jefferson noted
that besides destroying his crops and livestock, Cornwallis "carried off also about
30. Slaves," 27 of whom he believed had died "from the small pox & putrid fever
then raging in his camp."[32] He and his compatriots expected idemnification
from the British for their property.

The Americans' southern flank in the war was covered by Louisiana's Spanish governor, the general Bernardo de Gálvez, who led a group that took back
West Florida (Mobile), though not East Florida (Pensacola), for Spain. A number of Gálvez's troops were black—battalions of *pardos* and *morenos* constituted
about a third of Spain's fighting force in the Americas generally—and a number
of them were what might fairly be called Cubans, though a distinct Cuban
national identity did not yet exist.

Negotiations for war's end began in April 1782, culminating in the signing
in November 1783 of the Treaty of Paris. The British side of the negotiations
was led by the man George III believed the "fittest Instrument for the renewal
of . . . friendly intercourse": the slave trader Richard Oswald, who had lived in
Virginia and unlike most other Britons had a realistic notion of what America
and the Americans were like.[33] Oswald seems to have been chosen in part because
of his acceptability to American negotiator Benjamin Franklin, to say nothing of
another American negotiator, Oswald's former factor Henry Laurens, who arrived
late in the process. Oswald allowed his old friend to insert at the last moment a
clause prohibiting the "carrying away any Negroes or other property of the American Inhabitants." When the treaty was ratified by the Confederation Congress in
Annapolis in 1784, Laurens was its president.

Among its other accomplishments, the Treaty of Paris retroceded East Florida from Britain to Spain; Oswald knew from experience that Florida was, in
Laurens's words, "a Paradise from whose Bourn no Money e'er returns."[34] Africans had been imported to Florida as plantation slaves during twenty years of
British rule, and during the War of Independence the territory had been a haven
for Loyalist planters fleeing the war with their slaves. Now it would be Spanish again, and again San Agustín could be a haven for the escaped enslaved of
Georgia and Carolina.

Though the Treaty forebade the carrying away of human property, Sir Guy
Carleton, the Irish commander-in-chief of British forces in North America, considered that those who had crossed behind British lines were free, and as soon
as the spring weather of 1783 permitted, he began a flotilla that between April

and November took some three thousand of Britain's black allies to Nova Scotia, beyond the reach of re-enslavement. Their names were recorded in a document called *The Book of Negroes*; descendants still live in Canada, mostly in Halifax. But life was difficult in Nova Scotia, and more than twelve hundred of them went on to Sierra Leone in 1792.

Other black soldiers opted for military careers in the Black Carolina Corps, formally organized in 1779. A career outfit, it was evacuated to Jamaica following the defeat at Yorktown in 1781. Its success spurred the further Africanization of Britain's army in the Caribbean, leading in 1795 to the creation of the West India Regiment—a standing infantry of free black and enslaved soldiers. In order to fill out its ranks, the British army on occasion resorted to buying African captives off the slave ships and putting them to work as soldiers. Buying some 13,400 slaves for this purpose between 1795 and 1808, at the considerable cost of about £925,000, the British government became one of the largest customers of the same African trade that many in Parliament were working to abolish.[35]

As peace negotiations got under way, some French aristocrats remained in North America, where they were the toast of society. The Marquis de Chastellux, a major general at Yorktown under Rochambeau, took Jefferson up on his invitation to visit him at Monticello in April 1782, where Jefferson was living in what he said was retirement from public affairs. Chastellux remained at Monticello for four days with his entourage of ten, six of whom were servants.[36]

Martha Wayles Jefferson had to provide hospitality for them. She had been pregnant almost constantly for ten years, throughout the war, and though she was, in Chastellux's description, "amiable," she was in the habit of retiring early and seems to have been depressed, as she was, in Chastellux's words, "expecting her confinement at any moment" in the pregnancy that would finally kill her. Chastellux and Jefferson stayed up after Mrs. Jefferson had gone to bed, talking about, among other topics, their mutual enthusiasm for the poems of Ossian— about which, more later.

Martha gave birth in May for the last time, and died in September. Jefferson, who attended her for four months continually as she declined, was prostrate with grief on his wife's death. This has provided a dramatic scene in many Jefferson biographies, though his obvious agency in her repeated pregnancies has often gone circumspectly unmentioned.

There is no clue in Jefferson's papers that he saw himself as playing any part in his wife's death through continual impregnation in the face of her continually weakening condition, despite Jefferson's clear awareness of the mechanics of sexual reproduction. Nor was Jefferson unaware of what we now call family planning, as per his description of Native American women in *Notes on the State of Virginia*: "The women very frequently attending the men in their parties of war and of hunting, child-bearing becomes extremely inconvenient to them. It is said, therefore, that they have learnt the practice of procuring abortion by the use of some vegetable; and that it even extends to prevent conception for a considerable time after."[37]

Let us be clear that we are not guilty of the present-day bugaboo of "presentism" by noting that women in Jefferson's day were expected to be pregnant constantly. Our point is to call attention to the difference between the mindset of Jefferson's world and that of ours: it was commonly considered women's duty to produce babies nonstop, whether it killed them or not. We differ, however, with the interpretation offered by Jon Meacham, who suggests that Martha Wayles Jefferson's fatal continuum of pregnancy (Meacham suggests she may also have had tuberculosis) was evidence of "no shortage of physical passion between them."[38] We propose an alternate interpretation: that her repeated, debilitating pregnancies might be evidence that a dutiful wife had no right to say no.

On her deathbed, according to the later recollections of the enslaved women who attended her while dying, she exacted an oath from Jefferson never to remarry, which would have compromised their daughters' inheritance. But we don't know what Martha Wayles Jefferson thought, confined to die in her bed on that isolated mountaintop. Jefferson, so conscious of his own immortality through writing, burned her letters, thus erasing her voice from historical memory. We have not even a picture of her.

The forlorn widower returned to public life, accepting the appointment to serve the presidentless, moneyless American Confederation as US Minister Plenipotentiary—basically, the trade representative—to France in 1784, where he remained until 1789. John Adams, who unlike Jefferson was an experienced diplomat, performed the same function in London.

Chastellux, who helped get Jefferson's daughter Patsy into a good school in Paris, published in 1786 an account of his travels that helped promote the Jefferson mystique in France—an early flash of the enduring legend of the mountaintop sage of Monticello. In it, he noted the abject condition of Virginia's poor whites and connected it to the Virginia slaveowners' desire for "increase":

Humanity [suffers] from the state of poverty in which a great number of white people live in Virginia. It is in this state, for the first time since I crossed the sea, that I have seen poor people. For, among these rich plantations where the Negro alone is wretched, one often finds miserable huts inhabited by whites, whose wane looks and ragged garments bespeak poverty. . . . I have since learned that all these useless lands and those immense estates, with which Virginia is still covered, have their proprietors. Nothing is more common than to see them possessing five or six thousand acres of land, but exploiting only as much of it as their Negroes can cultivate. Yet they will not give away or even sell the smallest portion of it, because they are attached to their possessions and always hope to eventually increase the numbers of their Negroes.[39]

In Paris, where printing was much cheaper than in America, Jefferson in 1785 privately published *Notes on the State of Virginia*, first drafted in 1781 as an answer on the part of Virginia to a questionnaire put to the various states by François de Barbé-Marbois, the secretary of the French legation to the United States. The only book Jefferson ever published, it was intended to pitch the wonders of his state to the wealthy French. Jefferson printed two hundred copies privately and semi-anonymously (the author was "M. [Monsieur] J***") for individual distribution in elite circles only. When he sent one to James Madison, he wrote, perhaps disingenuously, "I shall only send over a very few copies to particular friends in confidence and burn the rest . . . in no case do I propose to admit them to go to the public at large."[40] But they did.

A French bookseller who acquired a copy after its owner unexpectedly died jobbed it out to a "hireling translator" and published it in French in 1786. The book was favorably reviewed in the *Mercure de France*, who proclaimed the barely anonymous author a *philosophe*. Jefferson, who disliked the translation, then allowed his English version to be published in London the following year.

In composing what amounted to an intellectual investment prospectus for the state he represented, Jefferson faced the problem of having to explain to the French why the enslaved of his country would never be freed. Most of his friends in France were abolitionists who expected the postrevolutionary United States to bring slavery to an end. But Jefferson's Virginia countrymen overwhelmingly had no intention of ever freeing their slaves and thus losing their property, and were touchy about the issue.

Jefferson did not make the true argument, which would have been that he and all his relatives, friends, and constituents would be paupers without slaves.

Rather, his justification was that the "negro" was inferior—something he seems to have truly believed—and moreover dangerous, and therefore had to be kept in a state of slavery for everybody's good. This problem, as Jefferson insisted throughout his career, was due not to the greed of the colonists themselves, but to British insistence on imposing slavery on the colonies in the first place, leaving the wealthy of Virginia no choice, so went the story, but to soldier on with their white man's burden of ever-increasing human property.

It's not an oversimplification to say that Jefferson despised blackness. The most inflammatory quote from *Notes* has been frequently reprinted in recent years after being largely overlooked, and we too will include it for purposes of clarity, with apologies to the reader:

> [T]he difference [of "the negro"] is fixed in nature, and is as real as if its seat and cause were better known to us. And is this difference of no importance? Is it not the foundation of a greater or less share of beauty in the two races? Are not the fine mixtures of red and white, the expressions of every passion by greater or less suffusions of color in the one preferable to that eternal monotony, which reigns in the countenances, that immovable veil of black which covers the emotions of the other race? Add to these, flowing hair, a more elegant symmetry of form, their own judgment in favor of the whites, declared by their preference of them, as uniformly as is the preference of the Oranootan for the black woman over those of his own species.[41]

With his evocation of "the Oranootan" copulating with black women, Jefferson provides an early instance of the fundamental racist trope that Felipe Smith calls the ape libel.[42] Because "negroes" were an inferior "race," Jefferson argued, they could not be freed. To do so would require their immediate deportation, he insisted, in order to avoid the amalgamation that would stain the purity he detected in the white "race":

> This unfortunate difference of colour, and perhaps of faculty, is a powerful obstacle to the emancipation of these people . . . The [Roman] slave, when made free, might mix with, without staining the blood of his master. But with us [in America] a second is necessary, unknown to history. When freed, he is to be removed beyond the reach of mixture.[43]

The notion of "racism" did not yet exist; the French term *racisme* was coined in the late nineteenth century. But if this call to maintain purity of blood is not racism, the word has no meaning. James Madison, who never freed any of his slaves in life or death, was a racist of the same stripe, who believed abolition impossible because of "the physical peculiarities of those held in bondage, which preclude their incorporation with the white population."[44]

With *Notes of the State of Virginia*, Jefferson definitively established himself as a founding theorist of white supremacy in America, laying out in condensed form key points of racialized thought that pro-slavery writers would consistently reaffirm and that would echo in the cant of modern day white supremacists. He linked his ideas to a deportation scheme that was, in effect, a foolproof way to avoid ending slavery, though he didn't package it like that. Quite the contrary: he pitched his impossible project as the only way slavery could be ended.

Jefferson insisted that manumission required the immediate deportation of the emancipated. This would be necessary, Jefferson explained, in order to avoid "convulsions which will probably never end but in the extermination of the one or the other race."[45] To avoid this conjectured race war of annihilation, emancipation required what is now called ethnic cleansing: Jefferson stamped that demand with a founder's seal and a philosopher's sigh.

The reviewer for the *Mercure* waxed enthusiastic about Jefferson's solution for the problem of slavery. That Jefferson would consider emancipation under *any* circumstances and would speak badly of slavery, even in abstract terms, was enough to trip the hair-trigger anger of many American slaveowners, which is perhaps why he had wanted to keep the book off the general market. It cost him some political support, especially in South Carolina.

Jefferson's plan was to deport flotillas of black youth, in wave after wave, year after year. He would "by degrees, send the whole of that population from among us," until the "race" itself was gone, and simultaneously replace them with white immigrant laborers—a plan for total removal that did not acknowledge the presence in the United States of free people of color. In *Notes on the State of Virginia*, he proposed:

> that they should continue with their parents to a certain age, then be brought up, at the public expence, to tillage, arts or sciences, according to their geniusses, till the females should be eighteen, and the males twenty-one years of age, when they should be colonized to such place as the circumstances of the time should render most proper, sending them out with arms, implements of household and of the handicraft arts, feeds, pairs of the useful domestic animals, &c. to declare them a free and independant people, and extend to them our alliance and protection, till they shall have acquired strength; and to send vessels at the same time to other parts of

the world for an equal number of white inhabitants; to induce whom to migrate hither, proper encouragements were to be proposed.[46]

To better understand what Jefferson had in mind, we flash forward to a February 4, 1824, letter he wrote to Jared Sparks, the Unitarian minister who published the *North American Review*. In it, the eighty-year-old Jefferson outlined a scheme for accomplishing the "colonization" that would rid the United States of its proliferating African Americans once and for all, before they got any more numerous, and proposed a timetable for accomplishing the expulsion of about a sixth of the nation's population:

there are in the US. a million and a half of people of colour in slavery. to send off the whole of these at once nobody conceives to be practicable for us, or expedient for them. let us take 25. years for it's accomplishment, within which time they will be doubled. their estimated value as property, in the first place, (for actual property has been lawfully vested in that form, and who can lawfully take it from the possessors?) at an average of 200.D. each, young and old, would amount to 600. millions of Dollars, which must be paid or lost by somebody.[47]

Jefferson went on to propose the creation of a fund, financed by the sale of western lands, for purchasing infants on the cheap, raising them as wards of the state, and deporting them—to "St. Domingo" (he did not ever use the name "Haiti"). But, he suggested:

the estimated value of the new-born infant is so low, (say 12 ½ Dollars) that it would probably be yielded by the owner gratis, and would thus reduce the 600,000,000 millions [*sic*] of Dollars, the first head of expence, to 37 millions & a half. leaving only the expense of nourishment while with the mother, and of transportation.[48]

Jefferson calculated that though it would take twenty-five years to accomplish the entire project, by the last nine years, the number of "breeders" (he used the word) would have diminished considerably. He imagined a fleet of fifty vessels recursively sailing away full of black youth and coming back empty for more until every last one of *them* was gone:

suppose the whole annual increase to be of 60 thousand effective births, 50 vessels of 400 tons burthen each, constantly employed in that short run, would carry off the increase of every year, & the old stock would die off in the ordinary course of nature, lessening from the commencement until it's final disappearance. in this way no violation of private right is proposed.[49]

The "private right" Jefferson was talking about was, of course, that of all those men who were created equal. Black people did not have "private right." But separating them from their children was not all that bad, thought Jefferson, because, as he explained in *Notes*,

> Their griefs are transient. Those numberless afflictions, which render it doubtful whether heaven has given life to us in mercy or in wrath, are less felt, and sooner forgotten with them. In general, their existence appears to participate more of sensation than reflection.[50]

This was the classic rationalization for minimizing the damage caused by systematically destroying African American families, and it was a libel: being simple creatures, they'd get over it. Accordingly, Jefferson concluded his letter to Sparks: "The separation of infants from their mothers . . . would produce some scruples of humanity. But this would be straining at a gnat, and swallowing a camel."[51]

Were the United States not purged of its black people soon, Jefferson warned Sparks, the demographics guaranteed armed slave resistance: "A million and a half are within [slaveowners'] control; but six millions, (which a majority of those now living will see them attain,) and one million of these fighting men, will say, 'we will not go.'" This did in fact happen, though the numbers were different: there were four million enslaved African Americans in 1860, not six million; and there were officially 186,097 soldiers and sailors who fought in the US Army and Navy against the Confederacy, in effect saying, "we will not go."

Confiscate all African American children from their mothers and ship them off to thrive or die: *that* was Jefferson's vision of a final solution for the Negro problem. Presumably such a massive expulsion as Jefferson contemplated would have required a fully totalitarian state apparatus to implement, and would have resulted in the death of many of the deported; mortality rates were high in the few miserable "colonization" attempts that were made.

Jefferson had not suddenly gone mad in his dotage. This had been his idea all along, as he explained to Sparks: "This was the result of my reflections on the subject five and forty years ago, and I have never yet been able to conceive any other practicable plan. It was sketched in the Notes on Virginia, under the fourteenth query."[52] If this kind of massive deportation couldn't be achieved, he insisted throughout his career, emancipation could not take place. This conviction would be strengthened by the Haitian Revolution that erupted in 1791 and by Gabriel's unenacted rebellion of 1800, and would be taken as gospel by pro-slavery Southerners. It would spur the founding of the American Colonization Society, whose ostensible mission was to deport all free people of color.

Having outlined the "physical" reason for exile in *Notes*, Jefferson proceeded to the "moral" reason, pursuant to which he described a long list of inferiorities attributed to "them," which we will not quote here. This was perfectly in line with the thinking of many European intellectuals. Citing David Hume, the leading light of the Scottish Enlightenment, Immanuel Kant had written in *Observations on the Feeling of the Beautiful and the Sublime* (1764) that "The Negroes of Africa have by nature no feeling that arises above the trifling. Mr. Hume challenges anyone to cite a single example in which a Negro has shown talents and asserts that among the hundreds of thousands of blacks who are transported elsewhere from their countries [etc] . . . "[53] But the point was less urgent to Kant, whose wealth did not consist of black people, than to Jefferson and Madison.

A mere seventy-five years later, as Southern states left the Union, pro-secessionist radicals argued to their unconvinced countrymen some of the same points as Jefferson's: the "negro" was inferior and not the equal of whites; emancipation would result in a race war to the death, or in the purity of the white race being sullied by the horror of mongrelization; and slaveowners' property rights must be respected.

There was, however, a solution of sorts to the perceived problem of black overpopulation, and it was highly profitable: if Virginia's black people could not be emancipated and deported, they could be sold away into the new territories.

All the states had prohibited the African slave trade by the time non-importation cut off exterior commerce during the independence struggle, so Africans had not been entering the colonies for years. With independence achieved, South Carolina and Georgia, whose labor forces had massively taken flight or died, reopened their slave trades. As Charles Town's slave market boomed, it changed its name in 1783 to the less regal Charleston. According to James McMillin, "between 1783 and 1787 nearly one hundred Charleston merchants handled slave sales ranging from one person to cargoes of more than four hundred Africans."[54] But there was soon a glut on the market as slavers from multiple territories, most numerously

British but also from Rhode Island, tried to get in on the action, depressing point-of-sale prices in America and raising point-of-supply prices in Africa.

The slave trade continued being a cash business for the captains who brought in the cargoes, so an intermediate class of British factors—still very much active in the independent republic—brokered the sales to the planters on easy terms, with up to two years to pay.[55] Though some of the factors became wealthy, there wasn't much money coming into the territory. The large market for American indigo died with independence, never to return, because Britain ended the subsidy that had made it profitable. The rice economy recovered only slowly.

A boom in slave sales meant a debt problem as well. The eagerness of planters to buy slaves drained the supply of specie from the economy, and many individuals were carrying excessive debt burdens. "The great quantity of negroes now pouring in upon us, occasions every planter to wish an increase of his stock," said Thomas Bee before the South Carolina Enquiry into the State of the Republic in 1785. "The sight of a negroe yard was to[o] great a temptation for a planter to withstand, he could not leave it without purchasing; in short, there seemed to be a rage for negroes, without any consideration how they were to be paid for."[56] Then Charleston's economy crashed, and in 1787, drowning in debt, the South Carolina legislature prohibited slave importation after a spirited debate.

South Carolina's closure of the foreign slave trade increased the traffic to Georgia, where the trade remained open until 1798, with an illicit trade continuing afterward.[57] More Africans entered Georgia after independence than before, but not so many as the planters would have liked: less credit was available to Georgia planters from merchants, so the state's economy incurred less of a debt burden than it might have, but since less labor was imported, production came back only slowly. During Georgia's period of importation, two revolutionary developments charted the nation's course:

In Philadelphia, the Constitution. In Savannah, the sawtooth cotton gin.

22

The Fugue of Silences

Mr. Madison thought it wrong to admit in the Constitution the idea that there could be property in men.[1]

—from James Madison's notes, August 22, 1787

The bargain between freedom and slavery contained in the Constitution of the United States is morally and politically vicious . . . The consequence has been that this slave representation has governed the Union.[2]

—John Quincy Adams, 1820

LIKE THE FUGUES OF J. S. Bach (1685–1750), the United States Constitution is an exemplary eighteenth-century machine. Like the Bible, it has been taken as scripture by those who imbue it with mystical authority.

Negotiated and agreed on in 1787 at Philadelphia, ratified the following year, and effective as of March 4, 1789, with a ten-amendment Bill of Rights that became effective December 15, 1791, the Constitution is synonymous with the American republic. It prescribes a carefully contrived system of representation that regulates our national life to this day.

It's the oldest constitution in effect among the world's nations today, and the hardest to amend. It's remarkably terse, which has contributed to its enduring quality. The later constitutions of some other nations go on for dozens or even hundreds of articles, making promises that cannot be achieved and specifying points of law rather than general principles, with the result that they have to be rewritten at intervals.

Anecdotal evidence would suggest that many twenty-first-century Americans confuse the Constitution, which is the source of US law and was largely drafted by James Madison, with the more poetic Declaration of Independence, which has no legal force and was drafted by Thomas Jefferson. The president swears to uphold the former, but not the latter.

There is much that the Constitution does not do. It does not state that all men are created equal, nor does it guarantee life, liberty, and the pursuit of happiness. It does not create a democracy; *democracy* was a dirty word, synonymous with mob rule, when the Constitution was written. With seven articles and ten amendments that have grown to twenty-seven, the US Constitution is a carefully composed fugue of silences that stipulates and limits government's powers.

Until the adoption of the Thirteenth Amendment on December 6, 1865, the Constitution did not prevent individuals from enslaving or trading in the enslavement of other individuals. Its rhetorical discretion was noted at the time by the Philadelphia physician and Declaration of Independence signer Dr. Benjamin Rush, a cofounder of the first American abolitionist society, who sarcastically wrote, "No mention was made of *negroes* or *slaves* in this constitution, only because it was thought the very words would contaminate the glorious fabric of American liberty and government."[3]

The silences went beyond euphemism. As ratified in 1788, the Constitution neither explicitly prohibited nor permitted slavery, but merely acknowledged its existence as a fact, without even naming it or defining it. But by means of that acknowledgment and its otherwise careful limitation of powers, it gave tacit permission to the long-established practice of enslavement.

The Constitution implied that there was a class of people—persons "held to service"—for whom rights might not apply. It nowhere suggested that enslaved people had any rights at all. It left the way clear for state and local government, and, in practice, for individual slaveowners and slave traders, to construct the world enslaved people would live in.

We are slaves to Britain! the rebels had shouted. It had been absurd for slaveowners to complain they were being subjected to "slavery," but it was the strongest, loudest thing they could say, the most potent word in their political lexicon, the most extreme rhetoric they could deploy. When it came time to write their Constitution, however, the word *slavery* vanished from the vocabulary, as had the word *negro*, though there was a considerable body of states' law dealing with "negroes," which the Constitution left untouched.

In its strategic silence, the Constitution perhaps resembled that genre of painting so popular in the parlors of the eighteenth-century plantocracy, as described in John Michael Vlach's *The Planter's Prospect*. These canvases, which provided bread and butter for skilled American painters, typically depict a static scene organized around an accurately rendered vision of the grand mansion. A pink, chubby, perfectly dressed family poses in front, on their expansive grounds, perhaps with topiary hedges.

No one is seen working in the idealized plantations of these paintings, though in reality these places were never still but were run by squadrons of slaves. There is nothing in the images to indicate how such a complex system might actually run, or who actually did the work, or what the work was—not so much as a child with a watering can—let alone who did the hard offstage agricultural labor that paid for it all.

We see no one singing in these paintings, nor are there fiddles, banjos, or bones players. These paintings are lattices of silence. Black people are entirely absent from this visual representation of a life that depended at every moment not merely on their labor, but also on their skills.

The enslaved workers who made it all run were as absent from the Constitution as they were from the paintings.

As we have emphasized, slavery is a central fact of American history, not a sidebar. Nor, despite the textual silence, was it a sidebar issue to the Constitution. In devising a national government and a system of representation, the Constitution created lasting political institutions. But the major sticking point was cutting a deal over slavery. How to compromise on an issue about which there could be no compromise? How to speak of a human right to own other people as property? How to stipulate the freedom to enslave?

And there was a problem that would only get worse: how to work constructively with violence-prone countrymen who became instantly belligerent the moment slavery was criticized, or even mentioned?

As early as 1775, John Adams had argued the need for the North American colonies to "set up a Republican government, something like that of Holland."[4]

Upon independence, the former colonists did not form a new nation called America, though that subsequently became its de facto common name, as if the rest of the Americas did not exist. Borrowing a nomenclatural model from the Dutch United Provinces—whose emblem, a lion with nine arrows representing nine provinces in his paw, is echoed in the thirteen arrows in the talons of the eagle in the great seal—they were the United States. They were a crazy-quilt confederation with distinct histories of governance and political identities, and nowhere more so than in the states' differing approaches to slavery.

A collection of individual, independently functioning states would inevitably work at competitive cross-purposes with each other, and would lead to currency wars, tariff wars, even shooting wars. The Articles of Confederation governing the thirteen ex-colonies' alliance had failed. State banks each issued their own money, which complicated interstate commerce considerably. There was no provision to raise funds to run a national government. Against the background of a sharp credit squeeze, Shays' Rebellion—an armed antitax and anti-debt revolt by disaffected elements in rural Massachusetts, including many unpaid war veterans from mid-1786 to mid-1787—pointed up the need for a stronger government to repress insurrections, as well as to find a mechanism for settling the war debts. Jefferson, who was in Paris and thus in no danger from Shays' Rebellion, applauded it from afar, prompting his remark so beloved of the twenty-first-century far right: "What signify a few lives lost in a century or two? The tree of liberty must be refreshed from time to time with the blood of patriots and tyrants."[5]

Meanwhile, a continuing external military threat imperiled American shipping and provided ample potential for conflict—especially with Britain, which did not in practice recognize American sovereignty on the high seas. Spain was in control of the Gulf Coast from Florida to Texas, and of all of Mexico and Cuba. With Indian attacks and slave rebellion as constant worries, a common defense was necessary. Or, to look at it from another perspective: a substantial military force would be needed if the United States was to seize neighboring territory, as South Carolina's elite hoped to do in expanding their empire of slavery, and as some acquisitive New Englanders hoped to do with Canada, which had declined to declare independence as the fourteenth colony.

The most memorable achievement of the Congress of the Confederation was the poorly drafted Northwest Ordinance, which formally annexed the territory northwest of the Ohio River. It allowed for the settling of present-day Ohio (which became the seventeenth state in 1803), Indiana (the nineteenth, in 1816), Illinois (twenty-first, 1818), Michigan (twenty-sixth, 1837), Wisconsin (thirtieth, 1848), and part of Minnesota (thirty-second, 1858). Britain had restricted immigration to these territories in 1763, following the end of the Seven Years' War, to the frustration of would-be settlers, especially those who had participated in military action against the French and Indians to keep the territory in British hands.

Article VI of the Ordinance provided that "There shall be neither slavery nor involuntary servitude in the said territory otherwise than in the punishment of crimes, whereof the party shall have been duly convicted"—a phrase that would echo in the Thirteenth Amendment of 1865. This was notwithstanding the fact that there were already slaveholders in the territory, but it provided for no enforcement, and there was in any case no federal government to speak of under the Articles of Confederation. The ordinance seemed to confirm the admissibility of slavery south of the Ohio, and it even contained a fugitive slave clause, the first appearance of that explosive notion in American law.[6]

Article VI was inserted at the last minute in the proceedings by Nathan Dane of Massachusetts, with no prior discussion of slavery and no debate.[7] It's something of a mystery exactly why and how this happened. The immediate model for Article VI was the Land Ordinance of 1784, which provided a mechanism for new states in the Western territories previously claimed by New York and Virginia to enter the United States upon attaining a population of twenty thousand free inhabitants.* The Land Ordinance was largely drafted by Jefferson, who wanted to name the new states Cherronesus, Metropotamia, Saratoga, Polypotamia, Illinoia, Assenisippia, Michigania, and Sylvania, and who, four years before the publication of *Notes*, already had his eye on possible territories where emancipated black people could be deported. His draft contained a clause prohibiting all slavery in the new territories after 1800, and though that clause was removed at the behest of delegates from farther south, it included a significant exception that echoes down to the twenty-first century: convict labor would be permitted. The Land Ordinance has been pointed to as Jefferson's principal attempt at taking any kind of antislavery action (as opposed to rhetoric); if so, it was also his last. It can also be seen as establishing the template for the ruinous competition for territorial expansion between free-soil North and slavery South. With its language regarding convicts, it might also be interpreted as the first faint stroke of a uniquely American regime of carceral labor.

No slaves were freed as a result of the Northwest Ordinance, and once the Constitution was adopted, it no longer had legal force. Its major long-range impact seems to have been discouraging the immigration of slaveholders to the Northwest as a new, non-slave system began to assert itself there. The free Northwest of Ohio and beyond became a magnet for European immigration

---

*Raised to sixty thousand in the Northwest Ordinance.

and a bulwark of antislavery politics; it was the region from which Lincoln, Grant, and Sherman emerged.

The die was cast, then, for a larger country divided into free and slave states. The ordinance was approved on Friday, July 13, 1787, which was also the day that at the Constitutional Convention in Philadelphia enslaved people were transformed into political capital.

The story of the Constitution's making in 1787 has been told any number of ways, typically suffused with a cue-the-kettledrums aura of religiosity and an assumption of American triumphalism. Constitutional historians have tended to portray their subject as the most important political document in world history, in the greatest nation in history. In extreme cases this has involved elevating the framers to a sort of secular sainthood, as in the post-Reagan years, when a school of constitutional interpretation called "originalism" emerged in American jurisprudence. Most prominently associated with archconservative Supreme Court Justice Antonin Scalia, originalism is a fundamentalist movement that seeks in effect to construe the Constitution as static and unchanging by mind-reading the intentions of the presumably divinely inspired Framers—a word Scalia writes with a capital F, the way they did it in the eighteenth century. His opinions are shot through with variations on phrases like: "The Framers recognized . . . ," "The Framers contemplated . . . ," "The Framers viewed . . . ," and "The Framers' experience . . ."[8] This is a peculiarly subjective lens through which to view a document created by so many people, at such sharp cross-purposes with each other.

"Aware that the South would not join a Union that prohibited slavery," writes Scalia's generally dissenting colleague, Supreme Court Justice Stephen Breyer, who does not capitalize "framers," "the framers in effect postponed the question of slavery's continued existence by writing into the Constitution a series of compromises."[9] But if we were to follow the notion of original intent from the point of view of the South Carolina Framers, we would see the Constitution as protecting the right to own and trade in slaves.

The deliberations for the Constitution began on May 14, 1787, before most of the delegates had arrived. They were done in secret, behind closed doors, with the press excluded. The official minutes were poor, so historians have to rely largely on the nightly recaps written by policy wonk and principal drafter James Madison while many of the other framers were busy drinking.

Slaveowners were on the defensive. When Vermont broke away from New York during the War of Independence to become an independent republic from 1777 to 1791, its constitution abolished slavery outright—the first such constitutional prohibition in the Americas. In 1783, a judicial decision interpreted the 1780 constitution of Massachusetts as abolishing slavery. Pennsylvania, Connecticut, and New Hampshire had all introduced phase-outs. Even Jefferson, in drafting a radical new constitution for Virginia in 1783—it was not even considered, much less adopted—had proposed: "The General assembly shall not have the power to . . . permit the introduction of any more slaves to reside in this state, or the continuance of slavery beyond the generation which shall be living on the 31st day of December 1800; all persons born after that day being hereby declared free."

Even so, white supremacy was assumed. Washington, who chaired the Convention, brought his lifelong personal manservant Billy Lee. Madison, perhaps fearing a runaway, did not bring any of his slaves to attend him in Philadelphia, but his fellow Virginian George Mason brought at least two of his more than three hundred slaves.[10]

To achieve the truce that the Constitution represented, it had to be, and was, a pro-slavery document.[11] It was made such largely at the insistence of South Carolina but done with the acquiescence of all. South Carolina's delegates to the Constitutional Convention supported a strong national government as long as they entered it on the most advantageous terms possible. The Lower South had suffered from foreign occupation during the War of Independence more than anywhere else. South Carolina and Georgia were militarily the weakest of the colonies, in no small part because so much of their population, being enslaved, was motivated to fight for the slaveowner's enemy; slaveowners remained at home to suppress slave rebellion and defection rather than fight.

Exposed on its southern flank to Spanish Florida, vulnerable to Indian attack and to slave uprisings, South Carolina needed the protection of a larger entity that could provide its defense. But even so, South Carolina's delegates were determined to protect slavery and the African slave trade, and they arrived ready to walk if they didn't get what they wanted.

Virginia—the largest, most populous, and wealthiest state—took the lead at the Convention. Delegate James Madison had seized the advantage in the constitutional negotiations by arriving first with a draft all prepared. His "Virginia Plan" was put forth on May 29 by Virginia governor Edmund Randolph, the American-born son of an English aristocrat and an aide to Washington during the War of Independence.

"Many of the delegates were stunned," writes Richard Beeman, "by the revolutionary character of the proposal so boldly laid before them."[12] Madison's plan radically reshaped the structure of what until then had been a weak confederacy into a national government that would be superior to the states. With Beeman's choice of the word "revolutionary," he places the accent of revolution where John Adams would have placed it—not on the military act of separating from a colonial master, but squarely on the civilian idea of making thirteen competing states into one self-governing republic.

This had not been the grand design everyone was working toward in the long, grinding civil war by which the colonies obtained independence from Britain. The wealthy rebels in each colony had seen themselves as leaders of sovereign states, not provincial officials of a larger entity. Subordination to a federal republic would take power away from them personally, and from their—note the word again—states.

Immediately the question arose of how states would be represented in this supra-state government. The Virginia Plan proposed two ways the "rights of suffrage" could be calculated: they would be "proportioned to the Quotas of contribution"—that is, they would get votes based on how much in taxes each state put into the kitty—"or to the number of free inhabitants, as the one or the other rule may seem best in different cases."

Population or wealth—whichever way it went, Virginia was on top. South Carolina definitively favored voting based on wealth. Max Farrand's compilation of the existing deliberation records reads:

> Gov. Rutledge [John Rutledge, of South Carolina] moved . . . that the proportion of representation ought to be according to and in proportion to the contribution of each state.
> Mr. Butler [Pierce Butler, of South Carolina] supported the motion, by observing that money is strength; and every state ought to have its weight in the national council in proportion to the quantity it possesses.[13]

Wealth as the direct basis for apportioning political representation: now *that's* original intent. As incorporated via the three-fifths clause, it sought to make the new nation into a plutocracy. The Constitution, in somewhat veiled form, made the idea of voting wealth structural to the new nation, capitalizing the enslaved as a way to do so, even as the colonies' transformation into a constitutional republic enhanced the resale value of the Chesapeake's enslaved population.

According to James Madison's notes:

On the motion of Mr. [Edmund] Randolph, the vote of saturday last authorizing the Legislre. to adjust from time to time, the representation upon the principles of *wealth* & numbers of inhabitants was reconsidered by common consent in order to strike out "Wealth" and adjust the resolution to that requiring periodical revisions according to the number of whites & three fifths of the blacks.

Madison also noted the response by Gouverneur Morris of New York:

A distinction had been set up & urged, between the Nn. & Southn. States. . . . Southern gentlemen will not be satisfied unless they see the way open to their gaining a majority in the public Councils. . . . If the Southn. States get the power into their hands, and be joined as they will be with the interior Country they will inevitably bring on a war with Spain for the Mississippi. This language is already held. The interior Country having no property nor interest exposed on the sea, will be little affected by such a war. He wished to know what security the Northn. & middle States will have agst. this danger.

Pierce Butler retorted, "The security the Southn. States want is that their negroes may not be taken from them which some gentlemen within or without doors, have a very good mind to do."[14]

When we speak of the Framers, we do not often speak of Founding Father Pierce Butler, who in a show of unconvincing modesty in a letter to a friend wrote that he had "some small part in frameing" the document.[15] Though he was a South Carolina delegate, the very wealthy absentee plantation owner lived, attended by his slaves, in his Philadelphia mansion. In the four-man South Carolina delegation, he was the number-two eminence behind the state's governor, John Rutledge, whose nickname was "Dictator John." One of the eight foreign-born of the fifty-five delegates to the Constitutional Convention, and one of the Constitution's thirty-nine signers, Butler pushed the limit in the negotiations to safeguard slavery.

Butler took a few pages of notes at the Convention, on the final page of which he—surely reflecting the tedium of the proceedings—doodled and drew cartoons, preserved today as part of the documentation of the framing of the Constitution. An opinionated, theatrical debater, Butler wore a powdered wig, a velvet neckcloth with a silver buckle, and a gold-laced coat as he delivered outspoken orations calculated to provoke.[16] He was a proponent of a strong national government, an electoral college system, and slavery.

To placate the Carolinians, the Scottish-born Pennsylvania delegate James Wilson proposed a compromise of sorts, one that took advantage of the prestidigitation of turning people into property. His proposal substituted for the phrase "quotas of contribution" the language that became known as the "three-fifths" clause, allowing slaveholding states to be represented based on three-fifths of their enslaved inhabitants. The measure was immediately seconded by South Carolina's Charles Pinckney, who in a previous plan had been the first to suggest a three-fifths figure.

The only compromise South Carolina made was that they didn't get to vote on behalf of 100 percent of their enslaved inhabitants, only 60 percent of them. Butler wanted to hold out for 100 percent representation. But neither was

Pierce Butler: Notebook from the Constitutional Convention, last page. Philadelphia, 30 May 1787–16 July 1787.

three-fifths an arbitrary formula; Pinckney knew it was the maximum the South could get away with. The three-fifths clause did not mean, as some have complained, that the enslaved were considered only three-fifths human. Politically, the enslaved were zero-fifths human. The three-fifths clause was a politically acceptable accounting gimmick for figuring out how much to rig the national vote on behalf of slaveholders, and it distorted political realities in the United States for as long as slavery lasted.

Earlier in this volume we have spoken of slaves as money. With the three-fifths clause, we might consider that, at least in one sense, the transformation of slaves into money was complete. To recapitulate:

Condition One, *medium of exchange*: from their first appearance in the colonies, slaves had been exchanged for anything money could buy, and moreover were a fundamental part of the collateral that numerous distinct credit systems were based on.

Condition Two, *retains its value*: by virtue of owning descendants in perpetuity, slave property did not die, but had eternal life the way real estate or gold does, and even provided an annual increase to counter interest and inflation (though the inclusion of slaves in the monetary system contributed to inflation). More simply: if people are money, children are interest.

And Condition Three: slaves were now *units of account* for what was literally political capital. At the level of national politics, the South voted its wealth, and that wealth was slaves, quantified and multiplied by three-fifths. Thanks to the demands of the South Carolinians, the slaveowners' privilege of voting their collective human wealth was enshrined into the Constitution. Though based on population, the three-fifths clause was explicitly understood to be a way of basing voting power on wealth—but only one kind of wealth: slaves.

No other region's principal form of wealth was taken as a basis for representation. Massachusetts delegate Elbridge Gerry bristled that "The idea of property ought not to be the rule of representation. Blacks are property, and are used to the southward as horses and cattle are to the northward; and why should their representation be increased to the southward on account of the number of slaves, than horses or oxen to the north?"[17]

Wilson's pragmatic purpose in proposing the three-fifths clause was to enlist the large slaveholding states in resolving the large state / small state debate and thereby break up the logjam that had divided the convention along the lines of those two blocs. Rhode Island, the smallest state, had boycotted the convention. The holdout was Connecticut, whose delegates ultimately proposed the formula that gave the United States its Senate—the American analog of the House of Lords, with two votes per state—and, corresponding to the House of Commons, a lower House of Representatives, based on population and, unlike senators, directly elected. The result of this compromise is that today a vote in Wyoming (pop. 563,626 in the 2010 census) has more national influence than one in, say, New York (pop. 19,378,102).

The balance of free versus slave states would prove an even thornier issue than the size of the states. There were seven mostly free states, assuming Rhode Island was in (slavery still existed in some Northern states, but not in large numbers), and there were six slave states (Delaware, Maryland, Virginia, North Carolina, South Carolina, Georgia). They would each get two senators, tilting the balance toward the free states.

But the South would get extra weighting in the House of Representatives and a guarantee that they could import more, and since the House of Representatives was the only body authorized to initiate budget legislation, the South had disproportionate power in that as well. South Carolina's three-fifths weighting also gave it disproportionate clout in the presidential selection process, via the electoral college's arbitrary formula of adding the number of senators and representatives to make the number of presidential electors. It was an enduring compromise: the Confederate Constitution retained the three-fifths clause in 1861.

In looking at the Constitution from the point of view of South Carolina, we are not attempting to reduce the many varied interests and motives of the new nation to those of the most politically extreme state, nor to deny the crosscurrents of opinion in every territory. But in order to understand what subsequently happened, it is necessary to understand the Constitution according to South Carolina's original intent: all slavery, all the time, and if you don't like it, you are the enemy.

A national government, announced Pierce Butler to the Constitutional Convention, "was instituted principally for the protection of property."[18]

It was Butler who proposed the fugitive slave clause to the Constitution (and took credit for writing it, though he probably did not), something that had not existed in the Articles of Confederation.[19] The immediate background for it was a 1783 Massachusetts court case that freed ten slaves out of thirty-four abducted four years previously from South Carolina plantations by an invading British privateer. The privateer had in turn been captured by a Spanish vessel (at the time allied with American independence), then recaptured by the British, and finally taken over by American warships and brought into Boston. When the Massachusetts court freed the ten enslaved men who had not yet been returned to South Carolina four years later, there was a hue and cry from down south.

Full protection of fugitive property, in Massachusetts or anywhere in the nation, was on the list of South Carolina's nonnegotiable demands at the Constitutional Convention. All the delegates knew that full well, which is perhaps why no one opposed Butler's fugitive slave clause. There is no record of any delegate—not Franklin, Madison, Mason, nobody—objecting to it. Reworded by the committee chaired by the antislavery Gouverneur Morris before being incorporated, it read in the evasive language characteristic of the Constitution regarding slavery:

> No Person held to Service or Labour in one State, under the Laws thereof, escaping into another, shall, in Consequence of any Law or Regulation therein, be discharged from such Service or Labour, but shall be delivered up on Claim of the Party to whom such Service or Labour may be due.

The fact of acknowledging the existence of a "person held to service" gave constitutional permission for the existence of slavery. Of the various clauses protecting slavery in the Constitution, the fugitive slave clause was the only one that required non-slave states to be proactive in enforcing it, and it implied that no state could prohibit slavery entirely on its terrain. It gave rise to the Fugitive Slave Act of 1793, and then to the Fugitive Slave Act of 1850 and the subsequent *Dred Scott* decision (1857) that accelerated the nation's downward spiral to war. By then, posses of people-snatchers were abducting free blacks from the North to sell them down South.

The fugitive slave clause meant that no state could become a haven for marronage. There was, however, still such a haven to South Carolina's southern flank in Spanish-controlled East Florida. To take that out would require a strong national government; South Carolina was incapable of doing it alone. So much manpower was needed to repress the black majority of South Carolina that little was available for external military ventures.

The most important non-mention of slavery in the Constitution from our point of view is one of the least-known by the general public, the first paragraph of Article One, Section Nine, which we take the liberty of reproducing for a second time:

The Migration or Importation of such Persons as any of the States now existing shall think proper to admit, shall not be prohibited by the Congress prior
to the Year one thousand eight hundred and eight, but a tax or duty may
be imposed on such Importation, not exceeding ten dollars for each Person.

Though vaguely enough worded that "importation of persons" could apply
to indentured servants, it was a twenty-year guarantee that the African slave
trade could not be banned or prohibitively dutied. (No one ever figured out
what the framers meant by "Migration.") It did not mean that the slave trade
would have to be prohibited as of 1808; it meant that the slave trade could not
be prohibited by the federal government before then.

The "importation of persons" clause is singularly out of place in the Constitution. It's the sort of thing that would normally be the subject of legislation,
concerned as it was with then-current conditions. But its presence in the Constitution made the twenty-year guarantee of being able to reopen the slave trade in
some sense structural to the new nation.

In practice, South Carolina merchants didn't want importation to be open
at that time. The same South Carolina legislature that sent four delegates to the
Constitutional Convention to argue for the protection of the slave trade in 1787
also voted to suspend South Carolina's slave trades, both foreign and interstate,
for three years, though they subsequently changed their mind about the interstate trade the following year.

South Carolina's legislature, home to the most practiced slave-dealers in the
thirteen colonies, turned the spigot of the foreign and domestic slave trades on
and off as market conditions dictated, though not without tremendous clashes of
internal interests in the process.[20] Seesawing between prohibiting and facilitating the foreign trade was partly due to the fluctuations of intrastate labor politics. Charleston and the Lowcountry coastal gentry, who controlled the South
Carolina legislature, had plenty of slaves. It was the new settlers out west who
wanted more of them. The black-to-white ratio in the Lowcountry was 3:1, but
upcountry it was 1:4; the Lowcountry was twelve times as black as upcountry.[21]
If an African trade were to dump vast numbers of new Africans onto the market,
the cash value of Lowcountry planters' human capital would drop. It would only
make sense for them to allow the African trade if there was a vast new market
opening up that South Carolina could not supply with its own slaves, but could
service via importation and re-exportation.

The question was taken up at the Constitutional Convention on August 21,
1787. Such records as we have of the debate over this measure, as summarized

by James Madison and more vaguely by the Constitutional Convention's bad note-taker James McHenry, make clear that everyone understood the stakes of prohibiting or permitting the foreign slave trade. According to Madison's summary, Rutledge of South Carolina put it bluntly: "Religion & humanity had nothing to do with this question—Interest alone is the governing principle with Nations—The true question at present is whether the Southn. States shall or shall not be parties to the Union."[22]

By this point, the three-fifths clause had been approved. With that in hand, the four South Carolina delegates drove home their right to expand their disproportionate franchise with all the Africans they could import. They backed their demand with the ever-present threat to walk, insisting that, as South Carolina's Charles Pinckney put it, "South Carolina can never receive the plan if it prohibits the slave trade. In every proposed extension of the powers of Congress, that State has expressly & watchfully excepted that of meddling with the importation of negroes."[23]

Georgia was South Carolina's ally in this; Virginia, on the other hand, was an adversary to South Carolina in this showdown, with Maryland as Virginia's ally. Continuing importation of Africans would do nothing to profit Virginia slaveowners; quite the contrary. George Mason made a speech whose fire burns through Madison's paraphrase, beginning with the standard disclaimer that "this infernal trafic originated in the avarice of British Merchants. The British Govt. constantly checked the attempts of Virginia to put a stop to it." That said, he went on to point out that "the evil of having slaves was experienced during the late war. Had slaves been treated as they might have been by the Enemy, they would have proved dangerous instruments in their hands," meaning that had Britain been more adept at exploiting the enslaved population, much more damage could have been done.

Mason argued for uniform conditions: "Maryland & Virginia he said had already prohibited the importation of slaves expressly. N. Carolina had done the same in substance. All this would be in vain if S. Carolina & Georgia be at liberty to import." What Mason described did in fact subsequently happen: "The Western people are already calling out for slaves for their new lands; and will fill that Country with slaves if they can be got thro' S. Carolina & Georgia."[24] Mason went on to catalog the ills of slavery for a society: "Slavery discourages arts & manufactures. The poor despise labor when performed by slaves. They prevent the immigration of Whites, who really enrich & strengthen a Country. They produce the most pernicious effect on manners. Every master of slaves is born a petty tyrant. They bring the judgment of heaven on a Country . . ."[25]

The key point was expressed by South Carolina's Charles Cotesworth Pinckney on August 22. The son of Charles Pinckney and indigo doyenne Eliza Lucas Pinckney, he was referred to as "General Pinckney" to differentiate him from his cousin Charles Pinckney, who was another of South Carolina's four delegates to the convention. General Pinckney described correctly what would happen in the future. In Madison's paraphrase: "S. Carolina & Georgia cannot do without slaves. As to Virginia she will gain by stopping the importations. Her slaves will rise in value, & she has more than she wants. It would be unequal to require S.C. & Georgia to confederate on such unequal terms."[26]

Virginia's slaves will rise in value. She has more than she wants. That was the economic argument, in a nutshell. Ending the African trade would be a bonanza for Virginia, which stood to dominate the domestic slave trade. Mason noted that the Carolinians were poised to profit if allowed to import; Pinckney countered by pointing out that if importation were not allowed, Virginia would have that lucrative market cornered.

Virginia's interstate slave trade was already going on. A few months after Pinckney's words, the Richmond *Virginia Independent Chronicle* carried an advertisement by Moses Austin & Co. If the name seems familiar, that's because he was the father of Stephen F. Austin, who later brought Southern slavery to Texas and for whom the Texas capital was named. The senior Austin, who began the American lead industry, was at the time a dry goods merchant, and though he was not a full time slave trader, on December 26, 1787, he was offering to dispose of troublesome slaves by selling them South, probably to Georgia:

W A N T E D, ONE HUNDRED NEGROES, From 12 to 30 years old, for which a good price will be given. They are to be sent out of the state, therefore we shall not be particular respecting the character of any of them—Hearty and well made is all that is necessary.[27]

The question of slave breeding (Virginia) versus slave importation (Carolina) to supply the demand for labor in whatever new territories might be annexed in the next twenty years was so financially momentous that it almost derailed the Constitution. McHenry's notes from the Constitutional Convention summarized the situation:

[The three-fifths clause] gave the slave States an advantage in representation over the others.

The slaves were moreover exempt from duty on importation.

They served to render the representation from such States aristocratical.

It was replied—That the population or increase of slaves in Virginia exceeded their calls for their services—That a prohibition of Slaves into S. Carolina Georgia etc—would be a monopoly in their favor. These States could not do without Slaves—Virginia etc would make their own terms for such as they might sell.

Such was the situation of the country that it could not exist without slaves—That they could confederate on no other condition.

They had enjoyed the right of importing slaves when colonies.

They enjoyed as States [*sic*] under the confederation—And if they could not enjoy it under the proposed government, they could not associate or make a part of it.[28]

Then, on Saturday, August 25, in Madison's words, "Genl Pinkney moved to strike out the words 'the year eighteen hundred' (as the year limiting the importation of slaves), and to insert the words 'the year eighteen hundred and eight.'"[29] Pinckney was prescient, as South Carolina's slave-importation bonanza would not begin until after the acquisition of Louisiana at the end of 1803, something no one could have predicted.

Charleston had built great fortunes by re-exporting Africans to the neighboring territories. Now it was poised to service the future market when the nation grew to the South and the West. No one knew exactly when, or under what conditions, that might happen.

23

Ten Thousand Powers

It appears that Mr. Henry is not at bottom a friend.

—James Madison to George Washington, October 28, 1787

WHEN THE SOUTH CAROLINA House of Representatives met to ratify the successfully negotiated Constitution in January 1788, former South Carolina governor Rawlins Lowndes congratulated Charles Cotesworth Pinckney by unleashing a blast of anti-Northern bitterness.

"Negroes were our wealth, our only natural resource," Lowndes said, "yet behold how our kind friends in the North were determined soon to tie up our hands, and drain us of what we had," with palpable sarcasm on the word "friends."

"We are at a loss, for some time," Pinckney responded, "for a rule to ascertain the proportionate wealth of the states. At last we thought that the productive labor of the inhabitants was the best rule for ascertaining their wealth."[1] Pinckney struck the already familiar tone of intra-sectional rivalry as he continued:

> your delegates had to contend with the religious and political prejudices of the Eastern and Middle States, and with the interested and inconsistent opinion of *Virginia, who was warmly opposed to our importing more slaves.*
>
> I am of the same opinion now as I was two years ago . . . that, while there remained one acre of swampland uncleared of South Carolina, I would raise my voice against restricting the importation of negroes. I am . . . thoroughly convinced . . . that the nature of our climate, and the flat,

swampy situation of our country, obliges us to cultivate our lands with negroes, and that without them South Carolina would soon be a desert waste. (emphasis added)

Yet, Pinckney insisted, there was a reason for South Carolina to have negotiated over this issue and to have joined the newly constituted republic: facing potential or actual threats from the English, the Spanish, the Native Americans, the free blacks of Florida, and its own captive labor force, South Carolina needed the other states to defend it.

We are so weak that by ourselves we could not form an union strong enough for the purpose of effectually protecting each other. Without union with the other States, South Carolina must soon fall. Is there any one among us so much a Quixotte as to suppose that this State could long maintain her independence if she stood alone, or was only connected with the Southern States? I scarcely believe there is . . . By this settlement we have secured an unlimited importation of negroes for twenty years. Nor is it declared that the importation shall be then stopped; it may be continued. We have a security that the general government can never emancipate them, for no such authority is granted; and it is admitted, on all hands, that the general government has no powers but what are expressly granted by the Constitution, and that all rights not expressed were reserved by the several states. We have obtained a right to recover our slaves in whatever part of America they may take refuge, which is a right we had not before. In short, considering all circumstances, we have made the best terms for the security of this species of property it was in our power to make. We would have made better if we could; but, on the whole, I do not think them bad.[2]

The two points had been made, yet again: one, without enslaved black labor, South Carolina would be desperately poor; two, without a defensive alliance, South Carolina could not survive. It was equally true in Georgia; as George Washington wrote in a letter of January 17, 1788: "if a weak state [Georgia], with powerful tribes of Indians in its rear and the Spaniards on its flank, do not incline to embrace a strong *general* government, there must, I should think, be either wickedness or insanity in their conduct."[3]

The word "slave" may have been silent in the Constitution, but not in the nationwide ratification debate. It required considerable persuasion to sell the ratification of the Constitution up North in the face of increasing antislavery sentiment. The provision for possibly ending the African slave trade after twenty years had to be touted as a step toward ending slavery, which it was not.

There was no debate in South Carolina as to whether the Constitution gave sufficient protection to slavery: it did. South Carolina had gotten what it wanted, and ratified the Constitution easily, despite protests from upcountry farmers who saw themselves as self-sufficient. David Waldstreicher writes that "strikingly few people" in the Lowcountry "criticized the Constitution for being insufficiently pro-slavery. . . . The relative absence of debate on the topic in North Carolina, South Carolina, and Georgia speaks volumes. . . . The only reason North Carolina did not ratify was because slavery-dominated districts did not outnumber those where small farmers predominated."[4]

The South Carolina Assembly voted in 1786 to move the capital to an upcountry site and to name it Columbia. It ratified a carefully drafted state constitution in 1790 that, like Britain, required property-holding and tax-paying in order to be able to exercise the voting franchise, with higher property-holding requirements for important officeholders. In effect, this excluded non-slaveholders from government. These requirements were partly expressed as a number of "negroes," so that a state representative was expected to "be legally seized and possessed in his own right of a settled freehold estate of five hundred acres of land and ten negroes, or of a real estate of the value of one hundred and fifty pounds sterling, clear of debt." The governor was required to have an estate of fifteen hundred pounds sterling.[5] From then until after the end of slavery, South Carolina's governor, US senators, and congressmen would not be chosen by popular vote but by the assembly, which was utterly dominated by planters; nor did the people at large have a vote in the presidential election.

The Constitution owed its existence to two Virginians: Washington, who chaired the convention and lent his prestige to it, and Madison, the principal drafter. But even so, Virginia, less in need of defense from invasion than South Carolina, was less eager to ratify. There was extensive sentiment in Virginia that the proposed Constitution gave too much power to a federal government. With eight states having ratified the Constitution out of nine needed, Virginia was widely seen as the swing state for ratification (though as it played out, New Hampshire became the ninth to ratify), and it was sharply divided.

The opposition was led by Patrick Henry and George Mason. Henry had declined appointment to the Constitutional Convention, worrying James

Madison, who with characteristic precision correctly predicted what Henry would do: "Besides the loss of his services on that theater [of the Constitutional Convention], there is a danger I fear that this step has proceeded from a wish to leave his conduct unfettered on another theatre where the result of the Convention will receive its destiny from his omnipotence."[6] Mason, however, had participated in the Constitutional Convention but did not like the result.

Henry saw Virginia as a "country" that would lose her sovereignty by demotion to membership in a "general" government. "What is become of your country?" he asked rhetorically. "The Virginian government is but a name." He warned that if you "give up your rights to the general government," then that government would have the terrible power to end slavery.[7] Sounding the tocsin of sectional antagonism, he warned that the Constitution would put slaveowners at risk for losing their property. "Among ten thousand powers which they may assume," thundered Henry (imagine exclamation points), "they [the general government] may, if we be engaged in war, liberate every one of your slaves if they please. And this must and will be done by men, a majority of whom have not a common interest with you. They will therefore have no feeling for your interests."[8]

Patrick Henry believed that the Articles of Confederation were adequate. An isolated provincial by then at the age of fifty-one, he was out of touch with the world beyond Richmond. James Madison, whom Henry directly confronted in the ratification debate, knew the complexities of American politics at that moment as well as anyone alive, and he knew the Articles of Confederation weren't working. Much of the country was in a state of near anarchy, with no visible control at any higher level than the local. A pro-Constitution essay in the Winchester, Virginia, *Gazette* of January 18, 1788, said plainly, "At the American Revolution there was not only an end to the power of the crown, but a total dissolution of government."[9] The South Carolinians, who were in favor of a national government that would defend them from external attack even as they demanded protection for slavery, were in much better contact with the real world of commerce than Patrick Henry. In a sense, Henry was arguing for imposing the decentralization of Chesapeake society on the nation.

The Constitution and Patrick Henry were on a collision course as regards rhetoric as well. The Constitution was everything Henry wasn't: concise and restrained. Henry's style was to sweep the listener away with cathartic discourse, the opposite of Madison's neoclassical rationality. The clash between Henry and Madison in the Virginia House of Delegates wasn't a fair fight, oratorically speaking. Madison was small, analytical, and a mumbler—"Mr. *Madison* added other remarks which could not be heard" is one of many such notations in the debate minutes—while Henry was an expansive, emotional orator who filled in the silences about slavery in Madison's document.

Henry, who literally talked for days, warned on June 17, 1788, in the Virginia Convention that had been called to debate ratification, that a national Congress could do the most horrifying thing possible: free Virginia's slaves. The Constitution did not give Congress the power of emancipation, but Congress could, in the reporter's paraphrase of Henry, "lay such heavy taxes on slaves, as would amount to emancipation; and then the Southern States would be the only sufferers. . . . He considered the clause which had been adduced by the Gentleman as a security for this property, as no security at all. It was no more than this—That a run-away negro could be taken up in Maryland or New-York. This could not prevent Congress from interfering with that property by laying a grievous and enormous tax on it, so as to compel owners to emancipate their slaves rather than pay the tax."[10]

In case of war, Henry warned on June 24, "may Congress not say, that every black man must fight?—Did we not see a little of this last war? . . . acts of Assembly passed, that every slave who would go to the army should be free." Then he looked into the abyss. "May they [Congress] not pronounce all slaves free?"[11] He continued: "The majority of Congress is to the north, and the slaves are to the south. In this situation, I see a great deal of the property of the people of Virginia in jeopardy, and their peace and tranquility gone away."[12] That the "property of the people of Virginia" consisted of other people of Virginia does not seem to have bothered Henry.

The old rhetorician knew when to deflate himself and jab his audience with something more vernacular. Though it does not appear in the official account of his speech, there is this tidbit in an 1850 account by Hugh Blair Grigsby, the nineteenth-century historian of the Virginia Convention and an influential thinker in secessionist circles:

> On one of the occasions which the reporter passes over with some such remark as, "Here Mr. Henry declaimed with great pathos on the loss of our liberties," I was told by a person on the floor of the Convention at the time, that . . . he suddenly broke out with the homely exclamation: "*They'll free your niggers!*" The audience passed instantly from fear to wayward laughter; and my informant said that it was most ludicrous to see men

who a moment before were half frightened to death, with a broad grin on
their faces.[13]

Whatever the truth of this secondhand account, "They'll free your niggers!" is
indeed a homely summary of what Patrick Henry was saying, and at the very
least, Grigsby's quoting of it suggests the continuity that later slaveowners saw
with Henry.

Ultimately, the opposition of Henry and Mason (along with Jefferson's
influence over Madison, exercised from Paris by letter) helped prompt the
insertion of the Bill of Rights in 1789. It is in no small part to Henry's resistance that the Constitution owes the Second Amendment in particular—the
one that promises "the right to keep and bear arms" in order to have "a well-
regulated militia"—and it too was, in part, about slavery, because in the South,
the militia was understood to be identical with the slave patrols that were constantly on guard.

The Constitution gave Congress a measure of control over the militia, which
Henry virulently opposed. He wanted assurances that Congress would not use
that control to disarm the militia. The Constitution empowered Congress "to
provide for calling forth the Militia to execute the Laws of the Union, suppress
Insurrections and repel Invasions." This mention of insurrections, while broadly
phrased, was made at a time when slave rebellion and Native American uprising
were an ever-present threat. Nor was the repelling of invasions by foreign armies
something the undisciplined American militias were capable of doing, as would
be demonstrated in the War of 1812.

The Second Amendment was intended in part to insure that Northerners could not interrupt or halt Southern repression of black people and Native
Americans—though many, notably including Jefferson, incorrectly thought
militias adequate for defending the country, too. The goal of slaveowners was
to make the entire South a prison from which no enslaved person could escape;
militias were the police force. What was intended by a militia, at least from the
point of view of South Carolina, was expressed by Alexander Hewatt in 1779
and agrees with the functions enumerated in the Constitution:

> As all white men in the province, of the military age, were soldiers as well
> as citizens, and trained in some measure to the use of arms, it was no dif-
> ficult matter to complete the provincial regiment. Their names being regis-
> tered in the list of militia on every emergency they were obliged to be ready

for defence, not only against the incursions of Indians, but also against the insurrection of negroes.[14]

When the Bill of Rights was ratified two years later, it did not lay a hand on slavery, nor did it extend a hand to Americans enslaved at the time the United States was born. The Fifth Amendment provided that "no person" could be "deprived of life, liberty, or property, without due process of law." At that time, there were 694,280 legally enslaved people, who lived in a far more abject relationship to the people who were legally their owners than the colonists had to their king, and to whom the Fifth Amendment would not apply.

Southern slavery democratized the divine right of kings. No matter how poor a plantation owner might seem to a London merchant, on the grounds of his plantation he was the head of a royal family where his word was law. Every man of property was a little king, with the power to order sexual reproduction or summary execution. With their labor to provide his income and the collateral of their bodies to secure his credit, he could be free to ponder great things and spend his days in politics. The South's down-home kings had the Constitution at their back, with a Bill of Rights that safeguarded their slave-patrolling militias from being disarmed by abolitionists up North who might at some future point take charge of the federal government, even though the South was disproportionately over-represented in Congress and in presidential elections.

The South got yet another benefit from the Constitution: Article 1, Section 8 contemplated (but did not mandate) the creation of a "District (not exceeding ten Miles square) as may, by Cession of particular States, and the Acceptance of Congress, become the Seat of the Government of the United States"—a neutral ground that would not be part of any state to house the federal capital. With so many Quakers in Pennsylvania, to say nothing of so many free people of color, and with Pennsylvania having passed the Gradual Abolition Act in 1780 (which granted birthright freedom to children born in Pennsylvania but did not affect those already enslaved), slaveholders did not consider Philadelphia a comfortable seat for a government that they expected to safeguard slavery. The Virginians knew where they wanted that federal district to be—right by where George Washington lived.

During the First Congress, Second Session, of 1790, Pennsylvania Quakers presented petitions calling for the abolition of slavery, triggering a strongly worded rebuttal. Offended by the Quakers' imputations, South Carolina representative William Smith responded to the petitions with an extended defense of his state. He asked rhetorically of the Quakers, "had any of them ever married a negro, or would any of them suffer their children to mix their blood with that of a black?" He then

> read some extracts from Mr. Jefferson's Notes on Virginia, proving that negroes were by nature an inferior race of beings; and that the whites would always feel a repugnance at mixing their blood with that of the blacks. Thus, he proceeded, that respectable author, who was desirous of countenancing emancipation, was, on consideration of the subject, induced candidly to allow that the difficulties appeared insurmountable.[15]

Jefferson in 1790 brokered a deal over dinner with Hamilton: Jefferson would get a Southern capital if Hamilton could begin his financial plan. As a result of the deal, Hamilton created the national debt and the Bank of the United States that issued bonds to back it, paid the veterans of the independence struggle what they were owed, and restored the United States' international credit, while Jefferson set out to create the federal city.

The one-hundred-square-mile District of Columbia was created out of sixty-one square miles of Maryland land on the north side of the Potomac, where the capital was sited, together with thirty-nine square miles of Virginia land south of the Potomac, including the town of Alexandria, whose harbor was designated by Washington, Jefferson, and Monroe as the Potomac's official port of entry in 1784. Building the new capital city of Washington out of swampland was good for business; it employed lots of slave labor, rented from Virginia and Maryland slaveowners. As construction began, the slave-selling business in Alexandria picked up from the federal stimulus.

Sixty years later, the Beaufort, South Carolina, arch-secessionist Robert Barnwell Rhett would call the Jefferson-Hamilton deal a "corrupt bargain" in which Jefferson sold out the South. For the political class of South Carolina, who saw themselves as rulers of a sovereign state, the creation of Washington City centralized power in the Chesapeake and legitimized a system of national debt, the payment of which, they believed, would be extorted from them in the form of tariffs. Indeed, the First Congress in 1789 passed a tariff that South Carolina and Georgia saw as a transfer of wealth from South to North, prompting Pierce Butler in 1790 to warn that, in William C. Davis's paraphrase, "the doctrine of protective tariffs, if pursued, might one day destroy the Union."[16]

During the thirty-one-month interval between the Constitution taking effect and the Bill of Rights taking effect, the French and Haitian Revolutions erupted. It was one long upheaval: American independence was a French-supported project that occurred in parallel with France's revolution, though the American side erupted first. The two movements were inextricably tied together, with communication between the two and an overlapping cast of characters that included Jefferson and the Marquis de Lafayette.

In Europe, where American independence was seen primarily as a victory for France against England, the fall of the Bastille on July 14, 1789, was a far greater shock. Not only had the French monarch been powerful, but France was wealthy: the island colony of Saint-Domingue was the most profitable piece of ground on earth, contributing perhaps as much as 40 percent of France's annual income with its products.[17] In 1789 it supplied "about 60 percent of the coffee sold in the western world"; only Jamaica could compete with it as a producer of sugar; and it produced indigo, cotton, and tobacco. It was a high-volume consumer of kidnapped Africans; forty thousand arrived in 1789 alone, after a six-year period that had seen Saint-Domingue's agricultural production double. As such, it generated a vast cash flow for the trans-African slave trade at its height. This capital "fertilized" the crops, as C. L. R. James put it: "though the bourgeoisie traded in other things than slaves, upon the success or failure of the traffic everything else depended." The great revenues from Saint-Domingue created the prosperity that was the source of the power France projected internationally. But it was not royal power; the fortunes of the slave trade were made by the bourgeoisie.[18]

Some of the bourgeoisie of Saint-Domingue were free people of color, though they were discriminated against. Stewart King, who analyzed Domingan notarial records, estimates that as many as 30 percent of the slaves in Saint-Domingue were owned by free people of color, who were approximately half the free population.[19] There were about thirty thousand whites and about thirty thousand free people of color in Saint-Domingue, and approximately half a million slaves, about two thirds of them African-born.[20] No comparable-sized piece of ground in Africa had ever sustained such a population. They were angry, and among them they had a considerable body of military knowledge to draw on.

In the hodgepodge of African nations compacted together under the harsh discipline of the plantation, the Senegambians of Saint-Domingue, from an Islamized region, brought a concept of *jihad*. From farther south in Africa, the Fon-speakers from Ardra (in present-day Benin) followed traditional African practices and called their spirits *foddun* (from which, *vodou*), alongside representatives of other traditional African practices. From farther south yet, in West

Central Africa, the most numerous group, the Bakongo, whose military techniques seem to have predominated, had been Catholicized, while continuing
their traditional practices. The body of spiritual practices called *vodou*, which
developed along with the Haitian nation, became an umbrella concept, an *e plu-
ribus unum* of African religion that allowed for different traditions to continue
within an overall framework of *nanchons*, or nations. Under this umbrella, the
spirits multiplied.

24

The French Revolution in America

Suppose a negro man of 25. years of age costs £75. sterling: he has an equal chance to live 30. years according to Buffon's tables; so that you lose your principal in 30 years.[1]

—Thomas Jefferson, letter to George Washington, June 18, 1792

BEING ANTI-MONARCHIC AND PRO-REPUBLICAN to the bone, Thomas Jefferson was sympathetic to the French revolutionaries, who in turn idolized him as a hero of the American revolution.

They misunderstood Jefferson so badly that in 1788, while Jefferson was United States Minister Plenipotentiary in Paris, Jacques-Pierre Brissot de Warville invited him to become a member of the organization he had founded. Inspired by Thomas Clarkson's Society for Effecting the Abolition of the Slave Trade in Britain, the *Societé des Amis des Noirs* (Society of the Friends of the Blacks) was the first French antislavery society.

With the insincerity that was Jefferson's political hallmark, he declined Brissot's invitation, using what the editors of Jefferson's papers, speaking of another occasion, refer to as a "polite diplomatic fiction."[2] In it, he distinguished abolition of slavery from abolition of the slave trade:

> I am very sensible of the honour you propose to me of becoming a member of the society for the abolition of the slave trade. You know that nobody wishes more ardently to see an abolition not only of the trade but of the condition of slavery: and certainly nobody will be more willing to

encounter every sacrifice for that object. But the influence & information of the friends to this proposition in France will be far above the need of my association. I am here as a public servant; and those whom I serve having never yet been able to give their voice against this practice, it is decent for me to avoid too public a demonstration of my wishes to see it abolished.[3]

When the Bastille fell, Jefferson was in Paris, preparing to leave for home. He'd been packed since April, and he decamped in September 1789 for his mountaintop in Virginia with his daughter Patsy, and—though he had told Brissot that "nobody would be more willing" than he to "encounter every sacrifice" to end slavery—he brought home as well Patsy's enslaved attendant, the pregnant fifteen- or sixteen-year-old Sally Hemings, who was the deceased Martha Wayles Jefferson's half sister (one of six half siblings Martha had owned) and thus Patsy's illegitimate aunt.

Much has been written about Hemings in recent years, and we will not summarize her story once again here. It is ironic that she has come to define Jefferson in the modern popular image, with her captivity cast as a love story in some narratives. The fact that she was, as was typical of enslaved concubines, only one-quarter black made her acceptable to Jefferson for cohabiting. As he explained in *Notes*, elaborating on his pseudoscientific notion of black inferiority: "The improvement of the blacks in body and mind, in the first instance of their mixture with the whites, has been observed by every one, and proves that their inferiority is not the effect merely of their condition of life."[4]

There was in the last third of the twentieth century a long historiographic scandal over Jefferson's parentage of Sally's children Beverly, Harriet, Madison, and Eston—who, far from being "removed beyond the reach of mixture," were seven-eighths white. We consider the issue of Jefferson's paternity of them to have been resolved and will forbear discussing the literature on the subject here.[5] For us, the key point is not whether Jefferson fathered Hemings's children, but that he *owned* the children, and could sell them if he wanted.

Returning home from France to what was now a constitutional American republic, Jefferson brought an extraordinarily large cargo of goods he had purchased. The list has delighted Jefferson biographers ever since, with its furniture, cheeses, musical instruments, gadgets like the portable copying machine he had commissioned in London, and 680 bottles of wine. All of it would ultimately be paid for by his slaves, who produced all his revenue.

Jefferson answered Washington's call to join his administration and became the first secretary of state, a position that brought him into frequent conflict with his great enemy, Alexander Hamilton, whom Washington named secretary of the treasury.

The Antillean colony of Saint-Domingue stopped being profitable for France in August 1791, when, in the instability after the French Revolution, with radicals on the ascendant and talk of liberty in the air, another revolution began. A little more than two years after the fall of the Bastille, the enslaved Boukman Dutty—a visionary troublemaker who had been traded into the colony illegally from British Jamaica—led a brilliantly organized, intensely violent August 1791 rebellion on the northern plains of Saint-Domingue.[6] It was the beginning of a complicated struggle, in two main phases with a tense interregnum, that continued until January 1, 1804, when Jean-Jacques Dessalines issued the Declaration of Independence of the Republic of Haiti, taking the new country's name from the indigenous Taíno language.*

The military aspect of Boukman's experience was informed by both African and European techniques of war, and by the body of African spiritual practices that in Haiti came to be collectively known as vodou.

By the time the US Bill of Rights went into effect on December 15, 1791, the sugar plantations of the northern plain of Saint-Domingue lay in ash heaps. The consequences were immediate: Europe's sugar and slavery industries were remade overnight. The principal supplier of sugar abruptly disappeared from the world market, though it would re-emerge to a lesser degree under Toussaint Louverture, who reinstated the plantation system with conscripted labor.

Cuba stepped in to fill the breach in sugar supply. The island had received its first shipment of African slaves in the 1520s, but for most of that time it had principally been a transshipping center for silver and gold from Mexico and Peru; without a plantation system, it had not been a major importer of slaves. Though Africans had been in Cuba for almost three centuries by then, the first four decades of the nineteenth century would be Cuba's peak period of

---

*Since the nation of Haiti did not exist until January 1, 1804, we use "Saint-Domingue" to refer to the territory prior to that date; contemporary reports often refer to "St. Domingo," not to be confused with the city of Santo Domingo on the Spanish-speaking side of the island. We call the people "Domingans," reserving the word "Haitian" for those in or coming from Haiti after the existence of that republic. We refer to the entire conflict as the Haitian Revolution, while acknowledging that the name obfuscates the multi-threaded nature of the conflict.

importation of kidnapped Africans—a tremendous source of revenue for those who supplied the captives—as well as Havana's peak of prosperity, as sugar plantations proliferated.

The Domingan slaveowners were internationally notorious for sadism toward the enslaved. The uprising was everything they had feared, and the convulsive violence of it was made even worse in the telling of it by slaveowners, who were the sources of much of the printed discourse around it. "Their standard was the body of a white infant impaled upon a stake," read a pamphlet widely read in France and in England, though there is no corroborating evidence that such a baby on a pike existed. The message hardly needed reinforcing: the natural state of the "Negro" was to be a baby-murdering, devil-worshipping savage. Accounts circulated in the slaveholding South of the spectacular violence directed against the bodies and plantation properties of the whites in the northern agricultural plain of Saint-Domingue. Word spread through the black Americas what had happened: the enslaved heard it through the inter-plantation grapevine, and they heard their aghast masters talking about it.

The United States' 1778 treaties with Louis XVI, which created the framework pursuant to which France substantially helped the United States win the War of Independence, committed the American republic to recognize France's claim on Saint-Domingue. No one in Washington's administration—not Hamilton, and certainly not Jefferson—wanted to see slave revolt there. The United States weighed in, and by 1792 had proactively spent some $726,000 in "supplies, arms, and equipment" to support the Domingan planters against the black rebels.[7]

In a letter to President Washington, Secretary of State Jefferson attempted in 1792 to answer some questions about American agriculture posed by the English agricultural expert Arthur Young, whom Jefferson knew from Paris. In calculating the relative value of hired versus owned laborers, he observed that "our families of negroes double in about 25. years, which is an increase of the capital, invested in them, of 4. per cent over & above keeping up the original number."[8]

This is unambiguous: Jefferson was describing African Americans as self-reproducing merchandise that could meet a capital returns target. The consequences for Jefferson's personal economy of this calculation were that, in Henry Wiencek's words, "he had realized that he was making 4 percent profit every year on the birth of black children."[9]

In reply, Young disputed Jefferson's figures for wheat—because, he said, it was impossible to raise as much wheat as Jefferson projected without proper land management (not something Virginia was known for), which meant letting land lie fallow, which in turn would call for more cows and sheep to graze it than Jefferson projected. He scoffed at Jefferson's projection of £60 profit annually from slave-breeding, noting that "to have a considerable value in slaves, is a hazardous capital; and there is no man in the world who would not give 60 *l.* a year on six thousand acres, to be able to change slaves to cows and sheep: he cannot otherwise command labour, and therefore must keep them; but the profit in any other light than labourers, is inadmissible."[10]

Young may have understood the economics of wheat-raising better than Jefferson, but as he acknowledged in his letter, he was not on the ground in Virginia. The English economist does not seem to have fully understood how Virginians were wringing multidimensional profits from their labourers over and above their capacity to labor. Which is to say, he did not comprehend the nascent slave-breeding industry. In the process of explaining it to him, Jefferson seems to have improved his own comprehension of it.

In a response to Washington about Young's reply, Jefferson pleaded inexperience with macroeconomics, as he had not already had these figures on the ready but had to create them from scratch. He wrote, "I had never before thought of calculating what were the profits of a capital invested in Virginia agriculture"—an extraordinary admission, it might seem, for a debt-burdened owner of a large slave plantation.[11] But then, Hamilton, not Jefferson, was the money man in the Washington administration; though Jefferson was a compulsive record-keeper who kept minutely detailed lists of expenditures, he "abandoned any effort to balance credits and debits in 1770," writes Alan Pell Crawford.[12] Other large slaveowners who were more adept financial managers than Jefferson, like Charles Carroll of Annapolis, had been calculating their profits on "natural increase" all along.

Slaveowners knew that their wealth increased with every enslaved birth, of course. The revelation for Jefferson was to think of it in terms of capitalism. It was a subtle perceptual shift that seems obvious to us now: translate that knowledge into a dollar figure that could be compared with other investments as an abstract rate of return. In comparing those figures, Wiencek suggests, Jefferson had realized that raising slaves was his best business. Wiencek's interpretation of this correspondence as a pivotal moment in Jefferson's thinking was attacked vociferously, and, in our opinion, incorrectly, by Hemings family biographer Annette Gordon-Reed, who legalistically argued that Jefferson "was not speaking about his slaves at Monticello—he was speaking about farms in Virginia generally."[13] But that seems a false distinction: Jefferson's phrase was "*our* families of negroes," emphasis added. He identified personally with what he was describing.

More to our point, however, is that, as Gordon-Reed indicated, Jefferson was telling Young (and Washington) that slave reproduction was increasing Virginia's capital stock by 4 percent every year, whether there was a good crop or a bad one. That had obvious implications for him, both as a Virginia politician and as a large slaveowner. Laden with debt and entirely invested in the human capital of slaves, Jefferson was representative of the slaveowning class.

Alexander Hamilton was not interested in monetizing slaves. Along with Aaron Burr, he was a member of the New York Manumission Society, which kept lists of slave traders and urged they be boycotted and which played a role in urging the end of slavery in New York.

Hamilton and Jefferson were the public faces of the England-France split of the country, which meant something close to civil war. Neither were pro-democracy ideologues. Hamilton loathed the idea of democracy, which he referred to as "poison" in a letter written the last night of his life, while, as Lucia Stanton notes, "democracy" was "a word Jefferson rarely used and never in the way we do today."[14]

The Federalist money of New England and New York was pro-British, while Republican Virginia was mostly pro-French. The Jeffersonians painted President Washington as an aristocrat and monarchist mouthing pro-British words supplied to him by the manipulator Hamilton, who was understood to be a threat to slavery.

Washington, the father of the Constitution, didn't want political parties. All the specifications in the Constitution about representatives and senators didn't contemplate that they would be members of one of two political parties. More than any other individual, Jefferson was responsible for creating a party system in the United States, and he did so in direct opposition to Washington, while he was Washington's secretary of state. Washington, perhaps understandably, took it as a personal betrayal.

Jefferson had watched the workings of parties in revolutionary France. He created his own propaganda organ out of patronage by giving printer Philip Freneau a job in the Department of State, thereby supporting the publication of

Freneau's highly partisan *National Gazette.* As of October 31, 1791, it published unsigned attacks by Jefferson and Madison, among others, against Hamilton, Washington, and the policies of the very administration from which Jefferson was a political renegade.

When the French Republic was declared to exist in 1792, the radical Girondins were in power, though they were soon to be displaced (and many of them executed) by the more radical Jacobins. Believing in the radicalism of the American revolution, the more idealistic of the Girondins dreamed of a political union between the American and French republics, a free trade zone where *citoyens* of one country would be citizens of the other. The Girondins had no strong hierarchy, but their de facto leader was the writer Jacques-Pierre Brissot de Warville, he who had previously invited Jefferson to join his abolition society; they were sometimes known as Brissotins.

Brissot had traveled in the mid-Atlantic and Upper South of the United States, where he attempted to help organize antislavery societies, and published a narrative of his observations in 1791. A significant chunk of his book is about his contacts with slavery in America. He wrote of Jefferson's home state: "Every thing in Maryland and Virginia wears the print of slavery; a starved soil. Bad cultivation, houses falling to ruin, cattle small and few, and black walking skeletons; in a word, you see real misery and apparent luxury, insulting each other."[15] Still, Brissot idealized America and he admired Jefferson, who had advised Lafayette during the drafting of the Declaration of the Rights of Man—betraying, as some saw it, America's independence ally Louis XVI.

Brissot, momentarily in a position of power in 1793, dispatched the loose cannon Citizen Edmund-Charles Genêt as the Minister Plenipotentiary to America, advising him to trust Jefferson over all other Americans. Genêt's father had been a courtier to Louis XV, and he had grown up at Versailles, so he had the necessary skills and contacts for the mission Brissot entrusted him with: to escort the royal family—Louis XVI, Marie Antoinette, and the young Dauphin—out of France to a safe exile in America. But before Genêt could depart, the Jacobin faction pressed the momentous vote on death for the monarch, with Brissot as one of 387 convention members voting for regicide. Eleven days after guillotining King Louis XVI on January 21, 1793, the Girondins declared war on Britain and the Netherlands.

Genêt went on to the United States alone, with a diplomatic brief, basically, to be a saboteur—to export the French revolution, consolidate the alliance with the United States, and, in the words of Genêt's biographer Meade Minnigerode, "to do all the harm he could to England and Spain in America."[16] He was also supposed to collect Louis XVI's $2 million war debt from the Americans so they could use it in the war in Saint-Domingue. (Hamilton had been making timely payments, but the French wanted the principal.) The charming, thirty-year-old Genêt's instructions gave him a budget of sixty thousand *livres*, with the laughable instruction to draw it from the United States Treasury—meaning, he was supposed to get it from Alexander Hamilton—to be deducted from the American war debt to France.

On his way to America, Genêt paused his voyage so that his vessel, the *Embuscade* (Ambush), could engage in privateering against British merchants. He took several prizes before being blown off-course and landing on April 8, 1793, in Charleston rather than the intended destination of Philadelphia. Despite the urgency of his diplomatic mission, the delighted Genêt determined to travel up the coast from Charleston by land.

The day after Genêt arrived in Charleston, the April 9, 1793, issue of *The Apollo; or Chestertown Spy* (Maryland), was headlined by the shocking, just-arrived news of the execution of Louis XVI eleven weeks earlier. A smaller, more locally oriented, article was also significant:

> On Tuesday last the *Corner Stone* of the AFRICAN CHURCH, was laid
> in Fifth Street, between Walnut and Spruce Streets, Philadelphia, by four
> of the members of the Church. One of them afterwards kneeled down
> upon the stone and prayed in a fervent manner, for the success and useful-
> ness of the undertaking.
> This church will be forty-six feet in front, and sixty feet in depth.

The Bill of Rights' guarantee of freedom of religion gave protection to the movement of free black people toward becoming churched. The Free African Society, founded in Philadelphia in April 1787, was a mutual aid organization that aimed to create a nondenominational black church.

With the disestablishment of the Anglican church, or any other, guaranteed by the Bill of Rights, the murderous religious divisions that had long plagued

Europe and carried over to the colonies—between Catholic and Protestant, between Anglican and evangelical—were moderated. Instead, there was a division between white and black that extended into the spiritual sphere. The church whose construction was announced in the *Spy* was the African Episcopal Church of St. Thomas, founded by the Free African Society's Absalom Jones. After a split along Anglican/Methodist lines, the society's Richard Allen founded the African Methodist Episcopal Church. Both churches taught reading to children.

"Mother Bethel," the A.M.E. church, which began as the Blacksmith Shop Meeting-House, was consecrated on July 29, 1794, as a great wave of evangelization was sweeping over First Amendment America, with numbers of African Americans taking to Jesus as their liberator. Methodism was still associated with antislavery, and abolition societies already existed in the 1790s, as per the notice in the *Chestertown Spy*, enlarged and reproduced here.

> ❋❋❋❋❋❋❋❋❋❋❋❋❋❋
>
> *⁎* The Members of the ABOLITION SOCIETY, are requested to meet at the METHODIST MEETING-HOUSE in Cheltertown, on *Friday* the 3d day of *May* next, precifely at Eleven o'clock, A. M.
>
> *By order of the Prefident,*
> ABRAHAM RIDGELY, Sec'ry.
> *Cheftertown,* April 23, 1793.

There were no such societies in the Lowcountry, where such a thing would not have been tolerated. Nor were the enslaved there allowed to preach, as Frederick Law Olmsted quoted a slaveowner in 1853, "unless a white man hears what they say."[17]

Charlestonians were known for extending a generous, courteous welcome to foreigners of a certain social rank, with which they hoped to win over ambassadors for the goodness of slavery. Genêt was given a superstar's welcome in South Carolina, where he met leading men of the state—"Dictator" Rutledge, Senator Ralph Izard, Thomas Pinckney. While not many of the Federalists in Charleston turned out to greet him, most of the Southern elite supported the republicans in France. It comported flatteringly with the Charlestonians' view of their own importance that the emissary of the greatest nation in the world had come to see them first.

With South Carolina governor William Moultrie's full permission, Genêt commissioned four privateers (one of them named the *Citizen Genêt*), which began attacking English shipping and bringing the prizes into Charleston harbor.[18]

That activity, which Jefferson ultimately made him stop, carried the possibility of bringing down retribution or even a declaration of war against the United States by the British navy, the world's most powerful.[19] It provided the direct motivation for the passage by the next Congress of the Neutrality Act of 1794, which prohibited freelance warmongering.

Genêt wrote that Izard told him—though he disregarded the advice—that Jefferson and Madison "pretend to be great republicans . . . They will do everything in their power to secure you on their side and will be friendly to you as long as your country or yourself may be serviceable to their ambitious views. Place no confidence in them." When Genêt answered that "I shall have no other friends in America but those who will be friendly to France and to the cause of liberty," Izard replied, according to Genêt, "oh[,] then[,] I see that you are going to fall into the snares of Mr. Jefferson and his party, and very probably will become their victim."[20]

Jefferson indeed befriended young Genêt. The Virginia trio of Jefferson, Madison, and James Monroe saw American support for republican France as essential. In a letter to James Monroe of June 4, 1793, Jefferson, looking forward to dual citizenship for all, wrote: "France has explained herself generously. . . . she wishes to promote [our prosperity] by giving us in all her possessions all the rights of her native citizens, and to receive our vessels as her vessels. This is the language of her new minister. Gr. Britain holds back with the most sullen silence and reserve."[21]

Washington took Jefferson's advice to receive Genêt, but did it standing in front of portraits of the murdered Louis, who had supported him in the War of Independence, and Marie Antoinette, who had not yet gone to the guillotine. By recognizing Genêt, the pro-British Washington was not merely recognizing the French Revolution, but actively harboring a hostile agent against Britain.[22]

Genêt proposed a commercial treaty—a family compact, he called it—that Jefferson was in favor of but Washington shot down, which would have ultimately had the effect of making the United States France's ally against Britain in war.

The radical Montagnard faction of the Jacobin Club came to power in France, on June 2, 1793. The execution of King Louis XVI was the beginning of the ascent to power of the *terroristes*—Danton, Marat, Robespierre—as the Montagnards began liquidating all opposition, with the Girondins as their main political targets. Genêt, who like all transatlantic diplomats had to contend with a lag of five weeks minimum, and often months, to receive word from home, continued prosecuting his agenda. Meanwhile, Brissot and twenty-one other Girondins went to the guillotine on October 31, 1793; one of the charges against Brissot was his responsibility for Genêt's mission.

According to Genêt's account, the popularity of the French Revolution in the United States brought a group of Philadelphians to ask him for advice on what to name their Jacobin club, the constitution of which had been drawn up by Pennsylvania secretary of state Alexander Dallas. Genêt diplomatically suggested they call it the Democratic Club.[23] Soon every American city had a club with a variety of names, collectively remembered as the Democratic-Republican societies, which were in favor of the French Revolution and which began the formalization of the opposition into a Democratic-Republican party, with Jefferson as its leader.

In Saint-Domingue, the Jacobin revolutionary civilian commissioners Léger-Félicité Sonthonax and Étienne Polverel came into open confrontation with General François-Thomas Galbaud du Fort, the Royalist head of the French fleet and an absentee landowner in Saint-Domingue, who had assumed authority. After Galbaud attacked Cap Français, sending two thousand or so sailors and newly unchained political prisoners to run riot in that city on June 20, 1793, they were driven away by an army of black freedmen fighting on the side of Sonthonax and Polverel. In a battle that lasted several days, the city of Cap Français—Saint-Domingue's largest port, and a center of arts and culture—burned to the ground. Galbaud evacuated with about ten thousand people, whom he brought to Baltimore first; by August, his fleet had dropped anchor in New York, from which base his ships began cruising up and down the coast. Genêt tried to have Galbaud arrested, but he had broken no US law.

Refugees had fled Saint-Domingue with the first insurrection in 1791; now, in a new wave, more refugees traveled down the Antilles—Guadeloupe, Puerto Rico, Trinidad—or to next-door, British-controlled Jamaica, while the largest number sailed up the Gulf Stream to the East Coast of the United States.

Only a few went to New Orleans at the time, though later the US-controlled New Orleans would become a magnet for what Nathalie Dessens describes as the ultimate "convergence zone" of a "real Saint-Domingan diaspora" that kept in touch with family, friends, and business connections, both by correspondence and by travel.[24] But New Orleans was not an immediate destination in 1793: it was not as accessible by sail as Atlantic North America because of the loop current in the Gulf. Moreover, the Spanish government of Louisiana was not welcoming to French refugees, some of whom were evangelists for revolution.

A convoy of 137 ships carrying Domingan refugees arrived in Norfolk, Virginia, in July 1793; from there, they went to cities up and down the coastline. Many went to Charleston, where there was already a community of French-speaking Huguenots. Bringing a new wave of Catholicism to the city, they effectively took over an Irish church there.[25] John E. Baur notes that "St. Domingue's creoles, many of them republican, tended to go to the Southern states, while French-born Royalists generally settled in New England and the Middle Atlantic states."[26] About four thousand Domingans went to New York.

In Philadelphia, the nation's capital and largest city, refugees who began arriving from Saint-Domingue in the spring were widely believed to have brought the city's first yellow fever epidemic in 1793, which killed over 10 percent of the town's population, causing many residents to flee, while the Free African Society cared for the sick and dying. Erupting out of the dockside area, it paralyzed the city and the US government. Dr. Benjamin Rush identified the disease on August 19, and it abated in mid-October, when the weather cooled and mosquitoes stopped biting (though their agency as disease vectors was not yet realized), and it did not spread anywhere else.[27]

During this crisis and in the months before, French privateers had been openly using the United States as a base. Their vessels, fitted out in the United States, had been taking British prizes—and Spanish, and even American—and bringing them into American harbors—Charleston, New York, Wilmington, Boston. This was inviting war with Britain, but, as Jefferson insisted in a cabinet meeting, "the French have by treaty a right to come into our ports with prizes."[28] Finally, realizing that Genêt's attacks on British shipping from a US base could put them at war with England, Washington, Hamilton, and Jefferson concurred that he had to stop passing out letters of marque to privateers.

The summer of 1793 stands out for the electric political turmoil in Philadelphia. The mounting death toll from the epidemic, combined with the convulsive energy emanating from the Terror in Paris and from Saint-Domingue, kept the town agitated, as political clubs increased in number and in aggression. Washington's government was nearly overthrown, as Adams angrily reminded Jefferson in an exchange of letters twenty years later:

> You certainly never felt the Terrorism, excited by Genet, in 1793, when ten thousand People in the Streets of Philadelphia, day after day, threatened to drag Washington out of his House, and effect a Revolution in the Government, or compell it to declare War in favour of the French Revolution, and against England. The coolest and the firmest Minds, even among the Quakers in Philadelphia, have given their Opinions to me, that nothing but the Yellow Fever . . . could have saved the United States from a total Revolution of Government. I have no doubt You was fast asleep in philosophical Tranquility, when ten thousand People, and perhaps many more, were parading the streets of Philadelphia. . . . What think you of Terrorism, Mr. Jefferson?[29]

Jefferson rationalized the mass guillotinings in Paris, even though some of his friends had fallen victim. But then the Jacobins brought terror to Jefferson, in the form of an emancipation proclamation.

The black army was the strongest force in Saint-Domingue, and it was better to be with it than against it; the French navy was an enemy; and Britain and Spain were both trying to take the colony over. Needing allies, Sonthonax and Polverel offered freedom to slaves who would join them—at first within a limited geographic range, then widening its scope. Justified by strategic considerations, and consistent with their own revolutionary principles, they unilaterally abolished slavery by proclamation in the northern province of Saint-Domingue on August 29, 1793. Over the next two months the decree was at least theoretically extended to the rest of the island, though the commissioners did not control all the territory. They needed as unified a force as possible: in September, the British invaded Saint-Domingue from their base in Jamaica, attracting the support of pro-British planters.

Though Jefferson was alarmed by Genêt's reckless actions, he was the administration member identified with the French. He had tried to resign before; now, in the wake of the turbulence that trailed Genêt, his opposition to the Washington administration made his position untenable. Jefferson left the post of secretary of state on December 31, 1793, announcing his return to Monticello. Vice President John Adams's comment in a letter to his son John Quincy Adams attributed Jefferson's resignation to his not making enough money as vice president to support his "habit" of expensive living, adding:

> Jefferson thinks by this step to get a reputation of an humble, modest, meek man, wholly without ambition or vanity. He may even have deceived himself into this belief. But if a prospect opens, the world will see and he will feel that he is as ambitious as Oliver Cromwell, though no soldier.[30]

It was time to make some money. As Jefferson prepared to leave public life, he wrote the iron merchant Caleb Lownes, asking for sixty to ninety days' credit on an order for iron rod, to be made into nails: "I suppose one ton will serve me the first quarter of the year by the end of which I shall be ready to work up two or three times as much every quarter."[31] He was going to go into business for himself, installing a cottage-industry nail factory with a workforce that Jefferson described as "a dozen little boys from 10. to 16. years of age."[32] They were given extra rations of meat and fish, and a suit "of red or blue" for the best workers.[33] Needless to say, they were kept away from reading and writing, and spent their formative years in captivity, living together and making nails together all day until they were sixteen, when they were transferred to field labor. From 1794 to 1797, while Jefferson was at Monticello and supervising it daily, his slave-labor nail factory was a profitable operation.[34]

Sonthonax and Polverel's declaration of emancipation was ratified and extended to all those enslaved in French territories on February 4, 1794, by the National Convention in Paris. It was the most radical achievement of the French Revolution: the immediate emancipation of all slaves, with no period of transition. When the ratification was confirmed, the general Toussaint Louverture stopped fighting under the Spanish flag in Saint-Domingue and came over to fight under the French.

Slaves in Saint-Domingue had risen up and killed not only their masters, but slavery itself. Speaking of a hypothetical war that might pit the United States allied with France against Britain, Ralph Izard, who had lived in both London and Paris, and who had welcomed *citoyen* Genêt to Charleston with open arms, wrote:

By a decree of the Convention of France, all the Slaves in their Colonies are emancipated. A joint war with France, under the present circumstances, would occasion a prodigious number of the lower order of Frenchmen to come to this Country, who would fraternise with our Democratical Clubs, & introduce the same horrid tragedies among our Negroes, which have been so fatally exhibited in the French Islands. Are the inhabitants of South Carolina ignorant of these things; or is it the will of God that the Proprietors of Negroes should themselves be the Instruments of destroying that species of property?[35]

From Georgia up to Virginia, slaveowning whites entered a new era of panic that at times crossed over into mass hysteria over the prospect of black revolutionary infiltration from the island. "Our town swarms with strange Negroes," wrote the Norfolk County commandant Colonel Willis Wilson from Portsmouth, Virginia, to Governor Henry Lee in August 1793. In a panic, Wilson demanded that Lee send troops to defend against the "many hundreds [of] French Negroes" in the Portsmouth streets.[36]

The looming post-Sonthonax fear in the slaveowners' collective imagination of infiltration by black warriors augured rising prices for suppliers of domestically born people. No one wanted a foreign slave trade now, not even South Carolina.

By this time, Jefferson was positively bullish on the profits to be made from reproduction of the enslaved. In April 1794, he wrote to Madame Plumard de Bellanger, a friend from Paris whose relative, J. P. P. Derieux, was living in Charlottesville and doing poorly. Blaming Derieux's bankruptcy on the Haitian Revolution, Jefferson politely asked Madame Plumard to send her relative money. He promised to see to it that her money would be put in the most conservative investment possible, the capitalized womb: "I think I may pledge myself that it shall be every farthing of it laid out in lands and negroes, which besides a present support bring a silent profit of from 5. to 10. per cent in this country by the increase in their value."[37]

Exiled Domingan planters, many of whom clung to the belief that they would return to claim their rightful real and human property, told terrifying tales that became further elaborated in the telling, further radicalizing US slaveowners.

But the exodus from Saint-Domingue to North America did not only bring paranoia. The Domingans were the world leaders in plantation technology. They brought skills, techniques, and knowledge everywhere they went, to say nothing of arts and culture. In eastern Cuba and Puerto Rico, they introduced the cultivation of coffee, subsequently a mainstay for those mountainous territories, along with a creolized music and other cultural paradigms that still resonate in those islands today. In South Carolina, they showed the few farmers who were still growing indigo new chemical reagents they could use in the process.

In Baltimore, which conducted much maritime trade with Saint-Domingue under Toussaint's leadership, the Domingans' influence was profound. Their boatwrights, both enslaved and free, knew French boatbuilding techniques, plus they knew all about building pirate ships, and Baltimore was heavily invested in the pirate-ship business. We can read "French" as meaning "Domingan" in the advertisement in the June 17, 1795, issue of the *Maryland Journal and Baltimore Universal Daily Advertiser* that offered a "New Vessel for Sale[:] . . . built at Baltimore and launched the latter part of last month. She is built with live-oak and cedar, nailed and finished *after the French manner* (emphasis added), being calculated for extraordinary sailing."[38] The Domingans brought new ideas of construction and finish to what was becoming a uniquely Baltimorean style of boat: the steeply raked, low-draft, fastest-thing-on-the-water vessel that would later become known as the Baltimore clipper.

With virtually all of Antillean trade being illegal according to the laws of one or another European country, vessels had to be fast and light, so everything was sacrificed to speed in this new model, which carried less freight than state-sanctioned merchant marines. These vessels were narrow and shallow, so they could go places large ocean-going vessels couldn't. The crew slept on deck. Many were fitted with "sweeps" (oars), so they could drop their sails and creep unseen when they set sail at night, in the dark of the moon.[39] With their strongly raked masts, they could outfly any ship if they were to its windward.[40] They looked dashing; the Baltimore boatwrights prided themselves in the quality of their construction.

Though the major influx of Domingans did not come to Louisiana until 1809, the professions of journalism and law there were begun by Domingans; they founded newspapers and participated in the writing of the state's constitution of 1812, which was debated and written in French, then sent to Washington in translation.[41] Stars of Saint-Domingue's theater scene took refuge in New Orleans, where their language was understood. The first great US piano virtuoso and arguably the greatest nineteenth-century US composer was the Domingan-descended New Orleanian Louis Moreau Gottschalk. Naturalist and artist John James Audubon was Domingan-born.

One celebrated refugee of the Haitian Revolution went to Spanish-controlled Florida. The black, Domingan-born general Georges Biassou was an early leader of the slave uprising—he had received a blessing from Boukman himself—and was subsequently Toussaint Louverture's superior officer in the Spanish army. Toussaint went over to the French army after the National Convention ratified Sonthonax's emancipation proclamation, but Biassou remained with the Spanish. The two wound up fighting each other before Biassou ultimately evacuated.

Biassou was a fully commissioned general of the Spanish army in good standing when he arrived in Florida in early 1796 with an entourage of twenty-three, including five family members and one slave. "The black general strolled through the streets of St. Augustine in fine clothes trimmed in gold," writes Jane Landers, "wearing the gold medal of [Spanish King] Charles IV, a silver-trimmed saber, and a fancy ivory and silver dagger."[42] As slaveowning planters in Florida—many of them English speakers who had come in from the north—watched in horror, Biassou and his men received land grants and began clearing the ground for plantations. They spoke of more of their black countrymen being on the way, though Spain wasn't about to let that happen.

A black man who had killed slaveowners was living in comfort, with full military authority, in Florida. Nothing could have been more calculated to disturb the Georgians and Carolinians, who for their part were experiencing an agricultural revolution that would create a vast new market for slaves.

The Lynx, a replica of a privateer from the War of 1812, flying the fifteen-star flag (1795–1818).

⇒ Part Four ⇐

The Star-Spangled Slave Trade

25

The Cotton Club

The experiments made in planting Annual Cotton has generally prov'd successful in respect to quantity and quality. But unless some engine be found as will take out the Seed agreeably to that Sort which is rais'd in the West Indias, no great quantity can be obtain'd. That of the West Indias will not produce Cotton here and is easily divested of its' Seed; But the Sort which grows here is far more difficult, and at present is no otherwise cleans'd than by a tedius picking.[1]

—Thomas Causton, letter to the Trustees of Georgia, 1741

COTTON CROPS HAD BEEN grown in the North American colonies every year from 1607 forward, but American cotton was not wanted by the English during colonial days, nor was mass production of cotton textiles yet possible.

British policy was protective of its woolens industry. But Britain was running out of land on which to raise sheep for wool, and a series of industrial inventions caused the manufacture of cotton textiles to overwhelm the older woolens manufacture.[2] Machines could card the cotton (untangle its fibers) and comb it (align the fibers, making a more compact, tightly weavable yarn). Hargreaves's spinning jenny (1764) spun the yarn into thread multiple strands at a time. All the different machines were combined under one roof into a single, integrated textile factory, and then there were a thousand such factories. Remembered as the Industrial Revolution, its input was cotton, and cotton's input was enslaved children.

Cotton's desirability for manufacturers rested on its unique strength: each cotton fiber (the "lint") is a single cell. First the fibers grow long, then, after seventeen days, the cellulose walls begin to thicken. There are only four species of domesticated cotton, which emerged independently in isolated parts of the world. Of the two that would grow in the Americas, one, *Gossypium barbadense*, became known as long-staple, or "Sea Island," or "black-seed" cotton, while the other, *Gossypium hirsutum*, was short-staple, or "upland," or "green-seed" cotton. The two were genetically isolated from each other and did not easily interbreed.

The fibers of *G. barbadense* were longer and stronger, and it was easier to separate the fibers from the seeds and the lint; but in North America, it would only grow on the Sea Islands and inland for thirty miles or so. This was the crop that Thomas Causton was lamenting would not grow in Savannah, but in 1786 it was successfully raised for the first time in Georgia with seed brought from the Bahamas. The fibers could be removed from the seed mechanically by means of a roller gin—a machine with rollers that plucked the fiber off, preserving its length and orientation.[3]

The other variety of cotton, *G. hirsutum*, which today accounts for more than 90 percent of the world cotton crop, could be cultivated across a much broader area, and it had a higher yield than long-staple; unfortunately, as Causton noted, it was too labor-intensive to clean by hand. Planters were growing it in areas where Sea Island cotton would not grow, using several types of cumbersome, labor-intensive foot- or hand-and-foot-operated gins to pull the fibers from the seed.

A mechanical solution to that problem could open up vast new possibilities for cotton, and Thomas Jefferson wanted to find it. The US Patent Office, established in 1790, was his responsibility as secretary of state. He wrote in 1792 to William Pierce of New Jersey, who was advertising a machine that would mechanically tear the fibers from the boll and sweep the seeds away, but Pierce failed to answer the letter. The following year, however, Jefferson received a drawing of such a machine from Eli Whitney, a newly minted Yale graduate and mechanical prodigy from Massachusetts. While staying as a guest on the Mulberry Grove plantation near Port Wentworth, Georgia, Whitney built a prototype cotton gin. Jefferson expedited the patent, writing Whitney on November 16, 1793:

> The only requisite of the law now uncomplied with is the forwarding a model, which being received your patent may be made out & delivered to your order immediately.
>
> As the state of Virginia, of which I am, carries on household manufactures of cotton to a great extent, as I also do myself, and one of our great

embarrassments is the cleaning the cotton of the seed, I feel a considerable interest in the success of your invention for family use.[4]

Jefferson's term "family use" referred, as was customary, to his extended "family" of captives, as per Whitney's sales-talk answer to Jefferson: "It is the stated task of one negro to clean fifty [pounds] . . . of the green-seed cotton Per Day. This task he usually completes by one oClock in the afternoon."[5] Whitney's machine, a sawtooth, or "saw," gin, solved the problem of cleaning cotton by redefining it. The twenty-six-inch-long tabletop machine didn't pull the fibers off, leaving them intact and combable, like the roller gin; it used teeth to chomp them off, so it could not be used on long-staple cotton without destroying its value. It produced an inferior fiber, a third the length of roller-ginned Sea Island cotton, that was not what textile manufacturers wanted to use for high-value goods.

But massification was happening. While the *hirsutum* cotton processed by Whitney's gin was of lower quality, the South could turn out a tremendous amount of it. Having transitioned to highly productive steam-powered Watts-engine mills, Lancashire's textile businesses had the capacity to handle all the cotton the South could produce. The immediate consequence of Whitney's saw gin was to give upcountry South Carolina and Georgia their new staple crop—the two states produced the majority of United States cotton until 1821—but its long-term consequence was to create the cotton kingdom of the South.

It was not simply a switch that was flipped on in 1793: improvements and accommodations had to be made, including to the machines of Britain, which had to be refitted for the shorter-staple cotton. The power loom, first used in 1785, took until about 1820 to become reliable, but once it was, it gave Britain's textile industry capacity far in excess of the available supply of cotton thread. At first the gins were powered by horses, then by steam. Another invention, the screw press, compacted cotton into bales, which were then compressed into place in the holds of vessels by "screwmen"—highly paid, muscular artisans who used specialized equipment to apply enormous screw-pressure to the already compressed bales.

The success of the saw gin sparked new enthusiasm for premium long-staple Sea Island cotton as well, which, processed by the roller gin, sold for three times as much per pound as *hirsutum*, in much smaller quantities.

><

More or less concurrently with the rise of cotton, Spanish Louisiana became a late arrival to the longtime major staple crop of the hemisphere: sugar. Amid the market scramble caused by the Saint-Domingue rebellion, sugar was fetching high prices that caused explosive growth of canefields in Cuba to the south and east of Havana. The port of Matanzas, which the British had not even bothered with when they occupied Havana in 1762, would soon begin its career as the cultured, affluent "Athens of Cuba." Cuba was in constant communication with Spanish Louisiana, whose governor reported from New Orleans to the Spanish captain general in the strategic hub city of Havana.

Unlike Cuba, Louisiana could not make sugar. Louisiana freezes in the winter, and its nine months' growing season was thought to make sugar production unfeasible, since a crop of sugarcane was considered to require some thirteen to fifteen months of growth and several months of harvest. But in 1795, working with a Domingan sugar chemist, the planter Étienne de Boré found a way to produce a light, sweet syrup from the sucrose in Louisiana cane; the method required the labor force to work long hours in damp cold. There had been other such initiatives, but Boré's sugar crop, produced by forty enslaved laborers, was the famous one: after it brought him $12,000, sugar plantations sprang up along both sides of the Mississippi. By the following year there were ten sugar refineries in operation.

Sugar operations were large and capital-intensive: those with fortunes could make their fortunes larger, but it was much easier to get started in cotton. The sugar plantations of south Louisiana became the highest-priced farmland in the South as the area around the lower Mississippi filled up with slave labor camps and the mansions they supported.

The sugar regime had come to North America, creating a voracious new demand for labor. But there was a complication: the Pointe Coupée slave rebellion conspiracy was uncovered in the spring of 1795. The testimony from the promptly held trials made it clear that radical ideas from the French and Haitian Revolutions had reached Louisiana. According to the testimony, conspiracy leader Jean Baptiste said, "we could do the same here as at Le Cap [Cap Français in Saint-Domingue]."[6] Twenty-three people were promptly tried and executed, and Spanish authorities, already nervous about infiltration of Jacobin radicals into the French-speaking population they uneasily governed, banned slave importation, even as labor-hungry plantations were springing up along the banks of the river, where the conspirators' heads were placed at intervals, impaled on pikes.

But the planters were determined to acquire slaves, and their regime had only begun.

The pro-French turmoil in Philadelphia pushed the Federalists closer to Britain.

The 1794 treaty that John Jay negotiated with Britain at President Washington and Treasury Secretary Hamilton's behest resolved a number of issues stemming from the War of Independence and laid the groundwork for ten years or so of relative peace between Britain and the United States, which was a boon for American shippers. However, Jay, a pro-British Federalist who had been against American independence and who detested slavery, dropped a major sticking point from the negotiations: the issue of compensation for slaveowners for the loss of their slaves during the war. The treaty was then more easily resolved, but at the domestic political price of cutting the Southern claimants loose. Moreover, the treaty appeared to be an alliance with Britain, which in those tense times meant against France.

Beginning with Jefferson, who had filed a claim for compensation, Southern slaveowners were furious about Jay's dropping their demands, and they made their displeasure felt. Henceforth, US diplomats in negotiations with foreign powers, whatever their domestic position on slavery—even John Quincy Adams—maintained "a unanimity in favor of guarding slavery from foreign harm," in Ward M. McAfee's words, "even to the extent of claiming it as a constitutionally recognized national institution."[7]

In Nashville, the twenty-eight-year-old Andrew Jackson thought Jay's treaty had created an "alarming situation" and wondered, "will it End in a Civil warr[?]"[8] In Paris, Jay's treaty was seen as aggression. As the pro-French Democratic-Republican societies in the United States protested, the partisan breach in American politics widened. English and French alike identified the party of Hamilton as pro-English and that of Jefferson as pro-France.

Jay's Treaty seems to have been a spur for Manuel Godoy, the "Prince of Peace" in charge of Spanish affairs for King Carlos IV, to cut a deal with the Americans. On October 27, 1795, negotiations with Spain by Thomas Pinckney (Charles Cotesworth Pinckney's younger brother) yielded the Treaty of San Lorenzo, by which Spain acknowledged the United States' "right of deposit"—i.e., to place goods for transshipment—at the port of New Orleans, which meant that the cotton and sugar that was beginning to be cultivated in large quantities could find an outlet, along with all the other products that came from the grow-ing upriver population.

The Treaty of San Lorenzo temporarily resolved a part of the Florida con-troversy by ceding to the United States a portion of the territory that comprised about the lower third of present-day Mississippi and Alabama. This Mississippi Territory did not extend down to the Gulf Coast, but it included the Mississippi River port of Natchez. It was a tremendously useful acquisition for the busi-nesses of cotton and slaves, but the all-important coastal zone, including the port of Mobile, remained part of Spanish-controlled West Florida.

As part of organizing the Mississippi Territory, the Anglo-Americans marked an international boundary in 1798 by hacking out a neutral ground between their territory and that of the Spanish: a sixty-foot gash in the forest growth from the Mississippi River eastward all the way to Georgia—cut by slave labor, needless to say.[9] Foreign slave importation into the new territory was strictly forbidden; the labor would have to be purchased from domestic sources.

In Paris, the five-man Directory, three of them Jacobins, brought a more conser-vative government to power on November 2, 1795. The Royalist Charles Maurice de Talleyrand-Périgord, who had lived unhappily in Philadelphia after fleeing the Terror (unlike Genêt, he was never officially received by President Washing-ton), returned home on September 25, 1796, and became foreign minister for the Directory in July 1797, just before the Coup of 18 Fructidor (September 4) brought a disastrous group to power within the Directory. Authoritarian and incompetent, this new Directory repressed journalists and declared the state bankrupt, stiffing France's creditors, even as the Corsican general Napoleon Bonaparte was conquering Italy in the name of France.

At a time when candidates did not campaign for office in the public way we have since become used to, John Adams beat Thomas Jefferson in the 1796 presidential election, one that entailed a Virginia-South Carolina split: Adams's running mate was South Carolina Federalist Charles Pinckney, and South Caro-lina failed to support Jefferson. But Jefferson got the second highest vote total, so under the laws then in force, he, not Pinckney, became vice president, though he was Adams's political enemy. (Adams may have had occasion to recall the words of diplomat Arthur Lee, who in 1788 when sending a copy of the draft

Constitution to Adams in England, complained about the creation of the office of vice president, "whose sole business seems to intrigue."[10])

By then, the diplomatic break between France and the United States was complete. With Talleyrand as its would-be head, the Directory looked to restore the colonial project that the Seven Years' War had arrested thirty years previously: to control the North American continent, even as France expanded its empire to control the rest of the world. By 1796, six hundred US merchant ships were doing business in Saint-Domingue. But when French privateers started attacking, hundreds were lost. When three American diplomats (John Marshall, Elbridge Gerry, and Charles Cotesworth Pinckney) tried to resolve the issue, Talleyrand sent go-betweens to solicit an enormous bribe—$250,000—before he would allow them to be received as diplomats. This was the "XYZ Affair," so called because French diplomats' names were redacted from documents that, to Talleyrand's surprise, the Adams administration released to the public.*

American indignation over XYZ was the spark, though not the reason, for the Quasi-War with France, an undeclared war during the second half of the John Adams administration, from 1798 to 1800. The affair cost Talleyrand his post with the Directory, though he soon worked his way back into power via his alliance with the ascendant Napoleon.

The number-one reason for the Quasi-War, as enumerated by the Federalist Secretary of State Timothy Pickering (leader of a disunionist movement for New England to secede and establish a Northern confederacy), was "spoliations and maltreatment of [US] vessels at sea by French ships of war and privateers."[11] The pro-British Federalists began what has been remembered as "black cockade fever," wearing long trailing black ribbons from the back of their hats. As Republicans countered with red—or red, white, and blue—ribbons, Philadelphia divided into two color-coded camps.

Some Federalists believed that the democratic frenzy was the result of a conspiracy of a secret society of Illuminati, with French and Domingan membership. The Republican position was expressed by Virginia senator Henry Tazewell in a letter to Andrew Jackson: "The Contest between them [England and France] is a Contest of political principles. One or the other must be annihilated . . . Either monarchey or Republicanism must be rooted out of Europe, or the

---

*It was first referred to as the WXYZ affair, in which "W" was Caron Beaumarchais, who had acted as a go-between; Beaumarchais is also remembered as the librettist of Mozart's class-conflict opera farce *Le Nozze di Figaro*.

War will not cease. If England succeeds, Monarchy will become more formidable then ever to the liberties of mankind . . . If France succeeds liberty will at least for a time be emancipated from the despotism of Kings."[12]

Attempting to combat a prolonged period of domestic political unrest following the French Revolution and war with France, and pushed by Pickering, the Adams administration passed the Alien Act, with which they hoped to deport French people—they were never used for prosecution, but they motivated some French-speakers to leave the United States—and the Sedition Act, which they used against the highly partisan press.

In response, Jefferson drafted the Kentucky Resolutions of 1798, in which he argued that states could find federal laws unconstitutional and oppose them. He did this anonymously, while he was Adams's vice president and as such was in theory part of the administration that had promulgated the Alien and the Sedition Acts. His stalking horse was Kentucky state representative John Breckinridge, who introduced the resolutions in the Kentucky House as his own, keeping Jefferson's involvement secret.

Though the Kentucky Resolutions are largely forgotten today, they became a touchstone for antebellum separatists because in them Jefferson put the soon-to-be-a-buzzword "nullification" into the American political vocabulary: "[T]he several states who formed [the Constitution], being sovereign and independent, have the unquestionable right to judge of its infraction; and that a nullification, by those [states], of all unauthorized acts . . . is the rightful remedy." Madison in 1799 drafted a similarly anonymous, somewhat milder, document, the Virginia Resolutions, which did not use the word "nullification."

By the time Toussaint negotiated a British withdrawal in 1798, some fifteen thousand British soldiers had died during Britain's ill-advised campaign to take Saint-Domingue.[13] One of the great military debacles of British history, it marked in blood the point at which Britain turned away from its sponsorship of plantation slavery. By this time, Toussaint was firmly in control in Saint-Domingue, and, as life became more orderly there, some planters even began returning.

In France, the Coup of 18 Brumaire (November 9), 1799, definitively put an end to dreams of democracy and republicanism, deposing the Directory in favor of the French Consulate government. This left only one republic in the world: the United States. Talleyrand was the coup's chief political strategist and, as of February 7, 1800, its head was First Consul Napoleon Bonaparte, who had returned from a failed two-year mission in Egypt days before.

"The recovery of colonial power was the first of all Bonaparte's objects," wrote Henry Adams, and every "decisive event in the next three years of his career was subordinated to it."[14] Bonaparte's Consulate intended to re-establish France's lost colonial plantation empire in the Americas, but, in the words of biographer Steven Englund, "the measures proved to be such a failure that posterity has stopped seeing the policy as foundational."[15]

Napoleon's ascendancy was the definitive end of the abolition movement in France. A new French Constitution specifically exempted the colonies from metropolitan law, which was tantamount to re-legalizing slavery.[16] Saint-Domingue was still theoretically under the French flag, but Toussaint was in charge and had restored some of the colony's sugar production using conscripted labor. In order to re-establish French control of Saint-Domingue, it was necessary to pacify the high seas so as to have clear sailing for the fleet, which Talleyrand and Napoleon did by making peace with the United States—easily accomplished—and with Britain, which took longer.

Relations between Toussaint Louverture's government in Saint-Domingue and the United States were not bad under President Adams. Saint-Domingue, still in theory a colony of France, was exporting coffee and sugar again under Toussaint, and US merchants, especially those from Baltimore, were doing business in its port cities despite the problems. During the Quasi-War, Toussaint had taken the extraordinary step—for which, along with related offenses, he paid with his life—of brokering a separate peace with Adams, because supplies from North America were essential to Saint-Domingue's survival. An arrangement between the United States and Britain brought the British navy to patrol Saint-Domingue, allowing for commerce to continue, though the conservative British prime minister William Pitt the Younger was horrified by the idea of a black government.

The Adams administration went so far as to support Toussaint with the US Navy (the first intervention by the US military in another country's war) in a decisive 1800 battle in the south of Saint-Domingue between forces commanded by Toussaint's general Jean-Jacques Dessalines and those of André Rigaud.

As the United States entered into war with France, there was renewed fear in the South that slaves would once again become weapons of war in the hands of the enemy. Henry Knox, the former secretary of war, in the words of Alexander DeConde,

> urged Adams to raise an army for protection against a possible attack by "ten thousand blacks" recruited by the French. He feared that the invaders

would land at "the defenceless ports of the Carolinas and Virginia," where slaves would join them in a march of conquest.

Rumors spread saying that special Negro agents were distributing arms among the slaves in preparation for the French attack. These rumors were repeated in a Federalist pamphlet published in April. "Take care, take care, you sleepy southern fools," a Federalist gazetteer warned. "Your negroes will probably be your masters this day twelve month."[17]

Though Spain was the pre-eminent colonial power of the Americas, it was increasingly subordinate to France. Louisiana had been founded by France, but had been given over to Spain in 1762 as part of France's disgrace at the close of the Seven Years' War. Now Napoleon made a secret pact with Carlos IV, the Italian-born Bourbon king of Spain to recover Louisiana. Carlos, who flattered himself Napoleon's ally but was more like his stooge, was known as El Cazador (The Hunter), for the avidity with which he hunted game on his private preserve, to the neglect of affairs of state. In exchange for Louisiana, Napoleon swapped Carlos the Italian Duchy of Parma as a kingdom for his son-in-law. Key to this retrocession of Louisiana from Spain to France was Napoleon's promise not to alienate—not to give away or to sell—Louisiana.

Napoleon's intention in retaking control of Louisiana was to use it as a supply base for the plantation empire he was planning to re-establish on Saint-Domingue, where every bit of ground was to be used to produce cash crops. The English sugar islands were being provisioned from the United States, and in the absence of a French supply base, so would a French island colony have to be.

Hostilities between France and the United States ended on September 30, 1800, when Napoleon's brother, Joseph Bonaparte, signed with the Adams administration the Convention of Mortefontaine, named for the lesser Bonaparte's country estate. But, writes Henry Adams:

> The next day, October 1, [Louis Alexandre] Berthier [Napoleon's chief of staff] signed at San Ildefonso the treaty of retrocession [of Louisiana to France], which was equivalent to a rupture of the relations established four-and-twenty hours earlier. Talleyrand was aware that one of these treaties undid the work of the other. The secrecy in which he enveloped the treaty of retrocession, and the pertinacity with which he denied its existence, showed his belief that Bonaparte had won a double diplomatic triumph over the United States.[18]

Napoleon's plan to establish an empire in the Americas was moving forward. Meanwhile, Saint-Domingue's legacy of emancipation via violent rebellion was percolating throughout the slave societies of the hemisphere.

In Cuba, practitioners of the Kongo religion speak of Zarabanda, "Nsalabanda," the blacksmith god of iron and war. In Haiti, there is Ogou Feray, the creolized Yoruba blacksmith liberation-fighter *lwa*. In Richmond, in 1800, a well-planned conspiracy was discovered, led by one Gabriel, a literate, enslaved blacksmith who could split a grain scythe down the middle to make a pair of fearsome swords and had stockpiled a number of them. Gabriel had been sentenced to hang the year before, when he bit off the ear of a white overseer who had whipped him, but he was too valuable for his captor, Thomas Prosser, to lose, so Gabriel was allowed to take advantage of an archaic law that commuted his sentence to being publicly branded if he could quote a Bible verse. Let off on the condition of good behavior, with a brand burned into his skin, he was soon jailed again, forcing Prosser to post a thousand dollars to get him back, an indication of how lucrative the rented-out services of a blacksmith could be.[19]

Virginia had modernized its penal code as of 1796, reclassifying twenty-seven different kinds of offenses as punishable by prison time instead of corporal abuse and restricting capital punishment to murderers. To deal with the new prison population this change would generate, Jefferson's friend, the English-born architect Benjamin Henry Latrobe, the first professional architect working in the United States, received his first major American commission in 1797, to build the Virginia State Penitentiary in 1797. The first penitentiary to be built as such in the United States, it was an Enlightenment-era prison, part of an agenda that emphasized a notion, advanced by Jefferson, of reform over punishment, with the architectural innovation of individual cells that facilitated the carceral innovation of solitary confinement.[20] It quickly became a hellhole, was rebuilt in 1905, and was closed in 1992.

Gabriel's conspirators planned a surprise attack on that partly finished penitentiary, where the militia's weapons were stored but were only lightly guarded. After that, it was said, they would burn the city and hold Governor James Monroe hostage. Gabriel's plot was quite real, and could well have achieved those tactical objectives. Terrifyingly for the slaveowners, it was, like Boukman's uprising, widely networked among agents on different plantations. It grew out of routine socializing among the enslaved of the region, who might see each other in a number of ways, ranging from clandestine nighttime visits to church socials on Sunday.[21]

Gabriel and his network of conspirators were animated by an ideology that resonated fearfully in the post-Saint-Domingue world: with the bold paralysis of the apparatus of state and the violent chaos they intended to cause as leverage, they planned to demand freedom for the slaves of Virginia.[22] For the terrified slaveowners of Richmond, "the most commonly repeated notion of how far the slaughter of whites would go simply held that all whites would be killed," writes Lacy K. Ford, "except Quakers, Methodists, and Frenchmen, whom Gabriel planned to spare because they had tried to help the slaves win freedom."[23]

Much the same way that the Stono Rebellion was a clear demonstration of the threat posed by Spain, Gabriel's plan was understood to be a signal of the perceived vulnerability of the slave regime to the revolutionary abolitionism of the French, even though in fact the viciously anti-abolitionist Napoleon was now in charge there. As with the later scapegoating of "outside agitators" in the civil rights era, saboteurs were thought necessary to catalyze uprisings among enslaved laborers, who were believed to be otherwise inert. Quite possibly there had been a "Frenchman" or two trying to foment slave uprising, or perhaps it was a figment of the paranoia of the times; the implication of two unnamed Frenchmen by witnesses at the trial cast a pall of suspicion over all the "French" people in Richmond, whether French-born or merely Huguenot-descended. The press denounced "the French principle of liberty and equality," an idea that was self-evidently un-Virginian, because it was incompatible with slavery.[24]

Gabriel's rebellion was foiled by a spectacular storm—in Monroe's words, "checked by the extraordinary torrent of rain which fell"—on the night the assault had been planned for, which was interpreted by both conspirators and townspeople as divine intervention.[25] The plot was then betrayed by Pharoah and Tom, two enslaved informers fearful of the rebellion's consequences, who were subsequently purchased from their owners by the State of Virginia for five hundred dollars each and were not only emancipated as a reward, but also ultimately received an annuity of fifty dollars each a year.[26] Amid fears that the conspiracy might still be active and moving forward, Monroe initiated a manhunt for Gabriel, who was described by Prosser as "twenty four years of age, six feet two or three inches high, darkish complexion, long visage, with a gloomy insidious brow, short black knotty hair, some scars on his head."[27]

Monroe informed Jefferson on September 9 that "about" thirty prisoners were being held.[28] There was considerable concern that the new, untested penitentiary would not be able to hold them; adding to the tension, it also turned out that four thousand muskets delivered to the militia and stored in the penitentiary were shoddy goods that were "improperly constructed" and "badly executed."[29]

Though the conspiracy had not resulted in any bloodshed, trials began on September 11 and hangings began the following day. On September 18, thirteen men from Richmond petitioned the Henrico County court to move the executions somewhere out of sight, "as the frequent Executions that have lately taken place, has been extremely distressing to the view of our families—especially the female members."[30] In response, three of the condemned were halted "in the cart" on their journey to the gallows for a reprieve until the place of execution could be moved.[31]

With a price of three hundred dollars on his head, the "Black General" Gabriel escaped Richmond by boat, but ran aground four miles below Richmond. Taken up by a schooner that was going to Norfolk, he was brought back to Richmond under heavy guard on September 28, a few hours before Monroe's youngest child died after a few days' illness, overwhelming him "with grief," as he wrote to Madison the next day.[32]

Monroe and Gabriel—whom Monroe referred to not by his name, but as "this slave"—had what must have been a dramatic face-to-face: "From what he said to me," wrote Monroe, "he seemed to have made up his mind to die, and to have resolved to say but little on the subject of the conspiracy."[33] Gabriel attempted no defense at his trial but requested that his execution be postponed so that he could be hanged together with the others who would also be convicted. The request was granted, and Gabriel was hanged on October 10 together with George Smith, Gilbert, Tom, William, and Sam Graham.[34] By October 24, twenty-six people had been executed.[35]

With presidential voting about to begin October 31, it was a time of great political tension between Federalists and Democratic-Republicans. Jefferson was running for president again, and this time he was the leading candidate.

The poison-pen propagandist James Callender wrote to his employer, Thomas Jefferson, on September 13 from the Richmond jail, where he was serving his six-month sentence, that "nothing is talked of here but the recent conspiracy of the negroes."[36] Callender, who had fled Scotland one step ahead of the law in 1793, was one of only ten people convicted under President Adams's Sedition Act, for his book *The Prospect Before Us*. Funded by Jefferson, it was a sleazy work of character assassination that attacked Hamilton and Adams as monarchists while praising Jefferson in immodest terms.

Two days later, Monroe informed Jefferson that "the plan of an insurrection has been clearly proved, & appears to have been of considerable extent. 10. have been condemned & executed, and there are at least twenty perhaps 40. more to be tried, of whose guilt no doubt is entertained."[37] Twenty-six conspirators were hanged. Jefferson, whose preferred method of dealing with troublemakers on his plantations was to sell them to Southbound traders, wanted them disposed of by sale instead of hanging, and nine conspirators were, thereby realizing some income.

In the Richmond *Virginia Argus* of October 3, 1800, Callender—still loyal to Jefferson—responded to charges that had been levelled against him of having somehow been involved in Gabriel's rebellion by changing the subject back to vilifying Alexander Hamilton:

> If an idea so monstrous as that of promoting an African conspiracy can have entered into the head of any white man, he must have been a *Federalist*; for this plain reason. An insurrection, at the present critical moment, by the negroes of the southern States, would have thrown every thing into confusion, and consequently, it was to have prevented the choice of electors in the whole, or the greater part of the States to the south of the Potomac. Such a disaster must have tended directly to injure the interest of Mr. Jefferson, and to promote the slender *possibility* of a second election of Mr. Adams.
>
> I do not, for my part, believe that any white person whatever was concerned in the business. But if the country contains one man capable of conceiving such a project, it corresponds, in preference to the character of any other person, with that of Alexander Hamilton, the theoretical incendiary of Pittsburg,* and the grand Patriarch of American calamities.
> — JAMES T. CALLENDER.
> Richmond Jail.

Callender subsequently wrote a second volume of *The Prospect Before Us*, also funded by Jefferson.

Gabriel's plot sensitized electorate and politicians alike to the dangers of slave rebellion, with obsessive focus on the possibility of ideological contamination from Saint-Domingue. Virginia had a far greater slave population than

---

*Referring to the recent Whiskey Rebellion in Pennsylvania, which had erupted in response to a tax Hamilton had tried to impose.

anywhere else in the United States. Its 345,796 enslaved were overwhelmingly (322,199) in the eastern district, with only 23,597 of them in the non-plantation west of the state.[38] Virginia slaveowners had been terrorized by the nightmare that "the horrors of St. Domingo" could happen to them; now, they thought, it was coming closer.[39] The popular panic facilitated the adoption of the "Negro Acts," which had been previously been considered too harsh to pass. These were new state laws directed at slaves, and partly also at pro-emancipation evangelicals, particularly Methodists and Baptists. A suite of laws forbade masters from manumitting, removed rights of assembly for blacks and all assembly by them at night, and forbade religious instruction of slaves—though after pressure from evangelicals, the law was amended to allow religious gatherings if a majority of white people were present. A new military-style police organization, the Public Guard, was created as part of the militia in Richmond in 1801.[40]

President Jefferson wrote his minister to Britain, Rufus King, in 1802 that "the course of things in the neighboring islands of the West Indies appears to have given a considerable impulse to the minds of the slaves in different parts of the US. A great disposition to insurgency has manifested itself among them, which, in one instance, in the state of Virginia, broke out into actual insurrection," though of course Gabriel's conspiracy did not break out into actual insurrection but was merely planned. Jefferson, who thought the many hangings resulting from Gabriel's conspiracy—"between 20. and 30. I believe"—too severe, affirmed that they had caused public revulsion: "so extensive an execution could not but excite sensibility in the public mind." In other words, as terrified as the Virginians were, the repression was too grisly. The purpose of Jefferson's letter to King—at the request of the Virginia legislature, he noted—was to ask him to make inquiries in London into the possibility of using the English Sierra Leone colony not only as a "receptacle" for "insurgents" but also for future "emancipated negroes."[41]

Richmond's African American burial ground was rediscovered in the 1990s, and there is now a state historical marker for this potter's field at Fifteenth and Broad. The wide expanse is partly covered over by I-95 and was for years partly buried under a Virginia Commonwealth University parking lot. Before that, it had been the dog pound, and, before that, the site of the Richmond City Jail. The lot was transferred to the city in response to community initiatives,

A circle marks the approximate site of the execution of Gabriel. Richmond, June 2013.

resodded, and rededicated. It is now a flat, grassy memorial space framed by the interstate high overhead on one side and rail cars on the other.

To mark the gallows where Gabriel and five coconspirators were hanged in 1800—not that the exact spot is known—there is nothing more than a yellow cord strung around ground-level wickets, making a barely perceptible circle of power in the immensity of the field. To one side are two large trees with sashes tied around them, and, when we visited, small altars in the African manner. No one is allowed to play sports or picnic on the large field, respecting the space's memorial status as the trucks and train cars roll by above. It's walking distance from where Patrick Henry made his "Liberty or Death" speech, a quarter-century before Gabriel.

26

The Terrible Republic

Slaves! . . . Let us leave that qualifying epithet to the French themselves:
they have conquered to the point of ceasing to be free.[1]
—Haitian Declaration of Independence

GEORGE WASHINGTON DID NOT live to see Thomas Jefferson become president, nor were the two men on speaking terms when Washington expired, along with the eighteenth century, on December 14, 1799. Washington's widow, Martha Custis Washington, is said to have thought Jefferson "one of the most detestable of mankind."[2]

Lacking South Carolina's support, Jefferson had lost the 1796 election to John Adams. Open campaigning was at the time thought to be beneath the dignity of a presidential candidate, but as 1800 came around, lest anyone in South Carolina think the emancipation/deportation proposal of *Notes on the State of Virginia* meant that he was soft on slavery, Jefferson let it be known via Charles Pinckney that he "authorized his friends to declare as his assertion" that the Constitution did not give Congress the right to "touch in the remotest degree the question respecting the condition or property of slaves in any of the states."[3]

After a complicated election, culminating in a protracted standoff over a tie vote with Aaron Burr in the House of Representatives, Jefferson prevailed over the incumbent Adams, becoming president on March 4, 1801, with Burr as vice president. For the next twenty-four years, the presidency would be occupied by a "Virginia dynasty" of Jefferson and his protégés—actually, a Piedmont dynasty, from the Shenandoah Valley above the fall line of the James River, where Jefferson, Madison, and Monroe were relative neighbors. During those years (and subsequently, for that matter) foreign and domestic policy alike would reflect the concerns of the Southern states, and specifically Virginia: protecting slavery (which meant expanding it); preventing slave rebellion (which meant isolating Haiti); free trade (with the significant exception, in Virginia's case, of protectionism for the domestic slave trade); hard money (though an all-metal currency regime was utterly unworkable); a weak federal government (though once the Republicans took power, they came to like wielding it); and a budgetary conservatism that excluded projects for the public good.

Jefferson's ascent to the presidency was the first peaceful transfer of political power to another party in recorded history. He seems to have truly believed, as he expressed in an 1819 letter, that his election was a "Revolution of 1800" that was as significant a revolution as the one his younger self had personified with the Declaration of Independence.[4] The new Democratic-Republican party, usually just known as Republicans but sometimes as Democrats, attempted to implement Jefferson's philosophy of governance, which proved to be impractical.

Jefferson wanted an agrarian republic, where the "chosen people of God" would "labor in the earth." For the general operations of manufacture, "let our workshops remain in Europe," he wrote in *Notes*, though he subsequently founded a nail factory. He didn't want there to be *cities*, which he compared to "sores" on a body, and to that end he starved Washington City of infrastructural funds during his presidency, so that the capital consisted of two magnificent buildings in a malarial, muddy swamp.[5]

Jeffersonian democracy, as it came to be called, held that states' rights were paramount, and central government was at best a necessary evil. Debt was an evil to Jefferson, something to be cancelled as quickly as possible. Banks were an evil. Slavery was a great evil, but we have no alternative to the riches it brings.

Keeping a standing army was, as Madison expressed it during the Virginia ratification debate, "one of the greatest mischiefs that can possibly happen."[6] Jefferson attempted to defend the country from foreign aggression entirely by commercial sanction, a method he called "peaceable coercion." There would be nothing peaceful, however, about the coercion employed domestically to repress slave escape or rebellion. The constitutionally sanctioned "well-regulated militia" could put down rebellions and apprehend black people traveling without a pass, selling them to a trader if no one claimed them.

As president, Jefferson committed to his theory of governance by paying down the debt quickly rather than investing in defense. Moreover, in spite of having a long coastline to defend, he dismantled what military readiness the nation had, reducing the army from five thousand to three thousand, and, in a backhand blow to New England, mothballing the successful United States Navy that Adams had built.

A compulsive tinkerer, Jefferson couldn't resist refitting the navy, though he had no firsthand knowledge of naval affairs. He was taken with the idea of light, portable gunboats carrying a crew of twenty or so. These were heavily used in the Barbary War that the US Navy fought from 1801 to 1805 in Mediterranean North Africa, although the navy also relied on frigates and brigs in that war. Jefferson's remarkably bad idea was to make the entire navy into a fleet of the theoretically cheaper gunboats, relying on them as a domestic defense force.

Unfortunately, in that capacity the gunboats were almost useless; vessels that plied the relatively placid Mediterranean couldn't go to war in the stormy Atlantic, and they were dangerous and demoralizing for the sailors who manned them. They also turned out to be unexpectedly expensive. Some of them, however, were built in Virginia.

President Jefferson pardoned James Callender from his Sedition Act conviction and gave him fifty dollars, one-quarter of his fine, but Callender interpreted the gesture, wrote Jefferson, "not as a charity but a due, in fact as hushmoney."[7] Believing himself entitled to the postmastership of Richmond, Callender turned viciously on Jefferson, publishing their correspondence. In an article published in the Richmond *Recorder* on September 1, 1802, he broke the story that Jefferson "keeps, and for many years past has kept, as his concubine, one of his own slaves. Her name is SALLY . . . There is not an individual in the neighbourhood of Charlottesville who does not believe the story; and not a few who know it. . . . The *African venus* is said to officiate, as housekeeper at Monticello." Callender's role in American history ended the following year, when he drowned while drunk in three feet of James River water on July 17, 1803.

The years of Jefferson's and, subsequently, Madison's administrations were years of war between England and France, a war in which the United States was in many ways a participant, even as it declared its neutrality.

In this chaotic maritime war, American merchant vessels fell victim to seizures by predators of both countries. Jefferson had no effective response, and piracy became more common, a situation Jefferson's gunboats did nothing to abate.

The federal government had for years been trying to stop piracy, which overlapped with the slave trade. Responding to antislavery petitions, Congress passed the Act of 1794, subtitled "An Act to Prohibit the Carrying on the Slave Trade from the United States to any Foreign Place or Country," which went so far as to provide for money penalties, though not imprisonment, for outfitting vessels for the foreign slave trade. A subsequent congressional measure in 1800 authorized the taking of slavers as prizes, and in the last days of the Adams administration, the US Navy began capturing slavers in the West Indies. In the days of the gunboats, however, enforcement dropped off. During Jefferson's first term, by one estimate, US slavers carried 16 percent of the African slave trade, up from 9 percent the previous decade.[8]

Jefferson's policy toward Toussaint Louverture was markedly different from that of the non-slaveowner John Adams. He refused even to write a personal letter for his new consul to Saint-Domingue to carry to Louverture, as was diplomatic custom, nor would he direct the credentials to Louverture's attention, sending them merely to "Cap Français," an insult that Toussaint was quick to perceive.

Saint-Domingue had never declared independence from France, though Toussaint had infuriated Napoleon by sending him a new constitution for Saint-Domingue and declaring himself Governor for Life. As Jefferson described it in a November 24, 1801, letter to James Monroe, in Saint-Domingue "the blacks are established into a sovereignty de facto, and have organized themselves under regular law and government." Jefferson wrote in the context of wondering whether Saint-Domingue might be a possible colony on which to offload black people "exiled for acts deemed criminal by us, but meritorious perhaps by him." By "him," Jefferson meant Toussaint Louverture, but apparently could not bring himself to write the name, referring to him merely as "their present ruler."[9]

On this issue, at least, Jefferson and the First Consul coincided. Jefferson's explicitly racialized hatred of Toussaint was shared by Napoleon, who referred to Toussaint as the "gilded African," while Jefferson, in a letter to Burr, referred to Toussaint's men as "the Cannibals of the terrible republic."[10] But Jefferson still didn't know about Napoleon's secret plan to occupy Spanish Louisiana when, four months into his presidency, Louis-André Pichon, the French minister to Washington, broached the possibility of an armed French intervention in Saint-Domingue to prevent Toussaint's declaring independence. Jefferson replied that, given the hostility between Britain and France, Britain had to sign on first. Pichon reported Jefferson's words back to Paris: "in order that this concert may be complete and effective, you must make peace with England, then nothing will be easier than to furnish your army and fleet with everything and to reduce Toussaint to starvation."[11]

To Pichon's delight, the new President Jefferson, a veteran political intriguer with no military experience, had just conditionally greenlighted a hypothetical invasion of the Americas by Napoleon Bonaparte. But once Jefferson realized the implications for Louisiana, he withdrew his support.

Napoleon instructed Talleyrand in a letter of November 13, 1801, how to spin for British consumption his forthcoming invasion of Saint-Domingue: with racism. A black republic, it was assumed, would be a pirate state and a center of terrorism. Napoleon matter-of-factly wrote of "the course which I have taken of annihilating the government of the blacks in Saint-Domingue." Without his intervention, he warned, "the scepter of the New World would sooner or later fall into the hands of the blacks . . . the shock that would result for England [would be] incalculable, even as the shock of the blacks' empire, as relates to France, has been confused with that of revolution."[12]

The British saw Napoleon's plan for what it was. "The acquisition [of Louisiana]," reported Rufus King, Jefferson's envoy to Britain, paraphrasing British foreign secretary Lord Hawkesbury, "might enable France to extend her influence and perhaps her dominion up the Mississippi; and through the Lakes even to Canada. This would be realizing the plan, to prevent the accomplishment of which, the Seven Years' War took place."[13]

With the Treaty of Amiens on March 25, 1802, Britain and France made a peace that was more or less a capitulation on Britain's part. Though Prime Minister Henry Addington would declare war on France less than a year later, for the time being, the peace cleared the way at sea for French intervention in the Americas. While negotiations with Britain were in progress, Napoleon wasted no time in preparing his trusted brother-in-law, General Charles-Victor-Emmanuel Leclerc, to lead an expedition of some thirty thousand men, the largest fleet that had crossed the Atlantic to that date. "Troops were directed to ports, and shipyards in France, Holland and Spain intensified their activity in armaments," wrote Lieutenant General Baron Pamphile de Lacroix, who served in Leclerc's campaign. "The purpose of these armaments could not be doubted; they were self-evident . . . the most superficial observer could conclude, without mental effort, that immediate action was being taken to put Saint-Domingue back under the power of the metropolis."[14]

Cap Français in Saint-Domingue was only to be the first landing. While Leclerc's fleet was crossing the ocean during the brief window of peace between France and England, Jefferson's minister to France, Robert Livingston, correctly reported to Rufus King on December 30, 1801, that: "I know . . . that the armament, destined in the first instance for Hispaniola, is to proceed to Louisiana provided Toussaint makes no opposition."[15]

Bonaparte's intention was to invade the hemisphere under cover of subduing a slave rebellion, portraying his move internationally as a preemptive expedition against black terrorists, confining the English-speaking population along the East Coast and eventually driving them out, while controlling the rest of the hemisphere through puppet Spanish and Portuguese kings. Accordingly, Leclerc's brief was to subdue the *noirs* of Saint-Domingue, ship their leaders back to France in irons, and then proceed immediately on to Louisiana. Needless to say, Leclerc never complied with the latter instruction, because the black army of Saint-Domingue, together with the *Aedes aegypti* mosquito, beat the French. Leclerc's men died of yellow fever even more often than they died in combat with an organized if ill-equipped black military whose soldiers were, terrifyingly, not afraid to die.

When Leclerc's fleet appeared in Cap Français, Domingan general Henri Christophe burned the newly rebuilt town on February 4, 1802, torching his own house first and repositioning his forces in the mountains. After Leclerc betrayed Toussaint on June 7, kidnapping him to France to die in a freezing mountain prison cell after inviting him to a meeting, the command passed to Jean-Jacques Dessalines, who had formerly served as a general for the French.

At the time Dessalines took charge, Bonaparte still believed he was winning. He wrote to his minister of the marine, Denis Decrès, on June 19, 1802: "My intention is to take possession of Louisiana with the shortest delay, and that this expedition be made in the utmost secrecy, under the appearance of being directed on St. Domingo."[16] In July, the news arrived in Saint-Domingue that Napoleon had signed a decree reinstating slavery in Guadeloupe, and the resistance against France intensified. Dessalines gave an order that he is remembered for: *koupe tèt, boule kay*—cut off heads, burn houses.

The South was terrified.

Negro News.

" A curse will light upon the limbs of men,
" Domestic fury, and fierce civil strife;
" Shall cumber all our peaceful shores;
" Blood and destruction shall be so in use,
" And dreadful objects so familiar,
" That mothers shall but smile when they behold
" Their infants quarter'd with the hands of war."

North-Carolina.

RALEIGH, OCT. 19.

FRENCH NEGROES.

An important letter from a gentleman in Fayetteville, to the editors, dated 15th inst. follows: A letter received here yesterday, by a young gentleman of the Academy, from his father, a very respectable man in Georgetown, (s. c.) dated 11th inst. says:—" This town and neighborhood are all in great alarm, four French frigates from St. Domingo, were the whole of yesterday employed in landing brigand negroes at Mr. Alston's sea-shore plantation, Waccamaw; and it is said they have not landed less than 1000. The militia are marching from all directions against them. I presume those are the frigates that were some time ago at New-York, and finding that they could not effect their design there, steered round to take advantage of a more defenceless place."

Columbia.

WASHINGTON, OCT. 20.

FRENCH NEGROES.

☞ We stop the press to publish the following.
Extract of a letter from a gentleman in Georgetown, (S. C.) dated 10th Oct. to a gentleman in this place.
" The infernal French are disgorging the whole of their wretched blacks upon our shores.

An express arrived this afternoon to the Brigadier General, with information that a French frigate was landing negroes about 32 miles from this place. Every inhabitant of the town was ordered to equip himself and march to oppose them; which they did this afternoon with the greatest cheerfulness, and I believe would have gone with more pleasure, had they to combat with the French."

New-York.

NEW-YORK, OCT. 23.

FRENCH NEGROES.

Extract of a letter from a respectable gentleman in Georgetown, (S. C.) to a merchant in this city, dated the 15th inst.

" Three French frigates left the Hook the day we did, and we have just heard of their landing their negroes on Long-Bay. We are all summoned to turn out with the different companies, and the orders are, not to take a single negro, but shoot them all—we are informed they have landed about 1000; by to-morrow morning there will be soldiers enough at the place to prevent more landing—if they get scattered among our negroes, it will be a dreadful thing."

Massachusetts.

BOSTON GAZETTE, NOV. 1.

MORE OF THE FRENCH NEGROES.

Extract of a letter from a gentleman residing in the vicinity of Georgetown, (S. C.) to his friend in this town, dated 11th Oct. 1802.

" We expect to have the trouble of taking care of about a 1000 negroes, which the French have landed on our coast."

The sources from which we derive the intelligence under our mail head, respecting the attempt of the French to pollute our Southern shores by landing the refractory negroes from their colonies, are too authentic to be doubted. Their views in this outrageous transaction, cannot be questioned; and should they succeed, the most dreadful consequences must ensue.—How long will the patience of our democrats bear with the insolence of that nation, and how many times must they be told, before they will believe, that the destruction of this country, ever since the reign of democracy commenced in France, has been their avowed design, and the object of their unceasing pursuit? Will they, with this glaring instance before them, with their eyes open, proceed to fill up their elections with men who have even avowed their attachment to that proud and insidious nation; and who have always been ready to second all their attempts to subject us to their malignant views? Will the citizens of this district any longer submit to be deluded by that system of political sorcery which has been but too successfully practised on their unsuspecting credulity? No, let those who have not yet become familiarized to the schemes of wickedness, who have not yet learnt to calculate the quantum of individual compensation which they are to receive in return, for the ruin which they shall effect—reflect a moment, and this day, while they have it in their power, blast the wicked hopes of those men who have ever been coadjutors in these designs.

Articles warning of an imaginary invasion of "French Negroes" in the Courier of New Hampshire, November 11, 1802.

Fear of "French negroes" was general, not just in the slaveholding South but in Cuba as well, where slaveowners were prohibited from importing slaves who had lived in foreign colonies, and in Spanish Louisiana.[17] A 1797 insurrection plot in South Carolina that may or may not have been real was attributed to "French negroes." Five years later, as the carnage in Saint-Domingue mounted, a more serious eruption of popular fear had its origin in New York, where, writes Lacy K. Ford, the rumor began that "the French planned to release incendiary black 'brigands' up and down the Atlantic coast." An unidentified ship in the waters near Georgetown, South Carolina, in 1802 set that heavily black area "on the razor's edge of alarm," so that "the sighting of a single black man, allegedly of French background, traveling without a pass on a Saturday evening prompted the rapid spread of reports that an armed brigade of French-speaking Caribbean insurrectionists had finally come ashore at Georgetown."[18] In a fit of panic, the state militia was mobilized to resist a phantom invasion. The panic was transmitted in the popular press, as newspapers published accounts describing the imaginary landing of "French negroes."

While this panic was occurring, the French invaders were dying by the thousands in Saint-Domingue. With Leclerc's forces dwindling, he embarked on a campaign of genocide, reporting to Napoleon on October 7 that "we must destroy all the mountain negroes, sparing only children under twelve years of age. We must destroy half the negroes of the plains, and not allow in the colony a single man who has worn an epaulette."[19] There were no further communications from Leclerc, who died on November 2 of yellow fever. His successor, General Donatien-Marie-Joseph de Vimeur, the vicomte de Rochambeau, was the son of the French general who had saved the United States at Yorktown and had served his father as an aide-de-camp during the American war. He attempted to continue Leclerc's genocide, importing some five hundred bloodhounds from Cuba trained to rip their victims apart, though most of the dogs were apparently eaten by starving French troops.[20]

Napoleon, who never hesitated to make a far-reaching decision fast and act on it at once, effectively gave up on his American plan when he learned of Leclerc's death; though he retained Martinique and Guadeloupe, he was determined to spend no more money on Saint-Domingue, where some fifty thousand French soldiers had perished. Already assembling the resources for his coming campaign to conquer Europe, he cut off support for the American venture, leaving his soldiers to twist in the wind without reinforcements. Rochambeau was captured by the British while ingloriously fleeing the island and remained imprisoned for more than eight years.

In Paris, the US ambassador Robert Livingston had been instructed by Jefferson to try to purchase New Orleans and the Floridas. West Florida, with Mobile and Pensacola, was already interdependent with New Orleans for trade, and controlled the access to the sea of the rivers that emptied into the Gulf of Mexico. Without that access, frontiersmen had no outlet for their products. Then a crisis erupted: on October 18, 1802, the Spanish intendant at New Orleans, Juan Ventura Morales, suspended the "right of deposit" that allowed citizens of the United States to transship goods via that port.

Needing to look like he was doing something, Jefferson dispatched Monroe on an "extraordinary mission" to Paris in January 1803, though Livingston was already on the case. "The fever into which the Western mind is thrown by the affair at N. Orleans," wrote Jefferson in a hasty letter to Monroe, "stimulated by the mercantile, & generally the federal interest, threatens to overbear our peace."[21] Three days later, he wrote Monroe again: "The agitation of the public mind on occasion of the late suspension of our right of deposit at N. Orleans, is extreme."[22]

Livingston was no stranger to land deals; as the great-grandson of the landowner and slave trader Robert Livingston, he had inherited the town of Clermont, New York, where the British had burned his mansion during the War of Independence. But he was astounded when Talleyrand offered him not only New Orleans, but the whole vast Mississippi watershed west and north of Louisiana, albeit with little geographical precision—or, more accurately, offered him France's claim to the territory. By the time James Monroe arrived to join him as a special envoy, sick from his ocean journey, Livingston had already made the deal, though Monroe received the credit for it in America. The price they agreed on for the territory was sixty million francs (approximately $15 million)—a bargain, but enough money that it could fund Napoleon's war in Europe.

Was it Napoleon's to sell? The North American purchase in effect legitimated Napoleon's claim to Louisiana. But it was exactly what Napoleon had promised Carlos IV he would never do. The furious Spanish king took the position that by alienating Louisiana, France had lost its claim and that therefore Louisiana was rightfully Spain's.

In Charleston, where newspapers had been chiding Jefferson for not acquiring New Orleans, the Louisiana Purchase was seen as a "greater treasure to the western part of the US than a mountain of gold."[23]

But it wasn't Florida.

Acquiring Louisiana was a coup, but Livingston and Monroe had failed to accomplish their mission. They were supposed to get the Floridas along with New Orleans, to lock in the whole Gulf Coast. Instead, they got the west bank of the Mississippi and the uncharted, undeveloped territory upriver.

Florida was an obsession, and a permanent security threat. Controlling the Floridas would secure the entire southeast of the continent from European invasion. It would allow full-scale removal of Native Americans to begin, so that slave-driven plantation agriculture could flourish outward from the slave-supply center of Charleston down into Florida, and through Georgia and Alabama, into Mississippi.

As President Jefferson explained to Congress, the Americans didn't even have a map of Louisiana.[24] No sooner was the Louisiana deal done than Livingston and Monroe—and President Jefferson, and Secretary of State Madison—began claiming that Florida was part of the deal, though they all knew it was not. Florida was still a Spanish possession and had never been ceded to Napoleon. The United States' baldfaced attempt to claim rights to Florida became the subject of considerable diplomatic wrangling and was a major international issue through the War of 1812 and beyond. Jefferson's minister to Spain was his South Carolina campaign supporter Charles Pinckney, the Constitution framer from South Carolina, who—unfortunately but typically for an American diplomat—did not speak Spanish.

Historians have argued about exactly why Napoleon made the sudden strategic decision to make Louisiana available to the United States at a fire-sale price, but two motives are clear: one, he wanted money right then for his European war; and, two, he didn't want the British to have it. Empowering America would provide a check on British expansionism.

That's certainly what the British thought. They saw Jefferson, as they had since his days in Paris, as a French lapdog, and understandably resented his funding of Napoleon's war against them. The American Federalists, who sided with Britain against France, were furious.

President Jefferson wanted to get rid of the Indians by the old traders' device of predatory lending—ensnaring the chiefs in personal debt, then foreclosing on the commons of the tribes they represented. He advocated this method to General William Henry Harrison on February 27, 1803:

> to promote this disposition [on the part of the Native Americans] to exchange lands, which they have to spare & we want, for necessaries, which we have to spare & they want, we shall push our trading houses, and be glad to see the good & influential individuals among them run in debt, because we observe that when these debts get beyond what the individuals can pay, they become willing to lop th[em off] by a cession of lands.

He continued in a tone that perhaps illustrated how the doctrine of "peaceable coercion" applied at home:

> it is essential to cultivate their love. as to their fear, we presume that our strength & their weakness is now so visible that they must see we have only to shut our hand to crush them.[25]

The annexation of Louisiana was a political blockbuster. New England was cold to the acquisition, pointing out correctly that Jefferson had exceeded his constitutional limits in making it. But though it was opposed by New Englanders in both houses of Congress—with the significant exception of John Quincy Adams, a pro-expansionist who crossed regional and party lines to side with Jefferson—it approximately doubled the size of US territory overnight. It changed the national balance of power even as the innovations of the cotton gin and a method for making sugar from Louisiana cane made practical the cultivation of these two highly profitable slave-labor crops. Virginia was set to be the primary vendor for the large numbers of slaves that Louisiana planters would want. Jefferson was well aware that a commercial network already existed in which itinerant traders and small-time merchants bought Virginia slaves for trafficking down South, and he knew it was a handy way to get rid of troublemakers, because he took advantage of it repeatedly.

After Cary, one of the imprisoned teenage boys who worked in his slave-labor nail factory at Monticello, attacked another one, Brown Colbert, with a hammer, he was sent away under Jefferson's orders. "It will be necessary for me to make an example of him in terrorem to the others," he wrote to his son-in-law,

Thomas Mann Randolph Jr., from the White House on June 8, 1803. "There are generally negro purchasers from Georgia passing about the state, to one of whom I would rather he should be sold than to any other person. [I]f none such offers, if he could be sold in any other quarter so distant as never more to be heard of among us, it would to the others be as if he were put out of the way by death."[26]

Jefferson, then, was not only well aware of the Georgiamen and their southbound interstate slave trade, but also understood their process as a tool with which to terrorize—"in terrorem to the others"—his factory's workers, who were imprisoned children, and who had a cash value even as felons.

Louisiana's Anglo-American settlers were primarily from Kentucky, a territory that had been carved out of Virginia and settled by Virginians. While the Louisiana Territory was being organized, President Jefferson sent his proven ally John Breckinridge—now a senator from Kentucky—a top-secret letter on November 24, 1803, enclosing two cramped double-column pages of proposals for a markedly undemocratic rule of Louisiana by a pro-American oligarchy that he referred to as an "Assembly of Notables." As with the previous Kentucky Resolutions, Jefferson cautioned Breckinridge to pass the work off in the Senate as his own and not reveal his hand in it:

> In communicating it to you I must do it in confidence that you will never let any person know that I have put pen to paper on the subject and that if you think the inclosed can be of any aid to you will take the trouble to copy it & return me the original. I am this particular, because you know with what bloody teeth & fangs the federalists will attack any sentiment or principle known to come from me, & what blackguardisms & personalities they make it the occasion of vomiting forth.[27]

It was the first time that Congress had dared contemplate making any determination as to whether slavery should be allowed somewhere, but there was no alternative if the territory was to be organized. Breckinridge put forth Jefferson's proposals as his own, perhaps with some modification (no copy survives of his bill as introduced). Having amply demonstrated his loyalty, he became Jefferson's attorney general in 1805.

For our purposes, the most interesting feature of Jefferson's plan for Louisiana as contained in the Breckinridge-tendered proposal was that he wanted to prohibit the foreign slave trade but allow the domestic. There was no question that Louisiana would continue to buy imported slaves. The payday for Virginia slaveholders was that slaves could not be brought to Louisiana from Africa or Havana, but would have to be imported from the United States—a move that substantially revalued every Chesapeake slaveowner's holdings upward and substantially increased Virginia's share of the nation's capital stock.

But on the same day Jefferson wrote Breckinridge, South Carolina's governor James Richardson sent a message to his state's General Assembly calling for the reopening of the foreign slave trade to South Carolina.[28] The following day, Jefferson wrote Breckinridge again, adding text to his previous letter: "Insert in some part of the paper of yesterday 'Slaves shall be admitted into the territory of Orleans from such of the United States or of their territories as prohibit their importation from abroad, but from no other state, territory or country.' salutations. Nov. 25. 1803."[29]

Jefferson's added clause was specifically aimed at denying South Carolina the right to import slaves for reshipment to New Orleans. Though Jefferson's general plan became law, the prohibition of importation from South Carolina did not survive; when the Louisiana bill came before the Senate, James Hillhouse, a Connecticut Federalist, attached an amendment that prohibited slaves from "without the limits of the United States," but made no other distinction. With legal obstacles removed, South Carolina unilaterally and legally reopened the African slave trade in order to service Louisiana with freshly imported Africans rebranded as domestic product, undercutting the Virginia slaveowners substantially.[30]

The United States formally took possession of Louisiana from France on December 20, 1803, twelve days before Commander in Chief Jean-Jacques Dessalines issued the Haitian Declaration of Independence that proclaimed the existence of the Republic of Haiti on January 1, 1804. It largely consisted of an extended and strongly worded cry of hatred for France, but nevertheless offered an olive branch to the rest of the hemisphere that acknowledged the fear that Haitians would become exporters of terrorism:

> Let us ensure, however, that a missionary spirit does not destroy our work; let us allow our neighbors to breathe in peace; may they live quietly under the laws that they have made for themselves, and let us not, as revolutionary firebrands, declare ourselves the lawgivers of the Caribbean, nor let our glory consist in troubling the peace of the neighboring islands.

But then Dessalines went from town to town, personally supervising the execution of the French remaining in the territory—while exempting the Polish soldiers who had fought on the side of the Haitians, who were made honored members of the new society, and the many US captains who were happily doing business in the ports of the new republic. Dessalines served as Haiti's first president for less than three years before being murdered by other Haitians, and ultimately (unlike the Catholic Toussaint) became a *lwa* of Haitian vodou.[31]

James Wilkinson was upset to see the black militiamen of New Orleans in uniform and carrying weapons. A traitor who acted as a Spanish secret agent while commanding the US Army, Wilkinson had previously proposed that Kentucky declare independence from Virginia and become allied with Spain instead. But he nevertheless was tolerated by Jefferson, who made Wilkinson the head of the US Army in Louisiana.

Jefferson's Virginian-via-Tennessee protégé, W. C. C. Claiborne, a blue-blood descendant of Kent Island's William Claiborne, became the territorial governor of Louisiana. Claiborne, who spoke neither French nor Spanish, had since 1801 been governor of Mississippi, a position awarded him by Jefferson. As the Americans took charge in Louisiana, Claiborne's agent Dr. John Watkins, who had reconnoitered the country, pointed out in a report of February 2, 1804, the most important political issue:

> No Subject seems to be so interesting to the minds of the inhabitants of all that part of the Country, which I have visited as that of the importation of brute Negroes from Africa. This permission would go farther with them, and better reconcile them to the Government of the United States, than any other privilege that could be extended to the Country. They appear only to claim it for a few years, and without it, they pretend that they must abandon the culture both of Sugar and Cotton. White laborers they say, cannot be had in this unhealthy climate.[32]

The "Kaintucks"—a minority in Louisiana—had a marked preference for American-born slaves. But the Creoles of Louisiana wanted slaves from Africa. They didn't want English-speaking slaves, they didn't want Protestant slaves, and they didn't want to pay the much higher prices charged by the speculators who brought slaves from Virginia and Maryland.

Claiborne wrote to Madison on March 10, 1804, of unrest on the part of both planters and slave traders:

> In a Paper which was received by the last Mail from the Seat of Government, it was stated that a Law had passed the Senate prohibiting the foreign importation of Slaves into this Province. This intelligence has occasioned great agitation in this City and in the adjacent Settlements.
>
> The African Trade has hitherto been lucrative, and the farmers are desirous of increasing the number of their Slaves. The prohibiting the incorporation of Negroes therefore, is viewed here as a serious blow at the Commercial and agricultural interest of the Province. The admission of Negroes into the state of South Carolina has served to increase the discontent here. The Citizens generally can not be made to understand the present power of the State Authorities with regard to the *importation of persons:*—they suppose that Congress must connive at the importation into South Carolina, and many will be made to believe, that it is done with a view to make South Carolina the Sole importer for Louisiana.[33]

And, indeed, that is what happened. Louisiana was a colonized territory, and as such, it was subject to trade restrictions that benefitted the metropolis—principally Virginia, but Carolina had found a way to horn in.

Claiborne's power during the territorial era was frequently and not inaccurately described as dictatorial, though the picture that emerges from his letters is that of a man who has a French-speaking tiger by the tail.* Contemplating the impending prohibition of both the African slave trade and the interstate trade to Louisiana as of October 1, he wrote Secretary of State Madison on May 8:

> I am inclined to think that previous to the 1st of October thousands of African Negroes will be imported into this Province; for the Citizens seem impressed with an opinion, that a great, very great supply of Slaves is essential to the prosperity of Louisiana: Hence Sir you may conclude that the prohibition as to the importation Subsequent to the 1st of October,

---

*When in 1807 Jefferson tried to prevail on James Monroe to take the Louisiana governorship, he pitched it as the "2d office in the US. in importance." *PJMon*, 5:288.

is a source of some discontent; Nay Sir, it is at present a cause of much clamour.[34]

And on July 12:

At some future period, this quarter of the Union must (I fear) experience in some degree, the Misfortunes of St. Domingo, and that *period* will be hastened if the people should be indulged by congress with a continuance of the African Trade.

African Negroes are thought here not to be dangerous; but it ought to be recollected that those of St. Domingo were originally from Africa and that Slavery Where ever it exists is a galling yoke. I find however that an almost universal sentiment exist in Louisiana in favour of the African traffic. . . . Slaves are daily introduced from Africa, many *direct* from *this* unhappy Country and others by way of the west India Islands. All vessels with slaves on bord [*sic*] are stopped at Plaquemine, and are not permitted to pass without my consent. This is done to prevent the bringing in of Slaves that have been concerned in the insurrection of St. Domingo.[35]

The foreign slave trade into Louisiana was never again legalized. But under pressure from Jefferson to respond to Claiborne's urgent drumbeat that the citizens of Louisiana wanted more slaves, Congress legalized the domestic slave trade to Louisiana in March 1805, to be fully effective October 1.

That the black territory freed from France should call itself a republic was seen by whites as a grotesquerie.

For the slaveowners in the United States government to have diplomatic relations with slaves who had killed their masters was unthinkable; it would, they thought, amount to rewarding their actions. Although Haiti was the second republic in the hemisphere, the United States didn't extend diplomatic recognition to it until 1862, and then only because President Abraham Lincoln saw it as a potential site for "colonization," or deportation, of emancipated slaves.

Yet the Southerners owed the Haitians a lot. At a time when Washington, DC, was a squalid, barely built village and the US Army had only about three thousand troops, Haiti stopped the French troops' forward march into the Americas. To put it another way: though it was not their objective, Dessalines and his troops prevented Bonaparte's forces from invading Louisiana and controlling commerce on the Mississippi. Historians don't deal in counterfactuals—what might have happened—but it is tempting to imagine scenarios: if Leclerc had been able to comply with his orders to continue on from Saint-Domingue and occupy Louisiana with ten thousand men or more, controlling the great New Orleans gateway to the sea? Could the French have managed a permanent occupation that would have been hard to dislodge? Certainly the United States governing class had not expected to be able to expand across the continent so quickly and easily.

Spain's military involvement in Saint-Domingue was its last gasp as a world power, the prelude to losing its colonies one by one, and Saint-Domingue was the graveyard of British colonial expansion in the Americas as well. The expense and horrendous loss of life were a spur to the British in stopping the African slave trade—though not British colonial slavery, yet—via an act approved in Parliament on March 25, 1807, a mere three years after the establishment of the Republic of Haiti.

Britain could afford to get out of the slave trade. As profitable as slaving could be, British commerce was so large, and so diverse, that losing the slave trade didn't make a dent it. Trinidad, Britain's last-acquired Caribbean colony, was ceded to Britain by France in 1802. It had been Spanish, French, and now English in succession. The Africans who were subsequently brought to Trinidad were not brought as chattel slaves but as indentured workers from the British empire in Africa.*

New England merchants did a brisk business in Haiti, to the disgust and alarm of Southerners, trading arms along with other commodities and consumer goods. Napoleon, who refused to recognize Haitian independence, was furious about American commerce with Haiti; Jefferson, who hoped to have Napoleon's cooperation in taking over Florida, wanted to keep him happy. Congress passed sanctions against commerce with Haiti in 1806, amid arguments that to trade with Haiti against France's wishes was to recognize Haitian independence. That would be, Jefferson's son-in-law John Wayles Eppes shouted in the House, "a system that would bring immediate and horrible destruction on the fairest portion of America."[36]

Southerners were on permanent high alert for terrorism, and never backed down. The specter of Haiti informed all future discourse—every dinner-table

---

*The old ways persisted, however; Trinidad's carnival was a Mardi Gras, and when its characteristic musical form of calypso later appeared, it was in the French Creole tongue, as were many of the old *bombas* of western Puerto Rico, where Domingans also went.

conversation, every political calculation, every speech—about slavery in the Southern United States. The "French Negroes" were thought to carry the contagion of insurrection, and prophylactic measures were thought necessary to keep them from infiltrating; there was even concern, utterly unwarranted, that Haiti might attack the United States.

Here as on other occasions, Southern slaveowners revealed how terrified they were by the ferocity of black fighters. Haiti had a significant population of black men who had served in European and/or African armies or in colonial militias, and their military knowledge embraced both European and African military tactics and systems of organization.

The clock was ticking. The Constitution allowed the federal government to stop the foreign slave trade as of January 1, 1808, and President Jefferson wanted that trade shut down for good. Prohibiting the slave trade was easily represented to a panicked public as antiterrorism.

But it also partook of that other great issue: prohibiting the African slave trade protected the market so that a new class of American traders could come forward, supplied with homegrown captives born into slavery on Virginia and Maryland farms. The conditions were right for a massive forced migration of enslaved Chesapeake laborers down South, and it did not have to be a one-time drain: a continuing domestic slave-breeding industry was now possible.

This was something new. Taking the long historical view, African American historian William T. Alexander wrote in 1887:

> Slave breeding for gain, deliberately purposed and systematically pursued, appears to be among the latest devices and illustrations of human depravity. . . . That it was cheaper to buy slaves than to rear them, [had been] quite generally regarded as self-evident. But the suppression of the African slave trade, coinciding with the rapid settlement of the Louisiana purchase and the triumph of the Cotton Gin, wrought here an entire transformation. When field hands brought from ten to fifteen hundred dollars, and young slaves were held at from ten to fifteen dollars per pound, the newly born infant, if well formed, healthy, and likely to live, was deemed an addition to his master's stock of not less than one hundred dollars, even in Virginia and Maryland. It had now become the interest of the master to increase the number of births, in his slave cabins, and few evinced scruples as to the means whereby this result was obtained.[37]

The Spanish had had the most permissive slave regime ever to exist in the territories that now make up the United States. Under Spanish law, the enslaved had a right to have a hearing to establish a price by which they could purchase their freedom. This practice, called *coartación*, was hated by the planters, and it ended in 1807.

In Louisiana, both free people of color and the enslaved found themselves in transition to the hemisphere's psychologically harshest racial regime: the Anglo-American mode of slavery, which provided no path to freedom even for future generations of descendants. The Virginians brought them a kind of slavery that was not only lifelong, but perpetual.

27

I Do Not Threaten
the Government with
Civil War

[The] facility with which the sugar Planters amass wealth is almost incredible. It is not uncommon with 20 working hands to make from 10 to 14 thousand Dollars and there are several planters whose field Negroes do not exceed forty who make more than 20,000 Dollars each year.[1]

—Louisiana governor W. C. C. Claiborne, letter to President
Thomas Jefferson, July 10, 1806

GEORGIA, THE ONLY STATE to have legally imported slaves from Africa since the Constitution took effect, finally banned both African and interstate slave trade in 1798, at a time when maritime commerce was disturbed by war. During the years the trade was open, Charleston merchants and factors had sold large cargoes of slaves in Savannah, and a class of Georgia traders had grown up as well. Slave trading continued after the ban, but illicitly, not subject to legal regulation or protection.

In 1802 the South Carolina legislature renewed the prohibition against both the foreign and interstate slave trades. As had previously been the case in both Chesapeake and Carolina, it was a regional issue. About half the population of Charleston at this time was enslaved; upcountry, the enslaved population comprised only about one-fifth of the total.[2] Not only did the Lowcountry's large slaveholders, who were firmly in control, want to disempower their upcountry competition by denying them labor, they wanted to control the labor market so that upcountry would have to buy its labor from the Lowcountry, without having access to competitors from Virginia and Maryland.

Charleston newspapers published excited reports of the productivity of the new Louisiana Territory, with the clear implication being that Louisiana had insufficient slave labor. South Carolina could easily supply it, since Charleston had since the 1790s carried slaves to New Orleans via its commercial, albeit treacherous and irregular, coastwise shipping route around the Spanish-held Floridas to New Orleans.[3]

For South Carolina legislators, long attuned to fast-changing market conditions, it was time to act. "To the surprise of many political observers," writes Lacy K. Ford, "in late November 1803, just one year after its desultory rejection of inland cotton growers' pleas for a reopened slave trade, the South Carolina legislature suddenly began a serious reconsideration of the issue, undoubtedly prompted by both persistent backcountry pressure and the prospect of supplying legions of slaves to the lower Louisiana Territory for handsome profits."[4] The two interests cut a deal: the merchants of Charleston got the African slave trade, whose victims they could resell to Louisiana and Mississippi, and the upcountry planters got the interstate trade, which would allow them to buy enslaved laborers from the Chesapeake.

"The news had not been five hours in the city," wrote Charleston bookseller E. S. Thomas, "before two large British Guineamen, that had been lying on and off the port for several days expecting it, came up to town; and from that day my business began to decline."[5] For the next four years, available resources went to investing in slaves.

It was not yet clear what the laws of an American-controlled Louisiana would be, but in adjacent Mississippi, under Claiborne's governorship, Congress had since 1798 allowed the interstate but not the foreign trade, requiring planters to buy from American slave vendors. With the cotton boom underway, Natchez was already a developed slave market, and Louisiana could—and, as it happened, did—radically widen that opportunity. It was clear that though the interstate trade to Louisiana was at that moment prohibited, the territory was being set up as a market for Virginia slaves, and South Carolina wanted in on the action.

Beyond the simple lure of making sales, there was an additional, compelling reason for South Carolina to sell slaves to Louisiana: Louisiana had a hard-money supply, courtesy of the Spanish. Spain did its business the old-fashioned way, paying bills with silver mined out of the ground in Mexico. Claiborne reported from New Orleans to Secretary of State James Madison on June 16, 1805, that "Two Spanish Schooners from Vera Cruz, have arrived at this Port, and are consigned to the Marquis of Casa Calvo. They brought with them a large Sum in Silver, report says One Hundred thousand Dollars, but it is believed the real Amount is much greater. This money is said to be destined for the payment of the Pensions allowed to persons residing in Louisiana, and to meet the expences which the Marquis has or may incur as Commissioner of Limits."[6]

South Carolina had no such shipments coming in. Louisiana offered a chance for Carolina merchants to get silver, instead of paper that might depreciate or become worthless. The Creoles had silver Spanish dollars, and they were eager to buy slaves.

The previous peak of South Carolina importation of Africans was 1773, when an estimated eight-thousand-plus slaves were brought in. This time, when South Carolina reopened the African trade, they brought in far and away the largest single concentration of victims that came to North America in any comparable period, as this table of estimated embarkations (using the Eltis and Richardson numbers) shows:[7]

1804	7,643
1805	8,592
1806	15,551
1807	23,174
1808	498
total	**55,458**

Eltis and Richardson show an estimated 12.7 percent death rate, with 47,281 arriving alive. Some estimates of the traffic are higher; James McMillin believes that more than seventy thousand Africans—a phenomenal number—arrived into the Lowcountry during the four years from 1804 to 1807.[8]

Some of these newly arrived Africans were sent on to Jamaica, Barbados, or other Antillean territories, and it's unclear how many of them were re-exported to Louisiana. At least five thousand, believes Lacy K. Ford—more than 10 percent of the Eltis and Richardson estimate of Africans trafficked to South Carolina—but the number could be larger.[9] There was definitely a commercial corridor in slaves: Gwendolyn Midlo Hall's Afro-Louisiana database shows that between 1806 and 1810, 76 percent of captives that she was able to obtain documentation for who came into the port of New Orleans arrived from South Carolina, versus only 3 percent for other US ports of origin (a sample that does not include the migration of some ten thousand people, about a third of them enslaved, to New Orleans from eastern Cuba in 1809–10). Her statistics for 1811 and 1812 show 67 percent from South Carolina.[10] A committee report to Congress on February 17, 1806, stated flatly, "African slaves, lately imported into Charleston, have been thence conveyed into the Territory of Orleans; and, in their opinion, this practice will be continued to a very great extent, while there is no law to prevent it."[11]

Some of the Africans were taken past New Orleans to Natchez, though in the pre-steam days it was hard work getting a boat up the Mississippi River. The *Lucy* left Charleston on July 4, 1806, "carrying 50 negroes insured from Charleston to Natchez, the premium 7½ per cent."[12] During the Missouri Compromise debate of 1820, South Carolina senator William Smith, arguing in favor of unlimited slavery, entered into the congressional record the following passage about the importations of 1803–07, which shows how little the Carolinians were involved in the actual business of importation (as opposed to selling the captives):

> The whole number imported by the merchants and planters of Charleston and its vicinity were only two thousand and six. Nor were the slaves imported by the foreigners, and other American vessels and owners, sold to the Carolinians, only in a small part. They were sold to the people of the Western States, Georgia, New Orleans, and a considerable quantity were sent to the West Indies, especially when the market became dull in Carolina.[13]

So a number of the slaves brought into Louisiana through 1810 came from Africa through South Carolina via the coastwise trade. The manifests before 1818 were lost, but the one stray surviving manifest from 1807 is for a "new negro man"—i.e., African-born—coming to New Orleans from Charleston.

Probably Charleston was the source from which George W. Morgan received the cargo of thirty people—twenty adults, ten children—from two widely separated regions of Africa that he advertised in the *Orleans Gazette and Commercial Advertiser* of August 13, 1806, though they could also have been plucked by pirates off a ship headed for Cuba:

AFRICAN SLAVES.
JUST RECEIVED and for fale
by the fubfcriber,
Twenty prime young men, four boys,
and fix girls,
Of the Mandingo and Congo nations.
The whole together will be fold on
moderate terms.
GEORGE W. MORGAN.
2d Auguft, 1806.

But there was also competition from the Chesapeake, as per this February 5,
1807, advertisement from the same paper:

FOR SALE,
One Hundred and Three valuable
MARYLAND NEGROES,
Accustomed to plantation work—
these negroes will be sold by families,
the whole of them forming only two
gangs, taken from only two planta-
tions. For terms apply to
P. F. Du Bourg & C. B. Dufau,
January 24.   4t

Another advertisement in the same issue, reproduced here, shows the participation of Charlestonians in the business, offering "140 NEGRES BRUTS, DE
NATION CONGO" to francophone buyers:

140 *Prime Congo Negroes,*
NOW on board the Brig Ethiopi-
an, captain Walsh, from Charles
ton, being the first choice from a car-
go of Four Hundred,
FOR SALE AT AUCTION
BY
PATTON & MOSSY,
ON
FRIDAY 13th Instant,
TERMS OF PAYMENT,
Approved endorsed Notes at 6 and 12
months.

---

140 NGRES BRUTS, DE NATION
CONGO,
Actuellement à bord du Brig Ethio-
pian, Capitaine Walsh, venant de
Charleston : ces Nègres sont de
premier choix d'une cargaison de
400
A VENDRE A L'ENCAN
DE
PATTON & MOSSY,
VENDREDI 13 du courant,
Payables à six et douze mois, en
bonnes notes endossées à la satis-
faction du venduer.
Nouvelle-Orléans, le
5 Février 1807.

Re-exporting Africans was not a business that benefited most South Carolinians, nor did most of the money stay in Charleston. The Carolinians were middle-men, not suppliers. They had a harbor, but not a transatlantic shipping industry of their own, so the profits from carrying went elsewhere. As a "Planter from Pedee" wrote during the non-importation movement of 1769–70, "purchasing Negroes is in fact purchasing British manufactures."[14]

Charleston customs entries for 1806 show thirty-three slave ships from Africa as being owned by British proprietors, followed by thirteen from Rhode Island, then three from New Jersey, three from Charleston, and two from Ire-land.[15] Breaking down a customs count of 39,075 slaves declared as entering into Charleston between 1804 and 1807, Elizabeth Donnan found 19,949 of them entering on British ships, 7,958 on Rhode Island vessels, and only 2,006 imported by "merchants and planters of Charleston and vicinity," presumably the same 2,006 cited by Smith.[16]

The Carolinians tried to make their money on volume, in an unprecedented mass retailing experiment. Their greed was matched by that of the shippers, the largest number of whom were in Liverpool; they knew the market would be closing soon.

The Liverpool slavers' heaviest shipping period was the last ten years of the trade. During that time, they also sold slaves to the British Army, who pur-chased them for conscription into the West India Regiment, an arrangement that only ended with the end of the African slave trade. From January 1, 1806, through the prohibition of the trade on May 1, 1807—the height of the South Carolina importation—185 ships from Liverpool carried 49,213 Africans.[17]

In this free-for-all slave importation scene, people from widely different parts of Africa turned up in Charleston—from Kongo, Sierra Leone, the Gold Coast, and other regions. Omar ibn Said, an Islamic scholar from Senegal, a Fula, who arrived in Charleston in 1807, described his experience in a fifteen-page 1831 autobiography, one of fourteen manuscripts that he wrote in Arabic while enslaved:

> . . . there came to our place a large army, who killed many men, and took
> me, and brought me to the great sea, and sold me into the hands of the
> Christians, who bound me and sent me on board a great ship and we sailed
> upon the great sea a month and a half, when we came to a place called
> Charleston in the Christian language. There they sold me to a small, weak,
> and wicked man called Johnson, a complete infidel, who had no fear of
> God at all. Now I am a small man, and unable to do hard work so I fled

from the hand of Johnson and after a month came to a place called Fayd-il. [Fayetteville, North Carolina.][18]

The unilateral reopening of the slave trade by South Carolina caused much anger in the rest of the country, both in the Upper South and in the abolitionist strongholds. Newspapers in North Carolina, Tennessee, Maryland, and Virginia all strongly criticized South Carolina's decision, but the Carolina press became especially defensive when the criticism came from the North, as in this piece from the *Charleston Courier* of July 10, 1806, which takes on a mocking tone not unfamiliar in other eras of American politics:

> As to the epithet of thieves, which [an unnamed Philadelphia editor] applies to those who bring Slaves from Africa, we shall presently see whether we cannot apply it to the pure, the immaculate, and demure Philadelphian, and some other of the Northern cities, where they are bellowing out, humanity! humanity! humanity! Oh! the rights of dear insulted human nature!

As captives died awaiting sale, Charlestonians were irritated by the captains' practice of disposing of the corpses on the cheap by throwing them overboard, "in consequence of which," reported traveler John Lambert, "no body would eat any fish."[19] A city ordinance of 1805, printed in the *Charleston Courier*, noted that "since the importation of Slaves from Africa, several incidents have occurred of dead human bodies having been thrown into the waters of the Harbour of Charleston" and provided that not only should a fine of one hundred dollars be imposed, but that the offender's name should be published in "the several gazettes of Charleston, to hold up every such offender to public detestation."[20] Still, the numerous advertisements for luxury goods in the four pages of the previously mentioned issue leave no doubt that, bodies floating in the harbor or not, the Charlestonians were prosperous. But since all those goods had to be imported, either from the North or from Europe, their money quickly left the city again on northbound boats.

Looking forward to the January 1, 1808, expiration of the constitutionally specified guarantee that the African slave trade could exist, President Jefferson's Message to Congress of December 2, 1806, proactively called for its prohibition as of the first constitutionally permissible day. In defending the urgency of his proposal as necessary to forestall a final cycle of African expeditions, Jefferson also presented it as a moral issue:

> I congratulate you, fellow citizens, on the approach of the period at which you may interpose your authority constitutionally to withdraw the citizens of the United States from all further participation in those violations of human rights which have been so long continued on the unoffending inhabitants of Africa, and which the morality, the reputation, and the best of our country have long been eager to proscribe. Although no law you may pass can take prohibitory effect until the first day of the year 1808, yet the intervening period is not too long to prevent by timely notice expeditions which can not be completed before that day.

A bill was duly proposed the following day.

However moral it may have seemed to Jefferson to lament "violations of human rights," ending the transatlantic slave trade did nothing to end slavery itself. Instead, it replaced one inhumane slave trade with another. This action of Jefferson's has been praised as, in one historian's words, "his greatest act of humane egalitarianism."[21] Perhaps in his layers of intellectual complexity, Jefferson thought so himself; we will resist the temptation to psychoanalyze. But in practice, it was no such thing. It was an act to transform American slavery into a purely domestic industry, reducing the nation's dependence on foreign sources of supply for slaves and bringing the entire slave trade under Virginia's control. Nor was this an unforeseen consequence; it was the predictable, desired outcome, which is why South Carolina and Georgia opposed the bill, albeit unsuccessfully.

The bill was referred to a House committee of four Southerners (from Georgia, Virginia, Maryland, and North Carolina) and three Northerners, with Peter Early of Georgia as chair. In debate, Early answered John Smilie of Pennsylvania, who wanted capital punishment for slave importers, with words that put Jefferson's high-flown appeal in perspective:

> [Mr. Smilie] has said that, in the Southern States, slavery is felt and acknowledged to be a great evil, and that therefore we will execute a severe law to prevent an increase of this evil. Permit me to tell the gentleman of a small distinction in this case. A large majority of the people in the Southern States do not consider slavery as a crime. They do not believe it immoral to hold human flesh in bondage. Many deprecate slavery as an evil; as a political evil; but not as a crime. Reflecting men apprehend, at

some future day, evils, incalculable evils, from it; but it is a fact that few, very few, consider it as a crime.

It is best to be candid on this subject. If they considered the holding of men in slavery as a crime, they would necessarily accuse themselves, a thing which human nature revolts at. I will tell the truth. A large majority of people in the Southern States do not consider slavery as even an evil.[22]

This was a long way from Mason, Jefferson, Henry, and even Pierce Butler and Henry Laurens's protestations that slavery was an evil forced upon North America by Britain, one to which there was unfortunately no effective end in sight because free blacks could supposedly not live together with whites. South Carolina was the center of an expanding commercial empire, with slavery at the heart of that vision. To hear Carolina slaveowners tell it, slavery was a positive good for mankind. This sentiment, soon to be institutionalized by South Carolina's John C. Calhoun, had already become common.

What to do with enslaved people rescued from slave ships was a problem as well; should the federal government sell them at auction? When it was proposed that they be indentured for a term in a free state, Early responded by threatening civil war (while claiming the contrary), according to the minutes in the *Annals of Congress*:

> Mr. Early said the inhabitants of the Southern States would resist this provision with their lives. We want no civil wars, no rebellions, no insurrections, no resistance to the authority of the Government. Give effect then to this wish, and do not pass this bill as it now stands.
>
> Mr. Smilie. — This opens such a scene as I never expected to witness in this House. If it were not owing to the impulse of the moment, and the influence of passion, I should think it extremely reprehensible. Are we to be threatened with civil war? that our laws will be resisted at the peril of life? Sir, this is new doctrine. The gentleman must know that we are not to be terrified by a threat of civil war.
>
> Mr. Early said the gentleman from Pennsylvania (Mr. Smilie) had made a palpable misrepresentation of his sentiments. I do not threaten the Government with civil war. I only communicated the idea that military force would be necessary to carry the law into execution.[23]

The Senate added to the bill a prohibition against the coastwise slave trade for ships of less than forty tons burden, which made it impossible for small vessels intercepted at sea bearing slaves from the Antilles to claim that they were engaging in domestic coastwise trade. This infuriated the Southerners; Virginia's senior senator, the voluble, unhinged, but not unperceptive John Randolph, who owned some four hundred slaves, argued that (as summarized by the congressional reporter):

> The provision of the bill touched the right of private property. He feared lest, at a future period, it might be made the pretext of universal emancipation, he had rather lose the bill, he had rather lose all the bills of the session, he had rather lose every bill passed since the establishment of the Government, than agree to the provision contained in this slave bill. It went to blow up the Constitution in ruins. Mr. R[andolph] said, if ever the time of disunion between the States should arrive, the line of severance would be between the slaveholding and the non-slaveholding states.[24]

Over Randolph's objections, the forty-tons clause remained, setting in place a mechanism that favored larger operators in the coastwise slave trade.

The Senate version also included a requirement that the ship's captain submit a manifest naming each enslaved passenger to the customs collector or surveyor both at the port of departure and at the port of arrival, with the customs officer performing a roll call at either end. New Orleans was the principal port of arrival, but far from the only one; the trade stretched to Galveston. The result of this requirement is that both inward and outward manifests exist. Many have been lost, but even so, these filled-in, commercially preprinted forms constitute the best record of the trade.[25]

Jefferson signed the act prohibiting the African trade on March 2, 1807, to take effect the first day of 1808. Britain, meanwhile, having lost tens of thousands of men in its attempt to take Saint-Domingue, and under strong domestic pressure from abolitionists who had organized themselves into an effective political movement, put an end to its lucrative involvement in the slave trade by a measure that received royal assent on March 25, 1807. The British law did not have to wait until the first of the year to be effective so it took effect before the already passed American prohibition did. Though a British abolition law would have to wait until 1833, ending the transatlantic slave trade was a major turning point. Over the next decades, the British Navy enforced it at sea not only with respect to British ships, but stopping slave ships from other nations as well.

As the shutoff approached, South Carolina traders turned the spigot as wide as it would open. By the final year, the market was glutted, with fatal consequences for the Africans who piled up in holding pens. John Lambert reported that in 1807:

> the sales for slaves was extremely dull, owing to the high price which the merchants demanded for them. The planters, who were pretty well stocked, were not very eager to purchase, and the merchants knowing that a market would ultimately be found for them, were determined not to lower their demands; in consequence of which, hundreds of these poor beings were obliged to be kept on board the ships, or in large buildings at Gadsden's wharf for months together.[26]

Exhausted and sick, many of the captives died; McMillin believes that "as many as sixteen hundred newly arrived Africans may have perished on the Charleston wharf over four months."[27] By November, the major traders seem to have agreed to hold captives back from the market. With Jefferson having shut the African trade off, Virginia and Maryland traders settled into their newly protected domestic slave trade.[28]

William Dusinberre's comment about another president, James K. Polk, is equally applicable in the case of Jefferson: "His political conviction was congruent with what appeared to be his own financial interest."[29] For Jefferson as for other large slaveholders, the end of African importation was a crucial step in protecting and growing their net worth, which perhaps explains the support Jefferson received from Virginia and the South in general during his subsequent measure, unique in the annals of American history: a complete embargo of all overseas trade.

28

These Infernal
Principles

From the best information I could obtain, this city contains nearly three hundred houses, and about three thousand inhabitants, including all colours. There are several extensive mercantile houses established here, and one at least which imports goods directly from England. There are two printing-offices, and consequently two newspapers, which are published weekly . . . The gentlemen pass their time in the pursuit of three things: all make love; most of them play [gamble]; and a few make money. With Religion they have nothing to do; having formed a treaty with her, the principal article of which is, "Trouble not us, nor will we trouble you."[1]

—The traveler Christian Schultz, describing Natchez in 1808

US MERCHANT SHIPPERS WERE caught in the crossfire between implacable opposed forces that would not allow them to act without subterfuge. Both the belligerent conservative government in Britain and Napoleon's government in France were increasingly taking a policy that there were no neutrals, pursuant to which they claimed the right to seize American vessels.

Napoleon's Berlin Decree of November 21, 1806, prohibited trade with Britain and its allies, and allowed the capture of ships and the blockading of ports in service of that goal. However, it was not put into force against the United States for almost a year, so that in British eyes, the Jefferson administration was getting special treatment from Napoleon and was therefore not neutral but pro-French, as Jefferson had been deemed to be by the British all along.

Indeed, Jefferson acquiesced to the Berlin Decree "without effectual protest," as Henry Adams put it.[2] Britain responded with the draconian Orders in Council of November 11, 1807, an opaquely worded declaration of commercial war against neutrals that was squarely aimed at the United States, even as Bonaparte began applying the Berlin Decree to American ships.

Jefferson's "peaceable coercion" theory of defense was about to be sorely tested. Henry Adams, whose nine-volume history of the Jefferson and Madison administrations examines the matter in detail, wrote bluntly, "Jefferson and his government had shown over and over again that no provocation would make them fight; and from the moment that this attitude was understood, America became fair prey."[3] Both France and Britain were seizing American merchant ships, but Britain's bullying was more aggressive, leading to the galvanizing seizure of one of the few ships of the American navy, the *Chesapeake*, by the British ship *Leopard* off the coast of Norfolk, Virginia, on June 22, 1807.

Dramatizing the stakes was the fate of Denmark. In Europe, both powers pressured the Danish king to support them, the endgame of which was that Britain bombarded Copenhagen from September 2 through 5, 1807, destroying about half the city, killing some two thousand people, and confiscating some $10 million worth of merchandise in Danish vessels.[4] Adams wrote that "the annihilation of Denmark left America almost the only neutral, as she had long been the only Republican State." (Not counting Haiti, that is, but the United States, England, and France alike refused to recognize Haiti's claim to be a republic and considered it an outlaw that still rightfully belonged to France.) According to Adams, the undefended United States' "offences . . . had been more serious than those of Denmark, and had roused to exasperation the temper of England. A single ship of the line, supported by one or two frigates, could without a moment's notice repeat at New York the tragedy which had required a vast armament at Copenhagen."[5]

During the seven years of his presidency, Jefferson had discarded his previously declared Republican ideals of limited government one by one. Now, in the commercial emergency posed by Britain's Orders in Council, Jefferson imposed the Embargo Act, signed on December 22, 1807. His secretary of the treasury, Albert Gallatin, described it as "an act prohibiting the sailing of ships or vessels from the ports and harbors of the U. States to any foreign port or harbor"— in other words, nothing less than a self-imposed embargo on all US maritime commerce and travel.[6] This unparalleled real-world economic experiment was a hopeless attempt to resolve British and French incursions on US sovereignty at sea. It badly depressed the US economy, made Jefferson widely hated during his last year in office, and did nothing to dispel the tensions that ultimately erupted in the War of 1812.

When the prohibition against the slave trade kicked in on January 1, 1808, then, it happened against the backdrop of the general embargo, which had unleashed a panic in American (and European) commerce that made even the African trade seem a minor issue. Even had the slave trade not been specifically prohibited, there would have been no one to ship slaves from Africa to South Carolina. The merchants of Liverpool, who provided the bulk of the slave shipments, had been shut down from London, because Britain now prohibited their trade and would soon be sending its imperial navy to chase down slavers. Nor would Rhode Island's slave-trade specialists have been able to take up the slack, because even had their slave ships somehow not been prohibited along with all other foreign commerce by Jefferson's embargo, they would have been subject to confiscation at sea by the British navy, or possibly by French ships taking prizes for Napoleon.

While the embargo did stimulate American manufactures, it was received in New England as a plot by the French agent Jefferson to destroy American commerce. In New York, wrote the traveler John Lambert, "the grass had begun to grow upon the wharves."[7] But the full brunt of the embargo fell on the South, where two consecutive crops could not get to market. "Virginia society could neither economize nor liquidate," wrote Henry Adams. "Tobacco was worthless; but four hundred thousand negro slaves must be clothed and fed . . . with astonishing rapidity Virginia succumbed to ruin, while continuing to support the system that was draining her strength." With more than a little sarcasm, he added, "No episode in American history was more touching than the generous devotion with which Virginia clung to the embargo, and drained the poison which her own President held obstinately to her lips. . . . the old society of Virginia could never be restored . . . President Jefferson himself woke from his long dream of power only to find his own fortunes buried in the ruin he had made."[8]

The indecisiveness of Jefferson's solution prolonged the agony, as the external threat to commerce did not let up. Jefferson had begun his second term riding the popularity in the South of his greatest achievement as president: the annexation of Louisiana, to which New England's legislators had been opposed.

Now, even in the wake of the unpopular embargo, he still had support in Virginia. He was, in the final analysis, the slavery president, and he had given his home-state constituents the means of monetizing their inert labor force.

Not for another eight years, until the resolution of the War of 1812 finally ended the crisis of seizure at sea, would the coast be clear for something like normal commerce to resume—and for Virginia planters to take advantage of the great gift Jefferson had given them by selling large quantities of black Virginians down South.

Jefferson was humiliatingly forced to sign the removal of the embargo on March 1, 1809, days before a new president was inaugurated—another Virginian, Jefferson's protégé James Madison.

The election had not been an inspiring one from the point of view of New England. It was a Virginia versus South Carolina election, pitting the Republican James Madison of Virginia, principal author of the Constitution, against Federalist Charles Cotesworth Pinckney of South Carolina, he who at the Constitutional Convention had insisted on a full twenty years' protection for the African slave trade. In his first term, President Madison more or less continued the policies he had pursued as Jefferson's secretary of state—which had left a sectionally divided country, a damaged economy, a restless Louisiana that chafed under Anglo-American rule from the Chesapeake, an unresolved stalemate with an angry Britain, and an unbridled Napoleon—who, despite having dumped Louisiana, was still intent on controlling the Americas.

On the pretext of subduing Portugal for having engaged in commerce with its centuries-long trading partner England, Napoleon introduced his forces into Spain in 1807 with the intention of taking control of the ports of Lisbon and Cádiz, key bases for reaching across the Atlantic. With his troops installed in Iberia, he humiliated Carlos IV and his son Fernando VII before the world by installing his brother Joseph Bonaparte on the Spanish throne as King José I.

Napoleon's defenestration of the Spanish government was a green light for independence movements in Spain's American territories. But Cuba remained loyal to the Spanish crown, and in eastern Cuba (known as Oriente), the French speakers who had relocated as refugees from the Haitian Revolution came under suspicion.

Already there had been justified concern that the *franceses* might secede from the island and take over Oriente for themselves as per the model of the neighboring island Hispaniola, permanently divided between contentious French and Spanish speakers. Now the thirty thousand (a best-guess number) who had escaped the unraveling of Leclerc's genocide by fleeing as immigrants to eastern Cuba from Saint-Domingue were seen as potentially subversive by the loyalist Spanish government of Cuba. Those who did not take a loyalty oath to Spain or marry Spanish citizens found it expedient to leave for New Orleans, taking their slaves with them.

In the course of this flotilla, a report published by New Orleans mayor James Mather counted 9,059 people as entering New Orleans on some sixty ships, many of them privateers, mostly during the last three months of 1809. In this number, 3,225 of them (36 percent) were slaves, and only 962 of those were men over fifteen.[9] Since this took place after the January 1, 1808, cutoff, "importation of persons" was by then prohibited by federal law, so it took an act of Congress to disembark the enslaved passengers, who were impounded for months in the harbor of what was then called the Territory of Orleans. They were thus the last slaves to be legally imported into the United States.

As they had previously done in Santiago de Cuba, the newly arrived Domingans transformed the French part of New Orleans—the old part, which came to be known as the French Quarter for the language spoken there. New Orleans by then was well along in becoming two adjacent towns: a fast-growing English-speaking one and a much larger French- (and Spanish-) speaking one, separated by the no-man's-land ("neutral ground") of Canal Street (named for a canal that was never dug). While the Domingans' arrival helped push Louisiana's population a little farther toward the minimum of sixty thousand free inhabitants required for statehood, it also slowed the pace of Americanization of New Orleans for the next thirty years and brought a new layer of culture and skills to an already complex Afro-Louisianan population. Despite the peculiarity and isolation of Louisiana, it had been a colonial cousin of Saint-Domingue, Martinique, and Guadaloupe. Six of the twenty-three French slave ships that came to Louisiana were from Ouidah in present-day Benin, from whence the word *vodou*. Domingan vodou found fertile ground in Louisiana, since it was kin to practices that had been going on in Louisiana since the first contact with Africa.

≫≪

Ending the African trade signaled a major cultural shift in black America. Africans had been entering the colonies on an ongoing, though not continual, basis for almost two centuries.

There were 1,191,364 slaves in the United States according to the 1810 census, an increase of 33.4 percent over 1800. It seems reasonable to assume that fewer than one hundred thousand were African-born, with most of those in the Lowcountry. The next five decades would each show a growth of the enslaved population of never less than 24 percent—a tremendous level of growth for a population not being supplemented by imports and routinely devastated by high child mortality—but never again would the 1800 to 1810 rate of growth in the slave population be reached, combining as it did massive importation in combination with reproduction of the domestic population.

During that decade, the population of the southwestern corner of Mississippi quadrupled. Most of the new nation's frontiers pushed westward, but the expansion of plantations into Mississippi unrolled in a northeasterly direction. Natchez, in the southwest of the territory, was at the edge of a vast forest of uncleared land. The nearest Anglo-American towns to the east were hundreds of miles away. Nor was it easy to get to Natchez from New Orleans; as Christian Schultz was leaving Natchez downriver in April 1808, his boat passed one going the other way whose cargo of enslaved laborers were doing the hard upriver slog that required physically pulling the boat forward: "we met a brig at the Fausse Rivière, one hundred and sixty-five miles above New-Orleans, which was then forty-two days from that city. This vessel had part of her cargo of slaves on board, and was bound to Natchez; and though she had the advantage of extraordinary assistance from her slaves, she had performed only one half of her voyage. I have no doubt that her whole voyage from city to city took up more than eighty days."[10]

Natchez was already the second biggest slave market of the Deep South. Sitting at the end of the distribution line, it paid the highest prices. As had happened in the Chesapeake and Carolina, there was a political cleavage between the planters already established around Natchez, who had plenty of slaves and wanted to see the value of their holdings appreciate, and those on the frontier, who wanted to buy more slaves, cheap.

When Jefferson left office at the beginning of 1809, the US economy was in tatters from his embargo, with New England's shipping industry having suffered especially badly. As shipping resumed, Britain and France returned to impounding American vessels, and the new president, James Madison, continued to swallow the insults.

As when Madison had been Jefferson's secretary of state, the acquisition of Florida continued to be a strategic obsession. A new Native American group had formed there: the Seminoles were a composite people, most numerously a breakaway group of Creeks who had incorporated a number of black escapees into their ranks. These "Black Seminoles," as they were called, were largely Gullah people making use of Native American social identity while living in marronage.

All over the Southeast, settlers pushed onto Native American land, and they wanted more of it. In Congress, the perhaps twenty-one representatives and senators who clamored for war with Britain were overwhelmingly Southern and Western. Their Federalist enemies dubbed them the "War Hawks." Kentucky's thirty-four-year-old Henry Clay made his debut on the national stage when, after two weeks as a senator, on February 22, 1810, he announced, "The conquest of Canada is in your power . . . I verily believe that the militia of Kentucky are alone competent to place Montreal and Upper Canada at your feet."[11]

Clay was trying to appeal to annexationists in New England, but he also wanted the Native Americans, Spanish, and British cleared out of the way of the Southern river arteries that could carry Kentucky's products to the Gulf of Mexico via the West Florida ports of Mobile and Pensacola. When Madison invaded the short-lived, self-proclaimed independent Republic of West Florida, which the United States had no claim to other than conquest, Clay defended the action on Christmas Day, 1810, with these words:

> I am not, sir, in favor of cherishing the passion of conquest, but I must be permitted, in conclusion, to indulge the hope of seeing, ere long, the new United States, (if you will allow me the expression,) embracing, not only the old thirteen States, but the entire country east of the Mississippi, including East Florida, and some of the territories to the north of us also.[12]

Exposed to attack from without and within, the Chesapeake was leery of war. Virginia congressman John Randolph argued restraint because of "the danger arising from the black population," as the congressional recorder summarized it during a December 1811 oration. "The French Revolution had polluted" them, declaimed Randolph with his characteristic rhetorical extravagance, and was teaching them

> that they are equal to their masters; in other words, advising them to cut their throats . . . What was the consequence? Within the last ten years, repeated alarms of insurrection among the slaves, some of them awful indeed. From the spreading of this infernal doctrine, the whole Southern country had been thrown into a state of insecurity. . . . God forbid, sir, that the Southern States should ever see an enemy on their shores, with these infernal principles of French fraternity in the van! While talking of taking Canada, some of us were shuddering for our own safety at home.

He then evoked the fearful specter of Gabriel's rebellion, reminding everyone to be afraid of the slaves' potential for violence: "The night-bell never tolled for fire in Richmond that the mother did not hug her infant more closely to her bosom."[13]

South Carolina's twenty-nine-year-old John C. Calhoun, as new in Congress as Clay, was at the beginning of a career that would see him become the embodiment of pro-slavery doctrine. Calhoun was the first upcountry South Carolina politician to make a name on the national stage; if he was representative, upcountry was an angry place.

Calhoun was a brilliant writer and debater, and to judge from the extensive documentation that exists, he was an unhappy, strict man whose single goal in life was to become president. Harriet Martineau wrote in 1838 of Calhoun that "I know of no man who lives in such utter intellectual solitude. He meets men and harangues them by the fire-side as in the Senate. He is wrought like a piece of machinery, set going vehemently by a weight, and stops while you answer. He either passes by what you say, or twists it into suitability with what is in his own head, and begins to lecture again."[14]

George C. Rogers Jr. writes that "Calhoun considered diplomacy too slow—the tool of the effete coastal aristocrat."[15] Slavery was Calhoun's irreducible demand, and he treated it as synonymous with the human dignity of his people; an affront to slavery was an affront to a Southerner. He replied to Randolph by bragging about how much better South Carolinians were than Virginians at keeping their enslaved ignorant:

Of the Southern section, I, too, have some personal knowledge; and can say, that in South Carolina no such fears in any part are felt . . . however the gentleman may alarm himself with the disorganizing effects of French principles, I cannot think our ignorant blacks have felt much of their baneful influence. I dare say more than one half of them never heard of the French Revolution.[16]

The awareness of what had happened in Haiti may well have reached more enslaved ears in Carolina than Calhoun imagined; but in Louisiana, the enslaved had definitely heard of the French Revolution. Up the Mississippi from New Orleans, on the riverbank that had since 1795 become a home to the death camps of sugarland, the mulatto Charles Deslondes—not a Domingan, but fully aware of what had happened there—led the largest peacetime slave revolt in US history: the "German Coast rebellion" that began on January 8, 1811. The uprising was ruthlessly suppressed by South Carolina's Wade Hampton, who would later become a Louisiana planter.

Clay, who urged armed confrontation with Britain, was also one of the Southern and Western legislators who pushed to allow the twenty-year charter of the First Bank of the United States to expire in 1811, with unfortunate consequences when the war began.

It requires an effort for a modern person, accustomed to a national currency, to imagine the monetary situation of the early United States.

The Constitution gave the federal government monetary authority, reserving for it the exclusive right "to coin Money, regulate the Value thereof, and of foreign Coin." No state could "enter into any Treaty, Alliance, or Confederation; grant Letters of Marque and Reprisal; coin Money; emit Bills of Credit; [or] make any Thing but gold and silver Coin a Tender in Payment of Debts."[17]

"Bills of Credit" meant paper money. The Constitution explicitly prohibited the printing of money by the states, so there couldn't be, say, Massachusetts dollars and Virginia dollars. But, perhaps because the debate would have been endless, the Constitution was silent on the issuance of paper money by the federal government, and silent on its issuance by banks. The most desirable money— many would tell you, the only real money—was specie, minted gold or silver coins that were usable around the world as money, most commonly in the form of Spanish coins. President Washington signed the Coinage Act in 1792, which adopted the dollar as the monetary unit, "each to be of the value of a Spanish milled dollar," and allowed for the coining of money, expressed in dollars and bearing an image "emblematic of liberty." Foreign gold and silver coins continued in circulation and were legal tender until 1857.

But there weren't enough silver dollars to conduct daily commerce with, nor was moving all the available precious metal around in daily circulation the best way to use it. Paper money was a practical necessity. A bank would own a given amount of specie and would issue notes "backed" by it. The notes could be redeemed in person at the bank for their face value in silver, but for most transactions this was an unnecessary step. The system worked because at any given time, much paper would circulate, serving the needs of commerce, while only a relatively small amount of paper would actually be exchanged for specie. In order to be assured of being able to cover their obligations, banks were expected to maintain "fractional reserve" requirements at a reasonable level, though that requirement was frequently ignored.

The First Bank of the United States, the only federally chartered bank, was a creation of Alexander Hamilton, modelled in part on the Bank of England. It was not under the control of the Department of the Treasury, though the government owned 20 percent of it and Treasury had access to its books, and it had a monopoly on receiving deposits of the government's revenues, some 90 percent of which were tariffs collected at seaport customs houses.[18] It was well-run and profitable, and by 1811 its high-quality notes constituted about 20 percent of the nation's money supply.

The state banks, most of which were chartered after the First Bank of the United States was chartered in 1791, disliked the competition from a national bank that acted to some degree as a regulator on the amount of paper money they could issue, and they wanted the deposits of specie that were going to the national bank. Jefferson in particular had been vehemently opposed to Hamilton's bank, as he was to banks in general. The hard Jeffersonians were united in their ideologically based opposition to the bank; meanwhile, the state banks leaned on senators and congressmen to take their competition out. In a political triumph for South Carolina's Langdon Cheves, who was Speaker of the House, Congress refused to renew the bank's charter, overriding the objections of the only competent member of Madison's undistinguished cabinet, Secretary of the Treasury Albert Gallatin.

Without a national bank, then, the War of 1812 was fought without financing by a government whose principal source of revenue—customs duties—had been devastated by wartime conditions since the embargo of 1807. Nor was there much of an army. The military structure was plagued by a surfeit of officers, many of them incompetent, and a deficit of troops, who suffered unspeakable hardships. The militias were undisciplined, as they would demonstrate when they turned and ran by the thousands at the Battle of Bladensburg (August 24, 1814), opening the door for the burning of the federal city. The navy, the most competent branch of the military, had been crippled by Jefferson's gunboat debacle.

Napoleon's towering influence on the course of American history extended to causing the breach in which the Spanish colonies could move toward independence. In forcing Carlos IV's abdication in 1808, he put a definitive end to Spain's status as a world power. As Spain's empire disintegrated, the fortress-city of Cartagena declared independence on November 11, 1811, beginning a series of bloody South American independence wars.

The Lafitte brothers—French-born pirates who had relocated from Saint-Domingue to Cuba and then to Louisiana—received letters of marque from Cartagena giving them legal cover as privateers to do what they were already doing: preying on Spanish slave ships bound for Cuba. They sold the human merchandise by the pound, cheap, from their well-guarded grey-market base at Barataria, west of New Orleans. Mostly they sold to the French-speaking creoles of southern Louisiana, who preferred to get their slaves from pirates than from the Georgiamen.

Louisiana's colonial status ended on April 30, 1812, when it was admitted to the Union. It was the best way to secure the largely French-speaking state's dubious loyalty to the United States before going to war against Great Britain on June 18, four days before Napoleon declared war on Russia. By going to war against Britain, the United States effectively became an ally of Napoleon, who was quite popular in New Orleans.

Jefferson's presidency, which began with his great popularity, had ended in disaster; now Madison's was failing. "Successive generations of scholars have never ceased to wonder," writes J. C. A. Stagg, who edited Madison's presidential papers, "how the creative statesman who 'fathered' both the Federal Constitution and the Bill of Rights, to say nothing of the Republican Party of the 1790s, could be as incompetent and as unsuccessful as he seemed to be as a chief executive." Stagg describes an enduring image of Madison as "the weak and indecisive statesman who handled the disputes with Great Britain over maritime rights so badly that he lost control of his policies to a congressional faction of 'War Hawks,' whose members, after November 1811, stampeded him into a conflict which he did not want and which he then mismanaged to the extent that he remains to this day the only president ever to have been driven from the nation's capital by an invading army."[19] Stagg supplied this description in an attempt to dispel it as a stereotype, but while it is admittedly incomplete as a summary of Madison's presidential career, it is not incorrect.

Remembered by the ideologically neutral name of the War of 1812, this conflict was crucial to the development of the republic. It was effectively the United States' participation in the final stage of the Napoleonic Wars, and it can be seen as a second War of Independence, since one of its most important outcomes was the definitive acknowledgment by Britain of American sovereignty. In New England, where many were antiwar, it was a failed war to annex Canada. In the South, where it was a war against Native Americans and free blacks, it was an essential step in the expansion of slavery that would fill in the territory from Louisiana to Florida with plantations.

There were four main fronts to the thirty-two-month war with Britain:

1) Canada, which the United States repeatedly attempted to assault, without success;

2) the Chesapeake, whose commerce was blockaded by the British from the start of the war and which was invaded by an army that burned the White House and the Capitol. The blockade was not impermeable, however, as the British admiral John B. Warren wrote to headquarters: "Several large Clipper Schooners of from two to three hundred Tons, strongly manned and armed have run thro' the Blockade in the Chesapeak, in spite of every endeavour and of the most vigilant attention of our Ships to prevent their getting out, nor can any thing stop these Vessels escaping to Sea in dark Nights and Strong Winds."[20]

3) Alabama, a front not generally mentioned as such in summaries of the war, because it did not directly entail fighting with Britain but with Native Americans, who were massacred. In Alabama, the United States achieved its military goals with what has been remembered as the Creek War, undertaken as part of the War of 1812. It's something of a commonplace that no territory changed hands as a result of the War of 1812, but that's not so. Under cover of

war with Britain, the United States—in the person of the most effective general in the US Army, Andrew Jackson—grabbed a vast area of Native American land in Georgia and Alabama; and

4) the Gulf South, whose seaports of New Orleans, Mobile, and Pensacola were essential for control of trade with the interior. There the British were vanquished under the iron command of Andrew Jackson, in a tremendous victory for Southern slaveowners against the power that had dared offer freedom to their property.

29

The Hireling and Slave

No refuge could save the hireling and slave
From the terror of night or the gloom of the grave
Oh, say, does that star spangled banner yet wave [etc.] . . .
      —Francis Scott Key, "Defense of Fort McHenry," third verse

To DESCRIBE MORE FULLY the Jacksonian context, we will briefly backtrack our chronology to quote a journal entry by a clergyman from the year Andrew Jackson was born—1767—and the place: Waxhaw, deep in the wooded, swampy hinterlands on the North Carolina side of the border between the Carolinas.

The most detailed account we have of this frontier life, albeit a biased one, is that of Anglican pastor Charles Woodmason, who was appalled. Woodmason had been shunned by Charleston society for having accepted a commission as a Stamp Act collector in 1765. He changed his life after that; apparently motivated by spiritual concerns, he was ordained so that he could become a circuit-riding Anglican (or Episcopal) priest on the frontier, where the Church of England had no institutional presence but where there were New Light Baptists, Presbyterians, Dunkards, Quakers, and more. (He ultimately returned to Britain after being stigmatized as a Tory.)

> [I went to] the Settlement of Irish Presbyterians called the Waxaws, among whom were several Church People. . . . This is a very fruitful fine Spot, thro' which the dividing Line between North and South Carolina runs . . . a finer Body of Land is no where to be seen—But it is occupied by a Sett of the most lowest vilest Crew breathing—Scotch Irish Presbyterians from the North of Ireland—They have built a Meeting House and have a

Pastor, a Scots Man among them—A good sort of Man—He once was of the Church of England . . . His Congregation is very large—This Tract of Land being most surprisingly thick settled beyond any Spot in England of its Extent—seldom less than 9, 10, 1200 People assemble of a Sunday— They never heard an Episcopal Minister, or the Common Prayer, and were very curious.[1]

Woodmason's memoir leaves no doubt that if politics was the popular entertainment of the cities, religion was the great organized participatory experience for the unlettered people of the frontier, as per his outraged description of a New Light Baptist service:

> There are so many Absurdities committed by them [New Light Baptists], as wou'd shock one of our *Cherokee* Savages; And was a Sensible Turk or Indian to view some of their Extravagancies it would quickly determine them against Christianity. Had any such been in their Assembly as last Sunday when they communicated, the Honest Heathens would have imagin'd themselves rather amidst a Gang of frantic Lunatics broke out of Bedlam, rather than among a Society of religious Christians, met to celebrate the most sacred and Solemn Ordnance of their Religion. Here, one Fellow mounted on a Bench with the Bread, and bawling, *See the Body of Christ*, Another with the Cup running around, and bellowing—*Who cleanses his Soul with the Blood of Christ*, and a thousand other Extravagancies—One on his knees in a Posture of Prayer—Others singing—some howling—These Ranting—Those Crying—Others dancing, Skipping, Laughing and rejoycing. Here two or 3 Women falling on their Backs, kicking up their Heels, exposing their Nakedness to all Bystanders and others sitting Pensive, in deep Melancholy lost in Abstraction, like Statues, quite insensible—and when rous'd by the Spectators from their pretended Reveries Transports, and indecent Postures and Actions declaring they knew nought of the Matter. That their Souls had taken flight to Heav'n, and they knew nothing of what they said or did. Spect[at]ors were highly shocked at such vile Abuse of sacred Ordinances![2]

While Dr. Woodmason never adapted to such a performative religious experience, he did become a voice for the settlers, helping them draft a remonstrance when they organized as "regulators"—vigilantes—in their own defense against roving gangs of bandits. Plantation slavery had not been developed upcountry yet; according to Woodmason, that was because the hazards of warlordism made it hard for white settlers to bring in slaves:

> . . . the people wearied out with being expos'd to the Depredations of Robbers—Set down here just as a Barrier between the Rich Planters and the Indians, to secure the former against the Latter—Without Laws or Government Schools or Ministers—No Police established—and all Property quite insecure—Merchants as fearful to venture their Goods as Ministers their Persons—The Lands, tho' the finest in the Province unoccupied, and *rich Men afraid to set Slaves to work to clear them, lest they should become a Prey to the Banditti*—No Regard had to the numberless petitions and Complaints of the people—Thus neglected and slighted by those in Authority, they rose in Arms—pursued the Rogues, broke up their Gangs—burnt the dwellings of all their Harbourers and Abettors—Whipp'd and drove the Idle, Vicious and Profligate out of the Province, Men and Women without Distinction and would have proceeded to Charleston in a Regular Corps of 5000 Men, and hung up the Rogues before the State House in Presence of Governor and Council.
>
> For the Mildness of Legislation here is so great and the Clemency of the Cheif [*sic*] in Authority has been carried to such Excess that when a notorious Robber was with Great Pains catch'd and sent to Town, and there try'd and Condemn'd he always got pardon'd by Dint of Money, and came back 50 times worse than before. The fellows thus pardon'd form'd themselves into a large Gang, ranging the province with Impunity.[3] (emphasis added)

That was the world Andrew Jackson grew up in: militantly defensive, self-reliant, and deeply distrustful of government. As a young man, Jackson relocated to the western part of North Carolina, which was now being called Tennessee and was where many veterans of the war with the British were settling. Jackson set up shop as a lawyer in the frontier town of Nashville, which was becoming a business center for the settlers who were pouring into the area. By 1789, he was traveling down the hazardous Wilderness Road—a 450-mile forest path through Native American territory plagued by "land pirates"—to do business in Natchez.

Natchez was already functioning as a slave market in the late 1780s, when the region's agricultural output was still relatively minor, consisting mostly of tobacco and indigo. It had the distinction of having been a French town, a

Spanish town, a British town, and a Spanish town again, with elements of all those populations. It was the site of the Indian uprising that ended French colonial plans for Louisiana. A 1790 report called it "an English [meaning, English-speaking] settlement, subject to the Spaniards," and by then it had "many negroes," in the words of Mississippi historian Charles S. Sydnor.[4]

Jackson was a product of the militia system, in which he was a leading officer. Like other merchants, he bought and sold slaves as part of his commercial activity. He was also a horse breeder and a racing enthusiast; a lawyer, land speculator, and plantation owner; a pathological hater of English, Spanish, Creek Indians, and anyone who crossed him; and a master of intimidation—all of which was consonant with being a slave trader.

"Between court terms in Tennessee," writes Jackson's biographer Robert V. Remini, "Jackson frequently dropped down to Natchez, where he brought [to Natchez traders] such items as cotton, furs, swan skins and feathers for bedding, lime, pork, beef, boats, and"—the final word in the list seems discreetly tucked in—"slaves."[5] In Remini's delicate words, Jackson carried slaves "frequently" from Nashville to Natchez as a "courtesy" to "his friends," though that belies the physical effort necessary to transport a prisoner through 450 or so miles of wilderness in the late eighteenth century.

A young white man's first significant investment on the road to wealth acquisition might well be a young black woman, rather than what the slave trade called a "prime hand." Such seems to have been the case with Jackson when he was twenty, as per a November 17, 1788, "Bill of Sale from Micajah Crews to Andrew Jackson Esquire for a Negro Woman named Nancy about Eighteen or Twenty Years of Age." Nancy was the first slave that we have any record of Jackson having purchased, and her purchase was one of his first transactions of any sort of which we have a record. He may have purchased her with the intention of reselling her; we know nothing about what kind of use he put her to, nor do we know anything else about her. The bill of sale is the only indication that Nancy existed.[6] Between 1790 and 1794, writes Remini, Jackson purchased "at least sixteen slaves . . . They measured his steady progress toward economic security" while he pursued a career as a merchant and a real estate speculator.[7]

In July 1794, Jackson made a great real estate deal when he became co-owner of some five thousand acres of the lower Chickasaw Bluff, marvelously situated on the Tennessee side overlooking the Mississippi River, where the Wolf River empties into it. The land's previous owner, the trader John Rice, had bought it in 1783, while it was still part of North Carolina—though under then-current law North Carolina had no right to sell it, as it was Chickasaw land. Rice was killed by Native Americans on his way back from a Nashville-Natchez run in 1791, throwing the property onto the market. The lawyer and slave trader John Overton, a Virginia-born Nashville transplant, purchased it in partnership with Jackson, his lifelong close ally.[8]

Though the area was as yet unpopulated by whites, it was the best site for a town along a far stretch of the Mississippi. Four decades later, in 1830, when steamboats ruled the transportation economy, Overton retroactively credited himself with foresight: "I always . . . considered that at some day, the water privilege attached to the banks would be worth more than all the lots and lands about the place."[9] Jackson had little to do with the property, other than making a profit on his share when he sold it; a third partner, General James Winchester, gave the settlement its fanciful Nile-istic name: Memphis.[10]

The Mississippi Territory was organized in 1798, and the United States took over administration of it in 1801. The United States Army went to work building the Natchez Trace—a road of sorts, along the route of the Wilderness Road, to connect the town with Nashville. Fortunately for Jackson, his friend from Tennessee and former colleague in Congress, President Jefferson's protégé William Charles Cole Claiborne, was now the Mississippi Territory's first US governor. Claiborne, who addressed Jackson effusively in his letters, made Jackson's family emissary John Hutchings welcome, helped him find buyers for slaves and horses he had brought, and helpfully advised Jackson of the progress by mail. Claiborne wrote him on December 9, 1801:

> The Races in this District, commenced yesterday, and will hold for three days; Mr. Hutchings has attended the *Race* today, and will proceed from *thence*, to Mr. Green's, where he has left the Negroes & Horses. Mr. H. will be at my House, next Week; in the mean time, I will try to find a purchaser for your Horses, as for Negroes, they are in great demand, and will sell well.[11]

Claiborne wrote Jackson again on December 23, informing him of young Hutchings's accomplishment as a slave trader: "The Negro Woman he has sold for 500 dolls. in Cash, and I belive he has, or will in a few days sell the Boy, for his own price, to Colo. West."[12]

Jackson must have been an effective frontier businessman. A violent man and an eager duelist, he once challenged another lawyer for mocking his knowledge of the law. Whether dealing with slaves, soldiers, or politicians, he was an authoritarian leader who, in Remini's words, "could hate with a Biblical fury and would resort to petty and vindictive acts to nurture his hatred and keep it bright and strong and ferocious."[13] When in 1804 he advertised in the *Tennessee Gazette* for the return of a runaway slave, he made the extraordinarily vicious offer of "ten dollars extra, for every hundred lashes any person will give him, to the amount of three hundred."[14]

Jackson got a bad reputation when he killed Charles Dickinson in a May 30, 1806, duel. After Jackson's pistol jammed and did not fire during the first exchange, he was allowed to recock his pistol and fire a second shot. With a disadvantaged opponent, the gallant move would have been to fire the pistol into the air, shake hands, and considered honor avenged. But there was no doubt that Dickinson had intended to kill Jackson. Dickinson, who made his money on the interregional slave trade by, as Jackson later described, "purchasing Negroes in Maryland and carrying them to Natchez & Louis[ian]a," had put a bullet into Jackson that fractured a rib or two and, in Remini's words, "lodged in the chest cavity close to his heart and impinged on his left lung."[15] Streaming blood from his chest wound, Jackson took aim and shot Charles Dickinson in cold blood from a distance of twenty-four feet. The bullet entered Dickinson's intestines, and he lived with no hope of recovery, in mortal pain, until he expired about ten o'clock that night. The bullet in Jackson's body remained there the rest of his life, one of a number of excruciating pains he lived with. The duel had been over a quarrel stemming from a horse race with a $3,000 purse.

Like many other merchants, Jackson traded in slaves along with everything else—horses, cattle, dry goods, and especially land speculation, which was the foundation of a great many fortunes in Jackson's day. Jackson made much money selling Tennessee plots to land speculators in Philadelphia, for which he typically got paid in paper, which he traded for goods, which he then had to sell at his own stores. Slaves, however, were cash transactions, as we see in a letter from Jackson's nephew Donelson Caffery, who was attempting to get started as a merchant, apparently in partnership with Jackson. Caffery wrote him from Bayou Sarah in West Feliciana Parish on May 20, 1810, which was at the time part of the nominally Spanish-controlled area that was about to briefly declare itself the independent Republic of West Florida and would come under Claiborne's control by year's end:

> I am sorry to inform you that I fear from the situation of this Country business cannot be done to advantage[.] It is true Goods may be sold on credit, but contrary to the opinion I had form'd from the accounts of

people; There is no such thing as making collections . . . As soon as I can make sale of some Negroes, I will go to New Orleans to buy Groceries[.] it's the only business that can be done here for Cash.[16]

There are various instances of Jackson's using "negroes" in settlement of accounts. A 1795 letter to him requesting him to purchase land for one Joseph Anderson notes that "it would suit me to pay for it, either in a negro and Horses, or in Horses and some Money."[17] Jackson's slave-trading past became a political hot potato when he later ran for president. During the election of 1828, a pamphlet authored by a man with whom Jackson had been in litigation over land deals, Andrew Erwin, bore the memorable title of *Gen. Jackson's Negro Speculations, and his Traffic in Human Flesh, Examined and Established by Positive Proof.* It brought up a story about which Jackson had to issue a clarification: in a not unusual transaction for the time and place, the mercantile firm of Jackson & Hutchings in 1806 accepted a thirteen-year-old "negro boy" as partial payment to close out a three-year-old debt. In Jackson's words, "The negro boy was recd. & the account with Rawlings & Bradford closed." As was all too common in such stories, it had a sad ending: the boy, whose name was Charles, was kept at the Clover Bottom racetrack, run by Jackson's friends. One of them, William Preston Anderson, bet him in a race and lost him, and Charles subsequently died from an unspecified disease.[18]

Jackson was the partner with capital and credit in Coleman, Green, and Jackson, founded in 1810 to sell cotton and tobacco from Nashville to Natchez. After losing money on a cotton deal, the partners attempted to recoup the expenses by going into slaves, buying a group of them from a tavern dealer in Virginia. The men, as Jackson later noted, were received naked; it was not uncommon for a seller to palm off the expense of clothing them on the buyer. The junior partner, Horace Green of Natchez, took the slaves down to Natchez by boat in the summer of 1811, but no one was buying. Business was terrible. Britain was hammering at American shipping pursuant to its Orders in Council, and commerce was dead. It was clear that war was coming with Britain, and there would likely be a naval blockade that would prevent taking the cotton crop out of New Orleans.

Finding a weak market, Green traded a few of the unfortunate people for horses before Jackson arranged for John Hutchings to take them over and house them at his nearby plantation until he could come down personally to salvage what he could of the fiasco. Failing to sell the slaves himself, Jackson drove the unsold slaves back to Nashville, taking the unheard-of step of driving a coffle of slaves from the destination back to the point of origin, through Choctaw and Chickasaw territory.[19] From Natchez he wrote his wife, Rachel, on December 17, 1811:

> on tomorrow I shall set out from here homewards, on the Biopierre [Bayou Pierre][.] I expect to be detained Some days preparing the negroes for the wilderness[.] . . . I shall bring home with me from twelve to Twenty—I hope to be able to sell some of them on the way at good prices—but many of them I Shall be obliged to bring home and as most of that number will be females I leave you to point out to Mr. Fields [the overseer] where to have the house built for them.[20]

Meanwhile, an apocalyptic fear ran through the region. The New Madrid earthquake, with its epicenter in Arkansas, still believed to be the strongest earthquake ever to hit that part of the country, had struck on December 16, and the aftershocks were continuing. Navigating the Mississippi had become impossible, creating economic havoc in New Orleans. On the way back to Nashville with his coffle, Jackson, already in a bad mood, ran afoul of the federal Choctaw Indian agent, Silas Dinsmore, whose post on the road between Nashville and Natchez, as mandated by law, required passports for slaves being transported. Dinsmore was in the habit of confiscating undocumented slaves, thus creating a barrier for slave traders along the main trading artery. Jackson, who saw Dinsmore as a "highway robber," defied him, bringing his train through with a conspicuous show of arms. He subsequently began a campaign to have Dinsmore removed from his post, writing to Tennessee governor Willie Blount a letter that bluntly threatened arson and murder: "from the conduct of Silas in this as well as in other cases he must be removed, or our citizens will rise and burn his Tavern and Store with Silas in the middle of them."[21]

Jackson subsequently refused to pay his partner Green's invoiced expenses, charging that Green was padding the bill to pay his gambling debts, that his transportation and provisions expenses were too high, and that he had hired the "negroes" out in Natchez and pocketed the proceeds. Like a number of items of Jackson's correspondence, his letter to the arbitrator appears to have been composed in a fit of passionate anger, but from it we can learn something about the deal. Needless to say, it shows not a bit of concern for the victims of his business, who had been trafficked from Virginia to Natchez, then made to trek through the wilderness back up to Nashville. Jackson's concern was that he was being cheated on the money:

I also found from examining the ac[coun]ts of Negroes sent to Markett that the expence never averaged more from here than fifteen dollars a head except one wench and three children, who had been subject to the fits remained better than six months in the Natchez, she cost with her children twenty five dollars . . .

[F]rom every inquiry I have made on the subject, [I find] that fifteen dollars pr head is about the usual expence, and finding this to amount including the amount of the price of the Boat, and not taking into view the children at the breast, it makes the cost on each negro $44.66 2/3—this as I am advised is more than double what is usual . . .

Three months of provisions was talked of as necessary to be laid in as an outfit . . . let us take the soldiers ration for the Basis—there was 25 grown negroes with two sucking children they always count with the mother—then say 25 for three months will take 1125 lb. Beacon [bacon] . . . let us give $60 for cloathing (there was 13 wenches one habit each[,] the fellows recd naked) . . .

It was agreed on all hand that the Natchez was glutted with negroes . . . a sacrafice will be upon the negroes of at least $1500 if not $2000.[22]

The trip was, unsurprisingly, hard on the captives. Jackson wrote his sister-in-law, Mary Caffery, who was eager to purchase a laborer: "The negro fellows that I brought through with me owing to their exposure in the wilderness have all been sick and were the[y] *well* neither* of them is such that I could recommend to you."[23] Jackson never described the condition of the women and children, torn away from their families, who endured the round-trip forced march.

Given the documentation of this episode that exists, it appears safe to say that Andrew Jackson is the only US president that we know of who personally drove a slave coffle. But then, Jackson was also the first president to have been a merchant.

New England did not want the War of 1812; the Southerners did. They got what they wanted: under cover of war with Britain, a substantial chunk of the Deep South was made safe for plantation slavery when Andrew Jackson vanquished the Creek Nation and took its land.

*i.e., none.

Jackson was at home at the estate outside Nashville that he called the Hermitage when word arrived: a thousand or so Creek Indians had on August 30, 1813, committed a massacre of some 250 men, women, and children at Fort Mims in Alabama, in retaliation for a murderous attack on them by two settlers who had taken refuge there. They dashed out the brains of children, it was said, swinging them by their legs to bash their heads against the walls, and they slit open the bellies of live pregnant women. They carried off the slaves to be their servants—meaning, they stole the most valuable property there. Among the dead at Fort Mims were 160 unfortunate soldiers under the command of W. C. C. Claiborne's brother, Ferdinand L. Claiborne, who escaped harm.

Creek Indians were the very devil to white Tennesseans. South Carolina had fought the two-year Yamassee War against them almost a century before. Georgians had been fighting them since their colony was established. The people of Jackson's society considered it their duty to kill them as a matter of their own survival. For Jackson, the Indians were the flunkeys of the British, as were the Spanish; Britain and Spain were at this point allies, after the humiliation Napoleon had wreaked on Spain. With the United States at war with Britain at last, he sought to neutralize the British in the South by repressing their indigenous allies.

When word of Fort Mims arrived, the forty-eight-year-old Jackson was nursing a broken arm with a slug newly embedded in his shoulder, ten days after a seven-man gun battle in the town's streets against future senator Thomas Hart Benton and his brother. With a seemingly limitless tolerance for pain, he set out on horseback with his swollen arm in a sling to command a militia that would accomplish the white settlers' agenda: the ethnic cleansing of Native Americans from the entire South east of the Mississippi. It took Jackson multiple campaigns over many years to finish the job, which required his attainment of the presidency to complete. Remini describes Jackson's intention:

> Certainly by 1813, if not earlier, Jackson's course of action was fixed. He intended to eliminate all foreigners along the southern frontier as a necessary prelude to the systematic destruction of the Indian menace and the territorial expansion of the American nation.[24]

Jackson described his immediate mission unequivocally: "to *carry* a *campaign into* the *heart* of the *Creek nation* and *exterminate them*."[25] Though the Creeks were feared for their ambushes, they were unsuccessful at defending themselves against pursuit by organized armies hell-bent on killing them. The conflict had begun as a civil war among the Creeks, pitting the traditionalist Red Sticks, allied with Britain, against the more accommodationist Lower Creeks. Exploiting the division, Jackson ended by wiping out the Creek Nation, burning Native American towns wherever he found them and defeating a force he estimated at four thousand warriors; the Creeks had black slaves, who also participated in combat against US forces and were killed. As the defeated Red Sticks retreated to Spanish Florida, Jackson treated his allies among the Creeks as harshly as if they had been the losers, forcing hard terms on them and expropriating some twenty-two million acres of their land in what is now Alabama and southern Georgia.

Jackson did it without much in the way of resources with which to arm, feed, clothe, and pay his troops, who were frequently in a state of near or actual mutiny. Without a national bank, the federal government had to borrow from state banks, but the largest amount of specie was unavailable for Southern use, because it was in Massachusetts and Connecticut banks, who lent it to Britain instead. During the War of 1812, "New England banks were financial agents of the enemy," writes Henry Adams. "Boston bought freely British treasury notes at liberal discount, and sent coin to Canada in payment of them." Another embargo, from December 1813 to April 1814, cut off Southern exports, resulting in a net outflow of what specie there was from that region to New England.[26]

At the end of the Creek War, Jackson returned eighteen "negroes" who had been captured by the Creeks at Fort Mims to their lawful owners. In three Native American camps, his men found "one hundred and fifty scalps the greater part of which were females supposed to be taken at Fort Mimms."[27]

The enslaved of the Chesapeake began slipping away to the British invaders as soon as they arrived. They were particularly valuable defectors, because they could serve as guides to the area. This ongoing drain became formalized as a military strategy on April 2, 1814, when, much as Lord Dunmore had previously done, Admiral Alexander Cochrane, the new British commander, issued a proclamation from Bermuda "that all those disposed to emigrate . . . will have their choice of either entering into his Majesty's sea or land forces, or of being sent as FREE settlers to the British positions in north America or the West Indies."[28]

Cochrane was attempting to incite slave revolt. Knowing the white Southerners' fear of black violence—especially in Louisiana, which had so many white

survivors of Saint-Domingue—he imagined thousands of runaway slaves joining his troops. A diversionary force sent to harass coastal South Carolina and
Georgia under Rear Admiral George Cockburn included black West Indian
troops, with the explicit intention of instilling the fear that a British-supported
slave insurrection was under way.[29] One hundred thirty-eight of Pierce Butler's
slaves ran away, a loss for him calculated by Roswell King Jr. at $61,450.[30]

Unfortunately for the Americans, the British invasion came at a time when
Britain had a surplus capacity of well-trained, victorious soldiers. A beaten
Napoleon had abdicated on April 11, 1814, and in August, Cockburn's troops
landed in Maryland and marched toward Washington. After the Baltimore
militia turned tail and fled at the Battle of Bladensburg on August 24, the British entered the capital city. President James Madison left the debacle at Bladensburg, and returned to Washington to find the White House in the process of
evacuating. He fled to the countryside, humiliated.

British forces under Admiral Cockburn entered Washington, burning the
White House, the Treasury, part of the Capitol, and whatever was in the Library
of Congress up to that point, while sparing civilian property. Their targeted
arson in the capital city was widely believed to have been undertaken in reprisal
for the inexcusable American plundering and partial burning of York (Toronto)
in April 1813. A providentially violent thunderstorm blunted the British invasion of Washington, and they quickly retreated, having made their point.

The British offensive into the Chesapeake was stopped at Baltimore.

The War of 1812 is not well remembered today—except for its two most heroic
tableaux, both of which inspired familiar songs.

When the British forces continued on from Washington to Baltimore on
the night of September 13, 1814, they failed to get past Fort McHenry, which
controlled the access to the town at the mouth of the Patapsco River. The
Americans had plenty of gunpowder—the factory of E. I. du Pont de Nemours
was in nearby Wilmington, Delaware—and there was a prolonged cannonade
that stopped the British advance. "For two hours," writes Harold R. Manakee,
"houses in Baltimore, four miles distant, trembled on their foundations."[31]

One week after the battle, Francis Scott Key's lyric "Defense of Fort
McHenry" was published in full on page two of the two-page *Baltimore American
and Commercial Daily Advertiser* of September 21, 1814, though it subsequently

became better known as "The Star-Spangled Banner." To indicate how it should be sung, it was sufficient to place at the head of Key's lyric the name of the risqué and ubiquitous English glee club drinking song his words had been composed to fit: "*Tune* — Anacreon in Heaven," the final two lines of which read in the original:

> *And besides, I'll instruct you like me to entwine*
> *The myrtle of Venus with Bacchus's vine.*

Frank Key, a twenty-five-year-old lawyer from Georgetown,* was a slaveowner and, as he would demonstrate in his later career, a thoroughgoing white supremacist. As of 1806, he was the brother-in-law of Roger B. Taney, another politically savvy slaveowning Maryland lawyer. Out of the successful defense of Baltimore, as witnessed by Key from aboard a British ship, he spun a disastrous war into something victorious.

The third, or "vengeful," verse of Key's poem (quoted in this chapter's epigraph), which is *never* sung today, brags of terrorizing and killing "the hireling and slave," implying that the British soldiers were mercenaries and explicitly condemning the renegade ex-property who fought as enemies of the star-spangled banner.[†]

The tune was already being sung with a patriotic lyric, "Adams and Liberty," in praise of John Adams, but Key repurposed it—a political act, right there, which he had already attempted with an earlier lyric (in praise of Jefferson's actions against the Barbary Pirates) that had included the phrase "the star-spangled banner."

The other great heroic-tableau moment of the War of 1812 was, of course, kept alive in popular memory through Johnny Horton's 1959 recording of "The Battle of New Orleans," composed by songwriting Arkansas schoolteacher Jimmie Driftwood ("We fired our guns and the British kept a-comin' . . .") The war had been ended by the Treaty of Ghent before the battle took place, but no one in America knew that yet. For Andrew Jackson, the war against Britain was never over.

---

*Part of Maryland at the time Key was born, Georgetown was redistricted as the third town in the District of Columbia, along with Washington and Alexandria.

[†]*Hireling and the Slave* was subsequently the name of a lengthy 1855 pro-slavery poem that, according to the Oxford English Dictionary, furnishes the first known occurrence of the term "master race." Written by William J. Grayson of Beaufort, South Carolina, it was prominently serialized in *DeBow's Review.*

New Orleans, which Jackson was tasked with saving, was well on its way to becoming one of the world's great ports. The first steamboat arrived in New Orleans from Pittsburgh in 1811. The patrician Livingston brothers, early American practitioners of the political revolving door, were in the steamboat business with Robert Fulton (whose first steamboat was named the *Clermont*, the name of the Livingston estate). Robert Livingston, negotiator of the Louisiana Purchase and Fulton's principal backer, died in February 1813, but his brother Edward, in disgrace over missing funds during his tenure as New York district attorney, had relocated to yellow-feverish New Orleans in 1804—with, wrote John Quincy Adams in his diary, "one hundred thousand dollars of the public money."[32] After his first wife died, he married a nineteen-year-old aristocratic Domingan beauty and became the attorney for slave trader and pirate Jean Lafitte. As of 1814, Livingston and Fulton were offering infrequent but regularly scheduled steamboat runs up the Mississippi from New Orleans to Natchez and back, despite the tendency of the boilers to explode, scalding workers and passengers to death, and despite the many lethal obstacles that were so many wooden land mines in the still-uncleared river.

Sugar and cotton went downstream, and now slaves could be shipped upstream: New Orleans and Natchez were already the major slave distribution hubs of the emergent Deep South. With Alabama pacified by Jackson and Louisiana a newly minted state, an economic boom was already under way, especially in New Orleans, even under wartime conditions. New Orleans was going to get the benefit of joining the United States: military aid.

The Creek War had transformed Jackson's image from that of disreputable brawler to one of savior. He repeatedly asked James Monroe, who was doubling as secretary of state and secretary of war, for permission to seize Spanish-governed Pensacola, with the self-assigned task of driving the British and Indians away. Monroe responded "that you should at present take no measures, which would involve this Government in a contest with Spain."[33] Jackson did it anyway. "This will put an end to the Indian war in the South," he wrote when he informed James Monroe what he was about to do, "as it will cut off all foreign influence."[34] After leaving Pensacola, he wrote Monroe, "I flatter myself that I have left such an impression on the mind of the [Spanish] Governor of Pensacola, that he will respect the American character."[35]

Jackson had popular-hero status by the time he arrived in New Orleans to supervise its defense against the British, hatred and fear of whom united the town's Anglos and French in one of the few known cases of their agreeing on anything. After the shame of Jefferson's pacifism, when it seemed that the United States would rather swallow any insult from Britain or France than fight, and after more than two years of war in which the United States had fought and lost miserably, with the government's headquarters in the nation's capital a smoking ruin, here at last was a general who could not merely defend a town, but slaughter the enemy. While in New Orleans, Jackson censored the local press and became the first US general to impose martial law.[36]

The British had been so sure of their victory that some of the officers had brought their wives, ready to assume their colonial posts after the locals were subdued. But the British troops were caught in a crossfire between massive volleys from behind earthworks and bombardment from the ship *Louisiana*. The one-sided killing of so many British was unprecedented in the history of two wars fought between the United States and Britain.

The Kentucky militia that came down to fight as part of Old Hickory's motley crew didn't even have flints for their guns. As had previously happened with Washington at Yorktown, a combination of black soldiers and Frenchmen—in this case, the Lafitte brothers' well-trained, experienced pirate force—played key roles in carrying the day.

Jackson emerged from the slaughter covered in glory. The burning of the capital city was avenged. America would defend itself. The Mississippi River would remain open to commerce. Almost immediately the price of cotton went up sharply, giving an enormous shot in the arm to the nascent cotton kingdom and its associated slave trade.[37]

The slaveholders of the South paid a price for the war in lost slaves, because, as in the War of Independence, once again slaves had accepted the British offer of freedom. But after mediation by the czar of Russia, the British paid $1.2 million in compensation to the slaveowners, which they could use to restock their fields with young people. The slaveowners were the ones who had wanted to go to war in the first place, and as a class, they were the solid victors of the War of 1812. Jackson's land grab from the Creeks had made vast new acreage available for plantation slavery.

Many of the black soldiers who fought on the British side retreated to East Florida, which was still in Spanish hands and was only weakly guarded. Secretary of War William Crawford wrote Jackson on March 15, 1816, instructing him to remove a maroon community that occupied a fort built by the British in 1814 in West Florida: "It appears . . . that the negroe fort, erected during the war, at the junction of the Chathouchie and Flint rivers, has been strengthened since that period, and is now occupied by between two hundred and fifty and three hundred blacks, who are well armed, clothed and disciplined. Secret practices to inveigle negroes from the frontiers of Georgia, as well as from the Cherokee and Creek nations, are still continued by the negroes, and hostile Creeks."[38] Jackson's subordinate Edmund P. Gaines reported to him that "the Negroes are attempting to raise Corn . . . They have red Coats and are supplied with a large quantity of British muskets, Powder and other supplies."[39]

Free blacks wearing British redcoats, carrying guns, and teamed up with Indians: nothing could have provoked Jackson more violently. When gunboats from the US Navy attacked the "Negro Fort," a lucky shot from their first volley hit the fort's powder magazine. The spectacular explosion killed 270 of the 334 people in the fort—men, women, and children—and wounded all but three of the rest.[40]

Meanwhile, the number of cotton plantations was exploding. As large amounts of cotton shipped out of the port of New Orleans bound for Lancashire, tens of thousands of African Americans were forcibly relocated into the area—by oceangoing vessel, by flatboat, and in coffles.

A Jog of the Elbow

While the Bank is my goddess, its desks are my altars,
And all my "fine phrenzy" is spent on defaulters.[1]

—Nicholas Biddle, 1823

THE WAR WAS OVER, and at last Britain was respecting the American flag at sea. Money was flowing, albeit along unpredictable courses.

No energy was being consumed in partisan warfare; the Federalists had all but disappeared as a political force. Jackson didn't only crush the Creeks; his victory at New Orleans gave the coup de grace to the disgraced Federalist Party, members of which had been threatening New England's secession since 1793 and had openly sided with Britain during the conflict.

For the first time since the early days of the Washington administration, there was only one functional political party in the United States. At its head was Jefferson's former law student James Monroe, who as a teenager had crossed the Delaware with Washington and as an adult had taken credit for the Louisiana Purchase. It was Monroe who dispatched Jackson to New Orleans, and he came into peacetime a national hero. Facing no serious opposition in the presidential election of 1816, he became the third consecutive president from the Shenandoah Valley of Virginia.

After the extreme partisan battles during what some historians describe as the First Party System, the relative political tranquility of a one-party nation led a derrière-garde New England Federalist newspaper editor in 1817 to coin the sarcastic phrase "the era of good feelings," a term that passed into general retrospective use to identify Monroe's first (but not the second) presidential term. It was an era of especially good feelings for all those connected to the fast-growing commercial web spun out of cotton.

Monroe is the only US president to have an African capital city named after him: Monrovia, in Liberia, a country whose name betrays its intention as a destination of exile for manumitted ex-slaves. The American Colonization Society, which proposed to implement the self-deportation of free African Americans, was cofounded by Francis Scott Key, two years after he published "Defense of Fort McHenry." Over the years, a plethora of famous political names attached themselves to the society, including James Madison, Henry Clay, Daniel Webster, John Randolph, Andrew Jackson, and even Abraham Lincoln. The chimera of "colonization"—the white dream of mass black deportation that would comply with the vision Jefferson had projected in *Notes on the State of Virginia*—lasted until secession. Disclaiming any connection with abolitionism, it was a way of doing nothing about slavery. John Quincy Adams flatly called the Society a "fraudulent charitable institution."[2]

The word "colonization" implied that African Americans would somehow establish American colonies, which would have meant freeing slaves to go establish foreign beachheads for the slavemasters. The idea was widely hated by free black people, who were subject to various odious restrictions but for the most part had no intention of leaving their homes, and some three thousand people of color assembled at Mother Bethel in 1817 to protest the formation of the society. Harriet Martineau, who in 1834 visited James Madison in retirement at his Montpelier plantation a week after he had sold "a dozen of his slaves," wrote that "he accounted for his selling his slaves by mentioning their horror of going to Liberia, a horror which he admitted to be prevalent among the blacks."[3]

The idea of colonization was hated just as much by hard-slavery Southerners, who saw it as soft on abolitionism and tending toward keeping a smaller portion of the population enslaved, when what they wanted was to see as much of the population enslaved as possible.

The party of Jefferson and Madison had discovered the uses of executive power, shifting considerably from its radical anti-federal stance of the first years of the republic. As they began rebuilding the White House and the Capitol, the Republicans now saw the federal government as a functional entity able to make the "internal improvements" that the fast-growing nation needed. A reliable paper money was needed, and the government needed a fiscal agent to support its wartime debt, much of it owed to foreign financiers. To that end, the Second Bank of the United States was chartered, for twenty years as the first had been, in 1817. Much of its capital stock was drawn not from its shareholders' gold and silver, but from their holdings of public debt.[4] The bank was also heavily invested in British bills of exchange.

With the War of 1812 over, shipowners had surplus privateering boats to sell. But besides privateering, these fast, maneuverable vessels were also in use by slave traders, who bought used privateers and commissioned new vessels as well.[5] Baltimore-style "clippers," made in Baltimore and many other places as well, would be the vessel of choice for an African slave trade that no longer came to the United States but would still carry perhaps more than a million kidnapped Africans to Cuba and Brazil. The misery of the experience would have been heightened by the boats' characteristics: being light and fast made for even worse seasickness. This era of the slave trade was notorious for its tight-packing: the tiny below-decks compartments were typically only three feet or so high, so when the captives were put away at night, they rode lying down, packed tightly together; and since clippers "rode wet," taking on large quantities of sea water, they were damp and cold.[6]

With the Chesapeake unblockaded, coastwise vessels could freely ply the route from Baltimore to New Orleans; those CASH FOR NEGROES advertisements began appearing in newspapers around the Chesapeake as of 1815. But it was a slow expansion at first, because the Second Bank of the United States tightened credit in 1818.

South Carolina's Langdon Cheves, who had been a War Hawk and who had killed the First Bank in Congress, was named the Second Bank's director in March 1819. On the question of the balance of credit versus metal, Cheves was all the way at the hard-money end of the scale.[7] He was in favor of lavish personal spending coupled with extreme governmental restraint, and he was against the very concept of fractional reserves, the basis of modern banking. He continued tightening credit, accumulating governmental income in the form of inert specie while refusing to extend loans against it. That drove the Panic of 1819 into a depression the following year, during which he continued his extremely conservative management while many were ruined. Under his stewardship, the bank required each of its branches to make their own decisions with the capital they were allotted; by the time he resigned, Cheves had, in Howard Bodenhorn's words, "effectively taken a national organization and transformed it into a network of independent banks operating under the loose direction of the parent institution in Philadelphia."[8] The result was an uncoordinated interregional cash flow, and a differential of exchange rates from region to region—not a good basis for a national commerce.

Cheves resigned in 1822, proud of the soundness of his overcapitalized bank, and was replaced by board member Nicholas Biddle in January 1823. Biddle—who, in a poem he wrote at a lady's request shortly after he was named director, sang the praises of "that simplest, sublimest of truths — six per cent"—began letting credit out again, and organized specie shipments.[9] Precious metal could be purchased like any other commodity, and Biddle brought in shiploads of silver from Mexico—now independent from Spain, and more tractable. The silver entered the bank's system at its New Orleans branch, as New Orleans entered into its peak era of national influence. Biddle created a domestic exchange operation that could make capital easily mobile throughout the country, with a national currency supplied by him that was worth the same amount at any of the bank's national branches.[10]

The appropriation of the Creek lands was a textbook case of accumulation by dispossession. Now the formation of a new capital class could begin, with confiscated lands as the basis of new wealth—if enough slave labor was available to clear it and make it produce.

Alabama's liberation-for-slavery set off the great land rush remembered as "Alabama fever." The US land office did land-office business, privatizing the newly available territory taken from the Native Americans and handing out the land in vast quantities on liberal credit terms. For slave traders, the takeover of Alabama by the cotton kingdom was the beginning of a long boom.

Cotton was a different kind of crop from tobacco or rice, and its cultivation imposed a different kind of brutality on its laborers. The whip-driven regime of cotton was like nothing known in Virginia. Tobacco cultivation was artisanship by comparison; rice cultivation was task labor, in which individual workers had specific, differentiated tasks to attend to. But cotton was based on the uniform, infinite repetition of the same tasks, requiring much in the way of manual dexterity and endurance.

The society of the enslaved of the cotton kingdom was a far cry from the family structures that still existed in Virginia and Maryland; the plantation populations that worked the cotton fields were the isolated remnants of destroyed families, jumbled together like the prison population they were. In the first years of the boom, about a third of them came from Virginia or Maryland, but they also came from Kentucky, Tennessee, Missouri, and, increasingly, points south. The arrival of so many occasioned a new cultural collision among the enslaved, as black, English-speaking former Marylanders found themselves having to converse with Gullah speakers from the Lowcountry or French-speaking Louisianans—and, of course, until 1820 or so there were still some Africans coming in via piracy.

Some farmers left their played-out farms and set out for Alabama with their slaves; others went to market to buy as many slaves as they could get. Some planters traveled north to the Chesapeake, hoping to get better prices by buying slaves directly from planters who were selling; others formed small partnerships to travel around on buying trips—placing newspaper ads, visiting planters, attending auctions. They found eager vendors on the Eastern Shore of Maryland, where Easton began an annual slave auction in 1818, selling off its surplus young farmhands away from their families for the convenience of the Alabama-fevered.[11]

States farther North got in on the action. New York and New Jersey both still had slavery in 1819, and slaveowners in both states took advantage of the opportunity to sell slaves off to Alabama. The numbers were nothing like Southern numbers, of course; the 1820 census showed 7,557 slaves in New Jersey out of a population of 277,575, and by 1830 the slave count was down to 2,254. Most of the diminution was from manumission, but some hundreds of enslaved people in eastern New Jersey were trafficked down South. By that state's Act of Gradual Abolition in effect since 1804, they were supposed to give their consent to leave the state, but that consent was easily forged.[12]

The message was heard all through those states that still permitted slavery: raising slaves was a good business.

Florida—the prize that had eluded Monroe at the time of the Louisiana Purchase—was at last within reach. Spanish forces were stretched thin, engaged as they were in failing to suppress the independence wars being led in South America by Simón Bolívar and José de San Martín.

Monroe sent an eager Jackson to march some five thousand men into Spanish East Florida in 1818, in a de facto declaration of war on Spain without congressional consent. The expressed aim of Jackson's invasion was to stop Native American terrorists from making raids into US territory, though the skirmishes had been bidirectional, with Georgians also raiding into Florida for livestock and slaves. Jackson's Florida campaign was overtly a war on free black and indigenous people; his report of it made repeated reference to the enemy as "Indians and negroes":

> To chastise a savage foe, who, combined with a lawless band of negro brigands, have for some time past been carrying on a cruel and unprovoked war against the citizens of the United States, has compelled the president to direct me to march my army into Florida. I have penetrated to the Mickasuky towns and reduced them to ashes.[13]

Earlier we have spoken of the concept of an ongoing Gullah War; this was one of the major hostilities of its long course. Jackson's marauders burned hundreds of houses, destroyed forts, killed an unknown number of Native Americans, and hung two native leaders in front of their people.

Jackson almost started another war with Britain by executing two British subjects in front of the black and native populations, impressing on them that they could not look to Britain for an alliance. The Englishman Alexander Arbuthnot, who had accurately warned the Seminole chief Billy Bowlegs that "the main drift of the Americans is to destroy the black population of Suwannee," was hanged from the yardarm of his own schooner, while the Scotsman Robert C. Ambrister was shot by a firing squad. They were, Jackson wrote, "exciters of this savage [i.e., Native American] and negro war; legally condemned, and most justly punished."[14]

Jackson was burning to go on to Cuba, where there were no Indians but many Africans. Security of maritime commerce was not fully assured, he insisted, until Cuba also was under US control. "I will insure you cuba in a few days," he promised Monroe, if given the necessary support.[15]

Monroe was alarmed by the international implications of Jackson's aggression in Florida, though he wanted the territory. Secretary of War John C. Calhoun liked the idea of taking Cuba, but not of the war with Spain that it would entail, and denied Jackson the forces to continue. (Calhoun was apparently also afraid that Jackson's military ambitions might be Napoleonic and that he would take over civilian government.) He attacked Jackson in the closed meetings of the cabinet, demanding Monroe censure him—though Jackson only learned about that years later, when Calhoun was his vice president. The only member of the cabinet to defend Jackson's action was Secretary of State John Quincy Adams, who no less than Monroe saw Florida as essential to national security. Adams, who was far and away the most experienced diplomat of the time, proceeded to negotiate Jackson's win against Spain to an annexationist conclusion that resulted in major territorial gains for the United States.

The Adams-Onís treaty of 1819 ceded East Florida to the United States and ended lingering controversies about West Florida. It also promised that the United States would not try to annex Texas; Adams perhaps believed that to be a keepable promise, but Jackson certainly did not. The treaty also ceded Spain's claim on Oregon to the United States, extending the border to the West Coast, in a "joint occupation" with Great Britain, whose Hudson Bay Company competed with John Jacob Astor's company for the fur trade there.

Mississippi, as yet sparsely populated and with Natchez its largest city, became a state in 1819. Most of it was still Choctaw or Chickasaw land, and there was popular discontent from Georgia westward about the slowness of the process of Indian removal. In 1820, Calhoun called in Andrew Jackson, a firm believer in deportation of Native Americans, together with Thomas Hinds, a Mississippi veteran of the Creek War, to negotiate—more like, arm-twist—the Treaty of Doak's Stand with Jackson's former ally, the Choctaw chief Pushmataha, which conveyed Choctaw land to the United States with a chunk of land beyond the Mississippi River ceded to them in return.[16] (In practice, the Choctaw were unwilling to remove themselves, and it took until the 1830s, with Jackson as president, for their forced exile from the state of Mississippi to be accomplished.)

Memphis was developed into a town in 1819 by former Tennessee superior court judge John Overton, who would become for a time the richest man in Tennessee. Incorporated in 1826, it quickly became the regional distribution hub for large areas of Mississippi, Tennessee, Arkansas, and Missouri. As a slave-trade center that serviced the new plantations of the large, fertile region, it boasted Mississippi River connections to Natchez and New Orleans.

Grateful to Andrew Jackson, the politicians of Mississippi in 1821 named their newly created capital city for him. Located on the bluffs overlooking the Pearl River, at the site of a trading-post stop on the Natchez Trace, the town of Jackson connected by water to New Orleans via Lake Ponchartrain. Unfortunately, it wasn't easy to get to and from Jackson. The governing elite of Natchez, which was the only important commercial center in Mississippi at the time, blocked internal improvements that would have removed the sunken logs that booby-trapped the Pearl River, which was, said Senator Thomas Buck Reed in 1826, "useless to the inhabitants, or nearly so, from the want of resources in the State to adapt it for the purposes of commerce."[17] Roads were rudimentary.

Spain's empire continued to deteriorate; Mexico became independent in 1821, the same year the Spanish evacuated San Agustín for the second and last time pursuant to the Adams-Onís Treaty. The combat-averse Thomas Jefferson could not have imagined a less likely figure than Andrew Jackson to realize his dream of snatching the Floridas. Jackson had done it not by ensnaring the Indians in debt as Jefferson had imagined but by forcibly evicting them, even as he fought a war of repression against the free black people who lived among them. With the same stroke, he accomplished the Carolinian dream: now there was no free territory to the south that the enslaved of South Carolina and Georgia could escape to, or organize insurrections from.

The South had been made safe for plantation slavery. There was no more Native American threat, no more maroon havens, no more Spanish, no more British. It no longer needed the protection of the United States from enemies south and west. South Carolina could now afford to become even more uncooperative with the federal government.

Monroe sent Jackson to install the Florida state government, but he resigned after only nine and a half months in St. Augustine, amid complaints of dictatorial behavior, and went back to Tennessee to become a senator. The Americans built a new town near the site of the long-disappeared Huguenot community of Fort Caroline, called—what else?—Jacksonville.

Sectional politics resulted in one of the nation's historic political struggles, fought in 1819–20, over whether the sparsely populated territory of Missouri, acquired as part of the Louisiana Purchase and previously a slave territory under the French and Spanish, would be admitted to the Union as a free or slave state. The prize at stake was control of the Senate, which was crucial for the slaveholders. The House was coming under control of the North, because in terms of population the North was handily outpopulating the South through immigration. It had already outstripped the three-fifths constitutional advantage, and the gap was widening.

Another prize was the concession to sell slaves to Missouri pioneers; needless to say, Virginia was enthusiastically in favor of Missouri's annexation as a slave state. Senator Henry Clay of Kentucky began earning his nickname of "the Great Compromiser"—which was not a compliment in South Carolina—by leading through Congress the Missouri Compromise, which admitted Missouri with slavery to the Union as the twenty-fourth state in 1821. In exchange, Maine was detached from Massachusetts and admitted as the twenty-third state, thus maintaining the Senate in a stalemate.

But as part of the compromise, slavery was outlawed west of the Mississippi and north of a line at 36°30" latitude. The planter class of South Carolina, who could not expand their system into the West without slaves, was outraged; this, they shouted, was federal overreach. Frederic Bancroft wrote that slaveowners

> had not previously believed that their chief interest was in danger. The far-seeing were now convinced of this. The whole South was sure to be permanently sectionalized if the politico-antislavery North ever became thoroughly organized. The political strength of the North depended on the development of interests and the extent to which prejudices and fears could be excited. Formerly sectionalism had usually been mild and courteous. Henceforth it was rarely to be either mild or courteous.[18]

Missouri had been acquired as part of the Louisiana Territory by Jefferson, who in his retirement saw what would happen. His remark in a letter of April 22, 1820, to John Holmes of Maine, is well known: "A geographical line, coinciding with a marked principle, moral and political, once conceived and held up to the angry passions of men, will never be obliterated; and every new irritation will mark it deeper and deeper." But Jefferson was unambiguously on the slavery side of the question, agreeing with the Southerners that Congress had no right to legislate such matters for the states. Jefferson, ever the champion of exile for free black people, convinced himself that slaves trafficked to Missouri would be . . . *happier*:

> The cession of that kind of property, for so it is misnamed, is a bagatelle which would not cost me a second thought, if, in that way, a general emancipation and *expatriation* could be effected . . . But as it is, we have the wolf by the ears, and we can neither hold him, nor safely let him go. Justice is in one scale, and self-preservation in the other. Of one thing I am certain, that as the passage of slaves from one State to another, would not make a slave of a single human being who would not be so without it, so their diffusion over a greater surface would make them individually happier.

He finished the letter by absolving himself and his generation and dismissing his juniors: "I regret that I am now to die in the belief, that the useless sacrifice of themselves by the generation of 1776, to acquire self-government and happiness to their country, is to be thrown away by the unwise and unworthy passions of their sons."[19]

During all this time, kidnapped Africans had been smuggled into American seaports, especially via Jean Lafitte's pirate/privateer operation in the Gulf of Mexico. With Napoleon gone and the British once again allies, the US Navy concentrated on eradicating piracy. The milestone in the closing of the African slave trade was the 1819 Act to Protect the Commerce of the United States and Punish the Crime of Piracy, which was amended in 1820 to include the foreign slave trade as piracy, a crime carrying the death penalty. The ruling families of South Carolina saw that as an insult, but the slaveowners of Virginia liked it, and they were in charge in Washington.

The domestic slave trade was going full tilt. Finally, the competition from African importations was completely gone. With the British navy no longer harassing American ships, there was now a safe, legal ocean corridor for shipping slaves South in the domestic slave trade.

The legally mandated domestication of the slave trade put a sharp cap on how fast plantations could expand; they could only grow as fast as the enslaved women of the South could turn out babies.

The demand was intense. Over the next twenty years, as the power looms of Lancashire sucked up all the cotton the South could grow, enslaved wombs were not merely sources of local enrichment but were also suppliers in a global system of agricultural input, industrial output, and financial expansion.

How well or how harshly to treat an enslaved mother was a principal issue in plantation management, affecting as it did the survivability of children. Those farmers more inclined to long-term profit from "increase" than to shorter-term profit from labor were obliged to "promote their health and render them prolific," as one writer put it.[20]

In a now-notorious letter of January 17, 1819, that was in another era routinely ignored by Jefferson biographers, the seventy-six-year-old ex-president, plagued by debt and frustrated by the death in infancy of some of his human capital, emphasized urgently that producing children was a specialized occupation, on a par with other skills enslaved laborers might have:

The loss of 5. little ones in 4 years induces me to fear that the overseers do not permit the women to devote as much time as is necessary to the care of their children: that they view their labor as the 1st object and the raising their child but as secondary.

I consider the labor of a breeding woman as no object, and that a child raised every 2. years is of more profit than the crop of the best laboring man. . . . I must pray you to inculcate upon the overseers that it is not their labor, but their increase which is the first consideration with us.[21]

By this time, the interstate slave trade that Jefferson had done so much to facilitate was taking off, and the market it created for his slaves' "increase" offered the only hope for escaping his crushing burden of debt. In telling the overseer to ease off on hard labor for "breeding" women, Jefferson laid out the financial tradeoff that careful farm managers had to consider in deciding how to apply their female labor: how much time women should spend working the land versus how much to spend reproducing. This could involve calculations against market prices for crops—high prices meant more field labor, low prices more birth labor. Or, since poor land required more labor to be applied to it, it could mean balancing the fertility of a patch of land against the fertility of an enslaved woman.

Jefferson's one-child-every-two-years quota was, it should be noted, not the worst: an even more rapacious owner could insist on faster breeding. Martha Jackson, born in 1850 and interviewed in Livingston, Alabama, recalled that her "Antie" was a "breeder 'oman [who] brought in chillun ev'y twelve month jes' lack a cow bringin' in a calf."[22] Indeed, Jefferson had established the two-year limit experientially, because, as previously noted, his own frail wife had died at the age of thirty-three from six pregnancies in less than ten years, her health growing visibly worse with each confinement.

Not that that was unusual: white or black, women commonly were pregnant that often, and they not infrequently died during and especially after childbirth. One might wonder: if the reproductive ability of enslaved women was so valuable, why did they consistently sell for lower prices than men? Perhaps because women weakened from repeated pregnancy were less productive in the field, but also because women were a riskier purchase, often dying in their twenties because the prevailing unsanitary methods of childbirth were so deadly.*

---

*Despite black women's lower level of nutrition and generally poorer conditions, they may have been less at risk in childbirth than white women in one respect. Black women, who sometimes gave birth in the field and who followed African birthing practices that required them to squat, were likely more frequently successful at expelling the placenta; the mistresses, who gave birth lying on their backs

In testimony during an 1839 court case in Warren County, Mississippi, about a farm at which "the policy is not to make large crops but to raise young negroes," Tobius Stephens "suggested rating 'breeding women' at half a hand," writes Christopher Morris: "[Stephens wrote] 'If breeding women are worked hard on the hills, it is likely to produce abortion & sickness.' A witness for the plaintiff thought the current administrator had not managed the plantation very well, and offered as evidence his observation of women working in fields.' "[23] Concern for the women's well-being was not the issue in the court case, needless to say; what was being decided was the financial acumen of the manager. Jefferson was nothing if not consistent in his promotion of a two-year cycle of commercial human reproduction. In a letter of June 30, 1820, to John Wayles Eppes, in the course of justifying a plan to sell off twenty enslaved people in families rather than only laboring men, he discussed his captives in terms otherwise applicable to livestock management, as per the use of the verb *stocking*: "I know no error more consuming to an estate than that of stocking farms with men almost exclusively," Jefferson wrote. "I consider a woman who brings a child every two years as more profitable than the best man of the farm. what she produces is an addition to the capital, while his labors disappear in mere consumption."[24]

An addition to the capital! The variant word *capitalism* had not yet been coined, but the term *capital* had remained in Jefferson's lexicon twenty-eight years after his "4 percent" letter to Washington, and it still applied to slaves. Jefferson understood clearly how the concept of capital applied to his society. Capital is money that makes more money, and slaves were property who made more property—including more slaves, who could be used as money when the need arose. It was therefore advisable to "stock" a farm with enslaved women, who would "breed" every two years, and in doing so would make a per annum capital growth target, as Jefferson had identified in his 1792 letter to Washington.

Eppes, the recipient of Jefferson's letter, was the recently retired US senator from Virginia and was Jefferson's son-in-law, having been married to Jefferson's daughter Maria (or Mary, or Patsy), who was his first cousin. Maria had died in childbirth-related complications sixteen years before, in 1804, as her mother Martha (or Patty) Wayles Jefferson had died from childbirth before her, and as her grandmother had died after giving birth to her mother.

---

according to then-current medical protocol, may have been less successful in expelling the placenta, with a correspondingly greater danger of infection or hemorrhage.

As Maria's confinement approached, Jefferson perhaps failed to reassure the frightened twenty-four-year-old when he wrote her from the White House: "You are prepared to meet it [childbirth] with courage, I hope. Some female friend of your mamma's (I forget whom) used to say it was no more than a jog of the elbow."[25]

Maria knew better, having watched her mother die and having given birth twice already. She gave birth in February and died in April. The bereaved Eppes took up with a woman who may also have been Jefferson's daughter, at least according to present-day Hemings family oral tradition and local belief. By the time Jefferson wrote his "addition to the capital" letter, Eppes was cohabiting with Betsy Hemings, whom Jefferson had given to Eppes and Maria as a wedding present.[26] If she was indeed Jefferson's daughter, she would thus have been the deceased Maria's half sister, making a creepy parallel with the way her aunt Sally had been the deceased Martha Wayles Jefferson's half sister. All the above-named (except for Jefferson himself) were descended from John Wayles. After Eppes died, Betsy Hemings was never sold, and she is buried alongside him. Whoever Betsy Hemings's father was, the Hemingses had provided the Wayles-Jefferson family with three generations of what Madison Hemings, Sally's son, referred to as "concubine" in a March 13, 1873, interview in the *Pike County* (Ohio) *Republican*, in which he declared Jefferson to have been his father and which is our only record of his thoughts.

Jefferson died on the same day as John Adams, on the mystically suggestive date of July 4, 1826, the fiftieth anniversary of the date of the Declaration. His unpopularity as president had begun to fade with the growth of a patriotic cult around the Founding Fathers, fueled by Henry Clay's popular mythologizing discourse.[27]

Jefferson had desperately hoped to grow his way out of the debt that tormented him in his final years. Like many Southern planters, he failed. When he died, the boom in Virginia-born slaves was only starting to get under way.

William Barry, who visited Monticello in 1832, wrote, "All is dilapidation and ruin."[28] Most of the gadgetry, maps, and fixtures in the interior of the present-day Monticello that is so impressively maintained by the Thomas Jefferson Foundation is a loving work of collection, restoration, and re-imagination. Jefferson's things were sold off, as were all his slaves but the ones descended from Betty Hemings. Among the other things that it is, the shrine that is present-day Monticello is a well-kept window into the practice of slavery, complete with (as of 2015) rebuilt slave cabins.

Lucy Cottrell, the woman in this picture, was fifteen on January 15, 1827, when she was put on the auction block—one of 140 people sold, along with the farm implements, crops, and livestock of Monticello. She was bought, together with her mother, Dolly, by the German-born University of Virginia modern languages professor George Blaetterman, who had been vetted by Jefferson before being hired. Blaetterman was booted from the faculty in 1840 for horsewhipping his wife—twice in a single week, "once on the public road." It was around 1845 that the family had a daguerreotype made of Blaetterman's granddaughter Charlotte in the arms of the woman who attended her, making Cottrell one of the first African Americans to have been the subject of a portrait photograph. After Blaetterman died, his widow took Lucy and Dolly Cottrell to Maysville, Kentucky, around 1850, where she freed them five years later.[29]

The woman holding the child in this picture, made from a daguerreotype taken ca. 1845, is Lucy Cottrell, formerly enslaved by Thomas Jefferson.

By the time Monticello was liquidated, the self-reproducing capital represented by slaves was about to be subjected to a new kind of profit-extracting process unknown in Jefferson's generation. Louisiana, the commercial giant of the South, created a new way of financing plantation agriculture: the property bank. After the Louisiana legislature chartered a bank called the Consolidated Association of the Planters of Louisiana in 1827, capitalized at two million dollars, that bank began to bundle mortgages—largely collateralized, as were most Southern mortgages, by slaves, who thus made up a large part of the "property" of the "property bank."[30] Shored up by a guarantee from the State of Louisiana, the bank began to sell bonds in the financial capitals of the North, and in England and Europe. Edward E. Baptist, who calls attention to this securitization process, writes that "a British bank could now sell a completely commodified slave: not a particular individual who could die or run away, but a bond that was the right to a one-slave-sized slice of a pie made from the income of thousands of slaves."[31] Florida, Alabama, and Mississippi followed suit.[32]

When Jefferson took office in 1801, the African slave trade was still open. When Monroe left office in 1825, that trade was a distant memory, and the domestic slave trade in African Americans was on the verge of its great boom era. Managing that transition was one of the achievements, if one wishes to regard it as such, of the Virginia Dynasty.

The liquidation of Monticello in which Lucy and the others were sold was supervised by Jefferson's eldest grandson, Thomas Jefferson Randolph, with the help of his brother-in-law Nicholas P. Trist, a young Virginia-born Louisiana sugar planter who had married Jefferson's granddaughter Virginia Jefferson Randolph. We will meet Mr. Trist again.

As the center of population gravity shifted westward, the stage was set for the change from a political machine based in Virginia to one with roots in Tennessee. Intending to follow James Monroe as the fourth consecutive Jeffersonian president, Andrew Jackson won the popular vote and a plurality of the electoral vote in the 1824 presidential election. But it was taken from him by John Quincy Adams in what Jacksonians branded as the "corrupt bargain,"* for the backroom agreement Adams was alleged to have made to appoint the ambitious Henry Clay to the post of secretary of state in exchange for his electors.[33]

Appointing Clay doomed Adams's presidency from the start. Enraged at the outcome of the election, Jackson declined Adams's invitation to serve as secretary of war. Instead, with a group of advisors that included the New York professional politician Martin Van Buren and communications-magnate-in-the-making Amos Kendall, he built a powerful political machine that reshaped the nation and trained its political firepower on Adams, whose every initiative was blocked in Congress. The next four years was a full-time campaign for a Jackson presidency.

Adams's career had been marked by his distaste for political parties, and he did not have a political organization. The Jacksonians had a populist platform: land and gold. Adams, a cosmopolitan, Puritan-descended intellectual who spoke the language of diplomacy in erudite phrases laden with classical references and did not have the popular touch, wanted a federal government that

---

*"Corrupt bargain" was already a well-worn phrase in Anglo-American political discourse by the time the Jacksonians hung it on Adams and Clay.

would make infrastructural improvements and improve education. But Jackson, a ruffian who spoke the plain language of a warrior, wanted a weak federal government that would distribute as much former Indian land and as much specie as possible to individuals in an expanding slave society. Adams thought Jackson "a barbarian who could not write a sentence of grammar and hardly could spell his own name," but he learned a rough lesson at Jackson's hands about communicating with the public.[34] At a time when newcomers with no inherited wealth were increasing the free population faster than established families could hand wealth down, Jackson's party harnessed the political power of this new force.

Presidential candidates still were expected to remain somewhat aloof from campaigning, though candidates for lower offices showed no such restraint and traveled a lively circuit of political barbecues. Jackson spent the next four years running for president while pretending not to, burnishing his heroic aura. The Port Gibson, Mississippi, *Correspondent* of November 3, 1827, reported his words as:

> I have saved your women and children from the tomahawk and scalping knife. I have protected your great emporium from flames, and from British myrmidons, and when all other resources failed, have obtained and annexed to your State, an extensive domain, adding wealth and numbers to your restricted limits.[35]

The Jacksonians assembled what became the Democratic Party, with institutional continuity to the one we have today, whose bases were Nashville in the South and New York in the North. John C. Calhoun, who had been vice president under Adams, switched sides and ran with Jackson, who was elected president by a landslide in 1828. As Jackson had done in the 1824 election and would do again in 1832, he carried every county in Mississippi.

following page: Three advertisements from the Natchez Mississippi Free Trader, *December 22, 1852.*

❧ Part Five ❧

The Slaveocracy

31

Swallowed by Millions

I do believe that Virginia is become another Guinea, and the Eastern Shore an African coast.

—William Lloyd Garrison, *The Liberator*, October 5, 1833

I have known what it is to be dragged fifteen miles to the human flesh market and be sold like a brute beast. I am from a slave-breeding state—where slaves are reared for the market as horses, sheep, and swine are.[1]

—Frederick Douglass, 1846

ALREADY THE DOMINANT COMMERCIAL American city, New York took a major step toward consolidating its supremacy at the beginning of 1818, when "packet" boats began running monthly between New York and Liverpool.

Packets left at a scheduled departure time whether they were full of cargo or not, making shipping more predictable, and they had to do it in all kinds of weather, fighting their way across from Liverpool to New York even if it was stormy and icy. Especially in winter, the westbound, or "uphill," trip from England to America, going against the Gulf Stream, was the most dangerous passage a sailor could make, anywhere in the world. Because vessels couldn't sail directly against the prevailing westerly winds, they had to "tack": set their sails at a forty-five-degree angle to the wind in a series of successive adjustments that allow the craft to make an arc in the windward direction. Accordingly, they traveled farther than they would have, and much slower, than if the winds had been in their favor. Ships sailing from England to America typically could expect to travel anywhere from four to seven hundred miles more than when they were going the other way.[2]

The Gulf Stream was also an obstacle for the American coasting trade southward down around Florida to New Orleans. North Carolina was a navigational menace, with sandbars outlining its shores; Capes Hatteras, Lookout, and Fear all posed dangers for passing vessels. But it was also where vessels began to have to go against the Gulf Stream. Then, going around Florida, there were coral reefs, shoals, keys, sandbars, eddy currents, and shallow water, to say nothing of the difficulty of passing through the Straits of Florida against the force of the current. Maritime insurers rated the accident rate from New York to New Orleans at 1¼ to 1½ percent, more dangerous than the trip from New York to Liverpool though not more dangerous than the trip from Liverpool to New York.[3]

New York's monopolization of the carrying trade was bitterly resented by the cotton growers of the South, but there was nothing they could do. Even from Charleston, the "great circle" northern route was the shortest way from America to England. Though wealthy planters were beyond-conspicuous consumers, there were so few of them that the South didn't buy enough imports to make regular direct round-trip transatlantic shipping from Liverpool to Charleston worthwhile—ships would have arrived in America with their holds full of ballast. The shipping profit from sending cotton out and receiving imported goods in return went to New York, where the products were handled.

Coasting packets took Carolina and Georgia cotton to New York, where it was loaded onto transatlantic packets. When ships arrived at New York carrying merchandise from Britain, the part of it that was destined for the Lowcountry traveled on a coasting packet, so British goods cost more in South Carolina than they did in New York. And needless to say, when specie was shipped from Britain to pay for purchases, it came to New York.

Baltimore had the best harbor in the Chesapeake, and some of the best shipping facilities in the country, but it had no chance of competing with New York for European commerce. Instead, it was perfectly positioned to specialize in servicing the expanding domestic market, and it grew with the republic. Its shipyards built the lightweight, high-speed schooners that began darting back and forth along the coast as packets, bringing regular news from one place to another. The run was especially profitable between Baltimore and New Orleans: since both cities were rich emporia, ships could go full in both directions.

Maryland, a border state with diversified agriculture that counted a number of Quakers in its population, was increasingly divided over slavery. On the Eastern Shore, there was much slave agriculture but also antislavery sentiment. In the northern part of the state especially, slavery was on the decline after 1820, as it was in Delaware. Limited terms of service were becoming increasingly common for Maryland slaves, raising them almost to the category of indentured servants. Slave-sale advertisements naming individuals generally specified whether they had a term of service or were "slaves for life."

Fast-rising Baltimore had slave labor, but it was not a slave society the way Richmond or Charleston was. Seth Rockman describes the diverse mix of the early nineteenth-century Baltimore workforce as "a continuum of slaves-for-life to transient day laborers—with term slaves, rented slaves, self-hiring slaves, indentured servants, redemptioners, apprentices, prisoners, children, and paupers occupying the space in between." He argues that the reason slavery remained viable in the dynamic Baltimore labor market at all was the enslaved laborer's capitalized value: "the perpetuation of slavery in a place like Baltimore owed less to the actual labor compelled from enslaved workers and more to the fact that plantation purchasers in Charleston, Augusta, New Orleans, and throughout the South were willing to pay hundreds of dollars for Baltimore slaves."[4]

One of those enslaved laborers in Baltimore was Frederick Douglass, who ultimately escaped on a boat leaving the port. Though he remembered that "going to live at Baltimore laid the foundation, and opened the gateway, to all my subsequent prosperity," while working as a hired slave at the Fell's Point shipyard he was beaten by "four of the white apprentices" in a fight "in which my left eye was nearly knocked out, and I was horribly mangled in other respects." He described the relations between classes of laborers there:

> The white laboring man was robbed by the slave system of the just results of his labor, because he was flung into competition with a class of laborers who worked without wages. The slaveholders blinded them to this competition by keeping alive their prejudice against the slaves as men—not against them as slaves. They appealed to their pride, often denouncing emancipation as tending to place the white working man on an equality with negroes, and by this means they succeeded in drawing off the minds of the poor whites from the real fact, that by the rich slave master they were already regarded as but a single remove from equality with the slave. The impression was cunningly made that slavery was the only power that could prevent the laboring white man from falling to the level of the slave's poverty and degradation.
>
> To make this enmity deep and broad between the slave and the poor white man, the latter was allowed to abuse and whip the former without

hindrance. . . . these poor white mechanics in Mr. Gardiner's ship-yard, instead of applying the natural, honest remedy for the apprehended evil, and objecting at once to work there by the side of slaves, made a cowardly attack upon the free colored mechanics . . . The feeling was, about this time, very bitter toward all colored people in Baltimore, and they—free and slave—suffered all manner of insult and wrong.[5] (paragraphing added)

The Baltimore waterfront was a key site for slave trading. There were twenty-four wharves along the harbor, to any one of which Maryland captains of local packet-boats coming from Easton, Chestertown, Kent Island, or other Eastern Shore points of origin might bring along a slave or two to sell. Most were sold without newspaper ads, but some surviving examples testify to the practice.

A valuable Servant for Sale.

A very handsome healthy MULATTO BOY, of general good character, nineteen years of age, and has 17 years to serve. He has been accustomed to farm work and the management of horses—he would make an excellent coach-man or waiter. He is the property of an in-solvent debtor, and must be sold. Enquire on board of the Easton Packet at Bowly's whf.

Baltimore American and Commercial Daily Advertiser *of December 21, 1818. This nameless "mulatto," sold in payment of a debt, might have remained in Baltimore, perhaps hired out at the shipyard by his new owner, or perhaps ultimately taken down South. In the latter case, it is doubtful that his freedom date seventeen years hence would have meant much.*

It is clear that there was already an export market for slaves out of Maryland by this time, though not much direct documentation of it survives. An 1816 grand jury report in Baltimore stated:

There are, in this city, houses appropriated to this trade, as prisons for the reception of the Negroes intended to be carried to other states. Slaves are crowded together, male and female, in one common dungeon. They are loaded with irons, confined in their filth, and subjected to various species of cruelty and tyranny from their keepers.[6]

The earliest shipment of slaves by water from Baltimore to New Orleans of which we have a record—though clearly not the first to take place—was in December 1818, when, in Ralph Clayton's description, "twenty-four slaves, boarded by six different shippers, were brought to the dock over a four day period" to be put on the brig *Temperance*.[7] In addition to slaves consigned from traders on the hard sail South, the packets might take migrating farmers transporting their labor forces, or passengers accompanied by enslaved personal servants.

Austin Woolfolk Jr. was only nineteen when he began running his CASH FOR NEGROES advertisements in the Baltimore press in 1816, almost as soon as the coast was clear of the British.[8] Working with his father, he had built up a stake in his hometown of Augusta, Georgia, by supplying slaves to planters relocating to newly available Alabama land.[9] There were no quantities of slaves available in cotton-mad Georgia, so he went northward in search of supply—to the farmers of Maryland's Eastern Shore, whose eagerness to sell slaves had already been amply demonstrated.

Woolfolk was not the first slave trader to offer cash in newspaper advertisements, but he became emblematic of the practice. Spending liberally on advertising, traders helped anchor the Upper South's newspaper industry, running ads in every issue, all season long, of every small-town paper in their regions of coverage. Most merchants handled a variety of merchandise, but Woolfolk, who embraced as part of his pitch the term "Georgiaman," dealt only in slaves, and unlike other slave traders, he did not run coffles, but only shipped captives by water.

To maximize profits, a slave trader had to cover both ends of the transaction: buy young people cheaply from farmers in Virginia and Maryland, transport them to the Deep South, and sell them there at premium prices. Woolfolk could bypass intermediaries by canvassing farms directly, offering farmers more for young African Americans than the Richmond-bound traders could. That meant having operations at both ends, with all the complexities of interstate law, taxation, and banking, all the complications of transport, and a large network of contacts. It meant a cash-flow-intensive business that had to respond quickly to changing political, economic, or weather conditions, and it entailed having offices and slave-processing facilities in different cities, with partners or agents in those cities. In Woolfolk's case, as with many merchants, his family provided them.

The Woolfolks developed the most effective network for canvassing the farms of the Eastern Shore for slaves to buy, establishing a base of operations headed by Woolfolk's brother Joseph at Easton. Once the harvest was in and farmers were ready to sell, Woolfolk's agents scoured the area, visiting every farm they could. Throughout the region they established temporary headquarters at one or another inn, distributed handbills, and took out CASH FOR NEGROES newspaper ads. They sailed the captives downriver to the Chesapeake Bay and on to Baltimore, where they were held in Woolfolk's jail until he had a full gang for shipment.

Woolfolk "generally consummated just a few sales at a time" when buying in Maryland, writes William Calderhead, "and from one to four slaves per purchase. Most chattels were in their teens and males outnumbered females by a ratio of 8 to 5. Slaves were not purchased in families, but on occasion a mother and child would be acquired as a unit."[10] But only "on occasion."

Like everyone else in his trade, Woolfolk routinely separated families. John Thompson, born in Maryland in 1812 on a plantation with about two hundred slaves, had as one of his earliest childhood memories a visit to the jail where his sister was about to be sold, as his mother wept:

> the first thing that saluted my ears, was the rattling of the chains upon the limbs of the poor victims. It seemed to me to be a hell upon earth, emblematical of that dreadful dungeon where the wicked are kept, until the day of God's retribution, and where their torment ascends up forever and ever.
>
> As soon as my sister saw our mother, she ran to her and fell upon her neck, but was unable to speak a word. There was a scene which angels witnessed; there were tears which, I believe, were bottled and placed in God's depository, there to be reserved until the day when He shall pour His wrath upon this guilty nation.[11]

The slave-buyers chatted up the locals to find out who might be going out of business, who needed cash, who might have an extra laborer to sell. It was much like what horse traders did, and not a few people who wound up doing this kind of work were former horse-traders who had moved over into trading in slaves; their successors would move back to selling horses again after emancipation. The working vocabulary of the slave trade overlapped that of the livestock business, as per the use of a term like "stock"—specifically a breeding term—to describe a labor force.

A few slave dealers advertised themselves as "negro traders," but most were identified more generically as brokers, commission merchants, auctioneers, et cetera. The network of the slave trade was not limited to the trader's own agents. The commerce spread its largesse around Maryland, and especially around Baltimore, through an informally organized network whose meeting-places were inns and taverns, some of which were especially known for their involvement in the business. "Bartenders were often used as agents," writes Ralph Clayton. "Their exposure to numerous travelers . . . placed them in an ideal position to act as go-betweens. A number of ads often reflected the seller or buyer's desire to have information left 'at the bar.' "[12] Clayton has compiled a list of Baltimore spots where traders did business: Mr. Lilly's Tavern, Fowler's Tavern, Fountain Inn, Sinner's Tavern, Mrs. Kirk's, the General Wayne Inn, William Fowler's, John Cugle's, the Columbian Hotel, the Globe Hotel, et cetera. This pattern was consistent throughout the South, where hotels commonly had secure lockup rooms that ranged from individual cells to full-fledged jails.

Slave jailing was an informally organized, widely distributed system of for-profit prisons. Traders in many towns maintained their own jails, which passing coffle-drivers could use, with the advantage of possibly being able to sell or buy through contacts there. In other towns, the local lawman might be happy to rent space in the town jail for a night. Speaking of the 1850s, Bancroft wrote:

> Every Southern city, and some mere villages, had slave-jails, slave-pens, or slave-yards, as they were variously called. They differed much in size and character. Some were carefully built, while others were old buildings, houses, sheds or stables, slightly altered. They usually had some of the characteristics of a poor barrack, a boarding stable and a prison. . . . At the best of the public ones, where slaves were fed and watched for any stranger, the usual charge was twenty-five or thirty cents a day—hardly as much as the feeding and care of a horse at any public stable. Their food was almost as plain as a horse's and they often had less that could be called a bed. They slept on the hard floor, and considered themselves fortunate if, in addition to their bundle of clothes, which they used for a pillow, they could get an old blanket.[13]

NOTICE.

WAS Committed to the Jail of Baltimore county, by John Waiter, Esq. a Justice of the peace for said county, on the seventeenth day of August, eighteen hundred and twenty-eight, as a runaway, a negro girl who calls herself ANN DORSEY, and says she belongs to Thomas Stabler, near Brookville, Montgomery county, Maryland—said negro is four feet eight inches high, about eighteen years old, (at which age she says she was to have been free.)   Had on when committed a yellow stripe home-spun cotton frock, and calf-skin shoes.

The owner of the above described negro is requested to come forward, prove property, pay charges and take her away, otherwise she will be discharged according to law.

DIXON STANSBURY,
Warden of Baltimore county Jail.

One of nine such advertisements in an issue of the Easton, Maryland, Gazette, October 18, 1828.

Local sheriffs were good contacts for Woolfolk's agents, because they were in a position to flip runaways, whose disgusted owners might authorize handing them over to Woolfolk in exchange for a cash settlement, or who might be sold unclaimed. Surviving records from Baltimore show fifteen handovers of runaways to him between 1829 and 1836: Liz, on August 10, 1835; Kitty, on November 5, 1835; Henry Hazelton, December 3, 1835, et cetera.[14]

Some "runaways" might be free people kidnapped off the street, as in the case of Fortune Lewis, who was abducted in 1822, taken to Woolfolk's jail, and sent to Washington, where he was able to prove his freedom and was released.[15] But such a happy resolution for the victim was unusual. The free black people of Baltimore—and, indeed, free black people throughout the North—lived with the knowledge that they could be kidnapped and sold.

Austin Woolfolk's early growth was slowed by national economic difficulties. Much as the First Bank of the United States had previously done in 1792, the Second Bank of the United States caused a panic soon after it was chartered.*

The depression remembered as the Panic of 1819 took two years to bottom out and two more to come back, though its effects were lighter in the newly wealthy Deep South. "Not till 1821 did [Woolfolk] ship more than one hundred slaves south annually," writes Calderhead. That was the year he moved into his Pratt Street quarters, complete with his own slave jail. "In the following year his scale of operations doubled, and for the next six years he shipped from 230 to 460 slaves south on an annual basis."[16]

Woolfolk's main source of supply was the farms of Maryland's Eastern Shore; like those of Virginia, their well-fed, hard-working young farmhands were established as a premium brand. Calderhead notes that "as for sellers, many who dealt with the traders once were inclined to do so again."[17] For those repeat vendors, selling slaves had become a regular part of their economic cycle— which is to say, they had become slave-farmers who sold perhaps one or two teenagers a year.

Like many traders, Woolfolk lived on his jail site, in a house that was part of a complex where dozens of people might be chained up at a time. The size

---

*Cycles of capitalism in the United States have been remarkably consistent: too much easy credit, followed by strain to the system resulting in the failure of key financial institutions, after which credit vanishes and the economy goes into a long tailspin.

of Woolfolk's operation made him the public face of the "negro-trader" and his name the terror of the enslaved. He had a kind of bogeyman status for enslaved children—except, unlike the bogeyman, he was real.

Frederick Douglass grew up in fear of Woolfolk. Like many who were born enslaved, Douglass had been separated from his mother at an early age and did not know the exact date of his birth, which he reckoned to have been in 1818. Before he was hired and sold away, Douglass was one of about a thousand people Edward Lloyd owned on Maryland's Eastern Shore, near Easton. That kind of estate took generations to accumulate; Lloyd was descended from seventeenth-century Maryland old money, and the core of his property is still in the hands of his descendants today. Lloyd was at various times a congressman, senator, and the governor of Maryland; it is ironic that he is most remembered for owning the plantation where Frederick Douglass was born and lived as a child.

Lloyd's captives labored on a network of neighboring agricultural prisons administered from a central location. Douglass, who described the brutalities of Lloyd's regime, recalled of the central plantation that "if a slave was convicted of any high misdemeanor, became unmanageable, or evinced a determination to run away, he was brought immediately here, severely whipped, put on board the sloop, carried to Baltimore, and sold to Austin Woolfolk, or some other slave-trader, as a warning to the slaves remaining."[18]

Woolfolk accounted for 53 percent of the 4,304 people documented as sent by the oceangoing trade from Baltimore to New Orleans between 1819 and 1831, but despite his outsized historical footprint, there were many other traders. A person with "Negroes of either sex to dispose of" might, for example, stop by the New Bridge Hotel and leave word for the Kentucky trader David Anderson, who accounted for 223 of the 1,400-plus people known to have been shipped by water from Baltimore to New Orleans between 1818 and 1822.[19]

Woolfolk knew better than to parade the grim spectacle of loading his ships before the eyes of the town. When it was time to sail, the captives were marched under cover of predawn darkness out of his complex, located near present-day Oriole Park, down seven or so blocks to Fell's Point. From there, they sailed around the peninsula of Florida, and many were ultimately sold out of the Woolfolk firm's New Orleans office at 122 Chartres Street. Others were taken to Natchez, where Woolfolk also sold slaves, as an advertisement in the Woodville, Mississippi, *Republican* that ran for three months in late 1826 / early 1827 announced:

NEGROES FOR SALE. The subscriber has on hand *seventy-five* likely young Virginia born Negroes, of various descriptions, which he offers to sell low for cash, or good acceptance; any person wishing to purchase would do well to call and suit themselves. — I will have a constant supply through the season. — I can be found at Purnell's Tavern.

Natchez, December 1st, 1826. "Austin Woolfolk."[20]

Frederick Douglass recalled:

When a child . . . I lived on Philpot Street, Fell's Point, Baltimore, and have watched from the wharves, the slave ships in the Basin, anchored from the shore, with their cargoes of human flesh, waiting for favorable winds to waft them down the Chesapeake. There was, at that time, a grand slave mart kept at the head of Pratt Street, by Austin Woldfolk [sic]. His agents were sent into every town and county in Maryland, announcing their arrival, through the papers, and on flaming "hand-bills," headed CASH FOR NEGROES. These men were generally well dressed men, and very captivating in their manners; ever ready to drink, to treat, and to gamble. The fate of many a slave has depended upon the turn of a single card; and many a child has been snatched from the arms of its mother by bargains arranged in a state of brutal drunkenness.

The flesh-mongers gather up their victims by dozens, and drive them, chained, to the general depot at Baltimore. When a sufficient number have been collected here, a ship is chartered, for the purpose of conveying the forlorn crew to Mobile, or to New Orleans. From the slave prison to the ship, they are usually driven in the darkness of night; for since the antislavery agitation, a certain caution is observed.

In the deep still darkness of midnight, I have been often aroused by the dead heavy footsteps, and the piteous cries of the chained gangs that passed our door. The anguish of my boyish heart was intense; and I was often consoled, when speaking to my mistress in the morning, to hear her say that the custom was very wicked; that she hated to hear the rattle of the chains, and the heart-rending cries. I was glad to find one who sympathised with me in my horror.[21]

A coastwise trip took three weeks or so, depending on the weather, versus seven or eight weeks to make the grueling walk from Maryland to New Orleans. Economic historians Herman Freudenberger and Jonathan B. Pritchett found that eight passages—"shipments" was the term—from Norfolk to New Orleans took an average of nineteen days in transit, at a cost of seventeen dollars per slave. But the transit time, they found, was only 18 percent of the time elapsed between receiving a certificate of good conduct (affirming that the enslaved person in question was not dangerous) and sale.[22] The time of actual transport was sandwiched between weeks of being held in pens at either end. Though an individual interstate trade could be a process of between two and three months, there were cases that took a year—a process of mental agony for the captive. Enslaved women were frequently pregnant, and on occasion women gave birth while in a holding pen or at sea.

The advantages of coastal speed over the overland trade were obvious. Coastal trade turned capital around quicker, essential in a cash-intensive business; market conditions could be responded to more quickly; a minimum of two weeks' expenses of provisions was saved; and, most important, the enslaved arrived in better condition—especially children, who had a hard time keeping up with a coffle's pace—which meant a higher price. There were relatively few onboard fatalities among these young people, who had, after all, been selected for their relative health and appeal.[23] Long months of confinement in pens, followed by weeks at sea, facilitated the spread of diseases, but these were not the Middle Passage crossings that averaged something like a 15 percent mortality en route.

The inward shipping manifests show a disturbing phenomenon one digit at a time: the number of children under ten sold away from their mothers and sent for sale alone. Louisiana put a stop to that in 1829 with a unique law that harmonized with the rules of the old Code Noir, prohibiting the sale of children under ten without their mother unless documented proof of orphanhood was furnished. "This statute markedly lowered the number of sales in Louisiana of out-of-state, unaccompanied young slave children," writes Judith K. Schafer. "Immediately before passage of this law, 13.5 percent of the slaves sent from Virginia to New Orleans were under the age of ten years. Immediately following passage of the act, shipments from Virginia of slave children under ten declined to 3.7 percent, and none of these were unaccompanied by their mothers."[24] Which is to say that, in Austin Woolfolk's heyday, until a regulation to control it was implemented, 9.8 percent of the involuntary passengers shipped south were motherless children under ten. For that matter, most of the rest of the passengers were little more than children, in the early years of their reproductive lives. Ninety-three percent of the enslaved people whose passage Freudenberger and Prichett could document were between the ages of eleven and thirty. But then, it was a young country. Black or white, people didn't live all that long. Over 40 percent of Baltimore was fifteen or younger in 1820.[25]

There were dangers connected with oceangoing ships: piracy and mutiny. Both happened to ships carrying slaves for Woolfolk. The mutiny happened on April 20, 1826, when the schooner *Decatur* left for New Orleans with thirty-one enslaved people on board. When the veteran captain made the mistake of allowing small groups of them on deck unchained, two men took him by surprise and threw him overboard. The mate, attempting to come to his aid, was also thrown overboard. The mutineers had hoped to escape to "San Domingo" (Haiti, which since 1822 had taken over the entire island of La Española), but lacking navigation skills, they instead floated aimlessly and were overtaken.[26]

Ultimately fourteen men from the *Decatur* were brought into New York, where, incredibly, they escaped into the city. Only one man, William Bowser, was apprehended, and he alone was tried for the murders of the captain and the mate.

Coffles came via the National Road to Wheeling, Virginia, all the time during coffle season, there to be sent down the Ohio River, which empties into the Mississippi. Recalling his days as a nineteen-year-old saddler in Wheeling, Benjamin Lundy wrote, "My heart was deeply grieved at the gross abomination. I heard the wail of the captive; I felt his pang of distress; and the iron entered my soul."[27]

After resettling a few miles away to raise his family on the other side of the borderline of emancipated Ohio, Lundy began an antislavery society and, in 1821, moved it to eastern Tennessee, where a manumission society existed. He took over a faltering antislavery publication, renamed it *Genius of Universal Emancipation*, and made it the first substantial antislavery publication in the United States. By 1824 he was publishing in Baltimore and traveling extensively. He wasn't only a propagandist, but also an organizer, helping found other antislavery societies. He traveled to Haiti in 1825—still thirty-seven years away from being recognized by the United States—to make an arrangement with the Haitian government to take emancipated people. When in 1826 he arranged for the American Convention for the Abolition of Slavery to be held in Baltimore, there were "directly or indirectly, eighty-one societies" represented, "seventy-three being located in slaveholding States."[28]

Lundy began hammering at Woolfolk in print. He reprinted the *New York Christian Inquirer*'s account of William Bowser's trial and execution:

One woman, [Bowser] said, who was confined in Woolfolk's prison, first cut the throat of her child, and then her own, rather than be carried away! . . . he was carried to the place of execution, when a few minutes before his exit he addressed the spectators in a few words, stating his willingness to die, and exhorting them to take warning by him to prepare to meet their God. As *Woolfolk* was present, he particularly addressed his discourse to him, saying he could forgive him all the injuries he had done him, and hoped they might meet in Heaven; but this unfeeling "soul-seller," with a brutality which becomes his business, told him with an oath, (not to be named,) "that he was now going to have, what he deserved, and he was glad of it," or words to this effect! He would have probably continued his abusive language to this unfortunate man, had he not been stopped by some of the spectators who were shocked at his unfeeling, profane and brutal conduct. In a few moments after this, the unfortunate man was launched into eternity.[29]

Lundy ended his peroration with the words, "Hereafter let no man speak of the humanity of Woolfolk."

In the South, such an insult against a gentleman would demand satisfaction in a duel, but Woolfolk did not pretend to be a gentleman, nor did he consider Lundy to be one. A few days after the article ran, Lundy was, as he put it in his memoir, "assaulted and nearly killed" when Woolfolk caught up with him on the street in Baltimore on January 9, 1827.[30] Woolfolk beat Lundy severely, stomping on his head and leaving his face "in a gore of blood" that left him with a long recuperation and permanent damage. According to the coverage in *Niles' Weekly Register*,* when Woolfolk was tried for the assault on Lundy, he denied having been in New York during the execution, but admitted

that he was guilty of a breach of the law, but in mitigation of the penalty they read several articles in the Genius of Universal Emancipation, which Lundy acknowledged he had written and published, in which the domestic slave trade from Maryland to the southern states was spoken of in the heaviest and bitterest terms of denunciation, as barbarous, inhuman and unchristian; and Woolfolk was called a "slave trader," "a soul seller," &c., and equally guilty in the sight of God with the man who was engaged in the African slave trade. . . .

Chief justice Brice, in pronouncing sentence, took occasion to observe, that he had never seen a case in which the provocation for a battery was

---

*A widely read Baltimore magazine, edited by the antislavery Quaker Hezekiah Niles.

greater than the present—that if abusive language could ever be a justification for a battery, this was that case—that the traverser was engaged in a
trade sanctioned by the laws of Maryland, and that Lundy had no right to
reproach him in such abusive language for carrying on a lawful trade—
that the trade itself was beneficial to the state, as it removed a great many
rogues and vagabonds who were a nuisance in the state—that Lundy had
received no more than a merited chastisement for his abuse of the traverser,
and but for the strict letter of the law, the court would not fine Woolfolk
any thing. The court however was obliged to fine him something, and they
therefore fined him *one dollar* and costs.[31]

Woolfolk won the battle but lost the war; this violent clash of slave trader
versus abolitionist was a propaganda victory for the burgeoning antislavery campaign, which in its early stages tactically consisted largely of attempts to prohibit
the interstate slave trade.

It was not surprising that Lundy should receive street justice at the hands of
a crude man like Woolfolk; physical threats and intimidation were a regular part
of the arsenal of defending slavery. But Lundy's protégé, William Lloyd Garrison, had the effrontery to call out the respectable merchant Francis Todd—from
Garrison's hometown of Newburyport, Massachusetts—in the *Genius of Universal Emancipation* issue of November 13, 1829. Todd had allowed his vessel to
be used to take eighty or so enslaved people from Herring Bay in Anne Arundel
County, Maryland, down to New Orleans at the behest of a Louisiana planter
who had purchased an entire plantation's worth of labor.

Garrison, who was only beginning his career, was not impressed that, according to Todd's testimony, the whole gang boarded cheerfully at the thought of
being transported South to work together rather than to be broken up and sold
separately; he wrote that Todd should be "SENTENCED TO SOLITARY CONFINE-
MENT FOR LIFE."[32] Todd sued him for libel, and Garrison was jailed for inability
to pay approximately one hundred dollars in fine and costs after his conviction;
ultimately, he was ransomed by a wealthy abolitionist. From his incarceration
(which he was allowed to pass under conditions more like house arrest), he wrote
a letter to Todd, printed in the Boston *Courier*:

> How could you suffer your noble ship to be freighted with the wretched
> victims of slavery? . . . Suppose you and your family were seized on execu-
> tion, and sold at public auction: a New-Orleans planter buys your chil-
> dren—a Georgian, your wife—a South Carolinian, yourself: would one

of your townsmen (believing the job to be a profitable one) be blameless for transporting you all thither, though familiar with all these afflicting circumstances?[33]

Garrison went on to publish *The Liberator*, which began on January 1, 1831, and he formed the New England Anti-Slavery Society one year later to the day. The most consistently outspoken voice of the movement, *The Liberator* continued for thirty-five years, during which it focused on the slave trade as emblematic of the evils of slavery, and as slavery's most vulnerable point. Local and state antislavery societies appeared, with the National Antislavery Society being formed in Philadelphia in late 1833.[34]

Abolitionism already had a decades-long history in Britain, going back to the days of the *Somerset* decision. Nicholas Biddle derided its presence in America as part of "the latest English fashions of philanthropy and dress."[35] Abolitionism was a much more radical position than merely being antislavery. One could be antislavery without actually intending to do anything about it, while barring free blacks from one's state and letting the South continue having slaves. Abolitionists, who were both black and white, and both male and female, wanted slavery extinguished, immediately, where it existed—converted to free labor, without compensation for the slaveowners. As such, abolitionism was a revolutionary ideology. If implemented, it would have had the effect of impoverishing many of the richest men in the United States, devaluing their capital suddenly to zero. It would destroy the basis of Southern credit.

Even John Quincy Adams, who as a congressman delivered up sheaves of abolition petitions to the House of Representatives, wrote in his diary after spending an afternoon with Lundy:

> Lundy . . . and the abolitionists generally are constantly urging me to indiscreet movements, which would ruin me and weaken and not strengthen their cause. My own family, on the other hand—that is, my wife and son and Mary—exercise all the influence they possess to restrain and divert me from all connection with the abolitionists and with their cause. Between these adverse impulses my mind is agitated almost to distraction. The public mind in my own district and State is convulsed between the slavery and abolition questions, and I walk on the edge of a precipice in every step that I take.[36]

Bona fide abolitionists were relatively few among the white population in the early days of the movement, though their numbers grew in the 1850s. The hard core of abolitionists, of course, were the enslaved themselves, along with free people of color, who constituted most of the first five hundred subscribers to *The Liberator*.[37]

During the summer of 1822, the city of Charleston was convulsed by the investigation of an alleged conspiracy headed by Denmark Vesey, an ex-sailor and free man of color who had cofounded Charleston's African Methodist Episcopal church, where he was known as a radical abolitionist preacher.[38]

Vesey, whose first name came from his origin (if not his birthplace, which is unknown) on the Danish Caribbean island of St. Thomas, came with a suspect background: he had been enslaved in Saint-Domingue for a time as a boy.[39] In South Carolina, he purchased his freedom from the sea captain Joseph Vesey with lottery winnings in 1799.[40] Vesey was alleged to have organized a plot, said to be French-influenced, to kill white people, supposedly on Bastille Day, and flee for Haiti. Scholars have argued as to whether the conspiracy actually existed—many now believe it did not—or whether it was only in the imagination of Charleston mayor James Hamilton Jr., who made political hay out of it along with Robert J. Turnbull and Robert Y. Hayne, all of whom would in a few years become known as Nullifiers. But whether there was a conspiracy or not, the repression of a known revolutionary and the destruction of the "African Church"—the AME, affiliated with Philadelphia's Mother Bethel—was real. One hundred thirty-five men were tried, and Vesey, sentenced to death on June 29, was one of thirty-five who were hanged, becoming a martyr. The AME church was burned by a mob, and its ministry exiled.*

Among the condemned was the African-born Jack Pritchard, or "Gullah Jack," a conjurer who was part of the AME congregation and who was alleged to have been Vesey's recruiter.[41] African power objects were seen as part of the alleged plot's military process, as expressed by South Carolina magistrate L. H. Kennedy's reference to "powers of darkness" in pronouncing sentence on Pritchard on July 9:

> In the prosecution of your wicked designs, you were not satisfied with resorting to natural and ordinary means, but endeavoured to enlist on your behalf, all the powers of darkness, and employed for that purpose, the most

---

*The 1891 building of the Charleston A.M.E., "Mother Emanuel," was the site of the 2015 Charleston Massacre of nine African Americans, including pastor and state senator Clementa Pinckney.

disgusting mummery and superstition. You represented yourself
as invulnerable; that you could
neither be taken nor destroyed,
and all who fought under your
banners would be invincible.[42]

When the brig *Sally* carried
twenty-five slaves from Charleston
to Mobile on February 12, 1823,
the manifest noted that they "were
cleared of [involvement in] the recently attempted insurrection in Charleston."[43]
The Vesey conspiracy provoked a series of retaliatory measures that included
the formation of a new repressive organization, the South Carolina Association. The Negro Seamen's Act provided for imprisoning free black sailors while
their ships were docked in Charleston; in open defiance of federal law, it put
South Carolina in the provocative position of detaining black British sailors. All
emancipation petitions were to be denied; the entry of free people of color into
the state was prohibited, as was all education for free or enslaved blacks. A kind
of security fence bearing a medieval name became popular in Charleston: the
chevaux-de-frise.

JUST RECEIVED,
AND FOR SALE AT THIS OFFICE,
A few Copies, of the Late
Intended Insurrection
AMONG
A Portion of the Blacks of Charleston.
(South-Carolina.)
September 24.   10 1f

Advertisement in the Augusta *(Georgia)*
Chronicle, *October 22, 1822.*

David Walker was probably in Charleston when the post-Vesey repression began.
If Vesey had a plot, he might have been part of it. Walker, the first militant African American writer, was born with free status (free mother, enslaved father),
probably in Wilmington, North Carolina (though there is no documentation),
probably in 1796 or '97, and he became literate, probably through Biblical education in the African Methodist Episcopal church in Wilmington.[44] When he
was grown, he moved to Charleston, where a small community of free blacks
worked as craftsmen and entrepreneurs. An evangelical Christian, he probably
attended the same AME church as Vesey and Gullah Jack. He moved on to less
repressive Boston, probably in 1825 or '26, where he married. He kept a used-
clothes store in Beacon Hill, where he sold second-hand sailors' uniforms. He
was a subscription agent for the short-lived *Freedom's Journal,* the first African
American newspaper; edited by Samuel Cornish and John Russwurm, it was
outspokenly abolitionist and anticolonization.

A chevaux-de-frise at the Miles Brewton House on King Street, Charleston, June 2013.

In the tradition of that foundational genre of American literature, the insurrectionary pamphlet, Walker published *Walker's Appeal in Four Articles; Together with a Preamble, to the Coloured Citizens of the World, but in Particular and Very Expressly to Those of the United States of America* in September 1830. It demanded the immediate overthrow of slavery.

Walker's Appeal explicitly talked back to Jefferson. As the idea of "colonization" for free people of color—which meant, deporting people like David Walker—grew, the legacy of Jefferson's philosophical racism in *Notes on the State of Virginia* was being, in Walker's words, "swallowed by millions of whites," adding that "unless we try to refute Mr. Jefferson's arguments respecting us, we will only establish them."[45] But beyond calling for black responses to Jefferson, Walker's treatise was a call to action for immediate self-emancipation:

> in the two States of Georgia, and South Carolina, there are, perhaps, not much short of six or seven hundred thousand persons of colour; and if I was a gambling character, I would not be afraid to stake down upon the board FIVE CENTS against TEN, that there are in the single State of Virginia, five or six hundred thousand Coloured persons. Four hundred and fifty thousand of whom (let them be well equipt for war) I would put against

every white person on the whole continent of America. (Why? why because I know that the Blacks, once they get involved in a war, had rather die than to live, they either kill or be killed.) The whites know this too, which make them quake and tremble.[46]

Walker smuggled quantities of his *Appeal* into the South, where anyone remotely connected with its circulation would be considered guilty of sedition. The first place the *Appeal* turned up was Walker's old home town of Wilmington, where the North Carolina legislature responded by meeting in a secret session to enact a slew of repressive measures against slaves but especially against free people of color. By the time Walker was mysteriously found dead on his own doorstep on June 28, 1830, the state of Georgia had a price on his head: $10,000 alive, $1,000 dead. The rumor spread that he had been poisoned, but no autopsy was done and no one stepped forward to claim the reward.

Walker's Appeal was blamed by nervous Southerners for the bloody revolt in Virginia on August 21, 1831, when at least fifty-seven people were killed in an uprising at Southampton, a few miles inland from Norfolk. Led by the mystical evangelical preacher Nat Turner and four other enslaved men, the conspiracy had at least seventy followers. Turner was hanged on November 11, following which his dead body was skinned.

Reaction to Turner's rebellion was swift. Louisiana, Mississippi, and Alabama all banned out-of-state traders for a time, though state residents could still bring slaves in, and could still sell them. The fear that Turner's collaborators might show up in their territory corresponded to a frequently expressed belief in the Deep South, not entirely unfounded but certainly exaggerated, that the interstate slave trade was bringing in "the dregs of the colored population of the states north of us," in the words of a correspondent to a Georgia newspaper.[47] Louisiana's prohibition lasted until 1834, when the immediate terror had passed and planters would wait no longer. Mississippi's new constitution, to take effect in 1833, included a ban on slaves introduced "as merchandize." There was an immediate outcry in Mississippi to lift the ban, and though it remained on the books, it was unenforced. The Mississippi legislature imposed a 2½ percent tax on slave sales, subsequently reduced to 1 percent. Mississippi's flourishing slave trade was thus unconstitutional but not illegal, and it continued in a gray era until the state again prohibited importations in 1837.*

---

* The *Groves v. Slaughter* case, which went to the US Supreme Court in 1841, turned on the repudiation by a slave purchaser in Mississippi of a promissory note he had given a slave trader in payment by claiming that the state Constitution prohibited the sale. The Court ruled in favor of the trader.

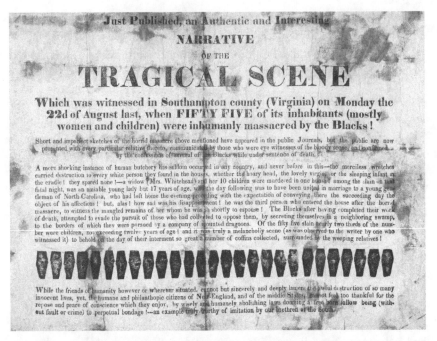

Excerpt from a broadside headlined Horrid Massacre in Virginia, *1831.*

In Maryland, where much of the state no longer used slave labor, the reaction to the Turner uprising was to prohibit almost entirely the growing trend of manumission in 1832. At the same time, Maryland's traffic to Louisiana, which had been drawing down the numbers of enslaved people in the state, stopped. These two reactions, writes Calderhead, "practically ended Maryland's chances of eventually becoming a free state."[48]

Nat Turner's vision was apocalyptic, but most of the enslaved were more pragmatic. Africans had believed they would return home after death; African Americans *were* home, in a high-security prison on perpetual lockdown. There was no place for most of the enslaved to escape to—no occupying armies to defect to as in 1775 and 1814, no foreign-held territory in Florida, no Indians left to hide out with.

In Virginia, where many whites were already alarmed by having so many black people in their midst, the result of Turner's rebellion was the debate of 1831–32 on the abolition of slavery, the only such debate in a Southern legislature ever. Among the many quotable statements of the session was the disapproving declaration by Charlottesville's representative Thomas Jefferson Randolph, grandson of the recently deceased ex-president: "It is a practice, and an increasing practice, in parts of Virginia, to rear slaves for market."[49]

Some individual slaveowners voluntarily impoverished themselves by freeing their slaves in the wake of the Turner rebellion. But after considering the matter, Virginia legislators unsurprisingly declined abolition, passing instead a repressive new slave code.

Thomas Dew, a respected academic who subsequently became the president of William and Mary College, published his much-read *A Review of the Debate in the Virginia Legislature of 1831 and 1832* in Richmond. In it, he argued that ending slavery would reward Turner's violence and legitimize the massacre. John Quincy Adams called Dew's 140-page landmark pro-slavery work "a monument of the intellectual perversion produced by the existence of slavery in a free community."[50] A full discussion of Dew's argument, which cites classical, Biblical, and European authors, is beyond the scope of our work, but we note two points:

1) Estimating the annual outflow of slaves into the Deep South market, Dew approvingly spoke of the fecundity of the capitalized womb as an economic engine for the state, affirming that "Virginia is in fact a *negro* raising state for other states; she produces enough for her own supply and six thousand for sale." (emphasis in original) He was if anything conservative in his figure of six thousand annually exported; Frederic Bancroft believed the number might be double that, and some estimates are higher.[51]

2) He reported that the post-Turner legislation was actually *good* for business, with more Louisiana and Mississippi planters journeying up to buy slaves in Virginia in the absence of a mechanism for importing:

> The Southampton massacre produced great excitement and apprehension throughout the slave-holding states, and two of them, hitherto the largest purchasers of Virginia slaves, have interdicted their introduction under severe penalties. Many in our state looked forward to an immediate fall in the price of slaves from this cause—and what has been the result? Why, wonderful to relate, Virginia slaves are now higher than they have been for many years past—and this rise in price has no doubt been occasioned by the number of southern purchasers who have visited our state, under the belief that Virginians had been frightened into a determination to get clear of their slaves at all events; "and from an artificial demand in the slave purchasing states, caused by an apprehension on the part of the farmers in those states, that the regular supply of slaves would speedily be discontinued by the operation of their non-importation regulations;" and we are,

consequently, at this moment exporting slaves more rapidly, through the operation of the internal slave trade, than for many years past.[52] (quotations in original, unsourced)

An inward manifest documenting the passage of six enslaved people from Charleston to New Orleans in 1832.

Even with Louisiana having closed its markets to outside traders from 1832 to 1834, there were still slaves coming into Louisiana, because New Orleans–based traders were still free to import, as per a manifest from September 24, 1832 (pictured), which shows the New Orleans trading firm Amidée Gardun et fils as "owners or shippers" of six people sent on the schooner *Wild Cat* from Charleston to New Orleans. One tries to imagine the stories behind the names and the descriptions by sex, age, height, and skin tone: Willis, Jack, Hector, Adam, Maria, and seven-year-old, three-foot-six Mary.

The business that Dew had enthusiastically described as "negro raising" was too important to stop. Meanwhile, Louisiana's cutoff of importation, combined with the wild Jacksonian credit boom and the new availability of Mississippi land, stimulated the slave market at Natchez beyond anything previously experienced.

32

Democratizing Capital

I leave this great people prosperous and happy.[1]

—Andrew Jackson, presidential farewell address, 1837

THE UPWARD TREND OF the American economy accelerated further, and again New York was in the lead, when governor DeWitt Clinton's great public works project, the Erie Canal, opened on October 26, 1825. Consolidating the power of New York City as a trade center, it was an audacious engineering feat that connected the Hudson River with the far western reaches of the country and tied New York State together by means of a commercial waterway.

The Erie Canal project needed as many people as it could hire. It was an economic stimulus even while it was being built, lifting all boats, so to speak, before the locks were even in operation. Whatever skills or labor a worker could offer was useful in such a massive undertaking: calculating, carpentry, cooking, driving mules, ditch-digging. The people who lived in the area prospered by selling the laborers food, liquor, clothes, lodging, and services.

It was one of the young country's proudest can-do moments. In the eight years it took to build, the canal employed some nine thousand wage laborers, many of them Irish, but also including free black laborers, including, from Saratoga, New York, the young Solomon Northup, later the author of *Twelve Years a Slave*. The Erie Canal was not built by slave labor. This was what a non-slave economy could do, and indeed by 1827 slavery ended in New York, following a period of gradual emancipation, providing the culmination of what some historians call "the first emancipation," that of the North.*

---

*Until 1840, out-of-state visitors could bring slaves to New York with them for a period of nine months.

The 360-mile Erie Canal supplied an unprecedented level of infrastructural improvement, connecting the vast land beyond the Great Lakes via the Lake Erie port of Buffalo to the state capital of Albany on the Hudson River, which ran 150 miles or so down to New York City.

By making it practical to get wheat from the western part of the state to New York's harbor for export, the canal caused the value of New York State's agricultural land to appreciate sharply, even as it created a path for distribution of finished goods from New York far into the interior—and it was a toll road, on which New York got paid coming and going. Because it was the only northern channel that crossed the Appalachians, it instantly became the major route to market for farmers and home manufactures across a large territory.

Fast-growing New York City had overtaken Havana in population sometime in the 1810s; now the Erie Canal, together with New York's control of the Liverpool route and its Wall Street stock market, made the city definitively the number-one commercial center in the United States. It caused a massive appreciation of property values to the west as far as Chicago, which in the early 1830s was the subject of a tremendous real estate boom based on its position as a hub for water transportation. Goods from St. Louis and the "northwest" could now be brought to market via Chicago and New York instead of New Orleans. By 1836, the State of Illinois was digging a canal to connect Chicago directly to the Mississippi River, though it did not open until 1848.

Private capital had been insufficient to build the Erie Canal. It was a project of New York State, financed without levying taxes. The state bank sold bonds, and happily for the investors, they were easily paid back by the toll receipts the state collected. Every state wanted that kind of success. In Maryland, the ninety-one-year-old Charles Carroll of Carrollton, the last surviving signer of the Declaration of Independence and the wealthiest man in Maryland, whose family's industrial arc had gone in two generations from colonial pig iron to republican railroads, turned over the first spade of earth on the Baltimore and Ohio, the nation's first "common carrier" railroad, in 1828.

A mania for infrastructural improvement seized the nation, but the political class of the South was dead set against this kind of project. It would be a bad precedent for the labor regime of slavery if the federal government paid large numbers of free people to work. They were rentiers, living off their capital, and their capital was also their labor. If anything was to be built in their territory, they wanted it built by slaves rented from them, and they certainly didn't want improvements elsewhere to be paid for by taxes or tariffs on them. Henry Clay's

"American System" of federally sponsored improvements, which counted among its successes the Second Bank of the United States and the National Road, was hated by Southern politicians and had been definitively stopped. With Andrew Jackson in the White House as of March 4, 1829, everyone knew that an extreme shift to limited federal government was about to begin.

Jacksonian rhetoric had freely levelled the charge of corruption against Adams, Clay, and the Bank of the United States. But Jackson's party was utterly corrupt. His campaign had freely promised governmental positions in exchange for support, and once in office, his administration began purging public employees, especially postmasters, in order to replace them with political hacks in what became known as the "spoils system."

Jackson continued the job of exiling Native Americans, conducted with the accustomed attitude of patronizing benevolence in the native negotiators were expected to, and some did, address him as "Father" and refer to themselves as "your children," as he took their homeland away. The urgency of the process was accelerated by a minor discovery of gold in Georgia in 1829.

Along with a number of other Native American groups, the so-called Five Civilized Nations (Choctaw, Chickasaw, Creek, Cherokee, Seminole) still inhabited the region; Jackson in 1830 signed the Indian Removal Act, which authorized him to "negotiate" for them to leave. A series of treaties were signed, and the first deportations began in 1831. During the decade, perhaps as many as a hundred thousand Native Americans were "removed" westward in the Trail of Tears. Evicting them was a money-maker: politically connected businessmen could receive a $10,000 contract for "Indian removal," which gave them an incentive to do it cheaply. The forced migration had perhaps a 15 percent mortality rate, which was about the same as the transatlantic slave ships—and indeed, much of the travel was by water, along river routes. More than three hundred Creeks died on the night of October 31, 1837, when the steamboat *Monmouth*, which was carrying them, collided with another vessel and sank.

The Seminoles, some of whom were black, would not leave and in 1835, a war began that lasted seven years. After capture, the Seminole chief Osceola, whose heritage was part Creek and part English and Scotch-Irish, was imprisoned in the old Spanish citadel at St. Augustine (by then called Fort Marion) and then moved to Fort Moultrie on Sullivan's Island, South Carolina.

No sooner had Native Americans withdrawn from a spot than a town sprang up; expansion onto the formerly occupied lands that Jackson had taken went as fast as the credit system would allow. Some 80 percent of the Chickasaw cession of the 1830s, sold cheap at the public land office, passed through the hands of speculators.[2]

The economic storm that raged during the eight years of Jackson's presidency and for another decade or so afterward drew its energy from a variety of sources. At the eye of it was Jackson, who opened up credit as wide as it would go and threw away the controls. The economy had been subject to the characteristic cycles of capitalism all along, of course, but the bubble of the 1830s was spectacular. Fueled by a conjuncture of forces international and domestic, it took the slave trade to new heights.

The boom-and-bust of the 1830s took place in the context of a radical economic experiment in decentralization and deregulation in which President Jackson took a wrecking ball to the country's financial structure, restructured it to operate without oversight, definitively abrogated a national role in the issuance of paper money, and shocked the system with abrupt rule changes. This is not to say that other crises would not have occurred had he not done that; but what *did* happen was the Panic of 1837, which led to the most severe depression in American history until the Panic of 1929.

It is ironic that the name of a man as autocratic as Andrew Jackson is associated with the word *democracy*.

"Jacksonian democracy," that great trope of American history, grew out of, and expanded the reach of, that other great trope, "Jeffersonian democracy." Jacksonians were loudly faithful to many of the ideals of the Jeffersonians. But whereas Jefferson imagined an agrarian rural republic of franchised property owners, Jacksonian democracy incorporated poor white men—the yeomanry of the Western frontier and the towns, the kind of person Jackson himself had been—into the franchise, thus promoting caste solidarity among white men of all classes at the expense of blacks. Indeed, it implicitly promised to poor whites that, being unenslaveable, they might someday become slaveowners, especially with so much land and credit available cheap. Enfranchising them invested them in white supremacy; Jacksonian democracy promoted white caste solidarity at the expense of black personhood.

Riches had never flown around so fast. Slavery could be incredibly profitable, especially when there was plenty of virgin Western land available and an unquenchable market for cotton that yielded cash returns as soon as slave labor could be applied to formerly native land. But even as a project for a racist democracy, or, as Sean Wilentz called it, "Master Race democracy," Jacksonian democracy had little appeal to the patricians of South Carolina; uninterested in democracy of any sort, they formed a separate power bloc from Jackson, who in many ways represented political continuity with the old Virginia dynasty.[3]

It is also ironic that Jackson's picture is on the twenty-dollar bill, because Jackson hated "ragg money" and wanted to get rid of it. Unfortunately, as his administration set out to, as the humorist Joseph Glover Baldwin satirically put it in a memoir of the era, "democratize capital," Jackson's actions made paper money less reliable than it had ever been, made government more economically inefficient, and drove the South to rely more on its human savings accounts.[4]

Jackson was a hard hard-money man. John Quincy Adams described Jackson's final presidential message as containing an "abundance of verbiage about gold and silver and the injustice of bank paper to the laboring poor."[5] Jackson would have liked silver coins to have been physically exchanged for every transaction, like when he sold slaves for silver in Spanish Natchez. There wasn't enough coin for the transactions of an expanding nation, but never mind, Jackson hated paper money, banks, and debt—a point of view that was understandable from a small-town merchant, but disastrous when applied to the nation's economic system.

Jackson especially hated Henry Clay, whose party was for a time called the Anti-Jackson party; in a coalition with the Adams followers, they became the Whigs, with Clay as their losing presidential candidate in 1832. In what has been remembered as the Second Party System, these two main parties and a welter of smaller ones attempted to be national parties, connecting North and South. That was an attempt to straddle the fundamental dividing line of American politics, which was overwhelmingly slavery versus free soil. In both cases, making a national party required accommodating the slavery interest. Antislavery people in the North were growing in number, while Southern delegates grew steadily less interested in compromise.

Whigs, who came in slaveowning and antislavery varieties, were modernizers. Most merchants were Whigs, in favor of banks and corporations, federally sponsored internal improvements, protective tariffs, and national currency regulation—what we now call "big government." Democrats, who saw all this as tyranny, were in favor of states' rights, limited federal government, an agrarian republic, hard money, and were for the most part aggressively or reluctantly pro-slavery, though there were antislavery Jacksonian Democrats as well.

Modern Americans are accustomed to thinking of Mississippi as the poorest of fifty states, but in 1831, when it was growing explosively with new plantations amid a landgrab and a slave boom, it had, in Biddle's words, "more rich proprietors than . . . any where else assembled."[6] Mississippi was the hottest lending location in the country, so in the spring of 1831, the Second Bank of the United States opened a branch—its last one, as it turned out—in Natchez. The Bank was not merely a presence in Natchez; it was aggressive, at one point concentrating 10 percent of its resources there.[7]

The Bank's arrival transformed the state's credit-hungry business environment. It was the legally mandated depository of federal funds, receiving federal income as it came in. By marketing federal debt to state and private banks, it controlled the money supply. It was far bigger than any state-chartered bank, and it kept something of a lid on the state banks by accepting their notes ("discounting," it was called, reflecting the percentage adjustments that had to be made when using paper obligations), and immediately redeeming them for specie. It thus acted as a kind of regulator on how much paper the state banks could issue; its national reach allowed it to move liquidity around and help keep the entire system flowing smoothly. Biddle called it a "commercial railroad"; it was the main channel of exchange at the national level.[8] The Bank was not unpopular, and it was powerful politically, being at the center of multiple webs of patronage—something Jacksonians wanted to monopolize. The paper money it issued could be exchanged for specie at any one of the Bank's national branches, but in fact it was not necessary to do so, because its paper was known to be high-quality and was easily accepted by everyone, including slave traders.

As competition from the Bank's new Mississippi branch forced the already existing State Bank of Mississippi (later called the Agricultural Bank) toward what would ultimately be liquidation, another bank appeared in the state: the Planters Bank. The Mississippi state legislature had chartered it in 1830, disregarding a state pledge made at the time of the first bank's charter not to charter another bank. It was theoretically capitalized at $4 million dollars, half of it subscribed to by the state and paid for with 6 percent state bonds. Its charter promised to "by a creation of revenue relieve the citizens of the State from an oppressive burden of taxes, and enable them to realize the blessings of a correct system of internal improvement."[9]

LOST

Somewhere between Smith's and Bowly's wharf, a Pocket Book containing about $33 in notes, as near as can be recollected, as follows:

One note U. S. Bank	$10
In notes of Cumberland Bank, Portland, about	15
One note Alexandria Bank	5
Small notes of Balt. banks about	3

with several bills and receipts of no use to any but the owner—The finder shall receive a reward of 5 dollars by leaving the book and contents at the store of

BRUNDIGE, VOSE & CO.

a 1   d4   **8⅓ Bowly's wharf.**

This lost-purse advertisement from the Baltimore American and Commercial Advertiser *of April 1, 1819, gives a sense of what managing cash was like, listing money from different banks separately; the Second Bank of the United States's note, the safest, most usable currency available, is listed up top as the largest denomination.*

Except for the national bank's notes, all paper money was local money, and negotiating it anywhere but its place of issuance was much like doing a foreign-exchange transaction today. As hundreds of banks appeared with licenses to print money, they all wanted to get as much of the money they printed into the public's hands as possible, crowding the other banks' paper out.

As the two state banks of Mississippi competed with the national bank to write mortgages, it was never easier to buy slaves on terms. The Natchez slave market soared; with Louisiana closed to out-of-state dealers in the wake of Nat Turner, the competition in Mississippi heated up. The banks' bulging loan portfolios were capitalized largely by slaves, who trudged down into Mississippi in coffle after coffle.

Both sides in the presidential election of 1832 made the bank their major campaign issue. The Bank's twenty-year charter was set to expire in 1836, but in the face of Jackson's harassment of it, and at the urging of Clay and Daniel Webster, Biddle, the Bank's president, proposed a recharter in 1832, gambling that Jackson would not dare kill it with the presidential election coming up, sneering at one point that "this worthy President thinks that because he has scalped Indians and imprisoned Judges, he may have his way with the Bank. He is mistaken . . ."[10] (ellipsis in original)

It was a bad idea to call Andrew Jackson's bluff.

We have previously noted Jackson's capacity for hatred. When Jackson hated, it was not only he who hated. It was a popular movement of hate, sanctioned by God, and it was a political mechanism of hate. To hate the Whigs was to hate the Second Bank of the United States, which was aligned with them to the point of having financially supported Henry Clay, who for his part had the bad idea of making the Bank recharter an election issue. Moreover, Jackson's first falling-out with the now-enemy Calhounites had been over the issue of the Bank, which they supported.

Destroying was what Jackson did best, and destroying the Second Bank of the United States was his obsession. Jackson saw the Bank as a federally sanctioned private monopoly, but whatever his ideological reasons for hating it, there was perhaps a more basic reason: it was the most powerful institution in the United States not under his control, and that alone was enough to seal its doom. The Bank's recharter passed Congress, but was boldly vetoed by Jackson a week later, who issued an economically incoherent veto message authored by his bank-hating advisor and political fixer Amos Kendall that stoked sectional rivalries—not simply South against North, but positioning Jackson on the side of the good West versus the bad East, understood to be associated with the South and the North, respectively that "it is obvious that the debt of the people in that section to the bank is principally a debt to the Eastern and foreign stockholders; that the interest they pay upon it is carried into the Eastern States and into Europe, and that it is a burden upon their industry and a drain of their currency."[11]

While Jackson was staring down the Bank, he also went up against the political chiefs of South Carolina. Four days after the veto, he signed the Tariff of 1832, or, as South Carolina politicians called it, the Tariff of Abominations. It was a laundry list of protectionisms with something for New England and something for the mid-Atlantic states; it had proved a vote-getter for Jackson nationally, who needed to shore up his political base in the North.

The slaveholding region saw it as a tax on them. Many in the South were not opposed merely to this specific tariff, but to tariffs in general, seeing them as tribute extorted by the North in a situation where the South produced the wealth but the North took the profits. In Mississippi, where nothing was manufactured and everything had to be imported, a writer to the Woodville *Mississippi Democrat* lamented that "there are ten spinning wheels and two looms in the county—such a thing as a slay, harness, shuttle or spindle is unknown, and if we want one of either we must send to yankee town for them."[12]

For South Carolina's politicians, Jackson's signing of the tariff was a blunt dismissal of their political importance. They resisted with a level of virulence and extreme rhetoric that astonished other congressmen. Indeed, the vehemence of their "discontent" was not entirely rational, unless it was understood that the point of it was polarization: the tariff was a smokescreen issue with which ambitious politicians hoped to focus Southerners' anger in order to drive a wedge against the North, with the ultimate end of fomenting disunion and provoking confrontation.

For two years or so, Calhoun had been promoting the doctrine of "nullification" that he had formalized, taking the name from Jefferson's 1798 Kentucky Resolutions. In Calhoun's vision, a state had the right to "nullify" a federal law within its borders, which also meant that the federal government had no right to impose tariffs. Never mind that federal revenue depended on tariffs, that was the idea: big slaveowners wanted a powerless federal government.

George McDuffie, from near the Georgia border, who had been "taken from labor in a blacksmith's shop by Mr. Calhoun" to become a landed cotton planter and Calhoun's loyal political lieutenant, was the grim-faced oratorical star of the 1832 South Carolina Nullification Convention.[13] McDuffie, who was known to be irritable because of the painful wounds dueling had left him, had come up with something retroactively called the Forty Bale Theory, which held that a 40 percent tariff equaled taking away forty bales of cotton for every hundred a planter produced. That was utter nonsense, but it had the advantage of simplicity, and the Calhounites used the aggressive messaging technique that in more recent times has become known as "repeat until true." Secession was threatened in congressional debates. Reprints of apocalyptically worded speeches, charged Representative John Reed of Massachusetts,

> were dispersed, thick as autumnal leaves, through the whole region of the South, with other incendiary tracts, all calculated, if not intended, to rouse the whole South to madness . . . We were told in this hall that the protective system [of tariffs] was a vampyre, by which the North was sucking the warm blood of the South; that the free States were prairie wolves, gorging their jaws by instinct in the blood of the South, whilst oppression,

robbery, and plunder were sounded to every note of the gamut. Is the result surprising?[14]

The argument over the tariff was in part a clash of factions in Jackson's government. Van Buren, who was Jackson's favored successor, had devised the tariff; Vice President John C. Calhoun made killing it his mission. As vice president under Adams, Calhoun had in 1827 cast the deciding Senate vote to kill a tariff, condemning it "as a sectional measure designed to impoverish the slave South," in Manisha Sinha's words.[15] But it was hard for Calhoun to stay ahead of the pack of radicals at home who were pushing him to the right. William C. Davis describes their objectives as to "defeat protectionism and contain the growth of central power in Washington," which was pretty much the same thing as maintaining the political power of slavery.[16] As always, the dynamics in South Carolina were different: in much of the rest of the country, the voting franchise had been expanding, but not in South Carolina, where a two-party system barely took root, and where, as Sean Wilentz put it, "they had no use for the democratic dogma that appeared to be sweeping the rest of the nation."[17]

Calhoun, Jackson's backstabbing former ally, had become his open enemy—both socially (after Calhoun's wife, Floride, ostracized Peggy Eaton, the wife of another cabinet member) and politically (after President Jackson belatedly learned that Calhoun had worked against him in the cabinet during his Florida conquest). Like Clay, Webster, and Benton, Calhoun had seen himself as a contender for the presidency. By now, it was clear that would never happen. But he could be president of an independent Southern nation, if one were to exist.

As a senator, Calhoun could more effectively promote nullification. He was appointed to the Senate by the South Carolina legislature—the state didn't have the bother of a popular vote—on December 12. He resigned the almost powerless office of vice president on December 28, 1832, finalizing his break with Jackson. The South Carolina legislature, meanwhile, passed a bill that committed South Carolina to raising a military force to resist the tariff. Calhoun insisted that nullification did not necessarily mean secession, but then again, it might. As he started a short-lived Nullifier Party, the thrilling idea of secession—which would make the most belligerent politicians of South Carolina into the rulers of a sovereign state, as they insisted they already were—was in the air. Not all of South Carolina was in favor of nullification, but Unionists were derided and intimidated. Sinha writes that "the election campaign of 1832 was the bloodiest in the state's history. Duels, which were usually personal affairs of honor, became the stuff of politics."[18] South Carolina went it alone; even in Mississippi the nullifiers lost.

Many years later, after Martin Van Buren had pivoted around to an anti-slavery stance, he wrote of the nullification standoff that "a more alarming crisis in the affairs of this country had never existed since the establishment of her independence."[19] But the nullifiers overplayed their hand when they went up against Jackson. He was pro-states' rights, but as the last president to have personally suffered the violence of the War of Independence, he was a Union man until death. He denounced nullification in a ringing proclamation in December 1832, written by Secretary of State Edward Livingston. Capitalizing on his immense personal popularity and vowing to use fifty thousand troops if necessary to enforce the law, Jackson rallied the country to his side state by state, leaving South Carolina isolated.

It almost came to the point of an armed intra-Southern clash. According to Van Buren, Jackson was ready to get on a horse and personally direct an invasion of South Carolina, using Upper South troops to take out the Calhounites:

> He had at this time . . . an inclination to go himself with a sufficient force, which he felt assured he could raise in Virginia and Tennessee, as 'a posse comitatus' of the Marshal and arrest Messrs. Calhoun, [Robert] Hayne, [James] Hamilton and [George] McDuffie in the midst of the force of 12,000 men which the Legislature of South Carolina had authorized to be raised and deliver them to the Judicial power of the United States to be dealt with according to law.[20]

South Carolina backed down. Jackson, who later expressed regret that he had not hung Calhoun when he had the chance, was re-elected president in 1832 by a landslide. In the wake of the nullification of nullification, a compromise tariff bill passed that would give South Carolina a climbdown from the failure of its insurrectionist posture by reducing tariff rates slowly. In the congressional debate over that bill, Representative Nathan Appleton, who as one of the founders of the New England textile industry and of the manufacturing center of Lowell, Massachusetts, was one of America's heaviest domestic cotton customers and one of Boston's richest men, asked point-blank:

> Does the South really wish the continuance of the Union? I have no doubt of the attachment of the mass of the people of the South to the Union, as well as of every other section of the country; but it may well be doubted whether certain leading politicians have not formed bright visions of a

Southern confederacy. This would seem to be the only rational ground for accounting for the movements in South Carolina. A Southern confederacy, of which South Carolina should be the central State, and Charleston the commercial emporium, may present some temptations for individual ambition.[21]

Two days before the beginning of his second term, on March 2, 1833, Jackson signed the compromise tariff that Southern legislators had voted for. But he also signed the revenue collection act that Northern legislators had voted for; known in South Carolina as the "Force Act," it allowed him to use the military to collect tariffs and to close any port he desired.

Though the South Carolina legislature passed an act nullifying the Force Act in South Carolina, there was no armed insurrection against the federal government—this time. The experience left South Carolina more isolated, and its politics even more extreme than before.

"I have had a laborious task here, but nullification is dead;" wrote President Jackson in a letter on May 1, 1833, "and its actors and exciters will only be remembered by the people to be execrated for their wicked designs to sever and destroy the only good government on the globe." The nullification struggle had been over the "Tariff of Abominations," not slavery; but nullification was thoroughly identified with slavery and secession, and the crisis had been a rehearsal for leaving the Union, as Jackson saw clearly. The letter continued with his much-quoted observation that "the tariff was only the pretext, and disunion and southern confederacy the real object. The next pretext will be the negro, or slavery question."[22]

For Jackson, as for Nathan Appleton and many other contemporary observers, the issue was the personal ambition of Calhoun and his argumentative countrymen.

Martin Van Buren's autobiography describes Jackson

> stretched on a sick-bed a spectre in physical appearance . . . Holding my hand in one of his own and passing the other thro' his long white locks he said, with the clearest indications of a mind composed, and in a tone entirely devoid of passion or bluster—"The bank, Mr. Van Buren is trying to kill me but *I will kill it!*"[23] [punctuation *sic*].

Stopping the Bank's recharter wasn't enough for Jackson. "The hydra of corruption is only *scotched, not dead*," he wrote James K. Polk on December 16, 1832, after learning of Biddle's plans to reintroduce a recharter.[24] In response, Jackson drove a stake through the Bank's heart to make sure the "Money Power," as he called it in his 1837 farewell address, was dead. The Bank's charter would be in force until 1836, but in September 1833, after two consecutive secretaries of the treasury had resigned rather than announce that the federal government would no longer deposit its funds in the Bank, Jackson's new secretary of the treasury, Roger B. Taney, did it. At the time Jackson killed the Bank, it was operating twenty-five branches throughout the nation, though its operations in New England were much less significant because New England had a powerful banking system already in place. Jackson was the first president of whom we can speak as having "managers," and there was a political payoff in destroying the Bank for one of them, New York's Martin Van Buren. Wall Street was happy; the Bank had been the last remaining power base of Philadelphia in US finance. Jackson and Van Buren's successful building of a national Democratic party was thus accomplished as a business alliance between slavery capitalism in the South and finance capitalism in the North.

In vetoing the Bank's recharter, Jackson abrogated the federal government's authority over paper money. He had hoped to do away with state banks next, but with the national bank gone, there was no alternative to state banks. But since the Constitution specifically denied to states the right to issue bills of credit, that left only private banks to print money. For the next thirty years, the United States had no uniform currency, as commercial institutions printed a massive uncontrolled emission of paper monies. This privatization of the money supply determined the commercial contours of the following decades, until the secession of the South provoked a new assertion of federal power by the Lincoln administration.

John Quincy Adams, whom Jackson defeated in the 1828 presidential election, was elected to Congress in 1830—the only ex-president to take such a step—and began a remarkable second career. His diary, which he began keeping at the age of twelve in 1779 and maintained for sixty-nine years until his death in 1849, is the most extensive by any American historical figure, and is a gripping record of the times and of a conscience. As it makes clear, he had always been antislavery; but as one of the major figures in increasing the territorial reach of the United States, he had been known as a pro-expansion president rather than an antislavery one. On his first day in Congress, however—December 12, 1831, only months after Nat Turner's rebellion—he took advantage of his appointment as committee chair to present "fifteen petitions, signed numerously by citizens of Pennsylvania, praying for the abolition of slavery and the slave-trade in the District of Columbia," and had one of them read out loud.[25]

It drove the Southerners in Congress mad. From then on, Adams delighted in presenting all the antislavery petitions he received. From the time he entered the House until he collapsed at his desk there in 1848 (remaining in the Capitol until he died three days later), no one in the US government opposed slavery more consistently or effectively.

Adams saw Jackson's shuttering of the Bank as a baby-with-a-loaded-gun scenario, writing in dismay, "His experiment is to stake the revenue, the credit, and the currency of the country upon the State banks."[26] Petitions and even deputations came in from around the country: no, *don't do this.* "They have all had interviews with the President," wrote Adams, "who treated them all politely, but declared his irrevocable determination never to consent to the restoration of the deposits, and never to assent to the chartering of a Bank of the United States."[27] Slave trader Jourdan M. Saunders approved of Jackson's action, writing his business partner David Burford on September 28, 1833: "We are looking out for hard times in the money market on account of the anticipated removal of the government diposits[.] The small [unclear: fry] are quaking[.] For my part I Glory in the Old Cocks [Jackson's] inflexible determination to rid the country of a growing evil[.]"[28]

The Bank's charter was to extend until 1836, but Jackson didn't wait until then to stop the flow of federal deposits to it. The federal government began depositing its tariff revenues into twenty-three non-networked state banks, a number later expanded to sixty, and then to ninety-three, and then to fewer, and to fewer, as so many of them failed. Referred to by Jackson's numerous enemies as "pet" banks, they were tools of the Jacksonian Democratic Party's immense patronage machine, with which Jackson put the financial power of the federal government at the service of his political party.

Biddle had maintained a conservative 2:1 paper-to-specie ratio in the bank, but these new banks—"wildcat banks," they were called—issued four, five, ten times as much paper money as they had specie to back it with. Sometimes they didn't have specie at all, just other banks' paper.

Biddle responded to Jackson's choke order by pursuing policies consistent with liquidation, contracting credit sharply at all the bank's branches, calling in loans and redeeming notes from state banks around the country, leading, predictably enough, to a panic in early 1834. Many criticized Biddle as trying to make the economy scream in a contest of wills, but his actions were consistent with Jackson's order.

In Mississippi, the Bank of the United States strained the Planters Bank's resources locally by taking away a major local source of credit and calling in its notes at the same time. The Planters Bank became one of the new depositories for federal funds, but unfortunately, when it finally received the first federal deposits, which came later than expected, "only a small percentage of the funds was in United States Bank notes or specie; a vast amount was in the paper of banks in Tennessee and Alabama, while the largest portion consisted of notes issued by the Planters Bank itself."[29] The government receipts that were being deposited were mostly revenues from the sale of public lands, which were being paid for in increasingly worthless paper.

Along with this, as a government depository, the Planters Bank also had the responsibility of paying out governmental obligations. If a government employee got paid with paper in Natchez, he no longer received paper money from the national bank, redeemable for silver coins at any bank branch in the United States. Instead, he got Planters Bank money, which, if he tried to use it in, say, New Orleans, would only be accepted at a discount from its face value.

Money, which had been moving in the direction of becoming a national commodity, became newly provincialized. Now that there was no national bank, and with lots of "virgin" land on the market whose new owners were in the market for slaves, the newly flush pet banks began competing aggressively to write mortgages. Meanwhile, state legislatures began granting bank charters freely as new operators got into the business. Against a backdrop of general inflation that was acutely felt by the increasing numbers of urban poor in the North, demand in Mississippi for slaves spiked, while supply remained constant.

Several bumper crops of cotton in a row had been sold into a growing industrial market in Britain. The British textile industry was continuing to expand, and there had been bumper crops of wheat in Britain, so British domestic consumers (who provided about half the market for British textiles), were relatively flush.[30] Industrial capacity was growing: power looms in Britain grew from 14,500 in 1820 to about 100,000 in 1833, even as they were growing in size and becoming more efficient.[31] This full-bore Industrial Revolution, which was creating wealth on a previously unknown scale, had enormous capacity to consume cotton. The French also bought American cotton, as did Lowell, Massachusetts, though its textile industry was tiny compared to the British juggernaut. Writing in humorist's hyperbole, Joseph G. Baldwin later recalled Mississippi during these "flush times":

> Emigrants came flocking in from all quarters of the Union, especially from the slaveholding States . . . Money, or what passed for money, was the only cheap thing to be had. . . . The State banks were issuing their bills by the sheet, like a patent steam printing-press its issues; and no other showing was asked of the applicant for the loan than an authentication of his great distress for money . . . Under this stimulating process prices rose like smoke.[32]

In these times, there was a double incentive to buy large numbers of slaves: 1) those in possession of cotton-growing lands could make big money fast, if only they could get enough labor; and 2) the most obvious way to capture and store the value of the easy money flying by was to lock it down in the form of slaves before it devalued.

In Britain, a frantic dance of the millions took place in the great ballrooms of the economy: London, with its huge financial centers; Liverpool, the shipping emporium; and Lancashire, the industrial capital—all dancing as fast as they could, taking in cotton and turning out cloth for the world. As Peter Temin has pointed out, there was a surfeit of silver on the British market, partly because the Chinese were accepting opium instead of silver in trade from Britain.[33] In another global trade first, Britain had addicted large numbers of Chinese to the product, flooding the market with opium cheaply grown in British-controlled India, sometimes shipped in Baltimore clippers built specially for the opium trade, in shipments sometimes financed by New England merchants, and licensed by the East India Company.[34] Eighteen thirty-four, wrote Karl Marx in an 1858 article in the *New York Daily Tribune,* "marks an epoch in the history of the opium trade": Britain's East India Company was prohibited from trading in China, and opium was thrown open to separate traders, who began smuggling it into China aggressively, increasing the volume of the trade dramatically and demanding silver in return, depleting the Celestial Empire of the metal as the opium-seller's customers multiplied.[35]

The growth of New England manufactures, together with the strong exports of cotton, shifted the balance of trade between Britain and the United States somewhat. As silver became cheaper on the British market, more of the silver

Britain paid for cotton and other staple crops remained in America instead of being sent back out. That east-to-west trade winds influenced the economic collapse does not, however, make Jackson's ideologically driven recklessness fade to insignificance. The global interconnection went both ways: the revenue derived from American cotton provided conditions for the storm to intensify.

Between 1830 and 1836, the number of state-chartered banks went from 329 to 730; they issued circulating banknotes and long-term bonds.[36] State governments borrowed heavily to finance internal improvements, most of which were never built. "From 1834 to 1836 the money supply grew at an average annual rate of 30 percent," writes Jane Knodell, "compared to 2.7 percent between 1831 and 1834."[37] Canal, railroad, and bank projects all moved forward, with the Deep South states investing especially heavily in banks. During that time American indebtedness to foreign creditors doubled, from $110 million to $220 million.[38] The state governments were on the hook for much of it. Intended to finance internal improvements, the money flowed through the American economic system; when it got to the South, it stimulated the market in slaves.[39]

Nicholas Biddle rechartered his bank under Pennsylvania state law as the United States Bank of Pennsylvania. Though it was still a giant in terms of capitalization, it was no longer the federal government's agent and no longer had the advantages of national branches. But once again, its most extensive operations outside of Pennsylvania were in Mississippi.[40]

Jackson, meanwhile, achieved the conservative dream of paying off the national debt in January 1835. Unfortunately, that left the Treasury empty. Treasury coffers relied on income from tariffs, and now that the Nullifiers had succeeded in getting the tariffs down though not removed, there was a sharp drop in federal income. But with the switch to what in theory was a debt-free federal government, it was time for some other source of revenue, and the only contender was land sales.

There were vast quantities of newly available, unplowed land to privatize. It couldn't go on indefinitely, but the federal government could make lots of money right now by selling the Native Americans' land cheap, as fast as the natives could be evicted. Having an inside track on this market was valuable; as always with the Jacksonians, patronage was crucial to political power.

The Jacksonians opened up the floodgates of massive land speculation and currency at about the same time. Between January 1835 and December 1836, some fifty thousand square miles were sold at a fixed price of $1.25 an acre.

Much of it was snapped up by speculators who flipped it, creating a real estate bubble, while banks issued paper money feverishly.[41] Banks that were politically allied with the administration to be under the control of Secretary of the Treasury Levi Woodbury had the free use of millions of dollars of public money, on which they were utterly dependent, as few of them had much in the way of assets otherwise.

The Whigs, wrote a nineteenth-century financial historian, "perceived that the system was exciting wild speculation, and that by it money was drawn from the great commercial centres and stored in remote banks to be loaned to the profit of those who had proved their loyalty to the administration and its 'revered chief.'"[42] One writer estimated in March 1837 that banknotes in circulation had been increased by $80 million since the veto of the bank charter in 1832.[43]

Field hands, meanwhile, might sell for $1,000 or more, so it was clear where economic power resided: in owning slaves. That was where the profit was taken, as gains made in dubious paper were converted into the safer instrument of laboring bodies.

Slave mortgaging was essential to the functioning of the Southern credit system, but the practice has not been much discussed by historians, and we do not have a good overview of the numbers. No one at the time seems to have compiled statistics about how much mortgaging was being done, whether of land or of slaves. Looking at South Carolina, Bonnie Martin found that "year in and year out . . . private mortgage contracts were quietly filed across the South, but no published tallies exposed the number of mortgages made or the amount of capital raised."[44]

The function of banks in the antebellum mortgage market was different than the way we think of it now. Most antebellum mortgages were funded not by bank capital but by private individuals in local networks. The credit networks of the time were informal, and often banks were not the lenders but merely the places of payment, where loans were facilitated by the issuing of paper. Martin writes that of the publicly recorded mortgages that she was able to analyze, "banks, churches, merchants, and building societies were only 19 percent of the lenders who accepted human collateral in South Carolina. Interpersonal lending accounted for 81 percent."[45] The financiers and banks made money, of course, and so did states and municipalities that collected taxes and fees and, through the court system, did buying and selling of their own.

It's clear that enslaved collateral was a significant part of the mortgage action: in the more than eight thousand mortgages she analyzed from Virginia, South Carolina, and Louisiana, Martin found that "the 41 percent of them that included slaves as all or a portion [of] the collateral raised 63 percent of the capital."[46]

The price of slaves fluctuated with the rise and fall of cotton, but over the long term, those fluctuations were superficial disturbances of steadily increasing prices.

The era between the War of 1812 and secession can be thought of as divided into two periods of bumpy boom followed by devastating busts. The first of these booms ended in the complicated series of events remembered as the Panic of 1837, the exact dynamics of which historians have argued about ever since.*

After what we now call a "dead cat bounce" in 1838, the economy in 1839 crashed a second time, harder, landing in a depression that bottomed out in 1842 and did not immediately recover. By then, more than two hundred banks had failed. But for the strongest, most disciplined traders, there was still business to be done. In a letter of November 16, 1839, that somehow wound up in print in an abolitionist tract of 1846, the small-scale slave trader G. W. Barnes, of Halifax, North Carolina, informed the big trader Theophilus Freeman of New Orleans of the names of and prices at which he had shipped six "girls" to him, then wrote: "I have a great many negroes offered to me, but I will not pay the prices they ask, for I know they will come down. I have no opposition in market. I will wait until I hear from you before I buy, and then I can judge what I must pay. . . . Write often, as the times are critical, and it depends on the prices you get to govern me in buying."[47]

The stimulus that got the economy pumping again was provided by the annexation of Texas in 1845, which stimulated the slave trade. It accelerated further with the discovery of gold in California in 1848 and the increasing penetration of railroads, and rose along with cotton to new heights. It dipped

---

*The title of Jessica Lepler's book *The Many Panics of 1837* conveys something of the fragmented, unsynchronized quality of the multisited crisis.

briefly with a Panic of 1857 that was caused in part, thought Natchez planter Benjamin Wailes, by "River lands at most unwarrantable prices & negroes at $1,500," though the South was actually the least affected by the downturn.[48] Then the slave trade went higher than ever, reaching unheard-of levels by 1860. That boom ended with secession, though the trade continued and even accelerated during the first three years of the war. But by then there was no longer any reliable money with which to compare prices, because the Confederacy was not part of the US financial system.

Not without a sense of irony, we will use white supremacist and onetime dominant-in-the-field-of-slavery historian Ulrich B. Phillips's data showing prices in four major slave markets, not including Natchez, the highest-priced large market. While Phillips's racist conclusions are thoroughly discredited, his numbers, in this case based on examining three-thousand-plus bills of sale, have been more or less generally accepted. As visually estimated by Robert Evans Jr. from Phillips's graphs, the curve of five-year average slave prices (for "prime male field hands") looks like this:

Years	Richmond	Charleston	Mid-Georgia	New Orleans
1830–35	529	592	883	942
1836–40	910	1,053	1,115	1,205
1841–45	530	590	685	745
1846–50	650	730	870	935
1851–55	835	930	1,180	1,250
1856–60	1,100	1,150	1,565	1,605

The effect of the post-1837 depression is clearly visible here, as is the economic tonic effect of annexing Texas in 1845. We see an impressive price rise over the fifteen years from 1845 to 1860, especially in Georgia. But a deeper wave was building that only broke with the ruin of war:

Slave prices inflated continuously as compared with the price of the cotton the slaves produced.

Here are Phillips's figures for the Georgia cotton belt, which incidentally give a sense of how profitable slave trading was.[49] With the importation of Africans no longer possible, the supply of African Americans onto the market could not keep pace with the amount of new cotton acreage continually being brought under cultivation, so the demand for labor always exceeded the supply. The degree of inflation slowed in hard times, but even then, the trend was upward.

Year	Price of a prime field hand expressed in pounds of ginned cotton
1800	1,500
1809	3,000
1818	3,500·
1826	5,400
1837	10,000
1845	12,000
1860	15,000–18,000

At these intervals, we see no depression, only slowed growth. The price of a field hand in Georgia fell from $1,300 to $650 between 1837 and 1845, but measured against the price of cotton, over the course of those years, the field hand appreciated in value from ten thousand pounds of cotton to twelve thousand. Over the six decades of antebellum slavery, even as agricultural innovations gradually increased per-hand productivity, slave labor was steadily becoming a more valuable property than the staple crops the labor produced.

The mere fact of holding slaves, then, brought substantial capital gains. The pressure of this curve, as we need not remind readers, was felt in unsubtle ways by enslaved women, who were pressured to bear children. Newborn black babies were worth more on paper all the time, their poor life expectancy actuarialized through traders' firsthand experience of discounting the substantial death rates. William Dusinberre believes that "about 46 per cent of slave children died before reaching the age of fifteen," compared with a 28 percent mortality rate for free children.[50] The higher mortality rate is no mystery, and it was needlessly high, as it turned on planters' reluctance to spend on the health and welfare of the enslaved.

Even clean drinking water was sometimes seen as an unnecessary expense, which might explain the higher death rates of the enslaved from cholera. "Good water is far more essential than many suppose," wrote a planter signing himself "A Citizen of Mississippi" in an article about plantation management titled "The Negroes" in *DeBow's Review* of March 1847, "or than I could be persuaded

myself until within a few years. . . . Cistern water not too cold will on any plantation save enough in doctor's fees to refund the extra expense."

But money spent on slaves' welfare came right out of the plantation's immediate profits. Some planters who could take the longer view—those who were
not being ground down by debt—could see that any money that was spent on
the health and welfare of the enslaved was of direct economic benefit to the
slaveowner, and could also be cited as proof of the slaveowner's purported kindness to his captives. "The great object," continued the Mississippi planter, "is to
prevent disease and prolong the useful laboring period of the negro's life. Thus
does interest point out the humane course."[51]

The word *humane* was frequent in slaveowner vocabulary. On some large
estates, children were taken off the various different parcels of land, away from
their parents, and raised together in a collective nursery that made easily visible
the slave-breeding nature of the Southern slavery project. A planter in North
Carolina told the British geologist Charles Lyell in 1842 that, given the frequent
necessity of breaking up families by sale, that "he defended the custom of bringing up the children of the same estate in common, as it was far more humane not
to cherish domestic ties among slaves."[52] That is, since domestic ties were only
going to be broken anyway, it was better not to create them in the first place.
Labor that was capital had no family.

Despite its shorter average life span, the enslaved black population of the
South grew faster than the white population, and faster than the small population of free people of color. The capitalized wombs of the South supplied boys,
who were sold to traders, who sold them to planters so they could produce the
cotton that would feed the steam-driven mills of Britain, France, and even New
England. And they supplied girls, who could pick as much cotton as the boys,
and who would themselves become captive baby makers. The slave-breeding
industry was going full tilt.

Old Robbers

The Slaver led her from the door,
He led her by the hand,
To be his slave and paramour
In a strange and distant land!

—Henry Wadsworth Longfellow, "The Quadroon Girl," 1842

THE STURDY BRICK DWELLING-HOUSE at 1315 Duke Street in Alexandria, Virginia, was built in the 1810s, when Alexandria was part of the District of Columbia. From 1828 to 1837, it was the home office and shipping entrepôt of Franklin and Armfield, the largest slave-trading company in American history, whose existence almost exactly coincided with the two terms of Andrew Jackson's presidency. Inscribed in the National Register of Historic Places in 1978, it now houses the Urban League of Northern Virginia and their Freedom House Museum.

The house was the master structure for a complex with three now-vanished courtyards. Enclosing the courtyards was a two-story multi-structure jail, "neatly whitewashed," in the words of Ethan Allen Andrews, an antislavery Bostonian who paid a surprise visit there in July 1835, and was readily admitted and given a tour by John Armfield. It had separate facilities for men (the west yard) and women (the east), a kitchen, a tailor's workshop, and a stable. Andrews allowed that the facility was clean and that the inmates "were well dressed, and everything about them had a neat and comfortable appearance, *for a prison.*"[1] (italics in original)

The 1830 census enumerated 145 people being held there, though the evenness of the numbers suggests that the census-taker might have accepted Armfield's word rather than count heads:

Age	Male	Female
Under 10	1	4
10–24	50	50
24–36	20	20

The captives were mostly strangers to each other, freshly and forcibly removed from their families and their familiar worlds. They were being held until the next ship sailed or until the annual coffle began marching. If they had been purchased during the off season, they might remain there for months. Andrews noted "that they are often chained at night, while at the depot at Alexandria, lest they should overpower their masters."[2]

Alexandria had formerly been a thriving port, but it was losing out to Baltimore. Federal law stipulated that public buildings could only be erected on the other, northern, side of the Potomac—that is, on the Maryland side—so Alexandria, on the Virginia side, got no federal offices. Instead, the slave trade was a key business for the town.

Across the Potomac, six miles away, the slave trade was disturbingly visible in Washington City. Coffles tramped through the streets of the nation's capital daily. Everyone knew where the slave jails were, and everyone walked past the open-air auctions.

Foreign diplomats were astounded to see such a thing in the country that propagandized so heavily its commitment to liberty. There was no comparable spectacle in Europe, where chattel slavery did not exist. Antislavery people saw it, not incorrectly, as a shameful proof that slaveowners ran their government. Many townspeople heartily disliked it, especially the women.

But slavery was fundamental to Washington City. Slaves built it, and slaves ran it on a daily basis. Starved of infrastructural resources by conservative politicians from Jefferson on, legally unable to govern itself, boasting a grand Capitol and the White House but lacking gaslight in its dark streets until 1848, Washington City was a dirty, disease-ridden fen that abounded with crooks, prostitutes, slaves, slave traders, and congressmen, the latter of whom typically lived in boardinghouses. About 6 percent of the city's residents were free black people in

1800, a percentage that grew after 1806, when Virginia began requiring manumitted slaves to leave the state.

The District of Columbia was the perfect site from which to command the slave trade from the Upper to the Lower South, with Alexandria as the port. Its water communication via the Potomac to the Atlantic made it practical to sail captives down to the Gulf of Mexico, up the Mississippi to New Orleans, and on to Natchez, leaving South Carolina out of the loop entirely. Financial and legal expertise was easily at hand in the nation's capital. It was adjacent to the largest, most prestigious, slave-selling territories—those of Virginia and Maryland. Alexandria rose as a slave-trade center with the building of Washington City. By 1802, an Alexandria grand jury grievance decried

> the practice of persons coming from distant parts of the United States into this District, for the purpose of purchasing slaves, where they exhibit, to our view a scene of wretchedness and human degradation, disgraceful to our characters as citizens of a free government. True it is that these dealers, in the persons of our fellow men, collect within this District from various parts, numbers of those victims of slavery, and lodge them in some place of confinement until they have completed their numbers. They are then turned out in our streets and exposed to view, loaded with chains as though they had committed some heinous offence against our laws.[3]

This was the world of small-time tavern traders. By 1806, if not earlier, slaves were being sold in Alexandria at the Indian Queen at King and Water Streets, which was licensed to sell horses and carriages. The Indian Queen then came under the management of Elias P. Legg, who had previously traded in slaves while he was tavernkeeper at the Bell Tavern, where he had done well enough to open his own operation. As Legg worked his way up to

CASH

Will be given for a few likely young NEGROES, with undisputed rights.— Apply at Eli Legg's tavern, upper end of King street.

JOHN L. ALFORD.

March 18 4t†

Alexandria Gazette, *March 22, 1817.*

buying a plantation, his tavern became for a time the main slave market of Alexandria.[4] An advertisement in the *Alexandria Gazette* of February 15, 1825, gives Tennessee—still a slave-importing state—as a destination:

SLAVES WANTED: The subscriber will at all times, pay the highest price in cash for slaves, either single or in families. Letters addressed to me in Alexandria, will be promptly attended to. Sixty or seventy slaves at this time, expressly to go to Tennessee. E.P. Legg.

Prior to 1812, a slave taken from Alexandria County to Washington County for the purpose of sale became free. Then Congress passed an act on June 24, 1812, that allowed slaveowners from one of the counties to remove slaves to the other, but did not allow a person from Alexandria to purchase a slave in Washington (or vice versa) for removal to Alexandria (or vice versa).[5] The exact legal situation of slave commerce between the two counties thus had a somewhat unsettled status under the law, but generally, the presumption was that while slaves could be sold in the District, they could not be brought into the District for the purpose of sale. The District of Columbia, then, major communications hub that it was, functioned mainly as a transshipment point for slaves bought in Maryland and Virginia (or kidnapped from the North), and destined for the South.[6]

As the interstate slave trade became big business, its largest player was Isaac Franklin (1789–1846), whose astute business sense allowed him repeatedly to time the market right. Born in territorial Tennessee, the grandson of a Huguenot, Franklin had two brothers who were already in the slave trade, with an office in New Orleans. They brought him in at the age of eighteen to make runs down the Cumberland, the Ohio, and the Mississippi, thus familiarizing him with the territory.[7]

Franklin had the good fortune to be from Nashville, which served as a base for both Andrew Jackson and James K. Polk. He built up his stake plying the same course Jackson had a generation earlier: trafficking slaves from Nashville to Natchez, which Franklin was doing by 1819, if not earlier. In 1824, during a Virginia slave-purchasing trip, he struck up a friendship with North Carolina slave trader John Armfield, a stagecoach driver who was doing the same.[8] The two became partners, and, in the classic merchant-family manner, Armfield married Franklin's niece Martha Franklin and moved to Alexandria.[9]

With good relationships at multiple banks, Franklin was the best networked and best capitalized slave trader. He understood clearly the implications of the country's demographic shift to the Southwest, and the advantages for a slave-trading firm of having a presence over the entire geographical footprint of the slave-labor system. By establishing a headquarters in Alexandria and sealing the partnership with a strategic marriage, Franklin connected his Nashville base to the nation's capital. From there, he connected by water with the nation's great internal port, Baltimore; the great exporting port, New Orleans, which was approaching the peak of its national influence; and on to Natchez.

Under the antiregulatory climate of the Jackson administration, Franklin brought a new level of professionalism to the interstate slave trade. Franklin and Armfield's business co-partnership was founded on February 29, 1828, and their first newspaper advertisement offering to buy slaves ran in May:

CASH IN MARKET.

The subscribers having leased for a term of years the large three story brick house on Duke street, in the town of Alexandria, D.C., formerly occupied by Gen. Young, we wish to purchase one hundred and fifty likely young negroes of both sexes between the ages of 8 and 25 years. Persons who wish to sell will do well to give us a call, as we are determined to give more than any other purchasers that are in market, or that may hereafter come into market.

Any letters addressed to the subscribers through the Post Office at Alexandria, will be promptly attended to. For information, enquire at the above described house, as we can at all times be found there.

FRANKLIN & ARMFIELD

There was, needless to say, no federal opposition to this perfectly legal trade, especially during the Jackson years (1829–1837). But because Congress made the laws for the District of Columbia, the slave trade in the District was a focal point of antislavery activism. Congressman Charles Miner of Pennsylvania, in his final days as a lame duck before vacating his seat, bravely introduced in 1829 a resolution into the House of Representatives—one that he knew would not pass—for the gradual abolition of slavery in the District. His speech in support of the measure, reproduced in the emerging abolitionist press, began:

Slave dealers, gaining confidence from impunity, have made the seat of the federal government their head quarters for carrying on the domestic slave trade.

The public prisons have been extensively used (perverted from the purposes for which they were erected) for carrying on the domestic slave trade.

Officers of the federal government have been employed, and derived emoluments from carrying on the domestic slave trade.

Private and secret prisons exist in the District for carrying on this traffic in human beings.

The trade is not confined to those who are slaves for life, but persons having a limited time to serve are bought by the slave dealers, and sent where redress is hopeless.

Others are kidnapped, and hurried away before they can be rescued.

Instances of death, from the anguish of despair, exhibited in the District, mark the cruelty of this traffic.

Instances of maiming and suicide, executed or attempted, have been exhibited, growing out of this traffic within the District.

Free persons of colour, coming into the District, are liable to arrest, imprisonment, and sale into slavery, for jail fees, if unable, from ignorance, misfortune, or fraud, to preserve their freedom.[10]

There was slave trading in all three towns of the District of Columbia. John Beattie's business at what became the 3200 block of O Street in Georgetown was established in 1760; in the nineteenth century, McCandless's tavern at M Street and Washington Avenue was a notorious slave-trade spot. Particularly visible in Washington, because of their location, were Robey's Tavern, at Seventh and Maryland, and, one block over and two blocks down, Williams's slave jail at Eighth and B Street (now Constitution Avenue). Williams's was where the kidnapped Solomon Northup regained consciousness after being kidnapped, and where he was beaten by trader James Birch (Burch, in Northup's spelling) before becoming one of the captives Birch regularly shipped to Theophilus Freeman, his partner in New Orleans.[11]

The US jail in Washington made money by housing captives in transit. Representative Miner noted that 742 people being trafficked by traders had been housed there during the previous five years, and told Congress of how, when visiting the jail, he saw a female prisoner with "three or four children with her— one at the breast," and asked her story:

She was a slave, but had married a man who was free. By him she had eight or nine children. Moved by natural affection, the father labored to support the children; but as they attained an age to be valuable in the market, perhaps ten or twelve, the master sold them. One after another was taken away and sold to the slave dealers. She had now come to an age to be no longer profitable as a breeder, and her master had separated her from her husband, and all the associations of life, and sent her and her children to

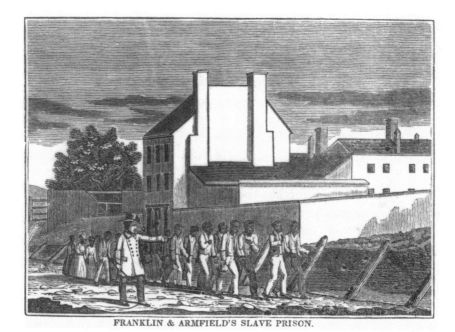

FRANKLIN & ARMFIELD'S SLAVE PRISON.

The house on Duke Street, as depicted in an 1836 abolitionist engraving. Armfield is characterized by his accessories: a broad-brimmed hat and a whip.

your prison for sale. She was waiting for a purchaser, and seemed to me to be more heart-broken than any creature I had ever seen.[12]

Though many slave traders were operating, Franklin and Armfield's operation quickly dominated the market. Armfield held down the Alexandria office on Duke Street, supervised the buying, and ran the shipping.

Armfield also drove a large annual coffle southward in the summer. Since the firm had its own jail, Armfield could afford to buy one or a few slaves at a time and pen them up at Duke Street until he had accumulated a coffle-full, then drive the coffle down to get a jump on the fall slave-selling season in Natchez. Most coffles contained fifty, sixty, or at most a hundred captives, but G. W. Featherstonhaugh estimated the coffle of Armfield's that he encountered as having three hundred, which, if not an exaggeration, is as large as coffles ever got, and represented a major logistical and security effort.[13]

By chance, Featherstonhaugh encountered Armfield a second time on a stagecoach. He described him as "a queer tall animal about forty years old, with dark black hair cut round as if he were a Methodist preacher, immense black whiskers, a physiognomy not without one or two tolerable features, but singularly sharp, and not a little piratical and repulsive." Armfield was dressed entirely in black except for "a huge broad-brimmed white hat, adorned with a black crepe," the latter perhaps worn in homage to Andrew Jackson, who perpetually wore mourning crepe for his deceased wife, Rachel. Featherstonhaugh quoted Armfield as saying of Jackson, "The old Gineral is the most greatest and most completest idear of a man what had ever lived." Armfield's enslaved valet, Pompey, explained to Featherstonhaugh that the trader was overfond of onions and brandy, which kept him feeling ill.[14]

Except for the summer coffle, Franklin and Armfield did all their trafficking by sea, connecting the Chesapeake, the source of wholesale supply, with the retail markets of New Orleans and Natchez. Franklin's first recorded slave sale in New Orleans took place in 1828, and the following year he took a two-year lease on a house with adjoining vacant lots at Esplanade and Casa Calvo (now the continuation of Royal Street) just below the French Quarter in the Faubourg Marigny, renewing it two years later. He seems to have kept his inventory of slaves for sale in a prison on the premises. A curiously ambiguous clause in his 1831 lease renewal stipulated that the lease was "as a dwelling house and not for the business which the said Isaac Franklin now carries on that is to say that of selling negroes, although it is not the intention . . . to deprive the said lessee of the privilege to Keep His slaves in the said house and therein to carry on his aforesaid business."[15]

Though the District of Columbia was an important slave-exporting outlet, it was quickly overtaken by Richmond. Virginia's capital city was the great intake center for the slave trade, where traders could buy locally raised people for trafficking down South. Because Richmond traders sold fast, in quantities, to busy, professional resellers in a high-volume, competitive market, they conducted a high proportion of their sales by open-outcry auction, the kind at which the people being sold were routinely and ritualistically stripped naked and examined, typically in another room or area off to the side. Richmond's power was supplemented by a big local market for rented slaves, since the town's tobacco factories always needed labor.

Having a partner in Richmond was the key to a successful national slave-trade operation, and Franklin's man was Rice C. Ballard, whom he and Armfield had encountered at Eli Legg's tavern in Alexandria. Ballard too had his eye on the long-distance interstate market; he was already selling slaves into New Orleans and Natchez by 1828, if not earlier.

Ballard's friends addressed him as "colonel," which was (and still is) the honorific of an auctioneer. Though Ballard was based in Richmond, he shipped slaves out of Norfolk, which was Virginia's major seaport, and where Franklin and Armfield's oceangoing brigs could make a stop. Franklin formed a second high-volume partnership with him that worked in parallel with his Armfield partnership.

Franklin was the business visionary, the senior partner, the big-picture guy, the strategist who directed the other partners by mail and made the far-flung parts of his organization work together. He handled the point of sale, where the money was made, and he handled the banking. He created a slave-trade operation that was national in scope in a way that no one had done before, or would do after him, from a base in Tennessee that was very near the president's.

Retail slave prices could vary by the day, and Franklin called the shots for when to buy and when to hold off. Besides watching market conditions carefully, he also paid close attention to crop forecasts, credit conditions, and political threats to the slave trade—and, most important, to keeping the firm's cash flow moving and maintaining its credit in A-1 condition.

Every year Franklin passed tens of thousands of dollars to Ballard and Armfield, in the form of drafts on any of eight or so northern banks. In return, they sent him young African Americans. He successfully addressed the problem of a decentralized slave supply network in the Chesapeake by building a region-wide web of slave-harvesting associates who combed the plantations of Virginia and Maryland, as per the firm's advertisement that ran in every issue of the *Daily National Intelligencer* and other papers during large parts of 1833 and '34. Their 1828 advertisement had solicited purchase of people between the ages of eight and twenty-five, but now the lower age limit had moved upward to twelve, presumably reflecting Louisiana's 1829 prohibition of children under ten:

CASH IN MARKET

We will pay Cash for any number of likely Negroes, of both sexes, from 12 to 25 years of age, Field Hands. Also, Mechanics of every description. Apply to

R.C. Ballard & Co. Richmond, Va.

J.M. Saunders & Co. Warrenton, Va.

George Kepheart & Co. Fredericktown, Md.

James F. Purvis & Co. Baltimore.

Thomas M. Jones, Easton, Eastern Shore of Md.

Or, to the subscriber, at their residence in Alexandria.

Persons having likely servants to dispose of, will do well to give us a call, as we at all times will pay higher prices in cash than any other purchaser who is now or may hereafter come into market.

All communications promptly attended to.

FRANKLIN & ARMFIELD

In shipping by water, Franklin and Armfield at first followed the prevailing practice of consigning slave cargoes to captains as necessary. But then, marking a new level of national reach and vertical integration for a domestic slave trading company, they went into the carrying trade, establishing their own packet lines. The firm may have purchased the brig *United States* as early as 1828. Three other brigs were subsequently added to the fleet: the *Tribune*, the *Uncas*, and, custom-built specifically for the needs of the domestic slave trade, the modern, copper-bolted *Isaac Franklin*.

By establishing a packet line, Franklin and Armfield brought the slave trade into the modern world, where time is money. At first, they announced they would sail every two months from Alexandria to New Orleans, but by 1835 they were sailing the first and fifteenth of every month, shipping over a thousand slaves that year. Other traders could board their captives at Duke Street for as long as necessary at twenty-five cents per head, per night. By consigning them to Franklin and Armfield for handling during shipment, the other traders in effect subsidized the firm's shipping costs. Franklin and Armfield's size and greater capitalization in turn gave them more clout for purchasing young people in the countryside, as they began to enjoy advantages of scale.

Franklin's firm, then, was a modern business that, as Bray Hammond described antebellum enterprise generally, was "served by waterpower, steam, and credit."[16] Franklin and Armfield proudly advertised that their vessels were fitted out as sail-steam hybrids in order to "steam up the Mississippi." Steam power was not usable on the open Atlantic until 1838, so the brigs had to unfurl their sails down the Atlantic and into the Gulf. It was not an easy sail down the coast, going against the Gulf Stream from North Carolina forward, but the last crawl was the worst. The sixty miles or so up the river from the alluvial "bird-foot" of lower Louisiana to New Orleans was a longtime shipping bottleneck that could take a month without steam. By steaming up the Mississippi as far as New Orleans, and then on to Natchez, the traders could save precious time, turn their money around faster, and have fewer of the people who constituted their cargo arrive dead. This faster, safer delivery gave them a previously impossible competitive advantage in that highest-priced of slave markets.

The Reverend Joshua Leavitt, a cofounder of the New York City Anti-Slavery Society, who was allowed to go on board the *Tribune* in 1834, reported that

> The hold is appropriated to the slaves, and is divided into two apartments. The after-hold will carry about eighty women, and the other about one hundred men. On either side were two platforms running the whole length; one raised a few inches, and the other half way up to the deck. They were about five or six feet deep. On these the slaves lie, as close as they can stow away.[17]

There does not seem to have been a standard security protocol for carrying slaves on the coastwise route. When Frederic Bancroft interviewed two people who had been carried south by sea, one of them, Nathan Ross, interviewed in Donaldsville, Louisiana, in 1902, recalled having been taken down to the James River to Portsmouth, Virginia, circa 1846, then put on a ship with thirty or forty others. He remembered that they were allowed to walk on deck and were only put into the hold at night and when it stormed. By contrast, seventy-two-year-old Washington Taylor, who had been taken to Richmond and put on a ship for New Orleans with some eighty others, recalled being kept in the hold all the time except when there was a storm; then, in Bancroft's summary, "they were let out, lest all should be lost if the ship sank."[18]

During the off season, Franklin and Armfield's brigs carried commodities and occasionally ballast. They offered passenger fares on their line, but it's not clear how successful they were, as slave ships carried a stigma. These runs were dangerous; the potential hazards included not only epidemic and rebellion, but shipwreck. The brig *Comet*, which probably belonged to Franklin and Armfield, left Alexandria in December 1830 with 164 captives on board, but went off course and broke up on the coast of Bermuda. The British governor of Bermuda set the captives free, but Franklin had insured seventy-six of them, and he collected $37,555, about a million 2014 dollars. That sum was left to the insurance companies to collect from the government of Great Britain, which in 1840 settled the claim.[19]

The *Comet* was followed two years later by the *Encomium*, whose forty-six captives were set free; by the brig *Enterprise*, which while taking seventy-eight African Americans from Alexandria to Charleston in 1835 was forced by bad weather to put in at Bermuda; by the *Hermosa* in 1840; and by the *Creole*—the most sensitive of the cases, since it put in at the Bahamas as the result of onboard slave rebellion, exactly what the slaveowners feared would happen if the enslaved had the incentive of being freed by the British. A diplomatic standoff ensued that lasted for years, as US diplomats to Britain defended slaveowners' rights and pressed for compensation for what was considered stolen property.[20]

With Franklin's nephew James Purvis as their agent in Baltimore, Franklin and Armfield poached Austin Woolfolk's business and even his agents, outcompeting him in every way. It didn't help Woolfolk that he had a reputation for dishonesty. His business fell off quickly, and by October 1832 he was reduced to running a strange newspaper ad that ran for weeks in the Baltimore *Republican & Commercial Advertiser*. It read:

> A. WOOLFOLK wishes to inform the owners of Negroes in Maryland, Virginia, and N. Carolina, that he *is not dead*, as has been artfully represented by his opponents, but that he still lives, to give them CASH and the HIGHEST PRICES for their NEGROES.

Hope Hull Slatter, the major Baltimore trader after A. Woolfolk, began operating in 1835 out of Owing's Globe Inn, at the corner of Howard and Market. He opened his jail on Pratt Street in 1838, digging a two-block tunnel beneath the city's streets to hide his coffles as they went from headquarters to wharf, and he continued selling slaves out of Baltimore until 1847, when he retired to Mobile.[21]

> CASH FOR NEGROES.
>
> I WISH to purchase from 75 to 100 Negroes, of both sexes, from the age of 8 to 25 years, for which I will pay liberal prices. I can always be found at Owing's Globe Inn, corner of Howard and Market streets, Baltimore; and in my absence at any time, a lien left at the bar will be attended to, immediately on my return.
>
> HOPE H. SLATTER
>
> N.B. I wish particularly to purchase several seamstresses and likely small fancy girls for nurses. I will also purchase several families. —Baltimore *Republican & Commercial Advertiser*, Feb. 2, 1835.

"Small fancy girls" meant light-skinned female children, salable as sex slaves. It was a discreet phrase, but not a mysterious one: everyone understood it.

⇒⇐

The New Orleans market specialized both in selling difficult-to-dispose-of "vicious slaves" to sugar plantations and in supplying high-priced craftsmen, skilled domestics, "body servants," and sex slaves (the light-skinned "fancy girls") for urban use. New Orleans was notorious for its slave auctions, but auctions seem to have constituted only about half of the sales; traders did much of their business by private sale out of their own retail showrooms, clusters of which were located in both the French- and English-speaking parts of town.

The Natchez market, by contrast, did not have regular auctions, but mostly sold retail, directly to cotton planters, out of a compound that housed several hundred captives at any one time. "From early in the century to 1860," wrote Frederic Bancroft, "the Natchez market, apart from its actual location, changed perhaps less than any other large market in the South, for its patrons were mainly of the planter class." Natchez purchasers were mostly end-users, as opposed to the resellers who dominated the market in Richmond and were also well represented in Charleston and New Orleans.[22]

Natchez was a split-level pair of towns. The city proper, high atop the bluff two hundred feet above the Mississippi River, was where the old Natchez aristocracy lived and where Isaac Franklin did his business; it connected socially and commercially with the rural planters. Down below, at the foot of the bluff, was Natchez-under-the-Hill, a sleazy row of taverns, gambling halls, brothels, and merchants who dealt with the river traffic. A traveler from Kentucky wrote of Natchez in an 1803 journal that "there are about 500 dwellings in this place. They are mostly Americans from South Carolina and Georgia . . . I suppose from what I have seen that Natchez is, or the inhabitants of the town are, as much given to luxury & dissipation as any place in America."[23] Natchez was the crossroads where the major water route, the Mississippi River, met the major land route, the Natchez Trace. As such, it was the principal destination for coffles as well as boats coming up from New Orleans. At the end of the slave-selling chain, Natchez consistently paid the highest prices. Natchez was Franklin and Armfield's cash cow.

Louisiana's post–Nat Turner prohibition on slave importation caused inventory problems. In a letter from New Orleans of February 28, 1831, Franklin wrote to Ballard in Richmond: "I will have a petition tomorrow before the house for our relief—should that fail god knows what will be the consequence. I will do the best I can for all concerned & if nothing better can be done I will declare myself a citizen of the state. I am much depressed & if we have to rely entirely on the Mississippi market we have more in this shipment than can be sold to

advantage." In November, facing a wipeout with the closing to out-of-state traders of the Louisiana market, Franklin conveyed "his entire lot of slaves" to his
brother and agent James R. Franklin in Natchez, who sold them all by December. After that, Franklin didn't sell into New Orleans again until 1834.[24]

Meanwhile, Natchez was heating up as a spot for sales. But epidemics were
a constant problem, especially after a global pandemic of Asiatic cholera reached
the United States in 1832. Symptoms "appeared almost simultaneously in Montreal, Philadelphia, and New York," write Kiple and King. For reasons that are
still unclear, but quite possibly related to the lower levels of sanitation available
to the enslaved, the ravages of cholera were more severe among the black population; many physicians in the hemisphere thought of it as a "negro disease."[25]

At first Franklin was afraid that the inmates of Ballard's slave jail in Richmond might die, but then he advised him to hold back from selling and wait
for prices to climb as the epidemic did its work: ". . . best hold on. The more
negroes lost in that country the more will be wanting if they have the means of
procuring them."[26]

On December 8, 1832, he wrote Ballard of casualties from cholera: "the last
two weeks we have Buried . . . 9 Negroes and 6 or 7 children and we have 7 or 8
Negroes sick . . . the way we send out dead Negroes at night and keep Dark is a
sin."[27] "Buried" was a euphemism, because he hadn't buried them; to the great disgust of the polite citizens of Natchez, he opted to dump their bodies in a swamp,
hoping not to be detected as he created a health hazard for the terrified town.

That a slave trader could easily bring an epidemic of deadly diseases into
town was part of the social stigma attached to the profession. Africans brought
in on the earlier transatlantic slave ships had passed through a period of quarantine in a "pest house," but there were no quarantines in interstate commerce.
Yellow fever, malaria, typhoid, smallpox, cholera: slave pens were a notorious
breeding ground for epidemics.

Frightened by the possibility of contagion in their midst, the citizens of
Natchez kicked the slave traders out of the city proper in 1833. They were banished only a mile out of town, to a site where slaves were already being sold: the
Forks of the Road, a crossroads where the ironically named Liberty Road, which
led east to Georgia, crossed Washington Road, which led to the Natchez Trace
and on to Tennessee. If Natchez was a crossroads, the Forks of the Road was the
crossroads of the crossroads.

Cue Robert Johnson: slave jails were often at the crossroads. However
you care to read the image of the crossroads in the blues, remember that in

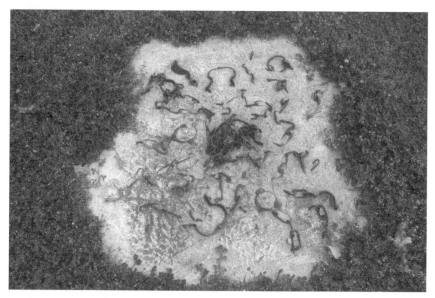

A display of manacles embedded in concrete on the ground, part of a memorial at the site of Natchez's Forks of the Road, March 2014.

Mississippi, the most notorious crossroads was the state's largest slave market, where Robert Johnson's great-grandfather's generation was sold.

Many locals referred to the Forks of the Road as Niggerville, as in an advertisement that ran in the Natchez *Free Trader* of February 26, 1835:

NEGROES FOR SALE.

THE subscribers offer for sale at Niggerville, one mile from Natchez, six carpenters and three blacksmiths. They will be first tried as to their capacity, in their different branches of business, with a full guaranty as to title and soundness of the same. To be disposed of either for cash, or on time, for good acceptances. All persons that may be in want of such mechanics, would do well to call and look at them before they are purchased elsewhere. EATON FREEMAN.
Niggerville, Feb. 26-30-3t.

In a letter to Ballard of April 24, James R. Franklin wrote from Natchez, "our negroes are getting much better but they have been very sickly. So much so the City Council Compells us all to leave the limits of the Corporation in two days. We shall have to take to the woods." By May 7, in the dreary woods amid sick and dying captives and sick himself, James R. Franklin's tone sounded desperate: "I do assure you it is dreadful I have 4 or 5 down at present," but he held out hope that he could still sell his diseased cargo: "I am in hopes all the fools are not yet dead and some one eyed man will buy us out yet." The term "one eyed man," which turns up at various places in the firm's correspondence, seems to have been a private but easily understandable joke: maybe some dickhead will buy our inventory of slaves before they all die.[28]

In a letter of February 2, 1834, James R. Franklin warned Rice C. Ballard not to ship any more "Negroes," giving him the bad news that smallpox had broken out on two or three plantations, and that slaves imported by their firm were suspected of having brought it. Then, amid a litany of complaints about uncooperative banks and piratical customs agents, he wrote: "I never wanted to leave any place so bad as I do want to leave this damn hole."[29]

"I have commenced upon a new years work, and am purchasing negroes much faster than usual at fair prices," wrote Franklin's associate Jourdan M. Saunders from the buying territory in Virginia to his partner David Burford in Nashville in April 1832.[30]

The boom was underway. Franklin wrote Ballard from Natchez that "the US Bank and the Planters Bank at this place has thrown a large amt of cash into circulation."[31] Franklin was positioned to scoop up that cash. In a letter of November 1, 1833, he urged Ballard to buy heavy, reminding him that "as to the money we can raise in a short Time any Amt that may be wanting." He went on to advise him that "we have sold all of our negroes for Good prices & Good profits accept [except] some old negroes say 18 in number . . . [they] will keep house until next Spring if they do not Die before that time[.] [We] could have sold as many more if we had of had the right kind. . . . [We sold] men from $8 to 900 Dollars[,] field women large & likely from 6 to 650 Dollars."

But then he complained, "We have no young Girl on hand . . . There are Great Demand for fancy maid[.] I do believe that a likely Girl and Good seamstress could be sold for $1000[.]" That complaint was also personal: "I was disappointed in not finding your Charlottsvill maid that you promised me[.] you must ship all the first rate house servants by the first shipment after you Receive this."[32]

"First-rate house servants" was, of course, a euphemism. The "fancy maid" was named Martha; according to a letter from James R. Franklin, she also answered to "Big Cuff."[33] Apropos the term *fancy*, Walter Johnson suggests that "the word 'fancy' . . . refers to appearances perhaps or manners or dress. But the word has another meaning; it designates a desire: he fancies. . . . The slave market usage embarked from this second meaning: 'fancy' was a transitive verb made noun, a slaveholder's desire made material in the shape of a woman."[34]

New Orleans was the capital for selling fancy girls, whose earnings could keep a riverboat gambler doubling as a pimp—not necessarily selling their services by the hour, but perhaps receiving regular rent on long-term concubinage contracts, beginning at as young an age as twelve. An anonymous 1850 booklet called *New Orleans As It Is* quotes a price of twelve to twenty dollars a month for a girl to pay her "owner"—until, it goes on to say, "she is cast off as a useless and worthless *thing*."[35]

The wealthy planters of Natchez could easily afford to purchase personal sex slaves as luxury goods. Franklin, Armfield, and Ballard certainly dealt in them, and, as slave traders commonly did, they raped them in the process. This was facilitated by the fact that traders generally owned the captives in their custody. Planters often retained ownership of their cotton until it was sold in Liverpool, moving it along through a series of consignments and commissions, by means of "huge" syndicates they formed for the purpose of marketing their cotton.[36] Not so slaves; they were generally sold outright as they moved through each stage of the distribution chain. Slave narratives commonly mention having been sold four or five times, and ten times over a lifetime was not unheard of.

Since traders were the legal owners of the slaves they were selling, they could mistreat them any way they wanted. The law was quite clear that slaveowners' power was absolute. The 1830 opinion of North Carolina Supreme Court judge Thomas Ruffin in the *North Carolina v. Mann* case that "the power of the master must be absolute, to render the submission of the slave perfect" echoed through the South with its sexual subtext intact.[37]

A trader was assumed to enjoy a surfeit of sex slaves; it was part of the culture of the slave trade, a notoriety that contributed greatly to the general disrepute traders were held in. A number of traders remained unmarried, preferring to enjoy the sexual benefits of being in the slave trade, cohabitating with enslaved women, who were frequently "mighty near white," until they perhaps left the trade for a more respectable life.

On the evidence of their correspondence, sexual exploitation was part of the corporate culture of Franklin and Armfield. These "fancy girls" were the highest-priced slaves, the premium class of the market, consistently outpricing even prime field hands. While Franklin waited to get the best prices possible for them they belonged to the firm. Wendell Holmes Stephenson, Franklin's admiring 1939 biographer, obtusely notes that Franklin was party to a sale in Natchez in which "Chloe Ann, yellow, aged sixteen, was sold on June 30, 1821, for $700, an unusual price for that period unless the slave were a skilled laborer."[38] It was not, however, an unusual price for a light-skinned sex slave.

The archetypal fancy girl was a "quadroon"—one-quarter black, three-quarters white—or lighter. Not that black women didn't have to do sex work, but their owners commanded a lower price for it. While awaiting sale in New Orleans, they might be sent from a slave jail for a night's work in the lower class of brothel to earn the trader some money. They didn't have to travel far for that; it was no coincidence that New Orleans had both the nation's largest slave market and was the leading city for prostitution—which also meant it was pimp city,* a profession that overlapped with gambling. New Orleans may have even outsyphilized her big sister city Havana. In some areas of the town, the brothels occupied "the windows and doors of every house as far as the eyes can recognize them," according to one writer.[39] The heavier the slave trade got, the lewder New Orleans grew.

Franklin seems to have raped a number of young women who were in his power. From this we can infer that the sexual use of young women did not harm the prices paid for them, or he probably wouldn't have done it. Quite the contrary: it might have been seen as adding value as part of the enslaving process, so that the girls, officially sold as seamstresses or maids, would arrive having been broken in and be more "compliant," a word that turns up in one letter of the Ballard correspondence collection, referring to a female sex slave. Franklin had the Charlottesville "fair maid Martha . . . and our white Caroline" on sale in 1832.

Franklin and his associates used their own peculiar lingo in intra-firm correspondence. Besides the previously noted "one eyed man," they referred generically to black people by the stereotypical name of "Cuffy" (Kofi, an Akan name).[40] Franklin jokingly referred to Rice Ballard as well as to himself as an "old robber." The firm's extant correspondence contains barely coded references to the sexual use of captive women, as per Franklin's notorious letter to Ballard of January 11, 1834. Written from New Orleans as the Bank of the United States was contracting credit, Franklin began with the gloomy news that retail prices for slaves had

---

*Pimp = *mec* in French, anglicized to *mack*.

not gone up there even though the Nat Turner–inspired importation ban that had closed the New Orleans slave market to him for more than two years was on its way to being lifted. He continued with an account of his depression in the face of low prices, continual rain and snow, the bad conditions of the coming sugar crop, and his fear of a concomitant downward pressure on the next year's market as surplus sugar hands would be sold rather than new ones bought.

Then Franklin transitioned into complaining that Ballard had not sent him "the Fancy Girl from Charlottesville," whom he had previously requested but whom Ballard had detained, asking "will you send her out or shall I charge you $1100 for her[?]" His spirits seemed to perk up as he began talking about the fancy girls they were passing between themselves. "I thought that an old robber [i.e. Ballard] might be satisfyed with two or three maids." In a postscript, he began fantasizing about another kind of business operation: "The old Lady and Susan could soon pay for themselves by keeping a whore house . . . let it be kept for the benefit of the consern . . . it might be . . . established at your place Alexandria or Baltimore for the exclusive use of the cosern [sic] and . . . [its] agents."[41]

Franklin's notoriety for his sexual use of "likely" girls was such that at a hearing over his estate after his death, attorneys for the plaintiff (Franklin's brother) against the defendant (Franklin's widow) tauntingly submitted as a cross-interrogatory for two witnesses the question: "in describing the domestic comforts [of Franklin's Fairvue plantation], . . . was there, at that place, several very likely mulatto girls [?]" One witness responded, "There were at the place several likely mulatto girls; the servants that he kept about the house were all of the likeliest description, both male and female," though he hastened to add that all was above board.[42]

Andrew Jackson owned about 160 slaves by the time he was elected president— which is to say, he was wealthy, but not super-wealthy. There's no question that Jackson had been a slave trader, but, like most of the domestic slave traders of his generation, he was a relative amateur at that business. Isaac Franklin was not. Even though Jackson was president, Franklin in some ways had better market information than his fellow Tennessean.

We do not know how Franklin arrived at his decision to quit while he was ahead. Perhaps he was merely reacting fast to the increasing financial disarray that he had a close-up view of, or perhaps he was activating a long-term plan, or perhaps both. But only seven years after starting Franklin and Armfield, Franklin announced his departure from the retail slave trade, and took quick, decisive steps to exit the business. Designating a New Orleans factorage firm to handle his affairs, he unloaded parts of the business onto his partners while retaining an ownership stake. His last known slave sale in New Orleans was on April 17, 1835.[43] An advertisement of March 6, 1836, in the *Daily National Intelligencer* for the firm's packet boat line the following year lists only Armfield's name, and at the close of the slave-selling season the firm's name listed Armfield first, as per the advertisement of April 5, 1836:

> FOR NEW ORLEANS. — The last Packet this season. — The Brig UNCAS, Captain BOUSH, will sail as above about the 20th instant. Persons wishing to ship will please to make early application to
> ARMFIELD, FRANKLIN, & CO. Alexandria

An advertisement in the same paper of November 7 shows that the partners had found a one-eyed man to take the brigs off their hands:

> WASHINGTON CITY AND NEW ORLEANS PACKETS. — The subscribers having purchased of Messrs. Armfield, Franklin, & Co. two of their splendid New Orleans packets, intend running them regularly between the two ports, leaving each place on the 1st of each month.
> The brig Tribune, Captain Boush, master, will leave this place on the 1st of next month, (December.) The brig Uncas, Nathaniel Boush, master, on the 1st January.
> Those wishing to ship had better have their servants at this place a day or two previous to the vessels sailing. Servants can be kept at 25 cents per day.
> Freight and passage as heretofore.
> WM. H. WILLIAMS & CO.

It wasn't easy turning off the largest slave-trading firm in the United States. But while Franklin didn't manage to extricate himself completely from long-running business issues, he was way ahead of everybody else. With perfect timing, he cashed out just before the Panic of 1837. Franklin exited the retail slave trade at the peak of the boom and managed a substantial, though not total, escape before the crash. He had moved many of his obligations onto other shoulders by the time Jackson's Specie Circular shook American finance, and did well when others were vulnerable.

Franklin was "a man of gentlemanly address, as are many of these merchants, and not the ferocious, Captain Kidd looking fellows, we Yankees have been apt to imagine them," as Joseph Holt Ingraham described him, without being so indelicate as to mention him by name. Ingraham, then a young clergyman with literary ambitions, went on to explain that slave traders' "admission into society, however, is not recognised. Planters associate with them freely enough, in the way of business, but notice them no farther."[44] Franklin was, however, a determined social climber, and after he became very wealthy, he changed direction dramatically at the age of forty-six, transforming himself from a despised slave trader to a respectable planter with an increasing fortune. Though he had created the basics of a functional corporate structure with interregional reach that had made him very wealthy, he seems to have been thinking not in terms of building a permanent, expandable company, but of enriching himself enough to jump to the next social station. From his new platform, Franklin worked nonstop to further develop the ample resources he had acquired during his career in the slave trade.

In 1830, Franklin acquired a prime tract of land about four miles from Gallatin, Tennessee—up the Cumberland River from Nashville, in a beautiful bluegrass region where buffalo had once run. First he put up an overseer's house, then slave quarters, then a mill and gin. After that, he built the mansion of Fairvue, which he filled with perhaps ten thousand dollars' worth of furniture; then a garden, a yard, an ice-house, and a stable where he kept blooded horses. He put his slaves to work raising cotton and food crops that he could sell downriver to Nashville.

Fairvue was the grandest house in Tennessee. After Franklin's untimely death, a neighbor testified:

> [The] house and everything about it is finished in most splendid and costly style; the mantle pieces are made of the finest Irish Kilkenny marble, which cost, as I understood from Mr. Franklin himself, $500 a mantle piece. The house, in part, is covered with fine cedar shingles, which were painted before they were nailed on; the other and flat part of the roof is covered with copper sheeting. This house has attached to it a beautiful yard, finely ornamented with a variety of shrubbery and a splendid garden, that is decidedly superior to any garden I have ever seen in Tennessee; the yard, garden and horse stables are beautifully enclosed with fine brick walls;

there are two large brick barns or stables, and a great many brick negro houses, and very splendid family vault, enclosed by a superior stone wall. I am well acquainted with the improvements of the hermitage, the house of Gen. Andrew Jackson, and consider those belonging to the Fairvue estate as decidedly superior to them.[45]

"Brick negro houses" were anything but common, but Fairvue was a grand showpiece. Those houses were the public face of Isaac Franklin. He had made the transition: he was no longer a slave trader—a man who raped light-skinned teenagers for amusement and dumped corpses in the swamp—but a reputable planter and a gentleman horse breeder.

Such a fine house would surely find a mistress. According to an unsourced but not implausible story in the privately printed *The Saga of Fairvue*, when Adelicia Hayes was brought by friends to see Fairvue, she wrote in the guest book with a fortune-hunter's frankness: "I like this house and set my cap for its master."[46] She had something to offer that he badly needed: respectability. He had something she wanted: that house. She was a twenty-two-year-old Presbyterian minister's daughter, which put her almost past marriageable age, and he was a fifty-year-Old Robber who had remade himself.

It was the first marriage for both of them. The evidence of Franklin's prior career was discarded: one of Franklin's associates, William Cotton, with Ballard's help, whisked Franklin's enslaved mistress Lucinda and their child away to be sold in Louisville. In their six years of marriage, Adelicia Hayes Franklin gave birth to a son who died in infancy and three daughters, none of whom lived to adulthood.

In his new career, Franklin continued to do business in slaves, because that was what planters did. But now his commerce was on a higher level than merely retailing flesh in a stinking slave mart; he was a financier, accumulating human capital through dispossession of smaller slaveowners.

There weren't a lot of different investment opportunities available in the all-slavery South. Savings most commonly took the form of slaves, which in turn were viewed by lenders as almost risk-free collateral. Large slaveowners therefore had lots of credit, collateralized by their slaveholdings, which they resold piecemeal to smaller fry. These well-capitalized individuals, whom Kilbourne calls "accommodation endorsers," thus lent out their credit.[47] Writing mortgages heavily collateralized by the debtor's slaves, they foreclosed on the weaker members of planter society as they went down, appropriating the bankrupt estates in the process. A neighbor recalled that "I have seen [Franklin], with his family, boarding at the St. Charles [Hotel], in New Orleans; he had a very large debt uncollected, both in Mississippi and Louisiana, and was in the habit of renewing notes from year to year, and taking mortgages, &c., which required his attention a great deal in the winter season."[48]

Most mortgage lending was done privately, using banks as "amplifiers," as Kilbourne put it.[49] At deal's end, the lenders either collected their interest or took over the collateral. In the latter case, they either sold the slaves and the land, taking a profit, or kept them, realizing a capital gain and commanding still more credit.

That's how Franklin came into possession of his other signature property besides Fairvue: some forty-eight hundred acres of prime land in East Feliciana Parish, Louisiana, that had formerly belonged to an unlucky man named Francis Routh. Franklin began acquiring the property, which Routh had acquired from different owners, by purchasing a one-half interest on May 29, 1835, when Routh's finances were faltering and Franklin was transitioning out of the slave trade. The property already had three developed plantations on it, with the French, Irish, and Scottish-nostalgic names of Bellevue, Killarney, and Lock Lomond (or Lochlomond). After Routh was ruined in the Panic of 1837, Franklin purchased the other half of the estate at two sheriff's sales on December 22, 1837, and January 7, 1838.[50]

An appraisal of February 26 valued the entire property at $159,507. Almost 60 percent of that value, $94,950, resided in the 224 individually named and expertly appraised slaves of the three working plantations. An enslaved man named Thomas Jefferson was worth $350; Plato Goodwin was appraised at $600; Nelly at $400, and her child French at $150; Catherine, one year old, at $100. Only two of them—fewer than 1 percent—were worth four figures, and unlike any of the others their professions were listed alongside their names: a blacksmith named Claiborne was worth $1,000. John Theodore, a carpenter, $1,500.

There were 134 slaves at Bellevue, the best-developed of the plantations. But there were only 47 at Lock Lomond and 43 at Killarney. This density of slave labor, low for a plantation, was because much of Franklin's Louisiana land was still undeveloped. He set to work building it up.

Bellevue became Franklin's residence when he was on the plantations, which was as little as possible. Although the main dwelling-house wasn't up to the luxurious standards of Fairvue, it did have the basic comforts, including a piano. He migrated north to Fairvue annually when the "sickly season" of summer settled into Louisiana and people began to die of yellow fever and other diseases, then returned south in mid-October to develop his Louisiana properties, which entailed putting up buildings and acquiring slaves and machinery.

After giving Routh and his family some "compassion money" and evicting them from the property, Franklin began developing a fourth plantation to be "sufficient for sixty hands" on some of the estate's uncleared land.[51] He set it up as a sawmill and gristmill, feeding it the timber that grew in profusion on his plantations-to-be, and tried selling Spanish moss harvested from the trees. He gave his newly developed Louisiana plantation a curious name:

Angola.

Wake Up Rich

INCENDIARY TRACTS AND PAPERS.—*The Mail brought by the Steam Packet Columbia, arrived this morning, has come not merely laden, but literally overburthened, with the Newspaper called "The Emancipator" and two Tracts entitled "The Anti-Slavery Record," and "The Slave's Friend," destined for circulation all over the Southern and Western Country. . . . If the General Post Office is not at liberty to act in this matter, it is impossible to answer for the security of the Mail in this part of the country, which contains such poisonous and inflammatory matter.*

—*Southern Patriot*, Charleston, July 29, 1835

EVEN TO SPEAK OF slavery, much less to criticize it, was likely to "excite the affections" of Southern congressmen.

The South erected an informational firewall so that its alternate reality could not be disturbed. The censorship of mail in the South was general; ideologically suspect literature was routinely confiscated. People in the South could rely only on Southern sources to tell them of the supposed horrors that the abolitionists were planning for them.

District attorney Francis Scott Key ran Benjamin Lundy out of Washington City in 1833 for having printed an article in the *Genius of Universal Emancipation* that said, "There is neither mercy nor justice for colored people in this district [of Columbia]." More than half the black people in Washington were free, and Key, one of the most prominent deportationists, was still district attorney in Washington two years later, in August 1835, when a white mob ran riot for two nights and destroyed black schools, churches, and homes.

A sensational pamphlet that described a plan for a Christmas Day slave uprising throughout the South created a panic in central Mississippi during the hot summer of 1835. It was widely believed that a criminal named John Murrell had a huge gang and planned to incite a massive slave rebellion to facilitate plundering the towns. Murrell, a murderous highwayman and notorious kidnapper of slaves, was serving ten years in the Tennessee State Penitentiary at the time for "negro-stealing," but that didn't stop the rumors. "Many Mississippians were led to believe that the state was indeed threatened with the fate of Santo Domingo," writes Edwin Arthur Miles.[1] In fact, there was no uprising, and no white people were killed by black people, but respected citizens formed extralegal vigilante groups that extracted confessions and lynched a dozen white men, five of them gamblers, and an unknown number of black people.[2] Similar groups hunted gamblers and other transients in towns and settlements up the Mississippi and the Ohio Rivers.

Eighteen thirty-five was the summer of abolition propaganda, when a mail campaign by the American Anti-Slavery Society sent tens of thousands of Garrison-published pamphlets down south via the postal system. "They have raised funds to support and circulate inflammatory newspapers and pamphlets gratuitously," wrote John Quincy Adams, "and they send multitudes of them into the southern country in the midst of swarms of slaves, which is causing great excitement and fermentation in all parts of the Union."[3]

Many Southern newspapers carried alarmed reports of the arrival of sheaves of abolitionist literature at the local post office. Charleston postmaster Alfred Huger wrote to his counterpart in the New York post office that

> the most respectable men of all parties gather'd about our doors and windows, and in a little time I was formally summoned to give up the "incendiary publications" which were known to be in my possession, and at the same [time] told with very little ceremony, that they would be taken from me, if I did not . . . I could only resolve that when the mail became the object of attack, I would make it the object of defence; but seeing plainly the excitement and exasperation which were every Moment increasing, I came to the determination to Separate the obnoxious papers, from the rest of the Mail, not doubting that otherwise, the whole might be destroy'd between the Office and the Rail-Road.[4]

Postmaster and key Jackson adviser Amos Kendall approved. In a letter to Huger that was published in various newspapers, he wrote, "We owe an obligation to the laws, but a higher one to the communities in which we live, and if the former be perverted to destroy the latter, it is patriotism to disregard them."[5]

Francis Scott Key would not be outdone in rooting out terrorism. "Are you willing, gentlemen, to abandon your country; to permit it to be taken from you, and occupied by the Abolitionist, according to whose taste it is to associate and amalgamate with the Negro?" he shouted in 1836.[6] It was part of his sensational prosecution of the young doctor Reuben Crandall for having possessed a trunkful of copies of *The Liberator* and *The Anti-Slavery Reporter* in his home in Georgetown. Key kept Crandall in jail for months, and though Crandall was found not guilty, he contracted tuberculosis in prison and died two years later. Key remained district attorney until the Whigs moved into the White House in 1841, using his position to suppress abolitionism wherever he found it.

Nor was the hostility only in slavery territory. In Boston, William Lloyd Garrison was nearly lynched after being captured by a mob that came to attack a meeting of the Boston Female Anti-Slavery Society. Abolitionist meetings were broken up by mobs in New York, where there was much Southern sympathy.

Meanwhile, traders continued trafficking young African Americans southward. On his first trip South in 1835, William Henry Seward saw a disturbing sight in Virginia, as summarized by his brother and biographer, Fredrick W. Seward:

> A cloud of dust was seen slowly coming down the road, from which proceeded a confused noise of moaning, weeping, and shouting. Presently reaching the gate of the stable-yard, it disclosed itself. Ten naked little boys, between six and twelve years old, tied together, two and two, by their wrists, were all fastened to a long rope, and followed by a tall, gaunt white man, who, with his long lash, whipped up the sad and weary little procession, drove it to the horse-trough to drink, and thence to a shed, where they lay down on the ground and sobbed and moaned themselves to sleep. These were children gathered up at different plantations by the "trader," and were to be driven down to Richmond to be sold at auction, and taken South.[7]

In New Hampshire, the young Jacksonian Franklin Pierce, a protégé of Levi Woodbury, was appalled at the formation of an Anti-Slavery Society in his home state in 1835. He wrote to a friend, "One thing must be perfectly apparent to every intelligent man. This abolition movement must be crushed or there is an end to the Union."[8]

James Madison died in 1835, leaving the legal ownership of his slaves to his wife Dolley. His writings bear witness that he had repeatedly agonized about the wrongness of slavery, though not as much as his slaves must have agonized about it. Madison did not leave Dolley in good financial condition, and the Panic of 1837 exacerbated her problems. It was a typical Southern widow's situation: Dolley Madison's slaves were her nest egg, and despite language in Madison's will forbidding her to sell them without their consent, she sold them off to pay her ne'er-do-well son's debts. Montpelier itself was sold to a Richmond merchant in 1844.

Along with the explosion of abolitionist propaganda in the 1830s came a new kind of argument, one championed by an emerging generation of free black abolitionists, that focused on the degradation forced on the enslaved. Frederick Douglass expressed it in his Fourth of July speech of 1852 in Rochester, New York: "The feeling of the nation must be quickened; the conscience of the nation must be roused; the propriety of the nation must be startled; the hypocrisy of the nation must be exposed; and its crimes against God and man must be denounced."[9]

Douglass was so radical that he called for full political rights for women. A nascent American women's-rights movement drew energy from women's activity in the antislavery movement, their largest participation in American politics up to that time. Often denied membership in men's political organizations, and without the right to vote, they formed "ladies'" political clubs, collecting signatures for the petitions that John Quincy Adams lay on the table by the hundreds in the House of Representatives.

The coffles marching through the nation's capital became the number-one target of the antislavery movement. The District of Columbia was Congress's responsibility, so grassroots organizations—local clubs—flooded both houses of Congress with petitions to close the slave trade in the federal capital. The term "slave-breeding" became a part of the antislavery polemic, the interstate slave trade the visible symbol of slavery.

In response to John Quincy Adams's continued presentation of abolition petitions, Speaker of the House James K. Polk in 1836 cut him off with the "gag rule" requiring that nothing relating to the subject of slavery could be introduced or discussed. The gag rule, which was reinstated every year with ever more restrictive language until 1844, became a cause célèbre for the antislavery movement. Adams, outraged, focused on breaking it, exposing himself to censure for receiving and submitting petitions. The more petitions he laid on the table, the more came in. By the 1837–38 term, there were 130,200 petitions calling for the end of slavery in the District of Columbia. Others called for abolition nationally, for abolishing the interstate slave trade, for lifting the gag rule, against the annexation of Texas, against dueling, and, during the winter of 1838–39, more than two hundred petitions for the recognition of Haiti, which was a busy trading partner of US merchants while officially remaining a pariah country.[10]

The arrival of master-race Jacksonian Democracy, the eruption of abolitionism as a movement, and the radicalization of the nullification movement combined to make a new, unapologetic attitude toward slavery that was felt especially along the southwestern frontier. In Mississippi, which had grown from twenty-six counties in 1832 to fifty-five in 1836 as former Choctaw and Chickasaw lands became occupied, Seargent S. Prentiss, newly elected to the Mississippi House of Representatives in 1836, introduced a resolution that the people of the state "look upon the institution of slavery, as it exists among them, not as a curse, but as a blessing, as the legitimate condition of the African race . . . and that they hope to transmit this institution to their posterity, as the best part of their inheritance . . . we will allow no present change, or hope of future alteration in this matter."[11]

In the decade between 1830 and 1840, as the plantation system exploded into the newly available lands, Mississippi's free population increased by a factor of 2.54 to 180,440 (free people of color were only 1,366 of them), but the enslaved population almost tripled, to 195,211.[12] Mississippi now had a black majority.

In Mississippi, as in Carolina, there was no doubt, at least among the slaveholders: God himself was pro-slavery.

"I am a nullifier!" shouted South Carolina's Robert Barnwell Rhett in 1837, in his first major speech as a congressman.

Having unsurprisingly outed himself as a Calhounian with that declaration, Rhett's speech pivoted into another kind of discourse as he unwound into over-the-top hyperbole. Rhett, who had no military experience, romanticized war and even annihilation in the service of the glorious cause of state sovereignty over the federal government, which in the case of South Carolina was to say, in the service of slavery. As he extolled martyrdom, which he had no intention of personally experiencing, he gave the House its sharpest taste yet of the belligerent, self-apotheosizing oratory of the new generation.

After shouting chains of rhetorical questions, Rhett spoke defiantly of the resistance that, he insisted, would have met Jackson had Jackson invaded South Carolina during the nullification crisis:

> Had South Carolina been invaded, upon the first gleam of the bayonet along our mountain passes, he would have seen and known what the chivalry of the South really was, not in bloodless tropes and metaphors, but in the stern realities of the tented field. Not only Carolinians, but thousands of volunteers from the whole South, whose names are upon the file, would have met you in that fierce contest [etc. etc.] . . . We knew the mighty inheritance for which we were to contend—that soil over which, for two centuries, we had been the lords; and those altars at which our fathers knelt and we had received our brides. We won it by the sword, and we were prepared to keep it by the sword.

Rhett had taken his political stage name just before running for office. Following a fashion in South Carolina to rename one's self after one's most illustrious ancestors, Robert Barnwell Smith and all his brothers changed their common laborer's last name to the more romantic-sounding Rhett. It was a Gaelic-style spelling of the name of a matrilineal ancestor, a Dutchman named Raedt, whose claim to fame was having captured Stede Bonnet, Charleston's only pirate of note.[13]

Margaret Mitchell took two of the Lowcountry's best-known pro-slavery political names for her fictional character of Rhett Butler in *Gone With the Wind*, but Robert Barnwell Rhett was no Clark Gable. Balding on top by his thirties, he tried to disguise it with a comb-over, his red face framed by a high-top starched collar. There is little favorable commentary about him. He was ambitious, arrogant, belligerent, and an implacable foe with a martyr complex who attacked no one as ferociously as those who almost agreed with him. His biographer William C. Davis speculates that there might have been favorable commentary about him in documents that were destroyed when Charleston fell, and concedes that "it is something of a struggle to present a balanced portrait of the man, especially since out of his own mouth he so often offends."[14] Rhett was self-righteous, utterly convinced of the rightness of slavery, and careless with the truth. To that we could add, again quoting Davis, "the inability to follow others and compulsion to enforce his own will, his unwillingness or inability to countenance any ideas but his own, and his constant scheming."[15] He was aggressively religious, having had a kind of born-again experience, while remaining within the Episcopal fold.

Rhett's view of history was decidedly odd and self-serving, believing as he did that Charles Pinckney, and not Madison, was the real father of the Constitution. One might be forgiven for thinking Rhett barking mad, but that is an insufficient explanation for the phenomenon he presented. He was arguably the single most influential individual in pushing the South to secession; he referred to himself as a "lucifer," a matchstick that lit the blaze.[16] Rhett had been a force in the nullification movement, and played an active if complicated role in Calhoun's increasing radicalization. Under his former name of Robert Barnwell Smith, he had for years been pushing Calhoun to the right from his position in the South Carolina General Assembly, a powerful body that chose the state's governor, senators, and representatives.

Rhett was from Beaufort, the wealthy town by the site of the former Huguenot settlement of Charlesfort and the Spanish Santa Elena, in the heart of the region that produced long-staple, or Sea Island, cotton. At Beaufort College in South Carolina the aristocratic young planters flatly rejected the notion of the Age of Reason, and believed fully in the natural right of the oligarchy.[17] Beaufort was Ground Zero of secessionism; the "secession house" in that town, owned in the 1850s by brother Edmund Rhett, was a central meeting place for the secession apostles who became known as the Fire-Eaters.

By the time Rhett arrived in Congress, he had not merely declared (in 1829), that "I am a Disunionist! I am a Traitor!" In the wake of the Force Act, he proposed what might lie beyond secession: a confederacy. He was the prophet of an independent slave nation, commanded from South Carolina. In what was perhaps a veiled dig at the most famous Jacksonian poet, Rhett declaimed at the States Rights and Free Trade Party convention of 1833 that "The star-spangled banner no longer waves in triumph and glory for me. Sir, if a Confederacy of the Southern States could now be obtained, should we not deem it a happy termination—happy beyond expectation, of our long struggle for our rights against oppression?"[18]

Rhett and his clan built the most powerful political clique in Charleston. Any serious politician needed a newspaper, and Rhett's brother-in-law John A. Stuart owned the *Charleston Mercury*, the most radical paper in the South. The family also came to control the *Columbia South Carolinian* in the state's capital. There were Rhett brothers in the state legislature, and they had control of the Bank of South Carolina.

Ironically, Rhett was a distant cousin of John Quincy Adams. When they were much younger, the two had met in private life. Describing Rhett's congressional speech, Adams drily noted his recent name change: "Robert Barnwell Rhett (Smith heretofore) moved a long amendment, and literally howled a nullification speech. I say howled, for his enunciation was so rapid, inarticulate, and vociferous that his head hung back as he spoke, with his face upward, like that of a howling dog."[19]

In an 1838 speech before Congress, Rhett explained his economic theory of the superiority of slavery: according to him, slaves were better off than free laborers, because they were both capital and labor, and self-interest would mandate their better treatment. In the midst of his lengthy lecture in political economy, he said, "there is but one state of society in the world, where labor and capital are identical in interest; and that is where domestic slavery exists . . . Labor, there, is capital, and capital is labor."[20]

According to Rhett, that was what South Carolina was fighting for, with God's full approval: for labor to be capital.

Of course, that meant there had to be a capital market. Rhett owned over a hundred slaves, whom he had bought pursuant to a promise not to sell them off. But his obsession was political power, and like many other slaveowning politicians, he was inattentive to his business as a planter, so he sold thirty-six people away to traders to cover his losses.

SALE OF SLAVES. — I will sell at public auction, on Monday, the 23d October, at 4 o'clock P.M. at the auction room of Edward Dyer, in Washington City, D.C. the following slaves, purchased by me upon the 22d of August last, from Rezin Orme, and who were warranted sound in bodies and in mind, to wit, Dorcas Allen, and her two surviving children, aged about seven and nine years, (the other two having been killed by said Dorcas in a fit of insanity, as found by the jury who lately acquitted her.)

Terms of sale cash, as said slaves will be sold on account of said Rezin Orme, who refuses to retake the same and repay the purchase money, and who is notified to attend said sale, and if he thinks proper to bid for them, or retake them, as he prefers, upon refunding the money paid, and all expenses incurred under the warranty given by him.

JAMES BIRCH

EDWARD DYER,

Auctioneer.

Four years before John Quincy Adams delivered the winning argument in the well-known *Amistad* case, he went up against District of Columbia slave trader James Birch, with less successful results. A diary entry of October 23, 1837, notes that:

There was in the National Intelligencer this morning an advertisement signed James H. Birch, and Edward Dyer, auctioneer, headed "Sale of Slaves"—a sale at public auction, at four o'clock this afternoon, of Dorcas Allen and her two surviving children, aged about seven and nine years (the other two having been killed by said Dorcas in a fit of insanity, as found by the jury who lately acquitted her). The advertisement further says that the said slaves were purchased by Birch, on the 22d of August last . . .

I asked Mr. Frye what this advertisement meant. He seemed not to like to speak of it, but said the woman had been sold with her children, to be sent to the South and separated from her husband; that she had killed two of her children, by cutting their throats, and cut her own to kill herself, but in that had failed; that she had been tried at Alexandria for the murder of her children, and acquitted on the ground of insanity; and that this sale now was by the purchaser at the expense of the seller, upon the warranty that she was sound in body and mind.[21]

Adams visited the slave jail and spoke to Dyer, letting the traders know someone in Congress was watching:

I learnt from Dyer that the woman had been the slave of a white woman who had married a man named Davis, who lived at Georgetown and was a clerk in the War Department; that this white woman had died, and had before her death promised Dorcas her freedom; that on her death-bed she had made her husband (Davis) promise her that he would emancipate Dorcas; that he did actually liberate her, but gave her no papers;

that she lived twelve or fifteen years at large, married, and had four children; that in the mean time Davis married a second wife [Maria], and afterwards died, without granting to Dorcas her papers of freedom; that Davis's widow [Maria] married a man by the name of Rezin Orme, and that he sold Dorcas and her four children, on the 22d of August last, for seven hundred dollars, to Birch, who is an agent for the negro slave-traders at Alexandria; that Dorcas and her four children were on the same day removed to one of the slave-prisons in Alexandria; that in the night of that day she killed the two youngest of her children—one, a boy four years of age, and the other, a girl under twelve months; that she attempted to kill the other two, but was prevented— their screaming having roused some person in the house, who went into the cell where she was confined and took her surviving children from her; that she was tried at Alexandria for the murder of her two children, and was acquitted by the jury on the ground of insanity.

Adams discussed the case with district attorney Francis Scott Key, who "appeared to interest himself," Adams thought, in the plight of Allen's desperate free black husband, and proposed a fund to purchase her freedom, to which Adams contributed fifty dollars. But, Adams wrote dejectedly on November 2, "if their freedom from Birch's sale should be purchased, they might still be reclaimed by Davis's creditors."[22] Eight days later, he wrote: "Upon conversing with [Mr. Key], I found he would give no assurance that Dorcas Allen and her children will be free if they should be purchased from Birch. By the law of the place, they are assets of the estate of Gideon Davis, upon which there never has been any administration; neither his widow nor her second husband . . . had any right to sell them."[23]

What ultimately happened is left a cliff-hanger in Adams's diary, but Key doesn't seem to have come through for Dorcas Allen. By November 13, she was with her husband, and her two children were back in Birch's jail. "Mr. Key told me," Adams wrote, "that if upon a writ of habeas corpus Birch's title should be disproved, still they were slaves; they could not be discharged."[24]

In his diary, Adams routinely referred to his Southern congressional opponents as "the slavers" and to their Northern supporters as "the serviles." On December 22, 1837, he recounted "banter" with Ratliff Boon of Indiana, who, recounts Adams, "said that if the question ever came to the issue of war, the Southern people would march into New England and conquer it. I said I had no doubt they would if they could, and that it was what they were now struggling for with all their might."[25]

The land-value bubble burst, but it was worse than that.

In a feat of election-year politicking, Congress passed, and Jackson signed, the Whig-sponsored Deposit Act, which directed that most of the federal government's surplus achieved from approximately $35 million in land sales be distributed beginning in January 1837 to the states in proportion to their number of electoral votes, a formula proposed by Calhoun.

Unfortunately for Mississippi, the state was only entitled to receive about a half million dollars in the distribution, but its deposit banks had ten million dollars' worth of revenues from land sales in the region and therefore were going to have to send away 95 percent of their capital.

Meanwhile, there was an explosion of commercial banking in which new institutions were chartered as if broadcasting seed, with no oversight. Florida banking operations of that time were satirized years later by Ellen Call Long, the daughter of Florida's governor during that era (former Jackson aide Richard K. Call, who had prosecuted the Seminole War):

> You want to know how it operates? Well, you see a man can mortgage his land or negroes; draw from the bank two-thirds (in money) of their value, which will be re-invested in more land and more negroes. One or two crops of cotton will redeem all obligation to the bank; so you see that it is the best thing afloat; a man can just go to sleep, and wake up rich.[26]

The riches obtained from this kind of maneuver, needless to say, were not in the form of gold pieces, but "negroes," who remained as capital in the planter's possession when the cotton was sold and who could always be used to collateralize a loan.

After Jackson promoted the obliging Roger B. Taney to chief justice of the Supreme Court, he named Secretary of the Navy Levi Woodbury to be his fourth secretary of the treasury. As speculators bought public land with increasingly questionable paper, Woodbury on July 11, 1836, issued the document that snapped the overextended banking system: the Specie Circular. Taking effect August 15, it announced an abrupt shift to hard money on the part of the government, which would henceforth require payment for public lands in specie.

The plan, apparently, was to remove all notes from circulation under $20 (a little more than $500 in 2014 dollars) and replace them with coins, with paper money being reserved for larger transactions. To make these coins a series of new mints was built, including the US Mint in New Orleans, one of the city's enduring landmarks.

This move created a demand for coin that sucked specie reserves out of eastern banks. As paper money spiraled toward worthless and banks suspended specie payments, silver and gold pieces were physically repositioned among the states. Biddle wrote in an unsigned piece in 1839 that "the monetary affairs of the whole country were convulsed—millions upon millions of coin were *in transitu* in every direction, and consequently withdrawn from useful employment. Specie was going up and down the same river, to and from the South and North and the East and West at the same time; millions were withdrawn from their usual and natural channels, and forced against the current of trade."[27]

The term that was used to describe the westward movement of specie was the same used for the westward movement of Native Americans: removal. The Specie Circular was not the only thing that brought down the American economy, but it was Jackson's crowning achievement to that end.

As Jackson was preparing to leave office, still riding a national wave of adulation, he warned, according to his biographer Parton, that a "paper money system and its natural associates, monopoly and exclusive privileges, have already struck their roots deep in the soil, and it will require all your efforts to check its further growth and to eradicate the evil."[28]

Paper money was . . . *evil*. No moral relativism: evil. Only gold and silver were good.

Fast-growing New Orleans had broken into three pieces. The French speakers (in the downtown "French Quarter") and the uptown Anglophone businessmen had long been at loggerheads, physically separated by Canal Street, which was a filthy, muddy, no-man's-land, or, as they say in New Orleans, "neutral ground."

Though immigrants generally did not come to the South, they did come to New Orleans, the second largest destination for them after New York. They encountered a vicious nativist movement; one New Orleans newspaper was called the *True American*.

The uptown Anglo-Americans in fast-growing New Orleans in effect seceded from the city (though historians have generally refrained from using that term in speaking about it) on March 8, 1836, separating themselves off from their French-speaking counterparts, whom they saw as receiving an excessive share of the public purse. The city split into three municipalities, each in charge of its own revenues.

The First Municipality, French-speaking and Catholic, was the old town below Canal Street (the French Quarter). The Second, English-speaking and Protestant, was the Faubourg St. Mary, uptown above Canal Street (today's Central Business District). The Third, French-speaking and Catholic (and unpaved and unlighted), was the Faubourg Marigny, downriver from the First below Esplanade. These municipalities, which were more or less antagonistic, each had their own police force, complete with hostilities between the respective departments, whose primary duty was slave patrol. Each municipality built its own levees and administered its own infrastructure.

The Anglo-Americans of the Second Municipality intended to corner railroad commerce. A proposed railroad, the New Orleans and Nashville, planned to link the major trade terminus of Tennessee with Carrollton, a suburb of New Orleans named for railroad hero Charles Carroll of Carrollton, who had died in 1832 at the age of ninety-five. "There is very little doubt," hummed an 1835 editorial in the *New Orleans Bee*, "of the New Orleans and Nashville railroad being completed in 3 or 4 years."[29]

The local spur line to Carrollton was built entirely within the Anglo-controlled part of town. In seceding from New Orleans, the Anglo-American Second Municipality made off with that new railroad link, which began operations on September 22, 1835. But the Nashville railroad was never built; the only part ever completed was the local link, from present-day Lee Circle to Carrollton. Though it never became a freight corridor connected to a mighty railroad, the link became instead the anchor of uptown New Orleans development. Carrying passengers (it even had a ladies' car), it made the far-flung Carrollton Hotel a chic place for downtowners to repair to for supper and encouraged the development of the territory in between. The space between New Orleans and Carrollton filled in alongside the train, whose track became the extension of the former stub street of St. Charles. The rail line became public transport through what became known as the Garden District, and is today the main streetcar line that connects downtown with uptown. The New Orleans streetcar line was thus approximately tied with New York (the Long Island Rail Road) as the first in the US to connect city with suburb by rail.

But the failure to connect to the national rail network betokened the beginning of New Orleans's long decline. Meanwhile, the breakup of the city left the English speakers without the year's biggest fun. Mardi Gras was a French thing, done at that time in New Orleans more or less on the Parisian model. The pre-Lenten carnival season was celebrated with masked balls galore in the French Quarter, the masks being the main difference between carnival balls and the year-round schedule of dances.

The first organized Mardi Gras parade that we know of in New Orleans took place in 1837, less than a month before the inauguration in Washington of President Martin Van Buren, which was only six weeks before the New Orleans *True American* published its sensational reportage on the failure of Hermann, Briggs, and Co.

Headed by America's most famous war hero, with Martin Van Buren, Amos Kendall, James K. Polk, Sam Houston, John Tyler, James Buchanan, and the young Franklin Pierce; Taney and Woodward on the Supreme Court; and Francis Scott Key as the capital's district attorney, the Jackson dynasty was the most powerful political force the United States had seen.

Van Buren's election was to be its consolidation. Matty Van, or the "little magician" (for his short stature and political cunning), the "red fox" (for his hair), "O.K." (Old Kinderhook, for his New York home town), or the "wily Dutchman" of the "Albany Regency," as one of Polk's correspondents unflatteringly put it, was the first president born after independence, the first presidential candidate to campaign openly, and the first professional politician to become president.[30]

But the chickens came home to roost on his head. Six weeks after Van Buren was inaugurated on March 4, 1837, his one-term presidency was wracked by economic convulsions as banks began suspending specie payments.

The winds of global trade had shifted again. The British financiers most heavily exposed to American debtors were insolvent; the Bank of England, which had its own problems, constricted credit. The invention of the telegraph was still seven years away, and steamships did not yet ply the Atlantic: the Panic of 1837 was in part a crisis of slow-moving financial information.

The panic seems to have begun in New Orleans when the cotton factorage firm Hermann, Briggs, & Co. failed. Perhaps because its proprietor Louis Florian Hermann was a German Jew, the New Orleans *True American* printed a sensational story about it that traveled far and wide, spreading the worry. Then J. L. & S. Joseph & Co., a New York firm that was Hermann, Briggs's creditor, failed too. Meanwhile, the price of cotton plunged in Liverpool to "a staggering fifty percent of what the cotton brokers had extended to the planters," writes Jessica M. Lepler. There was not yet class solidarity among bankers, so the directors of New Orleans's sixteen (!) banks did not take concerted action or even, apparently, talk to each other as the crisis accelerated. They all suspended specie payments in April, then the failure spread to New York on May 8.[31]

The 1840 census showed New Orleans as the nation's third largest city, with 102,193 residents, effectively tied with Baltimore's 102,313 for second place. New Orleans, the number-one port in the United States, was unlike the rest of the South in many ways. It was urban. It had a substantial business community and a local economy dominated by factors; a waterfront that shipped the world's greatest quantities of cotton and much sugar; and, since the plantations of Louisiana and Mississippi required enormous amounts of credit, it had a large banking sector, heavily capitalized by captive human beings.

But though the port's overall receipts continued to grow, the panic was the end of New Orleans's peak period of national influence, and its share of the nation's expanding commerce grew progressively smaller. In particular, New Orleans failed to get in on rail transport, the competition from which was cutting into the river trade more every year. The Mississippi River had formerly been the only way for a wide swath of the United States to get its goods to market. But as railroads slowly extended their reach—slowly, because laying a railroad was a big operation that required solid financing—the rivers would matter less. New Orleans continued growing, but it would never again be tied for second largest city in the nation.

New Orleans was, however, the largest slave market in the United States. At least half if not more of its sales, and probably most of its high-value deals, were conducted by private sale out of dealer showrooms. Some of the buildings are still there, though the spectacular main auction venues are long gone. Some dealers made slaves stand out on the sidewalk from nine to four, trying to entice buyers. The horrors of slave auctioning have been amply detailed elsewhere, and we will not describe these wrenching scenes here, citing as merely one example the testimony of the formerly enslaved Stephen Jordon, many years after he was sold in New Orleans:

> I tell you, people were miserable in that old slave-pen. They used to make them open their mouths so that they could examine their teeth; and they used to strip them naked, from head to foot, to see whether they were perfectly sound. And this they did to women as well as men. I tell you, my dear child, it used to seem to me so brutal to see poor women treated in that way by brutal and heartless men. I declare, child, I can't understand it, although I've been right in it. When they would put them naked that way they used to switch them on the legs to make them jump around so that buyers could see how supple they were.[32]

Dealers generally got better prices at private sale than at auction, but not necessarily. Auctions in New Orleans, typically conducted bilingually in French and English, were conducted to turn over large numbers of people as quickly as possible. It was a fast way to get rid of less desirable slaves or, on the other end of the profit scale, to maximize the value of a white-looking beauty or a first-rate cabinetmaker.

The New Orleans market sent large numbers of young men to the sugar plantations, which always wanted fresh victims, so the gender ratio of people sold in New Orleans skewed disproportionately toward males. But with so many wealthy people in the city, New Orleans also served the nation's largest market for domestic servants and skilled artisans, and it was the number-one retail market for fancy girls, with either Natchez or the horse-racing and gambling center of Lexington, Kentucky, perhaps a distant second in that category.

With so much money flowing through town, it was a great moment for architecture, not all of which survives. The St. Louis Hotel, which ran the length of the block from Royal to Chartres on St. Louis Street, is long gone. Frederic Bancroft visited its abandoned shell in 1902 and wrote of the "blaze of light" from the dome that illuminated the floor where slaves were sold daily.[33] With its front entrance on St. Louis Street, the British visitor J. S. Buckingham described it in 1839:

> The entrance into the Exchange at the St. Louis, is through a handsome vestibule, or hall, of 127 feet by 40, which leads to the Rotunda. This is crowned by a beautiful and lofty dome, with a finely ornamented ceiling in the interior, and a variegated marble pavement. . . . in the Rotunda, pictures are exhibited, and auctions are held for every description of good.

At the time of our visit, there were half a dozen auctioneers, each endeavouring to drown every voice but his own, and all straining their lungs and distorting their countenances in a hideous manner. One was selling pictures, and dwelling on their merits; another was disposing of ground-lots in embryo cities, and expatiating on their capacities; and another was disposing of some slaves.

These consisted of an unhappy negro family, who were all exposed to the hammer at the same time. Their good qualities were enumerated in English and in French, and their persons were carefully examined by intending purchasers, among whom they were ultimately disposed of, chiefly to Créole buyers; the husband at 750 dollars, the wife at 550, and the children at 220 each.

The middle of the Rotunda was filled with casks, boxes, bales, and crates; and the negroes exposed for sale were put to stand on these, to be the better seen by persons attending the sale. Often as I had witnessed this painful scene in the old times of the West Indies, and in several of the countries of the East, it had lost none of its pain by repetition; it appeared, indeed, more revolting here, in contrast with the republican institutions of America.[34]

The St. Louis was far from the only auction venue. Banks' Arcade, an enormous building that ran from Gravier to Natchez Street on Magazine, hosted them. (A small part of Bank's Arcade still stands, as do a number of now repurposed former slave dealer showrooms in New Orleans.) It was at Banks' on October 15, 1835, that a meeting of the "friends of Texas" promised financial and military support to the Anglo-American provisional "government" in Texas, in blatant violation of US neutrality laws.[35]

Mexico after its independence in 1821 prohibited slavery, but the territory was only sparsely settled; hoping to populate it, the Mexican government invited in settlers from the United States, giving them land. But once the settlers moved in, they declared it theirs. Moses Austin, who had become one of the country's major producers of lead, was a major promoter of the Texas colonization movement. With his eyes on Mexico's lead mines, Austin had sworn allegiance to the Spanish crown in 1798. His son, the Virginia-born, Missouri-raised land speculator Stephen F. Austin, brought slavery to Texas and fought to keep it.

It was an article of faith throughout the South that American slavery must expand into Texas and beyond. There was no question that Texas would be an ultimate destination for young African Americans who were being born and raised all over the cotton kingdom. Stephen Austin wrote his sister Emily from New Orleans in August 1835, the summer of the Southern abolition panic: "It is very evident that Texas should be effectually, and fully, Americanized . . . Texas must be a slave country. It is no longer a matter of doubt. The interest of Louisiana requires that it should be. A population of fanatical abolitionists in Texas would have a very dangerous and pernicious influence on the overgrown slave population of [Louisiana]."[36]

Andrew Jackson had mentored Sam Houston, the Scotch-Irish-descended, Virginia-born, Tennessee-raised land speculator, politician, and military leader. Houston had served under Jackson in the Creek War, and had been the Jacksonian governor of Tennessee, before fleeing to Texas to escape a disastrous marriage. He was one of fifty-nine signers of the Texas Declaration of Independence on March 2, 1836, four days before the massacre at the Alamo. As a general in the Texas army, he was the hero of the decisive Battle of San Jacinto that took Mexican general Antonio López de Santa Anna prisoner. On October 22, Jackson's protégé became the first president of the Republic of Texas.

There was much opposition in the North to annexing Texas, because it meant the expansion of US slavery. With Jackson's anointed successor Van Buren fighting hard to be elected president, annexation was too politically controversial and would provoke a sectional controversy instead of strengthening the national party the Democrats had built. James Hamilton of South Carolina printed a report in the *Telegraph*, a Jacksonian organ that presented "the Texans as a people struggling for their liberty, and therefore entitled to our sympathy," as John Quincy Adams disgustedly wrote in his diary. He continued: "The fact is directly the reverse—they are fighting for the establishment and perpetuation of slavery, and that is the cause of the South Carolinian sympathy with them."[37]

But for all his involvement in the Texas project, Jackson didn't annex the territory. Instead, one of his last acts as president was to recognize the independent Republic of Texas. Houston tendered an annexation offer, but John Quincy Adams stalled the annexation of Texas in Congress. Houston took it off the table in 1839, with the result that Texas and the United States dealt with each other for about ten years as independent nations.

Meanwhile, two real estate speculators from New York who intended to develop a town obtained permission to use Sam Houston's name. Incorporated on June 5, 1837, the town of Houston—a city named for the sitting president—served as the capital of the Republic of Texas until the capital was moved to

Austin in 1839. That year, the Texas Congress adopted the Lone Star banner, representing the territory's readiness to go it alone, as the national flag. It subsequently became, and remains, the state flag of Texas.

It sounds impressive: the Mississippi and Alabama Railroad Company. More familiarly known as the Brandon Bank, it was chartered in Brandon, Mississippi, in 1836—supposedly to build a railroad, but it never even tried. In 1837, with most of the state's plantation land already mortgaged, the Brandon Bank began making cash advances on cotton crops, paying $0.12 per expected pound. Unfortunately, by July 1838, the price for cotton was down to $0.083 a pound, and moreover, many farmers delivered no cotton to the bank at all. By the fall of that year, the bank's money was circulating in Jackson at 30 to 40 percent off face value.[38]

The sell-off of the public lands continued; John Quincy Adams wrote in his diary in June 1838 that "the thirst of a tiger for blood is the fittest emblem of the rapacity with which the members [of Congress] of all the new States fly at the public lands. The constituents upon whom they depend are all settlers, or tame and careless spectators of the pillage. They are themselves enormous speculators and land-jobbers."[39] The nation's economy seemed to recover in 1838, as banks warily resumed specie payments, but it didn't last. The US government was broke, and couldn't make the final payment on the redistribution of the long-gone surplus.

Three Mississippi bank commissioners traveled to Philadelphia, where they sold Nicholas Biddle $5 million in Mississippi bonds. Biddle sent the bonds on to London, where "the United States Banks' London agency sold $2 million of them to European investors and transferred the remaining $3 million to London and Amsterdam bankers as collateral security."[40] They wound up in the hands of the Rothschilds, the Baring Brothers, and others who knew quite well that they were purchasing shares in slaves.[41] James T. MacIntosh writes that "when the specie resulting from the sale of the bonds finally reached Mississippi, people celebrated in the belief that their financial woes were at an end."[42] Edwin Arthur Miles writes that the entire population "regarded those five millions as an especial Godsend . . . Wagon after wagon was seen conveying a portion of those five million in hard dollars to the vaults of the bank."[43] With that money in hand, loans were made supporting cotton production—which was to say, purchasing the bodies of young African Americans, trafficked from more settled regions of the country.

Several other states also indebted themselves wildly in the British and other capital markets. "In a very short period," writes Alasdair Roberts, "American states had accumulated obligations roughly equal to the combined national debt of Russia, Prussia, and the Netherlands."[44] Then, prompted by a bad wheat harvest in England that made Britain a food importer, the price of cotton in Liverpool crashed again in April 1839. Prices of slaves, so fundamental to the Southern economy, took a precipitous tumble—the only major slide in the dollar value of slaves during the antebellum decades. As mortgages crashed and liquidation sales put thousands of enslaved laborers for sale in a depressed market, the interstate slave trade slowed down. In Mississippi, the Union Bank lasted less than two years from its creation before its charter was withdrawn by Governor Alexander G. McNutt on July 10, 1840. By 1841, both of the Mississippi state banks had suspended interest payments on their $7 million worth of bonds. Eight states defaulted on their bonds, plus the Territory of Florida. All but Mississippi and Florida eventually resumed payment on at least some of them, though Louisiana, Arkansas, and Michigan repudiated part of them.

The Republic of Texas, which had no extradition treaty with the United States, quickly became notorious as a haven for busted farmers escaping their debts—G.T.T., gone to Texas—and for deadbeats and crooks of all sorts. Texas had no money to speak of, but when Texans did have money—often meaning, when they could borrow it—they tended to spend it on slaves. Sam Houston wrote General William G. Harding of Nashville on July 17, 1841, trying to explain why he hadn't paid back a $500 loan yet:

> I have offered every sacrifice in property, but there *is no money in Texas*, but our depreciated notes. I have upward of twenty five thousand dollars due me, and some of it for years, and I cannot collect as much as will pay one fourth of my land Tax! In addition, two valuable negro boys for which I had paid in cash $2100 previous to my visit to Nashville, ran away last spring to Mexico. Thus you see I am in bad luck![45]

The State of Mississippi's answer was simple: rather than impose a tax to pay its obligations, it flat-out stiffed its creditors. Alleging legal technicalities, Governor McNutt proposed debt repudiation to the legislature on January 5, 1841. It was blatant theft, based on a bogus legalistic argument, and it became a divisive campaign issue in the subsequent state election. The pro-repudiation forces won, and passed a constitutional amendment that forbade repaying the bonds. Occasioning litigation that dragged on into the twentieth century, the default ruined the name of Mississippi in Europe, and even affected the ability of the US government to borrow there, although the federal government had a clean credit record.

Bill collectors prowled Mississippi. When England threatened to invade the state on behalf of its burned creditors, John Quincy Adams moved on March 2, 1843, that any state that found itself at war as a result of repudiating its debts "will cease thereby to be a State of this Union, and will have no right to aid in her defense from the United States, or any one of them."[46]

When the Southern states seceded not twenty years later—repudiating debts in the process—British financiers were not eager to lend money.

35

The Slave Trade to Cuba and Brazil

The fruit, thus far, of the measures against the slave-trade, has been the substitution of small, sharp, wet clippers, for the large, clump, dry vessels, of double and treble the tonnage which would now be employed to transport the same number of persons; and there is no telling how far this process of reduction may be carried.[1]

—Nicholas B. Trist, 1839

AT SUNDOWN ON JULY 31, 1834, some 775,000 enslaved people (sources vary as to the exact number) in the British West Indies became free—technically, at least, though most remained as "apprentices" until 1838.[2] Twenty million pounds was allocated to compensate slaveowners for their lost property, but the newly freed Afro-Antilleans were not paid compensation for their stolen labor or their stolen persons. Some forty-seven thousand claimants filed for compensation as ex-slaveowners; the 6 percent of them who were absentees received 8.2 million pounds, or 41 percent of the money.[3] Britain's economy was large enough and diverse enough to be able to easily buy out the slaveowners, something that would have been impossible in the American South.

The end of slavery in Jamaica was followed by a sharp drop in sugar production there, subsequently cited by Southerners as a boilerplate cautionary tale: there was no production without the whip. Meanwhile, Cuban sugar planters, who continued using the whip, had their greatest opportunity since Saint-Domingue disappeared from the market forty years before.

Cuba didn't have a domestic slave trade. Like every place else that raised sugar, the growth rate of its enslaved population was negative. Cuba's slave market clamored for more Africans. Now that Britain was no longer trying to stop American commerce and was, pursuant to treaty, respecting American vessels at sea, blockade runners and privateers were no longer called for. But the Baltimore shipyards still did business building their fast-sailing boats, which could elude capture by the British Navy better than any other vessel. Even as Baltimore traders were shipping African Americans down South, the city's maritime industry was doing a big business illegally servicing the African slave trades to Cuba and Brazil with impunity, in the absence of any will to prosecute. Its prolific shipyards turned out schooners with special-shaped hulls for the thoroughly prohibited African slave trade, which was operating massively to Cuba and Brazil.

Fernando VII of Spain—remembered as the "Felon King," he dispensed with Spain's short-lived constitutional government to restore absolute monarchical power—accepted a payment of £400,000 from Britain in return for criminalizing the African slave trade to his domains as of May 30, 1820.[4] After he signed the compact, Spain and Britain set up a Mixed Court in Havana with officials from both countries to emancipate Africans from captured ships. In Brazil, the world record-holder for numbers of African slaves by far, a similar Mixed Court of Portuguese and British was established.

Fernando all but laughed in Britain's face. Cuba's prosperity—*his* prosperity—depended on a constant flow of slaves, with the creole and Spanish planters of Cuba for a market. The global cholera epidemic had reached the sugar plantations of Cuba, where by 1833 thousands of slaves had died and "nearly depopulated . . . several estates," intensifying the demand for labor, even as new lands continued to be converted to sugar.[5]

Participation in this trade by US citizens was defined by US law as piracy and punishable by hanging. But President Jackson didn't care, and he wasn't in an enforcing mood. His consul in Havana was Nicholas Philip Trist, whose credentials, both as a Jacksonian and as a staunch pro-slavery man, were impeccable for this important patronage position.

Well-educated and suavely mannered, Trist was a link between the worlds of Jefferson and Jackson. He had been tutored in law personally by his wife's grandfather Thomas Jefferson in their hometown of Charlottesville. He had been Jackson's private secretary in 1831 and was a lesser member of Jackson's unofficial circle of advisors that the Calhounites dubbed the Kitchen Cabinet.

He arrived in Havana in 1833, the year before General Miguel Tacón became the Spanish captain general of Cuba, and remained there until 1841, bringing Virginia Jefferson Randolph Trist there to live with him. Trist, who gave slave captains of various countries permission to fly the star-spangled banner, seems to have come to an understanding with Tacón.

As the British captured slave ships, they sent most of the slaves thus emancipated to Sierra Leone, but some thousands were also brought to Havana, where they were supposed to be set free. Unfortunately for them, Tacón and his colleagues, principally including monopolist fishmonger Francisco Martí ("Pancho Marty"), had a business reselling the *emancipados* back into slavery, until the British in 1835 realized what was happening and stopped handing them over. One formerly emancipated African woman wound up being the property of Trist, who hired her out, collecting $2.50 a week for her services.[6]

Now that slave ships were illegal pursuant to Fernando's deal with Britain, they had to make payoffs, which, it was charged, made their way up the Spanish political channels. A slaver who played the game got preferential treatment, including a privilege no one else had: to enter the harbor after dark. Tacón took a cut from the traders, reportedly a half-ounce of gold per captive.[7] Slavers could well afford the payoffs; by 1840, Cuba was producing 21 percent of the world's cane sugar.[8] Trist estimated in an 1839 letter that Tacón was making more than $200,000 a year from the slave trade, "a sum which, however respectable in itself, does not appear of very startling magnitude when compared with the value of twenty thousand slaves, which is about the number landed within the region."[9]

We don't have a number for what Trist made. It seems unlikely that he turned the US consul's office into a slave-trading clearing house as a purely charitable act. But though his household finances had been damaged by Jefferson's impoverishment, he did not leverage his activities into permanent wealth: he constantly complained about his debts, he continued as a government functionary, and he was poor later in life. Working for perhaps the most anti-British president ever, he seems to have seen his enabling activity as a patriotic, proslavery act, designed to give the British navy as much trouble as possible.

According to the British commissioner J. Kennedy in Havana, Trist in 1836 "declared he would not even open a letter from us in future."[10] The British commissioners repeatedly complained to the US government about Trist, and he was finally recalled to Washington. Horace Greeley's antislavery the *New-Yorker* reported in October of that year that *"Mr. N.P. Trist,* Consul at Havana, has been ordered home by the President, to make answer to the serious accusations against him. The charge of fitting out *slavers* from Havana with American papers is the most formidable."[11]

After John Quincy Adams interceded, Alexander Hill Everett was sent to Havana to investigate Trist's dealings with the slave traders. What he found was shocking: Trist had been registering slavers as US ships and allowing them the use of the American flag, along with false bills of sale and blank registries with his signature that could be filled out to show Spanish or Portuguese ownership. John Quincy Adams thought it "perfectly conclusive of the guilt of Trist in conniving at, aiding and abetting, by all means in his power, the African slave-trade by Americans, Portuguese, and Spaniards."[12] The British commissioner J. Kennedy told Everett that "prior to 1836 we have no account of any vessel sailing hence under the United States flag to Africa, to be employed in Slave Trade," but in October 1836 five American vessels left Havana for Africa, a month after arriving from the United States—apparently from Baltimore—"equipped for the slave trade," carrying lumber with which the crew would construct a belowdecks level once the vessel reached Africa. Eleven American-flagged vessels sailed from Cuba for Africa in 1837. As it became clear that the traffic could be conducted with impunity, it picked up: in 1838, there were nineteen American-flagged slave ships; and in 1839, twenty-three.[13] The post of Portuguese consul in Havana was vacant for almost two years, and Trist filled in, authorizing Brazilian slave deals as well, thus servicing the two major African-buying territories.

Newly built boats sailed from Baltimore to Havana, then on to Africa with an American captain, or an American pretending to be the captain, or sometimes a foreign captain pretending to be an American, with an all-Spanish or Portuguese crew or even with an American crew, often switching flags once they arrived in Africa and took on captives. Without the American flag on the way back, the ships were susceptible to boarding and confiscation by the British navy, but the danger of being captured before the return voyage had been eliminated, and if caught, the crews were not criminally chargeable: only the ship and the human cargo were subject to confiscation. Many traders thought the rewards great enough to justify the risk.

Trist brokered one deal in 1838 for a Spanish slave trader in Cuba to buy a Baltimore schooner that sailed for Africa with a Spanish crew, under an American captain and flag, with the name *Ontario of Baltimore* painted on her stern.[14] The British captain's report read, "Her sale was, no doubt, effected at Havana, although the bill of sale mentioned it to have taken place in Brass [present-day Nigeria]. In this instance the American flag gave unqualified protection to the slave trade." At some point, the flag was taken down; the captain apprehended the *Ontario* "with 220 slaves on board. She was under Spanish colors, but had no papers whatever."[15]

General Tacón remained at his post for fifteen years; the money from his wide-open clandestine slave trade paid for a building spree of historic dimensions in Havana, adjacent to the old city in what is now called Centro Habana. Pancho Marty built one of the largest and finest theaters in the world, Havana's Gran Teatro Tacón, which opened during Carnaval on February 18, 1838, with five floors corresponding to social classes.[16] According to a British Commissioners' report to Parliament in 1839:

> an astonishing number of new estates have been opened throughout the island within the last two years. In the district of Cienfuegos, of 40 estates now working there, 27 have been of recent formation . . . many [new plantations] have been commenced by American and some even by British subjects, who will thus, of course, give considerable impetus to the Slave Trade by means of their capital, industry, and skill.[17]

The British rear admiral George Elliot, tasked with enforcing the ban on the slave trade, asked for clarification of his orders on February 6, 1839:

> The probable object of using the American flag will be to protect the vessels up to the time of the cargo being ready for shipment; then to go through the farce of selling the vessel to a Portuguese or Spaniard.
>
>   But, in case of the capture of vessels with *slaves on board, under the American flag,* I should beg to know what is to be done with the man passing for the American captain?[18]

A week later, he wrote: "the use of the American flag is becoming rapidly more general in the protection of the Spanish slave-vessels." Elliot began capturing ships whose captains claimed to be naturalized US citizens. "Several of the slave-dealers," he wrote, "have declared their intention to have an American sailing-master in each vessel, and American colors."[19]

The traders sold slaves into the Republic of Texas, which was a haven for illegal slave trading. Hugh Thomas writes that Charles David Tolmé, the British consul in Havana, "in 1837 thought that 1,500 slaves might have been secretly carried to Texas in the previous few years."[20] The Virginia-born Sam Houston put a stop to that, when on December 19, 1836, he signed a "Proclamation Against the Slave Trade," which declared that "the importation or admission of Africans or negroes into this Republic" was "forever prohibited and declared to be piracy," with one significant exception: if they came from the United States of America.[21] In other words, he locked down Texas as a market for the US domestic slave trade.

The *Baltimore American* of July 4, 1838, reported that "A noble corvette ship, the Venus, Captain Wallace, pierced for 18 guns, built in this city on foreign account, is also ready for sea. She is, we learn, the sharpest clipper-built vessel ever constructed here, and according to the opinion of nautical men, must out-sail any thing that floats." Her Majesty's judge in Havana saw this item reprinted in the *Diario de la Marina*, when the ship arrived in ballast with a cargo of bricks after making the twenty-four-day sail from Baltimore to Havana, quoting it in a report that continued:

> The Venus is destined for Mozambique, and is arranged to bring as many even as 1,000 negroes; in which case, it is said, she would clear to the speculators from $100,000 to $200,000 in her first voyage—her cash price being estimated at $50,000, and the expenses of cargo and slaves at another $50,000.
>
> On the subject of vessels going equipped under the American flag to the coast of Africa, there to be pretended to be transferred for the first time to some Portuguese or Spanish owner, I have had several conversations with the American consul at this place [Trist], a gentleman of high character and of considerable reading and observation. I regret, however, to say that I have received only the most discouraging replies on every point relating to the prohibited traffic; and to add, that this seems the general feeling here of the American community. They all seem to declare that . . . England may as well think of closing up the work-shops of Birmingham, where they say the bolts and shackles are manufactured, as call on America to forbid the sailing of vessels equipped with them. In answer, I have not hesitated to express my disbelief of the shackles coming from Birmingham, and to declare my full conviction that at no port whatever, in England, would they allow any such articles to be shipped, had they any idea of their being intended for such a purpose.
>
> I regret to have also to inform your lordship that, during the suspension of the Portuguese consul, as I have previously stated, the American consul has been acting *pro tempore* in that character.[22]

The cargoes—the masses of imprisoned humans down in the hold—were getting larger; the *Venus* arrived back from Africa in Havana's harbor with 860 captives on board. Out of Havana, then, slave vessels carrying large numbers of Africans were being run by Spanish, Cuban creole, Portuguese, Brazilian, and United Statesian operators under the protection of the US flag. Some returned from Africa to Cuba, others to Brazil. The British captain Brunswick Popham wrote to Admiral Elliot that he did not want to exceed his instructions by arresting an American, "feeling that I should not be borne out, in interfering with a citizen of the United States; of which, it appeared to me, the American Government evinced no disposition to tolerate, *even in very extreme cases.*"[23] (emphasis in original) Popham closed his letter with:

> It has been mentioned by Spaniards and Portuguese slaving on this coast, that, were it not for the very active co-operation of the Americans, the slave-trade would very materially decline—in fact, be but feebly carried on. I do not doubt, from all that I hear, that the citizens of the United States (generally of Baltimore) are more deeply interested in the slave-trade to Havana and Brazil than is generally supposed.[24]

Among the papers dealing with the affair that were published as part of Van Buren's annual message at the end of 1840 was Trist's rambling defense, in which he professed indignation at the slave trade while demonstrating a close knowledge of it, and resorted to a change of subject to the classic y'all-do-it-too pro-slavery trope: insulting the British for profiting off the labor of a hypothetical girl working in the Lancashire textile mills.

Trist (for whom a middle school in Meraux, Louisiana, is named) figures in the best-known case of American slavery law from the period. He authorized the voyage of the *Tecora*, whose captives from Sierra Leone were transferred in Havana to the schooner *Amistad*, which coasted along toward Puerto Príncipe (Camagüey). The captives on the *Amistad* overpowered the ship and tried to sail back to Africa. But they didn't know how; the mates, hoping to have the mutineers all captured, brought the ship on a northwest course instead. They were ultimately captured by the US Navy floating off Long Island, New York.

The Cuban slaveowners sued to have their property returned. John Quincy Adams argued the case for two days in 1841 before the Taney Supreme Court and won the Africans' freedom, based on the notions that the United States had no jurisdiction and that they could not have been legally enslaved. He asked the court: "my clients are claimed under the treaty [of 1795, between the US and Spain] as merchandise, rescued from pirates and robbers. Who were the merchandise, and who were the robbers? According to the construction of the Spanish minister, the merchandise were the robbers, and the robbers were the merchandise. The merchandise was rescued out of its own hands, and the robbers were rescued out of the hands of the robbers. Is this the meaning of the treaty?"

Trist lost his post in 1841, with the coming of the Whigs. He faced no criminal charges for dozens of cases of using the American flag to cover blatant felonious activity, which would have made him an accessory to the slave trade that was defined as piracy by US law. As Adams remarked in the *Amistad* argument: "Say it was a Baltimore clipper, fitted for the African slave trade, and having performed a voyage, had come back to our shores, directly or indirectly, with fifty-four African victims on board, and was thus brought into port—what would be the assistance guarantied by our laws to American citizens, in such circumstances? The captain would be seized, tried as a pirate, and hung!"[25] Trist's guilt was never proved in a court, nor was he censured by Congress.

Successive administrations of the United States government turned a blind eye to American involvement in the African slave trade that had reopened following the Napoleonic Wars, and did little to enforce the law against it as US shipbuilders, captains, financiers, and officials facilitated the trade to Cuba and Brazil. But these African slave ships did not come to the United States. The government *did* effectively police the importation of Africans to the United States, because that was a protected market.

Without that protection, Virginia's economy would probably have collapsed. James Henry Hammond of Columbia, South Carolina, noted in his diary after dining with "Dr. Carter of Virginia" on February 12, 1841, that "he told me that in Virginia now planters realized nothing except from raising slaves and the increase in the value of their lands in consequence of improvements from marling [spreading quicklime]." Then, with a bit of snark, he added, "I suspect the rise in lands is rather imaginary."[26]

Heaps and Piles
of Money

*You cannot think (to return to the songs of my boatmen) how strange some
of their words are: in one, they repeatedly chanted the "sentiment" that
"God made man, and man makes"—what do you think?—"money!" Is not
that a peculiar poetical proposition?[1]*

—Fanny Kemble

PIERCE MEASE BUTLER HADN'T wanted his impulsive, high-spirited, strong-
willed, self-absorbed, talkative wife, Frances "Fanny" Kemble Butler, to come
South, but she wouldn't take no for an answer. In late 1838, she traveled to the
Sea Islands of Georgia to spend fifteen disturbing weeks as plantation mistress of
Butler Island. Her husband had inherited the property from his grandfather the
framer: Major Pierce Butler, the father of the fugitive slave clause to the Constitution, who in his day had been the second largest slaveowner—which is to say,
the second richest man—in Georgia.

Kemble was the superstar young actress who revitalized British theater, then
came to America for a year of performances in 1833–34 that inspired American
girls to wear their hair in "Fanny Kemble curls." Butler assiduously devoted
more than a year to courting the famous young woman nearly full-time, which
he could do because he did not work, or even have an identifiable profession
other than spending money.

previous page: Butler Island, Georgia, May 2013.

523

In spite of the sums she was earning from her performances, Kemble's finances were spread thin by her family's expenses, and the handsome, self-assured Butler seemed to offer, among other things, financial stability. But then she found out what being married to a slaveowner meant, in the context of a nineteenth-century marriage. Living with her husband in Philadelphia, she found that Mrs. Pierce Butler was expected not to have a stage career, publish her writing, associate with her former friends, or disagree with her husband in any way. Kemble had not declared herself to be an abolitionist before her marriage, but her diaries suggest that she made a personal connection between her condition as a married woman and that of the enslaved. She lived out her contradictions in public, via her twin careers as writer and actress, in one of the high-profile marriage disasters of the century.[2]

Kemble had apparently believed Butler's assurances that he was one of the "good" slaveowners. But after he became the full owner of his grandfather's Sea Island estate following the death of his brother in 1836, she saw the reality. Kemble is most remembered today for *Journal of a Residence on a Georgian Plantation in 1838–1839*, her account of the months she passed there. A collection of privately circulated letters, harshly critical of slavery, she ultimately allowed it to be published in 1863 in London in the hope it might help keep Britain from siding with the Confederacy.

In it, to Butler's everlasting humiliation that his wife had gone so far out of his control, she matter-of-factly blew the whistle on slavery as a system of concubinage and breeding. She wrote of rewards and privileges for childbearing women that were "indirect inducements to reckless propagation . . . a woman thinks, and not much amiss, that the more frequently she adds to the number of her master's live-stock by bringing new slaves into the world, the more claims she will have upon his consideration and good-will."[3]

Kemble shared in the racism of the times, as in her ape-libel description of one of the enslaved who was possessed of a beautiful singing voice (in which, incidentally, she references the African American use of the word "brother"):

By-the-by, this individual *does* speak, and therefore I presume he is not an ape, ourang-outang, chimpanzee, or gorilla; but I could not, I confess, have conceived it possible that the presence of articulate sounds, and the absence of an articulate tail, should make, externally at least, so completely the only appreciable difference between a man and a monkey, as they appear to do in this individual 'black brother.' Such stupendous long thin hands, and long flat feet, I did never see off a large quadruped of the ape species. But, as I said before, Isaac *speaks*, and I am much comforted thereby.[4]

At the same time, she saw the mote when it was not in her own eye:

One of their songs displeased me not a little, for it embodied the opinion that 'twenty-six black girls not make mulatto yellow girl'; and as I told them I did not like it, they have omitted it since. This desperate tendency to despise and undervalue their own race and colour, which is one of the very worst results of their abject condition, is intolerable to me.[5]

Kemble was appalled by "the meritorious air with which the women always made haste to inform me of the number of children they had borne, and the frequent occasions on which the older slaves would direct my attention to their children, exclaiming, 'Look, missis! little niggers for you and massa, plenty little niggers for you and little missis!'" After Butler forbade her to continue carrying him requests for better treatment from the enslaved, she received a visit from the pregnant women whose owner she did not want to be, but whose labor supported her and provided a legacy for their two daughters:

The women who visited me yesterday were all in the family-way, and came to entreat of me to have the sentence (what else can I call it?) modified which condemns them to resume their labor of hoeing in the fields three weeks after their confinement . . Their principal spokeswoman . . . implored me to have a kind of labor given to them less exhausting during the month after their confinement, I held the table before me so hard in order not to cry that I think my fingers ought to have left a mark on it.[6]

Once Kemble saw what Butler's fortune really depended on—and realized that he too had been fornicating with enslaved women—the marriage was over, though ending it took years, created a public spectacle, and set in motion a life-long battle for the affections of the couple's two daughters. Divorce was uncommon in those days, and the law was not friendly to it. South Carolina did not allow divorce at all (until 1949).[7] The suit was filed in Philadelphia, where state laws were relatively liberal on divorce; but the presumption was that children belonged to the father, and Butler kept the daughters. In a legal narrative drawn up for Butler by his attorneys in the course of divorce proceedings, which Butler published and circulated privately, he expressed his view of marriage as a contract between unequal partners:

One reason, and perhaps the fundamental one, for the ill success which attended my marriage, will readily be found in the peculiar views which were entertained by Mrs. Butler on the subject of marriage . . . She held that marriage should be companionship on equal terms—partnership in which, if both partners agree, it is well; but if they do not, neither is bound to yield—and that at no time has one partner a right to control the other.[8]

He recalled that "although we resided in Pennsylvania, where slavery does not exist, the greater part of my property lies in the State of Georgia, and consists of plantations and negroes. Mrs. Butler, after our marriage, not before, declared herself to be in principle an abolitionist . . ."[9]

But that was before Kemble met Die, who

had had sixteen children, fourteen of whom were dead; she had had four miscarriages, one had been caused by falling down with a very heavy burthen on her head, and one from having her arms strained up to be lashed. I asked her what she meant by having her arms tied up; she said their hands were first tied together, sometimes by the wrists, and sometimes, which was worse, by the thumbs, and they were then drawn up to a tree or post, so as almost to swing them off the ground, and then their clothes rolled round their waist, and a man with a cow-hide stands and stripes them. I give you the woman's words; she did not speak of this as of anything strange, unusual or especially horrid and abominable; and when I said, "Did they do that to you when you were with child?" she simply replied, "Yes, missis." And to all this I listen—I, an English woman, the wife of the man who owns these wretches, and I cannot say, "That thing shall not be done again[."][10]

Once independent, she went back to work, paying her family's expenses by giving one-woman readings of Shakespeare plays.

Prices for slaves might go down, but there was always a market for them. After all the banks had suspended specie payments, and planters by the thousands had sworn never to deal with banks and paper money again, there were still hundreds of thousands of enslaved people, whose bodies were the most reliable store of value.

No free black youth in the North was entirely safe from the "negro stealers." One of the best-known slave narratives, meticulously adapted into an Oscar-winning movie in 2013, has as its full title *Twelve Years a Slave: Narrative of Solomon Northup, a Citizen of New-York, Kidnapped in Washington City in 1841 and Rescued in 1853, from a Cotton Plantation Near the Red River in Louisiana.* It describes how Northup was lured in 1841 from Saratoga, New York, to Washington, DC, with the promise of work. He was kidnapped and sold, becoming a captive of two slave traders infamous for their brutality. At the shipping end was James Birch of the District of Columbia, the same trader who had put Dorcas Allen and her children up for sale. After protesting that he was a free man from New York, Northup received a severe beating from Birch, described in detail, with the threat never again to say such a thing or he'd be killed. "I doubt not he understood then better than I did," Northup wrote, "the danger and the penalty of selling a free man into slavery."

While imprisoned in Washington, a woman named Eliza arrived, with a son Randall and a daughter named Emily, who, recalled Northup,

> was seven or eight years old, of light complexion, and with a face of admirable beauty. Her hair fell in curls around her neck, while the style and richness of her dress, and the neatness of her whole appearance indicated she had been brought up in the midst of wealth. She was a sweet child indeed. The woman also was arrayed in silk, with rings upon her fingers, and golden ornaments suspended from her ears. Her air and manners, the correctness and propriety of her language—all showed evidently, that she had sometime stood above the common level of a slave. She seemed to be amazed at finding herself in such a place as that.

After two weeks imprisoned in Washington, Northup and the pen's other captives were marched to a steamboat in the dead of night and taken down the Potomac, then transferred to stagecoaches and finally taken by rail to Richmond, where they were examined and where Northup was chained together in the pen with Robert, a kidnapped free-born black man from Cincinnati. They were put on an oceangoing brig that took on four more slaves at a stop in Norfolk; as they were sailing to New Orleans, Robert died of smallpox. Arriving there, they were taken charge of by Theophilus Freeman, one of New Orleans's largest slave dealers; Northup, who had contracted smallpox, was taken to Charity Hospital and managed to recuperate.

Northup watched as Freeman sold Eliza's son Randall away, then sold Eliza, refusing the buyer's offer, urged by Eliza's desperate pleading, to sell her daughter Emily to him as well:

> He would not sell her then on any account whatever. There were heaps and piles of money to be made of her, he said, when she was a few years older. There were men enough in New-Orleans who would give five thousand dollars for such an extra, handsome, fancy piece as Emily would be, rather than not get her. No, no, he would not sell her then. She was a beauty—a picture—a doll—one of the regular bloods—none of your thick-lipped, bullet-headed, cotton-picking niggers—if she was might he be d--d.
>
> When Eliza heard Freeman's determination not to part with Emily, she became absolutely frantic.
>
> "I will *not* go without her. They shall *not* take her from me," she fairly shrieked, her shrieks commingling with the loud and angry voice of Freeman, commanding her to be silent.[11]

As an unidentified formerly enslaved man, born circa 1845, recalled: "I've seen them sell women away from little children, and women would be cryin' and they'd slap 'em about cryin'."[12]

Biddle's United States Bank of Pennsylvania failed in February 1841. The settlement of its outstanding liabilities on behalf of creditors took years. To try to collect on its debts, the British trustees created the Bacon Trust, headed by John Bacon, which was assigned $12.5 million in assets to recover; 41 percent of them were in Mississippi and another 30 percent were in New Orleans and Mobile.[13]

Louisiana passed a measure allowing debtors to settle at twenty-five cents on the dollar, and in Louisiana, since slaves were considered "immovables," they could not be seized and separately sold. Neither of those conditions held in Mississippi, where the Bacon Trust became the biggest financier and "probably ranked among the largest slaveholders" in the state, says Richard Holcombe Kilbourne, who assembled its history out of a mass of archival documents.

The Bacon Trust's man on the ground, Joseph L. Roberts, actively managed as many as four plantations at a time.[14] The value of mortgage debt, he found, was often compromised by the prior removal of "the slaves which ma[de] mortgaged debts most safe." Once again, coined labor beat coined land: Roberts could not accept land in satisfaction of debts, because it was not salable; slaves, however were: "Negroes," he wrote, "c[ould] be sold & attain th[e] object but land not."[15] The Bacon Trust thus involved itself repeatedly in the person-selling business. Prices were still "dull," but, as Roberts wrote, "good Negroes I am told will sell readily altho they will not bring high prices." Accordingly, Roberts accepted slaves as security, sometimes large numbers of them, and sold them, sometimes at sheriff's sales, sometimes buying them back on his own account.[16]

In 1846, after Roberts had taken over a Louisiana plantation from a scam artist who had run the place down, his agent "reported a wretched state of things—Only 53 Negroes large & small; they received 60 Negroes with the place & their natural increase, inclusive of deaths, ought now to have made on the place at least 75 in number—several of the Negroes now there are sickly & inefficient from overwork & exposure—some frost bitten, some ruptured, some branded on their hips as runaways—all without shoes & most of them without winter clothing or blankets."[17]

The frost-bitten people who were property had to be discounted by the British banks' representative. Perhaps their fate was that nightmare of the enslaved: being sold at auction as "refuse slaves."

37

The Slave Power

A slave dreads the punishment of stripes more than he does imprisonment, and that description of punishment has, besides, a beneficial effect upon his fellow-slaves.

—Representative James K. Polk on the floor of the House,
April 27, 1830

THERE NEVER WAS A president of the United States from Mississippi. But Tennessean James K. Polk was the absentee owner of a plantation in Mississippi, for which he bought slaves on an ongoing basis while he was a congressman, and then while he was president.[1]

Polk's father, Sam Polk, was a land speculator in Tennessee, of the same generation as land speculator Andrew Jackson, who was an occasional visitor to the household when Jimmy Polk was growing up. Though Polk was as frail as Jackson was tough, the diminutive, sickly Scotch-Irish-descended lawyer was Jackson's loyal follower. Polk, who suffered all his life from bowel disorders, was apparently sterile and perhaps impotent as the result of an unfortunate operation to remove a urinary stone, performed without anesthetic when he was sixteen. His devoted and religious wife, Sarah Childress Polk, who had no children to occupy her, was instead an active participant in Polk's political career. She allowed no work or amusements on Sunday, would not serve spirits stronger than wine with dinner at White House functions, and would not sponsor balls with dancing. In order to cut down on the expenses of running the White House, which had to be borne by the president, she discharged its ten-member staff and replaced them with slaves who lived in the White House basement, which had drainage problems and frequently flooded.[2]

First elected to Congress in 1825, Polk carried Jackson's water in the House, and with his backing became Speaker for two terms. Hoping in vain to live to an old age in which his plantation income would support him while he lived in a big house in Nashville, he bought young people, typically one at a time, as the opportunity came along or as his farming needs seemed to require.

Polk kept a diary, intended for posterity, that does not mention slaves. But perhaps because he died suddenly, his correspondence was never sanitized, and it contains an extensive paper trail, including a number of letters that document the amount of time and money he spent buying slaves while in office as well as his injunctions to keep it secret. The title of William Dusinberre's book on the subject expresses it: *Slavemaster President: The Double Career of James Polk.* In his spare time, while directing a war of conquest that would expand slavery and thus sharply increase the valuation of existing slaveholdings, Polk also directed from the White House, via an overseer, a slave-labor plantation of which he was an inept absentee landlord.

In keeping with the common capital accumulation scenario of the South, Polk rarely sold slaves; he bought them in order to grow his value through their appreciation in price and increase in number. People frequently came offering deals on slaves to his brother-in-law, who bought for him. His collected correspondence contains frequent reference to the business of "negroes" until late in his life, as well as frequent references to their illness.

Polk's slaves were a miserable, unhealthy lot who couldn't even sustain "natural increase" over the years. Instead, Polk tried to increase his wealth by buying more slaves—which meant people twenty-one or younger. Every one of them would have been torn away from a family before being sold, so that the social composition of his plantation labor force followed the Deep South cotton-plantation model: a collection of young people bought like mules and cut off from their familiar lives, with few natural or local connections among them, in an atmosphere of violent, daily repression.

Like any absentee plantation owner, Polk had to rely on his overseer, who whipped the workers unmercifully. An overseer's worth was measured in short-term results—making the best crop possible *this* year—so his interest was at cross-purposes with the owner's stake in the workers' longevity. In 1832, during the cholera epidemic, Polk, then a congressman, received a letter from overseer

Herbert Biles, revealing that in spite of the entire work force being sick, Biles had made them produce twenty-five thousand pounds of cotton:

> I hav bad news to writ to you. Lucys youngist Child died on the 16th of the instant and the little orphin Child died yester Day and the other little girl I am afraid will go the same way. . . . Seasor has bean under the Doctr ever senc you ware hear with the Liver Complaint but is likley to recover. The rest of the niggars the most of them has bean sick. . . . I hav got out About twenty five thousand lb of Cotton and hav got on[e] lo[a]d Reddy to send down but the Colry [cholera] got to Memphis and Alarmed the people so that thay ware Afraid to gone thair.[3]

Polk's farm must have been a true horror. His slaves ran away much more than was usual on a well-run plantation. One of them, Gilbert, did it *ten* times. After Chunky Jack and Ben had absconded and been apprehended, Polk's brother-in-law and business advisor Silas M. Caldwell wrote him on January 4, 1834: "Your negroes here are very much dissatisfied. I believe I have got them quieted. Some others spoke of running away . . ." Caldwell's letter continued, reporting a crib death (which at then-current market rates meant a loss of perhaps $75 to Polk's net worth), and note the reference to the deceased child as "it," and apparently to the labor force as "stock":

> Elizabeths child died last night; she smothered it somehow. No person knew it was dead until this morning. It was a very fine child . . . I had it Buried to day. Maria has a fine boy about one Month old. I Bot you a very fine mule and Brot down with me. I gave $100 for it out of a drove. Your stock looks very well here, your negroes have plenty of Milk.[4]

Another brother-in-law and business adviser, James Walker, wrote Polk that "I am not sure that to sell some of your most refractory negroes to *real negro traders* would not be the best thing you could do to reduce the balance to subjection, and if *Chunky* Jack, could with propriety be sold it ought to be done."[5] (emphasis in original)

By September 1834, Polk had sold his Tennessee plantation and was already on the trail of acquiring more labor in expectation of getting some of that unplowed Mississippi farmland that Jackson had "negotiated" away from the Indians. Hours after having closed the deal, he wrote to Sarah, telling her to keep "the negroes" ignorant of it, and bragged about having gotten a new slave and hoping to acquire another, all without spending any cash:

I am resolved to send my hands to the South, have given money to *James Brown* to buy a place & have employed *Beanland* as an overseer. . . . I bought Mariah's husband a very likely boy—about 22 years old for $600. And paid for him with the notes I held on his master for land which I sold him several years ago. . . .

P.S. . . . The negroes have no idea that they are going to be sent to the South and I do not wish them to know it, and therefore it would be best to say nothing about it at home, for it might be conveyed back to them. . . .

N.B. Since writing it occurs to me, that I will have to go a day or two out of my way, with the hope of getting a negro in payment of a debt due me by Silliman to whom I sold land.[6]

Polk's whip-happy overseer Ephraim Beanland wrote him on October 4 that Chunky Jack had disappeared into Shawnee Town, opposite Memphis across the Mississippi River, a hidey-hole that would have been a terrifying place to a white farmer: "On last nite I got home from the Arkensis and I hearde of Jack but never co[u]ld get Site of him and it Is supposed that he is in Shauney villige which I was advised not to go theire for they is A den of thieves and to tell you the fact I donte [think] that you will ever git him."[7]

Walker, who together with partners ran a stagecoach line from Nashville to Natchez that relied on post office contracts and kept the family connection hidden through the use of a front man's name, advised Polk on October 15, 1839, of strategies for creating an annuity for the family of Polk's deceased brother:

The question . . . would be, in what kind of stocks the money could be invested with perfect safety. I should say not Bank Stock, for experience has proved that not a perfect safe investment. State Bonds bearing an interest of 6 pr. Cent would do and I think would certainly be safe. This investment could now you know be readily made. It is however probable, that a still better & more secure investment could be made, and the money and interest undoubtedly secured, by being upon land and negroes to double the amount.[8]

In order to keep Tennessee from falling to the Whigs, Democratic party enforcer Polk left the House to run for governor in 1839 for a two-year term; he was elected, but then was subsequently turned down by voters for a second term, then lost the next election two years later.

Isaac Franklin, who according to testimony "was warm and decided in his politics," was a "strong Polk man."[9] We have found no documentation of

Polk and Franklin having met, done business, or corresponded, but there is no way Polk didn't know Isaac Franklin, who had the finest house in his state, was one of his wealthiest supporters, was a kingpin of the trade of which Polk was such an eager customer, and moreover was a man who knew the value of connections.

Polk was the slave traders' candidate. Indeed, he was the embodiment of what the one-term antislavery Ohio senator Thomas Morris, in a speech of February 9, 1839, accompanying his presentation to the Senate of abolition petitions with "thousands of signatures," called the "slave power of the south." Morris juxtaposed this image with what he saw as the other great evil, the "banking power of the north." "The cotton bale and the bank note," he declaimed, "have formed an alliance; the credit system with slave labor." Morris noted the outsized capitalization of the South in slaves, noting Henry Clay's valuation of it at $1.2 billion and declaring that sum larger than the world's money (i.e., precious metal) supply, which was an exaggeration but not an unthinkable one:

> Permit me to tell the country now what this power behind the throne, greater than the throne itself, is. It is the power of SLAVERY. It is a power, according to the calculation of the Senator from Kentucky, which owns $1,200,000,000 in human beings as property; and if money is power, this power is not to be conceived or calculated; a power which claims human property more than double the amount which the whole money of the world could purchase.[10]

Meanwhile, the experience of slavery was getting worse as plantation management became more efficient. The antebellum cotton plantation of the Deep South was a much harsher regime than that of the Upper South; life as a worker there was hell on earth. Cotton planters extracted continually increasing amounts of labor through torture via a system not unlike modern time-metric monitoring of workers that Edward E. Baptist memorably calls "the whipping machine." Under this regime, failure to meet production targets was punished by vicious, lacerative whippings at the end of the long work day. And the production targets were continually increased, pushing the worker ever harder.[11] With this abusive, efficiency-conscious system in place, cotton production reached levels not seen again until mechanization.

⧓

Martin Van Buren's entire presidency was spent combating the post-panic economic depression, and he was beaten by a Whig in the 1840 election. The Whigs had decided that if the American people wanted a warrior president, they'd run one. Their candidate, Virginia's William Henry Harrison, hadn't beaten the English like Jackson had, but he'd massacred Native Americans in the battle of Tippecanoe twenty-nine years earlier and had cheated them out of some three million acres of land in what we now call the Midwest. This land was above the Missouri Compromise line and as such would be free soil, but Harrison had hoped to make it slave territory the way he'd tried to make free-soil Indiana into a slave state when he was its territorial governor in 1804. The ticket's rhyming, alliterative slogan, permanently engraved in American memory, was "Tippecanoe and Tyler too"; Harrison's running mate, John Tyler, was an erstwhile Jacksonian and a very conservative states'-rights man—a slaveowner whose family went back to the seventeenth century in Virginia, and whose father had participated in the ratification of the Constitution.

Looking back at Van Buren's term, Adams wrote in his diary:

> [Jackson's] personal popularity, founded exclusively upon the battle of New Orleans, drove him through his double term, and enabled him to palm upon this nation the sycophant who declared it glory enough to have served under such a chief for his successor. Both the men have been for twelve years the tool of Amos Kendall, the ruling mind of their dominion.[12]

Harrison was president for only thirty-two days before he caught a cold and died, occasioning the first vice presidential succession: Tyler took office on April 4, 1841. Adams and Clay were outraged that Tyler did not meekly assume the post of "acting president" but, with all but a month of a four-year term to serve, declared himself a full president, which has been the model for vice presidential succession ever since.

In later life, Tyler's states'-rights enthusiasm was directed toward the cause of secession, and in his final days he was elected a member of the Confederate House of Representatives. As president, not surprisingly, Tyler was an aggressive booster of Texas annexation. Adams referred to him in his diary as "the slave-breeder."[13]

"This was a memorable day in the annals of the world," Adams wrote on April 22, 1844. "The treaty for the annexation of Texas to this Union was this day sent in to the Senate; and with it went the freedom of the human race."[14] Adams had been a pro-expansionist, but not any more. For both abolitionists and slaveowners, Texas was about nothing but expanding slavery. That was the year the gag rule in the House of Representatives was finally overturned, and John C. Calhoun threatened that "if the annexation of Texas is to be defeated by the same sperit [*sic*] which has induced the reception of abolition petitions, it is difficult to say, what may be the consequence."[15]

Then a freak accident brought John C. Calhoun into the position of secretary of state as an emergency replacement for Tyler's secretary of state, Virginian Abel Upshur, who was killed, along with seven others, when an enormous wrought-iron gun on board a new steam-powered iron warship he had commissioned exploded at its public demonstration. (Tyler was on board but survived.) As secretary of state, Calhoun's support for Texas annexation merged entirely with his impassioned defense of slavery. In a classic case of diplomatic overreach, Calhoun portrayed the annexation of Texas as an act of self-defense for the Southern states against the possibility—for which there was no credible evidence—of the infiltration by Britain of abolitionists into Texas. He did this in a calculatedly offensive letter to British ambassador Richard Pakenham, which, when leaked by Senator Benjamin Tappan of Ohio and published on April 27, 1844, made explicit to the whole country in ringing, paranoid tones the notion that annexing Texas was essential to preserving slavery. Attempting to show that "in all instances in which the States have changed the former relation between the two races, the condition of the African, instead of being improved, has become worse," Calhoun reached for the census of 1840, citing figures from its demographic category of "deaf and dumb, blind, idiots, and insane Negroes."

Former president Martin Van Buren seemed like a favorite to be nominated in 1844, but he was against the annexation of Texas. Jackson, seventy-six and dying, took that as a betrayal. Had Van Buren been the one to run against Clay, Texas would not have been an issue in the election, because neither were annexationists. But Jackson wasn't about to let that happen, and instead he threw his support to James K. Polk.

After twenty-five years as a professional politician, Polk appeared to be a has-been. But he was pro-slavery, pro-expansion, and anti-tariff, and was thus the perfect presidential candidate for Southerners. For sectional balance, his running mate was George M. Dallas, former mayor of Philadelphia and James Buchanan's great rival in Pennsylvania.

The election turned on the issue of bringing Texas into the Union. William Seward described in a letter to Thurlow Weed a Whig rally at which "one of the banners, and the most popular one, was a white sheet, on which was Polk dragging a negro in chains after him."[16]

Louis Hughes recalled in his memoir that when he was being taken by coffle down South at the age of twelve,

> as we passed along, every white man we met was yelling, "Hurrah for Polk and Dallas!" They were feeling good, for election had given them the men that they wanted. The man who had us in charge joined with those we met in the hurrahing. We were afraid to ask them the reason for their yelling, as that would have been regarded as an impertinence, and probably would have caused us all to be whipped.[17]

The term Thomas Morris had popularized—the Slave Power—became a commonplace of abolitionist political discourse. A transform on Jackson's demonized "Money Power" of financial capitalism, it was a useful phrase with which to describe something that really did exist. Eric Foner writes, citing Marvin Meyers: "If . . . the Money Power was the 'master symbol' for the Age of Jackson, the Slave Power was equally effective as a symbol for all the fears and hostilities harbored by northerners toward slavery and the South."[18]

Only the abolitionists wanted to end slavery in the Southern states immediately; no ranking governmental official proposed such a thing, certainly not Adams. Despite the spectacularly belligerent reaction by the Slave Power to abolitionist literature, white abolitionists were few in number in the 1830s and '40s. But many non-abolitionist white northerners were antislavery, less because of compassion for black people than because they saw slavery as setting an unacceptably low floor for working conditions.

The sectional controversy over slavery was about its expansion to the new territories. Free labor did not want to go where there was slavery, and slaveowners felt locked out of any place where they couldn't sell slaves. Would the nation be a slave-labor nation with a free-labor section confined to the northeast, or a free-labor nation with a slave-labor section confined to the southeast? Or would it be all one way or the other: all-slavery or all-free? In 1844, Texas was the battleground.

Of the ten United States presidents up to that point, only two had been antislavery, both of them named Adams. Martin Van Buren, who grew up in a household that owned slaves who worked at the family tavern in Kinderhook, New York, had been "servile" to the Slave Power, in John Quincy Adams's words, while riding Jackson's power train.

As president, Van Buren had resisted the clamor for prohibition of slavery in the District of Columbia, but now he had been purged by his own party, from Jackson on down, over the annexation of Texas as a slave state.

For many observers, Polk's nomination represented the final takeover of the Democratic Party by the Slave Power, even though South Carolina, responding to John C. Calhoun's wishes, did not participate in the nominating convention and remained standoffish.

Both major parties held their 1844 conventions in Baltimore, an indication of how central the city had become to the country's communications. Polk's nomination was announced by the newly patented electrical telegraph, a machine that would make Samuel F. B. Morse's well-connected business partner Amos Kendall very wealthy. Committing from the outset to be a one-term president, Polk won the election, barely. He was what in another era was called a wonk—focused on his agenda, which was to take as much of Mexico's territory as he could, all the way out to California, and to settle the Oregon question with Britain.

The lame duck Tyler signed the Joint Resolution for Annexing Texas on March 1, 1845. It contemplated dividing Texas up into five states, each of which, needless to say, would get two senators.[19] After becoming president, Polk signed the Joint Resolution for the Admission of the State of Texas into the Union, which did not contain the five-state clause, on December 29.

Mexico's government had long since announced that it would consider the annexation of Texas by the United States to be an act of war.

Polk was eager to have a Mexican War.

The Mexican conquest was a warmup for the war that would be fought fifteen years later between Richmond and Washington. Many of the generals who fought in the later war, both Union and Confederate, knew each other from serving together in the Mexican War. Ulysses S. Grant, a junior officer in that war, later wrote in his memoir that "I was bitterly opposed to the measure [of annexing Texas], and to this day regard the war which resulted as one of the most unjust ever waged by a stronger against a weaker nation." Grant's quick summary of it will do for our purposes:

> Americans who had received authority from Mexico to colonize . . . paid very little attention to the supreme government, and introduced slavery into the state almost from the start, though the constitution of Mexico did not, nor does it now, sanction that institution. Soon they set up an independent government of their own, and war existed, between Texas and Mexico, in name from that time until 1836, when active hostilities very nearly ceased upon the capture of Santa Anna, the Mexican President. Before long, however, the same people—who with permission of Mexico had colonized Texas, and afterwards set up slavery there, and then seceded as soon as they felt strong enough to do so—offered themselves and the State to the United States, and in 1845 their offer was accepted. The occupation, separation and annexation were, from the inception of the movement to its final consummation, a conspiracy to acquire territory out of which slave states might be formed for the American Union . . . the Southern rebellion was largely the outgrowth of the Mexican war.[20]

Florida, the obsession of presidents from Jefferson to Jackson, finally became a state on March 3, 1845. Its first senator was a secessionist who would ultimately join the Confederate Congress: the sugar planter David Levy, who was already serving as Florida's territorial representative to Congress. Levy, who owned some thirty thousand acres in the Jacksonville area, and whose Sephardic Moroccan-born father Moses Levy had been a weapons dealer in Puerto Rico and made a fortune in shipping in Cuba, became the first Jewish US senator. The following year he married a politically connected Christian woman, changed his name to David Yulee, and raised his children as Christians.

The South's black-or-white two-caste system worked to the advantage of Jews. In the North, where anti-Jewish sentiment could be intense, they were Jews; in the South, they were white people. "For Southern Jews, loyalty to the Confederacy was often a matter of intense personal gratitude," writes Howard M. Sachar.[21] In Richmond, New Yorker Frederick Law Olmsted noted their presence with racialized distaste: "very dirty German Jews . . . abound, and their characteristic shops (with their characteristic smells, quite as bad as in Cologne), are thickly set in the narrowest and meanest streets, which seem to be otherwise inhabited mainly by negroes."[22]

Though more Jews went to the urban areas of the North than to the South—Robert N. Rosen estimates 120,000 in the North versus 25,000 in the South—Southern Jews played an important role as commercial interme- diaries in the emerging slavery nation.[23] The Jewish peddler, a fixture in many places of the world during the nineteenth century, and seen in every part of the United States, found a special niche among the plantations of the South.[24] Charleston, home of the first Reform congregation in the United States, had the nation's largest Jewish community in 1820—about seven hundred— until New York surpassed it. Until about 1830, Jews were part of Charles- ton's elite, and, like most of Charleston's white population, most of them were slaveowners.

Perhaps no story better illustrates how the explosive profits to be made in the cotton kingdom were foundational to American business than that of Chaim (or Heyum) Lehman, a twenty-two-year-old cattle dealer and wine merchant who arrived into New York's harbor on September 11, 1844. He was one of perhaps one hundred thousand Ashkenazi immigrants who came from Central Europe and the German states in the years between 1800 and 1860, transforming the Ameri- can Jewish community, which had previously been dominated by Sephardim.[25] Lehman had been forced to leave his Bavarian hometown of Rimpar, where the law required the departure of second and subsequent sons of a Jewish family. Changing his name to Henry, he sailed down to Mobile and traveled upriver, where he began a career as an itinerant peddler, one of many who sold dry goods and supplies to plantations and also served as conduits for news. The workaholic, well-informed merchant quickly built up enough of a stake to open a general store in Montgomery a few months before it became the state capital in 1846.[26]

With the banking system still in post-Jackson disarray and hard currency nowhere to be had, farmers paid for goods at Lehman's store in cotton, which he happily accepted. His brother Emanuel came over to join him; then in 1850 came another brother, Mayer. Though the Lehmans did not convert to Chris- tianity as some did, they assimilated; they ate pork, did business on Saturday, spoke English with Southern accents, and were pro-slavery.

We do not know whether Lehman ever sold slaves, but it would not be surprising if he did. It was certainly not illegal, it could be profitable, and few merchants did not at one time or another, in one way or another, become involved in a slave sale. Jacob Barrett, a Jewish merchant in partnership with his brother Judah in Columbia, South Carolina, and another brother, Isaac, in Charleston, sold:

> dry goods, groceries, provisions, liquors, (both at wholesale and retail,) hardware, crockery, shoes, hats and saddles. Besides all this, he sometimes bought a drove of hogs and made bacon for sale. He also speculated in negroes, horses and real estate. . . . a cargo of government soldiers' condemned coats or jackets, bought at a great sacrifice, were readily taken by the planters for their negroes at an advance of one or two hundred per cent. over cost. A gang of some twenty negroes from Charleston he soon disposed of at very large profits, keeping for his own use Armstead Booker, a good-looking, active carriage driver and barber, who attended to his horses and in the store, and Aunt Nancy, a first-rate cook, with her children.[27]

Barrett subsequently "married the daughter of his cousin, Jacob Ottolengui of Charleston, another speculator in Negroes, and claimed before the Civil War to have around a thousand slaves working his rice plantations near the Savannah River," in the words of Bertram Wallace Korn.[28]

All Southern towns of any size had Jewish residents in their business community. Some of them were, like other Southern merchants, slave traders, but the domestic slave trade was in no way a specialty of Jewish merchants. Jews were a tiny minority and were not disproportionately represented in the ranks of slave traders, nor were any of the biggest slave traders Jewish. Bancroft's list of seventy slave traders in Richmond lists only three Jews. The most important Jewish slave-trade firm was probably the Davis family of four brothers in Petersburg and Richmond, Virginia, who were named in Harriet Beecher Stowe's *The Key to Uncle Tom's Cabin*, quoting a letter from abolitionist Gamaliel Bailey: "The Davises, in Petersburg, are the great slave-dealers. They are Jews, came to that place many years ago as poor pedlers; and, I am informed, are members of a family which has its representatives in Philadelphia, New York, &c! These men are always in the market, giving the highest price for slaves. During the summer and fall they buy them up at low prices, trim, shave, wash them, fatten them so that they may look sleek, and sell them to great profit. It might not be unprofitable to inquire how much Northern capital, and what firms in some of the Northern cities, are connected with this detestable business."[29]

But a regionally bounded business like slaves wasn't Henry Lehman's interest, nor was tying up cash in long-term physical assets. He was into cotton and credit—which was inseparably bound up with the slavery industry, of course, but which was not the same thing. Slave property may have anchored Southern plantation mortgages, but it was the marketing of the cotton that consumed the credit from New York, which in turn consumed credit from London. It was the cotton, and not the slaves, that was shipped to Lancashire and sold by the pound, and in doing so, produced a hot cash flow. Handling that cash flow put Lehman in the fastest-rushing part of the global marketplace.

"In the years before 1845," writes Richard Holcombe Kilbourne, "the credit market was in many respects localized."[30] But with the regrouping of the economy after the prolonged post-Jackson depression and the annexation of Texas, the old institution of factorage became a principal provider of credit, and H. Lehman & Brother, as it was called at first, became a cotton factorage. Providing credit to cotton planters put the Lehmans in constant contact with New York banks—and, presumably, meant accepting slaves as collateral from planters. The firm in 1854 purchased a fourteen-year-old girl named Martha for $900, and Mayer Lehman ultimately owned seven slaves.[31] But he did not invest his profits in growing large holdings of enslaved people, the way planters did; he was a more modern kind of businessman. After Henry died of yellow fever in 1855, Emanuel moved to New York and established an office at 119 Liberty Street, while Mayer remained in Montgomery. The two became major financiers of the cotton trade in time for the boom years before secession. The Lehman brothers connected the slave-labor agriculture of the South with the financial world of New York in a direct way.

Lazarus Straus, a friend of the Lehmans from Bavaria, came over in 1848. Beginning as a peddler based out of Oglethorpe, Georgia, he moved to the small town of Talbotton, where he opened a store stocked with goods he managed to get on credit in Philadelphia, then in 1854 sent for his family.

Sam Houston arrived at the Hermitage a few hours too late on June 8, 1845: Andrew Jackson had died. As Houston's son watched, he lay his head on the dead Jackson's chest and mourned.

Jackson left his thousand-acre plantation and the approximately 150 slaves who worked it to his wastrel adopted son. As an anecdotal account of how he was remembered by one local African American, we turn to the memory of an elderly, formerly enslaved woman from the Nashville area, a former washer-woman whose name apparently went unrecorded when she was interviewed in 1929 or 1930 by a team from Fisk University:

> Did anybody ever tell you about old General Jackson? He was mean . . . In General Jackson's old place they had a whipping room, and they say now you can hear strange noises out there in that old house. I used to wash out there, after the War, but I never would go to the room to try to hear anything.[32]

38

Manifest Destiny's Child

*We have bought at this place, a very likely girl, 13 years old well grown &
smart, active &c. for $405.00, and Col. Campbell has just left with her for
home. I consider it a fine bargain.[1]*

—Letter from John W. Childress in Nashville to President Polk
in Washington, July 22, 1846

AS THE PROSPECT OF annexing Texas for the cotton kingdom created a speculative boom in young African Americans, the price of slaves shot up by about 30 percent. Anticipating the sustained bull market that did in fact set in, President Polk bought a total of nineteen people, quietly, from his perch at the White House between 1845 and 1848.[2] Except for a dip occasioned by the Panic of 1857, slave prices never went down again, but surged higher than ever.

In an article supporting the annexation of Texas, the Democratic Party propagandist John L. O'Sullivan coined the term *Manifest Destiny*, a phrase that has never gone away.[3] O'Sullivan's article is notable for its fusion of antiblack and anti-Mexican racism in a way that would become a permanent part of the social landscape of the American Southwest. In attempting to deny that annexing Texas was about slavery, O'Sullivan asserted in wordy prose typical of the era the principle that became known as "diffusionism": that the Upper South would become free of its slaves by selling them to Texas. Expecting, as many did, that Texas would be carved up into several states, he used the metaphor of waste water to describe the enslaved population, as he anticipated the day when slavery would no longer be necessary and black people could be flushed into Mexican society:

That [annexation] will tend to facilitate and hasten the disappearance of Slavery from all the northern tier of the present Slave States, cannot surely admit of serious question.

The greater value in Texas of the slave labor now employed in those States, must soon produce the effect of draining off that labor southwardly, by the same unvarying law that bids water descend the slope that invites it. Every new Slave State in Texas will make at least one Free State from among those in which that institution now exists . . . it is undeniably much gained for the cause of the eventual voluntary abolition of slavery, that it should have been thus drained off towards the only outlet which appeared to furnish much probability of the ultimate disappearance of the negro race from our borders.

The Spanish-Indian-American populations of Mexico, Central America and South America, afford the only receptacle capable of absorbing that race whenever we shall be prepared to slough it off—emancipate it from slavery, and (simultaneously necessary) to remove it from the midst of our own. Themselves already of mixed and confused blood, and free from the "prejudices" which among us so insuperably forbid the social amalgamation which can alone elevate the Negro race out of a virtually servile degradation even though legally free, the regions occupied by those populations must strongly attract the black race in that direction. (paragraphing added)

The project branded as Manifest Destiny was thus based in an utterly racist vision of ethnic cleansing—not only of Native Americans, but of African Americans.

The boundaries of Texas were not yet defined. The Republic of Texas's claims extended south to the Nueces River, but Polk went farther south and west, to the Rio Bravo del Norte (or Río Grande). Insisting on having the wide strip between the two rivers that was still populated mostly by wild horses (grassland then, barren and dusty now), he sent troops under the command of General Zachary Taylor, a wealthy Virginia-born Louisiana sugar planter who owned 147 slaves—even though Polk distrusted Taylor because he was a Whig. Taylor positioned his men on the banks of the Rio Grande and provoked an incident, creating the pretext to invade Mexican territory and take as much of it as possible, all the way out to California.

Polk asserted a new level of executive power, daring Mexico to fight and daring Congress to stop him. He signed the congressional act declaring war on Mexico on May 13, 1846. Almost at once, he advised his cabinet that he intended to acquire not only Texas, but California and New Mexico (the latter territory included the present states of Arizona, Utah, Colorado, and Nevada) as well.

There was also a legacy of conflicting claims to Oregon, but the South did not want a war with cotton-consuming Britain over it, so there wasn't one. Occupied with the fighting in Mexico, Polk compromised with Great Britain to divide up the Oregon territory, the lower part of which was already receiving American settlers in covered wagons. Ratified on June 18, 1846, the Oregon Treaty gave up American claims to "54°40' or fight" that would have extended American ownership up to Alaska, accepting instead the forty-ninth parallel (the present US-Canada border) that definitively brought present-day Oregon and Washington, including the highly desirable Puget Sound harbor, under US control. Oregon would not be a slave territory, but when it applied for admission to the Union as a state in 1858, its constitution forbade free black people from entering the state, as well as denying the ones who were already there the rights to testify in court, make contracts, and own property. Similar prohibitions would forbid the entry of free blacks into the free-soil states of Illinois, Indiana, and Iowa.

In August 1846 Polk asked Congress for an appropriation of two million dollars to support negotiations with Mexico in anticipation of victory, but antislavery members of the House on August 8 tacked onto the appropriations bill the proviso that would make Pennsylvania representative David Wilmot's name execrated throughout the South. The Wilmot Proviso prohibited slavery in any territory to be acquired from Mexico, following the theory that Wilmot explained in 1847: "Keep [slavery] within given limits . . . and in time it will wear itself out. Its existence can only be perpetuated by constant expansion."[4] When the Wilmot Proviso passed the House, eighty-five to seventy-nine, it wasn't on a party-line vote, but a sectional vote, North versus South, a harbinger of things to come. It failed in the sectionally balanced Senate. The South was furious that it had been proposed at all.

Antislavery politicians had no influence in the Senate, the Supreme Court, and certainly not in the executive branch. But free states dominated the House of Representatives. As the slave states slipped farther and farther behind in population, they became more insistent on keeping their balance of senators, which meant: add more slave states. As Wilmot had argued, slavery could only be perpetuated by constant expansion.

Though pressed by his duties as commander in chief of a war of conquest, Polk found the time to advise his recently widowed sister Eliza that she should invest what little money she had in buying people. In a letter of August 16, 1846, he suggested she move in with their mother and "apply [the money she had saved] to an increase of your [slave] force on your plantation, so as to enlarge your yearly income."[5]

"The Mexican War occupies much of my time at present," Polk wrote, in a classic understatement, to a correspondent on October 7.[6] A letter written to him two days later documents how his farm made twenty-five dollars, less commission, on a deal to acquire a girl who could be put to childbearing. With his hands full, Polk was more reliant than ever on his brothers-in-law, and one of them, Robert Campbell Jr., wrote him about some recent and planned purchases, including one in which he posted a small profit at a widow's expense through flipping the ownership of an enslaved boy in exchange for a "likely" girl at the beginning of her reproductive years. Bragging on his deal, Campbell discussed the children like they were mules:

> I have Sold the boy Jim that I bought for you [that] I gave $392 for to the Widow Colbern for $450 & bought a girl (Jane) 20 lb heavier for $425 and likely[,] 12 or 13 years old[.] it is one of the best trades I have made[.] I would have given the boy for the girl even[.][7]

General Winfield Scott, who like Taylor was distrusted by Polk as a Whig, bombarded the historic city of Veracruz for eighteen days in March 1847. When the troops entered the city to occupy it, they found starving people and rotting corpses. As Mexico capitulated, Polk didn't have the ideal negotiator at hand. But Secretary of State James Buchanan recommended his clerk, the number-two man at the State Department, who ran the department during Buchanan's extended absences: Nicholas P. Trist.

Trist's political credentials were impeccable, and after his years in Cuba he spoke Spanish. As negotiations dragged on, Polk fired him, but he remained on the job, negotiating the Treaty of Guadalupe Hidalgo with no official status whatever. Moreover, he didn't comply with his instructions, which had been to secure Alta and Baja California both: Mexico retained Baja California, which the United States had, after all, not conquered. Trist did manage, however, to secure the grand harbor at San Diego as the southernmost border of the territory to be acquired.

Polk was angry at losing Baja California, but he had a treaty, public support was waning, and the 1848 elections were looming. He made the deal, paying about $15 million for California and the New Mexico territory—about a third of Mexico, including its best farmland and the Northern California goldfields that would be discovered mere months after the purchase. Polk vindictively made sure that Trist did not receive his back salary for the time spent in the negotiations. It was the end of Trist's governmental career, and for the rest of their lives, he and Virginia Randolph Jefferson Trist lived in poverty.

The United States hoped to annex Cuba as well, and a suitor came calling to broker the deal. There were no tickets available for the sold-out performances in New York by Havana's opera company, the grandest in the hemisphere, of Giuseppe Verdi's new smash hit *Ernani*, but as noted in the *New York Herald* of June 28, 1847, they gave a special performance in honor of President Polk, while he was visiting New York. If Polk attended—there is no mention of it in his diary or letters—it is difficult to imagine that, with his chronic bowel complaints, he enjoyed the four-act Italian opera much, nor is it likely that such a spectacle was Sarah Polk's cup of tea. The company's impresario was none other than slave trader and fish dealer Pancho Marty, who had imported the best Italian talent to staff his troupe. The performance in honor of Polk was a demonstration not only of the riches and high level of imported culture in Cuba, but of who the right man was to make a deal with for Cuba—Pancho Marty.

The following year, John L. O'Sullivan began having meetings with Polk to urge him to acquire Cuba. In June 1848, Polk offered Spain $100 million for the island. Declined, thank you.

O'Sullivan, and a host of adventurers, made plans to take Cuba by conquest.

New Orleans could be a hellhole of disease in the warm months, and Isaac Franklin took ill there. After traveling back to his Bellevue plantation, he died suddenly, on May 4, 1846, at the age of fifty-six from what the doctor called "congestion of the stomach," which was likely cholera. A month later, after his distraught wife, Adelicia, had returned to Tennessee, she helplessly watched as two of their three daughters died two days apart from sudden cases of "croup and bronchitis."[8]

At the time of Franklin's death, he was possibly the richest man in President Polk's home state of Tennessee. He owned ten thousand acres of land in Tennessee, Louisiana, and Mississippi, plus claims in Texas, railroad bonds, and a large, continually increasing number of slaves. His estate was managed by his father-in-law and John Armfield as trustees, each receiving a 2½ percent commission, so that Armfield was still working for Franklin. By 1851, when the trustees got rid of the responsibility and turned his estate over to the widow, it was worth almost

$710,000 (perhaps $21.5 million in 2014). Sixty-nine percent of the value of Franklin's six Louisiana plantations was in its more than six hundred slaves, who were worth $363,927.80 out of the estate's total value of $525,674.85.

During the five years of Armfield and Hayes's trusteeship, the slaves registered thirty deaths and eighty births, realizing a profit from "natural increase." The deaths and births were broken out and inventoried in separate schedules in the estate proceedings, in which one can see that the average age at death was twenty-nine, all but four of the deceased having died before the age of fifty. The births—eighty children of four or younger—were listed by name, mother, age, and color: "Madison, child of Caroline, 3, black; Bradley, child of Martha Winchester, an infant, black; Milly, child of Matilda Trottman, 4, griff; Len, ditto, 1 . . ."[9]

What would they be worth in a few years? An April 1857 article in *DeBow's Review* cheered the high prices fetched at a sale of children in Texas, with terms of one and two years, and 10 percent interest. DeBow printed the names, ages, and prices fetched: "Caroline, 11 years old, $1,100; Frank, 9, $805; Little Allick, 7, $810; Catharine, 10, $700; Flora, 6, $695; Sarah, 9, $890; Dick. 7, $650; Sam, 3, $450; Phoebe, 10, $655; Ben, 6, $405."[10]

In his will, made in 1841, Franklin directed how many more hands were to be purchased for each of the plantations, and specified how the executors were to improve his holdings with two more plantations, called Panola and Loango, to be developed alongside the four already existing on the land. It's not clear why Franklin wanted to have two plantations (Loango and Angola) named after Central African slave markets on opposite sides of the Kongo River, since he didn't do business in Africans. But Angola is what the biggest antebellum slave trader called his plantation. The prison by that name today on those same grounds in East Feliciana Parish is Franklin's infamous bequest to Louisiana's cultural life.

So New Orleans saxophonist Charles Neville was right when he said that the land occupied by the Louisiana State Penitentiary was formerly a "slave-breeding plantation."[11] Neville spent three and a half years there for having had two reefers. Any Louisiana musician can sing you:

Now six months ain't no sentence
One year ain't no time
They got boys in Angola
Doin' nine to ninety-nine.

Isaac Franklin left a large footprint. His idyllically situated Fairvue mansion today anchors a beautiful, upscale residential development, with more than

Isaac Franklin's former mansion of Fairvue, now a private residence, March 2014.

eight hundred large homes, a golf course, a country club, and Franklin's mansion and tomb.[12]

A tale of two plantations: at the other end of the desirability scale from Fairvue, Isaac Franklin's Louisiana land ultimately passed to the State of Louisiana, retaining the name Angola to cover all five previously distinct plantation tracts. In the last decades of the nineteenth century, it was run as a plantation using convict labor. Since 1901 it has been home to the Louisiana State Penitentiary, known internationally as Angola—a singular institution even in the harsh annals of American penology. The former agricultural prison has remained an agricultural prison: a self-sustaining plantation that forces its inmates to get their hands cut up, because at Angola they still pick cotton by hand instead of using machinery. Angola houses sixty-three hundred inmates—76 percent of them black and 71 percent serving life sentences—and it employs eighteen hundred people to keep them incarcerated. The continuity of Angola prison ties the historical slave trade to a living modern legacy of unequal treatment, income disparity, social pathology, and mass incarceration. The penal regime it imposes on convicts bears a chilling resemblance to the antebellum slave experience.

⤐⤏

Adelicia Franklin married twice more after Issac Franklin died. Her first remarriage, at Fairvue on May 8, 1849, was a major social event, as per ex-president Polk's diary entry:

> This evening Mrs. Polk and myself attended the marriage of Mrs. Franklin, a wealthy widow of this City. She was married at her own house to Mr. Acklin of Huntsville, Alabama. The supper and whole entertainment was upon a magnificent scale. I met at the wedding many leading Whigs & democrats, and was courteously and kindly treated by all.[13]

It was one of Polk's last social events. He had just returned to Nashville after leaving the presidency. On his trip home from Washington, worn out from prosecuting the war with Mexico, he noted in his diary the presence of cholera on the boat. At every stop he was given balls, public dinners, and received enormous numbers of visitors, despite suffering from "a derangement of stomach & bowels" and feeling "greatly wearied and worn down."[14] In New Orleans, Mayor Abdiel Crossman denied there was a cholera epidemic (there was) and insisted the fatigued ex-president come to a public dinner with 250 guests. As Polk continued on by riverboat, there was cholera on board again; various passengers died. Once in Nashville, he noted in his diary various people in the town being taken ill with cholera. His penultimate entry, on June 1, ends, "During the prevalence of cholera I deem it prudent to remain as much as possible at my own house."[15] But he too died of it, on June 15, a little more than ten weeks after leaving the presidency.

In his one term, Polk had reshaped the nation. In the process, he had reached the westward limits of slavery expansion. Slavery was exploding in eastern Texas, but it would grow no more to the West beyond that, though the Slave Power would fight hard in a losing battle for California.

While most of the value of Polk's estate consisted of slaves, he wasn't worth a tenth of what Isaac Franklin was worth. In his will, Polk, ever the politician, wrote that "Should I survive her [Sarah], unless influenced by circumstances which I do not now foresee, it is my intention to emancipate all my slaves, and I have full confidence, that if at her death she shall deem it proper, she shall emancipate them." But, as in the cases of Martha Washington and Dolley Madison, who like Sarah Polk were survivors of slaveholding presidential husbands, she didn't "deem it proper" to emancipate them. Wearing black for the rest of her life, she lived to be eighty-eight at Polk Place, the mansion they had occupied together for only three months, with her husband's tomb in the front yard. She had not been weakened by multiple childbirths and miscarriages like so many women of her era, and she was wealthy and savvy. In 1860, she cashed out, selling a one-half interest in her plantation, including all but six of her fifty-six slaves, to a relative for $28,500—over $800,000 in 2014 dollars.[16]

It was a fraction of what Adelicia Franklin got.

In terms of territorial gains, Polk's Manifest Destiny war with Mexico did very well, bringing under US control more than half a million square miles, sparsely populated even by Native Americans. As the Texans began slowly learning the Mexican ways of handling horses and cattle that became known as cowboying, and learned a new way of cooking, they called themselves "white people" in opposition to the Mexicans, whom they typically treated as an inferior "race."

The "white people" began expelling the Mexicans from their towns. For one thing, in a frontier society that was chronically short of women, Mexican men were taking enslaved women away, thereby robbing the slaveholders of the future increase that they saw as their due. A newspaper reported:

> MATAGORDA. — The people of Matagorda county have held a meeting and ordered every Mexican to leave the country. . . . [They] have no fixed domicile, but hang around the plantations, taking the likeliest negro girls for wives; and . . . they often steal horses, and these girls, too, and endeavor to run them to Mexico.[17]

The annexation of Texas kicked the Southern slave market into gear. But as the market for slaves heated up, no single firm dominated the trade the way Franklin and Armfield previously had. No slave-trading firm grew like Lehman and Brother did dealing cotton, and there was no major slave-retailing corporation that survived the war to trade in something else. Instead of the market consolidating after Franklin, it fragmented. Slave traders were mostly small shops, including many part-timers who left no records and a much less coherent paper trail than Franklin's company. Perhaps no one else had the ability to focus so many partners on a common set of business goals across the full geographic area, much less accomplish the complex task of keeping the money flowing smoothly at all times.

The 1840 census showed 2,487,355 slaves, and the 1850 census registered a 28.8 percent increase, for a total of 3,204,313. American slavery had never stopped growing since its beginnings in seventeenth-century Virginia. It could never stop growing, or the whole system would collapse of its own weight. More and more slave states were looking to export their young. People from every slave state could be found on sale in the market at New Orleans, where many were bought for Texas. But even so, the value of "Virginia and Maryland negroes" held as a premium brand, and shipments continued from Baltimore, Alexandria, Richmond, Norfolk, and lesser ports.

Austin Woolfolk's operation had been profitable; Freudenberger and Pritchett calculate that after the expenses of maintaining slave jails at both ends, feeding the captives for weeks, buying all the newspaper advertisements, chartering a vessel, et cetera, Woolfolk's firm had a 14 percent rate of return.[18] Woolfolk married, had five children, and was substantially out of the business by 1842, though he continued shipping slaves until 1846. He too moved to plantation land he had bought in Louisiana.[19] He died of tuberculosis in 1847, "reduced to a mere skeleton," as his uncle described it in a letter, in a tavern in Auburn, Alabama, leaving behind property in Louisiana, Alabama, and Maryland.[20] More than thirty years later, his son, Austin Jr., sued his own mother, Emily Woolfolk, over the partitioning of the estate, which even with slavery no longer in existence was still worth a six-figure sum.[21]

Baltimore's outbound slave shipments in the 1840s exceeded those of the previous decade, as more major traders got into the act. In Alexandria, the Franklin and Armfield headquarters on Duke Street were taken over by their former associate George Kephart, who was for a time the biggest dealer in Alexandria, then by "Price, Birch, dealers in slaves," James Birch's firm. Kephart's business declined by 1843, and from then until secession the biggest Alexandria slave trader was the firm of Bruin & Hill (Joseph Bruin and Henry Hill), whose slave jail at 1707 Duke Street is now on the National Register of Historic Places, though it's not open to the public. Bruin seems to have sent most of his victims South in coffles—for which, unlike oceangoing vessels, there were no manifests to survive for the historical record.

As abolitionists continued to bombard Congress with petitions to end slavery and the slave trade in the capital city, Alexandria in 1847 requested, and was allowed, to leave the District of Columbia and rejoin Virginia, so that the present-day District of Columbia is entirely on land ceded by Maryland.

Three years later, as part of a series of compromises that occupied the nation's political class for an entire year—the Compromise of 1850—slave trading, though not slavery itself, was at last prohibited in Washington.

39

A Letter from Virginia

The little Boy has one of his toes cut off. I don't think that will lessen his value . . . Doct Ingram has Known the Boy for a length of time and Says he never Gives him medicine but once for Belly Ache[.] he is Smaller than I like but it is hard to Buy at any price up here.[1]

—Sumterville, SC, purchasing agent A. J. McElveen to
Charleston dealer Ziba B. Oakes, November 7, 1853

IN HIS WILL, ISAAC Franklin directed that the income from his plantations support a school to be named the Isaac Franklin Institute, but his widow Adelicia got the court to void the provision, on the grounds that it would create a "perpetuity," which in this case would have rested on the perpetual reproduction of the estate's enslaved. Instead, she got the assets, including Fairvue.

The trustees' management of Franklin's estate terminated with the resolution of the widow's court proceeding. During the five years or so of their management, seemingly every receipt submitted for every expense was collected and printed as part of the 918-page legal document titled *Succession of Isaac Franklin*, which thus provides an unusually detailed snapshot of the mercantile realities of the time. The trustees bought laudanum, morphine, calomel (mercury chloride, a toxic compound then believed to have medicinal value and often used as a laxative), and a host of other preparations for when the "negroes" were sick. They bought "negro shoes" from the Tennessee State Prison, which used convict labor to make salable products. They sold cotton and lumber.

Adelicia was presented to Queen Victoria when she visited London and was complimented on her riding skills by the horsewoman Princess Victoria Eugenie of Battenburg. It was Adelicia who brought Spanish palominos to breed in Tennessee.[2] With her new husband, Joseph Acklen, she became a leading light of the Nashville social scene at her new thirty-six-room mansion on her estate called Belmont, which besides ten thousand square feet of living space had a bear house and a zoo, and where her daughter Emma died of diphtheria.

John Armfield too became a respectable planter, and was a principal benefactor at the founding of the University of the South at Sewanee, Tennessee. Franklin's former Richmond partner Rice C. Ballard became a planter as well, though he continued to be involved in the slave trade. He married and moved to Louisville, though he seems to have spent a great deal of time in Natchez, to judge from the letters he received there from his wife begging him for money.

Ballard became friends, and then a business partner with, a Natchez judge named Samuel S. Boyd, with whom he co-owned a string of cotton plantations worked by perhaps five hundred slaves in Mississippi, Louisiana, and Arkansas. Boyd and Ballard's man in New Orleans was a Louisville-based slave trader named C. M. Rutherford, whose office in New Orleans was at 159 Gravier Street, between Baronne and Carondelet, and who also sold slaves in Natchez.

It was advantageous for Ballard to keep a hand in slave retailing. He and Boyd at one point closed down a plantation and sold the entire labor force South, a few at a time. Ballard provided working cash for Rutherford to buy with, and Rutherford knew what Ballard liked, as when he offered him a woman "19 years old black likely and all rite as tall and likely as the one you wanted of white, price $700."[4]

Boyd was cruel to women. The Natchez attorney J. M. Duffield had owned a woman named Maria, and though he was fond of her and had a sexual relationship with her, he wound up through financial pressures losing her to Boyd's ownership. On May 29, 1848, Duffield wrote Ballard about Maria and her daughter (who may have been his daughter), asking him to intervene after she had been whipped "like an ox, until the blood gushes from her." Another letter from Duffield reported on August 5 that "Mr. Boyd will part with her now as her health is such that she must be a charge on any owner," as she suffered from

Slave Transfer Agencies.

D. M. MATTHEWS,
C. M. RUTHERFORD,
Slave Depot, (old stand,) No. 159
Gravier street.

Southern Business Directory, *1854.*[3]

"womb complaint dreadfully brought on by unkindness and injuries, bodily injuries, and . . . [now that she can leave Boyd,] she can now recover though she will probably linger out to several years." Unfortunately, Duffield didn't have any cash right then. He offered another slave as security, promising to pay "any price you might think she ought to bring, and perhaps prolong her life, which will soon be shortened where she is [now]."[5]

On February 27, 1853, Rutherford wrote Ballard from New Orleans about a troublesome slave named Virginia, which may have been the name her mother gave her or may have simply been where she was purchased. Virginia was being sent as far away as Rutherford could manage, along with her swelling belly and her two children, who, though he didn't need to mention it, looked like Judge Boyd. While Rutherford was trying to decide whether to "send her to Texas . . . or send her to Mobile," she kept trying to run away.

Meanwhile, it was good to know a judge. On April 2, 1853, Boyd came to Ballard with a dirty deal—the lucrative prospect of selling a whole plantation full of freed slaves back into slavery:

Have lately learned of an opportunity to buy a lot of negroes at a very reasonable rate, next January.

Old man Baldwin, of Jefferson County, directed his slaves to be sent to Liberia. This will be declared void at the present term of the High Court, and as nearly all the heirs reside in New Jersey, they do not want the slaves, & are willing they should be all sold together, to a good master, at a reasonable rate, according to the will, if it cannot be carried out. {Name indecipherable}, one of the Executors, has informed me he thinks they can be had at . . . $27000 for fifty two. He is to furnish me with a list soon, and will endeavour to obtain authority to close the trade.

The same day, Rutherford wrote Ballard that he'd decided to send Virginia to Texas, but it was going to cost: he had "a friend there I can send her to but the vessels will not take any negro unless under the charge of some white person." So eager were the partners to get rid of Virginia that Rutherford hired an escort to deliver her personally to Texas. From New Orleans, Rutherford handled her case to the point of final sale, offering easy terms, as Rutherford reported on April 19:

I have this morning shiped Virginia & children to S.B. Ewing Houston Texas with special instructions to sell her not to return to this place or Miss[issippi.] I gave her character and did not limit the sale when sold to permit account sales & nett proceeds to [factors] Nalle Cox & Co of this place for your benefit[.] I will give Nalle Cox & Co a copy of my letter of instructions[.] I had to hire a young man to go with her to Galveston.[6]

A letter from Boyd three days later that refers to Virginia only as "the woman" makes clear that she didn't go quietly: "Rutherford was to ship the woman & her children to Texas on Tuesday last, by the steamer Mexico. She gave him a load of trouble."

There exists a letter from the heavily pregnant Virginia to Ballard, written in the desperation of the moment.[7] The dimensions of her story are apparent, even though much is unknowable about the events referred to. A facsimile is available online;[8] we will present it here as we have transcribed it, adding full-stop periods, capital letters, and paragraphing for readability, with question marks indicating transcription queries, brackets around reasonable guesses, and Xs signifying missing bits of text.

Houston May 6th 1853

Dear Sir permit me to address you a few lines which I hope you will receive soon. I am at present in the city of Houston in a Negro traders yard for sale by your orders. I was present at the Post Office when Doctor Ewing took your letter out through mistake and red it a loud, not knowing I was the person the letter alluded to.

I hope that if I have ever done or said any thing that has offended you that you will for give me for I have suffered enough cince in mind to repay all that I have ever done to anyone[.]

You wrote for them to sell me in thirty days. Do you think after all that has transpired between me & the old Man)I don't call names(that its treating me well to send me off a mong strangers in my situation to besold without even my having an opportunity of choosing for my self. Its hard in deed and what is still harder—for the father of my children to sell his own offspring yes his own flesh & blood. My god is it possible that any free born American would brand his charites with such a stigma as that, but I hope before this he will relent & see his error for I still beleave that he is possesst of more honer than that.

I no too that you have influence and can assist me in some measure from out of this dilema and if you will god will be sure to reward you, you have a family of children & no how to simpathize with others in distress.

all I require or ask [is] for an agent to be appointed hear to see to me, XXXXX to Earn the money, honestly, to buy my XXXXX I have to work

Houston May 6th 1853

Col. Ballet
Waren County Waverton
Missisipi Magnolia

Dear Sir please [give] me to address you a few lines which I hope you will receive soon, I am at present in the city of Houston in a Negro traders yard, for sale, by your order I was present at the Post Office when Doctor Oam took your letter out through mistake and read it aloud, not knowing I was the person the letter alluded to. I hope that if I have ever done or said any thing that has offended you that you will forgive me, for I have suffered enough since in mind to repay all that I have ever done, to any one, you wrote for them to sell me in thirty days, do you think after all that has transpired between me & the old Man, I dont call names, that its treating me well to send me off a mong strangers in my situation to besold without even my having an opportunity of choosing for my self, its hard in deed and what is still harder, for the father of my children to sell his own offspring yes his own flesh & blood My god is it possible that any free born American would hand his charter with such a stigma as that, but I hope before this he will relent & see his error for I still beleave that he is possest of more honer than that I no too that you have influence and can assist me in some measure from out of this dilema and if you will god will be sure to reward you, you have a family of children & no how to empathize with others in distress, all I require or ask for an agent to be appointed hear to see to me and [ ] me to Earn the money honestly to buy my [ ] I have to work my finger ends off I will earn [ ] any ony dime I do think in justice

The first page of Virginia Boyd's letter.

my finger ends off I will earn XXXXXay evry dime I do think in justice [the] children should be set free XXXX[As] for my self altho my youthfull days [were worn] out in [t]he service and grattification of the [person that] now wants me & his children sold is it posible that such a change could ever come over the spirit of any living man as to sell his child that is his image[?] I don't wish to return to harras or molest his peace of mind & shall never try get back if I am steall with family.

I no that you have been prejudist a gainst me, by what {name unclear} told you one day you will find who is the rascal & who has injured you most I have no motive in saying to you any thing but the pure truth, when you come to know all that she has said relative to you & matters concerning your family you will prehaps not have so great a confidence in all the tales she fabricates[.] I wish you to reflect over the subject and see if some little could be shown me for that mercy & pity you show to me god certainly will show you[.]

What can I say more if I ever have spoken hastly that which I should not I hope you will for give me for I hope god has, I am humbled enough all reddy, hear a mong strangers without one living being to whom I have the least shadow of claim upon, my heart feels like it would burst a sunder[.] It will not be long ere I am confined, & the author of my suffering to be the means of my being thrown upon the charity to strangers in XXXX when I most need a simpathizing friend is XXXXX that XXX to receive for making so mXXXX for his sattisfaction.

Will y[ou le]t me hear from you & say what yo[ur feelings] are relative to the proposition I make[?] [I know you are an] honerable high minded man and in your XXXX moments you would wish justice to be done to all, & if I am a servent there is some thing due me better than my present situation.

I have writen to the Old Man in such a way that the letter cant faile to fall in his hans & none others. I use any precaution to prevent others from knowing or suspecting any thing. I have my letters writen & folded put into envelope & get it directed by those that dont know the contents of it for I shall not seek ever to let any thing be exposed, unless I am forced from bad treatement.

Virginia Boyd

Some of the elisions in Virginia Boyd's letter are accidental, some strategic. We can imagine the story; indeed, we have to in order to parse what we read. But there's much we don't know. Who is the "Old Man," the father of her children she's referring to? Presumably Boyd. She's signing Boyd's name as hers, with the clear indication that her children are to carry that name too. But Ballard was the one giving the sale order—apparently because Virginia was owned by the partnership, and Ballard handled slave sales.

Unlike Maria, Virginia at least got away from Boyd without being maimed. All three of the traders in the loop knew her; she indicates a personal familiarity with Ballard, who was a frequent visitor to Natchez, and to her co-owner—and who, she believes, has been turned against her by lies told by another enslaved female. We can make up stories about what *that* was about, but we don't know.

What else might we know about Virginia? According to Rutherford's earlier letter, she already had two children. She felt that her "youthfull days" were behind her. She might have been twenty-five, ready to be discarded as too old. What did she look like? She'd been the mistress of a slave trader, so she was presumably light-skinned. She wasn't a field hand; she had been accustomed to privileges, and perhaps had imagined the goal of freedom for herself and her children to be getting closer. She expected to be able to "choose for myself," suggesting perhaps that even her enslaved status had been in question at some point, but she has now been "humbled."

The level of literacy in her letter is at least as good as the traders'. There is no reason to assume that it was written by a scribe; its twists and turns seem the product of a coordinated mind, voice, and hand. Somehow, we don't know how, she had the ability to get letters sent by private channels out of the trader's yard—one to Boyd, apparently, and this one to Ballard. And, she warns, if "forced from bad treatment" she could write another one that would tell what somebody doesn't want known.

The blackmail threat did her no good. She was sold into the hard conditions of the Texas frontier. There's no known record of her further existence. Her plea to free her children was ignored; slave traders didn't set children free, they sold them, and they were inured to—perhaps even enjoyed—desperate pleas. Virginia was sold together with her younger child, whose gender we don't know, for a thousand dollars. If that child was Boyd's daughter, by light-skinned Virginia, she would have been "mighty near white"—a fancy girl, the slave trader's premium prize. In a typical slave-trader move, Virginia's older child, a girl, was kept back.

A letter of August 8 from Rutherford to Ballard said: "I recd a letter this morning informing me of the sale of Virginia & her Child reserving the eldest Child for $1000[.] I wrote Mr. Ewing not to sell the oldest child untill he heard from me . . . I recollect you wanted to reserve her before she went away which can be done now if you wish let me hear from you on the subject."

Five months after Virginia was disposed of, Rutherford wrote Ballard from Natchez:

> Since writing I have seen Judge Boyd[.] he tells me that he thinks you will want 10 to 15 more females[.] I have on hand I think 12 more but they are the kind you would not buy[.] I know they are such as I would not buy for you although they are large . . . you cannot buy anything like a fair woman here for less than $1000 any that you would have[.] I know a lot of Georgia negroes at Memphis that I think you could buy the women for $900 . . . I told the judge if you wished me I would go up there and buy you ten or fifteen & and charge you nothing but my expenses . . . Judge is in favor of my going if you say so.[9]

It may be that Isaac Franklin's fantasy of a company "whore house" was not such an exaggeration.

In 1856, the year the secessionist leader and former governor James Henry Hammond was elected senator from South Carolina, he wrote his twenty-two-year-old son Harry a remarkably candid letter regarding the disposition of two sex slaves in the latest version of his will.

Hammond was something of an outlier in sexual behavior, as his confessional diary reveals. He wrote some of the only antebellum letters that survive documenting a sexual relationship between two men (with Thomas Jefferson Withers), and confessed in his diary to molesting all four of his teenage nieces from the marriage of Wade Hampton II to his wife's sister. Hammond had purchased Sally Johnson, a "mulatto" seamstress, when she was eighteen, along with her (presumably lighter-skinned) one-year-old daughter Louisa, who became his concubine when she was twelve. He had children by both women—which is to say that, besides those children's complicated relationship to each other, they were his son's half siblings, as he explained in the letter to his son:

> In the last will I made I left to you, over and above my other children Sally Johnson the mother of Louisa and all the children of both. Sally says Henderson is my child. It is possible, but I do not believe it. Yet act on her's rather than my opinion.

Louisa's first child may be mine. I think not. Her second I believe is mine. Take care of her and her children who are both of your blood if not of mine and of Henderson. The services of the rest will I think compensate for an indulgence to these. I cannot free these people and send them North. It would be cruelty to them. Nor would I like that any but my own blood should own as Slaves my own blood or Louisa.

I leave them to your charge, believing that you will best appreciate and most independently carry out my wishes in regard to them. Do not let Louisa or any of my children or possible children be slaves of Strangers. Slavery in the family will be their happiest earthly condition.[10] (paragraphing added)

Among the greatest misfortunes Hammond considered himself to have suffered was that his captives died so frequently—"I have lost 89 negroes and at least 50 mules and horses in 11 years," he lamented in his diary. Perhaps, he wrote, he should move their quarters to a less unhealthy spot.[11]

following page: The Maxcy-Rhett house, informally known as "secession house," in Beaufort, South Carolina. By 1850, the political class of Beaufort was already determined to secede. June 2013.

40

Communists in Blackface

Give us SLAVERY or give us death![1]

—Edward Bryan, South Carolina, 1850

THE DISCOVERY OF GOLD in California was a turning point on the way to Southern secession.

President Polk announced the find to the nation in his year-end message of 1848. Some ninety thousand gold-seekers arrived in northern California in 1849, staking their claims and displacing and murdering Native Americans en masse: the native population of the region dwindled in short order from about 150,000 to about 30,000.

Lured by the boom, immigrants came from Latin America and Europe to California and to the United States in general, and this on top of the massive Irish potato-famine migration that began arriving in numbers in 1847. Asian trade developed, Hawaii's economy thrived, and Chinese workers, principally Cantonese, came to both Hawaii and California. As gold fever spread, men (who were perhaps as much as 95 percent of the early migrants) left home and family to go West; Nantucket found itself "drained" of "one-quarter of its voting population" in nine months.[2] A song from the period described the mania:

> *The people all went crazy then, they didn't know what to do*
> *They sold their farms for just enough to pay their passage through*
> *They bid their friends a long farewell, said "Dear wife, don't you cry,*
> *I'll send you home the yellow lumps a piano for to buy."[3]*

With the discovery of other mines in the West, billions of dollars' worth of new money was extracted over the ensuing decades. It was an immediate game-changer, with global implications. So much gold was sucked to Britain, the United States' creditor and the world's economic powerhouse, that it was easily able to consolidate its already in-progress shift to the gold standard.

Europe was troubled by a wave of revolutions. Beginning with a revolt in Sicily in January 1848 and a much bigger one in France the following month, insurrection spread to most of the continent. But it was put down within a year, and economic problems faded as the new money supply worked its way into the continent.

A mint was established at San Francisco as the United States issued unprecedented amounts of its own gold coinage:

Year	Amount of gold minted into coins[4]
1848	$3,775,000
1850	$31,981,000
1851	$62,614,000
1852	$56,846,000

The flood of coins brought down the price of gold and drove silver out of circulation. With a domestic supply of gold, the United States could at last ban foreign money—most especially, the "Spanish dollar"—from circulation in 1857. The total amount of paper money issued by banks, in circulation and on deposit, went from $231 million in 1848 to $392 million in 1854, and $445 million in 1857—and the paper was of higher quality for having so much more gold in the system.[5] Bankers and businessmen had a newfound sense of confidence and optimism, which made them more eager to speculate. The British were investing.

California was an immigration magnet. But it was as hard to get to San Francisco from New York as from Chile, and Chilean gold-seekers were indeed arriving. The Eastern US wanted a transcontinental railroad, and the United States government wanted control of the Central American portage crossing—whether in Honduras, Nicaragua, or, the ultimate choice, Panamá, the latter of which was then part of Colombia but would be pried away to become a zone of US influence.

It was the richest injection of precious metal into the global economy since the Hapsburgs had capitalized the world with gold and silver from Mexico and Perú. As the dimensions of the gold find became clear in 1849, the statehood of

California was suddenly an urgent matter, before some other country tried to move in or before the miners decided to declare themselves an independent republic.

Unlike Louisiana, which had been slave territory before Washington took it over, California had been free territory under Mexico, and even slaveowner President Zachary Taylor was against establishing slavery there. But there was a powerful economic interest in favor of it: slavery in California would, it was widely believed, make the value of existing slaveholdings appreciate sharply.

A few slaveowners moved with their slaves to southern California, hoping to establish it as slave territory and take over the government, as had happened in Texas. But moving a plantation's worth of captive laborers even a few hundred miles was a big undertaking, let alone the near-impossibility of taking coffles the fourteen hundred parched miles from Houston to Los Angeles.

Southerners saw gold mining as something that should be done by slave labor, purchased from them. But up in the north, the forty-niner gold miners, who drafted their own legal codes requiring small, continuously worked claims, weren't about to have slaves working on massive gold plantations. They didn't want slave labor or free black people, either one; for them, California was white man's country. When a group of Texans headed by Thomas Jefferson Green tried establishing claims on the Yuba River in the names of their sixteen slaves in July 1849, miners informed them that "no slave or negro should own claims or even work in the mines," and physically expelled them all.*[6]

The large state of California, extending all the way down to San Diego, requested annexation with a free-soil constitution in 1849, putting checkmate as they did so on the westward expansion of slavery. One delegate at the California constitutional convention, Henry Tefft, matter-of-factly referred to the slaveowners as "capitalists" when he warned the assembly that the young white male miner population "would be unable, even if willing, to compete with the bands of negroes who would be set to work under the direction of the capitalists. It would become a monopoly of the worst character. The profits of the mines would go into the pockets of single individuals."[7] A clause that would have barred free blacks from entering the territory was voted down.

In South Carolina, Robert Barnwell Rhett, outraged that a group of gold-digging migrants could declare themselves to define California and thus exclude slavery, derided the California constitution as "squatter sovereignty," *squatter* being the preferred aristocratic epithet for poor rural whites, who often lacked

---

*The *Oxford English Dictionary* notes the emergence in 1856, in the United States, of a new word: *vigilante*.

legal title to the land they lived on. The states were the owners of the territories, argued the Fire-Eaters, and the slave states must be allowed to bring their property to their property.

Henry Clay, together with Stephen A. Douglas of Illinois, attempted to placate the Slave Power with a grand compromise in January 1850 that was packaged by Mississippi unionist Henry Foote into a single "Omnibus" bill, which was then disassembled and recast into a series of laws known as the Compromise of 1850. It proposed admitting California as a free state and giving territorial status to Utah (later divided into Utah and Nevada) and New Mexico (later divided into New Mexico and Arizona), while disregarding Texas's claims to New Mexican territory.

In Clay's final grand speech after decades of fame as an orator, he attacked Massachusetts senator John Davis's charge that Texans were trying to establish the "breeding" of slaves in New Mexico, a territory that was useless for plantation agriculture but which Texas was intent on annexing as slave territory.[8] Davis, perhaps intimidated, denied having used the term, but Clay wouldn't let him off the hook. He rhapsodized about how kind slaveowners were to their slaves and how sale into the market only was a painful last resort. Then he demonized abolitionists. He thus discredited himself in the eyes of posterity as a pandering apologist for slavery, while failing to please the Fire-Eaters, who wanted much more than Clay was prepared to give. Clay was a Unionist, and for him the Union meant the compromises that only he was adroit enough to manage.

The Compromise of 1850 included prohibition of the slave trade in the District of Columbia. Since Alexandria had left the District and returned to Virginia precisely over this issue, the interstate trade was not seriously disrupted, and in any case, slavery was not abolished in the District. But the secessionist project that was already well under way considered compromise to be treason, and the Fire-Eaters screamed bloody murder anyway.

For the North, the most offensive compromise was a new Fugitive Slave Act. Aimed at shutting down the Underground Railroad that emboldened the enslaved to escape, and building on the constitutional requirement to hand over fugitive "persons held to service," it required lawmen to capture and deliver anyone in any state accused of being a fugitive slave, with no right of denial on the part of the accused. It gave kidnappers a legal apparatus.

Outraged by the "aggression" of ending the slave trade in the District of Columbia, Southern members of both houses of Congress met in a caucus and produced *The Address of the Southern Delegates of Congress to their Constituents.*

Clearspring, Washington County, Md.,   1850.

DEAR SIR: AN ACT of Congress, Approved by the President Sept., 18th., 1850, enables us to secure any runaway negro, who can be found and identified.

Having a description of your negro who escaped in 18   we have taken the liberty to address you; to ascertain whether you are willing to aid us, in our efforts to procure him. During the last 10 years we have made every effort in our power, to secure servants, whenever they have escaped from their masters. While engaged in this persuit, we have become acquainted with men in almost every town and city throughout Pa., who will give us all the information, they are able to obtain, regarding any negroes who have escaped, or may hereafter escape from their masters.

We propose sending each of these men a copy of your advertisement, if you will pay the postage, and the expense of printing. By having a proper number of advertisements circulated at this time, we think you will have a better chance to secure your servant, than when he first run off; as the law which was formerly very much against us, is now greatly in our favor. Our charge for postage and printing, is $5. A copy of each bill printed by us, will in all cases be sent to the owner. Should either your own servants, or your neighbors hereafter attempt to make their escape, we hope to be notified as soon as possible; and in all cases when the money is sent to pay for printing and postage, we will send advertisements to all parts of Maryland and Pennsylvania, and make every effort in our power to have the runaways apprehended.

P. S. Runaways can be apprehended in any of the Northern states, and we propose to extend our operations to every point where fugitives can be found.

KINSEL & DOYLE.

The Fugitive Slave Act stimulated Southern slave-catchers to expand their operations into the free-state North, as per this September 1850 mailing piece by Maryland firm Kinsel & Doyle, which boasts of its network in Pennsylvania. The legal occupation of fugitive-catcher easily served as a cover for illegal kidnapping operations targeting free people.

Mostly written by the aged, embittered John C. Calhoun, it warned of emancipation's awful consequences, expanding out into rings of ever more apocalyptic fantasy clad in the robes of prophecy. We offer one of its key passages as a glimpse into the routinely voiced Southern fear that white people would be on the receiving end of the violence of slavery:

> If [emancipation] ever should be effected, it will be through the agency of the Federal Government, controlled by the dominant power of the Northern States of the Confederacy, against the resistance and struggle of the Southern. It can then only be effected by the prostration of the white race; and that would necessarily engender the bitterest feelings of hostility between them and the North.
>
> But the reverse would be the case between the blacks of the South and the people of the North. Owing their emancipation to them, they would regard them as friends, guardians, and patrons, and centre, accordingly, all their sympathy in them. The people of the North would not fail to reciprocate and to favor them, instead of the whites. Under the influence of such feelings, and impelled by fanaticism and love of power, they would not stop at emancipation.

Another step would be taken—to raise them to a political and social equality with their former owners, by giving them the right of voting and holding public offices under the Federal Government. We see the first step toward it in the bill already alluded to—to vest the free blacks and slaves with the right to vote on the question of emancipation in this District. But when once raised to an equality, they would become the fast political associates of the North, acting and voting with them on all questions, and by this political union between them, holding the white race at the South in complete subjection.

John C. Calhoun.

The blacks, and the profligate whites that might unite with them, would become the principal recipients of federal offices and patronage, and would, in consequence, be raised above the whites of the South in the political and social scale. We would, in a word, change conditions with them—a degradation greater than has ever yet fallen to the lot of a free and enlightened people, and one from which we could not escape, should emancipation take place (which it certainly will if not prevented), but by fleeing the homes of ourselves and ancestors, and by abandoning our country to our former slaves, to become the permanent abode of disorder, anarchy, poverty, misery, and wretchedness.[9] (paragraphing added)

Frederick Douglass answered Calhoun's negrophobic blast, referencing the Fugitive Slave Act:

We say to the slaveholder, Insist upon your right to make Northern men your bloodhounds, to hunt down your slaves, and return them to bondage. We say, let this be insisted upon, the more strenuously the better, as it will the sooner awaken the North to a sense of their responsibility for slavery, not only in the District of Columbia, and in forts, arsenals, and navy-yards, but in the States themselves; and will the sooner see their duty to labor for the removal of slavery from every part of this most unhallowed Union. In any case, nought but slaveholders have anything to fear.[10]

John C. Calhoun died of tuberculosis in March 1850, "with treason in his heart and on his lips," in the words of his Senate adversary Thomas Hart Benton, who, like Henry Clay and Daniel Webster, was by that time largely a spent force.[11] When Calhoun began fomenting pro-slavery disunion, he was the only such figure on the national stage. His followers competed to be the most radical. In his final years, Calhoun had pushed aside Robert Barnwell Rhett, his longtime lieutenant, and had visibly passed his mantle to the man Rhett would come to hate most, Mississippi senator Jefferson Davis, who had war-hero status from the Mexican War.[12]

One of the first two senators from California was William Gwin, Andrew Jackson's old crony from Isaac Franklin's hometown of Gallatin, Tennessee. Gwin, who owned two hundred or so slaves, was an embodiment of the Slave Power. After becoming a congressman from Mississippi, he wrote Jackson on March 14, 1842: "I want a slaveholder for President next time regardless of the man believing as I solemnly do that in the next Presidential term the Abolitionists must be put down or blood will be spilt."[13] Relocated to San Francisco, he participated in California's 1849 constitutional convention, where, presumably understanding that the free-soil measure would pass, he acceded to it graciously. Though he failed in his quest to bring slavery to the state, he was a happy man: he was the first slave baron to become a gold baron, having bought a mine that struck it rich. He organized the pro-slavery Democratic political faction in the California legislature—the so-called Chivalry wing, informally known as the Chivs.[14]

Gwin's case was not typical. Slavery wasn't in control of the gold mines, and as the world's economy was transformed by the new money, the specie failed to go South. Ultimately, the California gold strike was the death knell for an archaic modality of agrarian capitalism. But the South had no way out; it was locked into holding its wealth in the form of slaves, with human fecundity still the road to monetary increase, while slavery was locked out of the Gold Rush.

Enormous tracts of land were coming on the market as East Texas cotton fields bloomed under the hands of trafficked-in slave laborers. Amid a generally inflationary environment, the price of slaves went up, up, up. But the largest movement of slaves South and West had already been completed; Texas and Arkansas were viable new markets, but Mississippi was already reaching its saturation point.

South Carolina's overfarmed cotton land was playing out. Planters migrated westward, a little at a time, drawn by the lure of cheap land and a better deal. "By 1850 more than 50,000 South Carolina natives lived in Georgia," writes Lacy K. Ford, "more than 45,000 lived in Alabama, and some 26,000 lived in Mississippi."[15] The cultural swath they cut as they brought laborers from the most Africanized population of North America remains a permanent part of American culture.*

South Carolinian politicians had been actively constructing an ideology for secession since the 1820s, if not all along, one that cast the Constitution as an instrument of oppression now that its original meaning had been perverted by abolitionists. By 1850, they were working to export the secession project to the rest of the South.

The more of a state's land was under cultivation by slave labor, the more its politicians were apt to favor secession. Most of South Carolina was covered by plantations, with only a few counties in the north of the state not primarily slave-driven. In the plantation counties, nearly all the white population's prosperity depended, one way or another, on the continuance—which meant, the exportation—of slavery. South Carolina, so heavily dependent on slave property, had the most concentrated core of support for secession, arguably followed in zeal by Mississippi.

In Maryland, only a minority were in favor of secession, though they were vocal. But slavery in Maryland was on the decline. Much of Maryland did not rely on slave labor; between manumission and sale of slaves down South, its enslaved population was actually decreasing. As Bancroft put it, "counting slave property as so much interest-producing capital, Maryland's course, viewed superficially, was spendthrift, for it was steadily eating into the principal."[16]

The enslaved of Maryland had the most chance to escape via the Underground Railroad; all they had to do was get across the border to Pennsylvania, then push on to Canada. From Baltimore, they might have a chance of slipping away on a boat, the way Frederick Douglass did. While the number of escapees via the Underground Railroad may have been statistically small, the existence of

---

*From its platform in Mississippi, the "Delta blues" reaches back across the southeast to South Carolina and Georgia. Georgia was the birthplace of the three singers who did the most to bring the vocal dynamics of the black church into the mainstream popular repertoire: Ray Charles, Little Richard, and James Brown.

a path to freedom was psychologically significant. The South was a prison, but the enslaved knew there was an escape to the North.

With the West Coast becoming all free-soil, Southerners were desperate for an outlet to the Pacific. As the "Great Debate" over the new western territories continued, Congress mulled the possibility of admitting a state of Deseret (ultimately admitted as Utah), and there was talk of war as slave-soil Texas attempted to annex free-soil New Mexico.

The march of slavery had been halted at Texas. California was a free state. Now the South's great obsession was its old dream of taking Cuba. A Cuban state in the Union would have two reliably pro-slavery senators. There was no way to make Cuba a free state; its slaves were creating too much wealth. Annexing Cuba would have dramatically boosted the values of extant North American slaveholdings—which is to say, the slave-breeding industry. The United States would not only annex Cuba, but also its enormous slave trade, which as part of the United States would no longer be supplied with Africans, but would have to buy slaves entirely from US sources. Virginia alone would not be able to supply such a demand.

Narciso López, a Venezuelan adventurer, briefly invaded Cuba in 1848, hoping to annex it to the United States as a slave state. With the backing of secessionist Mississippi governor John Quitman, who hoped to make Mississippi into a slave-breeding state for Cuba's market, right across the Gulf, and with a cheering section that included John L. O'Sullivan, the *New Orleans Delta*, and the New York *Sun*, López invaded Cuba a second time. He organized his venture at the same jumping-off point as Austin's Texas invasion: Banks' Arcade in New Orleans. The one-star flag he flew, based on the Lone Star flag of Texas, first flew on Fulton and Nassau Streets in New York above the offices of the *Sun*; it was later adapted to become the flag of Cuba, and, with the colors reversed, Puerto Rico.

Landing at the northern Cuban port of Cárdenas with some six hundred men in May 1850, López found taking Cuba more difficult than he had imagined. Nor did he learn until he had safely escaped back to New Orleans that a number of Cuban slaves had stowed away in his boats, hoping to escape the plantation; they were returned to Cuba. López faced indictment for violation of the Neutrality Act, and Quitman was ultimately forced to resign his post as governor.

López invaded Cuba a third time, in 1851. He was captured and publicly garroted in Havana, using a screw-turn device that crushed his windpipe as he sat in a chair. In the wake of López's failure, a secret society of Cuban exiles and Southern-rights supporters was formed in the United States to further the work of annexing Cuba and of the expansion of slave territory in general: the Order of the Lone Star, or OLS. Founded in Lafayette, Louisiana, with Pierre Soulé as its first president, the organization came to claim—almost certainly hyperbolically—some fifteen thousand members in ten states, with its greatest strength in the Alabama-Texas corridor.[17]

In response to the controversy over the Compromise of 1850, and growing out of a previous call by the late John C. Calhoun, Mississippi politicians announced a convention to be held at Nashville beginning June 1, 1850.

South Carolina was the only state to send a full delegation of four to the Southern Convention, also known as the Nashville Convention. Ostensibly held to discuss ways to preserve the Union, it was promoted by the South Carolinians to legitimize the idea of secession and, not incidentally, to position themselves as the leaders of the movement. Only nine of the fifteen slaveholding states sent delegates; most of those who attended were Tennessee locals.

We know what the room smelled like. The church where the convention was held had to replace its carpet afterward because of all the tobacco juice and cigar ash.[18] We know that the delegates were entertained by a troupe of Swiss bell ringers. The *Nashville True Whig and Weekly Commercial Register* noted that, in St. George L. Sioussat's paraphrase, "there was a noticeable identity in personnel between the southern advocates of the Nashville convention and the promoters of the expedition of General Lopez for the conquest of Cuba"—most notably Governor Quitman. "The refusal to admit Cuba as an independent Southern state into the Union," said the newspaper, "is another 'alternative,' vaguely hinted at by Mr. Calhoun . . . to which 'disunion' would be preferred by the extreme Southern factionists."[19]

Held in the city that was the heart of Jacksonism, the Nashville Convention drove another wedge into the crevasse between secessionists and Jacksonian unionists.[20] In a letter to James Buchanan, the late President Polk's close Tennessee ally Cave Johnson wrote: "Be not surprised if you should hear even me with my fifty or sixty negroes denounced for favoring the abolitionists because I will not yield to the mad projects of disunion that are now so freely talked of."[21]

Rhett's aggressive political strategy was much like South Carolina's: take the most extreme position and fight from there. He was disappointed by the lack of secession fever from the other states, whose more moderate members, including unionist Sam Houston, carried the day. Only the South Carolina, Mississippi, and Georgia delegates—the states with the highest concentrations of slave labor—had been strongly in favor of secession. But more significant than the results was that delegates from Southern states had convened to talk about remaining in the Union—which was to say, to talk about secession.

Louisiana did not send delegates to the Nashville Convention, but the excitable French-born Louisiana senator Pierre Soulé proposed to the Senate on June 24 the extension of the Missouri Compromise line out to the West Coast, as the convention had recommended. Soulé wanted to divide California into two states, with the southern, slaveholding one to be called "South California." Brandishing the by-now standard threat of disunion, he warned that not to leave South California open to slavery would be—he must have shouted it, because it was printed in all caps in the *Congressional Globe*—"TO EXCLUDE THE SOUTH FOREVER FROM ALL SHARE IN THE TERRITORIES, THROUGH SPOLIATIONS OF HER RIGHTS AND A DEGRADATION OF HER SOVEREIGNTY, WITHOUT AN ALTERNATIVE THAT DOES NOT END IN AN INGLORIOUS SUBMISSION, OR A RUPTURE OF THE UNION!"[22]

As the California debate dragged on, President Zachary Taylor became the second Whig war-hero president to die in office, succumbing suddenly from cholera on July 9, 1850, leaving behind an estate of 131 slaves to be divided among his three children by his lawyer, Judah P. Benjamin.[23] As the nation lauded him, the *Charleston Mercury* was spiteful.

Taylor was succeeded by Vice President Millard Fillmore, who cleaned house and brought in his own cabinet. Fillmore, from Buffalo, New York, had been a moderately antislavery congressman who voted against the annexation of Texas. But President Fillmore refused to submit the New Mexico constitution to Congress, because it would have brought in another free-soil state and thus would have disturbed the balance in the Senate. "What is there in New Mexico that could by any possibility induce anybody to go there with slaves?" asked Daniel Webster in Congress. "Who expects to see a hundred black men cultivating tobacco, corn, cotton, rice, or anything else on lands in New Mexico, made fertile only by irrigation?"[24]

Texas's motive for trying to take a big chunk of New Mexico may have been hostage-taking. The Republic of Texas had run up a heavy debt selling bonds that the State of Texas could not pay. Though Fillmore stood up to Texas's attempted annexation of New Mexico, threatening to send troops, Texas got a bailout from its debts as ransom.[25]

Fillmore signed the compromise into law, and California became a state on September 9, 1850, which is why Fillmore's name survived in San Francisco to become the name of a rock-concert palace in the 1960s; another of the city's main thoroughfares is named Polk. But signing the compromise into law meant signing the Fugitive Slave Act, which cost Fillmore much support in the North and likely the election of 1852, which he lost.

Slavery had lost the contest for western expansion. But if the intense polemic from Calhoun and his successors had done nothing else, it had made leaving the Union thinkable in the South, and whatever the specific political issue being fought over, it was all about slavery. Increasing numbers of people in the slave states had severed the emotional attachment with a country that could harbor unprosecuted abolitionists. The nation's churches had largely split into Northern and Southern over slavery. Slaveowners wanted Cuba badly, and the secessionists imagined that they were sure to have Mexico, Central America, all the way down.

When a second session of the Nashville Convention was called for November, the moderates stayed home. On November 14, 1850, the delegates heard the seventy-three-year-old veteran South Carolina politician Langdon Cheves deliver an oration that presented the case for immediate secession in fiery terms—*if* four states would do it. Since three were already in the bag, he was trying to convert just one of the attending delegations.

The South was not a particularly hospitable place for any Yankee, but for a Northern reporter deep cover was especially necessary. Joseph Holt Ingraham, a Maine-born Episcopal clergyman who discreetly published his letters under the name Kate Conyngham, saw Cheves as a "hale, white-headed old gentleman, with a fine port-wine tint to his florid cheek."[26] Cheves denounced abolitionists as communists, a term recently current from its use during the European-revolutionary year of 1848 in Marx's *Communist Manifesto* and which would carry racialized connotations in Southern rhetoric into the Jim Crow era, when the Communist Party was the only one to call for full racial equality. Cheves conflated communism with democracy, as well as with jacobinism and anarchy.

He denounced them all as equivalent to abolitionism, which he then dismissed with a minstrelic metaphor that referenced the old practice of blacking up one's face before engaging in group attacks:

> What we call the rights of man, or the admission of great masses to the power of self-government, has brought into action the minds of persons utterly unqualified to judge of the subject practically, who have generated the wildest theories. . . . This agitation has recently reached the United States. It has been introduced by European agents, and has brought under its delusions the subject of African slavery in the Southern States. It is of the family of communism, it is the doctrine of [the anarchist] Proudhon, that property is a crime. It is the same doctrine; they have only *blacked its face to disguise it.*[27] (emphasis added)

Sliding into his big finish, Cheves called for southern unity by evoking a master-race utopia:

> Unite, and your slave property shall be protected to the very border of Mason and Dixon's line. Unite, and the freesoilers shall, at their peril, be your police to prevent the escape of your slaves; California shall be a slave State; the dismembered territory of Texas shall be restored, and you shall enjoy a full participation in all the territory which was conquered by your blood and treasure. Unite, and you shall form one of the most splendid empires on which the sun ever shone, of the most homogeneous population, all of the same blood and lineage.[28]

Cheves's speech was no fluke: proslavery writers formulated the first generation of American anticommunist rhetoric. Southern ideology had coalesced into a vision of a worthy elite who governs while the unworthy multitude suffer, with South Carolina taking the philosophical lead.

Though the turnout at the Second Nashville Convention was disappointing, Rhett followed up by developing a plan with Quitman to call a secession congress in 1852. On May 7 of that year, Rhett abruptly resigned the Senate seat he had been recently returned to. Taking full control of the *Charleston Mercury*, the Fire-Eatingest newspaper in the entire South, he installed his son, Robert Barnwell Rhett Jr., as editor.

People were being convicted of abolitionism in South Carolina courts, though it was early yet in the building curve of hysteria that took nine more years to become cannonfire. It was not safe to voice even moderate antislavery views. The pro-secession British consul Robert Bunch wrote:

> Persons are torn away from their residences and pursuits; sometimes 'tarred and feathered'; 'ridden upon rails,' or cruelly whipped; letters are opened at the Post Offices; discussion upon slavery is entirely prohibited under penalty of expulsion, with or without violence, from the country.[29]

The Whig party barely outlived Henry Clay. It had divided into sectional wings, and by 1852 it was disintegrating. Former Whigs and antislavery Jacksonians met in the new Republican Party, which did not exist in the South.

The South Carolinian writer, editor, and statistician James Dunwoody Brownson De Bow began publishing his *DeBow's Review* in New Orleans in 1846. A deluxe business-news publication, with articles on scientific agricultural management and new developments in technology, it was a voice of the modernizing wing of the pro-slavery movement. Perpetually in financial straits, because its subscribers tended not to pay up, the composition and printing of the magazine was done in the North, where the cost was a third what it would have been in the South, and the quality better.[30] During the Pierce presidency, De Bow was placed in charge of the Seventh Census of 1850, the most detailed US census up to that time. As the 1850s passed, the *Review*'s pro-slavery, pro-secession positions became more extreme, as it looked toward a more industrial, technocratic, slave-driven South.

By the 1850s, in the wake of the Fugitive Slave Act, the antislavery movement was making itself felt in the popular arts. Harriet Beecher Stowe published *Uncle Tom's Cabin* in 1852—a bestselling book that reached even more people in its numerous unauthorized stage adaptations.

William Wells Brown, previously the author of *Narrative of William W. Brown, A Fugitive Slave* (1847), became the first African American to publish a novel, though it could not be published in the United States at the time. *Clotel, or the President's Daughter* (1853), was about fictional slave children descended from Thomas Jefferson, who was named in the book. Brown, at the time a fugitive from slavery—or, rather, from the Fugitive Slave Act—fled the United States for London, where the novel was published. He published other versions of it later, including an 1864 American edition that changed the fictional protagonist's parentage from Jefferson to being "the granddaughter of an American Senator."

Slave narratives became an established publishing genre. Solomon Northup, one of the few kidnapped free people to have descended into slavery and then been rescued, returned to his life in Saratoga, New York, and told his story in *Twelve Years a Slave* (1853), dedicated to Harriet Beecher Stowe. John Thompson, a literate slave who escaped Maryland via the Underground Railroad and became a whaler in New England and a stern Methodist preacher, self-published his autobiography in Massachusetts in 1856: *The Life of John Thompson, a Fugitive Slave; Containing His History of 25 Years in Bondage, and His Providential Escape. Written by Himself.* To out himself as a fugitive slave was a provocation in 1856, when lawmen anywhere in the United States were obligated to hand accused fugitives over without further proceedings. It was a public dare: here I am, come and get me.

Sentimental popular songs referred to the interstate slave trade: in response to Stowe's book, Stephen Foster's "My Old Kentucky Home," premiered in 1853 by Christie's Minstrels, was at first titled "Poor Uncle Tom, Good Night," before Foster rewrote it. It's now the state song of Kentucky, but they don't sing the third verse any more:

> *The head must bow and the back will have to bend,*
> *Wherever the darkey may go:*
> *A few more days, and the trouble all will end*
> *In the field where the sugar canes grow.*
> *A few more days for to tote the weary load,*
> *No matter, 'twill never be light,*
> *A few more days till we totter on the road,*
> *Then my old Kentucky Home, good night!*[31]

That's a song about a black man from Kentucky being worked to death in a sugar prison camp in Louisiana. Benjamin Hanby's tearjerking "My Darling Nelly Gray" (1856), which Hanby based on a story told him as a child by a black man named Joseph Selby, sang of an enslaved couple broken apart by a sale of the woman to Georgia:

> *O my poor Nelly Gray, they have taken you away,*
> *And I'll never see my darling anymore;*
> *I'm sitting by the river and I'm weeping all the day,*
> *For you're gone from the old Kentucky shore.*[32]

This genre of songs continued after the Civil War (James Bland's "Carry Me Back to Old Virginny"), when they were bowdlerized and, bizarrely, repurposed into a nostalgia for the Old South.

Anthony Burns, a self-emancipated twenty-year-old man who had escaped from Virginia via the Underground Railroad, was apprehended in Boston on May 24, 1854, by a US commissioner acting on the behest of a slave-catcher hired by Burns's former master. His case became a cause célèbre; one man was killed when a mob unsuccessfully tried to storm the courthouse to free him.[33] But he was extradited to Richmond, where he was put into isolation at Lumpkin's Slave Jail. The Boston journalist Charles Emery Stevens published a book about the case, which described the conditions under which Burns was held for four months:

> The place of his confinement was a room only six or eight feet square, in the upper story of the jail, which was accessible only through a trap-door. He was allowed neither bed nor air; a rude bench fastened against the wall and a single, coarse blanket were the only means of repose. After entering his cell, the handcuffs were not removed, but, in addition, fetters were placed upon his feet. In this manacled condition he was kept during the greater part of his confinement.
>
> The torture which he suffered, in consequence, was excruciating. The gripe of the irons impeded the circulation of his blood, made hot and rapid by the stifling atmosphere, and caused his feet to swell enormously. The flesh was worn from his wrists, and when the wounds had healed, there remained broad scars as perpetual witnesses against his owner. The fetters also prevented him from removing his clothing by day or night, and no one came to help him; the indecency resulting from such a condition is too revolting for description, or even thought. His room became more foul and noisome than the hovel of a brute; loathsome creeping things multiplied and rioted in the filth. His food consisted of a piece of coarse corn-bread and the parings of bacon or putrid meat. This fare, supplied to him once a day, he was compelled to devour without Plate, knife, or fork.
>
> Immured, as he was, in a narrow, unventilated room, beneath the heated roof of the jail, a constant supply of fresh water would have been a heavenly boon; but the only means of quenching his thirst was the nauseating contents of a pail that was replenished only once or twice a week. Living under such an accumulation of atrocities, he at length fell seriously ill. This brought about some mitigation of his treatment; his fetters were

removed for a time, and he was supplied with broth, which, compared with his previous food, was luxury itself. . . .

One day his attention was attracted by a noise in the room beneath him. There was a sound as of a woman entreating and sobbing, and of a man addressing to her commands mingled with oaths. Looking down through a crevice in the floor, Burns beheld a slave woman stark naked in the presence of two men.

One of them was an overseer, and the other a person who had come to purchase a slave. The overseer had compelled the woman to disrobe in order that the purchaser might see for himself whether she was well formed and sound in body. Burns was horror-stricken; all his previous experience had not made him aware of such an outrage. This, however, was not an exceptional case; he found it was the ordinary custom in Lumpkin's jail thus to expose the naked person of the slave, both male and female, to the inspection of the purchaser. A wider range of observation would have enabled him to see that it was the universal custom in the slave states. . . .

After a while, he found a friend in the family of Lumpkin. The wife of this man was a "yellow woman" whom he had married as much from necessity as from choice, the white women of the South refusing to connect themselves with professed slave traders. This woman manifested her compassion for Burns by giving him a testament and a hymn-book. Upon most slaves these gifts would have been thrown away; fortunately for Burns, he had learned to read, and the books proved a very treasure. Besides the yellow wife, Lumpkin had a black concubine, and she also manifested a friendly spirit toward the prisoner.

The house of Lumpkin was separated from the jail only by the yard, and from one of the upper windows the girl contrived to hold conversations with Anthony, whose apartment was directly opposite. Her compassion, it is not unlikely, changed into a warmer feeling; she was discovered one day by her lord and master; what he overheard roused his jealousy, and he took effectual means to break off the intercourse.[34] (paragraphing added)

Burns was sold at auction after four months to a planter, but his freedom was subsequently purchased by L. M. Grimes, a minister who had established a church for runaway slaves in Boston. Fugitive slaves had become pop culture by this point; according to Stevens, P. T. Barnum offered the newly freed Burns $500 to be an exhibit in his museum in New York, which Burns indignantly turned down, reportedly saying, "He wants to show me like a monkey!"[35]

≥≤

N.B. FORREST, Dealer in Slaves, No. 87 ADAMS STREET.

HAS just received, from South Carolina, twenty-five likely young Negroes, to which he desires to call the attention of purchasers. He will be in the regular receipt of Negroes from North and South Carolina every month.

His Negro Depot is one of the most complete and commodious establishments of the kind in the Southern country, and regulations, exact and systematic cleanliness, neatness and comfort being strictly observed and enforced, and his aim is to furnish to customers No. 1 servants and field hands, sound and perfect in body and mind.

Negroes taken on Commission. — Memphis *Eagle and Enquirer,* June 2, 1857.

The western Tennessee river port of Memphis was a jumpoff point for selling slaves into the new territories of Arkansas and Texas. Memphis was a mature slave market by 1852, when the thirty-year-old slave trader Nathan Bedford Forrest begins to appear in the city's records. The hotheaded Forrest was at least as rash a man as Jackson, but had even less education. He instilled fear in those around him, and he didn't stay business partners with anyone very long; for a year he worked in a partnership called Forrest & Jones; then, with the more established Byrd Hill, he cofounded Hill & Forrest; and by 1855 was partners with Josiah Maples in Forrest & Maples. He bought a double lot on Adams Street—named for John Adams, between Washington and Jefferson Streets—using 85 Adams for his house and 87 Adams for his jail, and soon he began to run the customary 500 NEGROES WANTED advertisements in the paper, while opening depots in other towns. He seems to have procured his merchandise in what had become the standard way: canvassing planters personally and via agents, buying people one at a time.[36] It was no longer necessary to go to the Eastern Shore of Maryland to find farmers willing to sell slaves. These were the high-priced years of the slave trade, and profits came fast.

In a mythologizing account written at the time of Forrest's funeral in 1877, Lafcadio Hearn, who was passing through Memphis at the time, wrote that Forrest was "reported to have been 'kind' to his slaves, yet to have 'taught them to fear him exceedingly.'"[37] White people were afraid of him, too. He did not hesitate to escalate to lethal action, as when he put a gun up to a tailor's head for having delivered a bad suit.[38] He made a lot of money in the slave business, some

FORREST & MAPLES,
SLAVE DEALERS,
87 Adams Street,
Between Second and Third,
MEMPHIS, TENNESSEE,

Have constantly on hand the best selected assortment of

FIELD HANDS, HOUSE SERVANTS & MECHANICS,

at their Negro Mart, to be found in the city. They are daily receiving from Virginia, Kentucky and Missouri, fresh supplies of likely Young Negroes.

Negroes Sold on Commission,

and the highest market price always paid for good stock. Their Jail is capable of containing Three Hundred, and for comfort, neatness and safety, is the best arranged of any in the Union. Persons wishing to purchase, are invited to examine their stock before purchasing elsewhere.

They have on hand at present, Fifty likely young Negroes, comprising Field hands, Mechanics, House and Body Servants, &c.

A broadside advertisement for Nathan Bedford Forrest's slave dealership in Memphis.

of which he invested in land, before winding it down in 1860 and getting out of it by 1861. Other traders continued in the business after the South seceded, but Forrest went to war, which allowed him to further develop the talent for blunt violence that had served him so well in slave trading.

41

Hiring Day

"SEPARATION OF FAMILIES? YES, indeed," said the fugitive Lewis Clarke at an antislavery meeting in Brooklyn in 1842.

> If the gentleman had been in Kentucky at New Year's time, he wouldn't need to ask that question. Of all the days in the year, the slaves dread New-Year's day the worst [of] any. For folks come for their debts then; and if anybody is going to sell a slave, that's the time they do it; and if anybody's going to give away a slave, that's the time they do it; and the slave never knows where he'll be sent to. Oh, New-Year's a heart-breaking time in Kentucky![1]

New Year's Day, a day for settling debts, was also the occasion of a great annual party thrown by white people throughout the antebellum South: slave-hiring day. ("Hiring" is the customary term, though "rental" might be more appropriate.) A single tavern might be the stage for renting hundreds of legal nonpeople. They stood in the seasonal bitter cold for as long as it took, while drink flowed freely from the bar for prospective purchasers. Those too poor to own slaves could come and gaze at the possibilities. For the enslaved, it was the day when they learned where they would be sent next, whether back to the same place as last year or to a new and dangerous job far away.

"To the slave mother New Year's day comes laden with peculiar sorrows," wrote Harriet Jacobs. "She sits on her cold cabin floor, watching the children who may all be torn from her the next morning; and often does she wish that she and they might die before the day dawns."[2] For some, this system made the traumatic experience of being auctioned off into an annual event. "Them ole red headed yaps would bid us off to the highest bidder and we couldn't do nothin' but pray," recalled a formerly enslaved Tennessean. "Yes, fine times for them, but awful for us po' niggers. Yes'm, they would cry you off to the highest bidder for the next year. One by one, we had to get up on that block, and he bid us off."[3]

All sorts of service occupations throughout the South were done by rented-out slaves, who on a year's contract typically earned their owners between 10 and 20 percent of their sale value besides relieving him or her of the necessity of housing, clothing, and feeding them. "Those wages must represent exactly the cost of slave labor," noted Frederick Law Olmsted;[4] they were typically paid to the slaveowner at year's end though sometimes monthly or quarterly, with a security deposit and a bond required. For an enslaved person, this could be

Hiring contract in Petersburg, Virginia, dated January 2, 1865, for "negro slave" Cely and her children Rosie and Mary.

a relatively advantageous situation, as it was much preferable to be enslaved in town than on a plantation, and it was way better than being sold down South. Or it could be atrocious.

Slave hiring was particularly common in Virginia, where there was less plantation work to do and where there was a variety of other kinds of work suited for slave labor. By the 1850s, Virginia's economy had diversified. After lying fallow, some of its worn-out tobacco land had been restored to productivity for other kinds of uses, though none had the income-generating power of tobacco.

Frederic Bancroft described "hiring" as "a restricted kind of slave trade," and emphasized the importance of prestige to both slaveowner and slave-hirer: "the hirer as well as the owner was popularly considered as belonging to the slaveholding class."[5]

It boosted the hirer's prestige to have a slave working for him. At the same time, it provided the owner a lucrative alternative to selling slaves, which would have indicated a drop in his or her social standing. If that had to happen, it was best to keep it on the down low. "Richmond was the best place in the State to sell nearly all kinds of slaves at good prices without publicity as to ownership," wrote Bancroft.[6]

Richmond might not have looked like much of an industrial city to a Northerner, but it was the most developed in the South. Meanwhile, the sale of so many young people to traders over the decades had brought in plenty of capitalized labor to work with. Virginia had the most railroad mileage of any Southern state—1,771.16 miles in 1860, more than four times that of Maryland. "The completion of several rail lines in Virginia coincided with a dramatic surge in the prices of tobacco, wheat, and corn," writes John J. Zaborney. "The railroads so reduced transport costs that Virginia farmers shipped more of their products, more cheaply, to Virginia's growing urban centers."[7]

Railroads made possible the cultivation of new lands, increasing the state's development. They also made it easier to ship slaves; as a visitor can still perceive today despite the subsequent destruction of the town's core, Richmond's teeming slave-mart district of the 1850s was located by the town's railroad center. A traveler in 1856 wrote:

> You notice . . . that every train going south has just such a crowd of slaves on board, twenty or more, and a "nigger car," which is very generally also the smoking-car and sometimes the baggage-car. You notice also that these slaves whom you constantly meet going south in the trader's hands are not old men and women or by any means malicious-looking ones. . . . but are

for the most part apparently picked slaves, boys and girls or young men and women, eighteen-twenty, twenty-five . . .[8]

The trade in Richmond was located in an approximately thirty-block area between Fifteenth and Nineteenth Streets in the low-lying part of town called Shockoe Bottom, for which the large, comfortable Odd Fellows Hall between Fourteenth and Fifteenth on Franklin served as an auction site. The extension of Fifteenth Street, between Broad and Franklin, was called Wall Street, and was also known as Lumpkin's Alley for its tenant Robert Lumpkin, who operated the best known of the city's many slave-trading posts, and was more informally known as the Devil's Half Acre. Lumpkin's Slave Jail has become emblematic of Richmond's slave trade, but Lumpkin was only one of dozens of traders, and his jail was one of several.

Records show that as of 1840 Lumpkin owned an eight-year-old girl named Mary, by whom he subsequently had five children. As the pending acquisition of Texas stimulated the Virginia trade, he bought three lots on Wall Street in 1844, which were assessed at $6,000 in 1848. Lumpkin was not the first trader to operate on that site; the Richmond trader Bacon Tait was operating there in the early 1830s, and he built the brick jail Lumpkin later used. Tait sold it to the trader Lewis A. Collier, who made further improvements but was ruined in the post-Jackson depression; the Bank of Virginia took possession of the property in 1844, and sold it to Lumpkin.[9]

As was typical of the larger slave jails, there were four buildings to the compound. One was a boardinghouse for visiting traders; another was a kitchen/canteen. The filthy Shockoe Creek ran through the property, and the slave jail itself was down at the bottom of the embankment, on the lowest, muddiest, least desirable piece of ground.[10]

Like other such jails, it had a whipping room; the Reverend A.M. Newman of Opelousas, Louisiana, who as a boy was sent to be whipped there in 1862, recalled that "on the floor of that room were rings. The individual would be laid down, his hands and feet stretched out and fastened in the rings, and a great big man would stand over him and flog him."[11]

Lumpkin lived in the main building, together with Mary, now his concubine—the "yellow woman" who had given Anthony Burns a hymnal—and their five white-looking children, Martha, Annie, Robert, Richard, and John. Martha and Annie were sent to be educated at Mrs. John C. Cowles's Female Seminary in Ipswich, Massachusetts, where they ran no risk of being sold as fancy girls if their father should fall into debt; ultimately, all five were sent to live in Pennsylvania, where Lumpkin owned property. He had freed Mary by 1857, when she appears as a free woman of color in Richmond court records.[12] However, while Mary may have been referred to in daily parlance as his "wife," the state of Virginia prohibited "interracial" marriages until the United States Supreme Court's *Loving v. Virginia* decision of 1967.

The prices in Richmond were the lowest of any of the major slave markets because it was primarily a wholesale mart for export, so some enterprising Virginians found it an attractive business proposition to buy slaves there specifically in order to rent them out locally, doubling their money in a few years.

Many small slaveholders lived on the income that one or a few enslaved laborers earned by working for others; this was an especially important nest egg for slaveholding widows, and even for mentally incompetent persons who had inherited slaves. Churches received income by renting out the services of captives. To transact all this business, there were specialized employment agents dedicated to renting out slave labor; every Southern town had them. Southern municipalities made money from taxes and fees on slave-rental, sometimes requiring the purchase of a numbered badge that had to be worn by a rented slave.

Even those people who were too old to be sold to a trader for export as cotton-field labor might still bring in a comfortable income locally as domestic servants or other types of workers. Hotel and boardinghouse guests were commonly attended to by rented slaves; Frederick Law Olmsted marveled at the quality of service he received in his hotel at Richmond, where a middle-aged enslaved man named Henry, who, according to the hotel owner, would have been worth $2,000 if he had been a little younger, "becomes your servant while you are in your room; he asks, at night, when he comes to request your boots, at what time he shall come in the morning, and then, without being very exactly punctual, he comes quietly in, makes your fire, sets the boots before it, brushes and arranges your clothes, lays out your linen, arranges your dressing gear, asks if you want anything else of him before breakfast, opens the shutters, and goes off to the next room."[13]

Every kind of work could be contracted for, from wet nursing to piloting a boat. "Fieldhands, washers and ironers, cooks, porters, waiters, house-maids, plain mechanics of various kinds and half-grown boys and girls were numerous in nearly all hiring markets," writes Frederic Bancroft.[14] For the enslaved, a job in even a small city was much preferable to field labor; besides making it easier to abscond, it allowed access to merchandise and opportunities to do business, which many did with great eagerness when they had the opportunity.

While visiting Macon, Georgia, in April 1907, Bancroft interviewed a formerly enslaved man named Henry G. Griffin, who was, he said, bought twice via mortgage, once at the age of eleven months and again at the age of sixteen years. At first he "worked in a store nearly like a clerk," as Bancroft put it; then, in Griffin's words, "I sampled cotton for E.A. Wilcox, who paid [to Griffin's "owner"] at the rate of $30 a month for me. All the sample cotton was given to the samplers. Sometimes there was 40 or 50 pounds a day." That gave him a steady stream of something saleable. Griffin was treated rather well, he recalled, meaning that he was not separated from his family and could make some money at his job.

Griffin took Bancroft sightseeing Southern style, to the barred windows of the brick city guardhouse on the east side of Fourth Street between Cherry and Poplar where, as was the norm in Southern jails, slaves could be sent for whipping. Speaking as an eyewitness, Griffin recalled that they were beaten in the most common slave-whipping position: stretched out face down with their hands and feet tied. Women, said Griffin, were stretched on the ground with a hole beneath their bellies, "so that there was no chance of striking their stomachs," wrote Bancroft.[15] Or, though Bancroft didn't put it this way, if they were pregnant, the valuable fetus would be protected while the mother was being— the customary term was "corrected."

The great peril of being hired out was that the hirer, who had no long-term stake in the laborer's well-being, might work him or her abusively hard, assign a dangerous job, or simply beat the daylights out of him or her. Accidents of all types were common, nowhere more than in the industrial jobs given to slaves. Underground mining was particularly dangerous, but many types of occupational accidents were common. Slaveholders typically required the hirer to take out insurance, so slave-hiring was a boon to insurance companies.

By custom, slave-hiring contracts were for one year, commencing on January 2 and ending on Christmas Eve, when the contract became payable. Then the hired-out people would return home for a brief, heartbreaking reunion with their families, perhaps learning that loved ones had died or been sold away during the year.

Some enslaved people, typically the highest skilled workers such as carpenters, were sometimes allowed to hire themselves out. The repeated laws against the practice make it clear how common it was for them to handle the transaction themselves and live in their own quarters in town, paying their "owner" his or her fee and keeping any surplus for themselves.

But many were merely transferred from abusive master to abusive master. John J. Zaborney cites the case of a slaveholder who wrote a letter to a man who had rented a woman named Delphia from him, which perhaps provides one demonstration of the workings of pro-slavery theology:

> I am sorry to hear that Delphia is so impudent but glad to be able to recommend a cure which I have often tried with certain success. Let the overseer take Delphia and give her fifty lashes, on her bare and repeat the dose morning after morning . . .
>
> . . . Delphia is . . . no inconsiderable part of your household and I humbly suggest that it is your duty to command her that she may keep the way of the Lord, to do justice and judgments (see Genesis 18 chap.) What is due from Delphia to you? Service, labour—ready, willing faithful service unquestioned obedience. If she fails in this she keeps no[t] the way of the Lord to do justice and judgment.[16] (paragraphing added)

In 1850s Richmond, the larger hirers of young enslaved males were the tobacco factories, which prepared raw tobacco for chewing or smoking. Zaborney estimates that about half the tobacco factories' labor force consisted of hired slaves in 1850, and two-thirds in 1860, by which time there were forty-nine tobacco factories in the town hiring about thirty-four hundred laborers.[17] The tobacco factories did not house workers, but gave them an allowance to rent lodgings in town, creating an entire class of enslaved urban consumers with a little pocket money.

Musicians at a Saturday night dance were commonly enslaved workers, whose musical skills sometimes allowed them an opportunity to make a few coins for themselves. But in one case the scale was much larger. The South's best-known concert attraction was a slave: Blind Tom (Thomas Wiggins). With a mental age of six or so, Wiggins was what was then called an idiot savant and might today be called severely autistic. Born in Columbus, Georgia, in 1849, he had an eidetic memory for sound. He could do little else but play piano, which he did all day, every day. He could reproduce verbatim an entire political speech in all its sonic detail without understanding any of it; he could simulate convincingly the sounds of a rainstorm on the piano, or a battle; he could play music after hearing it once, and was said to know some seven thousand pieces; and he composed music, of which we have no recording or piano roll, though some sheet music was published, presumably bearing a dubious relationship to what he actually played.

Tom's curious, extreme talent probably saved him from the common fate of handicapped slave children, an early death. His master, the Columbus lawyer known as "General" James Neil Bethune, made a fortune touring Wiggins, taking in over $100,000 a year from London concerts alone in 1866, with a guardian agreement negotiated in 1864 that allowed Bethune to retain 90 percent of his no-longer-enslaved client's earnings.[18] Until the end of slavery, Blind Tom did not play in the free-soil states, where he might have been subject to confiscation from Bethune. But he was a familiar figure on the concert circuit in the South. What a model for musical labor relations: the manager owned not merely the artist's contract but also the artist, and could sell him if he chose. Louis Hughes noted the impact of Blind Tom's concert in Memphis:

The "Oliver Gallop," a piece of sheet music published ca. 1860, composed by the autistic, enslaved piano virtuoso Thomas Wiggins, or "Blind Tom."

> People came from far and near to hear him. Those coming from the villages and small towns, who could not get passage on the regular trains, came in freight or on flat bottom cars. The tickets were $5.00 each, as I remember, Boss said it was expensive, but all must hear this boy pianist. Many were the comments on this boy of such wonderful talents. As I drove our people Home they seemed to talk of nothing else. They declared that he was indeed a wonder.[19]

After secession, fearing the worst should he be removed from Bethune, the frightened, mentally impaired, blind teenager declared himself in favor of the Confederacy, making him its best-known black supporter.[20]

following page: There are not many slavery-era paintings depicting slave auctions. The people conducting them did not want them portrayed, and an artist caught sketching might find himself in trouble. This 1862 painting by Lefevre Cranstone, titled Slave Auction, Virginia, *depicts eight women being sold, three of them with children, as men leeringly assess them. The painting was first exhibited in London in 1863.*

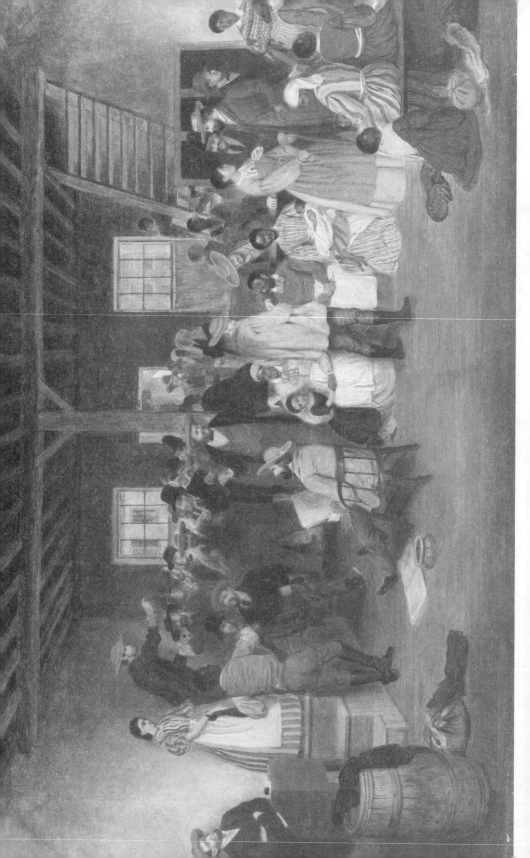

❧ Part Six ❧

The Revolution

Vanish Like a Dream

My soul is tormented with fears! Ah! they are dead! Their swords are red from the fight. O my brother! my brother! why hast thou slain my Salgar? why, O Salgar! hast thou slain my brother? Dear were ye both to me! what shalt I say in your praise? Thou wert fair on the hill among thousands! he was terrible in fight. Speak to me; hear my voice; hear me, song of my love! They are silent; silent for ever! Cold, cold, are their breasts of clay! Oh! from the rock on the hill, from the top of the windy steep, speak, ye ghosts of the dead! speak, I will not be afraid! Whither are ye gone to rest? In what cave of the hill shall I find the departed? No feeble voice is on the gale: no answer half-drowned in the storm!

—Ossian [James Macpherson], *Songs of Selma*

UPRIVER FROM THE GULF of Mexico port of Mobile, William Rufus DeVane King cofounded the town of Selma, naming it for the city in *Songs of Selma*, an over-the-top, internationally popular literary fraud.

Purportedly a collection of Celtic texts by an ancient Gaelic bard named Ossian, *Songs of Selma* was accepted by the reading public as genuine, but it was the fabrication of one James Macpherson, who seems to have dressed folktales up in ludicrously overwrought language. Marking a worldwide literary trend toward kitschy hyperromanticism, the *Songs of Selma* became a staple of a strain of pseudo-Celtic-nationalist mythology in spite of their bogosity.

King's family had done so well in the land scramble that they were the largest slaveholding family in the state, and King became Alabama's first senator in 1819. He was, according to an anonymous campaign biography, "about six feet high, remarkably erect in figure, and is well proportioned."[1] Some in Washington called him "Aunt Fancy" behind his back, while Andrew Jackson is known to have referred to King's good friend James Buchanan as "Miss Nancy."[2] Tennessee congressman Aaron Brown, in a letter to Sarah Childress Polk, referred to King as Buchanan's "wife."[3] Buchanan and King were a pair of lifelong bachelors who were not attracted to women, and it was "somewhat common," writes Robert P. Watson, for Washingtonians and others to refer to them mockingly as women.[4] Perhaps they were just good friends, but from our contemporary perspective, they look like a gay couple. And, yes, queerness—or gayness, or call it what you will—existed then, though it was less well understood in James Buchanan's rural southern Pennsylvania birthplace than in the big cities.

Buchanan and King met in 1834 and moved in together in 1836, maintaining a stable household in Washington. Both had nieces who posthumously burned a number of their uncles' letters to each other. They domiciled together until 1844, when King left the country to be Polk's minister to France.

If there had been same-sex marriage with community property, Buchanan could have been a large slaveholder, because King owned over a hundred slaves. Though Buchanan lived in the free state of Pennsylvania, he was from the state's south, the borderland with slave territory, and he was ardently pro-slavery, to say nothing of duplicitous. "I cannot rely upon his honest and disinterested advice," Polk wrote in his diary about Buchanan when he was Polk's secretary of state.[5] Polk's admiring biographer Robert W. Merry calls Buchanan "self-centered, devious, dishonest, and cowardly."[6]

The power couple's plan was for Buchanan to be president and King to be vice president. It went awry: Buchanan didn't get the nomination in 1852, losing on the forty-ninth ballot to the former Mexican War general Franklin Pierce, with Buchanan thus being edged out by the most pro-slavery New Englander. But King got the vice presidential nomination, apparently in the hope that Buchanan would help out in the battleground state of Pennsylvania. After the nominating convention in Baltimore, New Hampshire congressman Edmund Burke wrote to Pierce, addressing him as "General": "I think we did right in putting King on the ticket. You know he is Buchanan's bosom friend and thus a great and powerful interest is conciliated. . . . The slave states will fall into our laps like ripe apples."[7]

The Democrats won, but King was ill with tuberculosis, and he took the oath of office for vice president of the United States from his convalescence in Cuba, a political feat that has not been repeated since. Wasting away, he barely made it home to Selma in time to die, forty-five days after the beginning of his term, on April 18, 1853.

For the rest of Pierce's term, the office of vice president was vacant.

Even Franklin Pierce's biographers can't find much good to say about him. A Jacksonian in politics and a romantic in literary taste, Pierce was the only president from New Hampshire. Once in office, he named his close friend and campaign biographer, the perpetually broke writer Nathaniel Hawthorne, to the plum post of US consul in Liverpool. In the biography he wrote of Pierce, the New Englander Hawthorne had eagerly stoked sectional tension, disparaging "those northern men . . . who deem the great cause of human welfare as represented and involved in this present hostility against southern institutions." (At the risk of redundancy, we will remind our reader that "southern institutions" centrally included the legal right to force-mate adolescent girls and sell the resulting children.)

Hawthorne went on to explain Pierce's position on slavery: it was God's problem, not the president's. He characterized slavery as "one of those evils which divine Providence does not leave to be remedied by human contrivances, but which, in its own good time, by some means impossible to be anticipated, but of the simplest and easiest operation, when all its uses shall have been fulfilled, it causes to vanish like a dream."[8]

The country was torn in half over slavery, the Fugitive Slave Act was in effect, the Whig party was crumbling, Southern radicals were organizing to secede, and Hawthorne promised that one day slavery wouldn't be a problem.

Elected on a strongly pro-Southern platform that included the annexation of Cuba, Pierce named the Mexican War veteran and already-declared secessionist Jefferson Davis as his secretary of war, giving him on-the-job training in the management of armies. For his part, Davis was urgently interested in a southern route for the proposed transcontinental railroad, though it was a disadvantageous route from an engineering standpoint, and he enthusiastically promoted what became known as the Gadsden Purchase, negotiated in 1854 by James Gadsden, the Jacksonian US ambassador to Mexico.

Gadsden was a Charleston aristocrat. His grandfather, Christopher Gadsden, had built Gadsden's Wharf; a second cousin, Thomas Gadsden, was one of Charleston's most prominent slave dealers of the 1850s, though there was quite some competition for that title. Gadsden was an old-line Jacksonian who had served in the Seminole campaign. At a time when the secession project was already well under way, the $10 million Gadsden Purchase was the last major acquisition of territory by the continental United States, giving Washington control of what is now the southerly strip of Arizona and New Mexico. The reason for the Gadsden purchase, with its farthest-South-possible location, was the same reason a wealthy South Carolinian's name was on it: rail shipment would be the only practical way to export slaves from the South to southern California, as well as the best way to bring California gold back. A railroad was needed; the South wanted it.

The Compromise of 1850 that admitted California as a free-soil state had not removed the South's dream of slavery in a separate Southern California. Far from it: speaking of an elderly slaveowner in 1855 who wished to sell out, Frederick Law Olmsted noted that "he thought of taking them to Louisiana and Texas, for sale; but, if he should learn that there was much probability that Lower California would be made a slave State, he supposed it would pay him to wait, as probably, if that should occur, he could take them there and sell them for twice as much as they would now bring in New Orleans."[9] Olmsted also quotes a politician whose campaign in 1855 argued that "if slavery were permitted in California, negroes would sell for $5,000 apiece."[10] That was, of course, pure conjecture; but it was what slaveowners wanted to hear. With even Mississippi approaching saturation point for enslaved labor, population pressures militated for new territory to sell the ever-increasing human capital into. In other words, the slave-breeding industry was reaching critical mass for unraveling—unless the expansion of slavery territory could postpone the collapse. From California, it would have to expand outward into Asia, and this was discussed on occasion.

Describing the slave-labor "Colony under my lead" he would build in California, Gadsden wrote in an 1851 letter to General Thomas Jefferson Green in San Francisco:

> Negro Slavery, under Educated & Intelligent Masters can alone accomplish this:—They have been the Pioneers & basis of the civilization of Savage Countries . . . Let us feed our own People & add Cotton Corn & Rice to the Gold export . . . and No power can vie with that which is washed by the Pacific . . . Our Men could thus at the season for mining be employed in extracting the Gold, while the Women & Boys could raise their food & raiment . . . [I will] Make our Road as we go by an organised Corps of

Pioneers & Axe men & reach California with both Negroes & animals in full vigor to go to work.[11]

Meanwhile, schemes for expanding the empire of slavery into Latin America proliferated. As president, Pierce managed to remove Buchanan from his immediate sphere of intrigue by sending him to England in 1853 as ambassador to the Court of St. James, where he worked toward the longtime dream of the annexation of Cuba. He traveled to Ostend, Belgium, where he met with Pierre Soulé and Virginia's John Mason, the former of whom was then Pierce's minister to Spain and the latter minister to France, to formulate an aggressive document, largely written by Soulé. Published in October 1854, the Ostend Manifesto announced US plans to acquire Cuba—by purchase if possible, but if not, it warned, in a classic piece of Southern hyperbole, "by every law, human and divine, we shall be justified in wresting it from Spain, if we possess the power."

The manifesto also made a different case for the annexation of Cuba, that of self-defense against slave rebellion, invoking the possibility that an "Africanized" Cuba might become "a second St. Domingo," and arguing that taking Cuba would be justified "upon the very same principle that would justify an individual in tearing down the burning house of his neighbor if there were no other means of preventing the flames from destroying his own home."

Bankrolled by Cuban exiles, John Quitman, who by 1853 was the leader of the secret Order of the Lone Star, tried to organize an invasion of Cuba that never sailed. But another filibuster, the Nashvillean William Walker, a great admirer of Napoleon, invaded and took over Nicaragua in 1855. Walker had previously been acquitted by a sympathetic jury of violating the Neutrality Act for taking over Baja California and declaring it the Republic of Southern California. An anonymous correspondent to *DeBow's Review* called on Virginians to relocate with their slaves to Walker's Nicaragua, pooh-poohing the problem of yellow fever and exulting:

Here is a new State soon to be added to the South, in or out of the Union— here is the first piece of Mexico in fact, the whole of which, in a short lifetime, will fall into the hands of the white men of North America, and it behooves you to begin in time to secure your portion of the prize, for you are going to find it no easy task. I speak of Mexico (including of course, Central America in the same destiny) with absolute confidence. The expulsion of the Spanish masters has left that country to the red man—the Spanish Indian—an inferior and incompetent race, and the result is altogether analogous to the result of emancipation in the West Indies, just as the cause is similar. In both instances, the support of the strong will and high intelligence of the white man has been withdrawn, and, forthwith the red man and the black man, liberated but incapable and helpless, have sunk down from the position in which they had been held up and sustained, and lapsed rapidly towards their original and natural barbarism.[12]

The boosterism reflected the fact that every newly acquired slave territory revalued a slaveowner's human holdings upward drastically. President Pierce obligingly recognized Walker's Nicaraguan government in 1856, but Walker was driven out in 1857. He was captured and turned over to Honduras in 1860, where he was promptly executed by the Honduran government.

The great issue of Franklin Pierce's presidency was his signing of Stephen Douglas's disastrous Kansas-Nebraska Act on May 30, 1854, as pro-slavery bandits attempted to implement slavery in Kansas through murderous intimidation, with two rival state constitutions, one slave and one free, vying for recognition. The clashes were a precursor of the violence of the coming war over slavery, right down to the lethal participation of the abolitionist terrorist John Brown, who in 1856 was a commander in two battles in Kansas. It was after expressing his outrage in the Senate over a massacre in Lawrence that abolitionist Senator Charles Sumner was viciously beaten while seated at his desk on the Senate floor by South Carolina representative Preston Brooks.

Douglas's Kansas-Nebraska act sent shock waves through the North, because in declaring that Kansas and Nebraska could be slave territory, it effectively repealed the Missouri Compromise, which had been the basis of the entire deal between North and South since 1821. In doing so, it cut the fragile tethers of a frayed peace treaty loose.

Pierce left office unpopular, after one term, in 1857.

The oldest living Jacksonian still in a major position of power, the eighty-year-old Roger B. Taney, had been chief justice of the Supreme Court for twenty-four years when he handed down one of the most notorious decisions in the history of American jurisprudence: *Dred Scott v. Sandford*. The court had been deliberating the case for two years, but it held the decision until a slightly less old Jacksonian, sixty-five-year-old James Buchanan, was inaugurated as president in 1857.

It was Buchanan's fourth try to reach the presidency by appealing as cravenly as possible to the slaveowners' wish list; this time, it worked.

The annexation of Cuba—which would have been an enormous windfall for slave breeders—was Buchanan's major campaign issue. Had he been able to do it, he would have joined Jefferson, Jackson, and Polk in the pantheon of territorial expanders. Spain wasn't about to let it happen. Meanwhile, Cuban agriculture was changing, and a few planters were looking to emulate the US slave-breeding model for sale to their own voracious domestic slave market. A boosterish 1859 article in *Harper's* extolled the practice of one:

> In former times, before the introduction of machinery, the number of negroes employed was greater, and, in consequence of the short space of time allowed for the manufacture of sugar, the mortality among the laborers was excessive. Ten per cent. per annum used to be a common average of deaths on plantations managed by reckless and unwise agents; in such cases the negroes worked twenty hours out of the twenty-four during the season. Since the introduction of steam the negro mortality has been much less, and the number of hands employed has been largely diminished. A force of a hundred field hands will now suffice to work a very large plantation.
>
> Experience has also shown the mischief of overworking the men. Mr. Drake, of Havana, long since proved that by allowing his negroes a fair amount of sleep and nutritious food, they could not only perform far more work than the hands of his neighbors, *but could add yearly, by natural increase, a large sum to his estate.* On many estates in Cuba, it is known, though the female slaves are quite numerous, the natural increase is comparatively nothing.[13] (paragraphing and emphasis added)

President Buchanan did not acquire Cuba, but he began one of the most remorselessly pro-slavery administrations ever. Buchanan not only knew in advance from Taney what the *Dred Scott* decision would be; he improperly and without precedent interfered with the decision-making process, pressuring judges. Two days before the decision was announced, Buchanan lied in his inaugural address about not knowing what the result would be. He promised disingenuously that "to their decision, in common with all good citizens, I shall cheerfully submit, whatever this may be," though he already knew the outcome.[14] That was what we now call a "dog whistle"—a message to those who could hear it.

The ruling caused much anger in the free-soil states. Among other improper actions Buchanan took regarding the decision, he lobbied one court member from the North to support the majority ruling so as to make it look like less of a coup d'etat by the South.[15] The *Dred Scott* decision was political hardball; a blatant attempt to remodel American law to conform with the pro-slavery agenda, it far overreached the limits of the case. It was the first overturning of a federal law by the court, the previous *Marbury v. Madison* having struck down only a single clause. *Dred Scott* declared the Missouri Compromise unconstitutional.

The case had been making its way up the judicial pipeline since 1842. First it had turned on the enslaved plaintiff Dred Scott, who had been taken by his captor into the free states of Illinois and Wisconsin, and thus, Scott's lawyers argued, had become free. As the case progressed, it turned on a widow who wanted to keep Scott and his family enslaved; it became more complicated when the widow assigned the supposed ownership of Dred Scott to John F. A. Sanford,* a New York lawyer. Now, before the Supreme Court, Sanford was arguing that never mind that as Scott's owner he lived in the free state of New York, Scott as a slave was not a US citizen and therefore had no standing to sue. Taney agreed with him, delivering his rambling, expansive opinion on March 5, 1857. In what Frederick Douglass called a "hell-black judgment,"[16] Taney held that slavery was a constitutionally protected form of property, as he affirmed the constitutionality of the hereditary perpetuity of slavery unto the *n*th generation throughout the United States. In his opinion, charged with key points of pro-slavery ideology, he specifically addressed the Declaration of Independence's assertion that "all men are created equal":

> It is too clear for dispute that the enslaved African race were not intended to be included, and formed no part of the people who framed and adopted this declaration, for if the language, as understood in that day, would embrace them, the conduct of the distinguished men who framed the Declaration of Independence would have been utterly and flagrantly inconsistent with the principles they asserted, and instead of the sympathy of mankind to which they so confidently appealed, they would have deserved and received universal rebuke and reprobation.
>
> Yet the men who framed this declaration were great men—high in literary acquirements, high in their sense of honor, and incapable of asserting principles inconsistent with those on which they were acting. They perfectly understood the meaning of the language they used, and how

---

*The court documents referenced him as "Sandford," but that was an error.

it would be understood by others, and they knew that it would not in any part of the civilized world be supposed to embrace the negro race, which, by common consent, had been excluded from civilized Governments and the family of nations, and doomed to slavery. They spoke and acted according to the then established doctrines and principles, and in the ordinary language of the day, and no one misunderstood them. The unhappy black race were separated from the white by indelible marks, and laws long before established, and were never thought of or spoken of except as property, and when the claims of the owner or the profit of the trader were supposed to need protection.

Jefferson's famous phrase was not law. But in drawing on it, Taney explained the common Southern understanding of it, and he did so while ruling for the United States that "negroes" could not be citizens, whether enslaved or free. They had, he approvingly noted, for

> more than a century before been regarded as beings of an inferior order, and altogether unfit to associate with the white race either in social or political relations, and so far inferior that they had *no rights which the white man was bound to respect*, and that the negro might justly and lawfully be reduced to slavery for his benefit. (emphasis added)

Dred Scott declared that there was no safe haven in the United States where slavery could not exist; if slaves remained slaves when their masters took them into free-soil states, then all states were slave states. It also meant that free people of color had no access in any state to the courts, to contracts, or to owning property, since they could not be citizens and thus had no legal basis to exist as free people, anywhere in the country.

As the implications of *Dred Scott* sank in, the question emerged: why not just . . . enslave them all? After all, women were already slaves, noted Richmond's George Fitzhugh, a descendant of William Fitzhugh. In the *Dred Scott* year of 1857, Fitzhugh published *Cannibals All! Or, Slaves without Masters*:

> The husband has a legally recognized property in his wife's services, and may legally control, in some measure, her personal liberty. She is his property and his slave.

The wife has also a legally recognized property in the husband's services. He is her property, but not her slave.

The father has property in the services and persons of his children till they are twenty-one years of age. They are his property and his slaves.

After deciding who was and wasn't a slave, Fitzhugh warned the North that abolitionists were really Communists who were using the slavery issue as a Trojan horse:

Every one of the leading Abolitionists is agitating the negro slavery question merely as a means to attain ulterior ends, and those ends nearer home. They would not spend so much time and money for the mere sake of the negro or his master, about whom they care little. But they know that men once fairly committed to negro slavery agitation . . . are, in effect, committed to Socialism and Communism . . . to no private property, no church, no law, no government, —to free love, free lands, free women and free churches. . . .

Socialism, not Abolition, is the real object of Black Republicanism. The North, not the South, the true battle-ground. . . . The agitators of the North look upon free society as a mere transition state to a better, but untried, form of society.[17]

That was the kind of thing Southern men said to each other as their butlers brought them brandy, but Fitzhugh went further than most. It was not necessary, he explained, to have a racial boundary. Prefiguring the radical capitalism of Ayn Rand, he saw the "strong" as natural masters of the "weak." "It is the duty of society," he asserted, "to enslave the weak."[18] In the *Richmond Enquirer* of December 15, 1855, he wrote that anyone could be a slave if they were inferior: "Nature has made the weak in mind or body slaves . . . The wise and virtuous, the strong in body and mind, are born to command." Dispensing as it did with the Jacksonian notion of white caste solidarity, *that* was an extreme position, even in the South, and it was not a widely popular one: the color line was too useful, and too sacred, to be discarded.

But if Fitzhugh was a fringe theorist, he was widely read, and, writes Eugene Genovese, "the Southern intelligentsia certainly appreciated him. . . . The notion that slavery was a proper social system for all labor, not merely for black labor, did not arise as a last-minute rationalization; it grew steadily as part of the growing self-awareness of the planter class."[19]

As the genetic distinction between European and African continued to erode, the skin-lightening process was well underway in the upper echelons of enslaved society. Frederick Law Olmsted had noted in his much-read travel account that in Virginia, "I am surprised at the number of fine-looking mulattoes, or nearly white-coloured persons, that I see. The majority of those with whom I have come personally in contact are such."[20] Travelers' accounts of Southern slave auctions commonly mentioned seeing one or another "white"-looking person being sold as a "negro."

As slavecatchers kidnapped free people for sale down South, even white people began to feel personally threatened: if, for example, a white man's daughter were to be denounced as a fugitive slave, the local lawmen would be required to deliver her to the marshal without so much as a hearing. With the Fugitive Slave Act compelling the deliverance of an accused slave to a slavecatcher without due process, it seemed that there might be no place where free labor didn't have to compete with slave labor. It seemed that if the Southerners got their way, all labor would be slave labor, whether black, white, or, to use the then-current term, amalgamated.

Slaveowners incorrectly thought that the North would enslave them by making their black slaves into their masters. Increasingly, the laborers of the North correctly thought that the South wanted slavery everywhere.

43

A Snake Biting Its Tail

*Labor to supply the demands of the South can be obtained only from Africa;
and the laws of this country prevent the Southern people from obtaining
this labor, branding those engaged in furnishing it with the opprobrious
epithet of "pirates," and inflicting on them the punishment due to those
guilty of the crime of piracy!*

—Mobile *Daily Register*, January 1, 1858

THE COMING OF RAILROADS ushered in a new era of capitalism on a scale
impossible in the days when markets were linked only by water. Railroads
required enormous sums of money to create, with a national organization that
functioned simultaneously everywhere. But *Dred Scott* threw western expansion
plans into chaos, railroad bonds dropped in price, and there was a Panic.

The Ohio Life Insurance and Trust Company failed in August 1857, raising fears of a bank run. Then the SS *Central America,* which sailed from Panamá via Havana for New York, sank on September 12 in a hurricane 160 miles
off the coast of Charleston. Down with the ship went 425 people (153 more
were saved) and a double-digit number, perhaps fifteen or sixteen, tons of gold
from California that was headed for the New York banks.* Paper money could
be replaced in the system, but not metal money; the loss was by one estimate

---

*There are different estimates of the amount of gold on board, but it was substantial. The wreck was
found in 1988 and has not been completely excavated as we write. What has been brought to the surface
so far includes 43 gold bars of up to 54 pounds, "1,302 $20 double-eagle gold coins, 37 $10 eagle gold
coins, and 9,053 10-cent silver coins," some of which dated back to 1823. Winter, Michael.

equivalent to about 20 percent of the nation's gold reserves. In what has been remembered as the Panic of 1857, credit contracted sharply, and the banks stopped specie payments for three months or so.

The panic originated in New York in part as a consequence of the local shortage of coin and in part as a consequence of excessive speculation, with the buying of stocks to sell rather than hold having become a common financial activity. It was worsened by the credit contraction that banks imposed in response. The commercial crisis was strongly felt in the North, while the South to some degree escaped it. Unfortunately, this led some to believe that the South could go it alone. Certainly, some Southerners were ruined when cotton prices dipped that year, and the disruption of commerce from New York occasioned the loss of money by many planters. A German observer wrote:

> In 1857, the year of the commercial crisis in America, many planters were compelled to sell a portion of their slaves in order to raise ready money, which at that time was not to be had on the best security even at 50 per cent. interest; and I saw a planter bring a hundred slaves to market at one time, who certainly after that sale must have been obliged to leave half his plantation uncultivated. [1]

When a planter had a debt crisis, his captives were dispersed. As failures became larger, hundreds of people were occasionally sold at once, fragmenting an entire community each time. James Gadsden, of Gadsden Purchase fame, bought the Cooper River plantation of Pimlico in 1852; after his death six years later, his 235 slaves "accustomed to the culture of Rice and Provisions" were sold to thirty different buyers in a sale advertised throughout the South, all the way to Texas.

The Panic of 1857 was strongly felt in the West, leading New York businessmen to focus their commerce even more closely on the cotton-producing South, offering long credit terms, even as leading Southerners focused on finding ways to become economically independent from New York.[2] Slave prices dipped in 1857, but slaves held their value better than cotton, and prices quickly recovered and climbed with yet another bumper crop. As the economy rebounded, slave prices reached new highs, raising the entry barrier to planter status yet further.

There could be no quicker way to get the price of slaves down than to reopen the African slave trade, which would create enormous profits for Charleston slave merchants while investing a new generation of purchasers in the slavery system. An article in *DeBow's Review* pitched the idea as a solution to the problem of white social inequality in the South:

> At present prices, it is almost impossible that the mere laborer can ever [own slaves]. . . . However much he may wish a share in that desirable commodity of slave labor, it is done up in packages too large for common use . . . The foreign slave trade will bring slaves enough for all, and at prices which poorer men may purchase. . . . it will thus bring all the ruling race to the same social stand point; it will thus reintegrate and erect our social system; it will abolish the odious distinctions between slave owners and non-slave owners; it will increase the laboring element of our population; it will thus extend our capacity for production, and, in doing all this, will give the promise of a more abundant wealth, and open the prospect to a broader and a brighter future than was ever yet expanded to the eye of man.[3]

Though Virginians, needless to say, opposed reopening the African trade, it was an editorial priority of the Charleston papers, beginning about 1853. As South Carolina systematically attempted to expand its influence, measures promoting the importation of African labor appeared in the legislatures of South Carolina, Georgia, Alabama, Mississippi, Louisiana, and Texas—none of which succeeded, perhaps because they would have been in overt defiance of federal law. It was not a popular notion among the mass of Southern whites, who did not want new Africans complicating their society, nor even for all slaveowners, but for some, it would have been a bonanza, and it was a useful political cudgel. Though the trade was not reopened, the initiative was not without effect, as W. E. B. DuBois pointed out: "The agitation did succeed in sweeping away nearly all theoretical opposition to the trade, and left the majority of Southern people in an attitude which regarded the reopening of the African slave-trade as merely a question of expediency."[4]

In South Carolina, where reopening the African slave trade at critical moments was a political and commercial tradition dating back to colonial days, agitating to reopen the foreign trade was a way of putting pressure on Virginia. There was a tactical problem that went back to the negotiations over the Constitution: an independent Southern confederacy would need Virginia's heft, strategic location, and money, but reopening the foreign slave trade was a deal-breaker that would have devalued the Virginians' slave property.

Outside the cotton belt, there was always substantial political will to keep the African trade closed. The specter of a reopened African slave trade appeared in the Lincoln-Douglas debates of 1858, when the two men were contending for the position of senator from Illinois. Though neither of the two men was in favor of reopening the African trade, Lincoln went on the offensive. Stephen Douglas advocated "popular sovereignty" regarding slavery, which meant that each state was free to make its own determination about the institution.[5] In what became known as the "house divided" speech, Lincoln argued that the logical consequence of this would be the reopening of the trade: "For years he [Douglas] has labored to prove it a sacred right of white men to take negro slaves into the new territories. Can he possibly show that it is less a sacred right to buy them where they can be bought cheapest? And, unquestionably they can be bought cheaper in Africa than in Virginia."[6]

In spite of bumper crops, the overheating slave market was threatening agricultural prosperity. The Mobile *Daily Register* warned of dangerous levels of credit exposure:

[January 19, 1859.] *High Prices for Negroes.* — Our exchanges from all parts of the South and West, are teeming with notices of the extraordinary high prices at which negroes are now selling, either on the block or at private sale, and the question naturally presents itself, what is the cause of it? Can the present high price of cotton be the cause?

If so, a return in the value of the product of the negro, sufficient to justify a purchase, at the prices now ruling cannot be the case, and all reasoning based on the proposition, proves ephemeral, for the influx of slaves this season into the cotton and sugar growing States is enormous. It is supposed that from Augusta, Ga., alone, for the last three months, that the shipments South and West, by the trains, average 200, daily, while the tide of emigration by way of other points is proportionately as great. Some estimate the import of negroes into the cotton growing States alone, will increase the next crop 200,000 bales.

The present amount of home slave labor should be sufficient to till the lands now open and under cultivation, but with this large increase of laborers, new lands must be opened and cultivated, and their yield [must be on sale] in the market next season. Now will the demand for cotton be equal to the supply? . . .

If the negroes have been purchased on time, and we are satisfied that such is the case with a large portion of them, a decline of a few cents in cotton would produce a reaction that must, necessarily seriously embarrass the planting interest, that have purchased on these terms. It is too much the custom for planters to anticipate their crops in dollars and cents, and shape their liabilities accordingly.

The demand for laborers is good, but we do not think that it justifies the exorbitant and high rates which prevail, although the South was never more solvent than now.[7] (paragraphing added)

Capital for a new African slave trade would have been easily available in New York, where businessmen were still financing an African trade to Cuba. At least 350,000 Africans were carried to Brazil in the 1840s, and, writes Don E. Fehrenbacher, "at least half of those importations were achieved with American help of some kind."[8] But the British navy, which had been actively pursuing slave traders for thirty years, cut off the Brazilian trade sharply in 1850, finishing it entirely by 1852. Besides British coercion, there was a familiar economic logic to the shutdown: the established Brazilian planters had imported so many that they had more than enough for their needs. Now, as new plantations were carved out of the forest in southern Brazil, a domestic slave trade began from the old slave area to the new one, as a forced north-to-south migration began in Brazil.* Similar to the United States's interstate trade, this interprovincial trade was the only other sizable such trade in the hemisphere.[9]

After 1850, only Cuba was left importing Africans. It was done with extensive connivance from within the United States, whose ships were by treaty immune from belowdecks search by British cruisers. Slaving above the Bight of Benin had largely been stopped, but whole villages were still being ripped out of Yorubaland by Dahomeyan slave raiders and carried off to sugar mills in the area of Matanzas, Havana, and elsewhere, and the Central African ports continued selling slaves.

"We don't care for the English squadron," boasted an imprisoned slave ship captain in New York in an 1855 interview published in the antislavery *New York Evangelist* and reprinted in the pro-slavery *DeBow's Review*. "We run up the American flag, and if they come on board all we have to do is show our American papers, and they have no right to search us." The captain estimated that his brig had cost $13,000 to outfit and brought in $220,000 on one run to Cuba—a rate of return from which one successful venture could absorb the

---

*Brazil was the last country in the hemisphere to end slavery, in 1888, developing a mass abolition movement in the final years; Cuba, still a colony of Spain, ended slavery in 1886 in the face of growing independentist sentiment.

costs of several failed ones. Affirming that New York was the king of the trade, the captain was asked how he outfitted his ships:

> I can go down to South street, and go into a number of houses that help to fit out ships for the business. I don't know how far they own the vessels or receive the profits of the cargoes. I had rather not have American owners; I prefer Spaniards or Portuguese. But these houses know all about it. They know me. They see me sail out of port with a ship, and come back a passenger . . . They know [that] . . . when a cargo of slaves is landed, the vessel is often destroyed, not to be a witness against her officers and crew.[10]

The colonial-era delay of months on the African coast while assembling a cargo piecemeal was a thing of the past. The African side of the business had gotten steadily more industrial, so slavers in the 1850s were frequently able to pull up to their African destination port and choose a cargo of as many as twelve hundred people from among those held captive in what amounted to a wholesale warehouse maintained by factors. The captain continued:

> The boys and women we kept on the upper deck. But all the strong men— those giant Africans that might make us trouble—we put below on the slave deck.
>
> *Did you chain them or put on handcuffs?*
> No, never; they would die. We let them move about.
> *Are you very severe with them?*
> We have to be pretty strict at first—for a week or so—to make them feel that we are masters. Then we lighten up for the rest of the voyage.
> *How do you pack them at night?*
> They lay down upon the deck, on their sides, body to body. There would not be room enough for all to lie on their backs.
> *Did many die on the passage?*
> Yes, I lost a good many the last cruise—more than ever before. Sometimes we find them dead when we go below in the morning. Then we throw them overboard.

Mortality was decreasing on the voyages, because steam vessels now made the cruise from Africa to Cuba in as little as eighteen days. The year-end 1859 British report from Havana to Her Majesty's commissioners on the slave trade noted that Madagascar had become a new staging ground for East African Arab traders selling people principally from Mozambique (referring to Mozambique

Island, off the coast of the present-day country of Mozambique), to slavers
bound for Cuba:

> Such expeditions not unfrequently originate in the United States of
> America, from whence they take their departure; and there are at present
> here, we understand, agents from Boston and from New Orleans, who
> are engaged in completing the subscriptions for shares, which have been
> already in part filled up by American capitalists. One of these schemes is,
> for a ship of 900 tons to bring 2,000 slaves, under charge of an experienced
> slaver, who has made no less than thirteen successful voyages.
>
> It seems that negroes are to be had on the East Coast of Africa for
> about 28 dollars each; and even so, they are paid for in goods, upon which
> there is at the least 100 per cent. of profit.
>
> We learn that the ships to be employed in this unholy Traffic, with
> their goods for barter on board, and prepared with sufficient iron-fitting
> tanks for a supply of water, proceed from the United States, under Ameri-
> can colours, to a port in Madagascar; there the slave-deck is laid in safety
> and without hindrance, and there they take in their cargoes of human mis-
> ery, the victims being brought over from the opposite Coast of Africa in
> Arab vessels: and we have been told that such are the facilities and arrange-
> ments that a very large cargo of slaves can be completed in two or three
> days.[11]

The commissioners accounted for 12,744 Africans introduced illegally into
Cuba in 1858; of the twenty voyages that brought them, eleven were in American vessels. Certain that there was more traffic than they knew about, the commissioners rounded their estimate up by a third, to almost seventeen thousand.[12]

With Africans selling in Havana at $1,000 or more, the profits on such voy-
ages were immense; a merchant could afford to pay out bribes, and even burn the
ship if necessary. New York merchants especially were involved in the financing,
but a wide variety of US maritime centers participated in the trade, including
Baltimore and New Orleans. W. E. B. Dubois's list, compiled from congressional documents, shows vessels from Portland, Maine; Portsmouth, New Hampshire; Boston; Rhode Island; Mystic, Connecticut; and Philadelphia.[13]

The *Echo*, a brig carrying 475 slaves (out of about 625 it had started with),
was captured by the US Navy off the coast of Cuba in August 1858, and though
the captain and crew were found not guilty at their trials, the captives were sent
to Africa—not back to their homes, but to Monrovia, Liberia, where, inevitably,

a new composite culture was developing among people from various parts of Africa who had been left there.

The American ship *Haidee*, which had left Kilongo on the Angolan coast with 1,145 captives, brought the 903 of them who were still alive into the Cuban port of Cárdenas on September 8, 1859. Julián Zulueta, the enormously wealthy Basque trader who had commissioned the voyage together with partners, took them to an "estate" with "an escort of about 200 armed men. The bribes on this scandalous occasion are said to have amounted to about 200,000 dollars."[14] By the end of 1859, reported the British judge in Havana: "We have had information of the introduction of no less than thirty-nine cargoes, with 22,855 negroes; add to which one-third, as usual, and we have the enormous number of 30,473 landed here in this year."[15] Reporting from Luanda, where more than three centuries of the slave trade had depopulated the countryside, Her Majesty's acting commissioner wrote: "It is obvious that the only flag which the guilty adventurers in the Slave Trade now assume to cover their crime is the American."[16]

The slaveowners of the Lowcountry saw all this as another instance of Northern hypocrisy: Americans in free-soil states were building fortunes illegally in the foreign slave trade. But since none of the slaves came to the United States, Carolina planters were denied the use of cheap African labor, while they continued paying a protectionist markup on slaves to Virginia's benefit, and Carolina merchants were denied the use of their harbor as a slave depot.

Despite all the illegal African slave trading, with the exception of the well-known cases of the *Wanderer* in 1858 and the *Clotilda* in 1860, and perhaps a few others that left little trace, Africans were not imported directly into the American South. When in late 1859 President Buchanan sent a secret agent, Benjamin F. Slocumb, to travel from North Carolina to Texas as a potential slave buyer with a mission of looking for evidence of African slave vessels arriving, Slocumb found that "reports concerning the landing of Africans, except in the case of the yacht 'Wanderer,' were unreliable, in fact mere fabrications."[17] Joseph Bruin, the large New Orleans slave trader, told Slocumb there were none in town, as it was not a "Safe business," but that "about 100 [Africans] had been sold in and about New Orleans last Spring, and hurried away."[18] Some historians believe that some or many clandestine shipments of Africans came to the Gulf Coast from Havana, while others say that cargoes were smuggled along the Georgia coastline. It is certainly possible, but there is no direct documentation— there wouldn't be—and, moreover, there is no trace of them in documentation about the markets, where Africans did not, as far as we know, turn up. If such shipments did come, they presumably went directly to large plantations under high secrecy, but high secrecy was not all that easy in polemical, newspaper-heavy, nineteenth-century America. Africans for sale in the open market would have been news, and would certainly have been mentioned in slaveowners' and traders' letters. For the labor networks of the South to have been supplied with African bodies in any more substantial way would have had to have left traces that do not exist. Whether some Africans came in clandestinely via Havana or not, the slave-breeding industry remained well-protected.

The two African slave ships that we do know of were highly conspicuous. The *Wanderer* was outfitted by Charles Augustus Lafayette Lamar, a loose-cannon financier and speedboater from Savannah. Lamar was the son of New York bank president G. B. Lamar, who would shortly be part of a cocka-mamie plan, supported by pro-Confederate New York City mayor Fernando Wood, to have the city secede in sympathy with the South.[19] His voyage was an open secret, intended in rebuke and defiance of the federal ban. Lamar's investors included several major slave traders, who were all taking a consider-able risk since they were committing a capital crime. One was Nathan Bed-ford Forrest, whose business by this time reached from Texas to Georgia, and who bragged about his "interest" in the *Wanderer* expedition to a newspaper reporter in 1869.[20] Savannah historians Sheehy et al. write that Lamar "cal-culated that if he could maneuver this confrontation into his own back yard of Savannah, he could win. This victory would in turn undermine the federal law banning the importation of African slaves." Win or lose, "he hoped the importation of Africans would drive a wedge between the North and South and elect a Republican Party president—something he was sure would trigger secession."[21]

At the Angolan slave port of Benguela, 487 people were densely packed onto Lamar's *Wanderer*, a small, fast-sailing vessel built as a pleasure craft that flew the flag of the New York Yacht Club. They were young, in keeping with mar-ket requirements, and many were children. About 409 of them were still alive when the *Wanderer* came ashore on Jekyll Island, a little south of Savannah, on November 28, 1858. The crew was arrested immediately, but Lamar got the ship back and quickly disposed of the slaves. One African boy, the only remain-ing witness, was abducted at gunpoint from jail and never seen again.[22] The crew members were put on trial and acquitted. Secret agent Slocumb's previ-ously mentioned report to President Buchanan contains some information about what happened to the *Wanderer*'s captives: none of them went to Charleston, he reported from that city; some had passed through Mobile on the way to Louisiana; thirty were sold in Vicksburg by Nathan Bedford Forrest; and seven in Memphis, also by Forrest. Some wound up in Texas.[23]

Lamar, also a horse racer, owned the Ten Broeck Race Course in Savannah, where on March 2 and 3, 1859—a little more than three months after the *Wanderer* arrived—Georgia's all-time biggest slave auction was held to pay down the debts Pierce Mease Butler had incurred speculating in the stock market. The broker conducting the sale, Joseph Bryan, owned the largest slave jail in town, on Bryan Street facing Johnson Square, but even so, he couldn't manage an in-house sale of that size, so he moved it to Ten Broeck.[24] The people to be sold were housed in the stables.

A Northern newspaper reporter attempting to take notes at the sale would have been ejected if not violently abused, so Mortimer Thomson, writing for Horace Greeley's *New York Tribune*, went incognito, posing as a buyer. When his article, "Great Auction Sale of Slaves at Savannah, Georgia, March 2d and 3d, 1859," was published on March 9, it caused an international sensation and was a public relations disaster for Savannah. Writing under the name Q. K. Philander Doesticks, Thomson reported hearing at the auction strong sentiments in favor of reopening the African slave trade, and described the scene:

> For several days before the sale every hotel in Savannah was crowded with negro speculators from North and South Carolina, Virginia, Georgia, Alabama, and Louisiana, who had been attracted hither by the prospects of making good bargains. Nothing was heard for days, in the bar-rooms and public rooms, but talk of the great sale.

The community on Butler's Sea Island plantations numbered about nine hundred. Half of them were owned by the estate of Butler's deceased brother John, but Butler's 436 went to the auction block, there to be sold by what Southerners reckoned a "humane" method, in families, though of course such sales still broke family ties. So half the community would remain, and half would disappear. The auction realized $303,850 (about $8.7 million in 2014 dollars). The sale was particularly painful, since this community was so deeply rooted. "None of the Butler slaves have ever been sold before, but have been on these two plantations since they were born," wrote Thomson. "Who can tell how closely intertwined are the affections of a little band of four hundred persons, living isolated from all the world beside, from birth to middle age? Do they not naturally become one great family, each man a brother unto each?"[25]

Thomson reported as a conversation whose "sentiment" was "more than once repeated" a negative response by a prospective purchaser when asked if he would be buying a woman named Sally: "Well, Major, I think not. Sally's a good, big, strapping gal, and can do a heap o' work; but it's five years since she had any children. *She's done breeding, I reckon.*"[26] (emphasis in original)

The Ten Broeck sale is popularly remembered by the phrase "the weeping time," which also refers to the weather; four straight days of rain stopped when the sale ended. The auction was up in the grandstand, a room about a hundred feet long, where they lined up and waited their turn to go on the block. Thomson tells us that as "the wind howled outside, and through the open side of the building the driving rain came pouring in," auctioneer Thomas J. Walsh announced the terms: "one-third cash, the remainder payable in two equal annual instalments, bearing interest from the day of sale, to be secured by approved mortgage and personal security, or approved acceptances in Savannah, Ga., or Charleston, S.C. Purchasers to pay for papers."[27]

As the sale wound down, Pierce Butler moved among his former slaves carrying canvas bags from which he sorrowfully handed to each one of them four gleaming new twenty-five cent pieces, fresh from the mint, a dollar apiece, as if to say, it wasn't my fault. But when the sale was concluded, Butler's debts were paid, and he was a rich man again. He celebrated by going on an extended trip to the Mediterranean.[28]

Though Butler experienced the auction as a terrible humiliation, it turned out in the long run to have been a good business move: he cashed out his slaveholdings while they were still worth something. While it was not hard to tell in 1859 that war was coming, there was no reason for planters to believe the end of chattel slavery was around corner. Quite the contrary; it was a time-honored institution that had never been stronger. There were more slaves than ever; the cash value of the approximately four million people then enslaved in the United States embodied a phenomenal sum of money.

Though the Ten Broeck race course no longer exists as such, a historical marker was placed in a small commemorative area on the former site on March 2, 2008—another spot of sacred ground marked and acknowledged.

It was about the same time as the Ten Broeck sale—sometime in early 1859—that a "castle" of the Knights of the Golden Circle opened in Baltimore. Founded in 1854, and based in the free territory of Cincinatti, Ohio, the KGC was a pro-slavery secret society that had consolidated with the Order of the Lone Star, which had been somewhat directionless after the death of John

Quitman in July 1858.* The KGC wanted to secede from the United States and take over Mexico.[29]

In Virginia, the cherished diffusionist notion that the slave population would be eliminated by selloff had not become reality. Four and a half decades after the Battle of New Orleans, Virginia was still exporting slaves to the Deep South. Although planters had been living for generations off the earnings of slave-breeding, exactly as abolitionists charged, Virginia's slave population had increased by 1860 to 490,865, even though Maryland's and Delaware's had diminished.[30]

An editorial in the Richmond *Enquirer* of May 25, 1858, made clear the extent to which the Virginia economy still depended on the export to the South and West of domestically raised African Americans, as well as how alarming the loss of its protected status to a reopened trade would be:

> "If a dissolution of the Union is to be followed by the revival of the [African] slave trade, Virginia had better consider whether the South of the Northern Confederacy would not be far more preferable for her than the North of a Southern Confederacy. In the Northern Confederacy Virginia would derive a large amount from the sale of her slaves to the South, and gain the increased value of her lands from Northern emigration – while in the Southern Confederacy, with the African slave trade revived, she would lose two-thirds of the value of her slave property, and derive no additional increase to the value of her lands.[31]

The South Carolinians would make sure that the Virginia slave-breeders would not be able to sit their war out.

John Brown's attempt to ignite a slave rebellion at Harpers Ferry in what is now West Virginia, at the confluence of the Potomac and Shenandoah Rivers, began on October 16, 1859, and was suppressed two days later by Lt. J. E. B. Stuart under the command of Colonel Robert E. Lee.

---

*Quitman died of something later called "National Hotel Disease," which he along with several hundred other people contracted attending the inauguration of James Buchanan.

Frederick Douglass was one of perhaps eighty people who knew about John Brown's raid on Harpers Ferry in advance. Though he tried to talk Brown out of the suicidal act that lit the match for war, he didn't inform on him, which was enough to make him a conspirator. Douglass fled the country to Canada and on to London, returning home the following year.

Robert E. Lee's report, filed on October 19, described Brown's action not as Northern aggression, but as "the attempt of a fanatic or madman, who could only end in failure."[32] But Brown's attempt to start a slave rebellion galvanized the South, where it was seen by the political and intellectual class as proof of what the "Black Republicans"—a contemptuous name for the party of Chase and Seward—had in store for them. The *Charleston Mercury* noted on October 20 that three New York newspapers with different political affiliations

> all concur in opinion as to the desperate condition of the democratic party throughout the North, and the imminent prospect of a Black Republican Speaker of the House of Representatives and President of the United States being lifted to power. Let none, however, expect Seward to be the candidate of that party. We, at least, have never thought so; but we are confident some one less committed, yet equally Black Republican—such as [Salmon P.] Chase or [Supreme Court] Judge [John] McLean—would be put forward. . . . But whether Seward, or Chase, or McLean, to the South the difference is small. It is the candidate of a hostile sectional party, whose success must put the South, as unprotected tributaries, at the feet of inimical rulers.

It wasn't just about Lincoln. In the eyes of the *Mercury*, any "Black Republican" president would have been cause for war. The number of Southern vigilance committees grew.

John Brown wasn't hanged until December 2, and that wasn't soon enough for slaveholders, because he didn't stop talking until he was hanged, and never strayed from his calm, righteous tone. Brown's execution (witnessed by the wealthy, successful, well-connected, radical young actor John Wilkes Booth, a member of the Knights of the Golden Circle) elevated him to the status of martyr.[33] In his memory, new lyrics were put to an old campfire meeting song with the stirring chorus of "Glory, Hallelujah" to make the great song of the military campaign that ended slavery: *John Brown's body lies a-moulderin' in the grave* . . .

➤≈

After the *Wanderer,* only one more slave ship containing Africans is known to have arrived in the United States. On an unknown date in the summer of 1860, the *Clotilda* brought to Magazine Point on Mobile Bay 110 captives from Ouidah, in the Fon-speaking state of Dahomey. "Ouidah was a more cosmopolitan city than Mobile," notes Sylviane Diouf in her study of the *Clotilda* shipmates, which tells us that most of the captives were the people now called Yoruba (though that ethnonym was not yet in general use), practitioners of the orisha religion.[34] The *Clotilda*'s captives had been taken by the Dahomeyan king Glèlè; some were from Atakora, in what is now northwest Benin; others were Fon speakers from Dahomey; still others were Muslim.[35] One, Gumpa, who became known as Peter Lee, was a Dahomeyan nobleman who practiced vodun.[36] This ship, which could as easily have gone to Havana or Matanzas, was more or less representative of the dramatic, high-volume African cultural transplantation to Cuba that was by then in its final days and would prove highly consequential for twentieth-century Afro-Cuban culture.

One survivor of the *Clotilda,* Cudjoe Lewis, lived until 1935. One of the relatively few Yoruba to be brought to United States territory,* he described the slave raid in which he was captured, recalling that the warriors who killed the unsalable people and kidnapped the remainder were women—the Dahomeyan kings favored the use of female soldiers—and that as they took him to Abomey, they wore hanging from their belts the severed heads of the captives' unfortunate family members who had been slaughtered in the raid. After three days, the heads were decomposing, so the coffle stopped along the way for nine days as the soldiers smoked the heads over a fire to preserve them. The heads, along with the live slaves, were to be ceremonially sold to the king of Dahomey, a state organized for the purpose of slave-raiding.[37]

Most of the *Clotilda* captives remained enslaved in the Mobile area. With the end of slavery, many of them reassembled; in 1866, they established their community under Gumpa's leadership as African Town, which he led for thirty years or so. After Gumpa's son with his shipmate Josephina was born, writes Diouf, they had the baby tattooed on the chest with the image of a snake biting

---

*The bulk of Yoruba slaving happened after the fall of the Oyó empire to an Islamic jihad that began in the 1820s and culminated with the empire's collapse in 1836. By this time, the United States no longer allowed the African slave trade, but Yoruba were taken in numbers to Cuba, Brazil, and, as indentured servants, to Trinidad.

its own tail. Ultimately, as many vodouisants in Haiti have subsequently done, Gumpa became a Baptist.[38] Descendants still live in the area.

By the time the *Clotilda* sailed, the African trade was already feeling the heat of President Buchanan's program of stepped-up American anti-slave-trade enforcement off the African coast. But as we have previously emphasized, suppressing the slave trade was a different issue than abolishing slavery, which President Buchanan had no intention of doing. Many secessionists approved of his stopping the illegal African slave trade. They weren't making any money from it, and harassing it kept the ships of the tiny US Navy busy—far, far away.

44

Assignment in Paraguay

Both thy bondmen, and thy bondmaids, which thou shalt have, shall be of the heathen that are round about you; of them shall ye buy bondmen and bondmaids.

Moreover of the children of the strangers that do sojourn among you, of them shall ye buy, and of their families that are with you, which they begat in your land: and they shall be your possession.

And ye shall take them as an inheritance for your children after you, to inherit them for a possession; they shall be your bondmen for ever: but over your brethren the children of Israel, ye shall not rule one over another with rigour.

—Leviticus 25:44–46

PRESIDENT BUCHANAN CONDUCTED HIS administration in such a way as to leave his successor crippled.

Some of Buchanan's few biographers have defended him against the charge of being part of a Southern conspiracy. But however one cares to address the topic, the notion that Buchanan could have been unaware of having methodically put the Union in the most disadvantageous position possible does not pass the smell test. His contemporaries certainly thought that was what he was doing.

Buchanan announced at the beginning of his term that he, like Polk, would be a one-term president, in effect setting the secession clock ticking. He sent the US Navy as far away as he could, where its personnel would not be easily available for duty in the event that, say, Carolinians or Mississippians should declare independence, as their leaders were constantly threatening to do. In 1858, he ordered "a fleet of nineteen ships"—seven of them chartered merchant vessels—"of two hundred guns manned by twenty-five hundred sailors and marines" on an unprecedented mission to Paraguay (!), where a US sailor had been killed in a river incident three years previously.[1] Paraguay is a landlocked country, so the navy had to ascend three rivers. Most of the vessels stopped at Rosario, Argentina, and two continued on to the Paraguayan capital of Asunción, where they demanded an apology and extorted a new commercial treaty.

Following the completion of that expensive, time-consuming errand, Buchanan sent the navy to the African coast to police the slave trade—and indeed, for the first time, American enforcement did make a dent in it. The only captain ever hanged according to the legal penalty for engaging in the slave trade, one Nathaniel Gordon, was executed in 1862 under Lincoln, but he had been prosecuted and convicted during the Buchanan administration.

Riddled with procurement scandals, bribery, and "emergency loans," and spending extravagantly on military adventures, Buchanan's administration proved to be highly corrupt. Entering office with a $1.3 million surplus, Buchanan left behind a $25.2 million deficit, while government debt ballooned from $28.7 million to $76.4 million.[2] Buchanan's secretary of the treasury was Howell Cobb, his old Jacksonian friend and Georgia cotton planter, and at one time owner of a thousand slaves.[3] Ostensibly a Unionist and the ex-Speaker of the House of Representatives, Cobb in 1856 had published *A Scriptural Examination of the Institution of Slavery*, a Bible-thumping defense of divinely ordained property rights in slaves that execrated various individual abolitionists, in which he complained—this is a mere sample—that:

> Amongst the most successful schemes of mischief brought forth by abolitionists, may be reckoned what is familiarly called the Under-Ground Railroad: by this means, many owners have been deprived of their property by persons esteeming themselves, and being esteemed by their associates, pious.[4]

Asserting that enslaved women reproduced "like rabbits," the slave-breeding Cobb in 1858 told the Georgia Cotton Planters Association (of which he was secretary) that "the proprietor's largest source of prosperity is in the negroes he raises."[5] He was one of the key people informally known as the "Buchaneers" who helped make the Buchanan presidency a fiscal scandal of historic proportions. With him at the helm of Treasury, Buchanan ran his *entire term* on deficit financing, which Andrew Jackson would have regarded as a mortal sin if not treason. Such a thing might not seem so strange to modern readers, since the

Federal Reserve can now print money to meet the government's obligations, but this was an era in which there was no national paper currency. After three decades of a Jacksonian fiscal regime, the federal government was required to shift the physical location of pieces of gold and silver in order for federal spending to occur.

Besides the naval operations in Paraguay and Africa, Buchanan sent the US Army to Utah in 1857, to confront the theocratic Mormon state of Deseret. That was before there was a railroad to get the troops out there; they had to go on horseback, far from telegraph lines. Though hostilities ended in 1858, the army remained in Utah through the remainder of Buchanan's presidency.

Buchanan's vice president was Kentuckian John C. Breckinridge, the grandson of the man who had introduced Jefferson's anonymous Kentucky Resolutions that first branded the doctrine of nullification. As the Democrats split into Northern and Southern factions, Vice President Breckinridge ran for president in 1860 on the Southern Democratic ticket, with a platform that was essentially a threat that if he lost, the South would secede. He did, and it did. When Lincoln won the election, it was with a plurality of votes on a four-way split; his name had not even been on the ballot in the Southern states.

In his final, lame-duck State of the Union Address on December 3, 1860, Buchanan explained the problem to the nation—the abolitionists made them do it: "The long-continued and intemperate interference of the Northern people with the question of slavery in the Southern States has at length produced its natural effects."

By this point Northern bankers were refusing to buy Treasury notes for fear the money would go South; nor were they likely to invest in a situation in which the South was poised to repudiate its debts. Rhett's *Charleston Mercury* wanted a new government, now. There was no time to lose: strike while the South has the momentum and the North is in transition.

Many in the North had thought the Southern hotspurs wouldn't really secede. The plan to defeat the unprepared—and, the South thought, irresolute—North hinged on the idea of a quick mobilization. Howell Cobb had advised the secessionists to wait until the day of Lincoln's inauguration, which would have saved their old friend Buchanan considerable embarrassment, but they ignored his advice, so Cobb resigned as secretary of the treasury on December 8 to get in on the ground floor of the new country.

It was clear what Cobb had done, wrote Henry Adams in the *Boston Daily Advertiser* of December 13: "Everyone knows that [Buchanan] has neglected to

garrison Fort Moultrie; that Secretary Cobb has so managed the Treasury as
to weaken the new administration as far as possible; and that Mr. Floyd [John
Floyd of Virginia, secretary of war] has as good as placed large amounts of
national arms in the hands of the South Carolinians."[6]

As secession was declared in one state after another, Buchanan did nothing
to stop it. Instead, he let them go to form a slaveholders' confederacy that would
attack and invade the United States—once he was gone, and a less compliant
president inaugurated.

Before Lincoln took office in March, unidentified thieves removed all
the remaining specie from the federal treasury in Washington.[7] In William P.
MacKinnon's words, "By the time Abraham Lincoln took office in March 1861
the country's largest military garrison was in the desert forty miles southwest
of Salt Lake City, and the new administration could neither buy stationery nor
meet the federal payroll. The two circumstances were not unrelated."[8] What
little money the United States government had was in the form of pieces of metal
scattered around the far-flung country. That was how the South wanted it. Moreover, the secession of seven states from the Union meant that many Northern
creditors would be burned if not ruined, seizing up the nation's commercial cash
flow. Many of the merchants had been in favor of appeasing the South; but once
they were stiffed by their Southern debtors, they became staunch Unionists.[9]

The secession campaign was planned and executed by a wealthy group of men
who had been at war with the government years before they equipped an army
against it. Their propaganda machine ran full blast: disunion was the only permissible stance. With the *Charleston Mercury* leading the charge, newspapers
throughout the South hammered it home every day. When word of Lincoln's
election came, the Fire-Eaters were already mobilizing; Robert Barnwell Rhett
and others founded the Minute Men for the Defence of Southern Rights, an

*following page: This Currier and Ives print in response to Florida's secession on January 10, 1861,
depicts South Carolina leading Florida, Alabama, Mississippi, and Louisiana off a cliff. South
Carolina is shown as riding a pig in pursuit of a butterfly labeled "secession humbug," and saying, "We
go the whole hog . . . Old Hickory is dead, and now we'll have it." Georgia is depicted as deviating
from the path, though in fact it seceded on January 19, before Louisiana did (January 26). The rider
personifying Mississippi is saying, "Down with the Union! Mississippi repudiates her bonds!"—
referring to the self-ruination of Mississippi's credit on global markets almost twenty years before.*

THE "SECESSION MOVEMENT".

action group, in October 1860, while the Knights of the Golden Circle were establishing paramilitary forces elsewhere.[10]

South Carolina had been the state most likely to secede since the beginnings of the nation—indeed, had barely joined the United States except for reasons of defense, which had been moribund since the removal of the Spanish, the British, and the local Native Americans following the War of 1812.

"All the slaves in Maryland might be bought out now at half-price with a liberal discount for cash," wrote Henry Adams the week before South Carolina seceded.[11] Not all the slave states were determined to secede, however, and in order to evangelize on behalf of disunion, the governors of Mississippi and Alabama sent "secession commissioners" to the various slave states.

Alabama's commissioner to South Carolina, John Archer Elmore, arrived in time to address the first evening session of the South Carolina Secession Convention on December 17, 1860, warning them of what they already believed: that Lincoln's election was "an avowed declaration of war upon the institutions, the rights, and the interests of the South."[12] The directorates that sent out secession commissioners tried to send natives of the states they were sent to, so Mississippi's commissioner to North Carolina was North Carolina–born Jacob Thompson, President Buchanan's secretary of the interior. It was straight-up treason: Thompson was still a cabinet officer when he arrived in Raleigh on December 18 to deliver a barnburner of a speech characterized by the "message of emancipation, humiliation, subjugation, and ruin" that ran "through the commissioners' messages like a scarlet thread," writes Charles B. Dew in his history of the secession commissions.[13]

The South Carolina convention voted unanimously on December 20 to secede from the Union. Anyone who might have dissented had long since been weeded out. When it was Robert Barnwell Rhett's turn to ascend to the stage and take his turn signing the secession papers in the presence of three thousand cheering Carolinians, the most tireless and pugnacious disunionist of all "fell to his knees, lifted his hands upward toward the heavens, and bowed his head in prayer," writes his biographer.[14]

South Carolina sent out well-coached secession commissioners, focusing them on the idea of a constitutional convention at Montgomery. Their commissioner to Alabama was John C. Calhoun's son Andrew. Raised from birth at a high pitch of pro-slavery hysteria, the younger Calhoun had in November recalled that the Haitians had risen up "with all the fury of a beast, and scenes were then enacted over a comparatively few planters, that the white fiends [of the North] would delight to see re-enacted now with us."[15]

As the appeals to secede became more intense, they became less economic and more emotional: if you don't support the slaveowners, you will be the victim of the slaves. After winding himself up for several pages, Alabama secession commissioner Stephen F. Hale reached the boiling point of negrophobia that Haiti represented in this by now ritualized discourse, augmented as usual by the image of the violation of white women:

> The election of Mr. Lincoln cannot be regarded otherwise than . . . an open declaration of war, for the triumph of this new theory of government destroys the property of the South, lays waste her fields, and inaugurates all the horrors of a San Domingo servile insurrection, consigning her citizens to assassinations and her wives and daughters to pollution and violation to gratify the lust of half-civilized Africans. Especially is this true in the cotton-growing States, where, in many localities, the slave outnumbers the white population ten to one.[16]

But the economic argument predominated. In a December 27, 1860, letter to Kentucky governor Beriah Magoffin, Hale put it down squarely to property rights in human beings: "African slavery has become not only one of the fixed domestic institutions of the Southern States, but forms an important element of their political power, and constitutes the most valuable species of their property, worth, according to recent estimates, not less than $4,000,000,000; forming, in fact, the basis on which rests the prosperity and wealth of most of these States."[17]

Howell Cobb supervised the hasty, secretive drafting of the Confederate Constitution at Montgomery, Alabama, with a team that included his brother Thomas, Robert Toombs, Robert Barnwell Rhett, and Alexander Stephens. This constitution explicitly mentioned slavery—ten times. Cobb served as temporary head of the six-state Confederate States of America for two weeks, until Jefferson Davis was selected president of the self-declared new nation and was inaugurated on February 18, 1861.

Alexander Stephens of Georgia was declared vice president of the Confederacy. President-elect Lincoln had written Stephens on December 22 that, as the Republicans had insisted throughout the campaign, he had no intention of abolishing slavery where it existed, only of prohibiting its spread to other territories.

But of course, to stop slavery's expansion would have been to end it.

❋

So effective was the sermon *Mutual Relation of Masters and Slaves as Taught in the Bible* at the First Presbyterian Church of Augusta, Georgia, on January 6, 1861, that the congregation quickly raised the money to publish it.[18]

Its author, the twenty-five-year-old clergyman Joseph Ruggles Wilson, based his text on Ephesians 6:5-9; the passage begins, "Servants, be obedient to them that are your masters according to the flesh, with fear and trembling, in singleness of your heart, as unto Christ." Affirming that the Greek word translated as "servants" "distinctly and unequivocally signified 'slaves,'" Wilson saw slavery as a permanent Christian institution. Expounding the Southern churches' doctrine, which had occasioned a break with their Northern denominations' counterparts, he proposed that as servants of Christ, masters should treat their slaves with love and slaves should work hard. This was the doctrine known as "paternalism," in which slaves and master were portrayed as forming a big family—until it was time to sell some of the family.

Only fifteen days before Georgia seceded, Wilson told his parishioners to prepare for the upcoming victorious struggle, speaking of slavery as something to "cherish":

> We should begin to meet the infidel fanaticism of our infatuated enemies upon the elevated ground of a divine warrant for the institution we are resolved to cherish. . . .
>
> [The Apostle Paul] as much as says, that it is unnecessary to fear that this long-cherished institution will first give way before the enemies who press upon it from without. If slaveholders preserve it as an element of social welfare, in the spirit of the christian religion, throwing into it the full measure of gospel-salt allotted to it, and casting around it the same guardianship with which they would protect their family peace, if threatened on some other ground—they need apprehend nothing but their own dereliction in duty to themselves and their dependent servants.

He closed by anticipating prosperity for slaveowners and holiness for the enslaved:

> Oh, when that welcome day shall dawn, whose light will reveal a world covered with righteousness, not the least pleasing sight will be the institution of domestic slavery . . . which, by saving a lower race from the

destruction of heathenism, has, under divine management, contributed to refine, exalt, and *enrich* its superior race![19] (emphasis added)

We do not know whether Wilson's son, Woodrow, attended his father's sermon that Sunday during secession winter, because he had just turned four. But his subsequent writings as a historian and his adult actions suggest that he absorbed the racist message of his father, with whom he had a lifelong loving relationship.*

Rather than "submit" to the "Black Republicans"—so went the rhetoric—Mississippi seceded on January 9, 1861, followed by Florida (which had only been a state for fifteen years) on January 10, Alabama on the eleventh, and Georgia on the nineteenth.

On January 21, five Southern Senators withdrew from Congress. In his brief valedictory speech, Jefferson Davis, owner of 113 slaves,[20] said:

> It has been a belief that we are to be deprived in the Union of the rights which our fathers bequeathed to us, which has brought Mississippi to her present decision. She has heard proclaimed the theory "that all men are created free and equal," and this made the basis of an attack upon her social institutions; and the sacred Declaration of Independence has been invoked to maintain the position of the equality of the races.[21]

Davis went on to explain, as slaveowners frequently did and as the US Supreme Court had affirmed, that "all men were created equal" had not been intended to mean all men. Jefferson's youngest grandson, George Wythe Randolph, who as a boy stood by Jefferson's deathbed, apparently agreed: he was the Confederate secretary of war for eight months in 1862.[22]

Neither Virginia nor Maryland had seceded when, with Louisiana's P. G. T. Beauregard giving the orders, slavery "fired on the flag," in Ulysses Grant's words, on April 12, 1861, at Fort Sumter.[23]

Virginia did much business with the North and was decidedly ambivalent about seceding. The Confederate Constitution, signed as of March 11, offered

---

*When he was president of Princeton, Wilson kept out black students; as president of the United States, he implemented Jim Crow in the federal government, requiring job applications to include photos.

Virginia both a carrot and a stick. The document was modeled on the US Constitution, complete with a three-fifths clause, but with explicit protections for slavery written into it. However, even despite the latter-day clamor to reopen the African slave trade, the Confederate Constitution prohibited the foreign slave trade into the Confederate States with what might as well have been called the Virginia clause.

The carrot, then, was that a Confederate Virginia could continue to slave breed and thus retain a market capitalization of its enslaved population. With importation prohibited and conquest continuing, Virginia slaveowners could sell black people into new domains for the foreseeable future. But the stick was that since no foreign slaves could be traded into the Confederate States, if Virginia did not secede she would have no Southern market in which to sell African American youth.

Virginia gave in and joined the Confederacy. Facing the loss of the state's slave-breeding industry, a Virginia secession commission voted provisionally to secede on April 17—five days after South Carolina fired the first shot at Ft. Sumter, and after Lincoln had called for seventy-five thousand troops from all the states remaining in the Union. After Virginia ratified secession on May 23, West Virginia, where slave labor had never been much in use, seceded from Virginia, voting itself a Union state on October 24.

The day after Virginia seceded, Union troops moved into Alexandria, beginning the longest occupation of a long war. They surprised the Confederate cavalry eating breakfast at the Duke Street slave-shipping compound that had formerly been Franklin and Armfield's, and at that time was on its fifth owner, Charles M. Price, who had been a partner with James Birch in Price, Birch. "The firm had fled," wrote Virginian M. D. Conway, "and taken its saleable articles with it; but a single one remained—an old man, chained to the middle of the floor by the leg. He was released, and the ring and chain which bound him sent to the Rev. Henry Ward Beecher."[24] The "Slave Pen," as it was known, was repurposed as a prison for captured Confederates.

A divided Maryland did not secede, but continued to have slavery and was heavily occupied by the military. It was a fundamental priority for the United States to keep Maryland, because if Maryland went, Washington would be surrounded.

Kentucky did not secede. John C. Breckinridge was seated as a senator from Kentucky, subsequently enlisted in the Confederate army, and was formally expelled from the Senate as a traitor on December 2, 1861. Missouri, the most

The captured Price, Birch & Co., "Dealers in Slaves." Photograph: Andrew J. Russell, sometime between 1861 and 1865.

bitterly divided state, did not secede, but a faction announced a provisional Confederate government in the town of Neosho.

The capital of the Confederacy was moved from Montgomery to Richmond by a May 20, 1861, vote of the Confederate Congress. In eighty-two years, Richmond had gone from being the capital of Virginia's secession from Britain, to being the great wholesale center of the domestic slave trade, to being the Confederate capital. Prices for slaves remained strong, and slave sales continued until the city fell to the Union in 1865. Richmond versus Washington: the capitals of North and South were only a hundred miles apart.

Among the defects of Steven Spielberg's 2012 film *Lincoln* was the short shrift it gave Elizabeth Keckley.

Though depicted in the movie as a servant, she was the first African American couturier of note. Born enslaved in Virginia, and badly abused during slavery, after manumission Mrs. Keckley (as she was addressed) married and divorced, then opened her own dressmaker's shop as a modiste in Washington,

DC. At one point she had simultaneously as clients both Varina Davis (the wife of Jefferson Davis, at the time a Mississippi senator) and Mary Todd Lincoln.

She became the confidante of the unpopular Mrs. Lincoln and was frequently present in the White House. Her 1868 memoir, *Behind the Scenes, or, Thirty years a Slave, and Four Years in the White House*, was written with the abolitionist journalist James Redpath, who probably transcribed and tweaked her speech to create an "as told to" text. It would make a fine movie, complete with a unique, close-up view of Lincoln and his short-lived son Tad watching their pet goats play on the White House grounds. In it, Mrs. Keckley reported a conversation with Varina Davis:

> While dressing her one day, she said to me:
>
> "Lizzie, you are so very handy that I should like to take you South with me."
>
> "When do you go South, Mrs. Davis?" I inquired.
>
> "Oh, I cannot tell just now, but it will be soon. You know there is going to be war, Lizzie?"
>
> "No!"
>
> "But I tell you yes."
>
> "Who will go to war?" I asked.
>
> "The North and South," was her ready reply. "The Southern people will not submit to the humiliating demands of the Abolition party; they will fight first."
>
> "And which do you think will whip?"
>
> "The South, of course. The South is impulsive, is in earnest, and Southern soldiers will fight to conquer. The North will yield, when it sees the South is in earnest, rather than engage in a long and bloody war."
>
> "But, Mrs. Davis, are you certain that there will be war?"
>
> "Certain!—I know it. You had better go South with me; I will take good care of you. . . . Then, I may come back to Washington in a few months, and live in the White House. The Southern people talk of choosing Mr. Davis for their President. In fact, it may be considered settled that he will be their President. As soon as we go South and secede from the other States, we will raise an army and march on Washington, and then I shall live in the White House."[25]

The Yankees wouldn't fight. Varina Davis would live in the White House. New York would collapse without the money it stole from Southern cotton producers, and the poor would riot and burn down the mansions on Fifth Avenue. It was a common belief. Lazarus Straus's son Oscar, who would have been nine or ten years old at the time, vividly recalled hearing Georgia senator Robert Toombs speaking at Columbus's Masonic Temple: "He drew a large, white handkerchief from his pocket with a flourish, and pausing before mopping his perspiring forehead, he exclaimed: 'The Yankees will not and can not fight! I will guarantee to wipe up with this handkerchief every drop of blood that is spilt!' "[26]

Toombs's ghost must be mopping up the blood still. At the time he made that extravagant remark, he hoped to become the Confederate president, as did Howell Cobb. But Jefferson Davis had the most military credentials, and running a war was going to be pretty much the Confederate president's only job. Davis's older brother Joseph had for years been promoting him as the obvious chief executive of an inevitable Southern republic. In order to keep his talented sibling free of financial worries, Joseph had given him the plantation called Brierfield, twenty miles south of Vicksburg, whose captives were capably overseen during Jefferson Davis's extended absences by an enslaved man, Davis's longtime "body servant" James Pemberton.

Many in North and South alike believed that Lincoln would be no match as a warrior for Davis, who was unanimously named president of the Confederate States of America by the hastily convened Confederate Congress, which met in secret during its entire existence.

45

The Decommissioning of Human Capital

Every intelligent man knows that coined money is not the currency of the country.[1]

—Rep. Samuel Hooper (Massachusetts), arguing in favor of the
Legal Tender Act, February 3, 1862

After the Civil War was over, ole Marsa brought some money in a bag and says to his wife that it wasn't no count. What was it they called it? Confederate money? You know when the War ceased money changed—greenbacks, yes'm.[2]

—Unidentified informant, Fisk University, 1929–30

THE FEDERAL GOVERNMENT COST a million dollars a day, maybe more, to run.[3] There was nothing to run it with.

Lincoln did not merely inherit a ransacked treasury and a government in debt from James Buchanan and Howell Cobb. He inherited more than thirty years of Jacksonian hobbles on the financial powers of federal government. In the years since Jackson had first become president, the United States had become an industrial and financial power fueled by earnings from the massive export of cotton, but its enormous economic growth had not been matched by an increase in federal resources, which were limited by a welter of archaic constraints. Bray Hammond writes:

> To keep relations between the government and the economy "pure" and wholesome, tons of gold had to be hauled to and fro in dray-loads, with

634

horses and heavers doing by the hour what bookkeepers could do in a moment. This, moreover, was not the procedure of a backward people who knew nothing better; it was an obvious anachronism to which, in keeping it tied around the federal government's neck, a mystical virtue was imputed. Actually its only beneficiaries were handlers of gold and speculators in it.[4]

There had been no national currency since before the Panic of 1837. The nation's finances had taken the Jeffersonian small-government path instead of the Hamiltonian strong-government system of managed debt, and had ended up plucked clean. State power had been exalted and federal power demeaned, and the federal government had come apart. Cobb and Buchanan's systematic wasting of the Treasury had left the Jeffersonian-Jacksonian tradition bankrupted. The way was clear for the remaking of government along a Hamiltonian path—or possibly even Franklinian, since it necessarily entailed paper money, and lots of it.

With the slavery interest, which had been the hard core of resistance to a strong federal government, having decamped, Lincoln now asserted federal powers in a way that had never been politically possible.

In a desperate effort to fund the government's short-term obligations as it went to war, Treasury Secretary Salmon P. Chase, a lawyer who was not a banker and was a hard-money man, reluctantly issued US Treasury notes. These quickly became known as "greenbacks": the first federally issued paper money.

Greenbacks were not redeemable for gold or silver. They were what some economists call "fiat money"—money that is worth something because the government says it is. Conceived by Elbridge G. Spaulding, the congressman from Buffalo, New York, who introduced the Legal Tender Act, greenbacks were a radical experiment born of the desperation Buchanan had left behind. Bray Hammond suggests that they were in effect a bankruptcy settlement.[5] Though not convertible to specie, they were legal tender, meaning that their acceptance was mandatory for all obligations of the federal government.

Gold was coming in from California, where it was being found in creeks and rocks. Gold was coming in from England, which had become dependent on US wheat after its own crops failed, again. The federal government took in the gold and paid out greenbacks, which carried no interest and bore no date of maturity. They were simply intended to pass from one hand to another, and never be redeemed, only replaced.

There was a model for the Legal Tender Act: New York's free banking act of 1838, which dealt out money to the state's banks based on the amount of state bonds the bank had purchased and placed on deposit with the state. It

A greenback: the silver front and green back of an 1862 US dollar, with Salmon P. Chase's picture.

was a hard fight to approve the act in Congress, after years of hard-money fiscal orthodoxy had taught that paper money was a diabolical swindle. Many believed that, as Jackson had insisted, the Constitution forbade such a thing. Lincoln signed the Legal Tender Act on February 25, 1862, and the first notes went into circulation on April 5, after the government had gone a long three months without money; $150 million were printed, though $60 million replaced demand notes being withdrawn from circulation, leaving a net $90 million of new money. Two months later, Chase asked for, and received, another $150 million.

The obverse was a silvery gray, and the reverse was all green, giving the new paper dollar its nickname. Chase put his picture on the one-dollar bill, and Lincoln's on the ten.

There was, however, still a gold dollar in existence, so there were effectively two standards; the value of gold went up compared to the value of paper when the South won a victory, and down when the North won. The notes began depreciating, and after another $150 million were printed in the aftermath of Lincoln's call for three hundred thousand more troops, they depreciated more.[6]

The banks had wanted the Legal Tender Act, and it was followed by the National Bank Act of 1863, which created a national banking system. That year Chase's supporter John Thompson founded First National, the bank that subsequently became Citibank.* The banks took the greenbacks in from the government and they paid them out to customers; at least they had something to use for money.[7]

Greenbacks were popular. People wanted paper money; everyone was heartily sick of the patchwork system of privatized money issued by local banks, which was increasingly becoming irredeemable as the crisis of war deepened. Many newspapers wanted paper money and evangelized on its behalf. Now, for the

*In 1877, Thompson founded the bank whose successor still bears his friend's name: Chase.

first time since Jackson killed the Second Bank of the United States, there was a paper money that had the same value everywhere in the country. The new federal notes had the effect of knitting together the roughly two-thirds of the country's population* who were still flying the United States flag, because everyone had a stake in the survival of the currency, which meant, in the survival of the Union.

The bills depreciated substantially but did not become valueless. By 1863, they were trading at 61 percent of their face value, not bad considering the convulsions that the economy had undergone in wartime and the unresolved problems of a dual gold/greenback system.[8] There were only three issues of greenbacks, which were withdrawn from circulation at war's end, but the changeover had happened: though the course was not smooth, from then on the United States was committed to having a national paper currency.[†]

Greenbacks were as much an assertion of federal power as they were an economic innovation. Unlike the Confederate States of America, the United States had a functional government. As the Union created itself as a war machine, more initiatives issued from the federal government. Congress authorized, and Lincoln signed, an income tax. The Treasury sold the banks large amounts of long-term bonds. The Homestead Act was put into place—something that the South had been strenuously opposed to but that now could pass in the absence of their obstruction of it, though free black people were excluded. The Land Grant Act apportioned land to public colleges across the country. The National Bankruptcy Act was implemented.[9] The Yosemite wilderness was set aside as a national park. And spectacular new possibilities were opened up for corruption as vast amounts of Western land were granted to railroads, ushering in the age of the tycoons.

We will not attempt to replay the great conflict in these pages. For our purposes, we think of it as two successive, overlapping wars.

The first we could call the War of Southern Conquest, which was started in the expectation of a quick takeover of the US government by force. Its advance was quickly stopped, and it was definitively over by the time of the double Confederate losses at Gettysburg (July 3, 1863, which ended the South's invasion of the North), and Vicksburg (the next day, which ended the South's control of the Mississippi River). The Southern leadership—Jefferson Davis in particular—had

---

*Union population: ~23 million; Confederate: ~9.1 million (~5.1 million free, ~4 million enslaved).
†Convertibility to gold was restored in 1879, and ended under President Nixon in 1971.

no plan B, and it seems as though they wanted to prolong the misery as long as possible. Having committed to the total war that treason against the republic signified, expecting to pay the maximum penalty in the case of a Northern victory without a negotiated settlement, they dug in and continued fighting against a much larger, better equipped enemy, as the corpses mounted.

But they still had their slaves. And property rights in human beings still had multiple benefits, one of which was allowing the owners to avoid combat. After the Confederate Congress passed the first conscription act in April 1862, providing for three years of compulsory service (though one could hire a substitute), it passed on October 11 the so-called "Twenty Nigger Law," which exempted from the draft one white man per plantation with twenty or more slaves—in order to guard against rebellion. Overseers were also granted exemption.[10] It stimulated a wave of desertions, already ongoing, by the poor whites of the South, who were overwhelmingly the ones dying on the battlefields in support of slavery. A catchphrase was popularized that has persisted in subsequent conflicts: rich man's war, poor man's fight.

The Confederate regime acted very much like an occupier on its own territory, especially in those rugged pockets with fewer slaves and consequently less interest in defending slavery. To fund its military operations, it imposed "tax-in-kind," giving army officers the authority to take anything they wanted in a government-sanctioned banditry—everything from the horse that pulled the wagon, to the ham in the smokehouse and the corn in the garden plot, to the cloth women had woven to make clothes for their children. By 1862 already in Davis's Mississippi, crops were not being planted for lack of manpower and supplies. Young men were conscripted on pain of death into the Confederate Army where they were miserably treated; unlike their officer class, Confederate troops frequently went without uniforms, tents, shoes, or food, even in the war's early days, though they were well-supplied with ammunition. Nor did it escape their notice that many planters were occupying themselves not with fighting so much as with blockade-running their cotton to market. What, then, united the South's poor yeomanry with its wealthy elite? Why did perhaps as many as a million Confederate soldiers experience untold misery and mass death to fight for the rights of 347,525 slaveowners?

One dependable, long-term force that held the white classes together was a culture of negrophobia: the visceral fear of annihilation in the race war they were certain would follow emancipation. This deeply embedded, centuries-old belief was unsubtly stoked at every turn. The War of Southern Conquest was from the beginning portrayed as the defense of white women and children against conjectured mass violence by black marauders, stoked against whites by monstrous abolitionists. But there were also poor yeoman farmers who regarded the Confederacy as a plague on them. There were Union volunteers from every slave state, and even in hardcore Mississippi, Jones County announced its independence from the Confederacy.[11]

African Americans were entirely on one side in this war. But at the outset of hostilities, they weren't allowed to fight. US law prohibited black soldiers from enlisting in the army (though there were already black sailors in the navy), and Lincoln did not at first attempt to change it, so African American volunteers were turned down. The war went badly for the North during this time.

Despite the South's insistence that the "Black Republicans" would force abolition on them, Lincoln had never proposed to end slavery in the Southern states. He had begun by insisting that it was not a war about slavery, but to preserve the Union. But on September 22, 1862, prodded by Seward and Chase as the carnage dragged on, and as Frederick Douglass had been urging all along, Lincoln issued the preliminary Emancipation Proclamation, followed by the definitive proclamation on January 1, 1863. It only applied to those enslaved in the seceded territories; Maryland, Delaware, New Jersey, Kentucky, Missouri, and the District of Columbia, as well as some occupied territories, continued to have slavery while remaining in the Union, with New Jersey using the euphemism of "apprentices." But the Emancipation Proclamation transformed the meaning of the war.

Only after the North committed unambiguously to emancipation could the war be decisively won. Lincoln had not previously claimed to be prosecuting a war on slavery, but now that was unquestionably what it had become. This, then, was the second phase of the war, which we will call the War on Slavery.

Artist Francis Bicknell Carpenter, who painted an imagined scene of Lincoln reading the proclamation to his cabinet, wrote that Lincoln told him, "I felt that we had reached the end of our rope on the plan of operations we had been pursuing; that we had about played our last card, and must change our tactics, or lose the game." Why had Lincoln not started that way? According to Carpenter, Lincoln told him that "it is my conviction that had the proclamation been issued even six months earlier than it was, public sentiment would not have sustained it. Just so, as to the subsequent action in reference to enlisting blacks in the Border States. The step, taken sooner, could not, in my judgment, have been carried out." In short, political will.[12]

Effective January 1, 1863, the Emancipation Proclamation's effect was somewhat symbolic, since it did not apply to those still held enslaved in Union territory and mostly applied to areas the Union did not control, but it nonetheless marked a change in the purpose of the war. The Fire-Eaters had long charged that the North was planning to impose abolition on them. Now, for the first time, it was a policy goal. And in allowing for the enlistment and arming of black soldiers, the Emancipation Proclamation was not symbolic at all. "I further declare and make known," it read, "that such persons of suitable condition, will be received into the armed service of the United States to garrison forts, positions, stations, and other places, and to man vessels of all sorts in said service."

Lincoln's game-changer came as a shock to the Confederates. What Patrick Henry warned against had finally happened: enslaved assets—the property whose value had governed every Southern political initiative since colonial days—were no longer legally recognizable as such. In a long message to the Confederate Congress on January 12, Confederate president Jefferson Davis— who was never president of a functional government, but was commander in chief of a losing war—denounced the "execrable measure" by which "several millions of human beings of an inferior race, peaceful and contented laborers in their sphere, are doomed to extermination, while at the same time they are encouraged to a general assassination of their masters."[13] Up till that point, the Confederate hierarchy had considered the possibility that a negotiated outcome to the war might yet result in a reunited nation on their terms. No more.

Slaveowners' wealth had crumbled to dust. There would be no more securitizing Southern banks' collateralized slaveholdings by Northern banks, nor would European lenders buy into enslaved assets that Washington had pronounced worthless. Lincoln had been the wheat candidate; Britain, which had suffered bad harvests and needed Northern wheat, was siding with the North despite considerable Confederate sympathy in Lancashire. Nor did France save the day for Jefferson Davis, as it had for George Washington; instead, with the United States otherwise occupied, France invaded Mexico in 1861.

The Emancipation Proclamation decommissioned the capitalized womb. Labor was no longer capital. African American children were no longer born to be collateral. Their bodies were no longer a better monetary value than paper. The US economy was no longer on the negro standard. Not only were the slaves emancipated; so was American money.

The Emancipation Proclamation and the coming of the greenback were concurrent and were intimately related. Once the enormous appraised value of the bodies and reproductive potential of four million people was no longer carried on the books as assets, dwarfing other sectors of the economy on paper and generally distorting the economy, the financial revolution of a national paper

This engraving depicting three enslaved laborers was used on several different Confederate notes.

money was able to happen. The end of the slave-breeding industry was crucial to the remaking of American money.

The Confederacy, meanwhile, was not receiving gold from California or from wheat sales to Britain. Instead, it took in its supporters' accumulated savings in gold and silver and in return, it gave them some seventy varieties of engraved notes, many of them bearing pictures of slaves working. Some had a written promise on the notes to pay them back with interest once the war was over. These notes were not usable to pay import duties; only specie and bond coupons were allowed for that. Among the many notes featuring the picture on this page was a one-hundred-dollar Confederate note issued at Richmond on December 11, 1862, whose hopeful legend promised an excellent rate of return: "Six Months after the Ratification of a Treaty of Peace between the Confederate States and the United States of America, the Confederate States of America will pay to the bearer on demand One Hundred Dollars with interest at two cents per day." The back side of the bill was blank.

The South's banks were forced to buy worthless Confederate bonds on pain of being labeled treasonous to the Southern cause, so they effectively had their assets confiscated by the Confederacy. Unsurprisingly, the Southern banking system did not survive the war.[14] With it went the commercial network that had connected the South's slave-driven finance with that of the rest of the country.

There was still money to be made by the intrepid. Cotton had become a cash market, attracting middlemen willing to take personal risk in pursuit of high profit. Despite the difficulty of shipping, the sky-high prices that cotton fetched encouraged farmers to keep planting it instead of food. After Joseph Acklen died on the Angola plantation in 1863, his widow, Adelicia (previously Isaac Franklin's widow), is said to have slipped into Louisiana from Tennessee to negotiate the illegal sale of twenty-eight hundred bales of cotton to an English merchant for an exorbitant sum of gold, said to be $750,000 or more, which she subsequently collected in person in London.[15]

Despite the worthlessness of Confederate money, some people made a profit with it. When New Orleans was occupied by the Union in 1862, Julius Weis, a merchant in Natchez, managed to sell his firm's inventory of ready-made clothing to Confederate soldiers for Confederate money, "which was then nearly at par," he recalled. "I took $15,000 of this money and bought a piece of property in Memphis, which I sold after the war for a like amount of greenbacks."[16] Still having "faith in the ultimate success of the Confederacy," he spent another $18,000 in Confederate money for "a fine-looking mulatto, to whom I took a fancy."[17]

After the Southern rebellion began, the Lehman Brothers were well-positioned, having a New York office, and after the Union occupied the factorage capital of New Orleans in 1862, they established an office there. They became blockade runners, exporting such cotton as they could sneak out of the South.

"Six months after the ratification of a treaty of peace between the Confederate States and the United States, the Confederate States of America will pay two dollars to bearer." Judah P. Benjamin on an 1864 two-dollar Confederate bill, one of at least seventy issues of paper money during the Confederacy. Poorly printed, this note was cut out with scissors. The back is blank.

Blockade runners have been much romanticized, with tales of how they brought in British-made guns to the Confederates; but much of what the blockade runners brought back was luxury goods, because some of the wealthy continued to make money. After the war began, Charley Lamar became a blockade runner, slipping in and out of Charleston harbor on moonless nights in unlighted ships painted the color of water, past what Isidor Straus counted one night as twenty-one blockading steamers.[18] The Strauses too went into blockade running. After a local grand jury excoriated what it called the "evil and unpatriotic conduct of the representatives of Jewish houses," Lazarus Straus moved his family from Talbotton to Columbus, Georgia, the Confederacy's second most important industrial center after Richmond, in 1863, when Confederate money was trading five cents to the dollar in gold.[19]

New Orleans's Jewish community, tightly connected with that of Charleston, had perhaps doubled in size in the years preceding secession, and numbered about four thousand in 1861. Its merchants were clustered in the area of Canal Street, the dividing line between the town's Anglo and Creole populations. It contributed the Confederacy's most brilliant legal mind: Judah P. Benjamin, a St. Croix–born former sugar planter, former slaveowner, and a cosmopolitan attorney. He had been the second Jewish US senator (in 1852) and was a second cousin of the first Jewish senator, David Levy/Yulee, though neither he nor Yulee were practicing Jews. A key advisor of Jefferson Davis, he became the attorney general of the Confederacy, then its secretary of war, then its secretary of the treasury.

The role of Jewish merchants as financial intermediaries irritated General Ulysses S. Grant. "The Jews seem to be a privileged class that can travel anywhere," he wrote to Assistant Secretary of War C. P. Wolcott in 1862. Then and today, this complaint of "privilege" was a central tenet of anti-immigrant rhetoric, with which Grant was unfortunately familiar, as his political background included a strong nativist streak and he had in the winter of 1854–55 briefly joined a lodge of the xenophobic "Know-Nothing" movement in Missouri.[20]

Grant's General Order No. 11 of December 17, 1862, ordered the expulsion within twenty-four hours of all Jews "as a class" from Kentucky, Tennessee, and Mississippi. It was an attempt to stop cotton smuggling, but what it meant was that Jews who lived in those states were expected to pick up and leave their homes overnight. Grant's order all too easily fell into a pattern of anti-Jewish language—some of it casual, some of it deeply believed—that fell on occasion from the lips and pens of antislavery figures that included William Tecumseh Sherman, William Lloyd Garrison, Henry Wilson, John Quincy Adams, and

Henry Adams. It was the culmination of a series of measures that on November 10 had included an instruction to railroad conductors not to accept Jewish passengers. General Order No. 11 had a predictably demoralizing effect on the seven thousand or so Jewish soldiers in the Union army, subjecting them to taunts from other soldiers and causing one Jewish officer, Captain Philip Trounstine of the Fifth Ohio Cavalry, to resign in protest. A Jewish protest to Lincoln quickly resulted in the rescission of the order on January 6, 1863, and Grant subsequently apologized for having issued it.[21]

There were about three thousand Jewish soldiers in the Confederate army, most of whom were poor immigrants. Jewish merchants in the South, meanwhile, found themselves denounced in the Confederate Congress and on the receiving end of accusations from townspeople of disloyalty and extortion. The worse the war went for the South, the more vulnerable to scapegoating they were.

It is instructive to unpack the first words of Lincoln's Gettysburg Address again:

> *Four score and seven years ago our fathers brought forth on this continent, a new nation . . .*

Lincoln thus dated the republic as beginning eighty-seven years previously—not from the 1789 Constitution, but from 1776, though the Declaration of Independence does not mention a new "nation." In affirming that the thirteen colonies were a nation in 1776 rather than a confederation of thirteen states, Lincoln was providing a revisionist take on the Declaration. He then attempted to reclaim the words of the Southern hero Thomas Jefferson:

> *. . . conceived in Liberty, and dedicated to the proposition that all men are created equal.*

With abolition now at last the official post-Emancipation Proclamation US policy, Lincoln was repudiating *Dred Scott*'s interpretation of Jefferson's "all men," declaring that the inspirational words might at last include those who had not been conceived in "Liberty." At last, liberty no longer meant liberty for slavery.

Everybody knows what happened to Lincoln.

A Weird, Plaintive Wail

Savannah, Ga., Dec. 22 [1864].
To His Excellency, President Lincoln:
   I beg to present you as a Christmas gift, the city of Savannah, with one hundred and fifty heavy guns and plenty of ammunition, and also about twenty-five thousand bales of cotton.[1]

(Signed.) W. T. Sherman, Major-General

When de war ended, I goes back to my mastah and he treated me like his brother. Guess he wuz scared of me 'cause I had so much ammunition on me.[2]
—Formerly enslaved Civil War veteran Albert Jones,
Portsmouth, Virginia, January 8, 1937

NOW THE WAR COULD be won: as with previous proclamations by Dunmore and by Sonthonax and Polverel, emancipation meant black soldiers in combat, even as it emboldened the many enslaved who heard about it throughout the South.

   Pursuant to the Emancipation Proclamation, 166 black regiments were created. The number of African Americans who fought is officially around 180,000, but it seems likely there were more than that. By war's end, about 10 percent of the US Army was black. Though they were not commanded by black officers, they were known as dedicated fighters. For them, the war was even more dangerous than it was for white soldiers.

   In his previously quoted message, Jefferson Davis announced his post–Emancipation Proclamation intention to treat all captured Union officers as guilty of "exciting servile insurrection," which was to say, to execute them. The

Confederate hierarchy construed all black soldiers to be guilty of that crime and deserving of death.

From the first encounters between black soldiers and Confederates in battle pursuant to the Emancipation Proclamation, the Confederates waged "black flag" or "no quarter" war. Atrocities were routine; taking no prisoners, they slaughtered wounded black soldiers, on occasion bayoneting them repeatedly or beating their brains out with clubs. Confederate soldiers frequently made every effort to kill black soldiers on the battlefield, murdering them in cold blood if they were captured, including, writes Gregory J. W. Unwin, "those who attempted to surrender and wounded men too weak to offer resistance."[3] Captured black soldiers who were not killed were frequently enslaved. Confederates also typically targeted for murder the white commanders of the black regiments; the knowledge that any whites associated with black troops would be flat-out killed was intended to drive a wedge between white and black Union soldiers.

Afraid of the consequences, the Union refrained from calling for no-quarter war in reprisal, thereby leaving their black troops to be sacrificed. There were thus two different war regimes operating, one for white prisoners and the other, even more horrible, for black prisoners. "Confederate war crimes far exceeded those of the Federals by every measure," writes George S. Burkhardt, who called attention to it in *Confederate Rage, Yankee Wrath.*[4]

Confederate violence in battle was genocidal toward black people, reaching a pitch comparable to the final moments of that other major bloody American war of abolition, the Haitian Revolution. The mere fact of a black man in a military uniform with a weapon was cognitive dissonance: in the Confederate worldview, this was not possible. As they saw it, the enemy was less than human, and was their own escaped property. In the words of a South Carolina woman: "Just think how infamous it is that our *gentlemen* should have to go out and fight niggers, and that every nigger they shoot is a thousand dollars out of their own pockets!"[5] The most notorious massacre, though not the largest, was committed by the troops of Nathan Bedford Forrest at Fort Pillow, an army post of no great strategic importance on a Tennessee bluff overlooking the Mississippi River, on April 12–13, 1864. Forrest had enlisted in the Confederate army as a private, but quickly became a lieutenant colonel, then one of the most celebrated Confederate generals. He was a cavalryman, said to be one of the best horsemen in the army, whose principal military technique was the aggressive assault.

After charging into Fort Pillow, the troops under Forrest's command killed in cold blood perhaps as many as five hundred Union soldiers who had surrendered (there is no definitive count) over a period of two days.[6] Most of them were black. The *New York Tribune* reported that five soldiers were buried alive.[7] Forrest's *New York Times* obituary in 1877 recalled the massacre:

> Without discrimination of age or sex, men, women, and children, the sick and wounded in the hospitals, were butchered without mercy. The bloody work went on until night put a temporary stop to it; but it was renewed at early dawn, when the inhuman captors searched the vicinity of the fort, dragging out wounded fugitives and killing them where they lay. The whole history of the affair was brought out by a Congressional inquiry, and the testimony presents a long series of sickening, cold-blooded atrocities . . . The news of the massacre aroused the whole country to a paroxysm of horror and fury.[8]

An 1865 interview with Forrest, conducted by a reporter for the New Orleans *True Delta* and reprinted in other newspapers, asked him if the investigators' (the "Yankees'") report of Fort Pillow was accurate. He answered, "Yes, if we are to believe anything a nigger says." Then he added, "When I went into the war I meant to fight. Fighting means killing. I have lost twenty-nine horses in the war, and have killed a man each time."[9]

There were many witnesses to the Fort Pillow massacre, which contributed to its visibility as a media event, but Fort Pillow was not an anomaly; the level of hatred displayed toward black soldiers was consistent wherever Confederates fought. A Virginia colonel described the wholesale slaughter of prisoners at the disastrous Battle of the Crater outside Petersburg, Virginia, in July 1864: "Our men, who were always made wild by having negroes sent against them . . . were utterly frenzied with rage. Nothing in the war could have exceeded the horrors that followed. No quarter was given, and for what seemed a long time, fearful butchery was carried on."[10]

Black troops made "Remember Fort Pillow!" into a battle cry and became increasingly disposed to give no quarter. Burkhardt quotes a New Jersey officer: "The Rebel prisoners are very fearful of being left to . . . colored troops as they fear their own acts of inhumanity will be repaid."[11] Forrest's troops continued their homicidal career in June, a little north of Tupelo, Mississippi, at Brice's Cross Roads, where Forrest scored his greatest victory of the war against an enemy superior in numbers. After routing a Union force of eight thousand under the incompetent direction of Brigadier General Samuel Sturgis, Forrest's men hunted down and killed members of Colonel Edward Bouton's Colored Brigade who had survived the battle. In April 1865, Forrest directed a massacre of Union troops near Selma while they were sleeping.[12]

The month after the Fort Pillow massacre, General William Tecumseh Sherman, who liked neither black people nor abolitionists, began his Atlanta campaign. Entering Georgia from Chattanooga on the north, he burned the strategic rail depot in Atlanta, a small town whose population had multiplied under the pressure of war. Some of Atlanta was torched by Sherman's troops, and some by the Confederate general John Bell Hood; about half the city went up in flames. It was tremendous news in the North.

Sherman followed up Atlanta on November 15 with his sixty-mile-wide, three-hundred-mile long March to the Sea without supply lines, forcing his sixty-two thousand troops to eat their way through the country as they tore up railroad tracks and burned industrial, governmental, and military facilities and cotton crops along the way. Sherman's march, tactically aimed at destroying what remained of the Southern railroad system and strategically aimed at stopping the war once and for all, has been traditionally portrayed in the South as an orgy of cruelty, acquiring a mythical reputation as Exhibit A of Northern aggression. Sherman's troops certainly caused suffering, in part because they destroyed food supplies as well as cotton, but they concentrated primarily on strategic targets rather than residences.[13] Some homes were burned, especially those of the planters; Sherman took special care to make sure that Howell Cobb's plantation was burned to the ground.

But the property that Sherman's troops fired was the least of the wealth they destroyed.

They burned slavery to the ground.

Whatever else Sherman's march symbolized, for the enslaved it was a march of liberation, as one of the war's best-known songs, composed by Henry Clay Work, recalls:

> *Hurrah! Hurrah! We bring the jubilee!*
> *Hurrah! Hurrah! The flag that makes us free!*
> *And so we sang the chorus from Atlanta to the sea*
> *While we were marching through Georgia.*

"Marching Through Georgia" took its place alongside the most popular anthem played by Northern military bands: the stirring "John Brown's Body," for which

Julia Ward Howe had written new lyrics, still familiar today, as "The Battle Hymn of the Republic." Noah Andre Trudeau quotes a letter written during the campaign by General William P. Carlin of the First Division that described what happened on one occasion when the band played that song:

> About a dozen young African-American girls came out of nearby houses, "formed into a ring around the band at the head of the column, and with a weird, plaintive wail, danced in a circle in a most solemn, dignified, and impressive manner," wrote Carlin years afterward. "What their meaning was I did not know then, nor do I now, but I, of course, interpreted it as expressive of goodwill to our cause."[14]

Carlin was hearing a ring shout, a collective song of spiritual power sung and danced in a moving counterclockwise circle. One of the oldest known forms of African American music, heavily Kongo in influence, the ring shout is known in the Sea Islands and points west, all the way to the Louisiana / Mississippi delta region, where it became part of the Baptist tradition of "rocks."*

Meanwhile, Jacob Thompson was plotting the mass murder of Northern civilians on behalf of the Confederacy. Funded with a million dollars in gold and sent by Judah P. Benjamin to be head of Confederate Secret Service operations in Canada, Thompson dispatched incendiary attacks on New York and Chicago. These terrorist attacks were to be coordinated with occupation by the former Knights of the Golden Circle, as of 1864 called the Sons of Liberty, whose membership was said, perhaps hyperbolically, to number in the hundreds of thousands.[15] That never happened; but had Confederate colonel Robert Martin been less inept in scouting locations and in using his "Greek fire" phosphorus firebombs, the plot for eight infiltrated Confederate officers to burn down New York City in a massive conflagration on November 25, 1864, might well have succeeded, in which case the Confederacy would have exacted a civilian death toll of possibly historic proportions.[16] The fires were set, but in closed spaces, where they burned out for lack of oxygen.

.

---

*We don't know exactly what Carlin heard, but we can get an idea from hearing latter-day ring shout groups, which were recorded as early as 1934 by Alan Lomax. An annual ring shout, known as Easter Rock, is still performed in Winnsboro, Louisiana. See Jackson.

The Confederate commander General William D. Hardee fled Savannah with
ten thousand troops rather than confront Sherman, and he did not burn the
town on leaving, nor did Savannahans put up resistance, so the fine houses of
Oglethorpe's jewel of a city were spared the torch. Instead, Sherman established
his headquarters there. A train of thousands of former slaves followed Sherman's
troops into Savannah, creating a refugee problem.

Not until Sherman's arrival in Savannah did the town's slave trade stop.
Some traders escaped the city with captives, while others were less successful,
and at least two traders, E. M. Blount and W. C. Dawson, fell victim to revolt,
as the horrified trader Henry Bogardus wrote his sister: "Blount's Negroes killed
him and Dawson is not much better."[17]

For the whites of Savannah, Sherman's occupation was defeat. But among
black Savannahans, as the Reverend James Simms recalled, "The cry went
around the city from house to house among our race of people, 'Glory be to
God, we are free!'"[18] Almost immediately, the black community of Savannah
organized the Savannah Education Association. The Montmollin building, previously a Savannah slave trader's headquarters, was occupied by a school. It still
had bars on the windows, and all they had to use for paper was the blank back
sides of a stack of bills of sale for slaves, which were thus lost to history, but at
least some children learned how to read and write.[19]

Sherman continued on to Charleston, which fell in February 1865 after
a siege of 545 days.[20] Charleston had already suffered a devastating fire in
December 1861; now, as most of the city's white population fled, Confederate troops set fire to the cotton in the warehouses and the ships in the harbor,
and blew up their explosives, generating a great blaze that killed at least 150
civilians before Union troops put it out.[21] In the chaos, two Northern journalists broke into the hastily abandoned slave mart on Chalmers Street. Charles
Carleton Coffin, who reported for the *Boston Journal*, took the gilt letters that
read MART as a souvenir. James Redpath of the *New York Tribune*, who had
previously announced that he was not only an abolitionist but a reparationist,
scooped up 652 letters to slave trader Ziba B. Oakes from his regional purchasing agents, which he donated to William Lloyd Garrison and which since 1891
have been in the Boston Public Library.

The people of Richmond had become accustomed to the sound of artillery
fire, but now they too had to flee Grant's army. "My line is broken in three places
and Richmond must be evacuated," wrote Robert E. Lee to Confederate president Jefferson Davis, who ordered the evacuation of the Confederate capital on

April 2, 1865. As Davis ran with the members of his government to board the Danville train, Robert Lumpkin hurried amid the chaos to evacuate the captives from his slave jail, setting out with one final coffle.

The classic account of the fall of Richmond is Coffin's report:

Mrs. Davis had left the city several days previous. . . . There was no evening service. Ministers and congregations were otherwise employed. Rev. Mr. Hoge, a fierce advocate for slavery as a beneficent institution, packed his carpet-bag. Rev. Mr. Duncan was moved to do likewise. Mr. Lumpkin, who for many years had kept a slave-trader's jail had a work of necessity on this Lord's day,—the temporal salvation of fifty men, women, and children! He made up his coffle in the jail-yard, within pistol-shot of Jeff Davis's parlor window, and a stone's throw from the Monumental Church. The poor creatures were hurried to the Danville depot. This sad and weeping fifty, in handcuffs and chains, was the last coffle that shall tread the soil of America.*

Slavery being the corner-stone of the Confederacy, it was fitting that this gang, keeping step to the music of their clanking chains, should accompany Jeff Davis, his secretaries Benjamin and Trenhold, and the Reverend Messrs. Hoge and Duncan, in their flight. The whole Rebel government was on the move, and all Richmond desired to be. No thoughts now of taking Washington, or of the flag of the Confederacy flaunting in the breeze from the dome of the national Capitol!

Hundreds of officials were at the depot, waiting to get away from the doomed city. Public documents, the archives of the Confederacy, were hastily gathered up, tumbled into boxes and barrels, and taken to the trains, or carried into the streets and set on fire. Coaches, carriages, wagons, carts, wheelbarrows, everything in the shape of a vehicle, was pressed into use. There was a jumble of boxes, chests, trunks, valises, carpetbags,— a crowd of excited men sweating as never before: women with dishevelled hair, unmindful of their wardrobes, wringing their hands, children crying in the crowd, sentinels guarding each entrance to the train, pushing back at the point of the bayonet the panic-stricken multitude, giving precedence to Davis and the high officials, and informing Mr. Lumpkin that his niggers could not be taken.

*It was not; there were still coffles wherever the Union had not entered, notably Texas.

O, what a loss was there! It would have been fifty thousand dollars out of somebody's pocket in 1861, and millions now of Confederate promises to pay, which the hurrying multitude and that chained slave gang were treading under foot,—trampling the bonds of the Confederate States of the America in the mire, as they marched to the station; for the oozy streets were as thickly strewn with four per cents, six per cents, eight per cents, as forest streams with autumn leaves.

"The faith of the Confederate States is pledged to provide and establish sufficient revenues for the regular payment of the interest, and for the redemption of the principal," read the bonds; but there was a sudden eclipse of faith; a collapse of confidence, a shrivelling up like a parched scroll of the entire Confederacy, which was a base counterfeit of the American Union it sought to overturn and supplant, now an exploded concern, and wound up by Grant's orders, its bonds, notes, and certificates of indebtedness worth less than the paper on which they were printed.[22]

Jefferson Davis was trying to get to Texas, to continue the war from there. Did Lumpkin think he was taking his coffle to Texas too? There was nowhere to take a coffle. Those fifty people weren't going to be anyone's property now.

In a dramatic show of defiance, the Confederate general Richard S. Ewell torched a large area of Richmond, definitively ruining many of the city's businessmen. It was done with the acquiescence of his superior, Confederate secretary of war John C. Breckinridge, who was present in the city. The Richmond *Whig*'s report of April 4, 1865 seemed to suggest that the city had been ridded of an occupier with the departure of the Confederate government of which it had been the capital—an occupier that destroyed much of Richmond as it fled:

By noon the flames had transformed into a desert waste that portion of the city bounded between 7th and 15th streets, from Main street to the river, comprising the main business portion. We can form no estimate at this moment of the number of houses destroyed, but public and private they will certainly number 600 to 800.

At present we cannot do more than enumerate some of the most prominent buildings destroyed.—These include the Bank of Richmond; Traders Bank; Bank of the Commonwealth; Bank of Virginia; Farmers' Bank, all the banking houses, the American Hotel, the Columbian Hotel, the *Enquirer* Building on 12th street, the *Dispatch* office and job rooms, corner of 13th and Main streets; all that block of buildings known as Belvin's Block, the *Examiner* office, engine and machinery rooms; the Confederate Post Office department building, the State Court House, a fine old building situated on Capitol Square, at its Franklin street entrance; the Mechanic's Institute, vacated by the Confederate States War Department, and all the buildings on that Square up to 8th street, and back to Main street; the Confederate Arsenal and Laboratory, 7th street.

At sunrise on Monday morning, Richmond presented a spectacle that we hope never to witness again. The last of the Confederate officials had gone; the air was lurid with the smoke and flame of hundreds of houses sweltering in a sea of fire.

Coffin reported that:

To prevent the United States from obtaining possession of a few thousand hogsheads of tobacco, a thousand houses were destroyed by fire, the heart of the city burnt out, —all of the business portion, all the banks and insurance-offices, half of the newspapers, with mills, depots, bridges, foundries, workshops, dwellings, churches,—thirty squares in all, swept clean by the devouring flames. It was the final work of the Confederate government.[23]

Richmond's slave trade had continued full tilt, with a large population in the traders' jails when the Union entered the city. Chaplain Garland White, an African American soldier who entered Richmond with Indiana's Twenty-Eighth Regiment, described his experience in a letter written shortly after leaving the city: "a vast multitude assembled on Broad Street, and I was aroused amid the shouts of ten thousand voices, and proclaimed for the first time in that city freedom to all mankind. After which the doors of all the slave pens were thrown open, and thousands came out shouting and praising God, and Father, or Master Abe, as they termed him."[24]

On April 4, Elizabeth Keckley visited Richmond, as she accompanied Mary Todd Lincoln on the steamer *River Queen* up the James, "the river that so long had been impassable, even to our gunboats," to join the presidential party, with Lincoln at the head, to examine the city's condition.

The Presidential party were all curiosity on entering Richmond. They drove about the streets of the city, and examined every object of interest. The Capitol presented a desolate appearance—desks broken, and papers scattered promiscuously in the hurried flight of the Confederate Congress.

> I picked up a number of papers, and, by curious coincidence, the resolution prohibiting all free colored people from entering the State of Virginia. In the Senate chamber I sat in the chair that Jefferson Davis sometimes occupied; also in the chair of the Vice-President, Alexander H. Stephens. We paid a visit to the mansion occupied by Mr. Davis and family during the war, and the ladies who were in charge of it scowled darkly upon our party as we passed through and inspected the different rooms.
>
> After a delightful visit we returned to City Point.[25] (paragraphing added)

Five days after Lee's surrender to Grant, on Good Friday, April 14, Lincoln became the first president in US history to be assassinated. John Wilkes Booth's conspiracy also gravely wounded Secretary of State William Seward and members of his family, and unsuccessfully targeted Vice President Andrew Johnson of Tennessee, who had been drunk at his swearing-in as vice president not six weeks previously on March 4, 1865.[26]

Booth was killed during capture, before he could be questioned. Eight people were convicted and executed for participating in his conspiracy; Jacob Thompson spent the rest of his life trying to clear his name of a rumored involvement in it. Was there a conspiracy involving Thompson's terrorist organization or other elements in the Confederate hierarchy? None has been proved, and Booth has often been portrayed as a fanatic in popular historiography, but that's too simple. Writing of the monk who assassinated the French king Henri III, the historian Geoffrey Treasure called him "not mad, but *exalté* [exalted]: a recognisable type, not an isolated individual but representative, doing what many wished to see done."[27]

If Calhoun, Rhett, Davis, Stephens, Cobb, Forrest, and their many colleagues were not "madmen," neither was Booth. If they were madmen, at what point did madness set in? At Forrest's wholesale butchery? At Rhett's bizarre paean to martyrdom? At Calhoun's insistence that slavery was a positive good for humanity? At Jackson's genocide and ethnic cleansing? At Jefferson's scheme to deport all black people?

The madness was there all along. It was the madness of slavery.

In the Civil War's final battle east of the Mississippi, for Columbus, Georgia, on April 16, 1865, the forces of Union general James H. Wilson, who had not received word of Lincoln's assassination two nights before, defeated those of former US secretary of the treasury, now Confederate major general, Howell Cobb.

On May 2, President Johnson signed a proclamation offering $100,000 for Jefferson Davis's arrest in connection with Lincoln's assassination, and a manhunt for Davis ensued.[28] Whatever the conspiratorial mechanism, Lincoln's assassination was a coup d'etat that carried a number of benefits for former Confederates who might reasonably have expected to hang for treason. Johnson was a pro-Union white supremacist who was uninterested in prosecuting Confederate leaders or in helping freedmen. He issued presidential amnesties and pardons for former Confederates, and restored confiscated lands—thus ensuring that there would be no "forty acres," as Rufus Saxton of the Freedmen's Bureau had promised, to compensate the destitute, largely illiterate mass of formerly enslaved for their multigenerational legacy of confiscated labor. There were no war crimes trials for the mass murder of black troops under cover of battle.

But the fundamental change had been made. The Southern economy had suffered its final, fatal collapse, the one long feared by slaveowners: their property had ceased to be their property. They were not compensated by the taxpayers for its loss, as the Jamaican slaveowners had been.

No more counting children as interest. No more multigenerational wealth accumulating from reproduction of enslaved humans to be passed on as legacies to slaveowners' children. No more paying debts in a bad year by cashing out and selling adolescents: the liquidity of the financial system vanished when ownership of the human capital was transferred from landowners to the laborers themselves.

No more forced mating. No more fancy girls. No more sex slaves.

The Ponzi scheme of the slave-breeding industry had crashed. Since laborers were no longer property, they were no longer mortgageable. Without enslaved women producing ever-increasing numbers of slave children to borrow against, the South suffered a massive credit implosion, whiplashing from a credit economy to a cash-poor cash economy, floating on a sea of bad debt.

Many proud families never forgot the humiliation of losing their slaves, and some were downright hateful about it. Some former masters found it demeaning to have to share a sidewalk with black people who did not jump out of the way. Others were surprised to find that they could no longer slap black workers with impunity. There were still black laborers, of course, but they would no longer work sunup to sundown to make an ever-increasing, whip-enforced quota for bacon and corn mush in return. Some planters decamped for Brazil, which had slavery and plenty of land, and others for Mexico; a Confederate diaspora fanned northward up to Canada and out to the far West.

The poor whites of the South had a miserable time of it in the economically devastated postwar years. As the Southern states rejoined the country they had repudiated, many formerly wealthy Southerners occupied themselves by suing each other over old debts for which the collateral had vanished. But others had found ways to keep their money, or even made money during the war. They could no longer live off human capital as rentiers, but the elite were still the elite, and elite families have remarkable staying power over multiple generations, in every society. Since the planters' estates weren't broken up and distributed to the freedmen, they still had their land, which would be the basis of new fortunes. They still had their education, their family webs, their control of local institutions, their business and political contacts—and they still had cheap black labor, which they kept as abject as possible by terrorizing them with a new racist regime that would come to be known as Jim Crow, enforced all over the former slave nation.

Many of the formerly enslaved, whose dispossession was so complete that they had not even family names, got little more out of Reconstruction than an assigned surname, which was the bare minimum necessary for the creation a civil identity. Their new Anglo-Saxon names were in many cases assigned to them: Williams, Johnson, Smith, Jones, Brown, Jackson, Jefferson, Washington.

Some of the elite who had the resources relocated with style—the so-called "Confederate carpetbaggers"—to New York, Chicago, and other urban centers.[29] Some renewed Northern commercial contacts or business partnerships that had been active before or even during the war and found that little stigma was attached to their former treasonous activities, which were now recast as Southern patriotism.

Southern gynecologist Marion Sims, who had developed his surgical innovations by practicing on enslaved women, went to Europe during the war, where he operated on women of social importance for high fees. Returning to America, he established a private practice on Fifth Avenue and presented himself as a popular vision of a fabulously wealthy doctor-celebrity. He was "instrumental" in founding the nation's first cancer hospital, Sloan-Kettering Cancer Center, though he died the year before the project came to fruition in 1884.[30]

Isidor Straus spent much of the war in Europe, returning to America at war's end with about $10,000 in gold he had made in London trading Confederate bonds.[31] His father Lazarus Straus relocated the family's retailing firm from Columbus, Georgia, to New York, where they became the owners of R. H. Macy's department store, then bought an interest in the store that became Abraham & Straus. Isidor Straus died in the 1912 sinking of the *Titanic*, together with his wife Ida.

Emanuel Lehman, already based in New York, also made money during the war selling Confederate bonds in England, at one point uncomfortably encountering his New York neighbor Joseph Seligman, who was selling Union bonds. After the war, Lehman Brothers put up $100,000 for Alabama's constitutional convention. Mayer Lehman moved up to New York, where he organized the first futures market in cotton; two of his former slaves came to New York to work for him as servants. The brothers parlayed their warehouses full of cotton into a business that continued through many transformations until the Panic of 2008, when Lehman Brothers filed for the largest bankruptcy in American history, intensifying a worldwide economic crisis.[33]

Widely suspected of being a planner of the Lincoln assassination, Judah P. Benjamin fled to London and became a barrister there. He wrote the standard legal work* on the sale of personal property, became legal counsel to Queen Victoria, and died, quite wealthy, in Paris in 1884.

Adelicia Hayes Franklin Acklen Cheatham, one of the wealthiest women in the United States, died at the age of seventy, in 1887, in New York's Fifth Avenue Hotel, of pneumonia contracted while on a shopping trip.[34]

J. D. B. De Bow, who in the South had been the most influential proslavery business publisher, started his *DeBow's Review* right back up in New York in 1866, but died the following year.

Howell Cobb's plantation was up and running again soon after the war. According to Cobb, the problem was that the formerly enslaved laborers were ungrateful, as per a December 1866 letter: "The truth is I am thoroughly disgusted with free negro labor, and am determined that the next year shall close my planting operations with them. There is no feeling of gratitude in their nature."[35] Cobb, who was as guilty of treason as anyone in the Confederate project, received a presidential pardon and died of a heart attack in New York City in 1868; his son continued the plantation.

Pierce Mease Butler's Georgia plantation survived the war intact. The places that had been occupied by the Union earliest—Louisiana, the Sea Islands, Alexandria, etc.—suffered less destruction, and the Union had occupied Butler's

---

*Still being updated today, it's known as *Benjamin's Sale of Goods*.

land from early in 1862, which likely saved it. Since the plantation was not broken up and distributed to the former slaves, Butler remained the owner. Though there was no longer slave labor, many of his former slaves returned to the plantation—presumably less because they loved the Butlers than because the plantation was their home, and was the ancestral home of their close-knit community, or perhaps, as in other cases involving slaves who returned to the plantations they knew, because they were starving. Without a doubt, they would have preferred a small plot of land of their own in what sociologist Jean Casimir, speaking of Haiti, has called a "counter-plantation" system: "a refusal . . . of the plantation system itself, [involving] the creation of a very different way of living, one focused on production for oneself and for surplus within a local market."[36] But that was not on offer.

Frances Kemble finally published her *Journal* of life on Butler's plantation as a book in 1863, in post–Emancipation Proclamation wartime. It became popular reading for abolitionists and caused a sharp rift with her pro-Confederate younger daughter Fan. After Pierce Mease Butler died of the archetypal Low-country disease, malaria, in 1867, Fan took the plantation over and tried to make it produce. But she couldn't make a go of it, blaming the labor force's disinclination to work as hard as necessary.

Jefferson Davis never surrendered. As long as Robert E. Lee continued, the war went on, but even after Lee surrendered on April 9, Davis did not; he was captured on May 10 in Virginia while trying to escape to Texas and was imprisoned for two years. He never asked for a pardon, never apologized, never swore allegiance, failed at his business initiatives, and spent much time being a traveling guest of honor until he died in a mansion in New Orleans's Garden District in 1889. In 1881 he published the stultifying 1,515-page *The Rise and Fall of the Confederate Government,* in which he insisted that "to whatever extent the question of *slavery* may have served as an *occasion*, it was far from being the *cause* of the conflict." The cause, he explained, was "sectional rivalry" and "political ambition" that "happened" to have "coincided" along the "line of demarkation" of slavery versus free labor. He also maintained that "African servitude among us [was] . . . the mildest and most humane of all institutions to which the name 'slavery' has ever been applied."[37]

Robert Lumpkin barely outlived the war. He died in 1866 at the age of sixty, his livelihood of slave trading destroyed. Shortly before he died, he named his former slave Mary executor of his estate and granted her the right to use the name "Lumpkin." Provided she did not remarry, she became the sole proprietor of his properties in Richmond and Philadelphia.[38]

Mary Lumpkin thus became the owner of the property she had lived on since she was twelve. Formerly known as Lumpkin's Slave Jail, it had been famous to every trader in Virginia, and notorious to the thousands of African Americans who had passed through it. It was nearly worthless. Desperate like everyone else for income in the charred ruin of Richmond, she rented it for $1,000 a year to the Rev. Nathaniel Colver, a Boston minister, to be used as the School for Former Slaves, subsequently Virginia Union University.[39] White landlords wouldn't rent their property for such a purpose, so the newly freed students had to go down the muddy embankment at Shockoe Bottom. Unfortunately, Mary also inherited Lumpkin's debts, and she died poor.[40]

Lumpkin's competitor, Silas Omohundro, whose slave jail adjoined his, had done something very similar before he died in 1864, leaving the use of his properties in Richmond and Pennsylvania to his formerly enslaved common-law wife, Corinna, with whom he had six children. Corinna fared better than Mary Lumpkin; she came to own her own confectionery.[41]

Louis Hughes did not escape from slavery in Mississippi until 1865; he went behind Union lines, and from there managed to rescue his wife and children. After moving around, the family settled in Milwaukee, where he worked as a nurse, and where, in 1897, he published his autobiography, *Thirty Years a Slave.*

Frederick Douglass's house in Rochester, New York, was burned down in 1872, apparently an arson. From late 1889 to mid-1891 he served as the US minister to Haiti; he died of heart failure in 1895, at the approximate age of eighty-seven. Though he was the leading African American literary and political figure of the nineteenth century, his writing was largely forgotten until a rediscovery that began in 1945, when historian Philip Foner edited a multivolume anthology of his work.

William Wells Brown largely devoted his post-emancipation years to activism on behalf of the temperance cause, and practiced medicine in Boston, specializing in homeopathy. On the occasion of his return to his birth state of Kentucky, he was kidnapped by the Ku Klux Klan, but escaped. He died at the age of seventy in Massachusetts.

After Harriet Jacobs escaped from Edenton, North Carolina, to Philadelphia with the help of a boat captain in 1842, she lived in fear of being captured, especially after the passage of the Fugitive Slave Law. She became well known in abolitionist circles with her self-publication in 1861 of *Incidents in the Life of a Slave Girl*, which came back from the printer shortly after the first wave of Southern states seceded. A vocal advocate of an emancipation proclamation, with great dignity she organized relief for the "contrabands"—the homeless, impoverished refugees from slavery who poured into Washington and other cities in the early days of the war. With the post–Emancipation Proclamation entry of black soldiers into the war, Jacobs was active in aiding convalescent soldiers in Washington, and together with her daughter founded a free school after the war. She was largely forgotten after her death, and had to be rediscovered; Jean Fagan Yellin's biography of her, from which we extract the above information, was published in 2004.[42] Indeed, Jacob's memoir was considered by many critics to be fiction until Yellin authenticated it in 1987.

Elizabeth Keckley founded the Contraband Relief Organization in 1862, attempted to raise money for Mary Todd Lincoln, and published her book in 1868. She died in poverty in 1907, a resident of the National Home for Destitute Colored Women and Children in Washington, for which she had helped raise founding funds.[43]

General Sherman went on to supervise the building of the transcontinental railroad during the Grant administration, which meant completing the killing of the buffalo herds and what Sherman referred to in an 1872 letter as "the final solution to the Indian problem," in which the West's Native Americans were slaughtered or moved onto "reservations."[44]

If anyone in the Confederate ranks might have seemed a candidate for hanging, it would have been Nathan Bedford Forrest. By the time he was pardoned by Andrew Johnson instead of being tried as a war criminal, he had already returned to violence. Not two years after the Fort Pillow Massacre, in the fall of 1866, he was sworn in at Maxwell House in Nashville as the Grand Wizard of the Invisible Empire of the Ku Klux Klan. Beginning as a posse of malicious night-riding pranksters, complete with a fanciful, carnivalesque pedigree that cast them as Scottish knights, the Klan quickly expanded into other states to become the nation's most notorious, though not the only, white supremacist paramilitary organization as Forrest prosecuted a race war. In what was arguably the largest terrorist campaign in US history, the Klan and similar organizations murdered thousands of people, black and white, as part of a successful effort to suppress Reconstruction and black self-determination.

President Ulysses S. Grant, inaugurated in 1869, believed that the sacrifice of so much blood in the war had to be redeemed by fully enfranchising the formerly enslaved. That was precisely the proposition the Ku Klux Klan was determined to reverse, but after Grant made clear his determination to prosecute the Klan, Forrest officially disbanded it in February 1869. By then much of their work had already been done.[45] In subsequent testimony before Congress, Forrest added perjury to his list of crimes by denying his involvement with the Klan.

With no more slave trading business to do, Forrest ventured his net worth on a proposed Memphis & Selma Railroad, which was never built.[46] As his railroad plan deflated, Forrest, thinking there might be war with Spain and that it might take place in Cuba (where slavery still existed, though it was fading), offered his services to—of all people—General Sherman, as reported in the *New York Times* of December 3, 1873: "I hereby tender you my services as a volunteer. I think I could enlist from 1,000 to 5,000 men who served in the Southern army during the late war, and at short notice, and who could rendezvous at New-Orleans, Mobile, Pensacola, and Key West, either as cavalry or infantry." Sherman politely explained that he did not believe there would be a war with Spain in Cuba; ultimately, there was one, but it happened twenty-five years later.

Forrest spent the rest of his life trying to live down Fort Pillow, for which his name was popularly held in contempt, though in the South there was no lack of apologists for him. In the perhaps sarcastic words of his *New York Times* obituary on October 30, 1877:

> His last notable public appearance was on the Fourth of July in Memphis, when he appeared before the colored people at their celebration, was publicly presented with a bouquet by them as a mark of peace and reconciliation, and made a friendly speech in reply. In this he once more took occasion to defend himself and his war record, and to declare that he was a hearty friend of the colored race.

Slave trader, war criminal, the KKK's top terrorist: if Nathan Bedford Forrest's reputation could be sanitized, anyone's could be. A high school named for Forrest exists in his hometown of Chapel Hill, Tennessee; another, in Jacksonville, changed its name in 2014.

Forrest's final business venture was a plantation that used captive labor, under the postbellum name of "convict leasing." He contracted in 1875 with the Shelby County jail to put 117 prisoners (39 of them white) to work for a term of five years (though he died in 1877), paying the jail ten cents a day for their otherwise uncompensated labor, employing seven guards to watch over them.[47]

The slaves of the South had been emancipated by then, of course. But the Thirteenth Amendment, adopted on December 18, 1865, to prohibit slavery, left a loophole: prisons. It reads in its entirety:

> Neither slavery nor involuntary servitude, *except as a punishment for crime whereof the party shall have been duly convicted*, shall exist within the United States, or any place subject to their jurisdiction. (emphasis added)

It has been argued that the framers of the Thirteenth Amendment did not intend to tolerate slavery, and that the phrase "except as a punishment for a crime" should be parsed as only modifying "involuntary servitude" and not "slavery." A clearer version had been proposed: "Slavery being incompatible with a free government is forever prohibited in the United States, and involuntary servitude shall be permitted only as a punishment for a crime."[48] But it was Thomas Jefferson's phrasing and vision that prevailed: the amendment's framers copied the more ambiguous language of the Northwest Ordinance of 1787, which in turn had taken it from Jefferson's draft of the Land Ordinance of 1784: "after the year 1800 of the christian era, there shall be neither slavery nor involuntary servitude in any of the said states, otherwise than in punishment of crimes whereof the party shall have been convicted to have been duly personally guilty."[49]

From Jefferson's ambiguity forward, convict labor has been part of American commerce, and, as twenty-first-century readers are well aware, it continues.

The entrance to Angola, the former Louisiana plantation of the nation's largest slave trader, Isaac Franklin. Located at the dead end of a twenty-two-mile road that goes only there, it is now the penitentiary of the number-one incarcerator state of the number-one incarcerator nation of the world, with Death Row situated on the part of the property adjoining the Mississippi border. On its grounds, imprisoned people are forced to perform unmechanized field labor; it is understood by many, including the prisoners, as a re-creation of the slavery experience. March 2014.

Coda

Again we have deluded ourselves into believing the myth that capitalism grew and prospered out of the Protestant ethic of hard work and sacrifice. The fact is that capitalism was built on the exploitation and suffering of black slaves and continues to thrive on the exploitation of the poor—both black and white, both here and abroad.[1]

—Martin Luther King Jr., "Three Evils of Society" speech, August 31, 1967

IF ANYONE READING THIS book in the future wants to know the American historical context in which it was composed, the drafting was finished in August 2014, while the national trauma of Ferguson was going on, and the finishing touches were made during the aftermath of the Charleston Massacre of June 2015.

Today, people are no longer sold like livestock in the public market, but the racism slavery engendered has been resilient, having become a seemingly systematic disfigurement of American society.

The post-emancipation history is a gloomy one. The only group that was brought to America against their will is still on the bottom. After the brief period of Reconstruction that saw much progress, including the establishment of black colleges, the freedmen were abandoned by the North to the mercy of Southern sheriffs by the time of the Hayes-Tilden Compromise of 1877. Their rights and possibilities were severely limited by ever more discriminatory "black codes" that locked white supremacy into place. While they were no longer legally treated as chattel, African Americans were systematically excluded from educational, professional, and housing opportunities, were frequently denied the possibility of relocating, were sometimes forced to labor, and were generally the victims of a nearly century-long postwar campaign of domestic terrorism. They suffered through peonage, debt servitude, sharecropping, and a sustained campaign of lynching.

The golden age of the American economy following the Second World War—in which the working class did better relative to the wealthy than at any other time in American history—pointedly excluded black people. African Americans' collective struggle took until the 1960s to result in full legal rights: enforcement of *Brown v. Board of Education*, the Civil Rights Act of 1964, the Voting Rights Act of 1965, the Housing Act of 1968.

The counter-revolution to this "Second Reconstruction" was immediate. African Americans were further ghettoized: black neighborhoods around the country were lacerated and even destroyed by the Eisenhower Interstate Highway System, whose construction began in 1956. The interstate rammed elevated highways through the poorer parts of many cities,* demolishing black business districts and isolating existing housing projects in cul-de-sacs, while black applicants were denied mortgages in the suburbs that the new highways facilitated. African Americans ended up clustered in the old city cores that the whites abandoned, with their children attending dilapidated, underfunded, black-only schools.

Beginning in 1971 with President Richard Nixon's "war on drugs," along with "three strikes" laws and other mandatory sentencing guidelines, and a plea-bargaining system that made jury trials practically a thing of the past, the US prison population exploded in size, including millions of nonviolent drug offenders. As we write, the United States has for some years been the world's number-one incarcerator by far, holding at present (according to the most commonly cited figure) around 25 percent of the world's prisoners. In what has come to be known as the "cradle-to-prison pipeline," black men are incarcerated at about six times the rate relative to population of white men, and black women at about double the rate of white women. The prison population is heavily skewed toward the South: ten of the top eleven American incarcerators are former slave states, with Louisiana number one and Mississippi number two. Private, for-profit prisons began in 1984, with their growth stimulated by a 1995 model "Prison Industries Act" introduced into state legislatures around the country in an organized campaign by the right-wing American Legislative Exchange Council (ALEC). Convicted felons have a hard time getting a job, and since

---

*Four examples: the Bronx, New Orleans, Miami, and San Juan, Puerto Rico.

felons are disfranchised in many states, black people have been disproportionately removed from the voting rolls.

Last hired, first fired: increased post-civil rights economic and professional
opportunities were countered by a redistribution to the wealthy that picked up
steam in the post-Reagan years. Education and medical care have been repriced
out of the reach of the poor, and increasingly require legal sophistication to navigate. The new inequality hit the long-term disadvantaged the hardest, a tendency
that accelerated dramatically in the post-*Bush v. Gore* years. The financial crisis
that began in late 2007 wiped out gains that had been made by many African
Americans, especially those targeted by predatory lending. "Plunder in the past
made plunder in the present efficient," writes Ta-Nehisi Coates, referring to the
twenty-first-century subprime mortgage crisis that disproportionately affected
black homeowners.[3] Meanwhile, police brutality and murder, a longstanding
problem, has emerged as a national issue in the age of video documentation,
when it is no longer possible to pretend it doesn't happen, while open-carry and
other firearm laws favor increased aggression by white supremacist hate groups,
whose numbers "skyrocketed" during the Obama presidency.[4]

To be sure, society does not look like it did when the Civil War Centennial
began in 1961. Some African Americans occupy high professional and political
positions. But the economic gap between black and white has not been bridged.
Black unemployment remained more than double that of whites in the fifty
years from 1963 to 2013, with African Americans earning on the average two-
thirds as much; 27.6 percent of African American households were in poverty
in 2013, compared with 9.8 percent for whites.[5] Multigenerational wealth and
multigenerational poverty seem to be nearly intractable forces, especially under
the protection of a government by the wealthy, for the wealthy.

In talking about this book-in-progress with friends and strangers, we have frequently heard people say: but slavery is still going on today.

The highly charged S-word—sometimes used metaphorically, sometimes
not—is a broad term that can take in many different kinds of inhumane practices; scholars today speak of "slaveries." Our brief in writing this book has not
extended to covering the postbellum forms of unfree labor, some legal and some
not, which have been amply documented elsewhere: the postbellum neoslavery of
convict leasing that made Birmingham, Alabama, a steel capital and continued

in the South until the Second World War; the prison-industrial complex of the modern mass incarceration state; contemporary migrant exploitation, sex trafficking, and other forms of coerced labor; sweatshop and agricultural labor; and present-day work of all kinds performed in an environment of social brutality and under surveillance.[6]

That people persist in describing these as "slavery" is perhaps a measure of the continuing weight of antebellum slavery and its burdensome shaping influence on our consciousness and our society, for which there have never been adequate reparations.

Over the years we have been researching our nation's history, we have seen repeatedly that no matter how bad we thought slavery was, it was even worse. There's no end to it.

No one living today can fully understand what the enslaved endured in the total-slavery world of the Old South, where the economy was dependent on the production of chattel laborers by female reproduction workers who could be forcibly impregnated for that purpose, with their sexual violation approved by law.

Unfortunately, the agenda of the slave society seems all too familiar to us in the twenty-first-century world.

Antebellum slavery required a complex of social, legal, financial, and political institutions structured to maximize profits that flowed only to a small elite, while leaving the rest of the population poor. It wanted no legal oversight beyond the local, no public education, and no dissent. For laborers, it wanted no personhood: no wages, education, privacy, clothing, human rights, civic identity, civil rights, reproductive rights, or even the right to keep a stable family. It existed at the cost of everything else in the society, including the most basic notions of humanity.

The history of the slave-breeding industry demonstrates how far the unrestrained pursuit of profit can go.

Acknowledgments

In visiting as many of the sites mentioned in this book as possible during the writing process, we were impressed over and over again by initiatives, many of them local, to make history known. From Gabriel's gallows circle in Richmond, to the manacles in the concrete in Natchez, to the museum at Charleston's Old Slave Mart and the Freedom Museum in Alexandria, to performative and ceremonial events like the Gullah-Geechee festival in Beaufort, Juneteenth in Galveston, and every Sunday in New Orleans, we salute those people in every community who are fighting to commemorate their local sacred places. We would also like to thank the workers of the National Park Service, who are tasked with managing heritage sites all across the country while being crippled by constant budget cuts.

We are indebted to the brave and singular work of Frederic Bancroft (1860–1945), who turned over the rock other historians would not look under. His *Slave Trading in the Old South* (1931) employed the then-novel device, learned from German anthropology, of field interviews. Besides collecting documentation, he spoke in 1902 with formerly enslaved people, former slave traders, and other firsthand witnesses to the slave trade, and demonstrated that the commercial exploitation of human reproduction was indeed central to the antebellum system of slavery. *Slave Trading in the Old South* has been largely vindicated and appears a more important work with every passing decade. Though scholars commonly cite Bancroft today, the disturbing implications of his privately published book were not incorporated into the mainstream narrative of American history until fairly recently. In composing our narrative, we have been informed by a critical reading of Bancroft, including some of his notes, sources, and the typescript of never-completed work by him in the Rare Book department of Bancroft's alma mater, Columbia University.

This book would not have existed without our nine months' residency in Chestertown, Maryland, at the C. V. Starr Center for the Study of the American Experience at Washington College, where Ned was a Patrick Henry Writing Fellow in 2010–11 and where Parts One through Three were drafted. In the years since the fellowship ended, Chestertown has continued to be a part of our lives. We are profoundly grateful to Washington College and to Starr Center director Adam Goodheart, and to Jill Ogline Titus, Michael Buckley, Lois Kitz, Jenifer Emley, Mitchell Reiss, the staff of Miller Library, and Kevin Hemstock of the *Kent County News.* To other friends and colleagues in Chestertown, more than we can name here: Peter Heck and Jane Jewell; Craig and Katie O'Donnell; Kenneth Schweitzer; Diane Daniels at the Historical Society of Kent County; the staff of the Kent County Public Library; Leslie Prince Raimond at the Kent County Arts Council, as well as to Vincent Raimond, whose spirit has now joined the great Spirit of the Place. Very particular thanks are extended to Ellen and Frank Hurst of next door, Cynthia Saunders from across the street, and Carol Mylander, just up the way—the best neighbors and friends newcomers could ever have. We would also like to thank posthumously someone we never met: J. A. Leo LeMay, whose former personal library is in the Fellows' residence. We failed in our attempt to read it all, but we tried.

Much of Parts Four through Six was drafted at Bobst Library at New York University, with thanks to Franses Angelica Rodriguez and to the Circulation Department, and at the Mina Rees Library of the CUNY Graduate Center. Our ongoing research overlaps from project to project, so we would like to acknowledge fellowships that Ned held before this book project began as such. Studies undertaken while Ned was a Cullman Center Fellow at the New York Public Library, a Tulane Rockefeller Humanities Fellow at the Stone Center for Latin American Studies at Tulane University in New Orleans, and a John Simon Guggenheim Fellow all contributed significantly to our understanding of the subject as reflected in this volume. A Knight-Luce Fellowship for Reporting on Global Religion allowed Ned to make research trips to Mbanza-Kongo in 2012 and Port-au-Prince in 2013, and the final stages of work on this volume were done while he was a New York Foundation for the Arts Fellow in Nonfiction Literature.

We must thank more people for their help, support, and conversation than we can possibly list, so if your name is not here, please accept our thanks anyway. First, very special thanks to Julie Skurski and to Jason King. Thanks to Donald Harrison, David Rubinson, Michael Zilkha, Kip and Nancy Hanrahan, Howard Hunter and Metairie (Louisiana) Country Day School, Sarah Hill,

Madison Smartt Bell, Ted Widmer, Roger Trilling, Lambert Strether, Gwendolyn Midlo Hall, Eric Weisbard, John Cummings, Ibrahima Seck, Ina Fandrich, Joyce Jackson, Robert Farris Thompson, C. Daniel Dawson, Bárbaro Martínez Ruiz, Nzinga Paiva, Henry Wiencek, Laurent Dubois, Peter H. Wood, Warren Whatley, James Shinn, Freddi Evans, T. R. Johnson, Joel Dinerstein, Felipe Smith, Christopher Dunn, Beverly Trask, Shawn Hall, Mark Bingham, Susanne Hackett, Garnette Cadogan, Scott Aiges, Pat Cruz, Michael Zwack, Louis Head, Colin Dayan, Jerry Carlson, Sybil Cooksey, Dylon Robbins, Nadia Ellis, Kandia Crazy Horse, Linda Goldstein, Karen Goldfeder, Ken McCarthy, Blanca Lasalle, Ben Socolov, Peter Gordon, and Ronald Robboy, as well as Ned's colleagues at *Afropop Worldwide*: Sean Barlow, Georges Collinet, Banning Eyre, Michael Jones, and Sam Backer.

Thanks go to our agent, Sarah Lazin, who helped us craft our ideas into a coherent proposal, and especially to our publisher, Chicago Review Press, which has published Ned's previous three books over the last ten years, and whose faith in us we have noted and appreciated. Our singular editor, Yuval Taylor, who developed Ned's previous books, is a valued and principled collaborator who has given us advice and editorial direction. Our gratitude goes to publisher Cynthia Sherry and to Michelle Williams, Mary Kravenas, Caitlin Eck, and Meaghan Miller.

We view this work as the continuation of a forty-year process of collaboration between the two of us that began long before either of us had published a book, and we are grateful to everyone who has helped us over the years. Thanks to the readers of our work, whose dialogue with us has been important to our understanding, and to the independent booksellers who have been a vital part of the process.

Picture Credits

▶13 Map Division New York Public Library ▶ 72 Map Division New York Public Library ▶79 Library of Congress ▶ 81 College of Arms London ▶ 96 Arents Tobacco Collection New York Public Library ▶ 97 Arents Tobacco Collection New York Public Library ▶ 102 Photo by Ned Sublette ▶ 112 Map Division New York Public Library ▶ 114 Arents Tobacco Collection New York Public Library ▶ 118 Library of Congress ▶ 120 Library of Congress ▶ 127 British Museum ▶ 157 Photo by Ned and Constance Sublette ▶ 169 Huntington Library ▶ 170 New York Public Library ▶ 189 Library of Congress ▶ 191 Library of Congress ▶ 218 Maryland Historical Society ▶ 259 Photo by Ned and Constance Sublette ▶ 271 Photo by Ned and Constance Sublette ▶ 291 The Gilder Lehman Institute of American History ▶ 326 Photo by Ned and Constance Sublette ▶ 344 Photo by Ned and Constance Sublette ▶ 351 New York Public Library ▶ 418 Kentucky Gateway Museum Center Maysville ▶ 444 Special Collections University of Virginia Library ▶ 483 Photo by Ned and Constance Sublette ▶ 522 Photo by Ned and Constance Sublette ▶ 550 Photo by Ned and Constance Sublette ▶ 558 Rice C. Ballard Collection Wilson Library University of North Carolina at Chapel Hill ▶ 563 Photo by Ned and Constance Sublette ▶ 568 David M. Rubenstein Rare Book & Manuscript Library Duke University ▶ 584 New York Public Library ▶ 591 Columbus State University Archives ▶ 593 Virginia Historical Society ▶ 625 Library of Congress ▶ 631 Library of Congress ▶ 662 Photo by Ned and Constance Sublette◀

Note: We have not hesitated to retouch newspaper advertisements in the interest of readability.

Notes

Chapter 1: The Mother of Slavery

1. Hughes, 5.
2. Virginia Code of 1849, 747.
3. In his history of Shelby County, Mississippi, John E. Harkins says that the planter's name was Edmund (not Edward). Harkins, 53.
4. Harkins, 53.
5. Historical dollar conversion figures are intended only as rough approximations. This and subsequent conversions are queried from Sahr.
6. Hughes, 12.
7. Tadman, 141, 147–51.
8. Ball, 37.
9. Featherstonhaugh, 1:122–23.
10. Humes, 33.
11. Rumple, 254.
12. *The Negro in Virginia*, 173.
13. Ball, 72–73.
14. Brown, William Wells 1849, 49.
15. Brown, William Wells 1849, 32.
16. Strouse, 88.
17. Clayton 2002, 133.

Chapter 2: Protectionism, or, The Importance of 1808

1. Eltis and Richardson, 4, 17.
2. Eltis and Richardson, 18.

3. McMillin, 118.
4. Letter, Thomas Jefferson to John Wayles Eppes, June 30, 1820. http://founders.archives.gov/documents/Jefferson/98-01-02-1352.
5. US Constitution, Article 1, Section 9.
6. For a detailed account of Jefferson's second term, see Adams 1889/1986.
7. Ingraham 1860, 523.
8. For a discussion of credit in the creation of money, see Ingham, 107–133.
9. DuBois, W. E. B. 1933, 44.
10. There are numerous references to slave purchases in Polk's letters (*CJKP*); William Dusinberre's *Slavemaster President* covers the subject in detail.
11. Conrad and Meyer, 105–06.

Chapter 3: A Literature of Terror

1. Brown, William Wells 1847, 4.
2. Jacobs, 79–80, 117–18. See also *HJFP*, 1:lxxvi.
3. Veney, 26.
4. Perdue *et al*, 11.
5. Harrower.
6. Follett, 48.
7. *CJKP*, 11:346.
8. Cade, 307.
9. *The Negro in Virginia*, 83–84.
10. *TAS*, supp. 2:5:1580.

11. *TAS*, supp. 2:5:1580.

12. *FWP*, North Carolina narratives, 11:2, 131.

13. Quoted in Cade, 306.

14. *TAS*, supp. 2:5:1453.

15. Genovese 1974, 464.

16. Smith, Daniel Scott, 86.

17. Talbot gives a thorough accounting of the *Mandingo* product line.

18. See, for example, Tadman, 121–25.

19. Sutch, 38–39.

20. Tadman, 124.

21. *FWP*, Texas narratives, 16:1, 218..

22. *The Negro in Virginia*, 171.

23. *FWP*, Arkansas narratives, 2:3, 369.

24. Talbot, 11.

25. Musgrave, 264–67.

26. Catterall, 1:75.

27. Olmsted 1861, 55n.

28. *FWP*, Florida narratives, 3:166.

29. *FWP*, Texas narratives, 16:1, 180.

30. *FWP*, Texas narratives, 16:2, 203–04.

31. *FWP*, North Carolina narratives, 11:1, 31.

32. Lemieux; Jones.

33. Swarns, 2012a.

34. Escott, 44.

35. US Census (1860), x.

36. US Census (1860), x.

37. Steward, 151.

38. George, 317.

39. Hartman, 85.

40. http://law2.umkc.edu/faculty/projects /ftrials/celia/celiahome.html

41. Purcell, 338.

Chapter 4: Natural Increase

1. Bancroft 1931/1996, 24.

2. Quoted in Lightner, 5.

3. Marx 1937, 67.

4. Deyle 2005b, 296.

5. Deyle 2005b, 289.

6. Frederic Bancroft, Letter to Winfield Hazlitt Collins, Dec. 13, 1921. *FBC*, Box 89.

7. *TWOTR*, ser. 3, 4:355.

8. Wright, Gavin, 2.

9. *FBC*, Box 88, 109D.

10. *TAS*, 19:298

11. Kilbourne 1995, 5.

12. Olmsted 1861, 55n.

13. Menard, 18.

14. Stephenson, 227.

15. Kilbourne 1995, 4.

16. Adams, Henry 1883, 59.

17. See, e.g., Rutherford, 371.

18. Graeber, 192.

19. *FBC*, Box 84, 2:5, 3.

20. See Jefferson, "Notes on Coinage," in *PTJ* 7:175–85.

21. Kemble, 78.

22. *SIF*, 559–60.

23. Stanton, 127.

24. Berinato.

Chapter 5: Little Shadows

1. Say, 1:318.

2. Hughes, 34.

3. Marx 1937, 67.

4. "The Impending Crisis in the Southern States of America" (1859), *The Economist*, Dec. 24, p. 1429.

5. Henson, 7.

6. Wiencek, 156–57.

7. Virginia Code of 1849, 458.

8. Mason, 13.

9. Quoted in *The Negro in Virginia*, 71–72.

10. Quoted in Camp, 559.

11. Stanton, 23.

12. Smith, Gene Allen, 103–04.

13. Ball, 47.

14. Jefferson 1788, 148.

15. Kiple and King, 88.

16. Kiple and King, 89.

17. See Kiple and King, 74–78.

18. King, Roswell, Jr., 1:527.

19. Watson, 16–17.

20. Ball, 63–64.

21. See Cade, 300. There is a child-feeding trough in the collection of artifacts at Whitney Plantation in Louisiana.

22. www.cdc.gov/mmwr/preview /mmwrhtml/00020119.htm.
23. See Grandin, 40–41n.
24. Mather, 422.
25. Barker-Benfield, 85–112.
26. *DeBow's Review* (1851). 11:3, 332–33.
27. *FWP*, Virginia narratives, 17:2.
28. Starobin, 11–12.
29. Zaborney, 121.
30. *FBC*, Box 88, 70.
31. Green, J. D. 10.
32. Watson, Henry, 13.
33. Mason, 20–21.
34. Northup, 250.
35. *FWP*, Arkansas Narratives, 2:1, 113.
36. Jacobs, 217.
37. Watson, Henry, 16.
38. *TAS*, supp. 2:5:1580.
39. Chesnut, 29.
40. Jacobs, 57.
41. *FWP*, South Carolina narratives, 14:1, 150.
42. In a letter by William Hayward. Truth, 139.
43. Bremer, 3:340.
44. US Census (1860), xvi.
45. *FWP*, South Carolina narratives, 14:1, 158.
46. Gudmestad, 42.
47. Perdue et al., 158.
48. Clarke.
49. Brown, William Wells 1863, 17.
50. McCullough, 55.
51. McCullough, 47.
52. *TAS*, 18:300.
53. Aptheker, 162.
54. Dunbar.
55. Bauer and Bauer, 338–419.
56. Quoted in Aptheker, 235.

Chapter 6: Species of Property

1. Letter, O.P. Temple to Frederic Bancroft, February 8, 1904, *FBC*, Box 88.
2. Rousey, 19–24.
3. Kilbourne 1995, 6.
5. See Adams, Henry 1883, 36–37, 269–71.
6. *A declaration of the immediate causes . . .* See also, for example, Townsend, 19; Davis, Jefferson, 107.
7. *FBC*, Box 88.
8. US Census (1860), "Agriculture," vii.
9. Letter, Thomas Jefferson to James Madison, April 27, 1809, *PTJRS*, 1:169.
10. Quoted in Dew, Charles B., 35.
11. Kilbourne 1995, 7.

Chapter 7: Rawrenock

1. Kingsbury, 1.
2. Luther, 357–58.
3. See Landers, 13; Pickett and Pickett, 22–27; Milanich, 62.
4. Treasure, 3ff.
5. Ribaut, 67.
6. Ribaut, 75.
7. Ribaut, 93.
8. Ribaut, 93.
9. Lowery, 37.
10. Mercado, 16.
11. Thurber, 106–07.
12. Bennett 2001, 21.
13. Laudonnière, 103–122.
14. Scott, William Robert, 2:3–8.
15. Andrews, 20.
16. Rankin, 3.
17. Scott, William Robert, 2:8, 60–65.
18. Mercado, 9–10.
19. Mercado, 92; Bennett 2001, 37.
20. Laudonnière, 138n; Bennett 2001, 38.
21. Bennett 2001, 38.
22. Solís de Merás, 122.
23. Wilford.
24. Scott, William Robert, 89.
25. Taylor, 278.
26. Smith, John 1624, 58.
27. Keller, 66.
28. For a discussion of the term "motley crew," see Linebaugh and Rediker, 27–28 and *passim*.
29. Andrews, 36.

30. Purchas, 4:1728.

31. Andrews, Kenneth R. 37.

32. See Bartels, 305–322.

33. Tombs, 204.

Chapter 8: A Cargo of Shining Dirt

1. Lemay 1991, 210.

2. Smith, John 1624, 21–22.

3. Tilp, 100.

4. Purchas, 4:1753.

5. Quoted in Lemay 1991, 184.

6. O'Brien.

7. See Linebaugh and Rediker's chapter on this interlude, 8–35.

Chapter 9: Our Principall Wealth

1. Lemay 1991, 24

2. Smith, Abbot Emerson, 12.

3. Fischer, 227; McCusker and Menard, 242.

4. Morgan, Edmund S. 1975, 126.

5. Bruce 1895, 1:186.

6. See Parent's chapter, "The Landgrab," 9–54.

7. Quoted in Tyler, Lyon Gardiner, 284.

8. Harrower, 39.

9. Morgan, Edmund S. 1975, 171.

10. Letter, George Washington to Robert Cary, February 13, 1764. *PGW*, A:7:286.

11. Kingsbury, 243; see also www .encyclopediavirginia.org/_20_and_odd_ Negroes_an_excerpt_from_a_letter _from_John_Rolfe_to_Sir_Edwin _Sandys_1619_1620.

12. Sluiter 1997, 376n.

13. Smith, John 1624, 117.

14. Quoted in Anderson, Adam, 2:217.

15. Bruce 1895, 1:58.

16. Thornton 1998, 421.

17. Sluiter 1997.

18. Thornton 1983, 63.

19. Thornton 1983, 63.

20. Quoted in Kingsbury, 243.

21. Morgan, Edmund S. 1975, 111, 113.

22. Morgan, Edmund S. 1975, 101–02.

23. Lucas, 73; Mann, Charles C.

Chapter 10: Maria's Land

1. Heath and Philips, 220.

2. Hibbard, 119.

3. Hall, Clayton Colman, 5.

4. Hall, Clayton Colman, 33, 40.

5. Lucas, 114.

6. Hall, Clayton Colman, 38.

7. Allan.

8. Hall, Clayton Colman, 61.

9. Tilp, 78.

10. Tilp, 12.

11. "Lord Baltimore's instructions to his colonists." In *The Calvert Papers*, 1:131.

12. Smith, John 1884, 615.

13. Adams and Pleck, 37–38.

14. Bunker 2010, 242.

15. Fischer, 240, 243.

16. Fischer, 366.

17. Walsh 2010, 10.

18. Griffey, 182.

19. For an account of the iconoclastic riots, see Eire.

20. Brugger, 21.

21. Harrison, 104.

22. Weeks, 13.

23. Weeks, 20.

24. Fischer, 226.

Chapter 11: Barbados

1. Quoted in Firth, 146.

2. Schwartz, 13.

3. *The Bowery Historic District*, Sec. 8, p. 9.

4. Fisher, 102–03.

5. Harlow, 5.

6. Harlow, 82, 86.

7. Price 1991, 297; Dunn, 61.

8. Price 1991, 299.

9. Price 1991, 297; Dunn, 61.

10. Ligon 2011, 188.

11. Harlow, 162–68.

12. Dunn, 10, 337–38.

13. Nisbet, 116.

14. Quoted in Harlow, 59.
15. Harlow, 84.
16. Bunker 2014, 412–13.
17. Quoted in Firth, 146.
18. Dunn, 288.
19. Dunn, 266; Harlow, 44.
20. Dunn, 245.
21. McCusker and Menard, 92.
22. Scott, William Robert, 17.
23. Garrard, 71.
24. *The Duke of York's Release.*
25. Aptheker, 165.
26. Hening 2:299–300.
27. "Great news from the Barbadoes,"
    339–341.
28. "Great news from the Barbadoes," 342.

Chapter 12: The Anglo-Saxon Model

1. Morgan, Edmund S. 1975, 386
2. Quoted in Fischer, 212.
3. Slotkin and Folsom, 17.
4. Morgan, Edmund S. 1975, 327.
5. Brown, Kathleen M., 177.
6. Morgan, Edmund S. 1975, 383.
7. Breen, 241.
8. Bailyn, 97.
9. Jordan, 75.
10. For an extended discussion, see Wright
    2006, 14–47.
11. Rawley, 84.
12. Hening, 2:270.
13. Price 1991, 296.
14. Morgan, Kenneth, 719–720.
15. Price 1991, 10.
16. Parent, 2.
17. Walsh 2010, 17, 233.
18. Davis, Richard Beale, 253.
19. Deyle 2004, 215.
20. Parent, 72.
21. Fitzhugh, William, 44.
22. Davis, Richard Beale, 175.
23. Goodheart 2011a, 304.
24. Davis, Richard Beale, 54.
25. Davis, Richard Beale, 373–77.

Chapter 13: Carolina

1. Nairne, 47–48.
2. This summary of South Carolina's
   political backstory substantially
   follows the contours of Eugene
   Sirman's.
3. Armitage, 607.
4. Armitage, 608.
5. Sirmans, 14.
6. McCandless, 10.
7. McCandless, 7.
8. Sirmans, 16.
9. Wood, Peter H., 24.
10. Gallay, 225.
11. Gallay, 23–31.
12. Our account of this indigenous
    political geography is indebted to Gallay,
    1–39.
13. Armitage, 610.
14. Donnan, 804.
15. Berlin, 17.
16. Gallay, 299.
17. Gallay, 6–7.
18. Crane, 45.
19. Le Moyne d'Iberville, 119.
20. Crane, 19.
21. See Gallay, 40–69, and Crane, 6–21.
22. Gallay, 56–57.
23. Crane, 112.
24. See Ingham, 107–33.
25. Ingham, 127–131.
26. Price 1984, 26–31.
27. Ingham, 129.
28. Gallay, 212.
29. De Quesada, 6.
30. Horne, 3.
31. Landers 1999, 24.

Chapter 14: The Separate Traders

1. Quoted in *DIST*, 4:68.
2. Scott, William Robert, 23.
3. Behrendt 2007, 68.
4. Parent, 79; Rawley, 86.
5. figures from Price 1991, 305.

6. Catterall, 1:53–54.

7. Thomas, Hugh, 236.

8. Furdell, 245.

9. Thomas, Hugh, 235.

10. Parent, 93.

11. Whatley.

12. Bourne, Michael, 46.

13. Rawley and Behrendt, 182;
Ridley, 27.

14. Morgan, Kenneth, 719–720.

15. Anderson and Gallman, 32.

16. Ortiz 1947, 268; Ortiz 1978, 358.

17. Morgan, Philip D. 1998, 81.

Chapter 15: Charles Town

1. At the Gullah Geechee Festival, Beaufort,
South Carolina, May 26, 2013.

2. Norris, 58–59.

3. Morgan, Philip D. 1998, 1.

4. Gallay, 200.

5. Donnan, 804–05.

6. Wood, Peter H., 57n.

7. Wilder, 50; Leder and Carroso,
20–30.

8. See Carney, 32ff. for an extended
discussion.

9. Bruce 1895, 1:331.

10. Wood, Peter H., 36.

11. See author's interview with Gwendolyn
Midlo Hall for *Afropop Worldwide Hip
Deep*, http://www.afropop.org/11166
/gwendolyn-midlo-hall.

12. McCusker and Menard, 181–82.

13. Mancall et al, 630.

14. McCusker and Menard, 235.

15. Norris, 17–18.

16. Norris, 93.

17. Quoted in Gallay, 328.

18. Gallay, 338.

19. Caillot, 125n, 146–68.

20. Quoted in Aptheker, 175.

21. Quoted in Aptheker, 181.

22. Quoted in Donnan, 805.

23. Donnan, 806.

Chapter 16: Savannah and Stono

1. Hewatt, 2:300.

2. Egmont Papers, http://fax.libs.uga.edu
/egmont/14203/index.djvu?djvuopts&zoo
m=100&page=ep142030229.djvu.

3. Baine, 101.

4. Wilson, Thomas D., 12.

5. Wilson, Thomas D., 38–40.

6. Greenberg, 28.

7. See Wilson, Thomas D., 107.

8. Pinckney.

9. *CRG*, 23:57.

10. Hewatt, 63–64.

11. Landers 2010, 1–3.

12. *CRG*, 22:2:232–36.

13. Thornton 1991.

14. Fromont, 11.

15. Epstein, 39, 59.

16. Quoted in Wood, Peter H., 321.

17. Wood, Peter H., 320.

18. Hill, William, 93.

19. Seabrook, 13.

20. Kly, 18ff.

21. Wood, Peter H., 322.

22. See Lepore for an account.

23. Aptheker, 190.

24. Smith, Josiah, ii; Aptheker, 190.

25. Smith, Josiah, 10–11.

26. Landers 1999, 35–45.

27. *CRG*, 23:332–3.

28. Greenberg, 35.

29. Hewatt, 2:114.

30. Zaborney, 10.

31. Pinckney, Eliza Lucas, memorandum of
January 1742.

Chapter 17: A Rough Set of People, but Somewhat Caressed

1. Letter, Henry Laurens to John Knight,
May 28, 1756. *PHL*, 2:204.

2. Rogers 1976, 479.

3. Melvin Gibbs, private communication.

4. Hancock, 205–208; Rogers 1976, 488.

5. Behrendt 2007, 68.

6. Sellers, Leila, 112.

7. Letter, Henry Laurens to William Fisher, Nov. 9, 1768. *PHL,* 6:149–50.

8. Sellers, Leila, 25.

9. Hewatt, 129–130.

10. Hewatt, 291–292.

11. Hewatt, 294.

12. Donnan, 810–11.

13. *DIST,* 4:375.

14. McDonough, 21.

15. Sellers, Leila, 97.

16. Letter, Henry Laurens to Samuel and William Vernon, June 15, 1756, *PHL* 2:219.

17. Rawley, 82.

18. Higgins, 206–217.

19. Sellers, Leila, 97–98.

20. McCusker, 220.

21. Letter, Henry Laurens to Smith and Baillies, August 25, 1763, *PHL,* 3:539.

22. "worthy Friend": see., e.g., Letter, Henry Laurens to Gabriel Manigault, March 2, 1772, *PHL* 8:202; Oswald: Hancock, 205, 213.

23. Webster, 4–16.

24. *New Georgia Encyclopedia,* www .georgiaencyclopedia.org/nge/Article .jsp?id=h-686.

25. Morgan, Philip D. 2010, 27.

26. Sellers, Leila, 97–98.

Chapter 18: Ballast

1. Chance, 54.

2. Robbins, 2.

3. See Sublette 2004, 45.

4. Robbins, 100–01.

5. Robbins, 110.

6. Robbins, 120.

7. Robbins, 108.

8. Robbins, 256.

9. Carroll and Carroll, 1:438

10. Carroll and Carroll, 1:438

11. Carroll and Carroll, 2:707–08.

12. Carroll and Carroll, 2:706.

13. For a genealogy see Reamy and Reamy, 28.

14. Lemay 2009, 342.

15. *PGW,* A:7:146.

16. *PGW,* A:9:111.

17. Cohen, Richard, 374.

18. Carson, 114.

19. *The Apollo; or, the Chestertown Spy,* April 9, 1793.

20. Cohen, Richard, 374–76.

21. Kelly, 360.

22. Wroth, 274.

23. Letter, Thomas Ringgold to Samuel Galloway, July 10, 1763, *TRP.*

24. Beirne, 79.

25. Robbins, 98.

26. Carroll and Carroll, 2:710.

27. See Minchinton for more about the forms slaving vessels took; Wax 1978.

28. Letter, Thomas Ringgold to Fowler, Easton and Comp., September 17, 1761, *TRP.*

29. Letter, Thomas Ringgold to Samuel Galloway, August 14, 1761, *TRP.*

30. Behrendt 1997, 55.

31. Letter, Thomas Ringgold to Samuel Galloway, September 17, 1761, *TRP.*

32. Parent, 62–64.

33. See Sublette 2004, Ch. 12..

34. See Walsh 1999.

35. Letter, Thomas Ringgold to Samuel Galloway, November 21, 1762, *TRP.*

36. Bosman, 91.

37. Herbert, 124, 200–205; Metcalf, 380.

38. Rappleye, 58–59.

39. Eltis and Richardson, 71.

40. Letter, John Adams to William Tudor, August 11, 1818. *WJA,* 10:345.

41. Letter, Thomas Ringgold to Samuel Galloway, December 15, 1760, *TRP.*

42. www.abdn.ac.uk/slavery/resource1b.htm

43. Morgan, Kenneth 2007, 67.

44. Letter, Thomas Ringgold to Samuel Galloway, November 1, 1762, *TRP.*

45. See *Voyage of the slave ship Sally,* http:// cds.library.brown.edu/projects/sally.

46. Letter, Thomas Ringgold to Samuel Galloway, May 6, 1764, *TRP.*

47. Beirne, 79.
48. www.thevalleyfamily.org/getperson.php
?personID=I1167639417&tree=fitzvalley.
49. Conger, 63.
50. Hazzard-Donald 2011, 195, 200; Hazzard-Donald 2012, 40.
51. Hughes, 108.
52. Hazzard-Donald 2012, 35.
53. See Samford.
54. Alabama narratives, 1:341.
55. Lemay 2006, 73.
56. Lemay 2006, 74.

Chapter 19: Newspapers as Money as People

1. April 17–24, 1704; see also Thomas, Isaiah, 13.
2. www.vagazette.com/our_newspaper/about_us.
3. Waldstreicher 2004, 76. This chapter draws on Waldstreicher's analysis of Franklin's economic ideas.
4. Brissot de Warville, 1:182.
5. www.vagazette.com/our_newspaper/about_us.
6. Waldstreicher 2004, 121.
7. Waldstreicher 2004, 88.
8. Waldstreicher 2004, 88.
9. Marx 1970, 55.
10. *PBF*, 1:149.
11. Waldstreicher 2004, 21.
12. Waldstreicher 2004, 79.
13. Quoted in Hawke, 82.
14. *Pennsylvania Gazette*, July 8, 1731.
15. Grubb 2006, 7.
16. See the discussion of the Law company in Sublette 2008, 45–55.
17. Hewatt, 2:57.
18. Wiencek 2003, 178–79.
19. Hewatt, 2:169.
20. *CRG*, 22:1: 203.
21. *CRG*, 23:245–46.
22. Hewatt, 2:171–72.
23. Hewatt, 2:100.
24. Hewatt, 2:54.

Chapter 20: Lord Dunmore's Blackbirds

1. Smith, Adam, 2:89.
2. For an extended discussion of the term "motley crew" and its application to this era, see Linebaugh and Rediker, 211–247.
3. Zobel, 26.
4. Linebaugh and Rediker, 216–17.
5. Zobel, 28–29.
6. Bailyn 1974, 35.
7. Bailyn 1974, 135.
8. Rogers, 493.
9. Gadsden, 111, 316.
10. Gadsden, 92, 95.
11. *PHL*, 5:24n.
12. Quoted in Morgan, Edmund S. 1959, 155.
13. Blumrosen and Blumrosen, 17.
14. Blackstone *et al.*, 1:123.
15. Blumrosen and Blumrosen, 9–11.
16. Blumrosen and Blumrosen, 15.
17. "The Somersett Case and the Slave Trade." *London Chronicle*, June 18–20, 1772.
18. *PHL*, 8:353.
19. *PHL*, 16:533.
20. Quoted in Blumrosen and Blumrosen, 24–25.
21. Quoted in Kelly, 376.
22. Nybakken, 13, 85, 114.
23. Bell, Malcolm, 1.
24. Quoted in Bailyn 1974, 157.
25. Quoted in Bell, Malcolm, 22.
26. Bell, Malcolm, 22–23.
27. *PHL*, 16:557.
28. Bell, Malcolm, 26.
29. Berkeley and Berkeley, 31.
30. Hewatt, 2:97–98.
31. McCrady, 3–4.
32. McCrady, 24.
33. Quoted in Willard, 233.
34. *DIST*, 153–54.
35. Purdie's *Virginia Gazette*, Dec. 29, 1775.
36. Bell, Malcolm, 33.
37. For a discussion of the conditions within Domingan society for men of color

participating in the Chasseurs-Volontaires, see King, Stewart, 65–77.

Chapter 21: The General Inconvenience

1. Jefferson 1997, 1:334–35.
2. Quoted in Unger, 13.
3. Burke, 51–52.
4. Bailyn, 18.
5. e.g., *Virginia Gazette*, November 19, 1736.
6. Fuller, 132; Carson, 43.
7. Carson, 43.
8. Willison, 268.
9. See Cohen, Charles.
10. Willison, 267–68.
11. *Maryland Gazette*, Aug. 16, 1770.
12. Quoted in Bunker 2014, 148.
13. Quoted in Willison, 485–86.
14. Tyler, Moses Coit, 389.
15. Boswell, 1:154.
16. Henry, William Wirt. 3:4.
17. Robinson, 84.
18. Wills, 332.
19. *Journals of the Continental Congress*, 5:429.
20. Letter, Thomas Jefferson to Angelica Schuyler Church, Nov. 27, 1793. *PTJ*, 27:449.
21. *PTJ* 1: 243–247.
22. Robinson, 80–83.
23. Malone, 131.
24. *MJQA*, 8:284–85.
25. *PTJ*, 2:350.
26. Anburey, 2:192–3.
27. Adams, William Howard, 279.
28. *Phocion* 9 (1796). *Gazette of the United States,* October 21. See also Chernow, 313.
29. Idzerda, 170.
30. Carroll and Carroll, 1443.
31. See Lewis, 83–99.
32. Letter, Thomas Jefferson to Dr. William Gordon, July 16, 1788, *PTJ*, 13:362–64.
33. Quoted in Hancock, 391.
34. Quoted in Hancock, 160.
35. Buckley, 4, 22, 35–36, 55.
36. Parton, 262.

37. Jefferson 1788, 186.
38. Meacham, 58, 144.
39. Chastellux, 2:438
40. Letter, Thomas Jefferson to James Madison, May 11, 1785, *PTJ*, 8:147.
41. Jefferson 1788, 147.
42. Smith, Felipe, 24.
43. Jefferson 1788, 154.
44. Letter, James Madison to Frances Wright, September 1, 1825.
45. Jefferson 1788, 147.
46. Jefferson 1788, 147.
47. Letter, Thomas Jefferson to Jared Sparks, February 4, 1824. *LOC* American Memory.
48. Letter, Thomas Jefferson to Jared Sparks, February 4, 1824. *LOC* American Memory.
49. Letter, Thomas Jefferson to Jared Sparks, February 4, 1824. *LOC*, American Memory
50. Jefferson 1788, 148-49
51. Letter, Thomas Jefferson to Jared Sparks, *LOC* American Memory
52. Letter, Thomas Jefferson to Jared Sparks, *LOC* American Memory
53. Kant, 110–11.
54. McMillin, 76.
55. McMillin, 76–80.
56. *DIST*, 4:482.
57. McMillin, 84–85.

Chapter 22: The Fugue of Silences

1. Farrand, 2:417.
2. *MJQA*, 5:11.
3. Letter, Benjamin Rush to John Coakley Lettsom, September 28, 1787, *DHRC* 13:262.
4. *PJA*, 2:178–79.
5. Letter, Thomas Jefferson to William Stephens Smith, Nov. 13, 1787, 12:356.
6. Finkelman 1986, 346.
7. Finkelman 1986, 349.
8. See Freytag v. Commissioner (90–762), 501 U.S. 868 (1991).
9. Breyer, 33.
10. Beeman, 309, 320.

11. David Waldstreicher's *Slavery's Constitu-tion* develops this theme at length, using the term "proslavery," as well as tracing the history of this interpretation of the Constitution.

12. Beeman, 91.

13. Farrand, 1:204.

14. Farrand, 1:603–605.

15. Bell, Malcolm, 231.

16. Lipscomb, xxiii–iv.

17. Farrand, 1:205–06.

18. Farrand, 1:580–81.

19. Hutson, 68.

20. See Ford, Lacy K. 2009, 82–83.

21. Bell, Malcolm, 88.

22. Farrand, 2:364.

23. Farrand, 2:364.

24. Farrand, 2:370.

25. Farrand, 2:370

26. Farrand, 2:371.26.

27. Reproduced in Deyle 2005, 37.

28. Farrand, 2:378.

29. Farrand, 2:415.

Chapter 23: Ten Thousand Powers

1. Farrand, 3:253.

2. Farrand, 3:253–55.

3. *DHRC*, 3:263.

4. Waldstreicher 2009, 119.

5. South Carolina State Constitution (1790), Art. II, Sec. 2.

6. Letter, James Madison to George Wash-ington, March 18, 1787. Quoted in *LDC*, 24:149–150.

7. *DHRC*, 10:1284, 1486.

8. *DHRC*, 10:1473.

9. *DHRC*, 8:311.

10. *DHRC*, 10:1341.

11. *DHRC*, 10:1476.

12. *DHRC*, 10:1477.

13. Grigsby, 157n.

14. Hewatt, 2:245.

15. *AC*, House of Representatives, 1st Con-gress, 2d Session, 1505.

16. Davis, William C., 17–19.

17. Trouillot 1990, 37.

18. See James, 45–55.

19. King, Stewart, 84.

20. James, 35, 56, 64.

Chapter 24: The French Revolution in America

1. "Notes on Arthur Young's letter to George Washington," *PTJ*, 24:95.

2. *PTJ*, 26:xli.

3. Letter, Thomas Jefferson to Jacques-Pierre Brissot de Warville, February 11, 1788. *PTJ*, 12:577–78.

4. Jefferson 1788, 151.

5. See Foster et al; see also Stanton, 93–104.

6. See Dubois 2004, 99–101.

7. Mathewson, 321.

8. "Notes on Arthur Young's letter to George Washington," *PTJ*, 24:98.

9. Wiencek 2012, 8.

10. *WTJ*, 7:114n.

11. Letter, Thomas Jefferson to George Wash-ington, June 28, 1793. *PTJ*, 26:396.

12. Crawford, 121.

13. Gordon-Reed.

14. Letter, Alexander Hamilton to Theodore Sedgwick, July 10, 1804. *PAH*, 26:309; Stanton, 87.

15. Brissot de Warville, 244.

16. Minnigerode, 146.

17. Olmsted 1861, 107.

18. Ammon, 44.

19. Letter, Thomas Jefferson to Edmond Charles Genet, June 5, 1793. *PTJ*, 26:195.

20. Minnigerode, 188.

21. Letter, Thomas Jefferson to James Mon-roe, *PTJ*, 26:190.

22. Minnigerode, 146.

23. Minnigerode, 220.

24. Dessens, 20.

25. Dessens, 67; Baur, 398.

26. Baur, 395.

27. *PGW*, C:14:55n.

28. "Cabinet opinions on relations with France and Great Britain," September 7, 1793, *PTJ*, 27:49–50.

29. Letter, John Adams to Thomas Jefferson, June 30, 1813, *AJL*, 347–48.

30. Letter, John Adams to John Quincy Adams, *AFC*, 10:4.

31. Letter, Thomas Jefferson to Caleb Lownes, Dec. 18, 1793. *PTJ*, 27:586.

32. Letter, Thomas Jefferson to Jean Nicolas Demeunier, *PTJ*, 38:341.

33. "red or blue": the recollection of former nailery slave Isaac Granger, quoted in Stanton, 7.

34. Stanton, 81–85.

35. Quoted in Brady, 609.

36. Sidbury 1997, 539.

37. Letter, Thomas Jefferson to Madame Plumard de Bellanger, April 25, 1794, *PTJ*, 28:59–60.

38. Quoted in Chapelle, 5.

39. Chapelle, 13.

40. Bruchey, 106.

41. Ward, 1292.

42. Landers 2010, 82.

Chapter 25: The Cotton Club

1. *CRG*, 23:158.

2. Hills, 41.

3. Lakwete, 47–48.

4. Letter, Thomas Jefferson to Eli Whitney, *PTJ*, 27:392–33.

5. Letter, Eli Whitney to Thomas Jefferson, *PTJ*, 27:433.

6. Quoted in Hall, Gwendolyn Midlo, 351.

7. McAfee, xi.

8. Andrew Jackson letter to Nathaniel Macon, October 4, 1795, *CAJ*, 1:17.

9. Sydnor 1938, 18–19.

10. *DHRC*, 8:34.

11. *Naval documents related to the Quasi-War. . . .* 1:1.

12. Letter, Henry Tazewell to AJ, July 20, 1798, *CAJ*, 1:53.

13. Geggus, 285.

14. Adams, Henry 1889/1986, 248.

15. Englund, 178.

16. Popkin, 214.

17. DeConde, 84.

18. Adams, Henry 1889/1986, 250.

19. *PJMon*, 4:398n; Egerton, 33–34.

20. *PJMon*, 4:345n.

21. Sidbury 2002, 210.

22. *PJMon*, 4:398n.

23. Ford, Lacy K. 2009, 51.

24. Schwarz, 87.

25. *PJMon*, 4:410.

26. Schwarz, 63, 10, 215, xxxiii.

27. *PJMon*, 4:412.

28. *PJMon*, 4:404.

29. *PJMon*, 4:421.

30. Schwarz, 81.

31. "Account of Richmond trials," September 18, 1800, http://founders.archives.gov /documents/Jefferson/01-32-02-0109.

32. *PJMon*, 4:420.

33. *PJMon*, 4:423.

34. Egerton, 108–11.

35. Schwarz, xxx–xxxii.

36. Schwarz, 54.

37. Schwarz, 64–65.

38. US census figures for 1800.

39. See Schwarz, 97, for one of many examples of the use of this phrase.

40. Rousey, 21.

41. Letter, Thomas Jefferson to Rufus King, July 13, 1802, *PTJ*, 38:54.

Chapter 26: The Terrible Republic

1. Jenson, 89.

2. Quoted in Henriques, 122.

3. Quoted in Beard, 375.

4. Letter, Thomas Jefferson to Spencer Roane, September 6, 1819, http://www .loc.gov/exhibits/jefferson/137.html.

5. Jefferson 1788, 175.

6. *DHRC*, 10:1272.

7. Letter, Thomas Jefferson to James Monroe, May 29, 1801. *PJMon* 4:516.

8. Drescher, 31.

9. Letter, Thomas Jefferson to James Monroe, *PTJ*, 35:720.

10. Letter, Thomas Jefferson to Aaron Burr, 31:22.

11. Quoted in DeConde, 323.

12. Letter, Bonaparte to Talleyrand, November 13, 1801, *CN*, 7:320.

13. Letter, Rufus King to James Madison, June 1, 1801, *State papers and correspondence bearing upon the purchase of the territory of Louisiana*.

14. Lacroix, 2:59–60.

15. Letter, Robert Livingston to Rufus King, *State papers and correspondence bearing upon the purchase of the territory of Louisiana*, 10.

16. Letter, Bonaparte to Denis Decrès, June 4, 1802, *CN*, 7:485.

17. Ferrer, 60–72.

18. Ford, Lacy K. 2009, 85–91.

19. Quoted in Stoddard, 342.

20. See "Canine Warfare in the Circum-Caribbean" in Johnson, Sara E., 21–48; also Ferrer, 159.

21. Letter, Thomas Jefferson to James Monroe, January 10, 1803, *PTJ*, 39:306.

22. Letter, Thomas Jefferson to James Monroe, January 13, 1803, *PTJ*, 39:328.

23. Quoted in Ford, Lacy K. 2009, 97.

24. *AC*, November 14, 1803.

25. Letter, Thomas Jefferson to William Henry Harrison, February 27, 1803, *PTJ*, 39:590–91.

26. Letter, Thomas Jefferson to Thomas Mann Randolph, June 8, 1803, *PTJ*, 40:505.

27. Letter, Thomas Jefferson to John Breckinridge, November 24, 1803, *WTJ*, 10:52.

28. Shugerman, 274.

29. Quoted in Scanlon, 152–53.

30. Scanlon, 153.

31. See Dayan, 30ff.

32. Claiborne, 2:10.

33. Claiborne, 2:25.

34. Claiborne, 2:184.

35. Claiborne, 2:245

36. *AC*, 9th Cong., 1st Sess., 515.

37. Alexander, William T., 180–81.

Chapter 27: I Do Not Threaten the Government with Civil War

1. Claiborne, 3:363.

2. Shugerman, 8.

3. Shugerman, 15.

4. Ford, Lacy K. 2009, 97.

5. Thomas, E.S., 35–36.

6. Claiborne, 3:96.

7. Queried from *The Trans-Atlantic Slave Trade Database*, www.slavevoyages.org/tast/database/search.faces.

8. McMillin, 48.

9. Ford, Lacy K. 2009, 121.

10. Shugerman, 282.

11. *AC*, H of R, 9th, 1st, 472.

12. *DIST*, 4:513.

13. Shugerman, 19.

14. Quoted in Sellers, 219.

15. *DIST*, 4:516.

16. *DIST*, 4:525.

17. Table appears in Brooke, 234.

18. Said, 793.

19. Lambert, 2:406.

20. *Charleston Courier*, Nov. 22, 1805.

21. Wilentz 2004.

22. *AC*, H of R, 9th, 2d, , 238–9.

23. *AC*, H of R, 9th, 2d, 477–478.

24. *AC*, H of R, 9th, 2d, 626.

25. The surviving inward bound manifests from the Port of New Orleans are in record group 36 of the National Archives in Washington, and they have also been digitized by ancestry.com.

26. Lambert, 2:406.

27. McMillin, 114.

28. McMillin, 113.

29. Dusinberre, 124.

Chapter 28: These Infernal Principles

1. Schultz, 2:133–4.

2. Adams, Henry 1889/1986, 984.

3. Adams, Henry 1889/1986, 978–9.

4. Adams, Henry 1889/1986, 973.

5. Adams, Henry 1889/1986, 973.

6. Quoted in *Richmond Courier*, December 29, 1807.

7. Lambert, 2:158

8. Adams, Henry 1889/1986, 1:1121.

9. *Moniteur de la Louisiane,* January 18, 1810.

10. Schultz, 2:137–38.

11. *AC*, Senate, 11th, 2d, 579–80.

12. *AC*, Senate, 11th, 3d, 63–64.

13. *AC*, 12th, H of R, 1st, 450–51.

14. Martineau, 1:244.

15. Rogers 1962, 394.

16. Calhoun, 2:8.

17. Article I, Sections 8, 10.

18. Temin, 29.

19. Stagg, 2.

20. Dudley, 2:308.

Chapter 29: The Hireling and Slave

1. Woodmason, 14.

2. Woodmason, 101–02.

3. Woodmason, 27.

4. Quoted in Sydnor 1938, 15.

5. Remini 1977, 55.

6. *PAJ* 1:15.

7. Remini 1977, 56.

8. Capers, 26–28.

9. Quoted in Keating, 173.

10. Capers, 31.

11. Letter, W.C.C. Claiborne to Andrew Jackson,, Dec. 9, 1801. *PAJ*, 1:261.

12. Letter, W.C.C. Claiborne to Andrew Jackson, Dec. 23, 1801. *PAJ*, 1:265.

13. Remini 1977:378.

14. *PAJ*, 2:41.

15. Letter, Andrew Jackson to Thomas Eastin, c. June 1806. *PAJ*, 2:106; Remini 1981, 1.

16. Letter, Donelson Caffery to Andrew Jackson, May 20, 1810, *PAJ*, 2:246.

17. Letter, Joseph Anderson to Andrew Jackson, December 3, 1795. *CAJ*, 1:18

18. Letter, Andrew Jackson to William Berkeley Lewis, August 5, 1828. *PAJ,* 6:486–87.

19. *PAJ,* 2:261–62, 286–290.

20. Letter, Andrew Jackson to Rachel Jackson, December 17, 1811. *PAJ,* 2:273.

21. Letter, Andrew Jackson to Willie Blount, Jan. 25, 1812, *PAJ,* 2:277–79.

22. Letter, Andrew Jackson to "an Arbitrator," Feb. 29, 1812, *PAJ,* 2:286–89.

23. Letter, Andrew Jackson to Mary Caffery, February 8, 1812, *PAJ* 2:281–82.

24. Remini 1977, 191–92.

25. Letter, Andrew Jackson to Willie Blount, *CAJ*, 1:416.

26. Adams, Henry 1889/1986a, 886–87.

27. Letter, Andrew Jackson to David Holmes, April 18, 1814, *CAJ*, 1:504–05.

28. *Niles' Weekly Register*, June 11, 1814.

29. Owsley, 130.

30. Bell, Malcolm, 182.

31. Manakee, 35.

32. *MJQA*, 8:188.

33. Letter, James Monroe to Andrew Jackson, October 21, 1814, *PAJ*, 3:171.

34. Letter, Andrew Jackson to James Monroe, October 26, 1814, *PAJ*, 3:173.

35. Letter, Andrew Jackson to James Monroe, November 20, 1814, *PAJ* 3:191.

36. Warshauer, 2.

37. Haynes, 234.

38. Letter, William Crawford to AJ, March 15, 1816. *PAJ*, 4:15–16.

39. Letter, Edmund P. Gaines to AJ, May 14, 1816. *PAJ*, 4:31.

40. *PAJ*, 4:15.

Chapter 30: A Jog of the Elbow

1. Quoted in Simpson, 65.

2. *MJQA*, 9:41.

3. Martineau, 1:192.

4. Kilbourne 2006, 12.

5. Chapelle, 108.

6. Chapelle, 111.

7. For a discussion of this balance in the Jacksonian era, see Green, George D.

8. Bodenhorn, 169.

9. Quoted in Simpson, 65.

10. See Bodenhorn, 169–177.

11. Calderhead, 198.

12. Gigantino, 281–296.

13. *Niles' Weekly Register,* Dec. 26, 1818, 313.

14. *Niles' Weekly Register,* Dec. 19, 1818, 311.

15. Letter, Andrew Jackson to James Monroe, June 2, 1818. *PAJ* 4:215.

16. Fortune, 260–66.

17. *Gales & Seaton's Register of Debates in Congress* (1829), 3:12.

18. *FBC,* Box 85, IV:i, 44.

19. Letter, Thomas Jefferson to John Holmes, April 22, 1820. *MCMTJ,* 4:324.

20. *American Cotton Planter,* 1:10, 295, October 1857.

21. Letter, Thomas Jefferson to Joel Yancey, January 17, 1819. Jefferson 1953, 43.

22. FWP, Alabama narratives, 1:222.

23. Morris, 70.

24. Letter, Thomas Jefferson to John Wayles Eppes, Jne 30, 1820. http://founders.archives.gov/documents/Jefferson/98-01-02-1352

25. Letter, Thomas Jefferson to Mary Jefferson Eppes, December 26, 1803. Rayner, 295.

26. Jacques.

27. Rasmussen and Tilton, 70.

28. Rudolph, 157.

29. "Family histories: a beginning" www.monticello.org/site/plantation-and-slavery/family-histories-beginning.

30. Lislet, 2:394–406.

31. Baptist 2014, 248.

32. Neu, 550.

33. An account from the Jacksonian perspective is Remini 1981, 94–99.

34. *MJQA,* 8:546.

35. Miles 1960, 17.

Chapter 31: Swallowed by Millions

1. Sheffield *Mercury,* Sept. 12, 1846.http://docsouth.unc.edu/neh/douglass/support5.html.

2. Albion, 9.

3. Albion, 11.

4. Rockman, 7.

5. Douglass 1855, 310–11.

6. Quoted in Clayton 2002, 44.

7. Clayton 2002, 45.

8. Clayton 2002, 59.

9. Calderhead, 197.

10. Calderhead, 198.

11. Thompson, John, 14.

12. Clayton 2002, 29.

13. *FBC,* Box 85, I:iv, 10.

14. "Flight to Freedom."

15. Clayton, 62.

16. Calderhead, 200.

17. Calderhead, 198.

18. Douglass 1845, 10.

19. Clayton 2002, 44.

20. Quoted in Sydnor 1966, 151.

21. Douglass 2000, 198.

22. *cf.* Freudenberger and Pritchett, 470–73.

23. Komlos and Alecke, 449.

24. Schafer 1997, 165–66.

25. Rockman, 39.

26. Clayton 1998.

27. Lundy, 15.

28. Wilson, Henry, 1:170.

29. *Genius of Universal Emancipation,* Jan. 2, 1827.

30. Lundy, 29; *Genius of Universal Emancipation,* Jan. 20, 1827.

31. "Law case." (1827.) *Niles' Register,* 32:206. May 19.

32. *LWLG,* 1:92.

33. *LWLG,* 1:93–94.

34. Bancroft 1900, 1:68.

35. Quoted in Kilbourne 2006, vi.

36. *MJQA,* 8:365.

37. Lightner, 90.

38. The article disputing the conspiracy's existence of the conspiracy is Johnson, Michael P.; for a rebuttal, see Paquette and Egerton.

39. Egerton 1999, 16–20.

40. Egerton 1999, 73–74.

41. Egerton 1999, 118–20.

42. *City Gazette and Daily Commercial Advertiser,* Charleston, August 21, 1822.

43. Quoted in Wesley, 163.

44. For a biography of Walker, see Hinks.

45. Walker, 18–19.

46. Walker, 71.

47. Quoted in Deyle 2005, 54.

48. Calderhead, 207n.

49. Quoted in Stowe 1853, 363.

50. *MJQA*, 9:23.

51. *FBC*, Box 85, I:iv, 2.

52. Dew, 50–51.

Chapter 32: Democratizing Capital

1. Currier, 311.

2. Miles 1960, 118.

3. Wilentz 2005, 198 *et passim*.

4. Baldwin, 82.

5. *MJQA*, 6:317.

6. Kilbourne 2006, 109.

7. Kilbourne 2006, 28.

8. Quoted in Kilbourne 2006, 47.

9. Quoted in *Sound Currency,* 232.

10. Letter, Nicholas Biddle to Joseph Hopkinson, February 21, 1834. McGrane, 222.

11. President Jackson's veto message. (1832). http://avalon.law.yale.edu/19th_century /ajveto01.asp.

12. Quoted in Miles 1960, 61.

13. Poore, 81.

14. January 22, 1833. *Gales & Seaton's register of debates in Congress,* 1205.

15. Sinha, 19.

16. Davis, William C., 17.

17. Wilentz 2005, 375.

18. Sinha, 44.

19. Van Buren, 542.

20. Van Buren, 544.

21. January 22, 1833. *Gales & Seaton's register of debates in Congress,* 1194.

22. Letter, Andrew Jackson to Rev. Andrew J. Crawford, *CAJ,* 5:72.

23. Van Buren, 625.

24. *CJKP,* 1:575.

25. *MJQA,* 8:434.

26. *MJQA,* 9:93.

27. *MJQA,* 9:93.

28. Letter, Jourdan M. Sanders to David Burford, September 28, 1833, *DBP.*

29. Miles 1960, 74.

30. *CSS* 1536; Hills, 117.

31. Roberts, 27.

32. Baldwin, 82–89.

33. Temin, 22, 80–88.

34. Marx, Karl. "Free trade and monopoly," *New York Daily Tribune,* September 25, 1858.

35. Marx, Karl. "Trade or opium?" *New York Daily Tribune,* September 20, 1858.

36. Roberts, Alasdair, 31.

37. Knodell, 542.

38. Kilbourne 2006, 59.

39. Roberts, Alasdair, 36.

40. Kilbourne 2006, 109.

41. Roberts, Alasdair, 10–11.

42. Bourne, Edward G., 17.

43. Bourne, Edward G., 14n.

44. Martin, Bonnie, 819.

45. Martin, Bonnie, 846.

46. Martin, Bonnie, 821–822.

47. Wilberforce, 22.

48. Sydnor 1938, 95.

49. Evans, 199; Phillips, 266.

50. Dusinberre, 6.

51. *DeBow's Review,* 3:5, May 1847.

52. Lyell, 1:147.

Chapter 33: Old Robbers

1. Andrews, E.A., 135–138.

2. Andrews, E.A., 142–43.

3. Quoted in *The Friend* 2:164.

4. Yagyu, 131–35.

5. 2 Stat. 755. See also, *Fenwick v. Tooker,* Circuit Court, District of Columbia, 4 Cranch, O. C. 641, Nov. term 1835.

6. Laprade, 31.

7. Stephenson, 15, 22.

8. Stephenson, 23; Yagyu, 141.

9. Stephenson, 23.

10. *The Friend,* 2:162.

11. Northup, 41–47, 75–78.

12. *The Friend,* 2:163.

13. Featherstonhaugh, 1:120.

14. Featherstonhaugh, 1:166–70.

15. Quoted in Stephenson, 70.

16. Hammond, 15.

17. Quoted in Jay, 157–58.

18. *FBC*, Box 88, 179A.

19. Stephenson, 40–42.

20. Gudmestad, 32.

21. Clayton, 83, 87, 98.

22. *FBC*, Box 88, XIV, B6.

23. Rothert, 433.

24. Stephenson, 76.

25. Kiple and King, 148.

26. Quoted in Yagyu, 105.

27. Letter, Isaac Franklin to Rice C. Ballard, December 8, 1832, *RCBP*.

28. Letters, James R. Franklin to Rice C. Ballard, April 24, May 7, 1833, *RCBP*.

29. Letter, James R. Franklin to Rice C. Ballard, Feb. 2, 1834, *RCBP*.

30. Letter, Jourdan M. Saunders to David Burford, April 3, 1832, *DBP*.

31. Letter, Isaac Franklin to Rice C. Ballard, Jan. 9, 1832, *RCBP*.

32. Letter, Isaac Franklin to Rice C. Ballard, Nov. 21, 1833, *RCBP*.

33. Letter, James R. Franklin to Rice C. Ballard, April 16, 1834, *RCBP*.

34. Johnson 2000, 17.

35. *New Orleans As It Is*, 43–44.

36. Kilbourne 2006, 17, 30.

37. *North Carolina v. Mann*, 13 N.C. 263

38. Stephenson, 65.

39. See *New Orleans As It Is*, 44; Schafer 2009 3.

40. For an extended treatment of these letters, see Baptist 2005.

41. Letter, Isaac Franklin to Rice C. Ballard, January 11, 1834.

42. *SIF*, 272, 282.

43. Stephenson, 92.

44. Ingraham 1835,

45. *SIF*, 299.

46. Warden. There are various versions, more or less similar, of this story and quote.

47. See Kilbourne 1995, 18–25.

48. *SIF*, 280.

49. Kilbourne 2006, 1.

50. Stephenson, 131–146.

51. Quoted in Stephenson, 152.

Chapter 34: Wake Up Rich

1. Miles 1960, 124.

2. Miles 1957, 48–58.

3. *MJQA*, 9:257.

4. Quoted in Gatell, 194.

5. Quoted in Miles 1957, 57.

6. Quoted in Finkelman 2007, 46.

7. Seward, 271.

8. Wallner, 28.

9. Douglass 1855, 445.

10. Fehrenbacher, 116.

11. Quoted in Miles 1960, 123.

12. comparison of US Census figures, 1830 and 1840.

13. Davis, William C., 4.

14. Davis, William C., 88, 671.

15. Davis, William C., 189.

16. Davis, William C., 165.

17. Davis, William C., 20.

18. Davis, William C., 75.

19. *MJQA*, 9:386.

20. *Appendix to the Congressional Globe,* 25th Cong., 2d Sess., 507.

21. *MJQA*, 9:417–18.

22. *MJQA*, 9:425.

23. *MJQA*, 9:427–28.

24. *MJQA*, 9:429.

25. *MJQA*, 9:455.

26. Long, 84.

27. "Suspension of specie payments." (1839). *The New-Yorker*, 8:5, 76, October 19. The attribution to Biddle is by publisher Horace Greeley.

28. Parton, 3:626.

29. Quoted in Miller, Edward L., 6.

30. *CJKP*, 1:472.

31. Lepler, 108ff.

32. Quoted in Albert, 105.

33. *FBC*, Box 85, I:iv.

34. Buckingham, 1:334–35.

35. Miller, Edward L., 72.

36. Quoted in Miller, Edward L., 32.

37. *MJQA*, 9:332.

38. Miles 1960, 140.

39. *MJQA*, 10:19.

40. Kilbourne 2006, 109.

41. *PJD*, 2:46n.

42. *PJD*, 2:42n.

43. Miles 1960, 149.

44. Roberts, Alasdair, 51.

45. *WSH*, 3:10.

46. Adams, Henry Carter, 395.

Chapter 35: The Slave Trade to Cuba and Brazil

1. *Public documents* 1841, 135. (26th Cong., 2d sess.)

2. Morgan, Kenneth 2007, 191–92

3. *The Legacies of British Slave-ownership* website databases information given in slaveowners' claims for compensation. www.ucl.ac.uk/lbs.

4. British Parliamentary Papers, *Correspondence relative to the slave trade*, 28:4.

5. *CBC* 1834, 2.

6. *CBC* 1839, 276.

7. Thomas, Hugh, 642.

8. Klein and Vinson, 87.

9. Letter, N.P. Trist to John Forsyth, 23 May 1839, Despatches from US Consuls in Havana, Cuba, 1783–1906, Record Group 59, National Archives, College Park, MD. Thanks to James Shinn.

10. *CBC* 1839, 275.

11. *The New-Yorker*, 8:5, 75, October 19, 1839.

12. *MJQA*, 10:440.

13. *CBC* 1839, 272–73.

14. *Message from the President of the United States*, 193.

15. *Public documents Printed by Order of the Senate* (1841), 171.

16. See Sublette 2004, 129.

17. *AP* 1839, 20:103.

18. *Message from the President of the United States*, 189.

19. *Message from the President of the United States*, 188–89.

20. Thomas, Hugh, 642.

21. *WSH*, 1:510–511.

22. *Message from the President of the United States*, 185–86.

23. *Message from the President of the United States*, 133.

24. *Message from the President of the United States*, 133–34.

25. Adams, John Quincy 1841.

26. Bleser, 32.

Chapter 36: Heaps and Piles of Money

1. Kemble, 219.

2. For an extended account, see Clinton.

3. Kemble, 122, 60.

4. Kemble, 218.

5. Kemble, 219.

6. Kemble, 183.

7. For more on antebellum divorce, see Goodheart 2011.

8. Butler, 9.

9. Butler, 13.

10. Kemble, 200.

11. Northup, 61, 85–88.

12. *TAS*, 18:253.

13. Kilbourne 2006, 108–09.

14. Kilbourne 2006, 127.

15. Kilbourne 2006, 137.

16. Kilbourne 2006, 138–39.

17. Kilbourne 2006, 134.

Chapter 37: The Slave Power

1. For more on Polk as slaveowner, see Dusinberre.

2. Bordewich, 281.

3. Letter, Herbert Biles to James K. Polk, November 23, 1832, *CJKP*, 1:529–30.

4. Letter, Silas M. Caldwell to James K. Polk, Jan. 4, 1834, *CJKP*, 2:219.

5. Letter, James Walker to James K. Polk, February 14, 1834, *CJKP*, 2:315.

6. Letter, James K. Polk to Sarah Childress Polk, Sep. 26–27, 1834, *CJKP*, 2:508–09.

7. Letter, Ephraim Beanland to James K. Polk, Oct. 4, 1834, *CJKP*, 2:514.

8. Letter, James Walker to James K. Polk, Oct. 15, 1839, *CJKP*, 5:261–62.

9. *SIF*, 296, 359, 360.

10. *Congressional Globe*, 25th Cong., 3d. sess., 167–68.

11. Baptist 2014, 135n *et passim*.

12. *MJQA*, 10:556.

13. *MJQA*, 11:382.

14. *MJQA*, 12:13–14.

15. Quoted in Sinha, 65.

16. Quoted in Stahr, 96.

17. Hughes, 13.

18. Foner, Eric, 91.

19. www.tsl.texas.gov/ref/abouttx/annexation /march1845.html.

20. Grant, 40–41.

21. Sachar, 72.

22. Olmsted 1861, 51.

23. Rosen, 34.

24. See Diner, 86–108.

25. Rosen, 17.

26. Chapman, 1, 5–12.

27. Scott, Edwin J., 82.

28. Korn, 41.

29. Stowe 1853, 151.

30. Kilbourne 1995, 3.

31. Chapman, 23.

32. *TAS*, 18:301.

Chapter 38: Manifest Destiny's Child

1. Letter, John W. Childress to James K. Polk, July 22, 1846, *CJKP*, 11:251.

2. Dusinberre, 53.

3. In the July–August 1845 issue of the *United States Democratic Journal*.

4. Quoted in Foner, Eric, 116.

5. Quoted in Dusinberre, 17; not included in *CJKP*.

6. Letter, James K. Polk to John Catron, Oct. 7, 1846. *CJKP*, 11:345.

7. Letter, Robert Campbell, Jr. to James K. Polk, Oct. 9, 1846. *CJKP*, 11:345

8. Stephenson, 116.

9. *SIF*, 482, 549.

10. *DeBow's Review* (1857), 22:4, 439.

11. In the film *Bayou Maharajah*, dir. Lily Keber.

12. For more about Fairvue, there is a "Historical Fireside Chat" video with area historians at www.fairvueplantation.com /history.php.

13. Polk, 4:429.

14. Polk, 4:408, 393.

15. Polk, 4:439.

16. Dusinberre, 79.

17. Quoted in Montejano, 28.

18. Freudenberger and Pritchett, 476.

19. Clayton 2002, 77.

20. Quoted in Clayton 2002, 77; *Reports and cases argued and determined . . .*, 140.

21. *Reports and cases argued and determined . . .*, 140–47.

Chapter 39: A Letter from Virginia

1. Drago, 61.

2. Warden, 8.

3. *Southern Business Directory* (1854), 163.

4. Yagyu, 334–35.

5. Yagyu, 343.

6. Letter, C.M. Rutherford to Rice C. Ballard, April 19, 1853, *RCBP*.

7. Letter, Virginia Boyd to Rice C. Ballard, May 6, 1853, *RCBP*.

8. http://www2.lib.unc.edu/mss/inv/b /Ballard,Rice_C.html#folder_191#1.

9. Letter, C.M. Rutherford to Rice C. Ballard, Dec. 14, 1853, *RCBP*.

10. Bleser, 19.

11. Bleser, 101.

Chapter 40: Communists in Blackface

1. Quoted in Sinha, 102.

2. Roske 1968, 243–45.

3. *Put's Original California Songster*, 7–8.

4. Based on Roske 1963, 211.

5. Roske 1963, 210.

6. Richards, 67–68.

7. Quoted in Richards, 76.

8. *Appendix to the Congressional Globe*, 31st Cong., 1st sess., 1409.

9. *The Address of the Southern Delegates*, 13–14.

10. *North Star*, February 9, 1849.

11. Quoted in Bordewich, 203.

12. Davis, William C., 308

13. Quoted in Sellers, Charles G., 2:24.

14. See Richards, 72–76.

15. Ford, Lacy K. 1988, 38–39.

16. *FBC*, Box 88, p. 11.

17. Keehn, 10–12.

18. Davis, William C., 273.

19. Sioussat, 329n.

20. Sioussat, 330.

21. Quoted in Sioussat, 321.

22. *Appendix to the Congressional Globe*, 31st Cong., 1st Sess., 1067.

23. Bauer, K. Jack, 314–15, 319–20; Zachary Taylor Partition of Heirs. Historic New Orleans Collection, MSS 137.

24. Webster, 43.

25. Bordewich, 309.

26. Sioussat, 302.

27. Cheves, 26.

28. Cheves, 30.

29. Quoted in Sinha, 211.

30. Skipper, 24–25.

31. Foster, Stephen.

32. Hanby, B.R.

33. Stevens, 44.

34. Stevens, 188–93.

35. Stevens, 216n.

36. Hurst, 36.

37. Quoted in Hurst, 38.

38. Ashdown and Caudill, 65.

Chapter 41: Hiring Day

1. Clarke.

2. Jacobs, 26.

3. *TAS*, 18:162.

4. Olmsted 1861a, 1:117.

5. Bancroft 1931/1996, 145–46.

6. Bancroft 1931/1996, 95.

7. Zaborney, 145.

8. Abbott, 100ff.

9. Laird, 5.

10. Corey, 47–48.

11. Corey, 48–50.

12. Craddock, 23–24.

13. Olmsted 1861a, 1:51–52.

14. Bancroft 1931/1996, 153.

15. *FBC*, Box 88, A183.

16. Quoted in Zaborney, 94.

17. Zaborney, 123.

18. Southall, 167.

19. Hughes, 78.

20. O'Connell, 113.

Chapter 42: Vanish Like a Dream

1. *Sketches of the lives . . .* , 36.

2. *MJQA*, 12:25.

3. Baker, 25.

4. Watson, Robert P., 248.

5. Polk, 1:297.

6. Merry, 100–01.

7. Letter, Edmund Burke to Franklin Pierce, June 6, 1852, quoted in Pierce, 114.

8. Hawthorne, 416–17.

9. Olmsted 1861, 58.

10. Olmsted 1861, 58.

11. Letter, James Gadsden to Thomas Jefferson Green, quoted in Parish and Gadsden, 174–75.

12. "Nicaragua." (1857). *DeBow's review, agricultural, commercial, industrial progress and resources*, 22:1, January, 105–09.

13. "Notes on Cuba." (1859). *Harper's Weekly*, Jan. 29, 72–73.

14. Buchanan.

15. See Finkelman 2013 for a narrative of the events surrounding Buchanan and *Dred Scott*.

16. Douglass 1857, 32.

17. Fitzhugh, George, 341–42, 368.

18. Fitzhugh, George, 278.
19. Genovese 1969/88, 129–30.
20. Olmsted 1861a, 1:140.

Chapter 43: A Snake Biting Its Tail

1. Quoted in *FBC*, Box 88, 109D.
2. Foner, Philip, 146.
3. Spratt, 487–88.
4. DuBois, W.E.B. 1904, 174.
5. See Satz, 270.
6. Lincoln, 132.
7. Quoted in *FBC*, Box 88, 26.
8. Fehrenbacher, 179.
9. See Graham, 291–324, Slenes, 325–70.
10. "Slave Trade in New York." (1855). *Debow's Review.* (1855). 18:2, 225–6.
11. *CBC* 1860, 11–12.
12. *CBC* 1860, 8.
13. Dubois, W.E.B. 1904, 308–316.
14. *CBC* 1860, 8.
15. *CBC* 1860, 13.
16. *CBC* 1860, 45.
17. Davis, Robert Ralph 1971, 273.
18. Davis, Robert Ralph 1971, 276.
19. Foner, Philip, 293–94.
20. Hurst, 330.
21. Sheehy et al., 144–46.
22. Sheehy et al., 146–47.
23. Quoted in Davis, Robert Ralph 1971, 275–7.
24. Sheehy et al., 164; DeGraft-Hansen.
25. Thomson, 5.
26. Thomson, 9.
27. Thomson, 11.
28. Clinton, 160–62.
29. Keehn is the source for all material in this volume about the KGC. Keehn, 32–45.
30. Zaborney, 7.
31. *FBC*, Box 88, p. 24.
32. Lee.
33. See Keehn, 1–2.
34. Diouf, 55. For more about the orisha religion in Cuba, see Sublette 2004, 206–234.

35. Diouf, 6, 55, 30–39.
36. Diouf, 151–52.
37. Diouf, 14.
38. Diouf, 48–49; Hurston, 655.

Chapter 44: Assignment in Paraguay

1. Behlolavek, 114.
2. Flaherty, 252.
3. Baker, 79.
4. Cobb, 15.
5. "Cotton Planters' Convention," *American Cotton Planter II*, 11:330, 1858.
6. Adams, Henry 2012, 15.
7. Flaherty, 268.
8. MacKinnon, 73.
9. See Foner, Philip, 306–11.
10. Sinha, 234–35; Keehn, 77–88.
11. Adams, Henry 2012, 16.
12. Quoted in Dew, Charles B., 27.
13. Dew, Charles B., 32.
14. Davis, William C., xiv.
15. Quoted in Dew, Charles B., 41.
16. Quoted in Dew, Charles B., 98.
17. Quoted in Dew, Charles B., 92.
18. Wilson, Joseph Ruggles, 3.
19. Wilson, Joseph Ruggles, 4, 5, 16, 21.
20. McPherson, 29.
21. *PJD*, 7:21.
22. Shackleford, 3.
23. *PUSG* 2:194–95.
24. Conway, 22.
25. Keckley, 70–72.
26. Quoted in Marcus 1955, 2:300.

Chapter 45: The Decommissioning of Human Capital

1. Quoted in Hammond, 188.
2. *TAS*, 18:208.
3. Mitchell, Wesley Clair, 82n.
4. Hammond, 23.
5. Hammond, 250–52.
6. Mitchell, Wesley Clair, 100–118.
7. Hammond, 170, 244ff, 355.
8. Hammond, 1970, 307.

9. Hammond, 360.

10. Matthews, 77–79.

11. For more about the Republic of Jones, see Bynum.

12. Carpenter, 20, 77; see also Masur.

13. *JDC*, 5:409.

14. See Bodenhorn, 231–33.

15. Cf. http://belmontmansion.com/mansion history; Lessing, 29–35.

16. Marcus 1955, 2:55.

17. Marcus 1955, 2:56.

18. Marcus 1955, 2:305.

19. Rosen, 270; Marcus 1955, 2:299.

20. Anbinder, 121.

21. Rosen, 431–32n.

Chapter 46: A Weird, Plaintive Wail

1. *New York Times*, December 26, 1864.

2. *FWP*, Virginia narratives, 17:42.

3. Unwin.

4. Burkhardt, 8.

5. Quoted in Burkhardt, 39.

6. Some pro-Confederate historians subsequently denied that a massacre happened at Fort Pillow. For a discussion by a historian who reluctantly concluded that there was a racially motivated massacre, see Castel, 89–103.

7. *New York Tribune*, April 18, 1864.

8. *New York Times*, October 30, 1877.

9. Reprinted in *Sacramento Daily Union*, 10 July 1865.

10. Slotkin.

11. Burkhardt, 147.

12. Burkhardt, 148, 231.

13. See Trudeau; see also Groce.

14. Trudeau, 162.

15. Foreman, 706.

16. Foreman, 724.

17. Sheehy et al., 128, 131.

18. Byrne, 91.

19. Sheehy et al., 130; Byrne, 99–100.

20. Roberts and Kytle.

21. Foreman, 753.

22. Coffin, 501–02.

23. This account comes from Coffin, 499ff.

24. www.in.ng.mil/AboutUs/History/Hoosier CivilWarStoriesMajGarlandWhite/tabid /1514/Default.aspx.

25. Keckley, 164–66.

26. See Stewart, 8–12.

27. Treasure, 97.

28. *PJD*, 11:581n.

29. See Sutherland.

30. For an extended treatment of Sims's bizarre career, see Barker-Benfield, 85–111; see also Goodson, 229–231; "Memorial Sloan-Kettering Cancer Center."

31. Marcus 1955 2:301.

32. Rosen, 371.

33. Chapman, 29, 23–24, 33–34.

34. Warden, 9–10.

35. Toombs et al, 684.

36. Casimir, 110–20; Casimir and Dubois.

37. Davis, Jefferson, 78–9.

38. Craddock, 26.

39. Craddock, 27.

40. Craddock, 41.

41. Craddock, 1.

42. Yellin, 63–64, 143–44, 162, 176–80, 245–47.

43. Fleischner, 323.

44. Quoted in Fellman, 452n.

45. Simkins, 607.

46. Hurst, 360.

47. Hurst, 370–1.

48. Armstrong, 875.

49. "Revised Report, Plan for Government of the Western Territory." *PTJ*, 6:607–09.

Coda

1. www.youtube.com/watch?v=j8d-IYSM-08.

2. Elk and Sloan.

3. Coates.

4. "Hate and Extremism."

5. Fletcher.

6. The term "neoslavery" was suggested by Douglas Blackmon, in *Slavery By Another Name*.

References

Pre-twentieth-century newspaper and magazine articles are cited in the relevant footnotes. Long titles of pre-twentieth-century books have been truncated. All internet links were current as of August 2015.

ABBREVIATIONS

AC   *Annals of Congress*, Washington.

AFL   *Adams Family Correspondence*, Belknap Press.

AJL   *The Adams-Jefferson letters*, UNC Press, Chapel Hill.

AP   *Accounts and Papers of the House of Commons*, London.

CAJ   *Correspondence of Andrew Jackson*, Carnegie Institution of Washington.

CBC   *Correspondence with the British Commissioners*, Harrison and Sons, London.

CJKP   *Correspondence of James K. Polk*, Vanderbilt University Press, Nashville.

CN   *Correspondance de Napoléon Ier.* Plon and Dumaine, Paris.

CRG   *Colonial Records of Georgia*, Chas. P. Byrd, Atlanta.

CSS   *Congressional Serial Set* (1911), US Govt. Printing Office, Washington DC.

DHRC   *Documentary History of the Ratification of the Constitution*, State Historical Society of Wisconsin, Madison.

DIST   Donnan, Elizabeth. *Documents Illustrative of the History of the Slave Trade to America*, v. 1–4. Carnegie Institution of Washington, Washington DC.

DPB   *David Burford Papers*, University of Tennessee.

FBC   Frederic Bancroft papers, Columbia University Library, New York.

FWP   Federal Writers Project Slave Narratives, Library of Congress *American Memory*. http://memory.loc.gov/ammem/snhtml.

HJFP   *Harriet Jacobs Family Papers*, ed. Jean Yellin, University of North Carolina Press.

JDC   *Jefferson Davis, Constitutionalist, His Letters, Papers, and Speeches.* Mississippi Department of Archives and History.

LDC   *Letters of Delegates to Congress, 1774–1789.* ed. Paul H. Smith, Library of Congress

LOC   *Library of Congress.*

LWLG	*Letters of William Lloyd Garrison,* Belknap Press.
MCMTJ	*Memoir, Correspondence, and Miscellanies from the Papers of Thomas Jefferson* (1830). Gray and Brown, Boston.
MJQA	*Memoirs of John Quincy Adams,* ed. Charles Francis Adams. J.B. Lippincott, Philadelphia.
NPTP	Nicholas Philip Trist papers, University of North Carolina Libraries.
PAH	*The Papers of Alexander Hamilton,* Columbia University Press, New York.
PAJ	*The Papers of Andrew Jackson,* University of Tennessee Press.
PBF	*The Papers of Benjamin Franklin.* Yale University Press, New Haven.
PGW	*The Papers of George Washington,* University Press of Virginia.
PHL	*The Papers of Henry Laurens,* University of South Carolina Press.
PJA	*The Papers of John Adams,* Belknap Press.
PJD	*The Papers of Jefferson Davis,* Louisiana State University Press, Baton Rouge.
PJMad	*The Papers of James Madison: Presidential Series,* University Press of Virginia.
PJMon	*The Papers of James Monroe,* Greenwood Press.
PTJ	*The Papers of Thomas Jefferson,* Princeton University Press, Princeton.
PTJRS	*The Papers of Thomas Jefferson: retirement series,* Princeton University Press, Princeton.
PUSG	*The Papers of Ulysses S. Grant,* Southern Illinois University Press, Carbondale.
RCBP	Rice C. Ballard papers, University of North Carolina libraries.
SAL	*United States Statutes at Large.*
SIF	*Succession of Isaac Franklin.* Louisiana Supreme Court, ca. 1851.
TAS	*The American Slave: A Composite Autobiography,* ed. George P. Rawick. Greenwood Publishing Company, Westport CT.
TRP	Thomas Ringgold papers, New York Public Library.
TWOTR	*The War of the Rebellion: A Compilation of the Official Records of the Union and Confederate Armies.* Government Printing Office, Washington.
WJA	*Works of John Adams,* Little, Brown, Boston.
WJM	*The Writings of James Madison,* Putnam's, New York, 1910.
WSH	*The Writings of Sam Houston,* University of Texas Press, Austin.
WTJ	*The Works of Thomas Jefferson,* Knickerbocker Press, New York.

Items marked with an asterisk (*) can be accessed via the *North American Slave Narratives* collection of the University Library of the University of North Carolina at Chapel Hill: http://docsouth.unc.edu/neh

Abbott, Lyman. (1915). *Reminiscences.* Houghton Mifflin, New York.

Adams, Catherine and Elizabeth H. Pleck. (2009). *Love of Freedom: Black Women in Colonial and Revolutionary New England.* Oxford University Press, Oxford.

Adams, Henry. (1889/1986). *History of the United States of America during the Administrations of Thomas Jefferson.* Library of America, New York.

———. (1889/1986a). *History of the United States of America during the Administrations of James Madison.* Library of America, New York.

————. (1883). *John Randolph.* Houghton, Mifflin, Boston.

————. (2012). *Henry Adams in the Secession Crisis.* Ed. Mark J. Stegmaier. Louisiana State University Press, Baton Rouge.

Adams, Henry Carter. (1887). *Public Debts: An Essay in the Science of Finance.* D. Appleton, New York.

Adams, John Quincy. (1841). *Argument of John Quincy Adams, Before the Supreme Court of the United States : in the Case of the United States, Appellants, vs. Cinque, and Others, Africans, Captured in the schooner Amistad, by Lieut. Gedney.* S.W. Benedict, New York. http://avalon.law.yale.edu/19th_century/amistad_002.asp

Adams, William Howard. (1997). *The Paris Years of Thomas Jefferson.* Yale University Press, New Haven.

The Address of the Southern Delegates in Congress, to Their Constituents. (1849). Tower, Washington.

Akam, Simon. (2013). "George W. Bush's great-great-great-great-grandfather was a slave trader." *Slate,* June 20. www.slate.com/articles/life/history_lesson/2013/06/george_w_bush_and_slavery_the_president_and_his_father_are_descendants_of.single.html.

Albert, Octavia V. Rogers. (1988). *The House of Bondage: or, Charlotte Brooks and other slaves.* Oxford University Press, New York.

Albion, Robert Greenhalgh. (1938). *Square-riggers on Schedule: The New York Sailing Packets to England, France, and the Cotton Ports.* Princeton University Press, Princeton.

Alexander, Adele Logan. (2010). *Parallel Worlds: The Remarkable Gibbs-Hunts and the Enduring (In)significance of Melanin.* University of Virginia Press, Charlottesville.

Alexander, Michelle. (2010). *The New Jim Crow: Mass Incarceration in the Age of Colorblindness.* The New Press, New York.

Alexander, William T. (1887). *History of the Colored Race in America.* Palmetto Publishing Company, Kansas City.

Allan, Christopher N. (1998). "Foreword to 'Supplement to early settlers.'" http://msa.maryland.gov/msa/speccol/sc4300/sc4341/html/foreword.html.

Altman, Ida. (1991). "Spanish society in Mexico after the conquest." *The Hispanic American Historical Review,* 71:3.

Ammon, Harry. (1973). *The Genet Mission.* W. W. Norton, New York.

Anbinder, Tyler. (1997). "Ulysses S. Grant, nativist." *Civil War History,* 43:2.

Anburey, Thomas. (1776–1783 / 1923). *Travels through the Interior Parts of America.* Houghton Mifflin, Boston.

Anderson, Adam. (1787). *An Historical and Chronological Deduction of the Origins of Commerce . . .* Logographic Press, London.

Anderson, Ralph V., and Robert E. Gallman. (1977). "Slaves as fixed capital: Slave labor and southern economic development." *Journal of American History,* 64:1.

Anderson, Richard G. (2003). "Some tables of historical U.S. currency and monetary aggregates data." The Federal Reserve Bank of St. Louis. http://research.stlouisfed.org/wp/2003/2003-006.pdf.

Anderson, Thornton. (1993). *Creating the Constitution: The Convention of 1787 and the First Congress.* Penn State Press, University Park, PA.

Andrews, E. A. (1836). *Slavery and the Domestic Slave Trade in the United States.* Boston, Light and Stearns.

Andrews, Kenneth R., ed. *English Privateering Voyages to the West Indies, 1588–1595.* University Press, Cambridge.

Aptheker, Herbert. (1943). *American Negro Slave Revolts.* Columbia University Press, New York.

Armitage, David. (2004). "John Locke, Carolina, and the 'Two Treatises of Government.'" *Political Theory,* 32:5.

Armstrong, Andrea C. (2012). "Slavery revisited in penal plantation labor." Seattle University Law Review, 35:3.

Artemel, Janice G., Elizabeth A. Crowell, and Jeff Parker. (1987). *The Alexandria Slave Pen: The Archeology of Urban Capitivity.* Engineering-Science Inc., Washington. http://alexandriava.gov/uploadedFiles/historic/info/archaeology/ARSiteReportAlexandria SlavePenAX75.pdf.

Ashdown, Paul, and Edward Caudill. (2005). *The Myth of Nathan Bedford Forrest.* Rowman & Littlefield, Lanham, MD.

Ashworth, John. (1995). *Slavery, Capitalism, and Politics in the Antebellum Republic; Vol. 1: Commerce and Compromise, 1820–1850.* Cambridge University Press, Cambridge.

Bailyn, Bernard. (1968). *The Origins of American Politics.* Alfred A. Knopf, New York.

———. (1986). *Voyagers to the West: A Passage in the Peopling of America on the Eve of the Revolution.* Vintage Books, New York.

Baine, Rodney M. (1988). "James Oglethorpe and the early promotional literature for Georgia." *William and Mary Quarterly,* Third Series, 45:1.

Baker, Jean H. (2004). *James Buchanan.* Henry Holt and Company, New York.

Baldwin, Joseph G. (1854). *The Flush Times of Alabama and Mississippi: A Series of Sketches.* D. Appleton, New York.

*Ball, Charles. (1859). *Fifty Years in Chains: Or, the Life of an American Slave.* H. Dayton, New York.

Bancroft, Frederic. (1900). *The Life of William Henry Seward.* Harper and Brothers, New York.

———. (1931/1996). *Slave Trading in the Old South.* University of South Carolina Press, Columbia.

"Banking on bondage: private prisons and mass incarceration." (2011). American Civil Liberties Union. www.aclu.org/files/assets/bankingonbondage_20111102.pdf.

Baptist, Edward E. (2014). *The Half Has Never Been Told: Slavery and the Making of American Capitalism.* Basic Books, New York.

———. (2004). "'Cuffy,' 'fancy maids,' and 'one-eyed men': Rape, commodification, and the domestic slave trade in the United States." In Walter Johnson, ed., *The Chattel Principle: Internal Slave Trades in the Americas,* Yale University Press, New Haven.

*Baquaqua, Mohammed Gardo. (1854). *Biography of Mahomma G. Baquaqua.* Geo. E. Pomeroy and Co., Detroit.

Barker, Gordon S. (2004). "Unraveling the strange history of Jefferson's 'Observations sur la Virginie.'" *Virginia Magazine of History and Biography,* 112:2.

Barker-Benfield, G. J. (2000). *The Horrors of the Half-Known Life: Male Attitudes Toward Women and Sexuality in Nineteenth-Century America.* Second edition. Routledge, New York.

Barnett, Jim, and H. Clark Burkett. (2003). "The Forks of the Road slave market at Natchez." *Mississippi History Now.* http://mshistorynow.mdah.state.ms.us/articles/47/the-forks-of-the-road-slave-market-at-natchez.

Bartels, Emily C. (2006). "Too many blackamoors: Deportation, discrimination, and Elizabeth I." *Studies in English literature 1500–1900,* 46:2.

Bassett, John Spencer. (1926). *Correspondence of Andrew Jackson.* Vol. 1. Carnegie Institution of Washington, Washington, DC.

Bauer, K. Jack. (1993). *Zachary Taylor: Soldier, Planter, Statesman of the Old Southwest.* Louisiana State University Press, Baton Rouge.

Bauer, Raymond A., and Alice H. Bauer (1942). "Day to day resistance to slavery," *The Journal of Negro History,* October.

Baur, John E. (1970). "International repercussions of the Haitian Revolution." *The Americas,* 26:4.

Beard, Charles Austin. (1915). *Economic Origins of Jeffersonian Democracy.* Macmillan, New York.

Beck, Carolyn S. (1988). "Our own vine and fig tree: The authority of history and kinship in Mother Bethel." *Review of Religious Research,* 29:4.

Beeman, Richard. (2009). *Plain, Honest Men: The Making of the American Constitution.* Random House, New York.

Behlolavek, John M. (2013). "In Defense of Doughface Diplomacy." In Quist, John W., and Michael J. Birkner, *James Buchanan and the Coming of the Civil War.* University Press of Florida, Gainesville.

Behrendt, Stephen D. (2007). "Human capital in the British slave trade." In Richardson, David, Suzanne Schwarz, and Anthony Tibbles, ed., *Liverpool and Transatlantic Slavery.* Liverpool University Press, Liverpool.

———. (1997). "Crew mortality in the transatlantic slave trade in the eighteenth century." *Slavery and Abolition,* 18:1.

Beirne, Rosamond Randall. *William Buckland 1734–1774: Architect of Virginia and Maryland.*

Bell, Jessica. "The three Marys: The Virgin; Marie de Médecis; and Henrietta Maria." In Griffey, Erin. (2008). *Henrietta Maria: Piety, Politics and Patronage.* Ashgate, Aldershot UK.

Bell, Malcolm Jr. (1987.) *Major Butler's Legacy: Five Generations of a Slaveholding Family.* University of Georgia Press, Athens.

Bennett, Charles E. (2001). *Laudonnière & Fort Caroline: History and Documents.* University of Alabama Press, Tuscaloosa.

———. (1982). *Florida's 'French' revolution, 1793–1795.* University Press of Florida, Gainesville.

Berinato, Scott. (2013). "Plantations practiced modern management." *Harvard Business Review,* 91:9.

Berkeley, Edmund, and Dorothy Smith Berkeley. (1969). *Dr. Alexander Garden of Charles Town*. University of North Carolina Press, Chapel Hill.

Berlin, Ira. (1998). *Many Thousands Gone: The First Two Centuries of Slavery in North America*. Harvard University Press, Cambridge.

Biggar, H. P. (1917). "Jean Ribaut's Discoverye of Terra Florida." *English Historical Review*, 32:126.

Blackmon, Douglas. (2008). *Slavery by Another Name: The Re-enslavement of Black Americans from the Civil War to World War II*. Doubleday, New York.

Blackstone, Sir William, *et al.* (1765). *Commentaries on the Laws of England*. Clarendon Press, Oxford.

Blake, John B. (1952). "The inoculation controversy in Boston: 1721–1722." *The New England Quarterly* 25:4.

Bleser, Carol. (1988). *Secret and Sacred: The Diaries of James Henry Hammond, a Southern Slaveholder*. Oxford University Press, New York.

Blumrosen, Alfred W., and Ruth G. Blumrosen. (2006). *Slave Nation: How Slavery United the Colonies and Sparked the American Revolution*. Sourcebooks, Naperville, IL.

Bodenhorn, Howard. (2000). *A History of Banking in Antebellum America : Financial Markets and Economic Development in an Era of Nation-Building*. Cambridge University Press, Cambridge.

Bogus, Carl T. (1998). "The Hidden History of the Second Amendment." *UC Davis Law Review*, 31.

Bordewich, Fergus M. (2012). *America's Great Debate : Henry Clay, Stephen A. Douglas, and the Compromise that Preserved the Union*. Simon & Schuster, New York.

Bosman, Willem (1705). *A New and Accurate Description of the Coast of Guinea, Divided Into the Gold, the Slave, and the Ivory Coasts*. J. Knapton, London.

Boswell, Samuel. (1904). *Life of Samuel Johnson*. Henry Frowde, London.

Bourne, Edward G. (1885). *The History of the Surplus Revenue of 1837*. G. P. Putnam's Sons, New York.

Bourne, Michael Owen. (1998). *Historic Houses of Kent County: An Architectural History: 1642–1860*. Historical Society of Kent County, Chestertown MD.

The Bowery Historic District. (2011). National Register of Historic Places Registration Form. www.nps.gov/history/nr/feature/places/pdfs/13000027.pdf.

Brady, Patrick S. (1972). "The slave trade and sectionalism in South Carolina, 1787–1808." *The Journal of Southern History*, 38:4.

Breen, T. H. (1977). "Horses and gentlemen: The cultural significance of gambling among the gentry of Virginia." *The William and Mary Quarterly*, Third Series, 34:2.

Bremer, Fredrika. (1853). *The Homes of the New World: Impressions of America*. Trans. Mary Howitt. Harper & Brothers, New York.

Breyer, Stephen. (2010). *Making Our Democracy Work: A Judge's View*. Alfred A. Knopf, New York.

Brissot de Warville, J.P. (1794). *New Travels in the United States of America, Performed in M.DCC.LXXXVIII*. 2d edition, corrected. J.S. Jordan, London.

Brooke, Richard. (1853). *Liverpool As It Was During the Last Quarter of the Eighteenth Century, 1775 to 1800*. J. Mawdsley and son, Liverpool.

Brown, Kathleen M. (1996). *Good Wives, Nasty Wenches, and Anxious Patriarchs: Gender, Race, and Power in Colonial Virginia.* University of North Carolina Press, Chapel Hill.

Brown, Vaughan W. (1965). *Shipping in the Port of Annapolis.* United States Naval Institute, Annapolis.

Brown, William Wells. (1847). *Lecture Delivered Before the Female Anti-Slavery Society of Salem.* Massachusetts Anti-Slavery Society, Boston.

*———. (1849). *Narrative of William W. Brown, an American Slave.* Charles Gilpin, London.

*———. (1853). *Clotel.* Partridge & Oakey, London.

*———. (1863). *The Black Man: His Antecedents, His Genius, and His Achievements.* James Redpath, Boston.

Browne, Gary Lawson. (1980). *Baltimore in the Nation, 1789–1861.* University of North Carolina Press, Chapel Hill.

*Browne, Martha Griffith. (1857). *Autobiography of a Female Slave.* Redfield, New York. http://docsouth.unc.edu/neh/browne/browne.html.

Bruce, Philip Alexander. (1895). *Economic History of Virginia in the Seventeenth Century: An Inquiry into the Material Condition of the People, Based upon Original and Contemporaneous Records.* Macmillan, New York.

———. (1920). *History of the University of Virginia 1819–1919: The Lengthened Shadow of One Man.* Macmillan, New York.

Bruchey, Stuart Weems. (1956). *Robert Oliver, Merchant of Baltimore:1783–1819.* Johns Hopkins University Press, Baltimore.

Brugger, Robert J. (1988). *Maryland: A Middle Temperament: 1634–1980.* Johns Hopkins University Press, Baltimore.

Buchanan, James. (1857). Inaugural address. www.presidency.ucsb.edu/ws/?pid=25817.

Buckingham, James Silk. (1842). *The Slave States of America.* Fisher, Son & Co, London.

Buckley, Roger Norman. (1979). *Slaves in Red Coats: The British West India Regiments, 1795–1815.* Yale University Press, New Haven.

Bunker, Nick. (2010). *Making Haste from Babylon: The Mayflower Pilgrims and Their World.* Alfred A. Knopf, New York.

———. (2014). *An Empire on the Edge: How Britain Came to Fight America.* Alfred A. Knopf, New York.

Burke, Edmund. (1775/1898). *Speech on Conciliation with America.* Scott Foresman and Company, Chicago.

Burkhardt, George S. (2007). *Confederate Rage, Yankee Wrath: No Quarter in the Civil War.* Southern Illinois University Press, Carbondale.

Butler, Pierce. (1850). *Mr. Butler's Statement.* J.C. Clark, Philadelphia.

Bynum, Victoria. (2003). *The Free State of Jones: Mississippi's Longest Civil War.* University of North Carolina Press, Chapel Hill.

Byrne, William A. (1995). "'Uncle Billy' Sherman comes to town: The free winter of black Savannah." *Georgia Historical Quarterly*, 79:1.

Cade, John B. (1935). "Out of the mouths of ex-slaves." *Journal of Negro History*, 20:3.

Caillot, Marc Antoine. (2013). *A Company Man: The Remarkable French-Atlantic Voyage of a Clerk for the Company of the Indies.* Ed. Erin M. Greenwald. Historic New Orleans Collection, New Orleans.

Calderhead, William. (1977). "The role of the professional slave trader in a slave economy: Austin Woolfolk, a case study." *Civil War History*, 23:3.

Calhoun, John C. (1853). *Works*, D. Appleton and Company, New York.

Calloway, Colin G. (2006). *The Scratch of a Pen: 1763 and the Transformation of North America*. Oxford University Press, New York.

The Calvert Papers. (1889). Maryland Historical Society, Baltimore.

Camp, Stephanie M. H. (2002). "The pleasures of resistance: Enslaved women and body politics in the plantation south, 1830–1861." *The Journal of Southern History*, 68:3, August.

Capers, Gerald M. (1939). *The Biography of a River Town; Memphis: Its Heroic Age*. University of North Carolina Press, Chapel Hill.

Carney, Judith. (2001). *Black Rice: The African Origins of Rice Cultivation in the Americas*. Harvard University Press, Cambridge.

Carpenter, Francis Bicknell. (1866). *Six Months at the White House with Abraham Lincoln: The Story of a Picture*. Hurd and Houghton, New York.

Carroll, Charles, of Annapolis. (1930). "Extracts from accounts and letter books of Dr. Charles Carroll, of Annapolis." *Maryland Historical Magazine* 25:1

Carroll, Charles, of Carrollton and Charles Carroll of Annapolis. (2001). *Dear Papa, Dear Charley: The Peregrinations of a Revolutionary Aristocrat, as Told by Charles Carroll of Carrollton and His Father, Charles Carroll of Annapolis . . .* ed. Ronald Hoffman. Univ. of North Carolina Press, Chapel Hill, v. 1–3.

Carruthers, Bruce G., and Sarah Babb. (1996). "The color of money and the nature of value: Greenbacks and gold in postbellum America." *The American Journal of Sociology*, 101: 6.

Carson, Jane. (1965). *Colonial Virginians at Play*. University Press of Virginia, Charlottesville.

Casimir, Jean. (2001). *La culture opprimée*. Imp. Lakay, Delmas, Haiti.

Casimir, Jean, and Laurent Dubois. (n.d.) "Reckoning in Haiti." www.ssrc.org/features /pages/haiti-now-and-next/1338/1395.

Cassell, Frank. (1972). "Slaves of the Chesapeake Bay area and the War of 1812." *The Journal of Negro History*, 57:2.

Castel, Albert. (1958). "The Fort Pillow Massacre: A fresh examination of the evidence," *Civil War History* 4.

Catterall, Helen Tunnicliff, and David Maydole Matteson. (1926–37). *Judicial Cases Concerning American Slavery and the Negro*. v. 1–5. Carnegie Institution of Washington, Washington, DC.

Catton, Bruce. (1965). "Horror taken for granted." *American Heritage*, 16:4, June.

Chance, J. F. (1902). "George I in his relations with Sweden." *The English Historic Review*, 17:65, January.

Chang, Cindy. (2012). "Louisiana is the world's prison capital." *New Orleans Times-Picayune*, May 13.

Chappelle, Howard Irving. (1930). *The Baltimore Clipper*. The Marine Research Society, Salem, MA.

Chapman, Peter. (2010). *The Last of the Imperious Rich*. Penguin, New York.

Chastellux, Marquis de. (1963). *Travels in North America in the Years 1780, 1781, and 1782*. Revised trans. by Howard C. Rice, Jr. University of North Carolina Press, Chapel Hill.

Chernow, Ron. (2004). *Alexander Hamilton*. Penguin, New York.

———. (2010). *Washington: A Life*. Penguin, New York.

Chesnut, Mary Boykin. (1981). *Mary Chesnut's Civil War*. Yale University Press, New Haven.

Cheves, Langdon. (1851). *Speech of the Honorable Langdon Cheves, in the Southern Convention, at Nashville, Tennessee, November 14, 1850*. Revised edition, 1851. Southern Rights Association, Nashville.

Chipman, Donald E., and Harriet Denise Joseph. (2010). *Spanish Texas, 1519–1821*. Rev. ed. University of Texas Press, Austin.

Chireau, Yvonne P. (2003). *Black Magic: Religion and the African American Conjuring Tradition*. University of California Press, Berkeley.

Claiborne, William C. C. (1917). *Official Letter Books of W. C. C. Claiborne,1801–1816*. State Department of Archives and History, Jackson, MS.

Clark, Ronald W. (1983). *Benjamin Franklin: A Biography*. Random House, New York.

Clarke, Lewis. (1842). "Leaves from a slave's journal of life." *The Anti-Slavery Standard*, 20 and 27 October 1842. http://docsouth.unc.edu/neh/clarke/support1.html

Clayton, Ralph. (2002). *Cash for Blood: The Baltimore to New Orleans Domestic Slave Trade*. Heritage Books, Bowie MD.

———. (1998). "Baltimore's own version of 'Amistad.'" *Baltimore Chronicle,* January 7. www.baltimorechronicle.com/slave_ship2.html.

Clinton, Catherine. (2000). *Fanny Kemble's Civil Wars*. Simon and Schuster, New York.

Coates, Ta-Nehisi. (2014). "The case for reparations." *The Atlantic*. June.

Cobb, Howell. (1856) *A Scriptural Examination of the Institution of Slavery*. Printed for the author, Perry GA.

Coffin, Charles Carleton. (1866). *Four Years of Fighting*. Ticknor and Fields, New York.

Cohen, Charles. (1981). "The 'liberty or death' speech: A note on religion and revolutionary rhetoric." *William and Mary Quarterly*, Third Series, 38:4.

Cohen, Richard. (2007). "Well calculated for the farmer: Thoroughbreds in the early national Chesapeake, 1790–1850." *Virginia Magazine of History and Biography*, 115:3.

Conger, Vivian Bruce. (2009). *The Widows' Might: Widowhood and Gender in Early British America*. NYU Press, New York.

Conrad, Alfred H., and John R. Meyer. (1958). "Economics of slavery in the ante bellum South," *The Journal of Political Economy*, 66:2.

Conway, Moncure D. (1864). *Testimonies concerning slavery*. Chapman and Hall, London.

Copeland, David A. (1997). *Colonial American Newspapers: Character and Content*. University of Delaware Press, Newark.

Corey, Charles H. (1895). *A History of the Richmond Theological Seminary*. J. W. Randolph Company, Richmond.

Corrections Corporation of America (2013). Form 10-K. http://ir.correctionscorp.com /phoenix.zhtml?c=117983&p=irol-reportsannual.

Craddock, Hannah Catherine. (2010). *Black Female Landowners in Richmond, Virginia, 1850–1877*. Bachelor of Arts Thesis, Duke University, Durham.

Crane, Vernor W. (1929). *The Southern Frontier, 1670–1732*. Univ. of Michigan Press, Ann Arbor.

Crawford, Alan Pell. (2008). *Twilight at Monticello: The Final Years of Thomas Jefferson*. Random House, New York.

Cuguano, Ottobah. (1787). *Narrative of the Enslavement of Ottobah Cugoano, a Native of Africa; Published by Himself, in the Year 1787.* In *The Negro's Memorial; Or, an Abolitionist's Catechism.* (1825). Hatchard and Co., London.

Currier, Edward. (1842). *The Political Text Book.* Warren Blake, Worcester MA.

Davis, Jefferson. (1881). *The Rise and Fall of the Confederate Government.* D. Appleton, New York.

Davis, Richard Beale. (1963). *William Fitzhugh and his Chesapeake World, 1676–1701: The Fitzhugh Letters and Other Documents.* University of North Carolina Press, Chapel Hill.

Davis, Robert Ralph, Jr. (1966). "James Buchanan and the suppression of the slave trade, 1858–1861." *Pennsylvania History*, 33:4.

———. (1971). "Buchanian espionage: a report on illegal slave trading in the South in 1859." *Journal of Southern History*, 37:2.

Davis, William C. (2001). *Rhett: The Turbulent Life and Times of a Fire-Eater.* University of South Carolina Press, Columbia.

Dayan, Joan. (1998). *Haiti, History, and the Gods.* University of California Press, Berkeley.

Dean, Adam Wesley. (2009). "'Who controls the past controls the future': The Virginia textbook controversy." *Virginia Magazine of History and Biography*, 117:4.

A Declaration of the Immediate Causes which Induce and Justify the Secession of the State of Mississippi from the Federal Union (1860). http://avalon.law.yale.edu/19th_century/csa_mis sec.asp.

DeBow, J. D. B. (1845). *The Political Annals of South-Carolina.* Burges and James, Charleston.

DeConde, Alexander. (1966). *The Quasi-War: The Politics and Diplomacy of the Undeclared War with France 1797–1801.* Scribner's, New York.

DeGraft-Hanson, Kwesi. (2010). "Unearthing the Weeping Time: Savannah's Ten Broeck Race Course and 1859 slave sale." www.southernspaces.org/2010/unearthing -weeping-time-savannahs-ten-broeck-race-course-and-1859-slave-sale.

Dessens, Nathalie. (2007). *From Saint-Domingue to New Orleans: Migration and Influences.* University Press of Florida, Gainesville.

Dew, Charles B. (2001). *Apostles of Disunion: Southern Secession Commissioners and the Causes of the Civil War.* University Press of Virginia, Charlottesville.

Dew, Thomas R. (1832). *A Review of the Debate in the Virginia Legislature of 1831 and 1832.* T. W. White, Richmond.

Deyle, Stephen. (2004). "The domestic slave trade in America: The lifeblood of the southern slave system." In Walter Johnson, ed., *The Chattel Principle: Internal Slave Trades in the Americas*, Yale University Press.

———. (2005). *Carry Me Back: The Domestic Slave Trade in American Life.* Oxford University Press.

Dilts, James D. (1993). *The Great Road: The Building of the Baltimore and Ohio, the Nation's First Railroad, 1828–1853.* Stanford University Press, Stanford.

Diner, Hasia. (2006). "Entering the mainstream of modern Jewish history: Peddlers and the American Jewish South." In Ferris, Marcie Cohen, and Mark I. Greenberg, eds., *Jewish Roots in Southern Soil: A New History.* Brandeis University Press, Waltham.

Diouf, Sylviane A. (2007). *Dreams of Africa in Alabama: The Slave Ship Clotilda and the Story of the Last Africans Brought to America.* Oxford University Press, New York.

Donnan, Elizabeth. (1928). "The slave trade into South Carolina before the revolution." *The American Historical Review*, 33:4.

Douglass, Frederick. (1857). *Two Speeches.* C. P. Dewey, Rochester.

*———. (1845). *Narrative of the Life of Frederick Douglass, an American Slave. Written by Himself.* Anti-Slavery Office, Boston.

*———. (1855). *My Bondage and My Freedom.* Miller, Orton, and Mulligan, New York.

*———. (1892). *Life and Times of Frederick Douglass, Written by Himself.* De Wolfe & Fiske, Boston.

———. (2000). *Frederick Douglass: Selected Speeches and Writings.* Lawrence Hill Books, Chicago.

Drago, Edmund L. (1991). *Broke by the War: Letters of a Slave Trader.* University of South Carolina Press, Columbia.

Drescher, Seymour. (2010). *Econocide: British Slavery in the Era of Abolition.* 2d ed. University of North Carolina Press, Chapel Hill.

Dubois, Laurent. (2006). "An enslaved Enlightenment: Rethinking the intellectual history of the French Atlantic." *Social History*, 31:1.

———. (2004). *Avengers of the New World: The Story of the Haitian Revolution.* Belknap Press of Harvard University Press, Cambridge.

Dubois, Laurent, and John Garrigus. (2006). *Slave Revolution in the Caribbean, 1789–1804: A Brief History with Documents.* Palgrave Macmillan, New York.

DuBois, W. E. B. (1904). *The Suppression of the African Slave-trade to the United States of America, 1638–1870.* Longmans, Green and Co., New York.

———. (1933). "Postscript." *The Crisis*, February.

Dudley, William S. (2002). *The Naval War of 1812: A Documentary History.* Naval Historical Center, Washington, DC.

The Duke of York's Release to John Lord Berkeley, and Sir George Carteret, 24th of June, 1664. (1664). http://avalon.law.yale.edu/17th_century/nj01.asp.

Dunbar, Erica Armstrong. (2015). "George Washington, slave catcher." *New York Times*, February 16.

Dunn, Richard S. (1972). *Sugar and Slaves: The Rise of the Planter Class in the English West Indies, 1624–1713.* University of North Carolina Press, Chapel Hill.

Dusinberre, William. (2003). *Slavemaster President: The Double Career of James Polk.* Oxford University Press, New York.

Egerton, Douglas R. (1993). *Gabriel's Rebellion: The Virginia Slave Conspiracies of 1800 and 1802.* University of North Carolina Press, Chapel Hill.

———. (1999). *He Shall Go Out Free: The Lives of Denmark Vesey.* Rowman & Littlefield, Lanham, MD.

Einhorn, Robin L. (2002). "Patrick Henry's case against the Constitution: The structural problem with slavery." *Journal of the Early Republic*, 22:4.

Eire, Carlos M.N. (1986). *War against the Idols: The Reformation of Worship from Erasmus to Calvin.* Cambridge University Press, Cambridge.

Ellis, Mark. (2001). *Race, War, and Surveillance: African Americans and the United States Government During World War I.* Indiana University Press, Bloomington.

Elk, Mike, and Bob Sloan. (2011). "The hidden history of ALEC and prison labor." *The Nation*, August 1. www.thenation.com/article/162478/hidden-history-alec-and-prison-labor.

Eltis, David, and Stanley L. Engerman. (2000). "The importance of slavery and the slave trade to industrializing Britain," *The Journal of Economic History*, 60:1.

Eltis, David, and David Richardson. (2010). *Atlas of the Transatlantic Slave Trade.* Yale University Press, New Haven.

Englund, Steven. (2004). *Napoleon: A Political Life.* Scribner, New York.

"The Episcopal Church in Virginia, 1607–2007." (2007). *The Virginia Magazine of History and Biography,* 115:2.

Epstein, Dena J. (1977). *Sinful Tunes and Spirituals: Black Folk Music to the Civil War.* University of Illinois Press, Urbana.

Evans, Robert Jr. (1962). "The economics of American Negro slavery," in *Aspects of Labor Economics*, Princeton University Press.

Ewald, Johann. (1776–1784 / 1979). *Diary of the American War: A Hessian Journal.* Trans. and edited by Joseph P. Tustin. Yale University Press, New Haven.

Fairholt, F. W. (1859). *Tobacco: Its History and Associations.* Chapman and Hall, London.

"Family histories: A beginning." (n.d.) www.monticello.org/site/plantation-and-slavery /family-histories-beginning.

Farrand, Max. (1966). *The Records of the Federal Convention of 1787.* Yale University Press, New Haven.

Farrison, W. Edward. (1949). "William Wells Brown, social reformer." *Journal of Negro Education*, 18:1.

Featherstonhaugh, G. W. (1844). *Excursion Through the Slave States.* John Murray, London.

Fehrenbacher, Don E. (2001). *The Slaveholding Republic: An Account of the United States Government's Relations to Slavery.* Oxford University Press, New York.

Fellman, Michael. (2013). *Citizen Sherman: A Life of William Tecumseh Sherman.* Random House, New York.

Ferrer, Ada. (2014). *Freedom's Mirror: Cuba and Haiti in the Age of Revolution.* Cambridge University Press, New York.

Figgis, John Neville. (1907). *Studies in Political Thought from Gerson to Grotius, 1414–1625.* The University Press, Cambridge.

Finkelman, Paul. (2013). "James Buchanan, Dred Scott, and the whisper of conspiracy." In Quist, John W., and Michael J. Birkner, *James Buchanan and the Coming of the Civil War.* University Press of Florida, Gainesville.

———. (1986). "Slavery and the Northwest Ordinance: A study in ambiguity." *Journal of the Early Republic,* 6:4.

———. (2007). *Slave Rebels, Abolitionists, and Southern Courts: The Pamphlet Literature.* The Lawbook Exchange, Clark, NJ.

Firth, C. H. (1900). *The Narrative of General Venables.* Longmans, Green, and Co., London.

Fischer, David Hackett. (1989). *Albion's Seed : Four British Folkways in America.* Oxford University Press, New York.

Fisher, Linford D. (2014). "'Dangerous Designes': The 1676 Barbados act to prohibit New England Indian slave importation." *William and Mary Quarterly,* 71:1.

Fithian, Philip Vickers. (1900). *Journal and Letters 1767–1774.* Princeton University Library, Princeton.

Fitzhugh, George. (1857). *Cannibals All! Or, Slaves Without Masters.* A. Morris, Richmond.

Fitzhugh, William. (1893). "Letters of William Fitzhugh." *Virginia Magazine of History and Biography,* 1:1.

Flaherty, Jane. (2009). "'The exhausted condition of the Treasury' on the eve of the Civil War.'" *Civil War History,* 55:2.

Fletcher, Michael. (2013). "Fifty years after March on Washington, economic gap between blacks, whites persists." *Washington Post,* August 28.

Fleischner, Jennifer. (2003). *Mrs. Lincoln and Mrs. Keckly: The Remarkable Story of the Friendship Between a First Lady and a Former Slave.* Broadway Books, New York.

"Flight to freedom: Slavery and the Underground Railroad in Maryland." [n.d.] Maryland State Archives, ww2.mdslavery.net/dsp_searchresults.cfm?fn=4&search=11.

Follett, Richard. (2007). *The Sugar Masters: Planters and Slaves in Louisiana's Cane World, 1820–1860.* LSU Press, Baton Rouge

Foner, Eric. (1970). *Free Soil, Free Labor, Free Men: The Ideology of the Republican Party Before the Civil War.* Oxford University Press, New York.

Foner, Philip S. (1941). *Business and Slavery: The New York Merchants and the Irrepressible Conflict.* University of North Carolina Press, Chapel Hill.

Ford, Lacy K. (1988). *Origins of Southern Radicalism: The South Carolina Upcountry, 1800–1860.* Oxford University Press, New York.

———. (2009). *Deliver Us from Evil: The Slavery Question in the Old South.* Oxford University Press, New York.

Ford, Timothy. (1785–6 / 1912). "Diary of Timothy Ford," *The South Carolina Historical and Genealogical Magazine,*13:3.

Foreman, Amanda. (2010). *A World on Fire: An Epic History of Two Nations Divided.* Allen Lane, London.

Fortune, Porter L. (1973). "The formative period." In McLemore, Richard Aubrey, *A History of Mississippi,* Vol. 1. University & College Press of Mississippi, Hattiesburg.

Foster, Eugene A. *et al.* (1998). "Jefferson fathered slave's last child." *Nature,* 396, Nov. 5.

Foster, Stephen. (1853). "My old Kentucky home, good night!" Firth, Pond and Co., New York.

Franco, José Luciano. (1977). "The slave trade in the Caribbean and Latin America from the Fifteenth to the Nineteenth Century." UNESCO, Paris. http://unesdoc.unesco.org/images/0002/000277/027738eb.pdf.

Fraser, Steve, and Joshua Freeman. (2012). "Creating a prison-corporate complex." www.tomdispatch.com/post/175531/tomgram%3A_fraser_and_freeman%2C_creating_a_prison-corporate_complex.

Freudenberger, Herman, and Jonathan B. Pritchett. (1991). "The domestic United States slave trade: New evidence." *The Journal of Interdisciplinary History,* 21:3.

Fromont, Cécile. (2014). *The Arts of Conversion: Christian Visual Culture in the Kingdom of Kongo.* University of North Carolina Press, Chapel Hill.

712   REFERENCES

Fuller, Randall. (1999). "Theaters of the American revolution: the Valley Forge "Cato" and the Meschianza in their transcultural contexts." *Early American Literature*, 34:2.

Fundamental Constitutions of Carolina. (1669). http://avalon.law.yale.edu/17th_century /nc05.asp .

Furdell, Elizabeth Lane. (2001). *The Royal Doctors, 1485–1714: Medical Personnel at the Tudor and Stuart Courts*. University of Rochester Press, Rochester NY.

Gadsden, Christopher. (1966). *The Writings of Christopher Gadsden, 1764–1805*. Ed. by Richard Walsh. University of South Carolina Press, Columbia.

Gallatin, Albert. (1960). *The Writings of Albert Gallatin*. Ed. Henry Adams. Vol. 1. Antiquarian Press, New York.

Gallay, Alan. (2002). *The Indian Slave Trade: The Rise of the English Empire in the American South, 1670–1717*. Yale University Press, New Haven.

Garrard, Timothy F. (1980). *Akan Weights and the Gold Trade*. Longman, London.

Gatell, Frank Otto. (1963) "Postmaster Huger and the incendiary publications." *South Carolina Historical Magazine*, 64:4.

Geggus, David. (1981). "The British government and the Saint-Domingue slave revolt, 1791–1793." *English Historical Review*, 96:379.

Genovese, Eugene. (1965). *The Political Economy of Slavery: Studies in the Economy and Society of the Slave South*. Pantheon, New York.

———. (1974). *Roll, Jordan, Roll: The World the Slaves Made*. Pantheon, New York.

———. (1969/88). *The World the Slaveholders Made: Two Essays in Interpretation*. Wesleyan University Press, Hanover, NH.

George, James Z. (1860). *Reports of Cases Argued and Determined in the High Court of Errors and Appeals, for the State of Mississippi*, v. 37, v.8. T. and J. W. Johnson & Co., Philadelphia.

Gigantino, James II. (2010). "Trading in New Jersey souls: New Jersey and the interstate slave trade." *Pennsylvania History: A Journal of Mid-Atlantic Studies*, 77:3.

Goodheart, Adam. (2011). "Divorce, antebellum style." *New York Times*, March 18.

———. (2011a). *1861: The Civil War Awakening*. Alfred A. Knopf, New York.

Goodson, Martia Graham. (2003). "Enslaved Africans and doctors in South Carolina." *Journal of the National Medical Association*, 95:3.

Gordon-Reed, Annette. (2012). "Thomas Jefferson was not a monster." *Slate*, Oct. 19.

Grady, Timothy Paul. (2010). *Anglo-Spanish Rivalry in Colonial South-East America, 1650–1725*. Pickering & Chatto, London.

Graeber, David. (2011). *Debt: The First 5,000 Years*. Melville House, Brooklyn.

Graham, Richard. (2004). "Another Middle Passage? The internal slave trade in Brazil." In Walter Johnson, ed., *The Chattel Principle: Internal Slave Trades in the Americas*, Yale University Press, New Haven.

Grandin, Greg. (2014). *The Empire of Necessity: Slavery, Freedom, and Deception in the New World*. Metropolitan Books, New York.

Grant, Ulysses S. (1990). *Memoirs and Selected Letters: Personal Memoirs of U.S. Grant, Selected Letters 1839–1865*. Library of America, New York.

"Great news from the Barbadoes: Or a true and faithful account of the grand conspiracy of the Negroes against the English." In Hughes, Derek. (2007). *Versions of Blackness: Key Texts on Slavery from the Seventeenth Century*. Cambridge University Press, Cambridge.

*Green, J. D. (1864). *Narrative of the Life of J. D. Green, a Runaway Slave, from Kentucky, Containing an Account of His Three Escapes, in 1839, 1846, and 1848.* Huddersfield: Printed by Henry Fielding, Pack Horse Yard.

Green, George D. (1972). *Finance and Economic Development in the Old South: Louisiana Banking, 1804–1861.* Stanford University Press, Stanford, CA.

Greenberg, Mark I. (2006). "One religion, different worlds: Sephardic and Ashkenazic immigrants in eighteenth-century Savannah." In Ferris, Marcie Cohen, and Mark I. Greenberg, eds., *Jewish Roots in Southern Soil: A New History.* Brandeis University Press, Waltham.

Griffey, Erin. (2008). "Devotional jewelry in portraits of Henrietta Maria." In Griffey, Erin. (2008). *Henrietta Maria: Piety, Politics and Patronage.* Ashgate, Aldershot UK.

Grigsby, Hugh Blair. (1890). *The History of the Virginia Convention of 1788.* Virginia Historical Society, Richmond.

Groce, W. Todd. (2014). "Rethinking Sherman's march." *New York Times,* Nov. 17.

Grubb, Farley. (2000). "The transatlantic market for British convict labor." *Journal of Economic History,* 60:1.

———. (2006). "Benjamin Franklin and the birth of a paper money economy." Federal Reserve Bank, Philadelphia. https://www.philadelphiafed.org/publications/economic-education/ben-franklin-and-paper-money-economy.pdf

Grunberg, Bernard. (1994). "The origins of the conquistadores of Mexico City." *The Hispanic American Historical Review,* 74:2.

Gudemestad, Robert H. (2003). *A Troublesome Commerce : The Transformation of the Interstate Slave Trade.* Louisiana State University Press, Baton Rouge.

Guerino, Paul, Paige M. Harrison, and William Sabol. (2011). "Prisoners in 2010." US Department of Justice. www.bjs.gov/content/pub/pdf/p10.pdf.

Hacker, J. David. (2011). "Recounting the dead." *New York Times,* September 20.

Hall, Clayton Colman. (1959). *Narratives of Early Maryland 1633–1684,* Barnes & Noble, New York.

Hall, Gwendolyn Midlo. (1992). *Africans in Colonial Louisiana: The Development of Afro-Creole Culture in the Eighteenth Century.* Louisiana State Unviersity Press, Baton Rouge.

Hall, Michael, G., and Lawrence H. Leder and Michael G. Kammen, eds. (1964). *The Glorious Revolution in America.* University of North Carolina Press, Chapel Hill.

Hammond, Bray. (1970). *Sovereignty and an Empty Purse: Banks and Politics in the Civil War.* Princeton University Press, Princeton.

Hanby, B. R. (1856). "Darling Nelly Gray." Boston, Oliver Ditson.

Hancock, David. (1995). *Citizens of the World: London Merchants and the Integration of the British Atlantic Community, 1735–1785.* Cambridge University Press, Cambridge.

Hanson, George A. (1876). *Old Kent: The Eastern Shore of Maryland.* John P. Des Forges, Baltimore.

Harkins, John E. (2008). *Historic Shelby County: An Illustrated History.* Historical Publishing Network, San Antonio.

Harlow, Vincent T. (1926). *A History of Barbados, 1625–1685.* Oxford University Press, Clarendon.

Harrison, Samuel Alexander. (1915). *History of Talbot County, Maryland, 1661–1861.* Williams and Wilkins, Baltimore.

Harrower, John. (1963). *The Journal of John Harrower, an Indentured Servant in the Colony of Virginia, 1773–1776.* Ed. with an introduction by Edward Miles Riley. Holt, Rinehart and Winston, New York.

Hartman, Saidiya. (1997). *Scenes of Subjection: Terror, Slavery, and Self-making in Nineteenth-century America.* Oxford University Press, New York.

Harvey, David. (2005). *The New Imperialism.* Oxford University Press, Oxford.

"Hate and Extremism." Southern Poverty Law Center. www.splcenter.org/what-we-do/hate-and-extremism.

Hawke, David Freeman. (1976). *Franklin.* Harper & Row, New York.

Hawley, Joshua David. (2008). *Theodore Roosevelt: Preacher of Righteousness.* Yale University Press, New Haven.

Hawthorne, Nathaniel. (1852 / 1897). *The Life of Franklin Pierce.* In *The Complete Works of Nathaniel Hawthorne,* v. 12, Houghton, Mifflin, and Company, Boston.

Haynes, Robert V. (1973.) "The road to statehood." In McLemore, Richard Aubrey, *A History of Mississippi,* Vol. 1. University & College Press of Mississippi, Hattiesburg.

Hazzard-Donald, Katrina. (2011.) "Hoodoo religion and American dance traditions: Rethinking the ring shout." *The Journal of Pan African Studies,* 4:6.

———. (2012.) *Mojo Workin': The Old African American Hoodoo System.* University of Illinois Press, Urbana.

Heath, James, and John Phillips. (1676). *A Chronicle of the Late Intestine War in the Three Kingdoms of England, Scotland and Ireland.* Thomas Basset, London.

Hemphill, William Edwin, Marvin Wilson Schlegel, and Sadie Ethel Engelberg. (1957). *Cavalier Commonwealth: History and Government of Virginia.* McGraw-Hill, New York.

Hening, William Waller, ed. (1819–23). *The Statutes at Large; Being a Collection of All the Laws of Virginia . . .* R. & W. & G. Bartow, Richmond.

Henriques, Peter R. (2006). *Realistic Visionary: A Portrait of George Washington.* University of Virginia Press, Charlottesville.

Henry, William Wirt. (1970). *Patrick Henry; Life, Correspondence and Speeches.* Charles Scriber's Sons, New York.

*Henson, Josiah. (1849). *The Life of Josiah Henson, Formerly a Slave, Now an Inhabitant of Canada, as Narrated by Himself.* Arthur D. Phelps, Boston.

Herbert, Eugenia W. (2003). *Red Gold of Africa: Copper in Precolonial History and Culture.* University of Wisconsin Press, Madison.

Hewatt, Alexander. (1779). *An Historical Account of the Rise and Progress of the Colonies of South Carolina and Georgia.* Alexander Donaldson, London.

Hibbard, Caroline. (2008). "'By our direction and for our use': The Queen's patronage of artists and artisans seen through her household accounts." In Griffey, Erin. (2008). *Henrietta Maria: Piety, Politics and Patronage.* Ashgate, Aldershot UK.

Hibbert, Christopher. (1993). *Cavaliers and Roundheads: The English Civil War, 1642–1649.* Scribner's, New York.

Higgins, W. Robert. (1964). "Charles Town merchants and factors dealing in the external negro trade 1735–1775." *South Carolina Historical Magazine,* 65:4.

Hill, J. Michael. (1993). "The origins of the Scottish plantations in Ulster to 1625: A reinterpretation." *The Journal of British Studies*, 32:1.

Hill, William. (1893). "Colonial tariffs." *Quarterly Journal of Economics*, 7.

Hills, Richard L. (1989). *Power from Steam: A History of the Stationary Steam Engine*. Cambridge University Press, Cambridge.

Hinks, Peter P. (2010). *To Awaken My Afflicted Brethren: David Walker and the Problem of Antebellum Slave Resistance*. Penn State Press, University Park PA.

Horne, Gerald. (2014). *The Counter-Revolution of 1776: Slave Resistance and the Origins of the United States of America*. New York University Press, New York.

*Hughes, Louis. (1897). *Thirty Years a Slave: From Bondage to Freedom: The Institution of Slavery as Seen on the Plantation and in the Home of the Planter*. South Side Printing Company, Milwaukee.

Hurst, Jack. (1993). *Nathan Bedford Forrest*. Alfred A. Knopf, New York.

Hurston, Zora Neale. (1927). "Cudjo's own story of the last African slaver." *Journal of Negro History,* 12:4.

Hutson, James H. (1980). "Pierce Butler's records of the Federal Constitutional Convention." *The Quarterly Journal of the Library of Congress*, 37: 1.

Idzerda, Stanley J. (1981). "Indispensable allies: The French at Yorktown." *The Wilson Quarterly*, 5:4.

Impact of the Federal Government on Maryland's Economy. (2010). Department of Legislative Services, Annapolis.

Ingham, Geoffrey. (2004). *The Nature of Money*. Polity, Cambridge UK.

Ingraham, Joseph Holt. (1860). *The Sunny South; Or, the Southerner at Home*. G. G. Evans, Philadelphia.

———. (1835). *The South-West. By a Yankee*. Harper and Brothers, New York.

Jackson, Joyce. (2006). "Rockin' and rushin' for Christ: Hidden transcripts in diasporic ritual performance." In *Caribbean and Southern: Transnational Perspectives on the U.S. South*, ed. Helen Regis. University of Georgia Press, Athens.

*Jacobs, Harriet A. (1861). *Incidents in the Life of a Slave Girl. Written by Herself.* Published for the author, Boston.

Jacques, Edna Bolling. (2002). "The Hemmings family in Buckingham County, Virginia." www.buckinghamhemmings.com.

James, C. L. R. (1938). *The Black Jacobins: Toussaint Louverture and the San Domingo Revolution*. Dial Press, New York.

Jay, William. (1853). *Miscellaneous Writings on Slavery*. J. P. Jewett, Boston.

Jefferson, Thomas. (1788). *Notes on the State of Virginia*. Prichard and Hall, Philadelphia.

———. (1953). *Thomas Jefferson's Farm Book*. Princeton University Press, Princeton.

———. (1997). *Jefferson's Memorandum Books*. Ed. by James A. Bear Jr. and Lucia C. Stanton.

Jennings, Thelma. (1990.) "'Us colored women had to go though a plenty': Sexual exploitation of African-American slave women." *Journal of Women's History*, 1:3.

Jenson, Deborah. (2011). *Beyond the Slave Narrative: Politics, Sex, and Manuscripts in the Haitian Revolution*. Liverpool University Press, Liverpool.

Johnson, Clint. (2010). *"A Vast and Fiendish Plot": The Confederate Attack on New York City*. Citadel Press, New York.

Johnson, Keach. (1953). "The genesis of the Baltimore Ironworks." *The Journal of Southern History*, 19:2.

Johnson, Michael P. (2001). "Denmark Vesey and his co-conspirators." *The William and Mary Quarterly*, 58:4.

Johnson, Sara E. (2012). *The Fear of French Negroes: Transcolonial Collaboration in the Revolutionary Americas*. University of California Press, Berkeley.

Johnson, Simon, and James Kwak. (2013). *White House Burning: Our National Debt and Why It Matters to You*. Vintage, New York.

Johnson, Walter. (2013). *River of Dark Dreams: Slavery and Empire in the Cotton Kingdom*. Belknap Press, Cambridge.

———. (1999). *Soul by Soul: Life Inside the Antebellum Slave Market*. Harvard University Press, Cambridge.

———. (2000). "The slave trader, the white slave, and the politics of racial determination in the 1850s." *The Journal of American History*, 87:1.

Johnston, J. Stoddard. (1898). *First Explorations of Kentucky*. John P. Morton and Company, Louisvillle.

Jones, Leslie. (2014). https://twitter.com/lesdoggg/status/463074782205190144.

Jordan, Winthrop D. (1968). *White Over Black: American Attitudes Toward the Negro, 1550–1812*. University of North Carolina Press, Chapel Hill.

Kant, Immanuel. (1960). *Observations on the Feeling of the Beautiful and Sublime*. Trans. John T. Goldthwait. University of California Press, Berkeley.

Keating, John M. (1888). *History of the City of Memphis, Tennessee*. D. Mason, Syracuse NY.

*Keckley, Elizabeth. (1868). *Behind the Scenes, or, Thirty years a Slave, and Four Years in the White House*. G. W. Carleton & Co., New York.

Keehn, David C. (2013). *Knights of the Golden Circle: Secret Empire, Southern Secession, Civil War*. Louisiana State University Press, Baton Rouge.

Keller, Mary Frear, ed. (1981). *Sir Francis Drake's West Indian Voyage*. Hakluyt Society, London.

Kelly, J. Rainey. (1965). "'Tulip Hill,' its history and its people." *Maryland Historical Magazine*, 60:4.

Kemble, Frances Anne. (1864). *Journal of a Residence on a Georgian Plantation in 1838–1839*. Harper and Brothers, New York.

Kennett, Lee B. (1995). *Marching Through Georgia : The Story of Soldiers and Civilians During Sherman's Campaign*. HarperCollins, New York.

Kilbourne, Richard Holcombe Jr. (1995). *Debt, Investment, Slaves: Credit Relations in East Feliciana Parish, Louisiana, 1825–1885*. University of Alabama Press, Tuscaloosa.

———. (2006). *Slave Agriculture and Financial Markets in Antebellum America: The Bank of the United States in Mississippi, 1831–1852*. Pickering & Chatto, London.

King, David. (2008). *Vienna 1814: How the Conquerors of Napoleon Made Love, War, and Peace at the Congress of Vienna*. Harmony Books, New York.

King, Roswell Jr. (1828). "On the management of the Butler estate." *Southern Agriculturalist*, 1.

King, Stewart R. (2001). *Blue Coat or Powdered Wig: Free People of Color in Pre-Revolutionary Saint-Domingue*. University of Georgia Press, Athens.

Kingsbury, Susan Myra, ed. (1933). *The Records of the Virginia Company of London*, Vol. 3, U.S. Government Printing Office, Washington.

Kiple, Kenneth F., and Virginia Himmelsteib King. (1981). *Another Dimension to the Black Diaspora: Diet, Disease, and Racism*. Cambridge University Press, Cambridge.

Kirby, Holly. (2013). "Locked up and shipped away: interstate prisoner transfers & the private prison industry." http://grassrootsleadership.org/locked-up-and-shipped-away.

Klein, Herbert S., and Ben Vinson III. (2007). *African Slavery in Latin America and the Caribbean*, 2d ed. Oxford University Press, New York.

Klein, Philip Shriver. (1962). *President James Buchanan: A Biography*. Pennsylvania State University Press, University Park.

Kly, Y. N. (1998). "The Gullah War, 1739–1858," in Goodwine, Marquetta L. (1998), *The Legacy of Ibo Landing: Gullah Roots of African American Culture*. Clarity Press, Atlanta.

Knodell, Jane. (2006). "Rethinking the Jacksonian economy: The impact of the 1832 bank veto on commercial banking." *Journal of Economic History*, 66:3.

Knollenberg, Bernhard. (1975). *Growth of the American Revolution: 1766–1775*. The Free Press, New York.

Knutsford, Viscountess. (1900). *The Life and Letters of Zachary Maculay*. Edward Arnold, London.

Komlos, John, and Bjorn Alecke. (1996). "The economics of antebellum slave heights reconsidered." *The Journal of Interdisciplinary History*, 26:3.

Korn, Bertram Wallace. (1961). *Jews and Negro Slavery in the Old South 1789–1865*. Reform Congregation Keneseth Israel, Elkins Park, PA.

Lacroix, Pamphile de. (1819). *Mémoires pour servir à l'histoire de la révolution de Saint-Domingue*, v. 2. Chez Pillet-Aîné, Paris.

Laird, Matthew R. (2006). *Preliminary Archaeological Investigation of the Lumpkin's Jail Site (44HE1053) Richmond, Virginia*. www.richmondgov.com/CommissionSlaveTrail/documents/LumpkinsSlaveJailFinalReport.pdf.

Lakwete, Angela. (2003). *Inventing the Cotton Gin: Machine and Myth in Antebellum America*. Johns Hopkins University Press, Baltimore.

Lambert, John. (1811). *Travels through Canada, and the United States of North America*. 3d ed. Baldwin, Cradock, and Joy, London.

Landers, Jane G. (1999). *Black Society in Spanish Florida*. University of Illinois Press, Urbana.

———. (2010). *Atlantic Creoles in the Age of Revolutions*. Harvard University Press, Cambridge MA.

Lanning, Michael Lee. (1997). *The African American Soldier: From Crispus Attucks to Colin Powell*. Citadel, New York.

Laprade, William T. (1926). "The domestic slave trade in the District of Columbia." *Journal of Negro History*, 11:1.

Latrobe, Benjamin Henry. (1905). *The Journal of Latrobe*. D. Appleton and Company, New York.

Laudonnière, René Goulaine de. (1586/1982). *A Foothold in Florida*. Translated from *L'Historie notable de la Floride* by Sarah Lawson. Antique Atlas Publications, West Sussex (England).

Leder, Lawrence H., and Vincent P. Carosso. (1956). "Robert Livingston (1654–1728): Businessman of colonial New York." *Business History Review*, 30:1.

Lee, Robert E. (1859). "Report concerning the attack at Harper's Ferry." http://law2.umkc
.edu/faculty/projects/ftrials/johnbrown/leereport.html.

Le Moyne d'Iberville, Pierre. (1981). *Iberville's Gulf Journals*. Trans. Richebourg McWilliams. University of Alabama Press, Tuscaloosa.

Lemay, J. A. Leo. (2006). *The Life of Benjamin Franklin, v. 2: Printer and Publisher, 1730–1747*. University of Pennsylvania Press, Philadelphia.

———. (2009). *v. 3: Soldier, Scientist, and Politician 1748–1757*. University of Pennsylvania Press, Philadelphia.

———. (1991). *The American Dream of Captain John Smith*. University Press of Virginia, Charlottesville.

Lemieux, Jamilah. (2014). "Once again, no one is laughing at 'SNL.'" www.ebony.com
/entertainment-culture/leslie-jones-weekend-update-slavery-842#axzz31dbezyXT.

Leone, Mark. (2005). *The Archaeology of Liberty in an American Capital: Excavations in Annapolis*. University of California Press, Oakland.

Lepler, Jessica. (2013). *The Many Panics of 1837: People, Politics, and the Creation of a Transatlantic Financial Crisis*. Cambridge University Press, New York.

Lepore, Jill. (2005). *New York Burning: Liberty, Slavery and Conspiracy in Eighteenth-Century Manhattan*. Alfred A. Knopf, New York.

Lessing, Lauren. (2011). "Angels in the home: Adelicia Acklen's sculpture collection at Belmont Mansion, Nashville, Tennessee." *Winterthur Portfolio*, 45:1.

Leveen, Lois. (2012). "The paradox of pluck: how did historical fiction become the new feminist history?" *Los Angeles Review of Books*, Sept. 30.

Lewis, James A. (1980). "Las damas de la Havana, el Precursor, and Francisco de Saavedra: A note on Spanish participation in the battle of Yorktown." *The Americas*, 37:1.

Lightner, David L. (2006). *Slavery and the Commerce Power: How the Struggle Against the Interstate Slave Trade Led to the Civil War*. Yale University Press, New Haven.

Ligon, Richard. (1673/2011). *A True and Exact History of the Island of Barbados*. Ed. Karen Ordahl Kupperman. Hackett Publishing Company, Indianapolis.

Lincoln, Abraham. (2012). *The Writings of Abraham Lincoln*. ed. Steven B. Smith. Yale University Press, New Haven.

Linder, Suzanne Cameron. (1995). *Historical Atlas of the Rice Plantations of the ACE River Basin—1860*. South Carolina Department of Archives & History, Columbia.

Linebaugh, Peter, and Marcus Rediker. (2000). *The Many-Headed Hydra: Sailors, Slaves, Commoners, and the Hidden History of the Revolutionary Atlantic*. Beacon Press, Boston.

Lippson, Alice Jane, and Robert L. Lippson. (2006). *Life in the Chesapeake Bay*, third ed. Johns Hopkins University Press, Baltimore.

Lipscomb, Terry. (2007). Introduction to Butler, Pierce. *The Letters of Pierce Butler 1790–1794*. University of South Carolina Press, Columbia.

Lislet, L. Moreau. (1828). *A General Digest of the Acts of the Legislature of Louisiana*. 2 vols. Benjamin Levy, New Orleans.

Long, Ellen Call. (1883/1962). *Florida Breezes; Or, Florida, New and Old*. University of Florida Press, Gainesville.

Lowery, Woodbury. (1904). "Jean Ribaut and Queen Elizabeth." *American Historical Review* 9.

Lucas, Paul Robert. (1984). *American Odyssey, 1607–1789*. Prentice-Hall, Englewood Cliffs, NJ.

Lundy, Benjamin. (1847). *The Life, Travels, and Opinions of Benjamin Lundy.* William D. Parrisk, Philadelphia.

Luther, Martin. (1910). "Address to the German nobility concerning Christian liberty." Trans. R. S. Grignon. In Harvard Classics, v. 36, P.F. Collier and Son, New York.

Lyell, Charles. (1845). *Travels in North America, in the Years 1841–2: with Geological Observations on the United States, Canada, and Nova Scotia.* Wiley and Putnam, New York.

Mackay, Charles. (1859). *Life and Liberty in America; Or, Sketches of a Tour in the United States and Canada, in 1857–8, Volumes 1–2.* Smith, Elder, and Co., London.

MacKinnon, William P. (2013). "Prelude to Armageddon." In Quist, John W., and Michael J. Birkner, *James Buchanan and the Coming of the Civil War.* University Press of Florida, Gainesville.

Malone, Dumas. (1967). "Mr. Jefferson and the traditions of Virginia." *The Virginia Magazine of History and Biography*, 75:2.

Manakee, Harold R. (1972). "Anthem born in battle." In Filby, P. W., and Edward G. Howard, comp., *Star-Spangled Books: Books, Sheet Music, Newspapers, Manuscripts, and Persons Associated with "The Star-Spangled Banner."* Maryland Historical Society, Baltimore.

Mancall, Peter C., Joshua L. Rosenbloom, and Thomas Weiss. (2001). "Slave prices and the South Carolina economy, 1722–1809." *Journal of Economic History*, 61:3.

Mann, Charles C. (2007). "America, lost and found." *National Geographic,* May. http://ngm .nationalgeographic.com/print/2007/05/jamestown/charles-mann-text.

Mann, W. Howard. (1963). "The Marshall Court: Nationalization of private rights and personal liberty from the authority of the Commerce Clause." *Indiana Law Journal*, 38:2.

Marable, Manning. (1981) *Blackwater: Historical Studies in Race, Class Consciousness, and Revolution.* Black Praxis Press, Dayton OH.

Marcus, Jacob Rader. (1955). *Memoirs of American Jews, 1775–1865.* 3 vol. The Jewish Publication Society of America, Philadelphia.

———. (1970). *The Colonial American Jew, 1492–1776.* Wayne State University Press, Detroit.

Martin, Bonnie. (2010). "Slavery's invisible engine: Mortgaging human property." *Journal of Southern History*, 76:4.

Martin, Eliza Layne. (undated). "Eliza Lucas Pinckney: Indigo in the Atlantic world." http:// cwh.ucsc.edu/SocialBiog.Martin.pdf.

Martineau, Harriet. (1838). *Retrospect of Western Travel.* Saunders and Otley, London.

Marx, Karl. (1937). *The Civil War in the United States.* Ed. Richard Enmale. International Publishers, New York.

———. (1957). *A Contribution to the Critique of Political Economy.* International Publishers, New York.

*Mason, Isaac. (1893). *Life of Isaac Mason as a Slave.* [n.p.], Worcester, MA.

Masur, Louis P. (2012). "The painter and the president." *New York Times,* July 25.

Mather, Cotton. (1912) "Lost works of Cotton Mather." *Proceedings of the Massachusetts Historical Society*, 3rd series, v. 45.

Matthews, James M. (1862.) *Public Laws of the Confederate States of America, Passed at the Second Session of the First Congress.* R. M. Smith, Richmond.

Matthewson, Timothy. (1979). "George Washington's policy toward the Haitian Revolution." *Diplomatic History* 3:3.

McAfee, Ward M. (2001). Preface to Fehrenbacher, Don E. (2001). *The Slaveholding Republic: An Account of the United States Government's Relations to Slavery.* Oxford University Press, New York.

McCandless, Peter. (2011). *Slavery, Disease, and Suffering in the Southern Lowcountry.* Cambridge University Press, New York.

McCrady, Edward. (1901). *The History of South Carolina in the Revolution.* MacMillan, London.

McCullough, David. (1981). *Mornings on Horseback: The Story of an Extraordinary Family.* Simon & Schuster, New York.

McCusker, John J. (1978). *Money and Exchange in Europe and America, 1600–1775: A Handbook.* University of North Carolina Press, Chapel Hill.

McCusker, John J., and Russell R. Menard. (1985). *The Economy of British America, 1607–1789.* University of North Carolina Press, Chapel Hill.

McGrane, Reginald C. (1919). *The Correspondence of Nicholas Biddle Dealing with National Affairs, 1807–1844.* Houghton Mifflin, Boston.

McMillin, James A. (2004). *The Final Victims: Foreign Slave Trade to North America, 1783–1810.* University of South Carolina Press, Columbia.

McPherson, James M. (2014). *Embattled Rebel: Jefferson Davis as Commander in Chief.* Penguin Press, New York.

Meacham, Jon. (2012). *Thomas Jefferson: The Art of Power.* Random House, New York.

"Memoirs of President Davies." (1987). *The Quarterly Register,* 9:4.

"Memorial Sloan-Kettering Cancer Center: The nation's first cancer institute." (1965). *CA: A Cancer Journal for Clinicians,* 15:3, 112. http://onlinelibrary.wiley.com/doi/10.3322/canjclin.15.3.112/pdf.

Menard, Russell R. (1994). "Financing the Lowcountry export boom: Capital and growth in early South Carolina." *William and Mary Quarterly,* Third Series, 51:4.

Mercado, Juan Carlos. (2006). *Menéndez de Áviles y la Florida: Crónicas de sus expediciones.* Edwin Mellen Press, Lewiston, NY.

Merkel, William G. (2003). "To see oneself as a target of a justified revolution: Thomas Jefferson and Gabriel's uprising." *American Nineteenth Century History,* 4:2, Summer.

Merry, Robert W. (2013). *Where They Stand: The American Presidents in the Eyes of Voters and Historians.* Simon and Schuster, New York.

Message from the President of the United States. (1840). Blair and Rives, Washington DC.

Metcalf, George. (1987). "A microcosm of why Africans sold slaves: Akan consumption patterns in the 1770s." *Journal of African History,* 28:3.

Michael, Ronald L. (1975). "Construction of National Road bed: Historical and archaeological evidence." *Bulletin of the Association for Preservation Technology,* 7:4.

Middleton, Arthur Pierce. (1953). *Tobacco Coast: A Maritime History of Chesapeake Bay in the Colonial Era.* The Mariners Museum, Newport News, VA.

Milanich, Jerald T. (1999). *Laboring in the Fields of the Lord: Spanish Missions and Southeastern Indians.* Smithsonian Institution Press, Washington.

Miles, Edwin Arthur. (1960). *Jacksonian Democracy in Mississippi*. University of North Carolina Press, Chapel Hill.

———. (1957). "The Mississippi slave insurrection scare of 1835." *Journal of Negro History*, 42:1.

Miller, Edward L. (2004). *New Orleans and the Texas Revolution*. Texas A&M Press, College Station.

Miller, Marcia M., and Orlando Ridout V. (2001). *Architecture in Annapolis: A field Guide*. The Vernacular Architecture Forum and the Maryland Historical Trust Press, Crownsville, MD.

Minchinton, Walter E. (1989). "Characteristics of British slaving vessels, 1698–1775." *Journal of Interdisciplinary History*, 20:1.

Minnigerode, Meade. (1928). *Jefferson: Friend of France, 1793: The Career of Edmond Charles Genet*. G. P. Putnam's Sons, New York.

Mitchell, Wesley Clair. (1903). *History of the Legal-Tender Acts*. Dissertation, University of Chicago.

Montejano, David. (1987). *Anglos and Mexicans in the making of Texas, 1836–1986*. University of Texas Press, Austin.

Moreau de St.-Méry, M.-L.-E. (1958). *Description topographique, physique, civile, politique et historique de la partie française de l'isle Saint-Domingue . . .* New edition, Vol. 1. Société de l'Historie des Colonies Françaises, Paris.

Morgan, Edmund S. (1975). *American Slavery, American Freedom*. W. W. Norton, New York.

———. (1959). *Prologue to Revolution: Sources and Documents on the Stamp Act crisis, 1764–1766*. University of North Carolina Press, Chapel Hill.

Morgan, Hiram. (2004). "'Never Any Realm Worse Governed': Queen Elizabeth and Ireland." *Transactions of the Royal Historical Society*, Sixth Series, Vol. 14.

Morgan, Kenneth. (2005). "Remittance procedures in the eighteenth-century British slave trade." *Business History Review*, 79:4.

———. (2007). *Slavery and the British Empire: From Africa to America*. Oxford University Press, New York.

Morgan, Philip D. (1998). *Slave Counterpoint: Black Culture in the Eighteenth-Century Chesapeake and Lowcountry*. University of North Carolina Press, Chapel Hill.

———. ed., (2010). *African American Life in the Georgia Lowcountry: The Atlantic World and the Gullah Geechee*. University of Georgia Press, Athens.

Morris, Christopher. (1995). *Becoming Southern: The Evolution of a Way of Life*. Oxford University Press, New York.

Mullen, Lincoln. (2014). "Mapping the spread of American slavery." http://lincolnmullen.com/blog/the-spread-of-american-slavery.

Musgrave, Jon. (2005). *Slaves, Salt, Sex & Mr. Crenshaw*. IllinoisHistory.com, Marion IL.

Nairne, Thomas. (1708 / 1988). *Nairne's Muskhogean Journals: The 1708 Expedition to the Mississippi River*. Edited by Alexander Moore. University Press of Mississippi, Jackson.

Naval Documents Related to the Quasi-War Between the United States and France. (1935). US Gov't Printing Office, Washington.

Neale, J. E. (1957). *Queen Elizabeth I: A biography*. Doubleday Anchor Books, Garden City, NY.

The Negro in Virginia. (1940). Hastings House, New York.

Neu, Irene D. (1961). "J. B. Moussier and the property banks of Louisiana." *Business History Review,* 35:4.

New Orleans As It Is: Its manners and customs – morals – fashionable life – profanation of the Sabbath – prostitution – licentiousness – slave markets and slavery, &c, &c, &c, by a resident. (1850). [n.p.], New Orleans.

Newman, Eric P. (1997). *The Early Paper Money of America.* Krause Publications, Iola WI.

Nicholls, Michael L. (2000). "Strangers setting among us: The sources and challenge of the urban free black population of early Virginia." *The Virginia Magazine of History and Biography,* 108:2.

Nisbet, Stuart M. (2009). "Early Glasgow sugar plantations in the Caribbean." *Scottish Archaeological Journal,* 31:1–2.

Norris, John. (1712.) *Profitable Advice for Rich and Poor.* J. Howe, London.

*Northup, Solomon. (1855). *Twelve Years a Slave: Narrative of Solomon Northup.* Miller, Orton & Mulligan, New York.

Nybakken, Elizabeth I. (1980). *The* Centinel*: Warnings of a Revolution.* University of Delaware Press, Newark.

O'Brien, Jane. (2013). "'Proof' Jamestown settlers turned to cannibalism." BBC News, May 1, www.bbc.co.uk/news/world-us-canada-22362831.

O'Connell, Deidre. (2009). *The Ballad of Blind Tom.* Overlook Duckworth, London.

O'Donnell, Craig. (2006). "Colonial town became port and travel hub." *Tales of Kent County,* v. 1. Kent County News, Chestertown, MD.

Oliver, Peter. (1967). *Peter Oliver's Origin & Progress of the American Rebellion: A Tory View.* Stanford University Press, Stanford.

Olmsted, Frederick Law. (1861). *A Journey in the Seaboard Slave States, with Remarks on Their Economy.* Mason Brothers, New York.

———. (1861a). *Journeys and Explorations in the Cotton Kingdom.* Sampson Low, London.

Onstott, Kyle. (1946). *The Art of Breeding Better Dogs.* Denlinger's, Washington, DC.

———. (1957). *Mandingo.* Denlinger's, Richmond, VA.

Ortiz, Fernando. (1947). *Cuban Counterpoint: Tobacco and Sugar.* Trans. Harriet de Onís. Knopf, New York.

———. (1978). *Contrapunteo Cubano del Tabaco y el Azúcar.* Biblioteca Ayacucho, Caracas.

Owens, Robert M. (2007). *Mr. Jefferson's Hammer: William Henry Harrison and the Origins of American Indian Policy.* University of Oklahoma Press, Norman.

Owsley, Frank Lawrence Jr. (1981). *Struggle for the Gulf Borderland: The Creek War and the Battle of New Orleans 1812–1815.* University Presses of Florida, Gainesville.

Papenfuse, Edward C. (1975). *In Pursuit of Profit: The Annapolis Merchants in the Era of the American Revolution, 1763–1805.* Johns Hopkins University Press, Baltimore.

Paquette, Robert L., and Douglas R. Egerton. (2004). "Of facts and fables: New light on the Denmark Vesey affair." *The South Carolina Historical Magazine,* 105:1.

Parent, Anthony S. Jr. (2003). *Foul Means: The Formation of a Slave Society in Virginia, 1660–1740.* University of North Carolina Press, Chapel Hill.

Parish, John C., and James Gadsden. (1935). "A project for a California slave colony in 1851." *Huntington Library Bulletin* 8, October.

Parton, James. (1874). *Life of Thomas Jefferson: Third President of the United States.* J. R. Osgood, Boston.

Peck, Douglas T. (2001). "Lucas Vásquez de Ayllón's doomed colony of San Miguel de Gualdape." *Georgia Historical Quarterly,* 85:2.

Perdue, Charles L. Jr., Thomas E. Barden, and Robert K. Phillips, eds. (1976). *Weevils in the Wheat: Interviews with Virginia Ex-Slaves.* University Press of Virginia, Charlottesville.

Phillips, Ulrich B. (1905). "The economic cost of slaveholding in the cotton belt." *Political Science Quarterly,* 20:2.

Pickett, Margaret F., and Dwayne. (2011). *The European Struggle to Settle North America: Colonizing Attempts by England, France and Spain, 1521–1608.* McFarland, Jefferson, NC.

Pierce, Franklin. (1904). "Some papers of Franklin Pierce, 1852–1862." *American Historical Review,* 10:1.

Pinckney, Eliza Lucas. (1740–62). *Letters and Memoranda, 1740–1762.* National Humanities Center. http://nationalhumanitiescenter.org/pds/becomingamer/peoples/text5/eliza pinckney.pdf.

Polk, James K. (1910). *The Diary of James K. Polk During His Presidency, 1845 to 1849.* A. C. McClurg, Chicago.

Poore, Ben: Perley [sic]. (1886.) *Reminiscences of Sixty Years in the National Metropolis.* Hubbard Brothers, Philadelphia.

Popkin, Jeremy D. (2009). "The French Revolution's other island." In Geggus, David, and Norman Fiering, ed., *The World of the Haitian Revolution.* Indiana University Press, Bloomington.

Price, Jacob M. (1991). "Credit in the slave trade and plantation economies." In Solow, Barbara L., *Slavery and the Rise of the Atlantic System.* Cambridge University Press, Cambridge.

———. (1984). "Sheffeild v. Starke: Institutional experimentation in the London–Maryland trade c. 1696–1706." *Business History* 28:3.

Public Documents Printed by Order of the Senate of the United States during the Second Session of the Twenty-sixth Congress, v. 3 (1841). Blair and Rives, Washington.

Purcell, Sarah J. (2004). *The Early National Period: An Eyewitness History.* Facts on File, New York.

Purchas, Samuel. (1625). *Purchas his Pilgrimes.* William Stansby, London.

Put's Original California Songster. (1868). Fourth edition. D. E. Appleton, San Francisco.

De Quesada, Alejandro. (2014). *Spanish Colonial Fortifications in North America 1565–1822.* Osprey, Oxford.

Raatschen, Gudrun. (2008). "Merely ornamental? Van Dyck's portraits of Henrietta Maria." In Griffey, Erin. (2008). *Henrietta Maria: Piety, Politics and Patronage.* Ashgate, Aldershot UK.

Rankin, Hugh F. (1969). *The Golden Age of Piracy.* Holt, Rinehart and Winston, New York.

Rappleye, Charles. (2006). *Sons of Providence.* Simon and Schuster, New York.

Rasmussen, William M. S., and Robert S. Tilton. (2003). *Old Virginia: The Pursuit of a Pastoral Ideal.* Howell Press, Charlottesville.

Rawley, James A. (2003). *London, Metropolis of the Slave Trade.* University of Missouri Press, Columbia.

Rayner, B. L. (1832). *Sketches of the Life, Writings, and Opinions of Thomas Jefferson*. A. Francis and W. Boardman, New York.

Reamy, Bill, and Martha. (2007). *Genealogical Abstracts from Biographical and Genealogical History of the State of Delaware*, Volume 1. Heritage Books, Westminster, MD.

Rediker, Marcus. (2007). *The Slave Ship: A Human History*. Viking, New York.

Remini, Robert V. (1977). *Andrew Jackson and the Course of American Empire, 1767–1821*. Harper and Row, New York.

———. (1981). *Andrew Jackson and the Course of American Freedom, 1822–1832*. Harper and Row, New York.

———. (1984). *Andrew Jackson and the Course of American Democracy, 1833–1845*. Harper and Row, New York.

Reports and Cases Argued and Determined in the Supreme Court of the State of Louisiana, vol. XXX, for the Year 1878 (1879), 30:1. F. Hansell, New Orleans.

Restall, Matthew. (2000). "Black conquistadors: Armed Africans in early Spanish America." *The Americas*, 57:2, Summer.

Ribaut, Jean. (1927). *The Whole & True Discouerye of Terra Florida*. Florida Historical Society, De Land, FL.

Richards, Leonard L. (2007). *The California Gold Rush and the Coming of the Civil War*. Alfred A. Knopf, New York.

Riddell, William Renwick. (1927). "Encouragement of the slave-trade." *Journal of Negro History*, 12:1.

Rideau, Wilbert. (2010). *In the Place of Justice: A Study of Punishment and Deliverance*. Alfred A. Knopf, New York.

Robbins, Michael W. (1986). *The Principio Company: Iron-making in Colonial Maryland 1720–1781*. Garland Publishing, New York.

Roberts, Alasdair. (2012). *America's First Great Depression: Economic Crisis and Political Disorder after the Panic of 1837*. Cornell University Press, Ithaca.

Roberts, Blain, and Ethan J. Kytle. (2015). "When freedom came to Charleston," *New York Times*, February 19.

Robinson, Donald L. (1971). *Slavery in the Structure of American Politics, 1765–1820*. Harcourt, Brace, Jovanovich, New York.

Rockman, Seth. (2009). *Scraping By: Wage Labor, Slavery, and Survival in Early Baltimore*. Johns Hopkins University Press, Baltimore.

Rogers, George C. Jr. (1962). *Evolution of a Federalist: William Loughton Smith of Charleston (1758–1812)*. University of South Carolina Press, Columbia.

———. (1976). "The East Florida Society of London, 1766–1767." *Florida Historical Quarterly*, 54:4.

Rosen, Robert N. (2000). *The Jewish Confederates*. University of South Carolina Press, Columbia.

Roske, Ralph J. (1968). *Everyman's Eden: A History of California*. Macmillan, New York.

———. (1963). "The world impact of the California Gold Rush 1849–1857," *Arizona and the West* 5:3.

Rothert, Otto Arthur. (1913). *A History of Muhlenberg County*. John P. Morton, Louisville, KY.

Rountree, Helen C., and E. Randolph Turner. (1994). "On the fringe of the Southeast: The Powhatan paramount chiefdom in Virginia." in Hudson, Charles, and Carmen Chaves Tesser, eds., *The Forgotten Centuries: Indians and Europeans in the American South, 1521–1704.* University of Georgia Press, Athens.

Rousey, Dennis Charles (1996). *Policing the Southern City: New Orleans, 1805–1889.* Louisiana State University Press, Baton Rouge.

Rudolph, Frederick. (2011). *The American College and University: A History.* University of Georgia Press, Columbus.

Rumple, Jethro. (1881). *A History of Rowan County, North Carolina.* J. J. Bruner, Salisbury, NC.

Rutherford, Donald. (2002). *Routledge Dictionary of Economics*, 2d ed. Routledge, London.

Sachar, Howard M. (1992). *A History of the Jews in America.* Knopf, New York.

de la Sagra, Ramón. (1831). *Historia económico-política y estadística de la isla de Cuba.* Imprenta de las Viudas de Arazoza y Soler, Havana.

Sahr, Robert. (2015). "Individual Year Conversion Factor Tables." Oregon State University College of Liberal Arts website. http://liberalarts.oregonstate.edu/spp/polisci /faculty-staff/robert-sahr/inflation-conversion-factors-years-1774-estimated-2024-dollars -recent-years/individual-year-conversion-factor-table-0.

*Said, Omar ibn. (1831 / 1925) "Autobiography of Omar ibn Said, Slave in North Carolina, 1831." Ed. John Franklin Jameson. http://docsouth.unc.edu/nc/omarsaid/omarsaid.html.

Salter, William (1876). *The Life of James W. Grimes: Governor of Iowa, 1854–58; A Senator of the United States, 1859–1869.* D. Appleton and Company, New York.

Samford, Patricia M. (2007). *Subfloor Pits and the Archaeology of Slavery in Colonial Virginia.* University of Alabama Press, Tuscaloosa.

Satz, Ronald N. (1972). "The African slave trade and Lincoln's campaign of 1858." *Journal of the Illinois State Historical Society*, 65:3.

Say, Jean-Baptiste. (1821). *A Treatise on Political Economy; or the Production, Distribution, and Consumption of Wealth.* Trans. C.R. Prinsep. Longman, Hurst, London.

Scanlon, James E. (1968). "A sudden conceit: Jefferson and the Louisiana Government Bill of 1804." *Louisiana History*, 9:2.

Schafer, Judith K. (1997). *Slavery, the Civil Law, and the Supreme Court of Louisiana.* LSU Press, Baton Rouge.

———. (2009). *Brothels, Depravity, and Abandoned Women: Illegal Sex in Antebellum New Orleans.* Louisiana State University Press, Baton Rouge

Schomburgk, Robert H. (1847). *The History of Barbados.* Longman Brown Green and Longmans, London.

Schuckers, J. W. (1874). *The Life and Public Services of Salmon Portland Chase.* D. Appleton and Company, New York.

Schultz, Christian. (1810). *Travels on an Inland Voyage.* Isaac Riley, New York.

Schwartz, Stuart B. (1985). *Sugar Plantations in the Formation of Brazilian Society: Bahia, 1550–1835.* Cambridge University Press, Cambridge.

Schwarz, Philip J., ed. (2012). *Gabriel's Conspiracy: A Documentary History.* University of Virginia Press, Charlottesville.

Scott, Edwin J. (1884). *Random Recollections of a Long Life: 1806 to 1876*. Charles A. Calvo, Jr., Charleston.

Scott, William Robert. (1910). *The Constitution and Finance of English, Scottish and Irish Joint-Stock Companies to 1720*. University Press, Cambridge.

Seabrook, Whitemarsh B. (1825). *A Concise View of the Critical Situation, and Future Prospects of the Slave-Holding States, in Relation to Their Coloured Population*. A. E. Miller, Charleston.

Sellers, Charles G. (1987). *James K. Polk, Jacksonian, 1795–1843*. Easton Press, Norwalk CT.

Sellers, Leila. (1934). *Charleston Business on the Eve of the American Revolution*. University of North Carolina Press, Chapel Hill.

Seward, William Henry. (1877). *Autobiography of William H. Seward from 1801 to 1834*. D. Appleton, New York.

Shackleford, George Green. (1988). *George Wythe Randolph and the Confederate Elite*. University of Georgia Press, Columbus.

Sheehy, Barry, and Cindy Wallace with Vaughnette Goode-Walker. (2012). *Savannah: Brokers, Bankers, and Bay Lane: Inside the Slave Trade*. v. 2. Emerald Book Co., Austin.

Shugerman, Jed Handelsman. (2002). "The Louisiana Purchase and South Carolina's reopening of the slave trade in 1803." *Journal of the Early Republic*, 22:2.

Sidbury, James. (1997). "Saint Domingue in Virginia: Ideology, local meanings, and resistance to slavery, 1790–1800." *Journal of Southern History*, 63:3.

————. (2002). "Thomas Jefferson in Gabriel's Virginia," 210. In Horn, James, Jan Ellen Lewis, and Peter S. Onuf, eds. (2002). *The Revolution of 1800: Democracy, Race and the New Republic*. University of Virginia Press, Charlottesville.

Simkins, Francis B. (1927). "The Ku Klux Klan in South Carolina, 1868–1871." *Journal of Negro History*, 12:4.

Simpson, Henry. (1859). *The Lives of Eminent Philadelphians, Now Deceased*. William Brotherhead, Philadelphia.

Sinha, Manisha. (2000). *The Counterrevolution of Slavery: Politics and Ideology in Antebellum South Carolina*. University of North Carolina Press, Chapel Hill.

Sioussat, St. George L. (1915). "The Nashville Convention." *Mississippi Valley Historical Review*, 2:3.

Sirmans, M. Eugene. (1966). *Colonial South Carolina: A Political History 1663–1763*. University of North Carolina Press, Chapel Hill.

Sketches of the Lives of Franklin Pierce and Wm. R. King, Candidates of the Democratic Republican Party for the Presidency and Vice Presidency of the United States. (1852). [n.p.]

Skipper, Ottis Clark. (1958). *J. D. B. DeBow: Magazinist of the Old South*. University of Georgia Press, Athens.

Slenes, Robert W. (2004). "The Brazilian internal slave trade, 1850–1888: Regional economies, slave experience, and the politics of a peculiar market." In Walter Johnson, ed., *The Chattel Principle: Internal Slave Trades in the Americas*, Yale University Press, New Haven.

Slotkin, Richard, and James K. Folsom, "Introduction," in Slotkin and Folsom, eds., *So Dreadfull a Judgment: Puritan Responses to King Philip's War 1676–1677*. Wesleyan University Press, Middletown.

Slotkin, Richard. (2014). "The Battle of the Crater," *New York Times*, July 29.

Sluiter, Engel. (1948). "Dutch-Spanish rivalry in the Caribbean area, 1594–1609." *The Hispanic American Historical Review*, 28:2.

———. (1997). "New Light on the '20. and Odd Negroes' Arriving in Virginia, August 1619." *The William and Mary Quarterly*, 3rd ser., 54: 2.

Smith, Abbot Emerson. (1947/2000) *Colonists in Bondage: White Servitude and Convict Labor in America, 1607–1776.* Clearfield Company, Baltimore.

Smith, Adam. (1799). *An Inquiry into the Nature and Causes of the Wealth of Nations.* A. Strahan, London.

Smith, Daniel Scott. (1979). "Averages for units and averages for individuals within units: A note." *Journal of Family History*, 4.

Smith, Felipe. (1998.) *American Body Politics: Race, Gender, and Black Literary Renaissance.* University of Georgia Press, Athens.

Smith, Gene Allen. (2013). *The Slaves' Gamble: Choosing Sides in the War of 1812.* Macmillan, New York.

Smith, John. (1624). *The Generall Historie of Virginia, New-England, and the Summer Isles . . .* Michael Sparkes, London. http://docsouth.unc.edu/southlit/smith/smith.html.

———. (1884). *Captain J. Smith's Works, 1608–1631.* Birmingham.

Smith, Josiah. (1741). *The Burning of Sodom.* Fowler for Phillips, Boston.

Smith, Lacey Baldwin. (1966). "Henry VIII and the Protestant triumph." *American Historical Review*, 71:4.

Smith, Mark M. (2005). *Stono: Documenting and Interpreting a Southern Slave Revolt.* University of South Carolina Press, Columbia.

Smith, Paul H., ed. (1996). *Letters of Delegates to Congress, 1774–1789*, v. 24,

Smith, William Russell. (1861). *The History and Debates of the Convention of the People of Alabama Begun and Held in the City of Montgomery, on the Seventh Day of January, 1861.* White, Pfister and Co., Montgomery, AL.

Smithers, Gregory D. (2012). *Slave Breeding: Sex, Violence, and Memory in African American History.* University Press of Florida, Gainesville.

Solís de Merás, Gonzalo. (1567/1893/1923). *Pedro Menéndez de Avilés: Adelantado and Captain-General of Florida: Memorial*, trans. Jeannette Thurber Connor. Florida State Historical Society, Deland FL.

Soodalter, Ron. (2014). "The plot to burn New York City." *New York Times*, November 5.

Sound Currency 1896: A Compendium of Accurate and Timely Information on Currency Questions. (1896). Reform Club Sound Currency Committee, New York.

Southall, Geneva Handy. (2002). *Blind Tom, the Black Pianist-Composer (1849–1908): Continually Enslaved.* Scarecrow Press, Lanham MD.

Spanish Documents Concerning English Voyages to the Caribbean, 1527–1568, Selected from the Archives of the Indies at Seville. (1928). Ed. Irene A. Wright. Ashgate, Farnham UK.

Spratt, L. W. (1858). "Report on the slave trade, to the Southern Convention." *DeBow's Review*, June.

Stagg, J. C. A. *Borderlines in Borderlands: James Madison and the Spanish-American Frontier, 1776–1821.* Yale University Press, New Haven.

Stahr, Walter. (2013). *Seward: Lincoln's Indispensable Man.* Simon and Schuster, New York.

Stampp, Kenneth. (1956). *The Peculiar Institution: Slavery in the Ante-Bellum South.* Alfred A. Knopf, New York.

Stanley, Amy Dru. (2012). "Slave breeding and free love: An antebellum argument over personhood." In Zakim, Michael, and Gary J. Kornblith, *Capitalism Takes Command: The Social Transformation of Nineteenth-Century America.* University of Chicago Press, Chicago.

Stanton, Lucia. (2012). *"Those who labor for my happiness": Slavery at Thomas Jefferson's Monticello.* University of Virginia Press, Charlottesville.

Starobin, Robert. S. (1970). *Industrial Slavery in the Old South.* Oxford University Press, New York.

State Papers and Correspondence Bearing upon the Purchase of the Territory of Louisiana. (1903). Government Printing Office, Washington, D.C.

Stephenson, Wendell Holmes. (1938). *Isaac Franklin, Slave Trader and Planter of the Old South.* Louisiana State University Press, Baton Rouge.

Stevens, Charles Emery. (1856). *Anthony Burns: A History.* John P. Jewett, Boston.

*Steward, Austin. (1857). *Twenty-Two Years a Slave, and Forty Years a Freeman.* William Alling, Rochester, NY.

Stewart, David O. (2009). *Impeached: The Trial of President Andrew Johnson and the Fight for Lincoln's Legacy.* Simon and Schuster, New York.

Stoddard, Lothrop. (1914). *The French Revolution in San Domingo.* Houghton Mifflin, Boston.

Stowe, Harriet Beecher. (1853). *The Key to Uncle Tom's Cabin; Presenting the Original Facts and Documents upon Which the Story Is Founded, Together with Corroborative Statements Verifying the Truth of the Work.* John P. Jewett, Boston.

———. (1852). *Uncle Tom's Cabin, or Life Among the Lowly.* John P. Jewett, Boston.

Strouse, Jean. (1999). *Morgan: American Financier.* Random House, New York.

Stuart, James. (King James I). (1604/1616). *The Works of the Most High and Mightie Prince, James.* James, London.

Sublette, Ned. (2004). *Cuba and Its Music: From the First Drums to the Mambo.* Chicago Review Press, Chicago.

———. (2008). *The World That Made New Orleans: From Spanish Silver to Congo Square.* Chicago Review Press, Chicago.

Sutch, Richard. (1972). *The Breeding of Slaves for Sale and the Westward Expansion of Slavery, 1850–1860.* Institute of Business and Economic Research, University of California, Berkeley.

Sutherland, Daniel E. (1988). *The Confederate Carpetbaggers.* Louisiana State University Press, Baton Rouge.

Swarns, Rachel L. (2012). *American Tapestry: The Story of the Black, White, and Multiracial Ancestors of Michelle Obama.* HarperCollins, New York.

———. (2012a). "Meet your cousin, the First Lady: A family story, long hidden." *New York Times,* June 17.

Sydnor, Charles S. (1938). *A Gentleman of the Old Natchez Region: Benjamin L.C. Wailes.* Duke University Press, Durham.

———. (1966). *Slavery in Mississippi.* Louisiana State University Press, Baton Rouge.

Tadman, Michael. (1996). *Speculators and Slaves: Masters, Traders, and Slaves in the Old South.* University of Wisconsin Press, Madison.

Talbot, Paul. (2009). *Mondo Mandingo: The "Falconhurst" Books and Films.* iUniverse, Bloomington.

Taylor, John. (1888). *Early Prose and Poetical Works of John Taylor, the Water Poet.* Hamilton, Adams & Co., London.

Thomas, E. S. (1840). *Reminiscences of the Last Sixty-Five Years, Commencing with the Battle of Lexington.* The Author, Hartford.

Thomas, Hugh. (1997). *The Slave Trade.* Simon and Schuster, New York.

Thomas, Isaiah. (1810/1970). *The History of Printing in America.* Weathervane Books, New York.

*Thompson, John. (1856). *The Life of John Thompson, a Fugitive Slave; Containing His History of 25 Years in Bondage, and His Providential Escape. Written by Himself.* Published by John Thompson, Worcester, MA.

[Thomson, Mortimer]. (1863). *What became of the slaves on a Georgia plantation? Great auction sale of slaves at Savannah, Georgia. March 2d and 3d, 1859. a sequel to Mrs. Kemble's journal. New York Tribune,* March 9.

Thornton, John. (1998). "The African experience of the '20. and odd Negroes' arriving in Virginia in 1619." *William and Mary Quarterly,* 3rd ser., 55:3.

———. (1991). "African dimensions of the Stono rebellion," *American Historical Review,* 96:4.

———. (1983). *The Kingdom of Kongo: Civil War and Transition, 1641–1718.* University of Wisconsin Press, Madison.

Tilp, Frederick. (1982). *The Chesapeake Bay of Yore: Mainly About the Rowing and Sailing Craft.* Chesapeake Bay Foundation, Alexandria, VA.

Tombs, Robert. (2014). *The English and Their History.* Penguin, London.

Toombs, Robert; Alexander Hamilton Stephens; Howell Cobb. (1913). "The correspondence of Robert Toombs, Alexander H. Stephens, and Howell Cobb," ed. Ulrich B. Phillips, *Annual Report of the American Historical Association for the Year 1911.* [n.p.], Washington.

Tourtellot, Arthur Bernon. (1977). *Benjamin Franklin: The Shaping of Genius: The Boston Years.* Doubleday, Garden City, NY.

Townsend, John. (1860). *The Doom of Slavery in the Union; Its Safety Out of It.* Evans and Cogswell, Charleston.

Treasure, Geoffrey. (2013). *The Huguenots.* Yale University Press, New Haven and London.

Trouillot, Michel-Rolph. (1990). *Haiti: State Against Nation: Origins and Legacy of Duvalierism.* Monthly Review Press, New York.

*Truth, Sojourner. (1884). *Narrative of Sojourner Truth; A Bondswoman of Olden Time.* Review and Herald Office, Battle Creek, MI.

Tyler, Lyon Gardiner, ed. (1907). *Narratives of Early Virginia, 1606–1625.* Barnes & Noble, New York.

———. (1884). *The Letters and Times of the Tylers.* Whittet & Shepperson, Richmond.

Tyler, Moses Coit. (1898/1970). *Patrick Henry.* Arlington House, New Rochelle.

Unger, Harlow Giles. (2010). *Lion of Liberty: Patrick Henry and the Call to a New Nation.* Da Capo, Cambridge, MA.

Unwin, Gregory J. W. (2008). Review of Burkhardt, George S., *Confederate Rage, Yankee Wrath: No Quarter in the Civil War*. *The American Historical Review*, 113:2.

Van Buren, Martin. (1973). *The Autobiography of Martin Van Buren*. Da Capo, New York.

*Veney, Bethany. (1889). *The Narrative of Bethany Veney, A Slave Woman*. Worcester, MA.

Ver Steeg, Clarence L. (1966). "Historians and the southern colonies." In Billington, Ray Allen, ed., *The Reinterpretations of Early American History*. Huntington Library, San Marino, CA.

Vlach, John Michael. (2002). *The Planter's Prospect: Privilege and Slavery in Plantation Paintings*. University of North Carolina Press, Chapel Hill.

Wainwright, Jonathan P. (2008). "Sounds of piety and devotion: Music in the Queen's chapel." In Griffey, Erin. (2008). *Henrietta Maria: Piety, Politics and Patronage*. Ashgate, Aldershot UK.

Waldstreicher, David A. (2004). *Runaway America: Benjamin Franklin, Slavery, and the American Revolution*. Hill & Wang, New York.

———. (2009). *Slavery's Constitution: From Revolution to Ratification*. Hill & Wang, New York.

Walker, David. (1830). *Walker's appeal in four articles; together with a preamble, to the coloured citizens of the world, but in particular and very expressly to those of the United States of America*. David Walker, Boston.

Wallner, Peter A. (2005). "Franklin Pierce and Bowdoin College associates Hawthorne and Hale." *Historical New Hampshire*, 59:1.

Walsh, Lorena S. (2010). *Motives of Honor, Pleasure, and Profit: Plantation Management in the Colonial Chesapeake, 1607–1763*. University of North Carolina Press, Chapel Hill.

———. (1999). "New findings about the Virginia slave trade." *Colonial Williamsburg Interpreter*, 20:2.

Ward, Roger K. (1997). "The French language in Louisiana law and legal education: A requiem." *Louisiana Law Review*, 57:4.

Warden, Margaret Lindsley. (1977). *The Saga of Fairvue, 1832–1977*. Margaret Lindsley Warden, Nashville.

Warshauer, Matthew. (2006). *Andrew Jackson and the Politics of Martial Law: Nationalism, Civil Liberties, and Partisanship*. University of Tennessee Press, Knoxville.

*Watson, Henry. (1848). *Narrative of Henry Watson, a Fugitive Slave*. Bela Marsh, Boston.

Watson, Robert P. (2012). *Affairs of State: The Untold History of Presidential Love, Sex, and Scandal, 1789–1900*. Rowman & Littlefield, Lanham MA.

Wax, Darold D. (1965). "Negro imports into Pennsylvania, 1720–1766." *Pennsylvania History*, 32:3.

———. (1978). "Black immigrants: The slave trade in colonial Maryland." *Maryland Historical Magazine*, 73:1.

Webster, Daniel. (1850). *Speech of Hon. Daniel Webster, on Mr. Clay's resolutions,: In the Senate of the United States, March 7, 1850 . . .* Gideon and co., Washington.

Weeks, Stephen Beauregard. (1896). *Southern Quakers and Slavery: A Study in Institutional History*. The Johns Hopkins Press, Baltimore.

Wesley, Charles H. (1942). "Manifests of slave shipments along the waterways, 1808–1864," *The Journal of Negro History*, 27:2.

Whatley, Warren. (2012). "The transatlantic slave trade and the evolution of political authority in West Africa." http://mpra.ub.uni-muenchen.de/44932/1/MPRA_paper_44932.pdf

Wiecek, William M. (1977.) "The statutory law of slavery and race in the thirteen mainland colonies of British North America." *William and Mary Quarterly*, 3rd ser., 34:2, April.

Wiencek, Henry. (2003). *An Imperfect God: George Washington, His Slaves, and the Creation of America*. Farrar, Straus and Giroux, New York.

———. (2012). *Master of the Mountain: Thomas Jefferson and His Slaves*. Farrar, Straus and Giroux, New York.

Wilberforce, Samuel. (1846). *A Reproof of the American Church*. William Harned, New York, 22.

Wilder, Craig Steven. (2013). *Ebony and Ivy: Race, Slavery, and the Troubled History of America's Universities*. Bloomsbury Press, New York.

Wilentz, Sean. (2004). "The details of greatness." *The New Republic*, March 29.

———. (2005). *The Rise of American Democracy: Jefferson to Lincoln*. W. W. Norton, New York.

Wilford, John Noble. (2013). "Fort tells of Spain's early ambitions." *New York Times*, July 22.

Willard, Margaret W., ed. (1925). *Letters on the American Revolution, 1774–76*.

Williamson, Samuel H., and Louis P. Cain. (2011). "Measuring slavery in 2011 dollars." www.measuringworth.com/slavery.php.

Willison, George F. (1969). *Patrick Henry and His World*. Doubleday, Garden City, NY.

Wills, Garry. (1978). *Inventing America: Jefferson's Declaration of Independence*. Doubleday, Garden City, NY.

Wilson, Henry. (1875). *History of the Rise and Fall of the Slave Power in America*. James R. Osgood, Boston.

Wilson, Joseph Ruggles. (1861). *Mutual relation of masters and slaves as taught in the Bible. A discourse preached in the First Presbyterian Church, Augusta, Georgia, on Sabbath morning, Jan. 6, 1861*. Steam Press of Chronicle & Sentinel, 1861. http://docsouth.unc.edu/imls/wilson/wilson.html.

Wilson, Thomas D. (2012). *The Oglethorpe Plan: Enlightenment Design in Savannah and Beyond*. University of Virginia Press, Charlottesville.

Winter, Michael. (2014). "Gold worth millions recovered from 1857 shipwreck." *USA Today*, July 14.

Wood, Gordon S. (1969). *The Creation of the American Republic, 1776–1787*. University of North Carolina Press, Chapel Hill.

———. (1992). *The Radicalism of the American Revolution*. Alfred A. Knopf, New York.

Wood, Peter H. (1975). *Black Majority: Negroes in Colonial South Carolina from 1670 Through the Stono Rebellion*. Alfred A. Knopf, New York.

Woodmason, Charles. (1766–8/1953). *The Carolina Backcountry on the Eve of Revolution: The Journal and Other Writings of Charles Woodmason, Anglican Itinerant*. University of North Carolina Press, Chapel Hill.

Wright, Gavin. (1991). "What was slavery?" *Social Concept* 6:1.

———. (2006). *Slavery and American Economic Development*. Louisiana State University Press, Baton Rouge.

Wright, Irene A. (2010). *Spanish Documents Concerning English Voyages to the Caribbean, 1527–1568*. Ashgate, Farnham, UK.

Wroth, Peregrine. (1908). "New Yarmouth." *Maryland Historical Magazine, 3:3.*

Wyatt, David R. (2009). *Slaves and Warriors in Medieval Britain and Ireland: 800–1200.* Brill, Boston.

Yagyu, Tomoko. (2006). *Slave Traders and Planters in the Expanding South: Entrepreneurial Strategies, Business Networks, and Western Migration in the Atlantic World, 1787–1859.* PhD diss., University of North Carolina, Chapel Hill.

Yarema, Allan. (2006). *The American Colonization Society: An Avenue to Freedom?* University Press of America, Lanham, MD.

Yellin, Jean Fagan. (2004). *Harriet Jacobs: A Life.* Basic Books, New York.

Zaborney, John J. (2012). *Slaves for Hire: Renting Enslaved Laborers in Antebellum Virginia.* Louisiana State University Press, Baton Rouge.

Zobel, Hiller B. (1970). *The Boston Massacre.* Norton, New York.

Index